The Underside of Things

Praise for the book

Badri Raina is an acute, eloquent and prolific observer of contemporary India. This anthology of his short essays holds up a mirror to the times we live in. His convictions are robustly secular and democratic, his vision humane and prose eloquent. Warmly recommended.
Harsh Mander

Badri Raina grips his pen with ferocious precision: there is anger at the state of the world, but because of his advocacy of the poetic imagination, Badri is not governed by rage. He writes with joy at the possibility of what will come, a society absent the toxicity of the present. Grim as they might be, events are capable of going the other way – not backward to the worst urges of humankind, but forward to better dreams. Sociology is not *au fait* of such hope; for that one needs literature. Badri reads the former, but writes with the spur of the latter. Onward! Unfurl the sails of the Imagination! Strike a course from madness to possibility…
Vijay Prashad

I have long admired Badri Raina for his astonishingly wide range of interests, his fierce independence of mind, and his coruscating prose. From politics to poetry and from communalism to cricket – Badri writes on these subjects, and more, with empathy, understanding and, always, a strikingly original point of view. This book will provide a revealing and most illuminating window into the torments of the times.
Ramachandra Guha

Badri Raina is superb when dealing with religious and communal prejudice, which he does with great humour. Yet, he seems no less at ease when tackling foreign affairs, equity, freedom and democracy on a global canvas. The range of his subjects is staggering and he writes not only with a fine literary flair but with a deep sense of history, politics and philosophy. He is an academic and a scholar of the classics (of more than one culture), but one whose writing is clear and easy to read. In fact the use and misuse of language is a recurring theme in his work. He is also able to tie together history, religion, gender, present-day reality and wit when exploring, say, fundamentalist battles over women's hair and headgear. These are essays you want to read.
P Sainath

Reading Badri Raina, not for a moment do I delude myself that this may represent the viewpoint of the Indian intelligentsia. He does not represent anyone, yet he represents the passion for justice in everyone, often buried so deep in the debris of mundane chores of life that we may not be even aware of it. He bridges gaping distances within South Asia with one stroke of his pen. 'He is one of us! He is our own', The Pakistanis feel, the Bangladeshis, the Adivasis, the Muslims, Sikhs, Christians...the thronging multitudes of India – all those who are lucky to have access to his poems and columns. Here is a heart that throbs with compassion, a mind with incisive insight, that cuts through superfluities and gets to the kernel of an issue with such wit and humour, sifting through the details so thoroughly, so effortlessly that you feel it was always obvious to you, allowing no pretentious sophistry, camouflaged prejudices or the so-called 'national interests' (very often the interests of the plundering classes), to distort and mutilate the truth. Nor have I doubted for a moment that he is a true Indian and a patriot, a nationalist, if ever there was one. But 'nation' for him transcends the narrowness of bigotry, defined by a largesse that wipes out antagonism and makes you believe that love and fraternity is possible between those who may appear to be sworn enemies. Badri's poems and columns are testimonies of what we always naturally shared in this subcontinent, and, extending far beyond it, on this, our planet earth. One feels deep respect for the ambience and the milieu that shaped and formed his heart and mind.
Fahmida Riaz

Badri Raina's commentaries on contemporary events have been the chief help in restoring my faith in the idea of a socialist future after the traumatic collapse of the Soviet Union. His humanism is too imaginative, authentic and articulate to be set aside with customary indifference.
Agha Ashraf Ali

Badri Raina always gets the details right, but he is always aware of the big picture. He understands, with empathy, how cultural particularities can shape our thinking, but he is always attuned to universal principles and values. In his language you can read the influence of Shakespeare, in his analysis the influence of Marx, but always grounded in a deep knowledge of India, its history, its geography, its politics and economy. He is always on the side of the oppressed, but would never surrender his intellectual independence. I couldn't imagine trying to understand South Asia without his help, and can't remember how I did before I encountered his writing.
Justin Podur

The Underside of Things

India and the World

A Citizen's Miscellany, 2006-2011

Badri Raina

Foreword by Mani Shankar Aiyar

Three Essays
COLLECTIVE

First Edition August 2012

ISBN 978-81-88789-85-6

Three Essays Collective

B-957 Palam Vihar, GURGAON (Haryana) 122 017 India
Phone: 91-124 2369023, +91 98681 26587, +91 98683 44843
info@threeessays.com Website: www.threeessays.com
Printed and bound by Glorious Printers, New Delhi

To all those who keep their faith in reason, and struggle against odds on behalf of equality, justice, peace.

Contents

2008

2009

2011

Editor's Note

The *Miscellany* comprises a selection of columns written by Badri Raina for the Znet website between May 2006 and December 2011.

Raina has been one of a group of 'Writers' for Znet, which is thought to be one of the premier sites of the democratic international left. Other Znet 'Writers' include, among many, Noam Chomsky, Robert Fisk, Robert Monbiot, Tom Engelhardt, John Pilger, Justin Podur, and Arundhati Roy.

Although Raina's columns bear on identifiable and isolable themes – the politics of cultural fascism, the operations of a class state, its institutions, and ideological elites, the status of left politics and other forms of resistance, the troubled issue of Kashmir, the nature of the problems in Pakistan, the workings of American imperialism in league with other states, including India and Israel, and so on – we have thought it best to avoid what might have been inadequate and overlapping classifications, and to offer the columns in the order and heat of their writing.

Raina's journalism began somewhere in 1988, and constitutes a fairly massive body of work spread across some of India's best known dailies and journals.

Out of this a selection of readings has been drawn up, so that anyone wishing to make connections and build an archive is helped. Here too, the contributions have been placed in chronological order.

We hope this unique record of interventions by an erstwhile university professor entirely on a voluntary and independent basis will be seen as something of an inspiring example of caring and conscientious citizenship.

Editor's Note

Acknowledgements

My thanks to many friends, chief among them James Bittner and Justin Podur, who insisted that these interventions had a somewhat more than contingent value, and asked to be preserved in book form.

Thanks to Znet for affording me the space to articulate these thoughts. It has been a privilege to be among Znet 'Writers.'

My wife, Shashi, has been a critical sounding board throughout the writing of these pieces. To her I say thanks for not tiring of my iterations. And thanks also for the arduous task of helping with the compilation.

My very special thanks to Mani Shankar Aiyar for actually offering to write a Foreword. It has been a deeply enriching experience to have been befriended by one of the finest and most caring minds of our times.

To Nalini Taneja and Asad Zaidi at Three Essays Collective I say thanks for taking on a task that might prove thankless in the extreme.

Foreword

Mani Shankar Aiyar

Badri Raina's mind resides at the trijunction of literature, history and economics, while his soul flies on the wings of philosophy, soaring from the Riga Veda to the dialectics of Hegel and Marx.

The first point of contact between him and me is that Raina earned his spurs with a pioneering work on the Dialectics of Charles Dickens that won kudos around the academic world, as much from the United States as from the United Kingdom (if not in adequate measure from his home country). My Senior Tutor at Cambridge was Graham Storey, one of the legendary scholars of Dickens.

More substantively, I can think of no one more relevant to an understanding of India at the start of the second decade of the 21st century than Charles Dickens – and the twist to his tale given by Badri Raina. For Dickens began writing of Britain sixty to seventy years into the British Industrial Revolution, which is where India stands today, six to seven decades into her Industrial Revolution. And many of the issues of development and displacement raised by Dickens – immortalized in the one sentence, 'Please, Sir, may I have some more?' – are perhaps more relevant to the India of Accelerated Growth than they were to Dickens' England two hundred years ago.

'More relevant' because the England of Charles Dickens was barely a democracy whereas ours is full-blown. Westminster at the time was home to a series of rotten boroughs. (Disraeli got one; Gladstone, elected by the Oxford graduates constituency never had to seek more than 300 votes for his seat in the Commons!) The franchise was restricted (till 1867) to those who owned at least some property. Catholics got the vote only in 1832. And half the electorate – women – had still to wait a century to exercise their franchise (for the first time in 1928). Slavery, although being phased out under the impetus of Wilberforce, was still rampant. Labour laws were regarded as the work of the Devil and in their stead there were Poor laws for those so shiftless as to not secure employment in the sweatshops that passed for factories. Britain was still victim to half-baked ideas that led to the enclosures which forced millions off the land, driving them to the grim slums of the metropolitan centres; and of the implacable Laws of Economics that starved to death and despair hundreds of thousands in Ireland's potato famine. Escape was to be found in the colonies where white trash suddenly became the Raj. Justice for the proletariat was secured through injustice masquerading as the mission civilisatrice for the conquered people. Thus democracy survived development.

Democratic India has none of the safety valves that the Mother of all Parliaments built into her system of democracy in the Age of Charles Dickens. Every Indian is truly equal every five years. He casts the singular vote that decides the fate of governments. While the classes do indeed rule the roost in between, at the end of five years, the *aam admi* has to be supplicated for fear of the condign punishment that he and he alone can administer. Our Oliver Twists cannot be brushed off. For all its faults, ours is a democracy that speaks from the ballot box, a democracy of the rally and the demonstration in the street, of the daily grilling of the powerful and their minions on TV screens beamed into the humblest hut, of the Right to Information Act and the thundering editorials that follow, of Rajghat and Jantar Mantar and the Ram Lila grounds, of a media panting to expose the evil in all nooks and crannies of our public life (but its own), the only democracy in which anti-incumbency, demolishing ruling establishments and routinely knocking out two-thirds of sitting members, is par for the course. So the ballot box is where revenge is wreaked – until the discovery is made, as it has been made in a third of our districts, largely in tribal areas, that power can also grow out of the barrel of a gun. Dissatisfaction with democracy is thus expressed at one end of the political spectrum in anti-incumbency voting and at the other end in Naxalite violence. The ratio at present is 1:3. As that ratio gets reversed, democracy is in danger and development is undermined. For the underlying cause of disaffection is our warped pattern of development which privileges a tiny sliver of the population to living standards that are the envy of the Gates' and the Buffets' while condemning at least four-fifths of our population to existence as dreary as the hovel at the foot of the flyover. The flyover is indeed the metaphor of our growth trajectory, enabling the successful Indian to sweep over the heads of the huddled masses.

In Dickens' England, democracy had not matured enough to nurture a revolution. That is why the six-decade crisis spluttered out. Even Ireland, ravaged by the potato famine, found salvation in the United States, opened to European immigration by the most thorough genocide of the native population ever that makes Hitler look amateurish and land stolen from the tribals on a scale now being emulated by Posco and Vedanta and all other 'drivers' of GDP growth. Dissent in Dickens' England could be stifled. And so the barricades of Paris of which Victor Hugo wrote so movingly in *Les Miserables* were eventually dismantled. And the cry of the Revolution of 1848 – 'A spectre is haunting Europe…Workers of the World Unite. You have nothing to lose but your chains. You have a world to gain' – was stilled. Killed by the inadequacies of, or even the complete absence of, democracy. Meanwhile, in the United States, almost exactly six decades into the US Industrial Revolution, the American Civil War, the bloodiest war fought anywhere in the world till then, broke out over the inequalities bred by the Industrial Revolution. And continental Europe, after Bismarck's unification of Germany in 1870 ushered in the Industrial Revolution, found itself sixty years later in the Thirties caught up in the fascist coils of Salazar, Mussolini, Hitler and Franco, all popularly acclaimed precisely for their repudiation of democracy.

Our democracy is at that juncture. Our single biggest achievement since Independence – the translation of Independence for our country into freedom for our people – is jeopardized by the relentless pursuit of accelerated growth to the exclusion of inclusive growth. One stark figure should suffice. While our GDP grows at over 8 per cent per annum, the Planning Commission confesses that poverty alleviation is proceeding at under 0.8 per cent per annum. That is the measure of how the successful Indian is being privileged over the unsuccessful Indian, with little recognition, outside the breadth of vision of people like Badri Raina, of why such skewed growth is unsustainable in a lively democracy like ours, where anti-democratic forces, with little or no understanding of democracy, are stoking the people's contempt for Parliament and its institutions with the coals of the social injustice which are apparent from Dickens two hundred years ago to Arundhati Roy and Badri Raina today.

Moreover, Raina, like me, is a holdover fossil from the Nehruvian era, one who understands that the bonding adhesive of our nationhood is secularism, indeed, secular fundamentalism of the kind to which I have confessed, not the lily-livered kind that sends ministers scuttling to the airport to appease the voice of dissidence when swathed in saffron. Raina also understands, as Nehru did, the connect between external independence and internal sovereignty. He also sees, as the Mahatma did, that the progress of the poor begins with the empowerment of the poor.

Raina's offerings in these volumes are not journalism as journalism is ordinarily understood. These are deeply engaged and wholly selfless exposures of habits of thought, political formations, and cultural power structures that seek to distort and reduce the finest human urges into structures of sub-human and sectarian power-lust.

The totalizing angst of these essays ought to be seen in the tradition of essay writing that we associate with such 19th century essayists as Thomas Carlyle, who never wrote as distant observers but from an anguished need to seek transformations of contemporary history towards more rational ends.

Yet, it is fair to say that his name is not a name that evokes instant public recognition. I hope this volume will lead to that public acclaim for Badri Raina which alone can save this country as we hurtle on the back of accelerated growth to the brink of the destruction of our democracy.

New Delhi-Chennai
9 June 2012

2006

Capital Punishment

The Rarest of the Rare Case?

In recent weeks, the Indian public mind (often cutely managed by a savvy media world), has been much drawn towards two happenings.

One of these concerns the propagation of 'Gandhigiri' (a rather unfortunate analogue of 'Chamchagiri' or sycophancy, and 'Dadagiri' or ganglordism) by a Mumbai film wherein Gandhi's preferred methods of non-violence are sought to be made applicable to everyday life. Interestingly, some polls have it that this film has done more to popularize Gandhi than anything that has been done hitherto. Some thought that.

The other happening relates to the confirmation of the death sentence on Afzal Guru who was one of the accused in the Parliament attack case

Amazingly, many of the very same social groups who are taken in by the Gandhian approach to problems – as depicted in the film – are also the ones hot for Afzal's death by hanging. Altogether a rather gruesome contradiction. One would think you can either have Gandhi or you can have hanging.

Here is what Gandhi had to say on the subject of capital punishment: 'I cannot in all conscience agree to anyone being sent to the gallows. God alone can take life because He alone gives it.'

Given the high regard in which the Supreme Court of India is held for its competence and probity, few ought to question the determination of guilt it has made in the case of Afzal Guru. After all, it is to that competence and probity that S.A.R. Geelani owes both his life and his freedom, having been earlier sentenced to death by the trial court in the very same criminal case.

Gandhi's allusion to 'conscience' here does, however, seem to rebuke a phrase in the text of the judgement delivered by the Honourable Court upholding the death sentence. The Honourable Court has averred that only the death sentence would satisfy the 'collective conscience' of the country in the matter. One must ask as to which order of conscience ought to have taken precedence in the matter of sentencing – one that abhors taking life or one that seeks it to propitiate popular sentiment. In that conundrum, we stand with the Mahatma.

As we also know, Gandhi's rejoinder to the Code of Hammurabi ('eye for an eye, tooth for a tooth') was a witty and telling one: eye for an eye and surely one day it would be a blind world!

Staying with Gandhi for a minute, perhaps his most discomfiting moment in relation to capital punishment was to come when the revolutionaries, Bhagat Singh, Sukh Dev and Rajguru were sentenced by the British to be hung.

The question has often been asked: Did Gandhi do all he could to seek their reprieve from King George, with whom he was then preparing to share the first Round Table conference? No easy answers here, although Gandhi did point out to the colonial government that the sentence was not an 'irreversible' one. He was on several occasions to plead that there is little he could do. What, however, is on record in the matter is the following statement from Gandhi:

> The government certainly had the right to hang these men. However, there are some rights which do credit to those who possess them only if they are enjoyed in name only. (Collected Works, Ahmedabad, Navjivan, Vol.45, pp.359-61, Gujarati)

The direction from 'Gandhigiri', then, is explicit enough: you may have the right to sentence Afzal Guru to death, but it would do you credit not to exercise that right.

The problem may be that India's highly meritorious forward classes are as severely brutalized by events as any in America. Thus a certain tribalism seems to have overtaken their view of things. It remains a thought, nonetheless, that the 'eye for an eye, tooth for a tooth' dictum does not obtain in most crimes committed. For example, no country yet has a law that decrees that an arsonist must be punished by an official bonfire of all his belonging, nor a rapist be punished by being required to offer his womenfolk for retaliatory rape (except in some tribal communities). The instinct, therefore, to seek death for murder seems to answer to some residual animality wholly repugnant to civilized life.

The most forcefully telling indictment of the practice of capital punishment that I know of is that of Albert Camus:

> What is capital punishment if not the most premeditated of murders to which no criminal act, no matter how calculated, can be compared. (cited in Wolfe Burton H. Pileup on Death Row, N.Y. Doubleday & Co.,Inc. 1973, p.419).

Clearly, as Michael Radelet points out, 'a civilized society must be based on values and principles that are higher than those it condemns.' (Facing the Death Penalty: Essays on Cruel and Unusual Punishment, N.Y., 1989)

It must have been on the basis of such an understanding of civilized life that the Hammurabi Code was opposed by Voltaire, Diderot, Thomas Paine, Adam Smith, and David Hume. Quite some gathering there, wouldn't you say? Immanuel Kant was to put that opposition on the clearly articulated anti-utilitarian perception/conviction that 'people are valuable in themselves, regardless of whether they are useful, or loved, or valued by others.' (cited in MacKinnon, Barbara, Ethics: Theory and Contemporary Issues, 2nd ed., N.Y. Wadsworth Pub., Co., 1998).

MacKinnon makes the further excellent observation that 'using the concern for life that usually promotes it to make a case for ending life is inherently contradictory' (p.133). But, when the blood is screaming, especially among the socially endowed, who cares for contradictions? Nonetheless, since capital punishment has indeed been abolished in many countries, the case for pushing the argument remains a strong one. It may perhaps be a useful reminder to the Hindutva lobby here in India that among those honourable countries is one named Nepal! Three cheers for Nepal.

As part of that case-building, it must be repeatedly underlined that the utilitarian argument – quite apart from the philosophical/humanist one – remains flawed and fallacious.

For example, the death penalty has nowhere deterred the crime of murder. In 1989, Senator Edward Kennedy stated before the House Judiciary Committee:

> Not one of those countries (western democracies) has capital punishment for peacetime crimes, yet everyone of them has a murder rate less than half of the United States.' Likewise, FBI statistics for 1976-1987 state: 'In the twelve states where executions take place, the murder rate

is exactly twice the murder rate of the thirteen states without the death penalty.'

(source: The Information Series on Current Topics: Capital Punishment, Cruel and Unusual?, Wylie:Information Plus, 1998.)

I have on purpose adduced above instances from the United States of America, since our own endowed social groups are rather more prone to acknowledging the truth of anything if it has a US of A label on it. This is a bit sad, because our own Fali Nariman, Shanti Bushan, justice Bhagwati and others have made telling critiques of the logic of capital punishment.

Even when the injunction about the 'rarest of rare' cases is accepted for argument, does the case of Afzal Guru meet that requirement? Here is a clue from what Shanti Bhushan has to say:

> Merely because someone colludes with the actual perpetrators does not mean he/she gets death penalty.
>
> The role of conspirators needs to be assessed. Hundreds were killed in Gujarat after Godhra. Does it mean there would be death penalty for all of them?

Let us recall, for example, that in the Gandhi assassination case, Nathuram Godse, who pulled the trigger, received the death sentence, but his brother, who was intimately part of the conspiracy, did not. Afzal Guru was neither a chief plotter nor a participant in the actual attack on December 13; if provenly anything, he was a sympathetic, small-time facilitator, although guilty nonetheless. Remembering that he seemed not to have received the benefit of legal representation through the trial, one must ask whether the death sentence fits the merits of his case. This speculation independent of the fact that we regard capital punishment for any offence as deeply offensive to the very raison d'être of human existence.

Speaking of which, let us not forget the other troublesome question, that of human error. Michael Radelet counted, since the turn of the century, 343 cases 'in which a defendant facing a possible death penalty was wrongfully convicted. Of these, 137 were sentenced to death, and 25 were actually executed' (Ibid.). Closer at home, Nariman and Bhagwati have persuasively pointed out that the executed Kehar Singh (Indira Gandhi murder case) may actually have been innocent.

As the government of India mulls over the mercy petition submitted by Afzal Guru's family, they would do well to keep all of those things in mind. Most of all, they should remember that in the very same case, as stated earlier, S.A.R. Geelani was pronounced guilty and sentenced to death, only to be subsequently exonerated from all culpability. To return to America: it should be recalled that just recently one of the 9/11 attackers, Zachariah Mossaveih, was not given the death penalty just on the basis that his childhood was too abused to render him wholly responsible. No insanity, mind you, just childhood abuse. This is when he was otherwise found guilty in the first degree.

Or take the case from Peru (*HT*, p.19, Oct.,15): 'Shining Path founder…Guzman, whose messianic communist vision inspired a 12 year rebellion that cost nearly 70,000 lives, was found guilty on Friday of aggravated terrorism and sentenced to life in prison.' Clearly, even Peru with a record more disreputable in many ways seems more enlightened and rational. Let us hope the President reads such news.

As to 'collective conscience', it can work at dangerous cross purposes among different sections of the population, and in different regions of India. If politics are to be a consideration, the largest and the most fruitful view must necessarily be taken of the matter. Such a course would not be out of sync with what far-sighted rulers have done repeatedly in history.

October 2006

India and Nepal

Replicating the wishful follies of the eighteenth century Bourbon monarch, Louis XVI, King Gyanendra Shah of Nepal has finally been denuded of all his powers. It hardly matters now what royal robes he wears; the emperor will henceforth be effectively without clothes. This being 2006 rather than 1793, he might just save his head.

All that has been accomplished by a revolutionary upsurge spearheaded by Nepalese youth. Undeterred by either the 'royal Nepalese army', the subterfuges of 'mainstream' Nepalese polticians, or the not so incipient royalist sympathies of the Indian and American establishments, the Nepalese people may have laid the groundwork for a Republic.

Having brought about a relatively peaceful overthrow of feudal despotism in their own country – in sharp contrast rather to the exertions of elite sections of Indian youth who are now engaged in counter-revolutionary activity to shore up privileges that accrue to them as a consequence of birth and economic status – their achievement may, in fact, bear far-reaching beneficial consequence for India's state and polity as well.

One of the declarations made by the new Nepalese government is that Nepal will no longer be a Hindu theocratic state but a 'secular' one. This causes an enormous problem for the Hindu right (led by the RSS) in India whose project ever since its establishment in 1925 has been to transform India into a Hindu Rashtra, even as it has also been their oxymoronic boast that India's preponderant Hindu majority *ipso facto* renders it a secular nation. The declaration in Nepal, however, clearly implies that the Nepalese state has not been a 'secular' state thus far, regardless of its preponderant Hindu population. A statement made by the senior BJP (the political/electoral front of the RSS) leader, V.K.Malhotra (*The Hindu*, May 20) regretting the Nepalese declaration is based on the assumption that 'Hindu' and 'Secular' are interchangeable concepts. Never mind that the anti-minority pogrom of 2002 in Gujarat under Narendra Modi busted this pretence sky-high.

Recorded ideological facts, however, belie this boast. Long before Jinnah the founder of Pakistan, stipulated that Hindus and Muslims constituted separate 'nations,'and asked for a separate Muslim state (1940), it was the Hindutva ideologue, Savarkar, who had expressed this theory first (1923). He laid the hypothesis that only those who were both born in India (*pitra bhumi*) and bore allegiance to forms of religion 'indigenous' to India (*punya bhumi*) could be considered 'Indian.' Muslims and Christians were thus excluded from 'Indianness', since their chief places of worship lay outside the territory of India. Following upon that, Golwalkar, the then RSS chief (or *Sarsangchalak*) in a pernicious book, *We, or Our Nationhood Defined* (1939), which unabashedly lauded the Nazis for having elevated 'race pride' to unprecedented heights, warned India's religious minorities in no uncertain terms that unless they learnt to subjugate themselves wholly and without demur to dominant Hindu culture, and venerated Hindu gods, all their rights, including those of citizenship, would be denied them in the stipulated Hindu Rashtra (Hindu theocratic state).

In fact, just recently, another deeply embarrassing chapter has been added to the Goebbelsian history of the RSS/BJP: In a volume (*RSS Aur Bharatiya Jan Sangh ki Sthapna ka Itihas* – RSS and the History of the Establishment of the Jana Sangh), one of several commissioned by the Hindu right to commemorate the silver jubilee of the existence of the BJP, the authors (both RSS insiders), Makhan Lal and J.K. Mathur, have forthrightly inscribed the truth that the RSS and the Jan Sangh – the predecessor of the BJP – were created to 'counter the Muslims.'Having in recent years charged India's secular historians of 'distorting' Indian history, the RSS now claims its own history has been distorted by its own historians! Never mind that they spoke the plain truth.

Ever since India's Independence in 1947, thus, the Hindu right in India, led by the RSS, has refused allegiance to either the secular Indian Constitution or the national flag, the Tricolour. This despite the fact that such allegiance was enjoined upon them by the post-Independence government led by Nehru as quid pro quo to the release of their leaders from incarceration which had resulted from suspicion of their involvement in the conspiracy to murder Gandhi in 1948.

When the eastern wing of Pakistan seceded in 1971 to establish an independent Bangladesh, despite a shared religious affiliation, the world had resonant proof that a common religion alone could not be a viable basis for state-formation. Much as the RSS then applauded Pakistan's break-up, the larger lesson was lost on it. It thus continued to view Nepal, a Hindu theocratic state, as an object of its own dreams, and the King as a veritable avatar of the Hindu god, Vishnu. The new development in Nepal has thus driven a stake not just through the Nepalese theocratic monarchy but the RSS as well, just at it has lent force to all those in India who have maintained that only a secular and pluralist India can be a modern and viable India. Furthermore, one of the chief accusations of the RSS against India's Congress Party (which had led the struggle for independence from colonial rule), has been that it has always engaged in pampering India's religious minorities, chiefly the Muslims. The RSS calls this the Congress's 'minorityism.' With news coming now from the new Nepal that provisions will be enshrined there as well for protective and enabling laws in the interests of Nepalese ethnic and religious minorities, the RSS has lost another one of its major propaganda mechanisms against India's secular parties.

All in all, the Nepalese events bear a resonance that stretches way beyond life in Nepal. Indeed, these lessons need not be restricted only to the RSS in India; they seem of equal relevance to large parts of the world where Islamic ideologues seek to deny secular, democratic forms of statehood, and perhaps also to the new crop of born-again Evangelists in America whose vision of statehood in recent years has not, after all, been too different from that of those whom they seek to defeat.

June 2006

India, Nepal, and Left Praxis

In an earlier piece suggestions were made with respect to the implications of the Nepalese revolutionary upsurge for the idea of the theocratic state.

That upsurge also has an important bearing upon the practice of left politics in India. It would be intellectually remiss of India's Maoists to simply ignore the enormous significance of the choice that their counterparts in Nepal have made. Just as it would also be somewhat snooty of the two main communist parties of India not to press the implications of the Nepal happening to strive for broader left unity.

First: it must be a question in many minds, although no enunciation of this is yet in evidence, as to why the Maoists in Nepal did not choose to push the revolution to its logical conclusion. The relevance of the question seems obvious enough, given that the Prachanda-led revolutionaries are deemed to be already in physical control of more than half of the territory of Nepal. It might then have been a strong impulse to bypass any collaboration with bourgeois-democratic forces, represented by the Parliamentary parties, whose clout among the masses has over the years been rather severely depleted both by their own internecine squabbles and their ambiguous stance on the feudal, theocratic monarchy.

Three primary considerations – one pertaining to objective, domestic conditions, and the other two to qualitative changes in international realities – may have weighed with the Maoist leadership in Nepal.

Considering Nepal's current stage of social development, an astute leadership with its ear to the ground may have concluded that carrying the armed struggle rapidly forward in the face of a continued dominance of feudal cultural forms and of a long-standing superstructure of religious conditioning could have jeopardized the end result for lack of requisite ideological preparation among all sections of the Nepalese polity. That only a miniscule of labour power in that country could be characterized as proletarian could also not but have been a factor.

Let us recall what Lenin wrote on such matters in 1920:

> With regard to the more backward states and nations, in which feudal or patriarchal and patriarchal-peasant relations predominate, it is particularly important to bear in mind: first, that all communist parties must assist the bourgeois democratic liberation movement in those countries...second, the need for a struggle against the clergy and other influential reactionary and medieval elements in backward countries; third, the need to combat Pan-Islamism and similar trends, which strive to combine the liberation movement...with an attempt to strengthen the positions of the khans, landowners, mullahs, etc.[1]

Obviously, this needs gloss and caveat. In the Nepalese context, the 'liberation' that Lenin speaks of did not originate from the bourgeois democratic parties but from the Maoists, although, for that reason, it would have been dangerously short-sighted of the Maoists to have disregarded the bourgeois-landlord parties altogether at the present stage of the struggle. Secondly, the upsurge was not against western imperialism directly but first through its lackey, the monarchy. That said, Lenin's description of backwardness would seem to fit the Nepalese social situation quite handsomely still. Secondly, in the case of Nepal, the 'khans' and the 'mullahs' would need to be substituted by the 'purohit'(priesthood) and the 'matts' (Hindu religious institutions).

On a wider scale, the Maoists would have made the evaluation that the international zeitgeist at the present historical moment diverges momentously from that which obtained either in the thirtees or forties or fifties of the last century when the revolutions were made in China and Cuba. It might thus have been a pretty bad idea to provoke bedlam in an already berserk American imperialism – and their obliging compradors next door – which nowadays seeks the least irrational reason to see red and drop the cluster bombs.

Most importantly, and this cannot be emphasized enough, the Nepalese Maoists seem to have grasped the far-reaching dividends of

---

1 Preliminary Draft Theses on the National and the Colonial Questions for the second Congress of the Comintern, published in *Communist International,* No.11, July 14, 1920.

another kind of praxis now being increasingly adopted by left forces worldwide. Assured of wide-ranging mass support, thanks to the unprecedented oppression wrought by 'globalisation,' they seem to have recognized that the most effective way at the present juncture to counter and neutralize imperialist designs is to acquire overground legitimacy through the ballot box. Clearly, American imperialism is most frustrated today by the fact that regime after regime in Latin America has successfully obtained such legitimacy, not to forget the Hamas in Palestine. Peoples' Democratic Revolutions (what Chavez calls the 'Bolivarian' phenomenon) clearly thus represent a powerful left response to a zeitgeist wherein the coordinates of the 'cold war' stand off are no longer available to hold off American imperialism. The latter is therefore best checkmated upon its own much-trumpeted terms, namely, 'democracy,' even as its own democratic credentials everyday suffer terminal degradation at home.

The Nepalese Maoists have thus, for now at least, paid a compliment to India's Communist Parties and taken the electoral/parliamentary route. In consonance with Lenin's stipulations, there is a recognition here that where social organization teeters on the feudal or the communal-fascist, communists have the all-important task of protecting the more progressive aspects of bourgeois development, while striving to forge mass awareness and mass movements that can promise further advances by bringing greater and more diverse numbers into the Peoples' Democratic Revolution. It is in this sense that the seventh continuous victory of the left coalition in West Bengal carries a symbolic import that may otherwise fall short of concrete socialistic transformations on the ground.

India's Maoists, engaged in armed resistance to the state, then, must answer some hard questions to themselves. There can be no gainsaying that their battles on behalf of the landless and the dispossessed tribal populations have been heroic. In many areas where they exercise near-total hegemony, they have, apart from the forcible appropriation of land, affected exemplary social reconstruction. They have established schools where none existed, and set up irrigation systems that the state has failed to provide six decades after national independence.

The larger question, however, remains. Given a world-wide endorsement of the legitimacy of state violence and the paucity of regimes willing any longer to aid armed revolutions in other countries on the one hand, and, on the other, the deepening of democratic consciousness among India's working people and oppressed masses, coupled with their willingness to agitate, is it not perhaps time to join those others in many parts of the world who are opting for the Peoples Democratic Revolutionary path? At a time when the left coalition wields some clout over governance in India, such a bold rethink would seem feasible for obvious reasons.

Were such an eventuality to come about, the task of all left forces would be to understand what assets they bring to the left collective – an exercise which would need to proceed without self-regard or any perceived loss of self-esteem. Clearly, large parts of the country, beyond West Bengal and Kerala, could become theatres of people's participation towards the forging of a truly democratic politics. A United Communist Party of India could genuinely aspire to transform the character of the Indian parliament; from whence much else could follow. Let me conclude with some further wise words from Lenin:

> Complete victory over capitalism cannot be won unless the proletariat, and following it, the mass of working people…voluntarily strive for alliance and unity.[2]

After all, the last thing that India's immiserated masses deserve is a communist movement fragmented in half a dozen different formations along diverse practices.

June 2006

2 Ibid.

Back to a Better Version of Reform

Although the custodians of 'ruling ideas' seek always to lend 'universal' weight to concepts that suit them, it remains a truism of common human experience that the same words across changing histories do not mean the same thing. The same script and the same words come to yield a different language. As we know, Derridean post-structuralist theory was to put this common perception on a sound theoretical footing, beginning some three decades ago, even as the redoubtable Raymond Williams was to catalogue semantic transformations of language -use in his painstakingly remarkable work, Keywords (1976).

When capitalism still struggled with older forms of social organization, the word 'love' was frequently used to imply love of other human beings or of god. Rarely did such loving have conquest for its telos; often its richness of content had to do with selflessness and sacrifice (witness the Hindi cinema of the 1940s and 1950s). Some sixty years after, the noun phrase 'I love' is likely to indicate for its predicate a new brand of soft drink, or shoes, or automobile.

As to other human beings, we now do not 'love'; we enter into 'relationships' with due thought to securing individual preoccupation and individual 'space.'

Think that the word 'sentiment' likewise has come to be dissociated from human contexts and attached to the stock market – bullish or bearish 'sentiment' as the case may be. Gone are the days when novelists wrote the novel of sentiment, or sportsmen and women played games for fun. Indeed, just as 'sentiment' has gone over to Wall Street and other bourses, 'players' now have reference to tycoons who plough the exciting world of capital.

Or the word 'subtle': often when Shakespeare used the word, as in a 'subtle Venetian', the inference to be drawn was one of fickleness and deception. Now we know subtlety to be a valorized virtue, a subtle argument always preferable to a blunt assertion. Likewise, at one time being 'competitive' carried largely negative connotations, implying a tendency to snatch and grab, till the culture of capitalism raised it to mean 'efficient.' To be competitive suggests a will to 'win'. And in a somewhat unsubtle American parlance, where the world is seen to be divided between 'winners' and 'losers', always better to be 'competitive.' Always better to win at any cost, one must add.

What about the word 'reform' that now screams at us routinely from newspaper leads and television sound bytes? 'Reform' we are meant to understand connotes just that single sum of political perceptions which came to be encoded in the 'Washington Consensus' of 1990. At the heart of its ten-point iteration resides the following article of belief:

> Development – economic, social and sustainable – without an effective state – not a minimal on – is central to economic and social development....states should work to complement markets, not replace them.
>
> (*World Bank Report*, 1997, p.18)

Thus 'reform,' allegedly applicable the world-over, is foregrounded uncontroversially as the single, inevitable precondition of the advancement of the human race. 'Reform' we are to understand requires neutering the state, replacing it by the market, transfering wealth from public to private control, eliminating investment in the social sector, and reducing fiscal deficit ideally by curtailing employment in the first place. And if such 'reform' exacerbates poverty and inequality we are equally to understand that this is but a necessary stage to the Eldorado that 'growth' untrammeled by social concerns promises to everyone.

And yet, at the inaugural moment of industrial capitalism (1830s onwards), the demand for 'reform' meant just the opposite of what it has come to mean today.

Assessing the humongous economic and social distress caused by the new dominance of manufacturing over agriculture (as England was coming to be the 'workshop of the world'), many distinguished writers and thinkers who endorsed the idea of 'progress' nevertheless enjoined upon the state to exert itself on behalf of the 'losers'. One of the first to write a three-volume history of the French Revolution, Thomas Carlyle veritably screamed his caution that if the new ruling class in Britain ignored 'reform' what had happened in France was surely waiting to happen in Britain. So did Charles Dickens, the Christian and Utopian Socialists, and the more canny among the ruling Whigs. 'Reform' became a battle cry not for the liquidation of the state but for the exercise of its powers to effect 'amelioration' in what Carlyle captioned 'the condition of England.' Even the good Tory, Disraeli, noted that, in fact, England was no longer one nation but two – torn between the haves and the have-nots, underlining a useful role for the state in the circumstances.

Fortunately, at that point neither the IMF nor the World Bank existed, and the neocons of the day had somewhat greater human sensitivity than their progeny of the 21st century. All that helped produce the great Reform Bills of 1832, 1867, and 1887. Together, through such legislative measures backed up by consonant executive actions, the state extended franchise, granted rights of unionisaton (where 'Combination Acts' had repeatedly sought to curb association), narrowed income disparities, raised wages, passed the first Education Act (1870) to regulate a brutalized and commercialized private school system, and reduced unemployment. Cunningly, such measures helped put British capitalism on a more secure footing. (See Patrick Bratlinger, The Spirit of Reform: British Literature and Politics, 1832-1867, Harvard University Press, Cambridge, Mass. 1977).

As the learned Indian Prime Minister comes away rather shell-shocked by what he has heard and seen in Vidharba, a cotton-growing region of the prosperous state of Maharashtra where farmers have been committing suicide by the hundreds, it is time perhaps for the great economist to recall that 'reform' need not mean just what the 'Washington Consensus,' inspired by trans-national corporations and their front international finance agencies, says it does. Certainly, the non-specialist intellectual, Nehru, seemed to have a far more canny understanding of the role of the state in devising 'reforms' appropriate to a country like India. What Manmohan Singh needs to recognize, especially after his traumatic Vidharba visit, is that the conditions that Nehru was addressing may have improved for some miniscule percentage of Indians under the aegis of the 'Washington Consensus' version of 'reform' but have worsened immeasurably for the majority. This recognition ought to be compelling enough to switch from the current notion of 'reform' to an earlier and better one.

Indeed, this will involve reforming the notion of 'reform' itself – much in the sense in which Martin Luther had sought to 'reform' the corrupted Church, to wit, to 'restore' the institution to a lost purity of purpose. In this case, the instituton of the state itself.

A continued uncritical devotion to the current notion of 'reform' could also, of course, produce the cosequence that Carlyle had spoken of in the 1830s: it could yield the French Revolution here at home, even if through the ballot box, although one can never tell. Our admittedly humane and piety-ridden head of government then has the task of persuading his scholarly Finance Minister and the rather jauntily free-marketing vice chairman of planning as well that the state has uses that do not pertain merely to fattening the fatsos and repressing the labouring, but sparing some thought towards those who produce wealth for the nation.

It is also noteworthy that the President of the party to which the Prime Minister belongs seems far more attuned to the Indian zeitgeist than the government he runs. Something for the government to think about before it is too late.

July 2006

We the People

In perhaps the first public statement he made after the event of December 13, 2001 when the Indian Parliament became the target of a terrorist attack, (although there are those who still speculate about who the real attackers might have been), the then Home Minister defined the occurence as an attack on 'democracy.' This was good to hear for two reasons: one, as an expression of Advani's commitment to the idea of democracy, (something that his infamous role in the vandalized demolition of the Babri mosque in 1992 had put into serious question) and, second, for the potential that such characterisation of the attack bore for addressing the problem of terrorism. As we know, George W.Bush was to characterize the attack on the twin towers in very similar terms.

Insofar as terrorism tends to be seen as a regimented mind-set that views democracy as chief anathema, it invites us to revisit the idea of democracy, inorder that we may remind ourselves of its defining substance and strength – things that we tend to lose sight of until they are violently challenged.

Consider that of the many ways in which the movement of world history may be conceptualised, the most meaningful, perhaps, would be to see how through the millenia the legitimising ground of social and political power has shifted from the primitive man's animal strength to the general will of 'we the people.' Defeating, through the ages, partial and irrational claims – physical male prowess, brahminical/papal fiat, the king's so-called 'divine right', the privilege of birth or the colour of skin, or the notion of endorsed inequality based on caste, race, gender or class – the idea of democracy has, in large parts of the world, attained to the acceptance of citizenship and universal franchise. That such an achievement has often proceeded through bloody contest and struggle and against every entrenched odd testifies to the inherent force of the idea of democracy.

This is not to say that with the democracies that now obtain in the world, history has come to an end; for the simple reason that so long as these democracies remain partial and inequitous, the idea of democracy cannot be said to have exhausted itself. Indeed, many of the contentions the world is now witness to may be ascribed to the unfinished agenda of democracy. For instance, do we know that half of the world's population – its women – still remain excluded from some 98% of ownership and political power, regional variations notwithstanding?

Clearly, though, history's will towards the enlargement and enrichment of the idea of equity and freedom seems, to borrow from the American poet, Whitman, like the grass which is unstoppable, regardless of how much we trample on it. This idea, however thwarted, now by the pampered bigot who bears proximity to the state, now by the full-blown terrorist, often indeed by the very people who derive legitimacy from it as they govern in sectarian, often brutal and self-righteous ways, must be inherently right as it aspires to a full human rationality. Clearly, if it has prevailed upto now, it cannot but prevail in the future as well, precisely as does the method we call science. That such 'positivist' faith flies in the face of 'postmodernist' dithering need not worry us too greatly here, since 'postmodernism' can be understood as only a new, enticing attempt to stop us in our tracks as we seek to assist the further march of the idea of democracy.

Like all other ideas, the rationality of the democratic idea expresses itself not mechanically but through the incessant enquiry and self-criticism of individuals and of whole groups, (since the time of Pericles' Athens) in or out of political control, and through the collective struggles against those that constantly seek to stifle it. The regimented terrorist and bigot – who is only a terrorist-in-the- making, or as recent times show, ensconsced in the seat of preeminent power – is thus understandably most in fear of this march of reason and enquiry. It follows, therefore, that nothing would please the bigot or the terrorist as much as to see democracy cower, and doubt its power to confront and defeat the regimented mind of its adversary, or to compel democratic states to pay the ultimate compliment to terrorism by becoming terrorising states themselves.

If the soundness of that premise is conceded, it follows that governments the world-over that protest democratic pretensions must resist the temptation to make their own contribution to the attack on democracy. This will require that sentient distinction is made between civic discipline and whatever measures may be needed to encourage each citizens' voluntary contribution to protecting democracy on the one hand, and, on the other, coercive laws which instead of reinforcing democracy add their bit to snuffing it out. For it must be recognized that however attractive such recourses seem in the short term, their long term fall out strengthens not democracy but terrorist impulse of one kind or the other.

After all, those well-known regimes in world history – especially of the first half of the last century – who sought to make terror the principle of governance were not defeated by counter-terror but by the power of democratic reason and resolve. (And when that resolve exceeded itself in the gratuitous use of the atom bomb in 1945, that excess left a poisonous residue which democratic struggles still contend with. Indeed, it is doubtful that the world has known a terrorist event worse than was visited on the innocent children, women, and men in Hiroshima and Nagasaki.)

This, above all, has been the outstanding reality of India's collective, democratic, and nonviolent success against colonisation – a lesson never to be forgotten. Could then there be a more trenchant historical irony than that ,on the one hand, our freedom movement should have galvanized in the struggle against the draconian Rowlatt Act (1919), whereby the then colonial government, after all, sought to cancel the fundamental freedoms of free expression and association, and, on the other, that the National Democratic Alliance led by Vajpayee should have, when we are independent, imposed upon ourselves a law (Prevention of Terrorism Act – POTA – now thankfully repealed) infinitely more sinister and suffocating? Or, that America's 'war on terror' should have yielded a slew of executive measures, and many clandestine fiats that have threatened to nullify the high principles of constitutional democracy and the ideal of 'freedom' itself in the United States? Indeed a fine instance that, ignoring such ideals, we soon enough become mirror images of those we paint our adversary 'others.'

The exercise of democratic reason and resolve, thus, crucially depends on the quality of credibility that governments are able to command. Uncritical and opportunist calls for national unity in times of crisis based on a sectarian and disingenuous appropriation of patriotism, even as we divide the nation and the world on exclusionist social and religious premises of the time can hardly be trusted to draw unqualified allegiance.

Likewise, the selective application of laws already in place where social, religious, or political prejudice is made the determinant of action cannot but yield resentment and disunity. A bigoted deriding of dissent on the unviable ground that the government of the day alone is the trustworthy custodian of national honour and well-being weakens the idea of democracy and engenders crippling residues for the future.

Finally, beyond reworking the mechanisms of the state-apparatus, beyond reformulating the laws of the land, beyond playing the blame game, beyond seeking outside approval, the answers to domestic or international discontent must be sought selflessly in the wrongs that may have been perpetrated at home and abroad. History helps us most when we face its lessons with honest willingness. And if we do not, its retributions can indeed be relentless.

Is it perhaps not the case that having demanded and won freedom and democracy from our colonisers, we in India kept the true substance of freedom and democracy confined to but a privileged few? The sort of question that remains alive in the great democracy of America as well when something like the Katrina episode cruelly exposes the narrow confines of its convictions and operations.

Do we strengthen democracy when we allow the organised gangster or professional shister close to the corridors of power to rob sections of the demos of the right to vote come election time? Or connive at polluting our electoral rules – that basic sacred text of democracy? Or when we seek to do a Florida in Mexico?

Do we strengthen democracy when we protect those who go about with impunity claiming absolute status for their particular version of truth, and who exercise brute terror to enforce that perception in contemptuous disregard for the Constitution that 'we the people' gave to ourselves as the agreed testament upon which to base our democratic practices and laws? Or those who oppress and deny whole peoples and countries inorder to favour others who do their bidding or serve their narrow interests? Until, with further twists and turns of cupidity, the latter come to be seen as the new adversaries? Do we strengthen democracy when our policy and governance blatantly favour those who already have several times more than they need while 'we the people' struggle against all odds to make two ends meet? Do we strengthen democracy when we restrict education to those who have the wealth to pay, consigning millions to the darkness and the drudgery of the struggle for existence? Or when we turn our faces on the millions of destitute children whom the mere accident of birth robs of the joys of childhood? Or when we slash taxes for the rich while increasing the burden on 'we the people,' even as we fight our causes in their name?

Do we strengthen democracy when we hoard our godowns or allow forward trading in food grains but, upon some esoteric economic principle, will not feed those who suffer starvation and malnutrition, and who then commit suicide by the thousands because they cannot pay their measly debts while the fatcats merrily refuse to pay back the millions they owe? And all because such considerations do not enter into our definition of democracy.

Do we strengthen democracy when we displace people from hearth and home because large dams and other ecological disasters have to be built inorder to meet the requirements of some self-evidently transcendant economic doctrine – even if, as a result, we further annihilate the core idea of democracy, namely, equity?

Do we strengthen democracy when we view such questions with suspicion and disdain while we ask that our people waive the flag and sing hymns to our national honour?

The question, therefore, must be asked: is it only the terrorist who aims shafts at our democracy, or are we, after all, the principal guilty party? Indeed, rather than be shelved for some leisurely, future time, the current crises of the world community require that we honestly confront and answer that question.

Should we do so with collective resolve, and with a will to embrace democracy in its full demand, we may yet stave off catastrophes that lie in wait; should we fail to do so, thinking that mere fatuous and self-regarding cunning, disingenuous rationalizations, or high-sounding accusations hurled at the other party will save us the day, or mount patently illegal and beastly wars upon the most innocent and the most helpless, we live in fool's paradise. Eventually, such failure will only make us the witting or unwitting accomplices of the terrorist, and no security arrangement, no stringent anti-terrorist legislation, no 'international opinion', and no divine dispensation will help us meet the wrath of democracy deflected from its true purpose and essence. If the demons of destruction then visit their wrath upon us, we will have only ourselves to thank for the eventuality.

July 2006

Indian Muslims

Prospects and Ways Forward

My chief concern here is to understand the situation of Muslims in India. But, to the extent that the issue is inevitably affected by the condition of Muslims world-wide, it is relevant to take note of factors that impinge upon that condition even at the risk of enumerating a critique that is by now often made and well-recognized. The truth needs as much repeating as the lie, especially when the lie has the backing of imperialist money and muscle.

First a word about the villainous propogation that a 'clash of civilizations' is now underway, globally.

Nobody but the indubitably partisan is any more taken in by the reification-in-reverse, as it were, whereby American imperialism, unimpeded by any concerted, state-level opposition, seeks to fetishize its untrammeled material ambitions in the resource-rich middle and west Asian regions principally as a purely ideological crusade on behalf of 'freedom.'

This despicable subterfuge requires that Islam be recast as a theoretical breeding ground of 'jihadis' ; this for the simple enough reason that the preponderant population in these oil-rich regions is Muslim. Thus, nationalists throughout this region engaged in a life-and-death struggle to secure the rights of sovereignty need to be christened 'terrorists.' Never mind that both Hamas and Hizbollah owe their political legitimacy to massive electoral victories, duly 'certified' by reputed international agencies. Never mind also that American imperialism is hard put to find any 'terrorist' Islamism in a Wahabi Saudi Arabia, even though all of the protagonists who brought the twin towers down were of Saudi extraction. Nor, for that matter, are the neocons able to see Pakistan as a centerpiece in the 'Islamic' terrorist business. Or Musharraf as a military dictator who seems determined to hijack the promise of Pakistani democracy for ever and ever.

Clearly, for an American President who is widely suspected by his own countrymen of having stolen both his electoral victories, the 'democracy' slogan is just one instrument of imperialist designs.

It needs to be recalled that the pioneers in the 'terrorist' way of doing things were the Israelis. Scholarship, including the Wikipedia, has given us an elaborate record of the modus operandi of the Zionist Irgun and Stern terrorist groups – spearheaded by such respectable worthies as Menachem Begin, Yitzhak Shamir, and Ariel Sharon – in their fight to dislodge the British from their mandate in Palestine. Those modus operandi included the cold-blooded murders of diplomats and United Nations' officials, not to speak of the bombing of the King David Hotel in which more than ninety innocent people were blown to smithereens and many more maimed for life. Scholarhip also records that these terrorists took their stand as much on religion as the jihadis of our day.

Is it also not rather cute that while a prospective Iranian nuclear capability is sought to be sold to the 'international community' as the central source of menace for the world community, the well-known Israeli arsenal is never mentioned. Remember that Osama bin Laden and the Taliban were not viewed as 'terrorist' material while the principal contradiction of American imperialism was with the Soviets in Afghanistan. Once, however, that contradiction shifted course, yesterdays' 'freedom fighters' became todays' 'terrorists.' Or that the 'war on terror' should have been launched in Iraq which was notably the one truly secular state in the whole region. That the invasion of Iraq has now successfully converted that country into a jihadi hub goes of course to speak to the criminal accountability of the Americans in the matter, and to an imperialist folly that bids fair to destroy civilized governance throughout the world. There must be some reason after all why already some 85% Lebanese today call themselves Hizbollah as opposed to some 50% before the current Israeli invasion. And that includes the Lebanese Christians as well. Or why Maliki, the puppet prime minister of a 'free' Iraq has felt humiliated enough now to take issue with the continuing brutalities of the Bush regime in complete disregard of the so-called Iraqi government.

Having said that, if there is a clash now underway it is between those who advocate adherence to the principles of the Westphalian Treaty (1645) that guarantees the sovereignty of nation-states and non-interference in each other's internal affairs, and to the United Nations Charter which was drawn up by the world community to establish peaceful co-existence among nations and a non-recourse to violence and war as instruments of the redressal of disputes, on the one hand, and those others whose desire for global domination seeks to make mince-meat of both the Westphalian Treaty and the U.N.Charter.

And this clash today is nowhere more in evidence than within America itself. Never have Americans been as vertically divided 'between the reds and the blues' since the Civil War as they are today. By the latest reckoning, some 60% Americans would be considered 'anti-national' by the Bush administration! Having now christened the term 'Islamic fascism' Bush has had to be at the receiving end of important articles in the American media that have asked whether this may not be a case of the pot calling the kettle black.

Same is true of people who inhabit the 'Muslim' world. Despite the heinous depredations wrought everyday by the neocon 'vision' of a new world order – whereby American Imperialism arrogates to itself the right to preemptive war, to regime changes in other countries, and to full-scale global dominance' in the middle and west Asian region, and wherever else people seek to resist that evil 'vision,' Muslims are everywhere divided between those who think such resistance can succeed only through an assymetrical guerrilla war, and those who still wish to adhere to democratic, institutional mechanisms to force reason and sanity upon an imperialism gone berserk, or who desire to see a consolidation of state-level resistance to American imperialism.

On each side, of course, it suits the war-mongers to homogenize disparate, dissident, contentious identities and positions and complex political and intellectual considerations into crusading binaries – the regime, as it were, of a born-again Christianity against the injunctions of Allah. That the vast majority of the world's population knows this to be, nonetheless, a war, on one hand, for the control of the world's material resources and, on the other, for resisting that imperial agenda is by now obvious enough.

Indeed, this contention between the homogenizing political project and the concrete pluralities on the ground that demand democratic cognition lies at the root of much that has gone on in India during the last two decades.

Since the implementation of the recommendations of the Mandal Commissiion by the V.P.Singh government (1989) 'recommendations that, deriving from the Constitution, recognized caste affiliation rather than an undifferentiated religious one as the basic social unit of identity among Hindus' a crusade on behalf of Brahminical Hinduism ensued.

Clearly, the object of that crusade has been to reconstitute Hindus across social contradictions as the dominant 'majority' that then seeks to supplant the notion that a majority in a republican democracy can only comprise franchised 'citizens,' a circumstance which, in turn, feeds directly into minority-bashing. Thus the Brahminical upper-caste crusade against affirmative action on behalf of deprived castes curiously yields the politics of communalism. This despite the fact that the BJP has never yet polled more than 26% of the national vote at any general election. Considering that not more than 5% Muslims have ever voted for the party, the BJP thus fails to draw the allegiance of some 70% or more of voting Hindus. As in America now, the chief political divide in India has been between high-caste Hindus who seek to force their vision of the nation on the Republic and the great majority of Hindus who refuse that fascist imposition. Hence the 'cultural nationalism' of the Brahminical minority remains in clash with Hindus whose allegiance to the constitutional scheme remains in place.

Likewise, despite the beleaguered attempts of religious Muslim leaderships to cast India's Muslims into a monolithic block, the often-peddled notion of a 'minority vote bank' remains an interested myth. At no point during India's political history of the last three decades have Indian Muslims voted enmasse for any one single political party. Muslims have tended to vote only for such candidates who they have thought equipped to defeat the Hindu right. Such a voting pattern has inevitably meant that Muslims have often voted against many Muslim candidates along a diverse spectrum of parties in diverse electoral constituencies.

Post the recent train blasts in Mumbai, majoritarian fascism seeks once again to replicate the imperialist myth that 'terrorism' is an exclusively Muslim phenomenon. Note that one has never heard the RSS, which is itself listed as a 'terrorist' organization in an important American website, speak of LTTE terrorism as Hindus terrorism. Nor does one ever hear Christian or Jewish terrorism mentioned, although Wikipedia conscientiously records elaborate instances of both. Consider also the deep irony that Independent India's most memorably high-placed losses to terrorism have all been perpetrated by non-Muslim agents: Mahatma Gandhi was assassinated by a Brahmin, Indira Gandhi by a Sikh, and Rajiv Gandhi again by a Hindu LTTE assassin. It should also be noted that the many instances of espionage against the nation-state that have come to light in recent years have all involved non-Muslims; surely, treason can hardly be argued to constitute an offence less heinous than a 'terrorist' act. Currently, as we know, a nationalist scion of the BJP – an ex-minister several times over – continues his refusal to share his self-confessed knowledge of espionage activity on behalf of the Americans. Yet, nobody seems particularly bothered.

Understandably, Indian Muslims once again find themselves under siege, as day in and day out they are hauled up at any odd hour of day or night to answer to the most far-fetched suspicions. Muslim intellectuals, therefore, once again debate among themselves what new political expression the thwarted history of the community should now draw on, given that successive governments, including secular ones, have tended to leave their genuine material aspirations in limbo. Be it education, employment (especially in the army, police and higher bureaucracy) or traditional livelihoods in skills and crafts, or their share in property ownership, Indian Muslims find themselves at the bottom of the social rung, just as Gujarat-like episodes that repeatedly bring to light the complicity of official mechanisms, including state-aaparatus, with 'majoritarian' rioters, city after city, with the honourable exception of India's southern states, leave them fearing for their life and limb. Consequent ghettoisation of the community, both in terms of living conditions and an ideological inwardness that willy nilly collapses into religious identity causes a paralysis of initiative that is often easy to deride but difficult to redress. Younger Muslims, not burdened by any direct memories of India's partition, who aspire to seek for a future as authentic Indian citizens beyond mere physical security chaff at the failure of political choices the community elders have thus far tended to exercise. Even as episodes like the demolition of the Babri masjid and the Gujarat genocide fan the impulse to violent reassertion. That such an impulse has not come to any significant expression is of course a defining tribute to the specific formation of Islam in India, but a circumstance that ought not, however, to lull us into complacence.

What, then, is to be done? Easier asked than answered. The first important thing to recognize here is that whatever it is that ought to be done does not have to be done by India's Muslims alone. The temptation, therefore, to be holier-than-thou must be resisted because such a frame of reference in itself bespeaks a flawed grasp of what is wrong in the first place.

The doing necessarily must involve the following agencies, at the least: various organs of the state; English and Hindi media agencies (both print and visual); secular Indians across the board (which is to say some three fourths of citizens); Indian Muslims, who, like Indian Hindus or Sikhs, are not a homogenous monolith.

Briefly, ritual protestations notwithstanding, it remains an ugly fact that the police apparatus in the northern states of India seems invariably to reserve its sub-liminal brutal antipathy for India's Muslims, a reality that has been repeatedly recorded whenever communal clashes take place. Just to cite one episode, at Hashimpora the Provincial Armed Constabulary (PAC) a decade or so ago shot in the head some forty five Muslims in cold blood and dumped the corpses, one by one, in a canal nearby. It still remains to be seen what punishment the judicial system metes out to these murderers. Even as it is true that working class factory protesters are also routinely caned and bashed by the PAC, the emotion that informs official violence against Muslim Indians in these states flows out of a mind-set that holds Muslims responsible for the partition of India, and thus regards them as guilty and inauthentic members of the republic, however just their cause.

The larger failure of the state clearly involves the complicity of governments in their disinterest in delivering, and seen to be delivering, the same kind of justice to rioters and killers that are drawn from the majority community as is promptly handed out to Muslims on the instant. There is perhaps no more blatant instance of this from recent history than the contrast in the way the findings of the Srikrishna Commission that enquired into the communal carnage in Mumbai prior to the 1993 bomb blasts, and the subsequent bomb blast accused case have been treated. The Srikrishna report which forthrightly held many senior officers and top-level political leaders guilty has remained rather unheard and shelved, while the state and the media that is equally complicit await with glee the judgement in the bomb blast cases.

Nor should it be overlooked that the massacre that took place in Gujarat in 2002 was followed by the refusal to file FIRs or file them in distorted ways, leading to the closure of thousands of cases even where eye-witnesses were willing to make disclosures. That some of the most gruesome ones were reopened and sent off for trial in other states, unprecedented in itself, testifies of course to the odyssey undertaken on behalf of the victims by civil society organizations like the Citizens for Justice and Peace, led by the outstanding Teesta Setalvad.

This predilection undermines in the gravest extent the faith that Muslims seek to repose in the secular democratic state. Such a collapse of credibility, needless to say, can in time become the prime factor for persuading Indian Muslims that they must seek justice by other means.

Wide interaction with Muslims reinforces the truth that this treatment is not the least of reasons why, unlike other sections of society, Muslim Indians have grave forebodings about mounting any organized public protests on issues of concern. Clearly, given this reality, it is grossly hypocritical and disingenuous to accuse Muslims of shying away from asserting their democratic rights through mass mobilization. Those elements within the state who still refuse equal 'citizenship' rights to Muslims are much happier if Muslim demands of the republic turn into a seething cauldron of resentment. Once thus isolated, they can then the more easily be labeled as a potential danger to the nation. It is a remarkable statistic that under the draconian anti-terrorist legislation (TADA, repealed by the UPA government), more than 90% detenues were Muslims; when it is recalled that the total conviction rate under this act was all of 1%, it can be understood what political uses the act was put to.

As to the media, it is a grave indictment that the only time they seem to notice Muslim life in India is when 'terrorism' is under discussion. It is an agonized Muslim complaint that even as ignorant anchors and suchlike cavalierly berate Muslims for not standing firmly against 'terrorism' they almost never deign to report any one of umpteen instances of common and organized Muslim condemnations of the phenomenon, barring the exception of the Urdu media. Any one who watches ETV Urdu, a profoundly thought-provoking channel that analyses and debates issues that concern the community and the nation in such programmes as *Hamare Masail*, will know the depths of prejudice and ignorance that vitiate the mainline English and Hindi channels about the lives of some 130 million Indians! Indeed, this writer would make it mandatory for these channels to watch ETV Urdu, and to order back numbers of *Hamare Masail* for an educative introduction to Muslim life in India.

Thirdly, the most momentous onus of transforming the Muslim and national situation simultaneously falls jointly on the vast and preponderant majority of secular Indians – Muslim, Hindu, Sikh and all others. Indeed, given the failure of both the state and the mainline media to come upto the stipulations of the Constitution, this onus may be understood to be decisive.

It is not as though some dramatic sleight-of-hand is here either proposed or expected. Indeed, this joint project is a long-term and difficult one, but such as is alone guaranteed to deliver a durable and long-lasting result. Secular Indians across communities must assume as a life-and-death enterprise the battle that the state has largely failed to win even some six decades after constitutional republicanism. I refer to the battle to deliver an uncontestable Indian 'citizenship.'

As a praxis, this project involves nothing less than a people's democratic revolution that takes in the best lessons of Gandhian tolerance and of Marxian humanism. A revolution that breathes unquestionable life to those articles of the Constitution that guarantee fundamental rights to all Indian citizens regardless of caste, creed, gender, ethinicity, or linguistic practice. And, among those fundamental rights, the rights of minority populations enshrined in Articles 25-30 of the Constituion.

For Indian Muslims this involves the recognition that their well-being is inextricably intertwined with the well-being of the oppressed and dispossessed among all Indian communities. Put more radically, this involves redefining the concept of Ummah to include not just members of the Muslim community but the community of the labouring and suffering among all communities. Were this leftward reorientation to be undertaken, there can be little doubt that, leading such an initiative in close alliance with all struggling Indians, Indian Muslims would be inaugurating a second movement for independence rather than merely be pursuing, or seen to be pursuing, community concerns alone.

Having said that, it is equally incumbent on left political forces in India – the only ones perhaps whose allegiance to the notion of a non-discriminatory 'citizenship' is provenly credible – to provide the sort of leadership that expands the notion of class to include social groups and minorities who have a common stake in resisting class rule, since class rule in India often finds its easiest methodologies in fanning isolated social concerns. Any one would immediately recognize that in West Bengal, Kerala, Tripura these deeply transformative practices have been underway over a long time. The point is for Indian Muslims in the northern states to indicate to the left that they are prepared to undertake those transformative struggles in the Hindi heartland states to the exclusion of the political options that they have thus far exercised with frustrating consequences.

Finally, and following from the argument thus far, the attempts now underway to forge exclusively Muslim fora, it must be said, is an attempt entirely in the wrong direction. Such an attempt, born no doubt of extreme anguish and disenchantment with political options exercised thus far, can have all of the following consequences:

- further ruinously ghettoize Muslim aspirations and politics;
- face crushing setback to morale through crushing electoral defeats;
- help reinvigorate forces that are constantly at work to supplant the very notion of secular democratic citizenship by a culturally homogenized one.

One look back at the experience of the Majlis-e-Mushawaraat experiment of the 1960s (the Faridi movement) should be enough to bring home the truth that these cosequences are inseparable from the very notion of political mobilization along sectarian lines.

Embedded in the very dilemma of Indian Muslims, therefore, there is a call – a call to forge a new consciousness that amalgamates a new future for India with a new effort on their own behalf.

August 2006

Vande Mataram
Patriot Test Yet Again

Some two decades into acclaimed and dedicated service to King and country, Cardinal Wolsey, Lord Chancellor of England, was finally confronted with his patriot test by Henry the VIIIth. He was ordered to intervene with the Pope in Rome for his consent to the annulment of the King's marriage to his elder brother's widow, Katherine of Arragon.

This was one thing that the good Lord Chancellor could not bring himself to do, since such a course flouted Church doctrine on the issue of marriage. The result: Wolsey fell into illness and out of favour, till his death in 'traitorous' disgrace.

Considering the post-9/11 like hysteria that is assiduously sought to be built by right-wing Hindu forces, led by the RSS, subsequent to the train blasts in Mumbai (whereby 'patriotic' Indians are everyday invited to look over their shoulder for the lurking Muslim 'terrorist'), it occurs to me that Wolsey's moving lament 'had I served my God with half the zeal I served my King, he would not have deserted me in my old age' must resonate touchingly among Indian Muslims today.

After centuries of incalculable contribution to the shaping of India's economic, cultural and spiritual life, after exemplary sacrifices made during India's struggle for freedom, and after proven heroisms in the three or four military confrontations with Pakistan, Indian Muslims are yet again under suspicion because they object to singing *Vande Mataram*. Among other rabid jingoists of the *Sangh Parivar*, its two noted Muslim mascots are the loudest in demanding that Muslims either sing the 'national song' or 'go to Pakistan.'

That Muslims are not being asked to go to Saudi Arabia, for example, is a dead giveaway, in the meanwhile. Clearly, it is not so much the tenets of

Muslim faith that are sought to be attacked as their alleged role in causing the partition of India in 1947 as a consequence of the 'two-nation' theory.

The interesting fact, however, remains that it was no Muslim but Savarkar, the head of the *Hindu Mahasabha*, who was first to propound the 'two nation' thesis in that seminal book of communalism, *Hindutva* (1923), a full sixteen years before Jinnah caught up with the idea.

India's secular historians have, of course, in recent decades made irrefutable substantiations of this fact. Since, nonetheless, their scholarship amounts merely to 'minority appeasement' in the eyes of the *Sangh*, let us cite from another modern Indian historian – one close to the RSS heart – namely R.C. Majumdar:

> one important factor which was responsible to a very large extent for the emergence of the idea of partition of India on communal lines... was the Hindu Mahasabha. (*Struggle for Freedom*, 1969, p.611)

It is of course another matter that neither for Savarkar, a self-proclaimed atheist, nor for Jinnah, a liquor-drinking, pork-eating, non-*namazi* western gentleman *manqué*, was the 'two-nation' hypothesis driven by any religious impetus. If in Savarkar's case the matter was entirely of ensuring Brahminical hegemony over the post-independence Indian state, Jinnah's exertions were dictated equally by the material interests of an entrenched Muslim landed and bureaucratic elite who feared loss of clout under a Hindu-dominated independent India. No wonder then that both were far better friends of the British colonizers than of the freedom struggle led by the Congress under Gandhi.

Thus, after the rejection of the Montagu-Chelmsford Reform proposals by the Congress, and the launch of the Non-Cooperation movement (1920) – the first major mass mobilization against foreign rule – 'Savarkar's call to the Hindus was one of 'no support to the Congress move'; while the Congress leaders were in prison, Savarkar 'encouraged Hindu participation' in the formation of Ministries in 'Muslim-majority provinces' (Pattabhi Sitaramaya, *The History of the Indian National Congress,* Vol.II, p.512).

And, again, when Gandhi gave the 'quit India' call in 1942, Savarkar was to issue the following edict as President of the Hindu Mahasabha:

> I issue this definite instruction to all Hindu Sabhaites in particular and all Hindu Sangathanists in general... holding any post or position of vantage in the Government services should stick to them and continue to perform their regular duties.

As to the RSS, its good collaborative behaviour throughout received the following commendation from the colonial Home Department:

> the Sangh has scrupulously kept itself within the law, and in particular, has refrained from taking part in the disturbances that broke out in August, 1942.

Another telling vignette, this time from the scion of the then socialist movement in India, N.G. Goray. He had this to say about the attack on the May Day march in 1938 in Pune:

> Who attacked the May Day procession? Who assaulted men like Senapati Bapat and Kanitkar? Who tore up the National Flag? The Hindu Mahasabhaites and the Hedgewar Boys did all this….They have been taught to hate the Muslims in general as Public Enemy Number1. (*Congress Socialist*, May 14, 1938).

Such, then, are the worthies who shamelessly and without let continue to berate Indian Muslims with questionable loyalty to the Indian state.

Why, it ought to be asked, do Muslims refuse to sing *Vande Mataram*? And why, equally importantly, do they view with suspicion the right-wing Hindu insistence that they do so?

The answer to the first question is indeed a very simple one. The holy *Koran* explicitly stipulates that believers are '*enjoined to serve Allah and to worship none but Him*' (*The Koran*, trans. N.J.Dawood, Penguin Classics, 1956, p.29). In other places the holy book makes it clear that the 'none' includes prophet Mohammed as well. The very title and first line of Bankim's *Vande Mataram*, on the other hand, declare '*Mother, I bow to thee.*' (Aurobindo's rendering)

Thus, it wouldn't matter much whether Indian Muslims are packed off to Pakistan or some other Muslim-majority nation: as per the injunction in the *Koran*, they could not bow in worship to any of those land masses either.

The answer to the second question posed above, however, involves both the political history and the content of *Vande Mataram*. And many Indians who, because of insufficient acquaintance with either, feel rather outraged at Muslim refusal of the song, need to be better informed on both counts.

Written sometime in 1875, Bankim incorporated the song into his novel, *Anandamath* (1882), a novel that glorified Hindu rebellion against 'tyrannical Muslim rule in the 18th century.' The song depicts India as the Mother Goddess, Kali or Durga, and includes in the body of the text the following:

> *Thou art Durga, Lady and Queen,*
> *With her hands that strike and her*
> *sword of sheen,*
> *Thou art Lakshmi, lotus-throned,*
> *And the Muse a hundred-toned,*
> *Pure and perfect without peer,*
> *Mother lend thine ear.*
> (Aurobindo's translation)

In R.C. Majumdar's words again, this was an unambiguous project to convert 'patriotism into religion and religion into patriotism.' It should be no surprise therefore that in 1937 the Congress Working Committee decided that only the first two stanzas would be sung, since Nehru had always been wary that

> What is called Nationalism can be defined as in fact the National communalism of the majority community which has been ruling and still aspires to rule this country. (Nehru, *Recent Essays and Writings,* Kitabkhana, Allahabad, Second Edition, 1937, pp.47-61; quoted in *Nehru On Communalism*, ed. N.L.Gupta, Sampradaykta Virodhi Committee, December,1965, p.9)

Apart, therefore, from the obvious fact that Muslims are not permitted by the tenets of their faith to bow to gods or goddesses other than *Allah*, the history of the *Vande Mataram* phase of India's anti-colonial struggle was one in which that struggle was sought to be given an explicity sectarian hue and substance. That this was no incidental, Tilak-like, politically expedient manoeuvre to mobilize the mass of Indians against foreign rule is borne out by the fact that the communal nationalism symbolized by Bankim's offering was to remain at the centre of Hindu Mahasabha and RSS blue-prints of the future Indian nation-state, to the extent of stipulating the requirements of Indian citizenship.

Nowhere was this more blatantly and perniciously stated than in Golwalkar's 77 page booklet, *We, or Our Nationhood Defined* (1938), a text that Jean A.Curran characterized as the RSS 'Bible'. Therein, Golwalkar wrote the following:

> The foreign races in Hindustan must either adopt the Hindu culture and language, must learn to respect and hold in reverence Hindu religion, must entertain no idea but those of the glorification of the Hindu race and culture, i.e. of the Hindu nation and must lose their separate existence to merge in the Hindu race, or may stay in the country, wholly subordinated to the Hindu Nation, claiming nothing, deserving no privileges, far less any preferential treatment – not even citizen's rights.

Is there any wonder then that Indian Muslims should view the current, revivalist insistence as yet another attempt to incorporate them into the kind of existence that Golwalkar stipulates above? This especially in view of the fact that Muslims have unfailingly demonstrated unflinching allegiance to the National Anthem, *Jana, Gana, Mana,* and to the National Tricolour, both of which were accepted by the RSS only as a *quid pro quo* to the lifting of the ban on it, following Gandhi's murder, and which, in fact, remain subordinate in its reckoning to the *Bhagwa.*

On a normative plain: one recalls that until a decade or so ago, it used to be mandatory for cinema hall owners to play the National Anthem before the commencement of the day's entertainment. This direction, however, had to be withdrawn because hardly any cinema-goer was seen to rise as the Anthem was played. Yet, it has never occurred to either the 'nationalist' Hindu-right or the state to question the allegiance and loyalty of those cinema goers, the overwhelming bulk of whom, after all, were bound to have been Hindu. Recalling that fact helps then to underscore the communal politics that informs the current, renewed insistence that Muslim Indians either sing the national song or 'go to Pakistan.'

That many Indians do not quite see the matter that way has been brought out by a recent poll conducted by one of the premier TV channels. Some 40% of those polled were of the view that there should be no compulsion to sing *Vande Mataram.* Given that Muslims constitute only some 13% of the population, it is clear enough that some thirty percent Hindus and other non-Muslims do not see the singing of the national song as any test of 'patriotism.' That indeed is a happy state of affairs. The question then might be asked: where would the RSS propose to 'send off' the 30 some percent Hindus and other non-Muslims who, like Indian Muslims, are of that persuasion. Clearly, 'Pakistan' does not seem an option here.

One may also add that for many left thinking people and atheists like the present writer, the 'nation' is not some mystical sensation but is constituted by the people who live and labour within a defined territory, sharing a common history. Such a perspective can have little trek with dubious versions rooted in an emotive iconography that constructs the 'nation' into gods and goddesses. Not for no reason did Golwalkar severly criticize the idea that after Independence India would be denoted a 'territory,' since 'territorial nationalism' contradicted the RSS 'vision' of a nationalism constructed on racial principles.

It is crucial, then, both for the state and the secular Indian citizen to recognize the efforts that are afoot to project Muslims as 'terrorists,' and to create within the country the same sort of paranoia as now obtains in America, U.K. and elsewhere in the West, (a circumstance that is eloquently testified to by the racial and religious targeting of Indian-Muslim passengers in a North-West Airliner.)

Every sane impulse, therefore, needs to be exerted to prevent the terrorization of the Muslim community if we wish to ensure that we do not become the agents of generating the very effects which are ostensibly sought to be forestalled. Even as instances of unforgiveable violence against innocent citizens are strenuously unraveled and punished, including violence committed lawlessly by state agencies, it is of fatal consequence that Muslims per se be both involved, as conscientious citizens, in that endeavour and, through multiple integrationist strategies freed of the fear that they now constitute the suspicious 'other' of the self-designated 'authentic' nation.

We must remember that already Islam in India is a fascinatingly eclectic phenomenon, involving the acceptance of practices severly forbidden by Wahabi dogma. Devotional forms of music – *naat, manqabat, qawwali, kashmiri sufiana kalaam* – or the tradition of *ziyarat* to the resting places of saints and Sufis, these are anathema to Arabic Islam. There may well come a day when some irresistible post-modernist gale might inundate other rigidities as well. That, nonetheless, is best left to time and tide rather than made the agenda of a fearsome, fascist *putsch* in pseudo-nationalist garb. India has need of great tolerance and wisdom in each of its citizens if the deficiencies thereof among organized social forces, not excluding the media, are to be prevented from destroying the pluralist republic.

August 2006

The Last Straw

Women Among Religions

When Jack Straw the other day encountered a Muslim woman, face veiled in niqab, it spelt in his mind the last straw for white-dominated multiculturalism in Britain.

Surely and soon enough the post-9/11 discourse centring on the ostensibly uncomplicated opposition between the benign forces of 'modernity' on one hand and of medievalist 'orthodoxy' on the other received fresh impetus. What doubt could there be that it was unambiguously the Muslim community that was obstinately obstructing the march of reason, nowhere more apparent than in the way they brainwash their womenfolk. Never mind that to this day most men, white or not, tend to be 'modern' when it comes to other women and 'medieval' in relation to their own!

There are of course those who raise questions. For instance, if the essence of 'modernity' resides in the march of reason and the regime of inalienable human rights, how self-evidently do the claimants of 'modernity' pass the test. Were one to cast an objective and non-racist eye on the record of the fair-skinned agents of world history since the Enlightenment, a pretty picture may not emerge. Nor indeed, were one to consider the record of religions, may the Church score a great deal higher than barbarisms of the non-christian kind.

The strong possibility then is that 'modernity' may, after all, find a referent only in the march of technology and money-circulation; and who doesn't know to what ends these continue to be deployed by the proponents of 'modernity.'

Furthermore, whereas it may seem on the face of it that women other than the Muslim ones exercise a wider range of life-choices, including sartorial ones, please let us not pretend that male-dominated power-structures among Jews,Christians, even Hindus have thought any differently about their women than have Muslim patriarchs. Upon scrutiny it may turn out that, in theory, there is rather little that sets them apart, although differential aspects of community histories in various regions and epochs have perhaps contributed to degrees of freedom or unfreedom which then are peddled as ontological judgements.

Having placed those queries on record, let us return to the subject of women's hair and apparel. A remarkable uniformity of injunction and purpose meets us here through the history of culture. First the Judaic past: 'It is not like the daughters of Israel to walk out with heads uncovered' And 'cursed be the man who lets the hair of his wife be seen.'

Again, 'During the Tannaitic period the Jewish woman's failure to cover her head was considered an affront to her modesty.'

The subject of 'modesty' as we know crops up everywhere; and, as we also know, Frederick Engels in 1884 was to make a definitive linkage between this overbearing concern with women's sexuality and the emergence of private property. More of that later. For now the ingenuous precursor of that argument is cutely contained in this further gem from ancient Rabbinical teaching on the subject: 'A woman who exposes her hair for self-adornment brings poverty.'[1]

Next, this from the redoubtable St.Paul, as we enter the evangelical Christian era: 'Now I want you to realize that the head of every man is Christ, and the head of woman is man…' 'Every man who prays or prophesies with his head covered dishonours his head. And every woman who prays or prophesies with her head uncovered dishonours her head.'

Should you ask why, a more explicit answer is provided:

> A man ought not to cover his head since he is the image and glory of God, but a woman is the glory of man. For man did not come from woman, but woman from man; neither was man created for woman, but woman for man. For this reason the woman ought to have a sign of authority on her head.

Were you still in some confusion, here is the clincher:

---

1 See Rabbi Menachem M.Brayer, *The Jewish Woman in Rabbanical Literature*, cited in Sherif Abdul Azim, *Women in Islam versus in the Judaeo-Christian Tradition:The Myth and the Reality*, Part 15 – The Veil, pp.77-78.

> The head covering is a symbol of woman's subjection to the man and to God.[2]

As is well-known, what may be called Hinduism is a vast and diverse set of practices drawn from an equally vast and diverse spectrum of texts, beginning from Vedic times (usually placed back to 1500 B.C.) with no single text occupying an undisputed canonical position. Yet, barring a few traditions – chiefly the Shaivite cults – there is a fairly constant refrain that the chief duty of the woman is to her man, and chastity her highest virtue. Indeed, as in the case of Ram's consort, Sita, even the highest of women could risk abandonment no matter how guiltless if a sufficiently strong suspicion was floated.

In the *Mahabharta*, especially in the 'Anuśāsana Parva', there are episodes where such teachings are drilled home in direct or narratively ingenious ways.

In one protracted interchange between Narada and the apsara Panchachuda, the latter acknowledges in great detail how women are frail, inconstant, sinful, and prone to 'transgress' at the slightest.

In another section, the sage Ashtavakra is heard to declaim:

> women can never be their own mistresses. This is the opinion of the Creator himself,viz, that a woman never deserves to be independent.

Text after text, it is unmistakeably enjoined that through her three phases of life, the woman's duty is to serve father, husband, son in return for protection by the male of the species, nowhere more authoritatively inscribed than in the Laws of Manu (*Manusmriti*).

What sets Hindu enunciations of these edicts apart, often, is the more evolved quality of tale-telling, as within sophisticated dramatic skeins voices are manipulated to carry a greater persuasive charge. Thus, for example, in another section of the 'Anuśāsana Parva', Sandili is made to detail proudly the qualities that reward her with entry into heaven:

> Verily during the absence of my husband, I never used collyrium, or ornaments, I never washed myself properly or used garlands or unguents, or decked my feet with lac-dye…[3]

---

2 1 Corinthians 11: 3-10.

3 Sections xxxviii, xx, cxxiii, trans., Sri Kisari Mohan Ganguli).

In more recent times, explicit connections are made between the woman's purity and the purity of the 'race':

> If a woman is pure she can save and purify man. She can purify the race. Hindu women have been the custodians of the Hindu race… . Hindu civilization has survived on account of the purity of Hindu women.[4]

Now, believe it or not, what the Quran has to say on the subject seems a pittance in contrast to the aforesaid. Remarkably, when it speaks of the desirability of 'modesty' it does so for both sexes:

> say to the believing men that they should lower their gaze and guard their modesty….And say to the believing women that they should lower their gaze and guard their modesty.

As to the veil:

> that they should drape their veils over their bosoms.

Muslim history of the period explains that these counsels were given in response to a situation where many complained of harassment, so that something like the following sounds like mere commonsense, however childish or unsustainable in the context of women's historical experience world-wide; 'modesty' is recommended inorder to prevent molestation – something we hear about every single day from diverse Hindu gurus and dharmacharies:

> … that they should cast their outer garments over their bodies(when abroad)so that they should be known and not molested.[5]

Nowhere in the Quran can one find a text that says women should cover their faces.

The fact of the matter, as Engles was to point out, is that 'monogamous marriage comes on the scene as the subjugation of the one sex by the other; it announces a struggle between the sexes unknown throughout the previous prehistoric period.' And at the heart of the struggle has been the 'express purpose…to produce children of undisputed paternity (who) could later come into the father's property as his natural heirs.'

---

4 Swami Shivananda, *Divine Life Mission*, Rishikesh.

5 *Quran*, 24: 30,31,4.

Thus, 'the right of conjugal infidelity also remains secured to him' ; and, 'should his wife recall the old form of sexual life and attempt to revive it, she is punished more severely than ever.'[6]

According to this highly plausible reading, then, the economies of surplus produced not only monogamous marriage but the male necessity and prerogative to police female sexuality if the political economy of surplus appropriation was to be consolidated. And in that process, the female hair, as indeed, female laughter, came to represent an unruly reminder of threats that lurked within the female to secure male possession of her.

If anything, it might seem a credit then that within Muslim social practice, marriage does not come accompanied with the baggage of sanctimonious authorisations and injunctions that obtain in Hinduism, for instance, or in Christianity, but is regarded as a 'contract' between equals wherein the terms are explicitly laid out. And either party is given the right to dissolve the marriage should it not work.

The whole troubled business of what women may or may not wear must then be seen with some informed attention to larger histories across religious communities that have spawned these conformisms.

Nor can the disparate data that obtains as to actual cultural use of apparel within one and the same community from place to place and time to time be understood in isolation from the imperatives of local histories of power. If, for example, during the Algerian or the more recent Iranian revolution women took up the veil as a revolutionary assertion against colonial/imperialist domination, they are obliged to wear it in southern parts of contemporary Afghanistan as a purely self-protective mechanism. Jack Straw would not have forgotten how expatriate Sikhs were to fight for recognition of their right to wear the turban, the beard, and the kirpan during the 1960s and then again the 1980s in Britain, until they succeeded in obtaining recognition as one of Britains' 'ethnic' communities, a recognition that brought concomitant policy rewards. Same was the story in Canada. So that may be the Muslim lady teacher who insisted on wearing her niqab was not so much succumbing to male brainwash as declaring a stance of defiance against a hegemonic denial of choice.

---

6 *Origin of the Family, Private Property and the State,* Ch.ii, The Family, 1884.

Let me conclude with a snippet from the cultural/political career of Mahatma Gandhi, since he seems again very much a point of reference for our chattering classes. Do recall that when he went to London to meet King George during the Round Table Conference, the King, infuriated, at having to meet a man who barely wore any clothes, (Jack Straw infuriated that the lady wore too many), sent his refusal to meet Gandhi unless the man agreed to dress 'properly'. We know what Gandhi's answer to that was, not too different from the Muslim woman teacher in the veil.

The question relating to 'modernity' then has to be settled on a terrain far more intricate, analytic, and totalized than merely on the basis of what women wear from time to time. For example, one real battle for 'modernity' in culture is currently underway in India, as a new institution called the Muslim Women's Personal Law Board defies the male-dominated All India Muslim Personal Law Board on the question of what a married woman (Imrana), raped by her father-in-law (now sentenced under criminal law to ten years in prison), should do – renounce her husband, who, according to the decrepit AIMPLB has now become her son, or go resume her life with him – something that both she and her husband want to do. Does it then matter whether or not the women who sit on that Board wear the veil or not?

November 2006

Irom Sharmila

I have before me a national English daily which is much given to spreading the word about the beauties of 'reform' and modern 'development' in India. Never a day passes when it does not remind us and the world how India is just about to breast the tape to superpowerdom. As in the case of other English Dailies (bar one), if and when it reports on farmers' suicides, atrocities on dalits, the wretched state of superstition in India's vast hinterland, or other such unpleasant details of national life, it does so with a quality of impatience very reminiscent of that dismissive gesture of Mr.Podsnaps' forearm in Dickens' *Little Dorrit* (a novel that Bernard Shaw recommended over Marx for an understanding of the workings of finance capital) which says: "do not bring such things to spoil my appetite."

Be that as it may, the November 17 issue of this avant garde daily announces that the government of the day is all set now to inaugurate a 'Look East' policy. We are informed that a two-day North-Eastern Council Meet has determined to plough the 'seven sisters' (Arunachal, Assam, Manipur, Meghalaya, Mizoram, Nagaland, Tripura) for purposes of exploiting their potential for 'export'.

Be it noted that some six decades after India's independence from colonial rule, these states remain largely bereft of roads, electricity, educational institutions, hospitals, not to speak of industry or other sources of steady employment, regional variations notwithstanding. Now, however, 'access corridors' from these regions to neighbouring countries are proposed to be opened, as well as 'air connectivity' within the region. Such are the charms of 'reform.' If you have no bread, eat cake. The question as to what percentage of North-Easterners might be equipped to participate in the bounties of 'access corridors' and 'air connectivity' hardly needs to be asked. The observation seems warranted that while our post-Washington Consensus ruling elites remain mortally opposed to pampering the 'creamy layer' among the downtrodden social groups of India, everywhere else it is the creamy layer for which now the Indian state opens its purse strings and, one might add, its system of justice.

Reading this 'Look East' news report, it just struck me that after all we do see only what we wish to see. Looking East, not one worthy in that two-day conference seemed to see Irom Sharmila of Manipur who continues to be on her soul-wrenching satyagraha since October, 2000, refusing food and water, against the draconian Armed Forces (Special Powers) Act,1958.

Through this six-year long odyssey, unparalleled since the days of Gandhi – and in some respects more heroic than any of the many fasts he undertook – this 'iron lady' has either been in one jail after another, or one hospital after another where she continues to be force-fed through nasal drips. It is doubtful that the British colonialists would have waited through a six-year long saga of self-mortification to address a public issue. Indeed, even a Cindy Sheehan seems to have pulled greater punch with the American media and public than our own Irom Sharmila Chanu. Such is our self-absorption in project superpowerdom. Soon this hero of substance might actually die, and Manipur go up in flames. What will that matter? After all we do have the AFSPA in place, an Act that allows all manner of control.

Now this Act empowers not just any commissioned officer but any warrant or non-commissioned officer operating in a 'disturbed area' to:

- 'fire even to the extent of causing death' if in 'the opinion' of such 'it is necessary for the maintenance of public order';
- 'to destroy any shelter from which armed attacks are...likely to be Made';
- to 'arrest without warrant any person...likely to commit a cognizable offence or against whom a reasonable suspicion exists';
- 'to enter and search without warrant any premises to make an arrest.'

Thus wherever AFSPA is in force, the right to protest, and the right to legal redress remain rescinded. Many activists who have simply wanted to document excesses committed by the army have been 'picked up, tortured and killed'.[1]

Since all appeals to that package of assurances we call the Constitution of India seem to have fallen on the deaf ear of a state that has vowed to keep such noises out of hearing range, Irom Sharmila's heroism may find resonance from a throwback to an unforgettably decisive chapter of India's struggle for freedom. There is of course only the hope that such recall might melt the wax in the ruling metropolitan ear drum, but no guarantee whatsoever, since Podsnappery now seems the endorsed religion of the state. Ergo, let the wretched of the land be made invisible, and the protesting voice be quelled so that Washington is saved embarrassment, and our burgeoning breed of CEOs allowed to carry on without guilt or hindrance. After all, if Singapore is our ideal, why need the absence of civil liberties be factored into our enterprises.

As the infamous Defence of India Act lapsed with the end of the first world war, the British, wishing to carry on keeping tabs on civil liberties in place, notified the Anarchical and Revolutionary Crimes Act (more popularly the Rowlatt Act) in early March of 1919.

This 'black act' provided

- for the trial of seditious crimes by benches of three judges without the right of preliminary commitment or of appeal;
- for relaxation of the rules of evidence;
- for detention without charges;
- for searches without warrants;
- and it stipulated that 'punishment or acquittal should be speedy.'

Now the parallels with our own AFSPA must seem uncanny – with one exception: as far as I have been able to determine, the Rowlatt Act fell rather short of our current day AFSPA in failing to authorize any rummy sergeant major to 'fire even to the extent of causing death.' That the niceties of the law did not inhibit an O'Dywer from causing the massacre at Jallianwala is ofcourse another matter. After all he was not murdering his own people!

Yet this 'black act' seemed to Gandhi the last straw that broke the obliging back: 'the idea of leading a campaign against the Rowlatt Act… possessed me' he wrote in his autobiography (p.201). The call to an

1 Subash Gatade, 'Irom Sharmila: Iron Lady of Manipur' Countercurrents.org, 17/10/2006.

all-India hartal followed, inaugurating the moment from whence the struggle for complete independence was never really to be turned back, notwithstanding prevarications and internal dissentions. In April, the non-cooperation movement – the first truly massive all-India mass uprising – was unleashed, involving the boycott of offices, courts, educational institutions, and the burning of foreign cloth.

As Gandhi was arrested, this is how he spoke of the Rowlatt Act in his Trial: 'a law designated to rob the people of all freedom. I felt called upon to lead an intensive agitation against it.'

Thus, Irom Sharmila's six-year long satyagraha which, recalling Jallianwala, began precisely on the day the Malom massacre took place wherein, on 2nd October,2000 the Assam Rifles shot dead ten unarmed Manipuris at a bus stop in Imphal on suspicion of being insurgents, invites us not only to revisit the history of March/April,1919 (which we proudly teach our school children as preciously unique heritage), but to ponder the thickness of skin and soul that our rulers seem to have acquired since independence, especially since the beginning of the Washington Consensus and the era of 'Reform.'

Indeed in recent years who is to say that the brutalities of our own state-apparatus vented on protesting adivasis, workers, dalits, displaced oustees have in any measure fallen short of those that the colonisers reserved for us. It has been made clear time and again that the chief function that our policing mechanisms now reserve for themselves is to secure from any form of public discontent the operations of our ruling economic bosses and, additionally, to facilitate the exertions of majoritarian goons who, now in Ayodhyay, now in Gujarat, congregate in menacing intention on behalf of 'cultural nationalism' and 'national security.'

The fact remains that having obtained freedom from colonial rule in 1947, and subsequently promising to all Indian citizens the equitable fruits of a democratic social order, our indigenous rulers set about ensuring that those fruits were confined to a 'creamy' metropolitan minority which is increasingly unwilling to 'look' beyond what fattens it further, insatiably. No wonder then that when they 'look East' they do not see Irom Sharmila or the AFSPA, but only an opportunity to now plough its resources for 'export' promotion.

Every government that serves a class-based state must necessarily, from time to time, resort to tactics that helps to keep in place its democratic legitimation. Thus, in the aftermath of the protests in Manipur (which included the shockingly desperate and bold stripping by women in front of the army personnel, inviting the latter to rape them), the Prime Minister set up the Justice Jeevan Reddy Committee to report on the AFSPA.

This Committee submitted its report in June,2005. To this day the report has neither been made public nor placed in Parliament. Reason? Among other things, the Committee opines that the AFSPA has 'become a symbol of oppression, an object of hate, and an instrument of discrimination and high-handedness.' Irom Sharmila never put it that strongly

There is another rather deeply ironic aspect to the situation to which attention ought to be drawn.

When Gandhi proposed the hartal against the Rowlatt Act in March,1919, most moderates were askance; (as luck would have it, Tilak was in London at the time). Gandhi, sensing the moment to capture leadership of the Congress, wrote as follows to Dinshaw Wacha (letter dtd., 25th, February 1919; see Sumit Sarkar, Modern India, p.188): 'Satyagraha is the only way, it seems to me, to stop terrorism.'

Gandhi had in mind what he saw as a dangerously undesirable development taking place among sections of the intelligentsia, namely, the willingness to engage in armed resistance to colonial rule (something that had begun to happen since the partition of Bengal in 1905). Given that such impulses were largely inspired by the Bolshevik revolution of 1917, Gandhi and the bulk of the Congress, given their class character, were understandably alarmed. Satyagraha was then in no small measure conceived as an alternate praxis.

Keeping in mind the continuing armed insurgencies in the North East, one would then have thought that the course adopted by Irom Sharmila should have received more than a cold shoulder by the government of the day. The treatment received by her, however, raises doubts that the state seriously wishes to see the end of insurgency. Just as the British saw in the Gandhian methods of mobilization a menace more intractable than the then armed challenge it was receiving, it does seem that Irom Sharmila spells a threat which the state wishes to quell, preferring to deal militarily with the insurgents rather than face a people's democratic revolt. And as a statement put out by the Human Rights Features Organisation succinctly states, 'it is precisely this contemptuous attitude in the face of suffering which demeans the world's largest democracy'.[2]

Nor is it a surprise that India's prime media channels which have lately been hotly pleading the cases of some notable victims in instances of murder should have evinced rather negligible interest in the six-year long satyagraha of Irom Sharmila. Is it not perhaps time that these influential channels gave to the North East the same quality of sustained attention that they have laudably given to Kashmir in recent years? Why is it that we either never seem to 'look' towards the East, or if and when we do, we 'look' but do not 'see.'

I may be pardoned for recalling what I had written in an article titled 'Sangma Treads Dangerous Ground' (*Mainstream*, April 14, 2001). The article was occasioned by Mr.Sangma's campaign to dub Sonia Gandhi a 'foreigner' who had to be prevented from becoming Prime Minister even if the Constitution recognized her rights as a 'citizen of India.' I had pointed out to Mr.Sangma that if the right to ascribe citizenship was left to the subjective whims of all and sundry, people of his countenance would have a hard battle on hand, since, knowing from experience as a teacher in Delhi University, I knew that students who came from the North East were hardly ever treated as Indians by 'mainstreamers.' Is it possible that Irom Sharmila suffers such disgusting neglect on account of subliminal impulses from which not even the government of the day is free? A truly disturbing thought that.

November 2006

2 Human Rights Features (Voice of the Asia-Pacific Human Rights Network, B6/6 Safdarjung Enclave Extension, New Delhi 110 029); Home Page: http://www.hrdc.net/sahrdc/ 15/11/2006

Sachar Committee Report on Indian Muslims

Right Wing Lies Exposed

India's majoritarian fascists, represented in parliament by the Bharatiya Janata Party (BJP), are in a blue funk. The findings of the 'Prime Ministers' High Level Committee' (set up on 9th March 2005) headed by former chief justice of the Delhi High Court, Justice Rajinder Sachar have in their Report submitted to parliament on 30th November,2006 nailed the long-touted right-wing disinformation about Indian Muslims as a skein of lies.

Drawing on every conceivable data source, governmental and other, and interacting widely across 15 Indian states where Muslims live in high concentrations, the Sachar Report records, on the basis of facts that few dare refute, a litany of exclusion, alienation and immiseration. This painstakingly comprehensive computation bids fare to inaugurate a paradigm shift in the way in which India's largest minority, some 14% of its population, are viewed. Already, all sections of opinion, barring of course the BJP, are busy making honest revaluations of a widely- held, error prone, and pre-conceived spectrum of imagined constructions of the Muslim community – its attitudes, realities, and aspirations.

First, a recap of some of the stunning findings of the Sachar Report:

- less than 4% Muslims graduate from school;
- contrary to right-wing calumny, only 4% go to madrasas, principally because in most areas of high Muslim concentration even primary state schools do not exist for miles; where they do exist, Muslims invariably prefer to send their wards to them, even when the dropout rate of Muslim children is much higher compared to other community

wards due to 'poverty' as these children are pressed into work by their indigent parents;

- the Muslim share in government employment is 4.9% (against a population of 14%); in a state like West Bengal ruled by the Left Front, their representation in state Public Sector Undertakings is exactly zero percent!
- Among India's Security Agencies (viz., CRPF, CISF, BSF, SSB &c.) Muslim representation is 3.2%;
- Just 2.7% are in place among District Judges;
- In towns that range in population between 50,000 and 2 lacs, Muslim per capita expenditure is less than that of India's Scheduled Castes and Scheduled Tribes! This is also the case in areas across West Bengal, Andhra Pradesh, Gujarat, Rajasthan, Madhya Pradesh;
- Not more than 3.% Muslims are able to get subsidized loans, and only 1.9% benefit from the Antyodaya Anna Yojana Scheme (programme to prevent starvation among the extremely poor);
- Only 2.1% Muslim farmers own tractors, and just 1% own hand pumps for irrigation;
- Here is another significant eye-opener: there is 'substantial demand from the community for fertility regulation and for modern contraceptives' ; over 20 million couples already use contraceptives; 'Muslim population growth has slowed down as fertility has declined substantially' ; all that puts paid to the nefarious fascist propaganda that there has been a Muslim conspiracy afoot since 1947 to reproduce mightily, and a danger that the Indian Hindus will be reduced to a minority!
- If Muslims do outnumber majority Hindus in any statistics, it is predictably as a proportion of the prison population (much like the blacks in America);
- Wherever Muslims are spoken to they complain of suffering the twin calumnies of being dubbed 'anti-national' and of being 'appeased' ; both accusations are perceived to be deeply calculated from ever allowing them to feel equal citizens of India;
- The Report also puts on record the little-recognized reality of caste hierarchies that have always existed among subcontinental Muslims. Thus, the Ashrafs, Ajlafs, Arzals respectively correspond to the Hindu

Savarnas, Other Backward Castes, and Schedule Castes respectively. Although, untouchability of the kind that afflicts the Hindu social order does not exist among Muslims, and although there is no bar to collective prayer in mosques, the reluctance to inter-dine and inter-marry is often only a concealed reality.[1]

It should not be hard to see that these findings – and many others – take the wind out of right-wing Hindu myth-making about the Muslim community in India, a reason why the BJP from day one has sought to oppose the very notion of setting up a Committee to unravel the facts of Muslim existence in India.

Let me mention just three of the many path-breaking recommendations that the Sachar Report makes to the Prime Minister who set up the Committee:

- it recommends that 15% of all government funds be allocated to Muslim welfare and development under all Central government schemes;
- it recommends the constitution of an 'Equal Opportunities Commission' to look into the grievances of deprived groups and for the elimination of anomalies with respect to reserved constituencies under the delimitation scheme; in an interview that Justice Sachar gave to the media channel, CNN-IBN, he elaborated that the 'Equal Opportunities Commission will have the power to pass order for compliance with it and to punish, either by compensation, or by other things for those who violate it. It has powers of adjucation and powers like a court.' These are of course projected stipulations at this point.
- The Committee makes no recommendation of 'reservations' for the Muslim community per se, but suggests that those among them who approximate in terms of social and occupational status the scheduled and backward classes among Hindus be classified as Most Backward Castes and proferred the same benefits that relevant articles of the Constitution make available to counterparts among Hindus.

1 The reality of caste hierarchies within Indian Muslims was perhaps first commented on by Ziauddin Barani (14c, Mohammad Tughlak's court) in his *Fatwa-i-Jahandari*; See also Ambedkar, *Pakistan or the Partition of India*, ch.X: 'Social Stagnation' and Zarina Bhatty, 'Social Stratification Among Muslims in India,' in *Caste: Its Twentieth Century Avatar*, ed., M.N. Srinivas.

II

Predictably, the BJP finds the Sachar Report 'full of prejudices' and seeks to launch on a Hindu-communalist blitz. Alongwith the Sachar Report the BJP seeks also to rope in, with heinously tendentious selectivity, a statement that the Prime Minister made last week to a meeting of the National Development Council (which includes all the chief ministers of state governments) inorder to scream 'Muslim appeasement' in a renewed effort to line up 'Hindu' vote behind the party. That the 'Hindu' vote in effect amounts only to propertied upper caste vote is by now well-recognized, although it will be the BJP's attempt to inveigle disaffected social groups among Hindus as well.

But first for record, this is what the Prime Minister said at that meeting:

> I believe our collective priorities are clear: agriculture, irrigation and water resources, health, education, critical investment in rural infrastructure, along with programmes for the uplift of SCs/STs. other backward classes, minorities and women and children. The component plans for SCs and STs will need to be revitalized. We will have to devise innovative plans to ensure that minorities, particularly the Muslim minority, are empowered to share equitably in the fruits of development. They must have the first claim on resources. The Centre has a myriad other responsibilities whose demands will have to be fitted within the overall resource availability.

The BJP, hardly surprisingly, has chosen to extrapolate from this admirably detailed, diverse and comprehensive enunciation a one-point agenda – namely, that the Prime Minister is after all prejudiced against the majority community! Just in passing, it never seems to occur to Hindutva ideologues that the SCs and OBCs, as well as a substantial percentage of STs who enjoy the benefits of 'reservations' are, after all, components of the majority community. Or that just as they comprise socially and educationally deprived sections among Hindus, similarly and correspondingly deprived sections exist among Muslims as well.

Most interestingly, it is often forgotten that, notwithstanding the accusation that affirmative action favouring the Muslims is now sought to be instituted on 'religious' grounds in contravention of articles 341and 342 of the Constitution, the note to those two articles is amenable only to the construction that reservations were indeed conceived ab initio on a religious basis. How else would one read the stipulation that

> A person who is converted to another religion cannot claim scheduled Caste status.
>
> (Notes on Articles 341 and 342, *The Constitution of India*, P.M.Bakhshi ed., VIth ed., p.285)

Clearly, the fact that caste hierarchies exist among Muslims was not to be granted recognition, although subsequently in 1956, the principle was extended to the Sikh community as well! It may well be the wishful conviction of the RSS that Sikhs are infact only a sect among Hindus, but the Sikhs have never taken kindly to that communal and patronizing propagation.

Yet, if in spite of the ammunition that the Sachar Report and the statement made by the Prime Minister may have provided to the majoritarian fascists, they seem visibly fighting now with their backs to the wall. Nothing testifies more eloquently to the changed social and political environment in India over the last two or three years. If the BJP senses this, regardless of the renewed communalist blitz they have launched, the reasons may be as follows:

- shocking as it might seem, the Sachar Report and its recommendations have not drawn the sort of 'popular' outcry among Hindus that the BJP might have expected; this seems owing to three factors: one, the incontestable content of the Sachar Report; two, the organizational and ideological disarray within the BJP, resulting just last week in significant electoral losses in Assembly elections in Maharashtra, Karnataka and Chhattisgarh; and, three, to the augumented credibility of the Manmohan Singh led UPA government. Nor does it seem on the cards that the BJP's energetic polemic is likely to change opinion in any major way.
- the Sachar Report has blown a very big hole into the time-tested right-wing Hindu propaganda that the Congress has always indulged in 'Muslim appeasement' ; anybody can see the impossibility of reconciling that bogus claim with the concrete findings of the Sachar Report, even when there is truth to the charge that centrist parties, including the BJP under Atal Bihari Vajpayee, have sought to appease the religious/priestly leaderships of both communities over

the years. The BJPs subsequent charge that if such be the state of the Muslim community it is only the Congress which is to blame now draws the obvious rejoinder: that may well be so, but now that the UPA dispensation appears serious about remedying the situation, why should the BJP oppose such a project. The fact is that many sections among Hindus who have thus far tended to take the BJPs version of things for granted feel that if further deleterious radicalization of desperate Muslim youth is to be averted, now is the time to attend to the substance of Muslim grievance.

- It is significant that a poll conducted just the other day by one of the premier media channels on whether or not the Prime Minister was right in saying that deprived sections, including the Muslim minority, should have 'first claim' on the nation's resources drew a 40% positive response. Such a response would have been unthinkable in the wake of the Gujarat episode of 2002.
- given the exertions of the UPA government on the question, more and more sections of Muslim organized opinion as well as general public articulation among Muslims can be seen to acquire a new energy, centring now on a new hope and the desire to participate both in terms of ideas and targeted action steps. From the BJP's point of view, this transformation has the potential to draw both the Muslim community and general public discourse away from the sort of jihadi-talk and 'Islamism' that suits Hindu-fascist politics.
- the BJP's isolation among the political party structures on the question is already complete; even its ally, the Akali Dal, has stated that it sees nothing wrong if deprived minorities are attended to in a special way. Given that low-caste Sikhs have been beneficiaries of affirmative action since 1956, such a position is consistent, after all.

III

The all-important question must now pertain to how sincerely and resolutely the UPA government pursues the new agenda it has laid out. Should the Sachar findings be allowed to go to cold storage and amount merely to a clever ploy, the consequences for the secular and democratic future of India will not but be cataclysmic. Indeed, the state may not get another opportunity in the matter.

If, on the other hand, the UPA follows up resolutely, without communal/electoral calculation, on the implications that flow from the Sachar Report it may truly inaugurate a transforming politics that bears the promise of putting secular democracy on a firm and concrete footing and, all importantly, of defeating the project of both Hindu and Muslim communalists to push Indian Muslims into the corner wherefrom the discourse of 'terror' and 'war on terror' could become mutually possible.

Finally, let it be said that the bulk of the Muslim community in India, insofar as they are either petty farmers, or agricultural workers, or artisans, or unorganized urban proletarians, owe their economic immiseration massively to the economics of 'reform' and 'structural adjustment' . Until the government seriously rethinks its adherence to the political economy of 'globalization' nobody need expect far-reaching transformations to happen in any hurry.

December 2006

The Saddam Murder

Finally the democratic deed is done. The benign imperialists have set Iraq and the world on the road to peace and justice.

They may have 'handed' him over to the Quisling regime, but, forestalling all potential risk, hung him within the precincts of the 'green zone' where the marauders hide from the wrath of the Iraqi people.

They hung him even as Muslims in the Arab world celebrated the Bakr Eid that recalls the sacrifice of his son, Issac, made by Abraham to God. The unseemly haste in dispatching him was not owing only to the Quisling's fear of holding him safe from the insurgents for any length of time. It was in pursuance of an evil, imperialist design.

The murder was made to coincide with Eid as a malicious insult to Islam. It betokened the declaration that the issue between the Bush regime and Saddam and the Arabs had nothing to do with Weapons of Mass Destruction or Palestine, but with underlining the nature of the 'crusade' of which Bush had spoken after the collapse of the twin towers at the hands of a dozen Americans of Saudi extraction.

Eid was chosen to emphasise that, whatever the world may think, the Bush regime was certainly involved in a 'clash of civilizations' – the Christian and the Islamic. Consider that just today the Bush spokesmen have characterized the conflict in Somalia as one between the 'Christian Ethiopians' and the Somali 'Islamists.'

That Saddam seemed finally to understand this is reflected in his letter – his last testament – to the people of Iraq. In that he was to draw a pointed parallel between the sacrifice made by Abraham and now by him.

Be it noted that Saddam was not murdered for what may have been considered his most major excesses. And for a reason. Here is how Robert Fisk has put it:

> Who encouraged Saddam to invade Iran in 1980, which was the greatest war crime he has committed for it led to the deaths of a million and a half souls? And who sold him the components for the chemical weapons with which he drenched Iran and the Kurds? We did. No wonder the Americans, who controlled Saddam's weird trial, forbad any mention of this, his most obscene atrocity, in the charges against him. Could he not have been handed over to the Iranians for sentencing for this massive war crime? Of course not. Because that would also expose our culpability. (Truthout, Dec.,30).

No. A thorn in the American side for refusing to play the politics of sectarian divisions in the middle-east, for running a secular state, for his old-world nationalism that kept Iraq unified, for his principled support for the Palestinians and his unambiguous hostility to the Zionists in Israel, and, most of all, for his willingness to trade his oil wealth for Euros rather than Dollars, the charge that he was hung for had to do with the killing of a hundred and some Shias in Iraq's Dujail province. This was construed into a 'crimes against humanity' offence by accusers in Washington who, alongwith many predecessor American regimes, are commonly known to have piled such crimes upon the world in mountainous heaps. Just in passing, Chile, Nicaragua, Ecuador, Grenada, Vietnam, Indonesia, Philippines, all have this story to tell. Not to repeat the fact that Saddams's own worst offences, as Fisk points out, had had the blessings and much material support of the accusers themselves! Consider also that, after all, the Pakistani airborne massacre in Baluchistan was not so different from the Dujail event. And yet the strongman in Rawalpindi need fear no chargesheet, at least not till he has his uses.

Does it also not seem rather monstrous that those who invaded Iraq on false pretences – for which they have been so comprehensively exposed and derided by the American people themselves – and killed off some one million Iraqis in the process should have the gumption to have hung Saddam for the Dujail killings? Where Saddam had no WMDs, the imperialist invaders thought nothing of using genocidal weapons like cluster bombs, white phosphorus, and dirty uranium in pursuance of a Christian crusade ordained by God many thousands of miles from Manhattan.

And, where the Bushies have been shown to have been in close oily embrace with the Bin Ladens for decades, (do recall that only one airplane was allowed to fly out of America after 9/11; it carried the entire Bin Laden clan!), Saddam not only had no trek with Al Qaeda but was proved, by none other than the CIA, to have actively kept them at bay.

II

Good-natured people are now busy asking, 'so what is done is done, but will the Saddam hanging help matters in Iraq?' The naivete here is touching. Let it be recognized that – the new Congress notwithstanding – the Bush administration does not for a minute wish things to settle down in Iraq or the Middle-East, not until all challenge to American corporate control over the material resources there is established, and not until it has ensured for the Zionists an unchallengeable sway as the sole arbiter and hegemon in the region.

That being the case, fresh waves of violence that undoubtedly will ensue from the Saddam murder will suit the imperialists just fine. They can turn around and say 'look we told you; there can be no reasoned or quick end to terrorism; thus the 'war on terror' must go on.' And did not Schindler once say that nothing suits business as well as war? And will not that other expansive and insidious industry benefit likewise from that occurrence, namely, the religion of the right-wingers who wish 'values' to be missioned out to the fallen world?

Remarkably, till this moment, neither CNN, nor BBC here in India have carried any news of what, if anything, the Russians or the Chinese have had to say on the Sadddam murder. But our own astute and forward-looking government has given evidence that it is indeed learning the tricks of how to be a superpower. Not by adhering to any noble principles or loyalties (remember that Saddam alone in the Middle East always supported the Indian cause in Kashmir, even in meetings of the Organization of Islamic Countries where not a second country spoke for India), but by practicing expediency, even if of an abject and supine kind. Our government finds the killing of Saddam 'unfortunate' and is 'disappointed' that it should have happened. That it did not move a lttle finger to persuade the United Nations to intervene in the larger world interest, including one might add, Indian interest, is obvious enough.

Some well-known and influential political commentators here have taken the view that, after all, saying anything stronger could have risked our relationship with the present Iraqi government and put a spanner in our interests in Iran. That is indeed begging a whole lot of questions. It can only be a hopelessly myopic travesty to call the present government in

Iraq either as a government chosen by the Iraqis, or as a government with any prospect even in the near future. As to Iran, the disingenuousness is breathtaking; it seems to have been forgotten that already India has twice voted against Iran in the IAEA on gentle American behest.

If indeed any 'disappointment' has been expressed, or if the Congress Party as a political forum has mustered courage to 'condemn' the Saddam murder, these forked procedures have, alas, much to do with the forthcoming elections in Uttar Pradesh where Muslims have decisive vote in many constituencies. Had that not been the case, and had other parties like the Samajwadi Party that now rules the state not been already more than strident in calling Bush a murderer, we may indeed have heard nothing even of 'disappointment' at what has transpired in Iraq. Rather a time for one to hang one's head in some shame. In olden and unfashionable times, people were executed for what was called 'equivocation' by the law. A famous instance that comes to mind is that of the Jesuit who was found culpable for the Gunpowder plot (the Guy Fox event). Now, be it Bush (Saddam has WMDs) or us, 'equivocation' makes for enlightened realpolick. Never mind what our idealistic education systems teach in schools about truth, courage, and honesty. All that is for the serving classes.

III

What, then, are the prospects in Iraq and the world?

Clearly, from Morocco to Turkey to Indonesia, many 'spontaneous combustions' ought to be expected. That clerics everywhere will ply the Eid angle is already in evidence. Indeed, one can hear many perfectly liberal Muslims express indignation at the timing of the murder.

In many places today people have come out in numbers to express that indignation, however hopeless it may seem. Within India it is encouraging to note that secular and leftward analyses of what has been happening since 9/11 have persuaded large swaths of Indian Muslims to see the contest as not being between 'civilizations' but between the imperialist project and common resistance to that project. Clearly this understanding will need to be driven home in other parts of the subcontinent and the Asian and West Asian regions.

Yet, if something qualitatively decisive has to happen, it is from the great American people that concerted initiatives must come. Without that happening the recent Congressional rebuffs to the Bushies may amount only to a pyrrhic occurrence. That rebuff needs to be built upon day in and day out. There is news that the good old fake Florida victory is up for Congressional enquiry. The world takes heart from such a turn, but it is the drive for impeachment which must now be seriously pursued if the world is to be spared further destruction. After all, any lookback at the depredations wrought by the neocon regime in moral and material terms worldwide must put poor old Nixon's misdemeanours into petty and forgiveable relief.

As to Iraq, things may now be only beginning. What happens to the Middle-East in the coming days is simply a frightening thought. Meanwhile, let not the Shias and Ahmedinejad gloat at the happening. It could be anybody's turn next.

December 2006

2007

Is Independence a Viable Option for Jammu & Kashmir?

On January 16, 2007, the Academy of Third World Studies at Jamia Milia Islamia University in Delhi organized an interactive meet to deliberate on the 'Kashmir Problem.'

Some well-informed and well-regarded 'Kashmir hands' were present alongwith some two dozen or so interested citizens, some of them Kashmiris. This writer among them.

Most short speeches were in the nature of informed comment on the positive or negative aspects of the peace process now in hand between India and Pakistan, on Musharraf's viability as party to that process, on the need to include the 'real' representatives of Kashmiris in that process, and on the desirability of curbing and whittling down the army and paramilitary forces in the valley. One speaker addressed the question relating to the disappearances of Kashmiris over the years as an acute human rights concern that needed to be examined. Another, in a different sort of key, shared his anguish at disappearance of another kind, namely, of Kashmiri cultural expression (language, folk forms of art, other syncretic histories).

The two presentations (brief oral ones) that the rather loaded audience seemed to respond to most, however, bore on, one, the formulation that militancy and violence could not justly be expected to be shut down till the right to 'self-determination' was granted; the second, coming from a venerated senior journalist and editor based in Jammu, that the overwhelming sentiment of the people was for 'sovereign, secular independence.' It was left unsaid whether this sentiment pertained only to the Kashmiris in the valley or to the whole state of Jammu & Kashmir.

One common perception seemed to lace most of the presentations – that the Indian state was the chief culprit and the chief impediment to a realization of Kashmiri 'independence.' The mention by this writer of a Poll that was conducted across the state some years ago that had seemed to raise questions as to what the concrete profile of sentiments across the J&K state really might be was laughed out of hand. Unfortunately, I did not at the time have details either of the agency that conducted that Poll or its date in hand, a lack that left me only the option of taking my chastisement with grace and goodwill. As you would anticipate, I do so now,(that is, have the details of the Poll in hand.) The Poll I refer to was conducted between April 20-28, 2002, not by the government of India or of J&K, but by the MORI International organization – a reputed agency by all accounts – and covered all regions, urban and rural, of the three provinces of the Jammu & Kashmir State. A subsequent Poll was conducted by Synovate India (2005), this time in the valley, and its findings as well are before me as I write.

Looking at the two findings, I am struck by the recognition that it is not the 'stated' positions just of the governments of India and Pakistan that reduce and monologise the deeply complex, contradictory and diverse nature of the problem but the 'stated' positions as well of many discrete groups of opinion who concern themselves with the 'Kashmir Problem.' The two Polls taken together seem to me to carry surprises of the kind that the recent Sachar Committee Report brought to the fore on the actual status of Indian Muslims. The Polls in question do not only suggest the frustrating complexity of ground realities in Jammu & Kashmir but, in doing so, help to evaluate the validity of solutions that are often the expressions of ideologlical preference rather than of any objective assessment. Since it would take inordinate length to fully explicate the findings of these Polls, I suggest that the reader access the texts of both the Polls on the Net by simply logging on to 'MORI Poll, Kashmir,2002' and 'Synovate India Poll, Kashmir, 2005'. In what follows I seek only to underscore the obvious centralities and to draw inferences that seem warranted.

One all-important caveat: every interested party to the dispute on J&K, it must be recorded, proceeds on one accepted principle – that whatever resolutions are debated or found must pertain to the entire state of Jammu & Kashmir rather than merely any discrete part. No faction of the Hurriyat organization, not even Syed Ali Shah Geelani, spokesman for the Muslim League, or indeed Pakistan has thus far contested this view, or openly argued that the state is represented just by the valley of Kashmir. Needless to say, unarticulated private predilections of any group of people in any part of the state cannot be authorized agenda as the problem is addressed.

II
What the Polls Tell Us

The MORI Poll conducted 'interviews in the Jammu and surrounding rural areas, Srinagar and its surrounding rural areas and in Leh; interviewers were set quotas for sex and religion…to match the population of each region.' The Synovate India Poll was concentrated within the Valley and Rajouri (also Muslim majority area).

First the easy part: in the MORI and Synovate Polls respectively, 6% and 3% (the latter figure especially significant since the Poll was exclusive to the Valley) preferred the Pakistan option. Let it be said, though, that whereas this may have come as some surprise to a section of the Hurriyat and to the Muslim League in Pakistan, those that have intimate acquaintance with Kashmiri Muslims and their continued secular divergence from Wahabi Islam that necessarily seems to require Islamic theocratic statehood the findings only function as confirmation of the reality of what is often called the culture of 'Kashmiriyat.'

It is an unfortunate occurrence that owing to the brutal onslaught by Muslim communalists in 1989-90, many Kashmiri Pandits have not only lost faith in 'Kashmiriyat' but gone over to the Hindu communalism of the RSS. I wish humbly to say, though, that during my wide, and, I might add, purposely unorganized interactions in the valley with students, teachers political workers, journalists, tradespeople (boatmen, hoteliers, taxi-auto drivers, shopkeepers) during 2002, 2003, 2004 while residing with a Muslim family in Rawalpoora, I was struck by the abiding 'Kashmiriyat' of people everywhere, combined with a deeply felt regret, tinged with a sense of grievance that seems understandable, at the exodus of the Pandits.

Anxious to resolve whether my experience in this area while I was there may or may not be an illusory sentiment, I took care to meet with the secretary of the Kashmiri Pandit Association in the valley. I can only say that I was moved by the elaborate details he gave me of the quality of inter-dependence that still exists among the seven or eight thousand Pandits who still reside there – not in ostracized ghettos as Muslims now do in many parts of Gujarat, but in their own houses and original mohallas – and Kashmiri Muslims. Of this I have written elsewhere in greater length.

It, therefore, comes as a happy reward to learn from the Mori Poll that 'people in all regions are in general agreement that 'the unique cultural identity of Jammu and Kashmir – Kashmiriyat – shouid be preserved in any long-term solution.' Overall, 81% agree, including 76% in Srinagar.' No surprise then that 'there is a widespread view, held by 80%, that allowing displaced Kashmiri Pandits to return to their homes in safety will help to bring about peace.'

That sentiment finds further confirmation in another finding in the Mori Poll: 'An overwhelming 92% oppose the state of Kashmir being divided on the basis of religion or ethnicity.' That should explain why not even the most sectarian of leaderships, whether among Kashmiri Muslims or Hindus, is able to propound positions that would argue such a division.

III
India or Independence?

The MORI Poll found that 'on the issue of citizenship, overall, 61% said they would be better off politically and economically as an Indian citizen.'

Remembering that the Jammu Province had in 1981 45% of the states population of which some 34% are Muslim, this Mori finding invites to be seen as more than remarkable. Clearly, the finding suggests that support for this option within the valley is not negligible.

That inference is rendered into fact by the finding on the question of the Synovate India Poll which tells us that 36.2% Kashmiris in the Valley and Rajouri (equally Muslim dominated) prefer the India option.

By no stretch of the imagination then can it be argued that the overwhelming sentiment in the state of Jammu & Kashmir is for 'sovereign, secular, independence.' However much as these findings might shock some knowledgeable peddlers of the 'Kashmir Question,' those are the facts. And collateral other facts germane to that finding are as under:

> There is also widespread consensus on the types of proposals which will help bring about peace in Jammu and Kashmir. More than 85% of the population, including at least 70% in each region, think the following will help to bring about peace:
>
> - Economic development of the region to provide more job opportunities and reduction of poverty-93%

- The holding of free and fair elections to elect the peoples' representatives-86%
- Direct consultation between the Indian government and the people of Kashmir-87%
- An end to militant violence in the region-86%
- Stopping the infiltration of militants across the Line of Control-88%.

One ought to supplement that with the further sentiment, expressed by 'at least nine out of ten' in Srinagar that scaling down security operations would be another big step towards peace.

Having said that, it also remains true that a clear majority, although barely so, within the valley express preference for the 'independence' option. If 36.2% prefer India, 53.9% wish to secede from the union (Synovate India). This even as only 16% say that the Hurriyat represents them better than the state government! And, even as 55% in the same Poll "think the de facto position of the Line of Control as the effective border should be made de jure as well."

The latter finding clearly suggests that 'independence' is not envisaged by Kashmiris in the valley as inclusive of Kashmiris across the Line of Control (or as a near-term option). Kashmiris will know that the dominant sentiment that obtains here is not, once again, a religious but an ethnic one: Kashmiris that live in what is called the POK are not Kashmiri-speaking, barring a sprinkling, and even within the valley there never has been much love lost between Kashmiri-speaking Muslim Kashmiris and those that are non-Kashmiri-speaking Mirpuris or Punjabis! If anything, it is the Pandits who tend to be missed as blood brothers! Wheels within wheels, you might say.

The question, then, to ask is whether above body of statistics can form a legitimate ground for resolving the 'Kashmir Problem' in favour of 'independence' given, especially, the fact that it is nobody's stated case that the 'Kashmir Problem' be solved on the basis of any partial sentiment in one part or other of the state of Jammu & Kashmir. Put another way, can 'independence' be thought to be a democratically legitimated option when the provinces of Jammu and Ladakh, and nearly half the people in the valley itself do not favour such a course, forgetting for the moment the nation-state level considerations in both India and Pakistan? Indeed, how is the desire for 'independence' of half the valley's population to be squared with the overwhelming opinion in the valley itself that no resolution that divides the state on religious or ethnic lines or that is deleterious to Kashmiriyat can be acceptable?

One may also say that however pristine our own doctrinal principles may seem to us (the right to secession, we recall, was at one time a part of the theoretical repertoire of the undivided left in India), history never offers circumstances fully to our taste. This writer is as aware of the endemically repressive nature of the state as any anarchist now arguing vociferously for its defeat vis a vis the aspirations of a section of Kashmiris. And yet it is nothing but another form of Idealism to carry on in the teeth of objective conditions that render such beating of violent wings an exercise in fruitless heroism that is accompanied by unsustainable human costs. Not only do a majority of the people of Jammu & Kashmir clearly not favour independence, but neither the government in Pakistan nor in India can be expected to overlook the historical fallout of granting secession on such a thin ground. However we might castigate what these two states have done in Kashmir, their worries with respect to a potentially domino effect in Baluchistan, North West Frontier Province, Manipur, Nagaland, Assam and who knows where else can hardly be underestimated. Nor is it so sagacious, after all, to think that the consequences for Indian Muslims in the mainland are a matter only of extraneous significance, or that the democratic gains of the last five or so decades may easily be protected from a right-wing fascist onslaught sure to follow secession on what will inevitably seem a two-nation basis.

There are other considerations: given the landlocked geology of the state, its economic and productive life has tended to depend heavily on import of basic needs. It must remain a question how an 'independent' valley may ensure a supply line with a number of expansionaist nation-states bordering it on many sides. Same when it comes to its physical security. Is it far-fetched to think that the 'independent' valley may become a playground for imperialisms of several kinds. It should not be forgotten that as far back as 1953 America had actively explored such a possibility through the exertions of one Mr. Adlai Stevenson. Nor can the other question be definitively answered: how long can the valley then resist the push to theocratise both state and polity in that 'independent' situation. Surely, both Kashmiris and the Indian state have big stakes in all this.

IV

Given that complex of considerations, it must seem a historical rationality that all parties to the dispute are increasingly reconciled to a resolution that leaves sovereignties intact but transforms the devolutionary ambit of local governance in drastic measure. The Mori Poll found that an 'overall 55% support "India and Pakistan granting as much autonomy as they can to both sides of Kashmir to govern their own affairs." Considering that the Poll shows that most in Jammu oppose this course it can be inferred that support for autonomy within the valley is much higher than 55%. Clearly, the 53% who favour independence must regard that as a very long-term telos, while autonomy remains the achievable objective.

Alongwith some highly regarded opinion-makers on Kashmir, this writer has on several occasions argued that the Kashmir problem can be traced back to the failure of the Indian state to live upto its commitments to the Delhi Agreement of 1952. Whereas disaffections in other states came to be willy nilly seen as issuing from flawed centre-state arrangements (it is instructive to recall that secession was not demanded first by the Kashmiris but by the DMK in Tamil Nadu), such expressions in J&K came, most regrettably, to be communalized chiefly because of the concerted campaigns of the RSS to render the Kashmir question into a Hindu-Muslim question relating to the Partition, and by the failure of the Congress, Nehru notwithstanding, to meet those campaigns with any firm secular conviction. It is that failure that was to translate into the heinous attempts made repeatedly by the Centre to deny the assertion of any genuine democracy in the state, till the dam burst in 1987. After all, the chief of the Hizbul Mujahideen was a candidate for the MUF in the elections of that watershed year.

One would think that far too much blood has by now bedrenched the hills and the valley of Kashmir. All things considered, and on all sides – included the main falange of the Hurriyat which is today willing to confront the rump that still seeks to toe the Muslim League line on the streets of Srinagar – it is about time that the details of creative 'self-governance' within existing sovereignties were worked out with unflagging will. Let every shade of opinion bearing on the contours of autonomy that takes secularism and Kashmiriyat as a 'basic structure', with no side excluded (including the Pandits who seek a 'homeland') sit around the table for as long as it takes. Since democracy is the proposed answer, such an answer must necessarily be democratically arrived at.

The Meaning of Modi

After the true purposes of the Nazi party began to reveal themselves in Hitler's Germany (1933-4), incidentally, purposes aided by the then Social Democrats, the feature of Europe subsequently was the certainty with which a widespread consolidation of opinion and resistance against the Nazis began to happen. Apart from government machineries in the democratic states, apart from the conscious and informed segments of civil society, ordinary citizens in nook and corner across Europe, recognizing the dimensions of what the world was faced with, took upon themselves the world-historical task on behalf of human decency and democracy.

It is a heartening feature of our contemporary times in India that the holocaust in Gujarat, justified not just by the Sangh Parivar but, most crudely in the Lok Sabha by our social democrat of old vintage, the truly fallen Fernandes, has similarly roused the conscience of the nation. Over the last three weeks or so, notwithstanding complicit governments in Gujarat and at the centre, India's vibrant media and public opinion across the board, including scions of the bureaucracy, have come forward and made themselves heard. If even those allies of the central government who, presumably,hold federal principals dear today demand Modi's ouster they do so in the knowledge that their demand is not for the removal of a failed chief minister but of the ideology that he has pressed into operation in Gujarat, an ideology that threatens to tear apart India as presently constituted. Gujarat of today, they recognize, is no mere local issue but a matter of 'general interest' to the body politic on which they wish to register their opinion. The pity is that their sound perceptions should still be thwarted by niggling parochial interests when the nation had hoped that the fascist threat would have overridden their petty considerations on behalf of themselves. Their heinous prevarications with the momentous history of our times are rendered particularly tragic now that the BJP-ruled government has conceded the demand for the application of Article 355 – a ringing admission that the fascist campaign run by the Parivar over the last two months has had to collapse in the face of the undeniable bloody exposures of Modi's Gujarat. This is indeed a fine triumph for the resolute opposition put up by the nation across the political spectrum in and outside the houses of parliament.

What are the long-term recognitions that Gujarat has so trenchantly brought to the fore? One, that no sane Hindu or Muslim wishes in the remotest manner to be identified with the perpetrators either of Godhra or the rest of Gujarat. There is reason to believe that this is not a case merely of tactical or pusillanimous distancing.The vast majority of Hindus and Muslims recognize with the deepest horror that the method behind the bigoted madness let loose on innocent children, women, and men in Gujarat (madness which Mr.Fernandes dismisses as routine) far from being the expression of any religious concern is really reminiscent of the ungodly partition days and of the Nazi era in Europe. Indeed, in doing the unspeakable things they have done, the genocidal killers of Gujarat have discredited the religious impulse itself.

What could be a more telling illustration of this than the item in the Bajrang Dal website which stipulates that Gandhi was no Hindu. By implication, Gandhi's assasin was. Clearly, the time has come,as rightly stated by Sonia Gandhi, when every Indian must ensure that the Gandhi/Godse contention is put to rest once and for all.

Secondly, Gujarat has nailed the lie that the RSS, the VHP, the Bajrang Dal and the BJP are discrete entities. The time is past when, between themselves, they could play snakes and ladders, hide and seek with 'majoritarian' predilections. And, it is a good thing that this exposure finally includes Vajpayee as well, his maudlin self-regard notwithstanding. 'Good' people in 'bad' outfits do not last that long – and certainly not at the very helm.

It has taken the decade from the Advani rath yatra to the Gujarat holocaust – inseparable events – to finally show up 'cultural nationalism' for what it is, a vicious, divisive, and anti-nationalist programme calculated to consolidate the interests of a minority elite among Hindus by sabotaging the inclusive and pluralist nationalism forged during the anti-colonial struggle. And it is not for nothing that this venomous thesis issues from those who not only had no part in that historic struggle but who, in overt and covert ways, aided the colonial exploiters. One of the glaring metaphors of their opposition to the genius and purpose of the Gandhi-led anti-colonial struggle was indeed the installation of the black cap against Gandhi's white khadi.

That the RSS was not to accord allegiance to the tricolour until the conditional lifting of the ban on it in 1949 is, of course, well known.

Further, as a result of Gujarat 2002 the BJP stands in stark opposition to the mainstream secular sanity of the majority community, a fact that helps to prick the pretense that it represents Hindus. Whereas the BJP has its own reasons for perking up at being called a 'Hindu Nationalist' party by foreign media, we have our own different reasons for disagreeing with that appellation.

Not having ever crossed 26% of the popular vote at any national election, we believe the BJP's claim to speak for Hindus is as mythical as its reinventions of India's history; and insofar as the party has never had the well-being – political, economic, cultural – of all Indians at heart, not even of all Hindus, its claim to being 'nationalist' is equally fake.

Gujarat, in my view, also affords the opportunity to revisit a contention that was at the centre of much debate during India's Constitution-making days – that which bears on the character and content of Indian secularism. The concept of *sarva dharma samabhāva* (equal respect to all religions) seems to have been adopted as a guiding principle by the state keeping in mind the rich multiplicity of religious belief and observance in India. Over the years, nonetheless, the state has not succeeded so much in safeguarding the ordinary citizens' freedom of belief and practice as it has in making the sama bhava ideal an instrument for appeasing the rather nastily politicized fundamentalist power-structures of 'religious' organizations.

Indeed, speaking of 'appeasement' – so much at the heart of the Hindutva propaganda machine – the only people who have been appeased in independent India are the economic fat-cats across denominations and the controlling fundamentalist cliques of obscurantist organizations. It is perhaps time, therefore, learning from the Gujarat experience, that the Indian view of secularism be reworked to mean not that the state regards all religions equally, but that it regards none; to say that the state protects the Constitutionl right to belief, practice, propagation only upto the point that no other constitutional injunction is thereby subverted, no law violated, and no impingement made on the secular rights of ordinary citizens – such as the right to privacy – which must always supercede all other rights. Wherever and whenever frenzy seeks to overtake those civic rights, the secular state must perform the true function of dharma, and protect the citizen from the invasions of the profane-in-religious-garb.

It is also time to recognize that the right to 'propagate' belief can have little meaning unless accompanied by the right to choose belief – something that only a secular-democratic rather than a theocratic state can make available. The overwhelming public response to the Gujarat carnage suggests that the nation is finding a renewed democratic assertion. This assertion must not rest till Modi as a specific political metaphor is set aside. The vast majority that abhors evil must never again fail to come together.

[NOTE: This piece was written immediately after the carnage that took place in Gujrat in 2002. It was carried again on the 5th anniversary of the massacre.]

February 2007

Kashmir Calling

Did you kill this man?
I did.

Did you know he was not a militant?
I did.

Then why did you do so?
For reward.

Do you know you committed a crime?
But, sir, he was only a Kashmiri.

Even as utterly bigoted and power-drunk rogues among the Special Operations Group Forces in Kashmir, under cover of immunity from the draconian Disturbed Areas and Armed Forces Special Powers Act, commit nonchalant murders in furtherance of petty preferment, (just as they do in the North East), a consensus of admirable sanity seems to gather mass in the very heart of darkness.

It is increasingly evident that a sharp precipitation of positions is now on hand, as forces inimical to peace and democracy seem for the first time in decades on the backfoot, although more strident and determined for that very reason.

If, however, intimations of some real hope greet us today, hope that does not for once promise merely to return Kashmir to yet another sterile stalemate, our thanks will seem due to three primary factors: first and foremost, the heroically unprecedented struggle of the people of Kashmir; second, bold and creative leadership in India and Pakistan, and, thirdly, vastly and decisively altered international geo-political configurations.

An Indian parliament resolution that says Kashmir is an 'integral part of India' (implying that there the matter ends) notwithstanding, the Indian establishment has come to acknowledge that a 'dispute' there has been. No small thing that.

Impelled by the Pakistan President's subsequent formulation that a resolution be sought by first excluding positions unacceptable to both countries, the Indian Prime Minister could bring himself round to say that short of jeopardizing sovereignty or redrawing territory, a process of negotiations could be engaged in that would lead to creative and imaginative mechanisms of devolution, rendering, as the Pakistan President had suggested, the Line of Control a formal construct merely. It must be noted here, though, that important and substantial differences remain to be sorted out here as to the kinds of activity that may be formalized across the LOC and the modalities for so doing.

That Pakistan under Musharraf has been willing to press ahead with speed came to be strikingly evidenced by the stunning, although historically and legally accurate, pronouncement that Pakistan had never made a claim to Kashmir, reiterating that the all-important consideration was that any solution must have the concurrence of the 'people of Kashmir.'

One may note here another far-reaching switch on behalf of the Pakistan President: if up until now the tangled question of who actually represents the people of Kashmir had seemed wholly unproblematic to the Pakistan establishment (to the extent that the armed Jamat-e-Islami-indoctrinated militants were thought to do so without contention), that question also came to be revisited critically by the President in his recent meeting with Mirwaiz Umar Farooq who leads what has come to be called the 'moderate' faction of the All Party Hurriyat Conference.

Boldly and justly, the President has come to recognize that, one, Kashmiri representation is not as monolithic a phenomenon as erstwhile ideological persuasions might have dictated, and, secondly, and all-importantly, that such sections as still seek to force a resolution through the gun cannot be participants on the negotiating high table. That this has been the Indian position is well known, but it is to be hoped that ways will be found to include Kashmiri militants in whatever parleys ensue, and that they will sieze the moment that history now seems to offer. Nor, it must be underlined, may Kashmiri Pandit organizations be left out, since the preservation of the syncretic Kashmiriyat that everybody – except the good old communalists on either side – wishes to nurture requires that they return and reassert the invaluable secular and composite traditions of Jammu & Kashmir.

In one shot, as it were, (although endless back-channel considerations, Pakistan's own altered situation in relation to 'terrorism,' and the international zeitgeist now clearly lay behind Pakistan's truly path-breaking disavowal here of violence as a legitimate form of redressal), a ringing follow-up has been added to the Pakistani acceptance, however laggard initially, of the Proposal that the Indian Prime Minister had made in Havana in September, 2006 – that a 'joint anti-terror mechanism' be set-up to confront 'terrorist' depredations. Needless to say, that the Indian proposal was to draw the same quality of fire from right-wing 'nationalists' in India as Pakistan's stipulation earlier of never having made a claim to Kashmir had drawn and continues to draw from the right-wing 'nationalists' in Pakistan. If the Pakistani President was seen to have treacherously abandoned a claim which, after all, had all these years legitimated three wars with India and the subsequent jihad, the Indian Prime Minister was seen to have at one go converted Pakistan from a perpetrator to a victim of 'terrorism.'

Subsequent events have demonstrated that the President and the Prime Minister have both been rather ahead of revanchist predilections: three attempts have been made on the life of the President of Pakistan, and in recent weeks, ten suicide bombings have occurred at crucial official establishments within and around the Pakistani capital. All this a reminder that often history does not respect dearly held doctrines as much as the sheer dynamic of change. It must be the force of that dynamic that not only has the 'joint anti-terror mechanism' been set up and now endorsed by the former chief of India's foreign intelligence service, the RAW, but its first meeting has also been scheduled for the 6th of March.

This fascinating skein of convergence has to it of course another all-important dimension. Having jettisoned the plebiscite option as far back as his visit to India during the NDA regime, the President of Pakistan has put it clearly to the moderate Hurriyat leadership that Pakistan is ready and willing to explore bold mechanisms of 'self-governance' and 'joint-management' so long as these fall 'short of independence.'

This of course need not be such a departure, since 'independence' for Jammu & Kashmir has neither formed a part of the old (and decrepit) UN resolutions of 1948, nor an option that Pakistan, just as India, has ever endorsed. As I have suggested in a recent article, Polls conducted in 2005 show that, contrary to general propagation, an overwhelming majority of Kashmiris across Jammu & Kashmir state also do not favour this option. Indeed, within the valley itself, if 53% asked for independence, 37 % wished to retain their Indian citizenship in contrast also to 3% who wish to opt for Pakistan. The question then must be what exactly India and Pakistan will bring to the table as they debate the concrete contours of 'self-governance and joint management.' Difficulties here must arise from the asymmetries between the objective histories and conditions that have obtained and continue to obtain in the two parts of Jammu & Kashmir. The structure of convergence between Indian and Pakistani realignments on both the major questions of old (UN resolutions, Plebiscite, Jihadi violence as 'freedom struggle' on the one side, and the non-negotiable status of J&K as 'integral part of India on the other) and on the desirability to pursue the 'peace process' as the only workable praxis, path-breaking in itself, may have remained a democratically insufficient precondition had not important 'separatist' groups, chiefly the Hurriyat led by Umar Farooq, also come to the conclusion that, one, violent struggle has run its course and, indeed, defeated its own purposes, and, two, that the coalescing of the Musharraf-Manmohan position on 'self rule' short of independence is something to work with.

Taken together with the political groups who have consistently participated in local assembly elections in J&K and advocated peaceful and democratic struggle on behalf of greater 'autonomy' (often a reference to the stipulations first of the Delhi Agreement signed between the Nehru and Abdullah governments in 1952 after the adoption of the Accession and the Jammu & Kashmir Constitution, and then again to the Accord reached between a returned Sheikh Abdullah and the Indira Gandhi government at the Centre, both of which concede Kashmir's 'special status' under the Instrument of Accession vide Article 370 of the Indian Constitution), the willingness now of the dominant section of the Hurriyat to explore this route lends to the new convergence a strength it may not have had heretofore. That the Mirwaiz-led Hurriyat means business, however risky to life and limb (it will be remembered that the latter's venerated father fell victim to a militant bullet) is borne out by the fact that the street-level opposition from the Jamat-e-Islami faction led by Syed Ali Shah Gilani was openly confronted recently in Srinagar city by cadres of the Mirwaiz group.

Note that this impulse finds now an echo on the other side of the Line of Control. Speaking on the occasion of what is called there the 'Kashmir Solidarity Day,' the Prime Minister (sic) of Paksitan Occupied Kashmir stated on feb.5 that 'negotiations are the best method' to resolve the dispute in the context of the changed international situation. Sardar Atique Ahmed went on to endorse the terms of the 'peace process' based as these are on Musharraf's 'proposals' and the Indian Prime Ministers's 'positive' response to them.

In all this, the Jammu & Kashmir Liberation Front led by Yasin Malik occupies a hitherto tantalizing position. Perhaps the most well-thought-of group from the 1989 days when armed militancy broke in the state, it went into armed struggle but returned to a non-violent and democratic praxis in 1994. Although, despite brutal victimization at the hands of the military and para-military forces and often gruesome revenge by both the jihadi militants and 'reformed' vigilantes doing service for the state, it remains committed to a democratic praxis, its formal demand also remains unaltered in favour of 'independence' rather than any form of autonomy or self-rule. What contributions the JKLF makes to the developing situation in the coming days will be a crucial factor. That this group sets great store by Kashmiriyat and espouses a secular and composite state and polity makes its political location an extraordinarily enticing and important one.

Clearly, the fairly radical rethinks outlined above must be seen as the products of a combination of historical urgencies. A heart-breaking yearning for peace within Kashmir deriving from a terminal disillusionement with the corruptions that came to afflict those that took to the gun, a deeply felt realization within Kashmir, India and Pakistan that no military solution exists, the willingness within the Indian establishment to recognize that burying the head in the sand will not make the problem go away, the realization within the Musharraf government that poisoned chalices often return to plague the inventor, especially as erstwhile bartenders now turn their face, a new self-assurance within civil societies in Pakistan that, Hindu right-wing nuisance notwithstanding, India harbours no assimilatory intentions towards the entity called Pakistan, the uninhibited impulses of younger generations in each country to enjoy and profit by what a newer world has to offer as the demons of India's partition come to be exorcised in public memory (exemplified most of all by Punjabis on either side taking the lead in forging people-to-people contacts), and, not the least, a drastic transformation in the attitude of imperialism towards contentions that do not suit its purposes, be it the balkanization of nation-states – this concatenation of shaping impulses now lead the Kashmir imbroglio in a direction that calls for a deepening of democratic practices, for just and legitimated institutions of governance, for a federalism that upholds at any cost the sanctities of local rule, and for the abjuration of recourse to all forms of violence.

Most of all, it calls for processes of healing that might over time bring a broken people back to normalcy and health.

Having said that, it should be no surprise that those political entities that constantly seek to locate the Kashmir contention in the history of India's partition in 1947 are up in outcry, fearing a terminal threat to their political future.

If in India the RSS is busy bemoaning 'Muslim appeasement,' complicity with 'terrorists' (notice that Afzal guru has not been promptly hung), sell-out of Indian 'nationalism' to a 'jihadi' Pakistan, and so forth (never mind that the most repeated and facile gestures of peace towards Pakistan were made by the Vajpayee-led NDA regime), in Pakistan the Jamat-e-Islami leader, Qazi Hussain Ahmed, accuses the Musharraf government (of which his political group is a part) of complicity in jettisoning the 'two-nation' theory upon which Pakistan had come into existence (February 5 meet). The Qazi underscores his communal thesis rather dramatically: look that on the one hand Musharraf is busy drawing a fence across the border with a Muslim Afghanistan while on the other he is keen to make friends with a 'Hindu' India in order to betray the Muslims in Kashmir!

Similarly, within the valley, Syed Ali Shah Gilani of the Jamat-e-Islami rues what he calls a 'nationalist', 'secular', 'democratic', 'even communist' conspiracy to cheat Kashmiris of their right to self-determination (which Gilani naturally expects must lead to merger with Pakistan).

And yet, theirs seems now a losing enterprise.

As the 'peace process' develops in the coming days, accompanied within Kashmir by drastic reduction in military and para-military presence, as well as exemplary punishment meted out to their murdering members, a question will arise as to the prospects of the Musharraf Presidency in Pakistan. Contrary to earlier misgivings, it does now seem in the light of many recent events and decisions there that his Presidency and the enlightened civil societies that back him may be crucial to the success of the far-reaching initiatives now underway.

Dependent as his regime is on the legislative support precisely of those political sections who oppose any form of entente on Kashmir, can it be India's wish that he take recourse to the Emergency provision in the current Pakistani Constituion that can, theoretically, enable him to extend the life of the current assemblies by a year, and then ask them to reelect him prior to a fresh election which will soon be due? Is there any guarantee that they will oblige? And if, conversely, he is compelled to jettison his uniform before the next election, can it be said what the political architecture of the establishment in Pakistan then will be? These are further reasons why an urgency attaches to the 'peace process.' The need, it will seem, is to move forward on the modalities of 'autonomy'/ 'self-governance' in ways that may spawn a momentum and a dynamic not then to be retracted.

As these modalities are worked out, it will be fatal not to extend the principle of devolution to all provinces of the state of Jammu & Kashmir – a massive but wholly necessary exercise that will test the resolve and political ingenuity of all parties to the question.

As to 'joint-management': much easier said than done. Given that Pakistan Occupied Kashmir remains for any real purpose a total hostage to Pakistani Army rule, with a dummy assembly in place, a drastic and open transformation of the systemic realities there must precede any consideration that Kashmiris on that side of the LOC can function as voluntary 'managers' of anything. It would seem that for now the furthest possibility suggested here by the Indian Prime Minister is a rational and plausible one – that in matters of some services, transport, health, commerce and trade – such management appears feasible of operation.

At a macro level, the call on both India and Pakistan is to free Kashmiris of the sense that they remain in a state of colonization – a sense that is shared by Indians in the North Eastern states and by the Baluchis and the Pushtuns in Pakistan. And to free them in ways that translate into sustained and assertive instruments of self-realisation, always aided rather than thwarted by the Central governments in the two countries.

It is a thought, finally, that failure no longer is an option that can be sustained for any length of time.

February 2007

Hanging the Corrupt by the Lamppost

On the 6th of March, a two-judge bench of the Supreme Court of India, hearing a fodder-scam related case, permitted itself a rather unusual but highly instructive majesterial 'observation.' Be it recalled that the fodder scam refers to alleged embezzlements from moneys allocated for the purchase of animal feed in Bihar during the chief ministership of Lalu Prasad Yadav – now a much, and deservedly, adulated Minister for the Railways in the central Cabinet.

It may not be out of place to note also that as part of an overall fright at the increasing insistence of the intermediate castes for a space in the metropolitan sun, the fodder scam has during the last decade or so come to be constructed by elite opinion makers as the chief symbol of corruption in Indian political life. There is a point in saying this because although other more impressive scams were to follow the fodder one – for example the scam related to petrol pump allotments during the Vajpayee regime – it has been the fodder scam and the representation of Lalu Yadav as an unduly aspiring country bumpkin figure that have been driven relentlessly as the central emblems in a narrative managed largely by fair-skinned proprietors of the upmarket English language media. And let not the 'observation' here that probity and uprightness still tend to be associated with English education and fair skin be taken amiss either. Among all partial truths, this truth has more validity than many. Nor may our colonial history alone be blamed for these predilections: the penchant for fair skin has always been with us since the Vedic times; all that the British did was to replace Sanskrit with English as an alternate hegemony.

But to return to the matter in hand. Honourable Justices Sinha and Katju on the 6th day of March vented their anguish thus, in open court it is important to add: 'The only way to rid the country of corruption is to hang a few of you from the lamppost'.

Predictably, this majesterial anguish has not failed to evoke a rather muted counter-anguish, to the effect that perhaps the 'country' whose future is so much and so admirably close to the heart of the nation's highest Judicial Bench may have expected the honourable Judges to mind their language somewhat.

Both orders of anguish, we think, invite a rather more considered attention.

II

That India is pretty shamefully high on the list of the world's most corrupt nation-states is hardly disputable. Taken together with several other indices that testify to a decline in systemic probities, the last two decades have generated among India's upmarket middle classes a weary disenchantment with the very idea of politics. That often democracy itself is identified as culprit is borne out by the high incidence of metropolitan refusal to cast a vote come hustings.

It rarely happens, of course, that India's 'forward-looking' urbanites stop to consider their own subtle complicities with the corruptions they bemoan, since the level of 'networking' arrangements at which they usually operate to generate 'prosperity' is peddled by the institutions they symbiotically patronize and are patronized by as smart promise for a conquering future. If anything, in recent years, this disenchantment of the new vanguard has off and on found reassuring resonance in pronouncements by the Judicial branch of the state.

Thus, the 'observation' made by Justices Sinha and Katju reflect in essence the dominant 'vanguard' sentiment that, one, corruption is the number one national malady, and, two, that its sources are located exclusively in the party/political apparatus of Indian democracy.

Since it is not so easy to eject the notion of democracy per se, the unstated assumption here is that an ideal democracy would be one that neatly bypasses or transcends the messy concrete of historical conditions. Such a depoliticized ideal requires a two-party system which could function without any primary social/ideological antagonisms to augument the wealth and clout of the nation, leaving reliable elites incharge both of ownership and management regardless of which of the two parties form the government. The point being that, as in America, whereas the two parties may designate themselves as discrete political formations/contestants, they could be trusted always to share an identical theory of the state.

The chastisement administered by the honourable judges needs therefore to be understood in a wider social/ideological context. It is instructive to recall that soon after Independence from colonial rule, it was Nehru who recommended the 'hanging by the lamppost' remedy for corruption. The difference however is that the object of his particular anguish at that point was the hoarder and the black-marketeer. Now, at a time when the same in corporate avatar pretty much have the reins of state in their hands, it is the countrified political class that has come to replace the same as objects of contempt. This in view of two momentous axes of social and political transformation that have been underway since the decade of the Sixties (speaking here of only the northern cowbelt states). One, an increasingly bold, often cynical, assertion by new countrified leaderships that time has come for them to partake of what the state has after all always offered the empowered, and, secondly, the attempts made by the Legislative and Executive branches, however coerced by mass upheavals, to put in place, reluctant inch by inch, an agenda of change that purports to make India's development and growth an inclusive one.

And there is the rub. Such attempts at equity have repeatedly drawn the ire of India's entrenched elites, and now and again of the courts. Investments and affirmative measures taken to benefit, however pitifully, those that have hitherto been left out, (dalits, intermediate castes, minorities, tribals especially) are not only characterized as 'appeasement' politics calculated to establish 'vote-banks' but regarded somehow as a deviation from the narrative of nationalist 'progress'. Put another way, when a government directs the state towards enhancing the interests of some eighty percent of the population, the exertion is seen as a 'reactionary' withdrawal from the march to glory which, like it or not, remains identical with the interests of the twenty percent. Following from this construct, public moneys which remain unprivatised are seen as a repository of all real and potential corruption, the assumption being that every privatized corporate rupee, unlike the fodder money, goes to build the nation with unimpeachable selflessness and efficiency. Some assumption you might say.

It will be seen that this ideological topsy-turvydom had informed the bulk of England's post-1832 history. The bourgeois-industrial classes who had brought England out of the stranglehold of the feudal landed gentry might have been expected to carry forward the slogans of freedom and equality beyond their own enclave, but of course that was not what they had meant at all. So that not for nothing have historians – English ones at that, lest it be thought that good old Marx is meant here – noted that British 'Liberalism' was, at bottom, a deeply conservative phenomenon. Through every sleight-of- hand, and failing that through the exertions of what Carlyle was to call the 'drill sergeant', the bourgeois industrial class was to ensure that the fruits of historical change spilt as little beyond its own boundaries as possible without furthering an actual revolution. And there was no dearth of high sounding moral icons wedded to the interests of this class that periodically never failed to bemoan the sleaze and corruption that accompanied even the most minimalist attempts at 'reform' (which then meant the opposite of what it has come to mean after the 'Washington Consensus of 1990; not the disappearance of the state but its active exertion on behalf of equity'). All this, *en passant*, since the issues here must require considerable detailing.

The point, however, is to ask the question whether in India today, as in many other places, 'corruption' is merely a moral and sui generic phenomenon. Throughout the history of communities it has been the case that a refusal by the empowered to examine social problems without a willingness to admit complex concatenations has yielded veritable catastrophes of simple-mindedness. (What better illustration on a wider canvas than the career of the Bush presidency in America.)

Recall that in Maoist times in China the Red Guard phase was meant precisely to decimate corruption more or less by the 'lamppost' means articulated by honourable justices Sinha and Katju. Yet, alas, today China we are told is as high as number three on the list of corrupt nations. Indeed, were the 'lamppost' route the most effective anodyne to corruption, the dictatorial regimes that used to proliferate Latin America or South East Asia, or the monarchical ones that still rule the roost in much of the Middle East should have been the world's most pristine and pure. Not so.

In the meanwhile, there is a real enough danger that accompanies the anguished pronouncement of the two honourable Judges, namely the power of example. Recall that only some months ago in an Indian city a whole congregation of deeply anguished women took upon themselves the task of chastising a ruffian who had for years caused no end of misery to the women of the town. Possessed by a sense of righteousness, they surrounded the fellow bang in the court premises and beat him to pulp and to death. To this day a deabate carries on whether the said women deserve punishment or reward. These righteous conflicts have of course been much the subject matter of a whole stream of popular cinema since the late eighties wherein organs of the state having been found to be all corrupt, the noble protagonist takes it upon himself, occasionally herself, to avenge iniquity and corruption. Nor must it be forgotten that several children in recent years have lost their lives while emulating the extraordinary heroisms of a Superman, or Spiderman, or Shaktiman on behalf of the victims of corrupt and unjust authority. Given the great and, no doubt, justified regard in which the people of India hold the Supreme Court, it is not inconceivable that the 'lamppost' observation may well double as inspiration to victims of corruption. And if and when that happens, not many would remember that honourable Justices Sinha and Katju had also said as part of the same 'lamppost' observation that 'the law does not permit us to do so.' Precisely from the standpoint that the existential burden of the Judicial system after all is to guard over and enforce the rule of law, without which democracy is inconceivable, the 'lamppost' sentiment must be regarded as considerably out of sync with that burden.

We were all taught at school the lesson that 'Rome was not built in a day.' It took centuries indeed. It seems we need to acknowledge and lump the reality that, ancient as we well might be, we are no more than a six-decade long nation-state. We need to accept that in a country as diverse in social, cultural, ethnic, linguistic (to name but a few counters only) expression, practice and history, as riven and unequal in material endowment and aspiration, as wedded to 'pre-modernist' modes and predilections, as unequally affected and challenged by capitalist 'modernism', the project of 'purity' cannot be an easy one. Nor does it help to make high-sounding denigrations of what political realities obtain for the moment. In a continental country in which nations, classes, castes and their political expressions collide with a mindlessly homogenizing capitalism, any ruling elite that wishes 'progress' to be continued to be made must needs be both highly absorptive and imaginative. There seems little scope for pique or educated anger to succeed as state policy.

It will be recalled that a recent eminent chief justice of the Supreme Court of India (alongwith others) has publicly conceded that at least some twenty percent of the judiciary (presumably the lower echelons) are corrupt. It is a thought that perhaps the most telling thing for the honourable Supreme Court to do might be to clear those Augean stables. Indeed what better example could it set for the political class, the Legislature and the Executive.

March 2007

Parvenu Nationalism

I recall that some two decades ago Frederic Jameson noted how literary/creative productions from the 'third world' tend to become 'national allegories.' And I also recall some noted Indian intellectuals taking umbrage at the suggestion that third worlders should have been thought, after all, to be parvenu nationalists, when in fact we, in India for example, existed and produced within an unassimilable multiplicity and plurality of identities and allegiances in true federal fashion. The irony being that the umbrage in itself constituted an instance of hurt nationalist pride.

I thought then and I think now how right Jameson was. Not so paradoxically, as the Indian ruling classes float the myth of our imminent approach towards super-powerdom, this pretence to a global destiny remains equally embedded in a parvenu nationalism. Lacking any accreted self-confidence, we, even in this day and age, continue rather to think as did the American nationalist icons of the middle of the 19c. Walt Whitman then instructed his people that a democratic America should acquire the self-confidence to transcend that feudal Shakespeare, (claiming that, even as he wrote, some 'two dozen Shakespeares walked on either side of the Mississipi'); we want the world to know that a Kalpana Chawla or a Sunita something may well have been born and bred as American citizens but must be understood to reflect the glories of India. Some right wing nationalists of course go far further to claim that even as early in history as the Ramayana (if that be historical), India knew all about nuclear secrets and flying machines. How else would one explain the occurrence of Ram flying back from Lanka in a *Pushpak Viman* (literally a flying object).

If, then, today India is in mourning at the failure of our cricketing gods, the phenomenon needs to be contextualized within the sort of parvenu sensibility suggested above.

Three clearly differentiated orders of involvement seem apparent: at the level of the state, the corporates, and the common masses.

In city and town, effigies of 'team India' are being burnt, as the widespread breast-beating suggests the observance of a national Moharram – not celebratory of the event in Karbala, but as castigation of a loss of national self-esteem and expression of national shame. The gods having failed, a national wake is underway. A happening that after all testifies to the successful penetration of parvenu nationalism among both India's newly educated but illiterate middle classes and emulating, what if impoverished, masses.

The houses and other luxury waterholes of 'team India' are under police protection. The mobs that were the other day berserk with glee at 'team India's' record-making victory against that unheard-of Bermuda are today manaical in frenzy at our losses, first to Bangladesh (a country the size of a medium Indian province – indeed a country that we, in the first place, had brought into being; imagine child being the father of man!) and then against Sri Lanka (several sizes even less).

The galling ignominy of it all; it is as though the Pentagon had prostrated to Peru and to Surinam, not to speak of Iraq or Vietnam, and at a point in our national destiny when India's super-power credentials are just about to be ratified by a so-exclusive one-off nuke deal with that political Yehova of our times, America. What may the latter now think of us, when 'team India' cannot vanquish even a Bangladesh or a Sri Lanka. It is as though the Indian emperor has been discovered to have infact no clothes whatsoever.

II

For a while now India's virtual sense of its super-power eligibility has rested on four pegs: its rate of economic growth; the burgeoning number of billionaires; the power and potential of Hindu heritage as daily projected by sundry sadhus, management gurus, spiritual counsellers and other godmen; and, not the least, by the ubiquitous images of 'team India' (which, if you still do not make out, refers to the Indian cricket team, and cricket, which if you still do not make out, being a game played with bat and ball between two teams of eleven members each).

It is on the basis of this four-fold credit-worthiness that Indians have been schooled to look away from farmers' suicides, abysmal child labour, horrendous atrocities on women and dalits, incrementing joblessness, absence of potable drinking water or electricity for some 60% of the population, a stinking lack of sanitation, millions of easily avoidable deaths by waterborne diseases and a concomitant absence of health services for more than two-thirds of citizens, fleecing corporates and corrupt politicians, fourishing criminal mafias, thick-skinned bureaucracies, brutal superstitions, inter-community massacres, a collapsing parliament, and much else.

Now, that famous growth rate of 9% that never seems to touch the lives of some 70% of Indians seems castrated by inflation and price rise, rendering even the middle-income sections chary and wary; the billionaires recede further and further into planetary isolation from the beleageuered commoners, even as the forex reserves sit like that proverbial pile of inert gold over which the state watches over like a King Cobra, letting not a brick be put to any general use; and, the ultimate rebuff that 'team India' , the icons of many a commercial enterprise as well as quotidian homestead dream, cannot hold a bat straight when it matters, or move a nimble foot, or run with nationalist alacrity between wicket and wicket. Thus the shame, the drowning shame of it all!

As to the godmen etc., whatever happened to all the pujas and yagnas that were everyday performed in all corners of north India to seal the victory of the eleven good men and true? Not all the jagrans (collective prayers) seem after all to have awakened the somnambulant deity to the frustrations and aspirations of doting millions. And what may be said of all the astrologers who have been appearing in flowing robes on TV channels to pronounce the imminent glories of 'team India'? A great big question mark thus hangs over the prowess of Hindutva which, to obviate the failure, will surely now be pressed into service in the forthcoming elections where it may have more success, as life and limb come to be at stake. To wit, now that the World Cup of Cricket is lost, atleast the assemblies at home might be subdued.

Then there is the other thing – oh, the money behind and before it all! Not only have 'team India' failed the masses and the middle classes, more to the point they have brought unforgiveable losses to the corporate state and the media channels that make it visible and potent. Indeed, the damage to advertising revenues, and to the plethora of ancillary employments generated thereof, must be unendurable – certainly more unendurable, it seems, than rapes, caste atrocities, or farmers' suicides. No 'terrorist' or organized or unorganized labouring class, it must be concluded, has done more harm to corporate earnings than our eleven knights in shining blue, whereupon the national logo (or is it some sponsor strip?) now hangs limp in hang-dog perfidy.

As to the BCCI (namely, the Board of Control for Cricket in India) – a set-up (the pun intended) whose revenues must exceed those of some Indian states – what does it now do, with no victors to burgeon its kitty? Indeed, wait till India's rumbustuous Parliament, routinely stymied with street-level in-house mobocracy, meets again: 'team India' will be its main agenda. Its weak-kneed surrender to Bangladesh and Sri Lanka cannot but be read as another aspect of the state's indifference to national security. And the poor minister of Agriculture, co-terminously head also of the BCCI, will need all the protection he can get. There is no telling what forms of chastisement will be recommended for the errant minister-head; that he will be asked to resign may safely be assumed. Will the CBI be directed to enquire into the weakening allegiance of 'team India' to the national interest? Entirely conceivable. And, as to the foreign coach of 'team India,' will he only be sent packing, or will a diplomatic row with his home country, Australia, be also warranted? After all, should Australia win the Cup, as is more than likely, could 'team India's' Australian coach be up for charges of internal sabotage? Who knows, this is India.

Meanwhile, you may be thinking what is this all about? You may think cricket a mere sport; you may raise eyebrows at the quality and status of India's self-perceptio[illegible]ounseling that w[illegible] rather forget about a lost game or two and begin to attend to m[illegible]r more substance. Indeed, you may do all that and prove yourself, thereby, if not an enemy of the people, then of the corporate state. In which case you will become a suspect at home, or a candidate for extradition.

The point is that with so little else to fall back upon, 'team India's' anti-national surrender leaves a whole nation in limbo. And what if even the 123 nuke deal with uncle Sam should fall through? How then do we persuade the world that we are a super-power? And, remember, there are no free lunches.

March 2007

Nandigram and the Left

However much the CPI(M), including the rather overly ebullient Chief Minister of West Bengal, may regret the police firing at Nandigram on March 14, the last word does not seem to get said on the issue.

Things have now come to a pass when as well-reputed a socialist as Surinder Mohan has called upon the Left-Front (LF) allies of the CPI(M) to withdraw their support to the government in West Bengal and begin to look to forge a 'genuine left movement after the defection of the CPI(M) from the camp.' Surinder Mohan, believing that 'those who sell their loyalties to the affluent vested interests cannot dismount from the tiger they have decided to climb, so easily,' considers the CPI(M) to have done so. (*Mainstream*, March 30-April 5, 2007).

Let me say forthwith that, my own questions or reservations about the CPI(M)-led government's policy directions notwithstanding, I stand staunchly by the Left Front (LF). I do so because I hold its history and role over the last three decades as having been pivotal in modulating India's centrist political culture to the good on a wide spectrum of national concerns, and for being indubitably the most credible organized force against majoritarian fascism.

I could supplement that with a rather more petty middle-class predilection: I think that by and large the austere and educated decency of left leaderships is often a heartening relief from the noisy abusiveness of much else that is increasingly on offer. In the Nandigram case, for instance, after all the defence put up by spokespersons of the CPI(M), and not all of that gratuitous, the March 14 killings of 14 civilians have drawn reiterated remorse from the party. This in itself seems refreshing when it is recalled that no regrets are forthcoming from Narinder Modi or anybody else from the Sangh Parivar for the unthinkable brutalities of Gujarat 2002 even five years after the carnage.

Much has gone wrong at Nandigram, and the fact that there is substance to some critiques of the CPI(M) in the matter cannot be denied. Indeed, the fact that this much is now acknowledged by party leaderships as well is not the least of reasons to refuse the deleteriously myopic (reactionary or romantic) invite to throw the baby with the bath water. Apologies, therefore, to Surinder Mohan of whom I do think highly. And to other friends who may have like thoughts in mind.

II

The attack on the CPI(M) has come from disparate quarters, and objectivity requires that these be sifted one from the other.

There are, first of all, those whose breastbeating bears less on the lives and interests of the Bengal peasantry, more on seizing upon the moment to see the back of the LF – something they have failed to effect through the democratic process over seven consecutive elections to the Assembly. Indeed, there is here much of the crocodile in evidence. It should not be forgotten that these are forces who till the other day bemoaned the 'flight of industry' from West Bengal, holding the CPI(M) especially culpable for having pampered the peasantry in order to consolidate its 'vote bank.' That their own erstwhile 'vote bank' among the city bhadralok is today impatient for industrial development seems suddenly a matter of secondary concern. Therefore, the less said here the better.

Greater respect is due to critics who are understandably disillusioned that an occurrence like the March 14 firing should have happened under a LF dispensation. Such disillusionement then reflects on the quality of expectation that wide sections of progressive Indians have come to associate with the general culture of left politics. Thus, whereas state violence vented on civilians may seem routine enough in many parts of the country, that it should have happened in West Bengal has shocked many. That a number of CPI(M) workers were killed, burnt, and evicted from Nandigram between January 3 and March 14 has justified the fatalities of March 14 as little as Godhra justified the Gujarat carnage, although the analogy is merely an argumentative one. I may hasten to add that, having read a full account of the events at Nandigram between January and March, I am able to sense the impotence that the state must have felt at its near-total exclusion from the area. The tragedy clearly lay in the gross ineptitude with which the state then chose to approach the problem.

A third category comprises non-party left ideologues of proven commitment who cannot reconcile their learned and idealized constructions of left praxis with the messy contradictions on the ground. Whereas it would be all-too-easy to dub their concerns as aspects of 'abstraction,' it must be remembered that they perform the all-important task of holding the practicing left to its own highest pronouncements. Having read carefully the findings of the Citizens' Committee which visited Nandigram to see the situation first hand, its crucial conclusion that 'the vast bulk of the villagers' were 'opposed to the take-over of land and most are refusing compensation' throws up a disquieting question – disquieting in that one is speaking in the context of a LF-governed state.

Clearly, the disjunct between the LF government and the inhabitants of Nandigram bespeaks a majesterial tendency to take people for granted, ostensibly because much benefit has accrued to them from LF governance in land policy. This paternalistic bent of mind underscores the pitfalls that often await those who succumb to the temptation to put arbitray markers to the dynamics of democracy. That dynamics, alas, rarely permits the luxury to do-gooders to rest on their laurels.

Indeed this hiatus in the CPI(M)'s democratic praxis is testified to by a slew of statements made not just by leaders of the CPI, RSP, Forward Block but by no less a person than Jyoti Basu who has squarely upbraided the Chief Minister for his cavalier attitude not just towards LF partners but members of his cabinet. If there be truth to these aspersions, I will need to add my insignificant citizen's voice to the caution that distinguished well-wishers of the left have expressed. Any time that a left political culture succumbs to a complacency that entices it into authoritarian impulses, the consequences can be not just contingent but far-reaching. In this regard, the lessons of the history of socialist regimes in the recent past can be forgotten at grave peril to the future of left politics. This is indeed a course that threatens to bring into question the very assumptions which inform the personality of the left; its status as an alterity in the terrain of economic principles already in jeopardy, the left stands to become a party to the obliteration of its status as a political alterity as well. Think that this sort of charge has been articulated formally by be CPI at the conclusion of its two-day state conference. The party introspects that the LF in West Bengal has failed to emerge as a model in the country; its only job seems to be merely trying to stay in power (*Hinduatan Times*, April 10, 2007). Somewhere in that inter-party polemic must reside a grain of truth.

III

Then the larger question: the Chief Minister of West Bengal is on record as having said that nobody should have any illusion that what the LF is 'doing' in West Bengal is 'capitalism'. I recall that Prakash Karat, now General Secretary of the CPI(M), writing in an issue of the *Marxist*, expressed himself similarly to the effect that it would be a theoretical absurdity to expect just one state in India to operate an economic system outside the Indian capitalist path of development.

The candour in these articulations is laudable. That, however, still leaves the question as to the quality and axes of equation the LF ought to have with the current phase of Indian capitalism. For example, is it to be understood that the state government has no choice in the matter of endorsing the proposition that the only capitalism possible now is one that inevitably passes through the SEZ (Special Economic Zone)? And I make no exception here for the SEZ idea as its contours and terms of operation might be modified in line with stipulations made by the left. Given that those stipulations as of this minute remain unendorsed by the UPA government, in its present form, to mention but one detail, the tax concessions proposed for SEZ investors (this according to a finance ministry estimate) would result in a revenue loss of some 1,60,000 crores! That being the case, wouldn't the cost-benefit status of SEZs in relation both to investible revenues and employment generation in the state sector seem dubious in the extreme? And are we to believe that the corporate SEZ investor will place employment generation ahead of the maximization of profit? Or create for us the sort of infra-structure which may be useful to the common Indian but useless to him?

The point is that during the tenure of the UPA government the left has from time to time made a stream of people-friendly interventions in economic policy initiatives dear to the heart of those at the apex of financial management (and dear to the heart of those that forged the Washington Consensus of 1990). Be it on the question of disinvestments in public undertakings, the operation of the FDI regime, convertibility of the currency on capital account, the scale of corporate taxation, corporate incursions into the retail market, futures trading in essential food items, Employees Provident Fund, opening up the Insurance sector, the scale of investments in the social sector, public investments to enhance the prospects of weaker sections, the pricing of petroleum products, or the operation of labour laws and worker's rights – the burden of left interventions has been to guide Indian capitalism away from globalised monetarism towards a humane welfarism. The central left endeavour has been to preserve the primary role of the state and to dissuade the ruling class from massive transfer of assets to private hands.

That being the record – and a most laudable one at that – why need the left bite at the SEZ apple at all? And then for the left to function as a facilitator to the SEZ investor certainly stands to be seen as comprising a turn around that neither benefits the people of India nor the future of left politics.

As to industrialization, it now turns up that West Bengal does in fact have waste and fallow land far in excess of the 1% spoken of by the Chief Minister. One is aware that inter-state competition in the matter of attracting corporate investment in industry is a reality. But does that necessarily mean that the LF enter into that competition on the terms set by the corporate sector? Surely, the LF in West Bengal is possessed of other forms of intellectual and governmental initiatives, together with the great asset of an unperturbed social milieu, that can be offered as LF USPs. And why should the LF be perceived to be taking away from those that it spent three decades of struggle and governance to give to (indicated are the magnificent achievements of according ownership and permanent tenancy rights to various sections of the farming community – achievements that have indeed placed the LF among international record books) and giving to those who are, in theory at least, still regarded as class enemies? And how credible does such a course render the left's harangues against precisely such practices in other parts of the country? It would be useless to pretend that public peceptions spawned by these contradictions do not yield transformed negative equations in social relations in ways that threaten to undermine the identity of the left per se.

It is also rather hard to credit wholly the proposition that little revenue and employment generation can be looked to via the small scale, and medium entrepreneurial and retail sectors that may be based on agricultural production. It is a question as to whether the big and basic industry route or a creative amalgam of the latter is more conducive to enhancing rural incomes and purchasing power. Certainly, where industry wishes to come, it ought to be within the resource of an LF leadership to inspire such industrialists to show something of the pioneering spirit which informed their initiatives at the dawn of independence. Surely, the left can hardly be seen to be consistent in demanding, on the one hand, higher taxation (including capital gains tax) on corporate incomes, and, on the other, offering to them incentives at home.

I think of Cuba that has no limousines, and none of the accoutrement of consumption that goes with the limousine culture. What it has though is the world's best health care system, and the world's best educational system. Where in the calculations of the LF in West Bengal do these priorities figure? And let me also say, excusable flourish I hope, where in the quality of left mass interactions is the glow, the communicated warmth, the seamlessness that is so radiantly apparent everytime a Chavez or a Castro meets with the throng of their people? Why is it that left public culture seems always one of 'telling' rather than of 'sharing?' Why has that smiling lightness of being given way to the unsociable sang froid of the bureaucratic visage? Why has the left's all-knowingness frozen into a stance of rigid top-downism? The Indian left, methinks, needs not only to boldly assert its opposition to a capitalism that aims to drink at the common Indian's jugular, but it also needs to put on a face that draws to it the armies of the destitute and the expectant so that at some point its present telos of humanizing capitalism metamorphoses into a conviction and an energy of another kind. That will require that it gladly grow beyond its own skin to forge alliances with the best of the social movements now on the ground, unmindful of being always in the front line. The left needs to sing a song that draws many a melody into one resounding symphony, always feeling most at home with the disabled drummer in the back of the orchestra, and always cautious that it is not seen to be anxious to be the loudest voice.

Meanwhile, we need to realize that one Nandigram does not render the CPI(M) obsolete, does not render it a found-out collaborator, does not cancel its historic struggle against sectarian and fascist politics. Remembering the grievous fault-lines of our history as a nation, that last by itself testifies to our continuing need for the CPI(M), and the LF. If the CPI(M) does not seem cognizant of our existence (nobody says hello to me even at close quarters), we must remain cognizant of its in the conviction that, acknowledged or not, its ear is open to the selflessly rational and the provenly caring.

Let the CPI(M) begin anew, acknowledge its own best self-criticisms, and put its best foot forward in the march towards the million footfalls.

April 2007

Kashmir Revisited

A reply to Nirmalangshu Mukherji

In a recent Znet article, Nirmalangshu – a leftist himself, one whom I regard highly – has raised some questions with respect to my article 'Is Independence a Viable Option for Jammu & Kashmir?' (Znet, January 24).

The questions relate, roughly, to three sorts of concern: an ontological, analogical, and interpretive one. The first of these is clearly of far-reaching import and interest, and the best thing I can do is to enumerate my own position as of now as honestly as I am able. The latter two, being essentially polemical, I shall address in their own place.

Nirmalanghsu assumes, on what grounds is not clear – which is why it remains an assumption – that the right of self-determination 'ought to be viewed' as 'basic and absolute.' Nirmalangshu's 'ought to be' seems located in the notion of a 'categorical imperative' that deserves to override 'historical contexts' (his phrase).

Let me say atonce that I can think of other rights that seem to me more pressing than that of self-determination, and, I might add, of far greater universal validity; yet none of those are to this day codified as any part of the regime of 'human rights.' I shall come to this.

The point I wish to make here is that however 'self-evident' our notion of rights, be it as general postulates of selfless rationality, or even as elements which do find expression in various republican constitutions, 'historical contexts,' alas, have variously either upheld them for brief sojourns of human sanity, or mauled them at the behest of concrete and dominant interests and agentialities. Indeed, not unoften have the very power-structures that struggled on their behalf become their chief demolishers subsequently. What better instance than the current history of the 'land of the free and the brave.'

Thus I am constrained to argue that any study of the history of rights tells us two things: one, that they have always been located in specific histories (being therefore contingent rather than ontological), and, two, that all rights regimes have in one way or another been inseparable from the concrete interests of classes and social groups.

Consider, for example, that in pre-Enlightenment Europe the only right that seemed extant was the 'divine right' of the monarch to rule his/her realm. For the most part there were either those who had 'privileges' (clergy, nobility &c) and those others who had none.

It can hardly then be denied that the notion of 'human rights' in the 18c issued as a collateral to the material ascendance of a new class. And, interestingly, those that formulated the 'self-evident' theory of rights seemed very little bothered to be slave-owners as well. Thus, liberty and equality could, it seemed, happily coexist with slavery. Or racism, or anti-semitism, or a wholescale denial of agentiality to a half of all humankind, namely women. Keeping them as chattel seemed another form of a 'self-evident' categorical imperative if the affairs of the world were to be carried on with reliable male proficiency, since such proficiency was argued (and indeed continues to be) as issuing from an 'ordained' scheme of things.

Let me clarify, lest my friend Nirmalangshu should construe what I have said as proof of my disdain for rights.

I am simply contesting his view that any rights either ever have been or are likely to be universally installed and then implemented as being 'basic and absolute.' Indeed, when he stipulates that they 'ought to be' who, one might ask, is the audience he addresses himself to? It hardly solves our problem to make that enunciation, or simply leave it to a Hegelian abstract to obtain their realization, especially since Nirmalangshu, as a philosophical anarchist, will make no concessions to the idea of the 'state'. More of that hereafter.

Let me now say that, far from being an enemy of rights, I would, if anything, desire their amplification in a direction which I hold to be more 'self-evident' than self-determination.

Is it not a curious and cruel irony that nowhere in the world's binding documents are indubitable and universal human needs – needs that truly override 'historical contexts' – codified as 'self-evident' human rights?

Be it gainful employment, sanitation, housing, clean drinking water, assured and nutritious food supply, education without bars, non-polluting environment, universal health services, recreational infrastructure for children, old age care, and much more in that line, neither an international rights regime, nor national governments, nor indeed many advocates of rights seem as exercised on their behalf as they justly, repeat justly, are exercised on behalf of custodial deteneus or other victims of political tyranny. This stunning lacuna that disfigures both the theory and practice of rights only suggests that the notion that any rights are 'basic and absolute' is no more than a misconceived, even if laudable, postulate.

The problem is complicated by the fact that Nirmalangshu clearly locates the notion of the 'basic and the absolute' over and beyond the operations of the real world which only offers, in our experience of history thus far, contested perceptions and claims among 'the people' (his phrase), and various forms of 'state' which always, at bottom, represent concrete social interests. The difference between him and me here seems to devolve around his lordly disdain for the idea of the 'state' and my willingness to acknowledge its existence. Thus, when Nirmalangshu accuses me towards the end of his diatribe of viewing 'the status of the Indian state as higher than the rights of people' let me remind him of my text in this regard: "The writer," I wrote in that article, "is as aware of the endemically repressive nature of the state as any anarchist now arguing vociferously for its defeat." Surely, Nirmalangshu seems unbecomingly reductive of my stated position – something he accuses me of being in some places.

Nirmalangshu's endorsement of self-determination on behalf of 'the people' (who are 'the people' in the context of Jammu & Kashmir'?) bears inevitably on the question related to the 'state'. There seems to be a suggestion here that once self-determination is achieved (since 'granted' would imply an acknowledgement of the existence of the state', perish the thought) they would be rid of the 'state' or formulate one that better suited their purposes. Since we are not here, emphatically, considering the end of class struggle in Kashmir whence the state would wither, it would be in order to ask where the telos of the new just state might be. Is it inconceivable that within that new state, other voices might come up demanding further acts of self-determination? Indeed, what is to be thought of the already existing demand of dominant (no one voice there as well) for a 'homeland' within the valley (indeed a state within a state)? If self determination is to be "basic and absolute" on what grounds may that demand be turned aside? Or shall it be said that those that make such a demand are not somehow eligible to be included among 'the people'?

Suppose that self-determination once achieved in Kashmir, five crore Gujaratis, (remember?) were to seek self-determined secession from the secular democratic Indian state inorder to reformulate Gujarat, de jure, as a Hindu Rashtra; or suppose that West Bengal, similarly often frustrated by Delhi's class rule (you might contest the polemic but that would be their self-determined position) were to take the same route inorder to establish a 'communist' state, how would Nirmalangshu respond or advise? Or Tamil Nadu on linguistic grounds, or the North East on ethnic/racial principles, and so forth? For all I know, Nirmalangshu's grounding in the 'basic and the absolute' would only oblige him to say yes to all that. Which is where we would part company altogether. Indeed, there have been strong voices arguing that India should adopt a Presidential system of governance. Why then couldn't such strong opinion be granted the due of a referendum on the issue, since in Nirmalangshu's schema the strongly expressed will must override the numerical – a basis on which he questions my interpretation of the MORI and Synovate Polls? I will return to the conundrum (for me at any rate) about self-determination in the context of his allusion to Iraq.

Nirmalangshu holds the Indian presence in Kashmir as analogous to the American presence in Iraq – an argument that is much in the rounds in predictable enclaves. I invite Nirmalangshu to think that the analogy is not only factually erroneous but potentially fraught in ways that bode nothing good for the Kashmiris.

Yet, Nirmalangshu's analogy, paradoxically, has an application that either escapes him or that he is unwilling to concede.

Let it be recalled that the Indian state did not 'annexe' Jammu & Kashmir. The then maharaja – like all the other maharajas that did so – signed an instrument of accession in accordance with the then prevailing legal schema (however flawed it may seem to us now). Indian troops were invited into the state to meet an aggression that came from the new state of Pakistan which, to meet the analogy that Nirmalangshu provides, like the Americans in Iraq, made their occupation of one-third of Jammu & Kashmir permanent. Let it also be recalled that it was India that offered the self-determination route in the United Nations before anybody in Kashmir asked for it, and that the resolutions of that international arbiter required certain conditions to be met inorder for self-determintion to become operational, chiefly the vacation by the aggressor of the territories forcibly occupied by it. That has not happened to this day (and let us hope the Iraqis have better luck with the occupying imperialists). In the meanwhile, let it also be recalled that the instrument of accession was duly adopted by an elected assembly in Jammu & Kashmir. Indeed, it is conceivable that had self-determination been effected anytime prior to 1953, 'the people' would have overwhelmingly voted for the Indian state.

That raises the further question: at what point in the history of Jammu & Kashmir are we to fix the position of 'the people' as wholly and indubitably authentic and final? In 1938 when Sheikh Abdullah rechristened the Muslim Conference as the National Conference? In 1944 when he shooed off Jinnah from the valley for his sectarian persuasions? 1947 when Kashmiris fought the aggressor side by side with the Indian troops? 1952 when the Delhi Agreement was signed between Sheikh Abdullah and Nehru? 1975 when Abdullah reached an Accord with Indira Gandhi? 1987 when Syed Sallah-u-din, since the chief of the Hizbul Mujahideen, thought it was ok to participate in the then elections? Or after 1989 when militancy began and the Pandits became refugees? Or now when all parties barring some 'external forces' (a phrase that Nirmalangshu uses chiefly to describe India) seem inclined to find a peaceful and democratic resolution, not excluding Pakistan? Now, when most Kashmiris desire fervently a return to that syncretic Kashmiriyat to which Gandhi sang hossanas in 1946? When Sheikh Abdalluh was jailed, when India arranged for elections to be stolen, or in the worst periods of atrocities by India's military in Kashmir? Tough one for me to answer.

Lastly, to the bit about Nirmalangshu's polemics. Nirmalangshu accuses me of 'imposing the condition' that 'whatever resolutions are debated or found must pertain to the entire state of Jammu & Kashmir.' In thus committing himself to the unscholarly act of selective quotation, I must confess, Nirmalangshu surprises me much (although I can understand why he found it necessary to do so, since the whole weight of his diatribe against my analyses of the Polls impinges on so doing).

Therefore, in fairness to myself, let me cite my complete text in this area of concern:

> every interested party to the dispute on J&K, it must be recorded, proceeds on one accepted principle – that whatever resolutions are debated or found must pertain to the entire state of Jammu & Kashmir.

It is then easy to see that Nirmalangshu's deletion of the first clause in the sentence, and its replacement by the wholly erroneous projection that somehow I it is who is imposing that condition changes everything.

It would have been far more becoming had Nirmalangshu verified for himself the truth-content of what I have infact said above; indeed, I challenge him to find one single stated position of any interested group in Kashmir that holds that the Kashmir dispute must be resolved only on the basis of the valley – a fact that reinforces everything I go on to analyse in the two Polls. And let me reiterate: only stated positions can form the matter for debate. As to personal or private predilections, those come dime a dozen, and may at best constitute matter for back-channel parleys. The theoretically abstract and the politically unarticulated may well lead into charming discourse; they cannot show the way to decision.

The further charge that Nirmalangshu makes, equally tendentiously, is that I seek an ethnic division of the valley (the POK question). Once again my only recourse is to the context in which I spoke of the linguistic difference between the Kashmiri-speaking Muslim in the valley and the non-Kashmiri-speaking counterparts across the Line of Control (LOC).

I cited the Synovate Poll which among other things showed that 55% in the valley "think the *de facto* position of the Line of Control as the effective border should be made *de jure* as well." And it was then as an effort to comprehend that stunning statistics that I alluded to the linguistic divide between Kashmiris on the two sides of the LOC as one rationale. I invite Nirmalangshu to cite a phrase in my article that says that in my view the two parts of Kashmir should be divided. I am amazed that as responsible an academic as Nirmalangshu should misread my gloss on the Synovate statistic as my position on ethnic division.

In the end, let me suggest to Nirmalangshu that we do exactly as he advocates – leave the matter to 'the people' to work out. Nirmalangshu may not approve of the modalities in which those deliberations are underway, or the macro-parameters within which work towards a resolution seems proceeding. Surely, if a convergence is happening that has the 'people's' assent (and let us not pretend that the only 'people' who qualify to be 'people' are the ones who continue to follow the violent path), what business have Nirmalangshu or I to 'impose' our theoretical or other constructions on all that?

April 2007

The Moral Highs of India's 'Cultural Nationalists'

India's Hindu right-wing is currently in the moral doghouse. Curious fate for an ideological set-up that stridently claims proprietary rights to the terrain of 'values'. It is another matter that some fifteen years after they razed the mosque at Ayodhya in a despicable act of profound irreligion, the more conscientious even among Hindu saints and sadhus now openly characterise the BJP as in fact an unprincipled jamboree of crass atheists for whom the building of the Ram temple has been nothing more than a cynical ploy to garner Hindu-communal votes. Objective and knowledgeable political analysts have of course long learnt to identify the Hindu right that routinely mouths the slogan of 'cultural nationalism' as a proto-fascist phenomenon.

But to be now repeatedly found out as perhaps morally the most bankrupt among India's major political formations must seem grievous and galling. Not because such bankruptcy is any surprise to the BJP itself, since its gestalt has always willingly replicated the low mercantile cunning of the successful retailer, but because its camouflage of pieties stands publicly shred to smithereens.

It all began some years ago (speaking, that is, only of recent times) when no less than the BJP party President was captured on hidden camera extending a copious palm to collar hefty wads of graft as earnest to pursuing a defence purchase deal.

This category of moral corruption was to be followed up during the NDA regime (National Democratic Alliance, led by the BJP) by several mega-scams which involved the allotment of choice urban plots of land to RSS cronies at throwaway prices, as also petrol pump dealerships likewise – something that continues to happen routinely wherever the party is voted to power.

During the tenure of the current UPA Government, the most notable instance has been the hidden-camera exposure of a slew of BJP Members of India's Parliament accepting moneys for raising queries in the House, whatever queries that is.

As of this moment, the high moral podium is occupied by two honourable BJP Members of Parliament (again) who have been caught running a most lucrative human trafficking racket. The investigating agencies have unearthed a plethora of fake passports and fake identities – instruments that have been used repeatedly to cart women abroad in the guise of spouses in lieu of astronomical dividends, some to join their real spouses, and many others, as it now turns out, as fodder for the blue-film industry. Most of the latter on false pretences. Wretchedly, one of these two MPs is not just from Gujarat but close to Narendra Modi.

Now, as is well-known, right-wing funda-mentalists the world over have always sought to identify free female sexual choice as the one indubitable source of 'immorality'. The literature here is copious. Hindu 'cultural nationalists' are of a piece here, although, arguably, the history even of savarna Hindu thought provides some more emancipatory traditions as well, until women began to become the political focus of a regimentation directed ostensibly against the 'invaders' – Mughal, Afghan, or colonial – i.e., Christian – but ploughed to cement a male-militarist majoritarian future. Note that the constitution of the RSS which came into coerced existence as late as 1949 offers membership only to the male of the species. Borrowing explicitly from both Italian fascism and Nazi racism, the RSS has held that women are best obliged to bear and rear the species, and to mind the hearth and the home.

Which is why the Hindu right-wing, much like the Taliban, approaches the matter in two complementary ways. On the one hand their vigilantes (currently with menacing frequency) trash art forms or reading materials that represent women as agents of free choice, bash consenting young men and women, be it at college, or in the public park, or in the new-fangled malls – men and women who might just be walking side by side or holding hands – and do positive violence to such couples, if not foment a communal conflagaration, should they be inter-community twosomes. On the other hand, however, where the sleazy shenanigans of top Hindu right-wing mentors come to light, recourse is made to aggressive denial and to invoking the conspiracy theory.

Not long ago, a highly placed RSS apparatchik who had been installed to mentor the BJP was caught, once again, on hidden camera (damn the dirty instrument) having a rather jolly time, refreshingly oblivious of the pieties of right-wingism. But, lo and behold, a friendly BJP state Government and its wholly subservient state-apparatus went to work and defaced the Compact Disc before submission to the enquiring authority. At which it was proved that the whole thing had been yet another attempt by frustrated 'pseudo-secularists' to blacken the shining moral face of the saintly Sangh Parivar.

And just the other day news has come that an honourable Minister in the BJP Government in Uttarakhand might have something to do with the call-girl career and subsequent murder of one Neelam. True to pattern, the honourable Minister disavows the least knowledge of this deceased wretch, even as a maverick channel dredges up evidence of acquaintance between the two going back some three years in the holy town of Hardwar.

Yet other instances have involved sex-rackets run by venerated sadhus who run fat-cat temples and matths, and sleaze, property-related violence and murder among saffron owners of various akhardas (literally plots of ground reserved for training of recruits in martial activity like wrestling and so on). In the racket that pertained to the Naranyanswami temple in Gujarat, indeed, the video-graphic evidence was too compelling to afford denial, although righteous indignation was expressed that the media were put upto the job out of spite. In most of these cases, not the one who is found out but the one who finds out is held guilty of immoral conduct.

II

Speaking of morality, you would think that lying constitutes a bad case of immorality. As we know, 'thou shall not lie' is one of the commandments. That, however, has never prevented either Christian or Hindu fundamentalists from lying with aplomb. The world has not forgotten Watergate, nor has the current Christian right in America minded one bit the lies that the Bush regime spawned one after the other preparatory to its Iraq invasion – and that it continues to spawn and defend with 'patriotic' self-righteousness.

During the course of the elections now underway in Uttar Pradesh, the BJP formally released a Compact Disc chokeful of venomous lies and abuse about Muslims. Once caught by alert segments of the media, the Hindu right-wing lied to its teeth to say the CD was not an 'authorised' one, and that no one in the BJP knew anything about what it contained! So blatant has this episode of abysmal lying been that regardless of the BJP's disclaimers the matter has found cognisance with the Election Commission of India which is to adjudicate what punishment to mete out to the party. There is, of course, no telling what the Commission might do.

Or take the matter of the Godhra train burning of 2002 – an occurrence that Modi, out-Goebbeleseing Goebbles, bled to the drop as his argument for the existence of the WMD among the Muslims of Gujarat, and using it without the least qualm to engender the massacre of some two thousand innocent lives.

It took the meticulous and non-partisan work of the Justice U.C. Bannerjee Commission to expose the propaganda that the affected coach of the Sabarmati Express which was carrying saffron kar sevaks back from their triumphant act of destruction and desecration in Ayodhya was set afire from the outside as an act of pre-meditated 'Islamist' conspiracy.

III

Finally, if the Gujarat carnage had not been enough proof of the moral timbre of the Hindu right-wing, let us talk about plain good old murder that brooks no mitigation.

It has now been officially reported by an upright police officer of the Gujarat CID (since removed), one DIG Geeta Johri, that the 'encounter' in which one Sohrabuddin was liquidated by the Gujarat Police in November of 2005 was, after all, a 'fake' encounter, and, to put it simply, an act of murder. And the ones committing that act were not exactly some low-level constables, but two IPS officers, Vanzara and Pandiya, both close to the Home Minister, Amit Shah, and in turn to Nero-Modi himself.

Within hours literally, under the say-so of the Supreme Court of India which was pleased to issue habeus corpus for the production of Sohrabuddin's missing wife, Kausar Bee, the Gujarat Government has had to spill further beans (terrified that should it not, the case will be handed over to the Central CBI); it now acknowledges that the good lady, witness to her husband's murder, has also been put to sleep, then burnt in the vicinity of the Vanzara house, and her ashes and remainders scattered in the nearby fields. Particularly piquant is the further fact (from the point of view of Modi's Hindutva followers who wish to think that

Hindus matter to him in some special way) that one Tulsi Ram Prajapati, an informer to the Gujarat Police, has likewise been liquidated to obviate any leaks. Some news channels report that another three or four Hindus have suffered the same fatal consequence. The case of referral to the CBI is now before the honourable Supreme Court for order.

Speaking of which, it is to be recalled that the father of the late Haren Pandya, the erstwhile Member of Modi's Cabinet who fell out as a 'dissident' and was one morning assassinated during his routine walk, to this day publicly holds none other than Modi guilty of his son's murder. Morality piling on morality, and murder on murder; in between bribery, sleaze, lying and violent vigilantism, leading upto murder. Not to speak of those magnificently 'nationalist' episodes during which minority Muslims are ostracised, terrified, maimed, burnt, and killed; or, as in the recent most case again, when a Christian school principal and preacher is set upon by the Bajrang Dal for expressing Christian views, and wounded to the bone. Or when whole dalit slum colonies are razed, dalit women raped and killed, and, in one case recently, four dalit young men ritualistically murdered inch by inch in public view to the accompaniment of animal grunts of approval from caste Hindus. All in the name of occupying the moral high ground.

IV

There is another aspect to the redoubtable moral timbre of the Hindu right-wing fraternity. When the moral chips come apart, the fraternity jells into a rabid and shameless cacophony. Not one of the Sangh-associated intellectuals musters the integrity to call a lie a lie, a sleazy act a sleazy act, an act of moolah corruption an act of moolah corruption, a murder a murder, not to speak of a pogrom a pogrom.

By contrast, the history even of the Congress party (no stranger to corruption) is replete with instances of high moral conduct, even of open revolt. A knowledgeable journalist (Pankaj Vohra, *HT*, April 30, 2007) has pointed out how the imposition of the internal Emergency in 1975 led to such a revolt by a clutch of younger Congress-men and women who came to be called the 'Young Turks'. Indeed, were one to go as far back as India's first election (1952) one would come across recorded instance of a stunning moral character (the like of which may not be available anywhere). This is one when Jawaharlal Nehru, electioneering in the then REWA State, at the end of his speech admonished the crowd not to vote for the Congress candidate sitting next to him because he was a corrupt fellow. Those were the days.

Or take the recent Nandigram episode where on March 14, fourteen people lost their lives to police firing. Such a thing may have happened but once in the thirty years of uninterrupted rule by the Left Front, yet the occurrence drew instant criticism from known left intellectuals, including humble ones like the present writer. (See my 'Nandigram and the Left', Z-net, April 11, 2007.) To this day, however, one hears nothing but rabid and disingenuous defences or justifications of the unspeakable Gujarat carnage of 2002. Even the needlessly lauded Atal Behari Vajpayee was to eat his hesitant words of paternal admonition in deference to the gang-up.

V

Where, then, does all that leave us and the Hindu 'cultural nationalists'? Certain all-too-real class realities need to be noted. India's comprador corporates and the media channels that speak for them may now and again be embarrassed by the communal politics of the Hindu right-wing, if not so much as a revulsion against Hindu communalism per se as an irritation at the disruption such politics causes in the even and unthwarted operations of the market, yet they manage to return to view the aberrations of the Hindu right-wing crassnesses with an ameliorative eye. The most handy manoeuvre employed is to say 'hamaam mein sab nange hein', ergo, who is there who is not naked in the bath. Translated, all politicians and parties are of one rotten fibre built. Of course, were the same irresponsible generalisation to be made about the media, a huge outcry would follow.

The fact is that, never sure of the temperament of the Congress (now bourgeois, now Third-Worldist, now anti-colonialist, now social-democratic, now seeking proximity to the superpower, now hell-bent on quotas, and usually reluctant to be easy on first-name terms with the media, often aristocratic in memory and gloating in its history), it is the BJP that offers the corporate world an uncomplicatedly congenial platform. Be it disinvestment in the public sector, be it transfer of assets to private hands, be it throwing open the market to global predators, or be it seeking a close relationship with Israel and America on the grounds of a common anti-Muslim agenda, backed up by militarism at home, or indeed be it unifying the nation around a sexy Hindu ethos as an insusrance against left-wing consolidation (notice the corporate executive suit and tie, and the *kalava* – sacred thread around the wrist worn by many Hindus) – the BJP fits the corporate bill. And it needs to be recognised that a great part of the Hindu right-wing bravado even in the teeth of shameful shenanigans, the least of which would be enough to do in any of the other political parties, owes to the assurance it always has that where the least misdeed of the Congress or the left, or the regional outfits led by the Other Backward Classes will be certified to draw corporate-media fire, its worst criminalities are slated to receive kid-glove disapproval. You would need to watch a lot of television with sustained attention to recognise the truth of this, because often the casting of tone, time, space and panel selection is so astute that the channel can claim perfect impartiality. Until of course something happens in the internal mechanics of any particular channel ownership in relation to the power structure that sides seem to change overnight.

It is therefore for ordinary citizens of India to carry forward the message that often those that claim closest proximity to church or temple or mosque are the ones who are farthest from god. This is a task that, of course, the left-wing must lead and carry forward relentlessly in close association with the dedicated and selfless civil society agents who sustain the people's agendas in admirable ways.

May 2007

The Year of the Indian Diet of Worms?

> The question of the relationship of political emancipation to religion becomes...the question of of the relationship of political emancipation to human emancipation.
> Marx

It has taken a long time in happening, but at long last modern India may be beginning to embrace a challenging rite of passage.

One among India's proliferating Television channels has picked up the courage to expose, without fear or favour, the criminalities practiced within the country's myriad Hindu religious establishments.

Having previously investigated the unlawful manipulations of moneys related to the Muslim institution of the Haj, as well as captured on candid camera Christian pastors of diverse Indian churches issuing fake certificates of baptism against graft, TV 18 has over the past week or so scooped through hidden camera the mind-bogling money-laundering shenanigans of seven of India's best known Hindu godmen.

The racket involves facilitating the conversion of large sums of unaccounted wealth into legitimate incomes by using the agency of elephantine religious institutions over which these saintly dharm gurus preside. Notably, the properties – land, buildings, and other assets – that these institutions possess always seem to lie outside the operations of India's investigating agencies, just as the crores of unaccounted liquidity that finds a haven therein seems never to attract the notice of any tax-levying/gathering authority.

Not surprisingly, some of these infamous seven also made brazen claims of having serviced politicians in the highest places. TV 18 has judiciously withheld those names, lacking any corroborative evidence.

Happily, a few other channels seem to have caught on, even if with a view to not losing out on competitive TRP ratings. Who said capitalism does not have its positive points.

While one of these other channels has been running the spectacle of a Naga sadhu receiving public chastisement from a young woman whom he tried to molest in her house next door, another has been projecting the unlovely greed of the priesthood in the Juna akhara in the holy city of Varanasi who have been shown to lay forcible claim to a temple *gaddi* (seat of authority) in far off Jammu city worth some eleven crores! Not unreasonably, local Jammu city citizens have been shown physically preventing the somewhat colonial take-over from afar to raucuous resolve.

Even as I write, TV 18 is repeatedly displaying the latest violent vigilantism of VHP (Vishwa Hindu Parishad) goons (and the channel is indeed calling them such) who are shown bashing in broad daylight – and in front of media cameras – two miserable looking Christian priests allegedly for indulging in conversion activity. The TV 18 story is justly emphasizing the point that while a case has been lodged against the two priests, the police has thus far refused to take cognizance of the criminal brutality vented on them on the pretext, would you believe, that no formal complaint has been lodged. To wit, next time around you might feel free to rob, molest, or kill in broad daylight, or indulge more extensive communal pogroms if you can ensure that no complaint will be lodged! As to what the whole country is witness to, thanks to TV 18, well, maybe the channel should think better of it. It is to be noted that Maharashra where this lynch mob has been busy breaking Christian bones is ruled by a Congress-led government. Furthermore, the poorpriests are at the receiving end of the law when infact no complaint has been lodged against them by the people they have been accused of converting – a requirement in law as per the police's own stipulation!

II

Back, however, to the seven godmen. The path-breaking exposure made by TV 18 as a sustained critique invites the speculation whether India (Brahminical North India in particular) may be on the threshold of its Lutheran moment. One is encouraged to ask that question in the light of the public response that TV18 has been relaying; in town and city, young and old express a range of disgust, stretching from saddened disillusionment, to anger and outrage. Many are heard saying that these self-proclaimed godmen should forthwith face the legal consequences of their clandestine criminalities; others admonish that no faithfuls must frequent the discourses they routinely deliver.

Hindu religious practice is, as is well-known, endlessly fractious and pluralist, primarily because its diversity of doctrine disallows the centralization of any single creed. There are ofcourse the four Shankaracharyas who rule over four authorized matths (it is another matter, again, that one of the four is currently involved in litigation over a charge of murder). Thus Hindu religious organization has no Pope. Yet, the godmen and miracle-workers who are ubiquitous in droves have tended to wield an influence that continues to hold in thrall the consolidation of the regime of 'public reason' – a concept that Archbishop Rowan was to characterize as the central edifice of the secular way of life (see his lecture given at the Pontifical Academy of Social Sciences, Rome on November 23, 2006). Not that Archbishop Rowan endorses that way of life without intellectual challenge, as is to be expected. Yet, it would seem that India's Brahminical North might just be saying, enough of Indulgencies and certificates of remission, enough of claims to supra-rational prowess: we have seen the ugly truth. Keep your fingers crossed; this here is a land where mystery and myth reign, and where the magical irrational, even if often gruesome and inhuman, has votaries among the very highly educated and accomplished. Indeed, we are not quite past the time when even among professionals with astronomical incomes, the need and pride of indigenism expresses itself in the most maddening forms of unreason.

III

Far be it for me to suggest that the Lutheran revolt was a revolt against Christianity, not to speak of religion. Perhaps unbeknown to the man himself, the stand he took against Church hierarchy and its totalitarian requirements was to be the ideological bedrock upon which the new European capitalist class could base its expropriating, secular future. After all, in routing for 'faith' as the true ground for 'justification' as against 'works', Luther was to accomplish a liberation for the new avant garde that a hypocritical and venal Rome had consistently denied, never mind that they were found to be the worst offenders against what they preached.

The doctrine of 'faith' in effect ousted Jesus and his ethical/socially radical teaching from the Bible. Think; how on earth could the new capitalist elite carry on the proper business of expropriation so long as the moral/humanist centralities of the Sermon on the Mount remained at the heart of the Christian way of life. Imagine the new entrepreneur admonishing himself to love his neighbour as himself, or to take to heart the teaching that heaven was as inaccessible to the rich man as the eye of the needle to the camel; or that it was such a rotten thing to lay your treasure upon the earth! As to 'faith' anyone could lay claim to it with subjective fervour that brooked no demonstration in life.

None of this might have happened if a Copernicus, a Galileo, a Bruno had not made frontal assaults on the reigning epistemologies of the religious view that swore by the revealed rather than by the empirically established. The European bourgeois classes, I am suggesting, were to be the product of a grounding in the new method of science. And in seeking to dethrone medievalism, they had crucially underlined the linkages between medieval religious doctrine and feudal political economy – properly the project of a radical and progressive class. Not for a minute, though, was it any part of this class to jettison religion per se. As Marx was resonantly to observe, the capitalist class may have taken up cudgels against a discomfiting form of christianity; capitalism cannot, however, ever live without the idea of religion as a crucial ally in thwarting inimical extensions of the democratic histories it helped to forge.

Since the exhaustion of its first progressive role in history, the capitalist class the world over has made the fullest use of religion to further its reactionary/sectarian/imperialist purposes, paying to the ousted medievalists the ultimate tribute of mimicry. After all, it is christian jihadis today who seek to vanquish islamic jihadis, just as it is Hindutva jihadis who seek to oust both islamist jihadists and secular republicans at one go.

Marx, it will be remembered, was to articulate the double life of the citizen in capitalist society with customary clarity and force of formulation in his rejoinder to Bruno Bauer (On the Jewish Question):

> The citizen of a 'free state' leads a double life. In his real life in civil society, i.e. economic society, he is isolated and at war with everyone else in defence of his private interests. And in his imaginary life as a citizen of the state, he is integrated into and at one with the world in theory but not in practice. It is this situation which gives rise to religious feelings. Religion is the heart's cry of alienated, atomized man, who overcomes the separation he experiences in every day life, but only on the level of fantasy. Religious ideas will finally evaporate only when we have put

an end to the atomism of society and chased away the fear and anxiety caused by the role of money.

IV

Be that as it may, however the empowered and entrenched capitalist class may have sought to extinguish its crucial, formative debt to the method of science, substituting reified technologies and fetishised commodities for the regime of scientific reason and integrity, if western 'successes' have remained autonomous of the life of church doctrine (one kind or another), this has owed to those decisive centuries when it made science its legitimating ground.

The story as far as India is concerned was to be vastly, and dismally, at variance with that western capitalist narrative.

Although the party documents of India's organized left routinely allude to the post-independence state as, variously, 'bourgeois-landlord' or 'bourgeois' state, I have often wondered whether India actually ever went through a bourgeois transformation, or can be said to possess a classic bourgeois class.

Is it not the case, overwhelmingly, that the professional and propertied elites who led the Indian anti-colonial struggle had next to no history of having taken on social or religious medievalism, with countable honourable exceptions in the southern states and in Maharashtra? Can it be said that their grounding in science had a fraction of the conviction or rigour that the bourgeois classes in England and Europe came to have? Did they not rather seek, dissenting rational voices notwithstanding (and these were often heroic in the teeth of the most abysmal denials of scrutiny into disabling traditions and forms of social and religious life), to incorporate the worst archives of superstitious myth-making, and ostensibly supra-rational ways of seeing into the anti-colonial movement, either to avoid causing divisions among the polity or to keep in place a reservoir of indigenisms which somehow represented that which was wholly our own?

India's affluent metropolitans, alas, it must be said, are the products of a collective history of which the radical challenge of science and rational enquiry into the patent chicaneries and unsubstantiated claims of diverse patterns of hierarchy and authority formed little part. Their claim to modernity thus remains a spurious skein and veneer, defined more by income-levels, gadgetry, trans-global mobility, proficiency in English, rather than by an intellectual history of dissent and interrogation. That charlatan godmen and sundry mountebanks should have for so long flourished among them should be no surprise.

Given also the fact that this class, and Indian capitalist transformation generally, has still not yielded that classical individualism which in the west was to lead to terminally radical histories (not necessarily all nice and fine, but suggestive of real breaks with the past), our elites are always on the lookout for a 'community' that is reassuring in an unquestionable sort of way. This reassurance spans both emotional needs as well as functions as divine insurance against menace to vested styles of comfort. It is this sort of congruence that explains the successes of Hindutva communalism among a seemingly avant garde class.

Just as it also explains the extraordinary clout that godmen and suchlike continue to wield among five-star icons and their myriad followers among the upwardly mobile. Nor should it be any surprise that some of the most influential godmen continue to have among their most devoted followers some of India's best-known scientists as well.

And another thing: to the extent that India's new middle classes have come to identify the politics of the left as the chief dissenter with respect to the capitalist path of development, and left mobilization as the only probable collectivity that questions both the content and desirability of their chosen praxis, godmen and their political proponents among the Hindutva organizations offer a totality that seems equipped to thwart with success the incursions from the left.

Let it not be, then, said that India's continuing tryst with organized religiosity is owing exclusively to the ignorant need of the impoverished masses for the proverbial opiate. In a significant historical reversal, in India it is the possessing and entrenched classes that consume and propagate the opiate with far greater political purpose than do the labouring. Indeed, frequently, among the latter responses to spurious and sickeningly opulent demonstrations of godmen-led religiosity are simply and sharply canny. Invariably, they have no difficulty in identifying such opulent establishments as just one other part of the power-structure that wears them down.

V

Keeping all that in mind, I return to the significance of the exposures now under way. I may be pardoned for divining in this new departure on behalf of TV18 (managed by Rajdeep Sardesai) the beginnings of a subversive idea whose time has come. As I have said, the continuing responses to the exposures (as I write this, the latest in the line now on the air is one Asa Ram Bapu – a horrendously puissant member of the godmen clan who counts the biggest guns among his *shraddhālus* (devotees) – who it turns out has been hogging land in some states on false pretences, and now finds a First Information Police Report lodged against him), bespeak a public willingness to acknowledge the fraudulent realities of godmen and the establishments they lord over, even if with some sense of loss.

In that sense, it just may be that the polity is poised, however hesitantly, to stand up before the Emperor, as Luther did before Charles V, and begin to nod with some courage Bartleby's immortal demur 'I would prefer not to.' History surprises us in uncanny ways; there is no telling how the dominoes might fall and, how that falling might begin to yield a new self-confidence to the 'public reason' of secularity.

Congratulations, TV18; we are with you.

May 2007

Pet Panacea of India's Ruling Classes

India's ruling think gurus are forever on the lookout for a smart panacea for what they perceive the country's ills. In arguing for a two-party political system, the idea seems to be to subdue the proliferation of organic discontent among the lower orders of the polity by imposing a mechanical structural arrangement from the top.

The line that is sought to be pushed here is that the multiplicity of political formations in India bears no significant relation to felt grievances on the ground, or to any respectable ideological persuasions that diverge from the 'mainlines' of India's party-political apparatus as reflected in the careers of the two 'national' parties.

Since such multiplicity is viewed as merely a capricious nuisance issuing from the limited purposes of individual sartraps in the 'peripheries,' a managerial answer is sought to be floated to bind these caprices into two oceanic organizations into which all the haywire streams can be assimilated. The problem of political waste, as it were, can then be resolved.

Charmingly simple as the two-party formulation seems, the informing impetus behind the offer is far either from innocent or benign. Indeed, it is something of a disappointment that as astute a student of the issue as Paranjoy Guha Thakurta (author of *A Time of Coalitions*), and one who is usually alertly critical of most right-wing emphases in India's political life, should have missed the calling to underline forthrightly the class-based design from which the two-party formulation, recommended most recently by the President of India himself, issues.

In a recent lead article in the *Hindustan Times* (May 18) he expends most of his text on indicating the unlikelihood of a two-party system consolidating any time soon in India rather than on critiquing the ideological source of the poser. Indeed, while stressing that something may be said 'in favour of many parties and coalitions co-existing in a heterogeneous, plural, deeply divided and highly hierarchical society such as ours,' he is willing to concede 'that a bipolar polity is better than a fragmented multi-party political system.' It is ofcourse possible that writing for the *HT* such a critique may have been inadmissible.

II

To put the matter baldly, the proponents of the two-party thesis do not have in mind formations that are ideological polarities. As in all other matters (militarism, technological ascendance, great consumerist prowess, centralized mega-markets – all that with a dash of 'values'), the idea is to emulate the political superstructure of the American system wherein the two parties are in fact one and the same – a tweedledom and a tweedledee that agree permanently on the nature and components of the base that is to be protected and furthered at all costs.

The substance of that base may be encapsulated briefly in the following unstated stipulations:

- that capitalism is provenly the only (and eternally) valid system of economic organization;
- that private ownership of the means of production and consequent expropriation by the owning class benefit all citizens;
- that all varieties of the socialist experiment must be understood to have 'failed' once and for all;
- that the ills that often accompany capitalist democracy (poverty, unemployment, malnutrition, waste, dearth of equitous health care, gender discrimination, racism, bigotry, insensate corruption and crime, and war, to name just a few) do not constitute 'failure';
- that these consequences do not flow from the capitalist system but, as Malthus, Darwin and others have so astutely pointed out, from 'nature';
- that the free-market is not the expression of man-made preference but reflects the principle of liberty that is autonomous, ordained, and thus above and beyond 'ideology';

- that the state must never interfere in the operations of the free market, but must at all times retain sufficient coercive apparatus to intervene whenever disgruntled sections of the polity seek to thwart those operations;
- that the state, however secular, must retain a regard for 'values' since, apart from their intrinsic worth, these come in handy as the cultural arm of control, discipline, and social punishment;
- and that all challenges to the authority of the state thus constituted must be unequivocally dubbed at the least, malafide, and, at their worst, 'terroristic', deserving of the severest reprisal, even if for the time being the requirement of reprisal involves the capitalist democratic state in contravening the noble principles of liberty from which it derives its legitimacy;
- that the informing principles of equality and fraternity must not be construed to mean that equality and fraternity can either be obtained or are even desirable of attainment.

Going down that table of substance, it should be obvious that the two major, 'national' parties in the Indian political system share most of its meat. It may be argued that the one area in which the Congress party has consistently made protestations of divergence from the BJP is the one that concerns allegiance to secularism. Yet, it is curious that not once in the sixty years of India's existence as an independent republic, especially during the dark moments of intense right-wing Hindu resurgence, has the Congress given a general call to the people to fill the streets in defence of secularism – a lack that is starkly underscored, for example, by recent events in Turkey (commonly perceived as an 'Islamic' nation). Not a day passes when hundreds of thousands of Turkish citizens do not materialize from all corners to make explicit their preference for separation of state and religion. Despite every vicissitude, the Congress remains wedded to a notion of secularism that, rather than disregarding religion in the operations of the state (not to speak of coming down with any heavy hand on its nefarious attempts to usurp the state), looks upon all religions with a benign and equitous concern – a stance that repeatedly leads to a policy of catering. It is hardly a secret that many distinguished Cabinet ministers reserve a corner, not just at home (which would be fine) but in their offices for a holy idol or two.

III

It is understandable, therefore, why the two-party slogan should receive instant favour from India's upwardly-mobile elites. Everyday contemptuous of politicians, their strongest desire is to evacuate Indian democracy of 'politics' in toto. An ideal democracy is visualized as one wherein managers and technocrats take over the state, wherein 'knowledge commissions' distribute enlightened and efficient governance to the hinterland, and wherein people at large are taught to keep their place and peace, if not through persuasion, then by the might of the regimented state.

Alas, sixty years of democratic practice, however guided, has brought home to the people of India the realization that the interests and predilections of the major parties do not necessarily reflect their felt needs and urges. Be it the issue of democratic rights and concrete equality in law, be it the matter of justice in relation to talent and opportunity, or of livelihood and stake in the environments which they traditionally populate, be it the matter of full and free cultural and political expression, or be it the question whether 'we the people' truly possess the Constitution that operates in their name – capitalist democracy, unbeknown to itself, teaches them that other and better things are desirable and possible.

And the agendas of those aspirations may not, as they patently do not, bear convergence with the hegemonic designs that inform the two-party slogan. Often they see in the major national parties a relay team that but carries further forward the same baton. And writ over that baton is often one and the same message as well.

It is just as well, then, to acknowledge (sooner the better) that India's democratic career and agenda has not arrived at the finishing line. By no stretch of the imagination has history ended. And also to acknowledge, crucially, that the plethora of political expressions that obtain are not simply the evidence of some naughty, pointless mischief, directed crudely at the best interests of the state, but projections of dissent and divergence that issue from concrete historical need.

In the years to come, it would be worthwhile to explore the possibility of gathering the chief contending features of that divergence into a broad coalition of right-wing, centrist, and left-wing forces. Perhaps such a process is already underway. But to hope or propagate that two parties, clones at best, may be trusted to answer the call of India's incomparably diverse and complex polity is to live in a cloistered complacence of potentially dangerous consequence.

Let it be understood that consensus about the political superstructure can happen only when a consensus exists in regard to the base. In a situation where some seventy percent of the population remain unfulfilled by the character of the base, it is folly to wish that what 'knowledge commissions' at the top believe to be knowledge is truly so.

Managers and technocrats but run the given; politics seeks to make the new. And in India there is a lot of making waiting to be done that would seem to lie beyond the will or ideological preference of the two major parties.

May 2007

New Ringtones from Condy Rice

History is a moral necessity for a nation which is the world's dominant power. It is the best antidote to delusions of ominipotence and omniscience.
Arthur Schlesinger

The longer you look back, the further you can look forward.
Winston Churchill

Recently, Sam Janus has been calling India. But this time around only one of its two faces has been anthropomorphic; the other massively metallic.

You would have understood my drift here: I allude to the converging visits of Condoleeza Rice and USS Nimitz, the former dripping with the sort of jaunty self-assurance that demarcates the swaggeringly ill-educated, the latter a blunt hunk of brute brinkmanship – a kind of hi-tech King Kong minus the living primates feel for beauty. Put in quotidian idiom, one a smiling bowl of cream cheese laced with arsenic, the other the stubb end of a raised baseball bat.

Which invites the reflection: when was the last time that American diplomacy (unavoidable oxymoron) had to it any depth of perception or the least touch of grace? I can only recall the years when John Kenneth Galbraith was ambassador here. For a second instance one might have to time-travel as far back as the American war of Independence when Benjamin Franklin was deputed to France to draw French support. How he loved France, and how the thoughtful French took him to heart!

II

Cutting to the point: Dr.Rice (and I am guessing the doctorate would have had to be in the canny areas of Law or Management; I would cut my oriental throat if it had anything to do with any of the Humanities) invoking the 'values of common humanity' (read the interests of the US establishment and those willing to be client appendages), pronounced in one non-chalant breath the utter irrelevance of the principle of non-alignment in International relations. It then seemed self-evident to the good doctor that all those nations who seek 'opportunity and prosperity and justice and dignity and health and education and freedom and democracy' (the articulation brooked no commas), now have only one rational option – that of aligning with Sam Dubya inorder to realize that wish-list. As the ever-sentient Indian daily, The Hindu, pointed out editorially, the doctor somehow forgot to add to that list 'motherhood and apple pie.'

Predictably enough, some well-recognized senior scribes who habitually speak on behalf of comprador corporates, who in turn routinely speak on behalf of Sam Dubya soon let loose their no-nonsense contempt for decrepit socialist ideals, analyzing with devotion the great benefits to be garnered from an unashamed 'strategic alliance' with the only superpower – a myth that is sought to be kept alive despite the ever-widening tatters.

The recalcitrant ones, few and far between, but still nagging like the toothache, however, have continued to bore in with disconcerting history lessons, taking none of Dr. Rice's wish-list on face value.

Thus, for 'opportunity and prosperity' they read 'exploiters of the world unite, you have nothing to lose but your profits';

for 'justice' they read Guantanamo, Abu Ghraib, extraordinary renditions, assassination plots, subversion and sabotage, and, for eloquent finale, Scooter Libby. Not to mention small things like spying on the critical and hounding the innocent at home.

For 'health' they read the 49 million Americans, including some 9 million children, still without health insurance and no 'universal health care' in sight; they also read the five hundred thousand children in Iraq consigned to horrible malnutrition-driven and medicine-less deaths through the regime of 'sanctions.'

For 'freedom' they read the unending line of client tyrants and dictators – 'our sons of bitches' in Roosevelt's forthright formulation – past and present: in the Philippines, in Indonesia, in Vietnam, in Pakistan, in Saudi Arabia, in Iran, Egypt, Mexico, Panama, Nicaragua, Ecaudor, Gautemala, Chile, Brazil, Columbia, Cuba (Batista, Batista), Haiti, Grenada, and on and on and on.

And, for 'democracy' they yawn and think the matter unworthy of mention. They recall how the seventh fleet was deputed to the Bay of Bengal to dissuade Indira Gandhi from aiding the freedom fighters in the then East Pakistan where the infamous butcher, General Yahyah Khan was busy hacking thousands in the streets of Dacca. They recall that all that was in the teeth of the stunning electoral victory obtained by the Awami League under Mujib-u-Rehman whose democratic right to rule Pakistan was liquefied in streams of blood. And they point to the fate that the electorally triumphant Hamas has had to suffer for not aligning with Dubya; and they point to Venezuela where, despite repeated, and repeatedly massive verdicts in favour of Hugo Chavez, Dr. Rice and her master are unable to see 'democracy' legitimately at work. And they point to the shameless media campaigns routinely conducted by Fox News and other obliging outlets against a plethora of other electorally victorious Latin American governments for keeping their own counsel on what policies to pursue. They remember with a pang the CIA-executed murder of Allende in Chile and the subsequent sufferings of Chilean patriots at the hands of Dubya's beloved Pinochet; and the equally beloved and brutish army generals in Argentina and elsewhere.

And they point Dubya to upright and conscientious American agencies that have shown how both his electoral victories were in fact stolen ones!

III

So, they say, thank you very much Dr. Rice; go catch up on some history. Or, if indeed, you are no innocent babe, desist from propagating the delusion that America has been or is a force for 'democracy' in the world – a self-inflicted pretence that now wears thin as tulle all across the globe. Imagine that your own good citizens at home believe none of your disingenuous homilies any more.

Far more honourable for you to put your cards on the table and say what imperialist interests you have in mind – 'military interoperability', 'structures of co-operative vigilance', drawing India into an anti-China, anti-Russia, anti-Iran, anti-Venezuela, anti-Cuba gang-up alongside the likes of Japan, Australia, Korea and suchlike. Then looting Asia as long as that lasts? Exactly as the honest Australian minister of defence has the other day admitted that his men are in Iraq on account of the oil! One truthful Christian there.

Indeed, as the erstwhile Indian diplomat, M.K.Rasgotra has recently put it, ensuring that the twenty first century becomes 'an American century in Asia' rather than an Asian century as some aspiring Asian ruling interests think it is destined to be. Oh woe the gluttony of the incautious!

IV

It is indeed true and heartening that official response from India (some consolation that Pranab Mukherjee is still Foreign minister rather than candidate for India's Presidency) has been a no-nonsense one. It says that India as a founder member of NAM remains committed to its ideals, and it says that NAM now has a great role to play in deepening South-South co-operation.

One ofcourse wishes that the Indian response had included two questions as well: if indeed the cold-war era is dead and gone, rendering NAM infructuous, would Dr.Rice kindly enlighten us why she thinks NATO still remains relevant? Or why America has been embroiled in battles dime a dozen since (complete with dirty uranium and phosphorus bombs, cluster killers and so forth)?

Something that raises the suspicion that there may be a Janus lurking somewhere within the Indian establishment as well, making the politically correct statements in public but smoothing the grounds for American corporates and embracing the USS Nimitz in private (with all the crimes the Nimitz emblematises). Ergo, NAM for a figleaf of legitimacy, but SAM for the real thing!

Charitably, the jury may be yet out on those posers. Clearly, how the Indian establishment modulates its equations with Iran, China, and Russia in the days to come, and how it eventually deals with the Hyde stipulations on the nuke-deal with Sam will yield some reliable answers to those anxieties. India's parliament had better be on its toes, and the mass of Indians ready and willing to take to the streets, just in case.

One thing is for sure: you cannot wrap the anaconda around your waistline and still hope to exit. Indians yearning for super-powerdom need thus to heed Schlesinger's admonitions and Churchill's cryptic as much as Dr.Rice needs to revisit the histories of predecessor American regimes. Self-inflicted hypnotism on either side will do the world no good.

July 2007

Vedic Mantra in the American Senate

Even as 'Potter Mania' overtakes India, the American Senate has been overtaken by Hindu-Vedic mantras. Fascinating conjuncture.

Fascinating because the conjuncture invites such diverse reads, depending on where and how we are located as historical subjects.

The most obvious read, of course, was instantly available in the Senate house itself. Two women and a man had this to say as Rajan Zed, the saffron draped Hindu priest, stood up to chant the good chant: "Lord Jesus, protect us from this abomination." And, "we shall have no gods before you."

And, remarkably, at the high-noon of 'born-again' assertion among wide swathes of American society, rather than applauding the three good Christians, the marshall was ordered to arrest them. Martyrs of an older vintage indeed.

II

A second read must be how the empire now writes back, not just in literary-historical form but in the matter of worship.

Clearly, if in the first instance – where it concerned British colonial hegemony – the empire has been writing back as an intellectually self-confident underdog, in the case of the American Senate the occurrence must be seen to issue from a position of clout. A clear case of Hindu NRI dollar endowments translating into spiritual capital.

It would be hard to imagine a more emphatic cementing of the Bush-Indian NRI nexus.

Interestingly, this is how a somewhat innocent Senate majority leader, Harry Read, has commented on the event:

> If people have any misunderstanding about Indians and Hindus, all they have to do is to think of Gandhi.

Poor Mr. Read hardly seems to have any idea that the last Indian that the dollar-guzzling Hindu-NRIs have in mind is Gandhi. More to their purposes the missile scientists and the anti-Muslim war-mongers.

III

Speaking of which, the thought must be in many minds how the gesture that the American Senate has made to 'Indians and Hindus' is amenable as a politics to truly peace-making purposes. Imagine what Gandhian strides could be made as between Huntington's 'civilizations' were the Senate now to make its podium available to a Muslim cleric as well. Looked at from a doctrinal perspective, Islam and Christianity, after all, share much more history and many more points of belief than they together do with Hindu 'transcendentalism' or 'mysticism.'

Alas, of course, such an eventuality seems hardly in the offing. Something that underscores the point that the Vedic incursion into the Christian senate has had less to do with faith, everything to do with advancing the 'strategic alliance' between India and the United States.

IV

Recalling Gandhi, we recall the all-religions prayer meetings he used to hold routinely. Surely, Mr. Read may be trusted to know this.

Now if Indians are to be identified with Gandhi, what could be more logical a follow-up to the path-breaking Senate initiative than for the Indian parliament to reciprocate by inviting a Christian padre and a Muslim cleric to replicate that initiative.

Clearly, we secularists and agnostics who oppose the admixture of state and religion are not too enthused by what the Senate in the United States has chosen to do. Nor would we anything but oppose were something similar attempted here.

But the question we ask is would Hindu NRIs who have been behind the Vedic assertion in the Christian senate welcome a reciprocal gesture by the Indian parliament? And if they would not – as is more than likely – how might that refusal, however expressed, be justified?

All of which speaks to the same text: in the first, last, and ultimate analysis, it is money that matters, stupid.

The gods of any denomination merely toe the line.

July 2007

Teach Them Not to Think

There is no such thing as a value neutral educational process.

(Richard Shaull, Foreword to *Pedagogy of the Oppressed*)

After the initial attempts by a section of Christian-bourgeois souls (Dickens, Carlyle, Chadwick, Mayhew, Mrs.Gaskell, even the honourable, although not Christian, Benjamin Disraeli who first enunciated the thesis that England was in fact not one nation but two – the rich and the poor), to seek reformative state interventions on behalf of the new urban poor who now swamped the industrial towns, towards the middle of the nineteenth century the inevitable exhaustion of goodwill followed.

Where a Dickens had made visits to Yorkshire schools (captured unforgettably in *Nicholas Nickleby*) in the thirtees and returned to raise a cry for amelioration, such sentiment expressed from outside the lived experience of the suffering classes, was to wear thin in a growing fright at the spread of what was to be christened 'mass culture.'

Dickens of course had repudiated the Chartists who had erroneously hoped he would go over to their side (a story rather less often recited about him). Some flavour of that history may be savoured in what G.M. Reynolds was to write in the *Weekly Newspaper* of June 8, 1851:

> This wretched sycophant of Aristorcracy – this vulgar flatterer of the precious hereditary peerage – is impudent enough to consider himself the people's friend! A precious friend indeed when he ridicules universal suffrage (the elementary principle of Chartism) and proclaims himself a thick and thin supporter of Lord John Russell's reform bill, even before he has seen it![1]

---

1 See my *Dickens and the Dialectic of Growth*, University of Wisconsin Press, 1986, p.145

Suddenly, as industrial England entered the fraught social contentions of the sixties, a whole falange of opinion-makers closed ranks to argue that writers, poets, 'creative' individuals of all description had best wash their hands off this fruitless business of meddling with social matters. It was best that they devoted themselves to their precious private visions of abiding truths above and beyond the piss and mire of this thing called history.

The ringing thesis here was to come from Matthew Arnold, who, in his perniciously influential *Culture and Anarchy* (1865) drew the first distinctions between 'high culture' and the culture of the 'populace' – the latter in his view constituting 'anarchy.' Pleading for an intellectual aristocracy, a return to the classics was advocated. The aesthetics of Liberalism was thus inaugurated; and specially endowed individuals were henceforth to seek for eternal verities and universal truths outside the concrete processes of social and political contention.[2]

II

A great discomfort with the equalizing philosophies (chiefly of Marx and Engles) had of course been steadily growing. Siezing the moment that Arnold articulated, Pareto, Mosca, Burckhardt were to float the new concepts of an 'elite' and a 'political class' that comprised individuals endowed by nature to be rulers of men. Elements of Darwin, and Carlyle's notion of the 'hero' were thus drawn into the stipulation that not equality but inequality was the true order of 'nature'. Needless to remind ourselves that Nietzsche was to put all that together famously to tell us how the chief business of history – and women – was to give us the 'superman.'[3] Thus educational processes had to be those that absorbed and disseminated the ideas of the ruling class. England's first Education Act of 1870 was to be the first pusillanimous policy decision towards consolidating inequality eventhough, don't you know, it was all about furnishing a sound education on the best principles of English 'humanism.'

As the manufacturers and the colonizers busied themselves in profit-making, education came formally to be regarded not as a rational aid to understanding how society came to be thus constituted, but in a forked programme to equip, on the one hand, the labouring classes with the

2 See Raymond Williams, *Culture and Society*, for a penetrating analysis of these ideological conjunctions.

3 See T.B.Bottomore, *Elites and Society*, Penguin, 1964 for a lucid account of these histories.

minimal skills that industry needed from time to time (more profoundly, as Marx was to point out and Althusser in our time was to nail, in order to keep in place the 'reserve army of labour' or in order to ensure the 'reproduction of the relations of production'), and, on the other, to make available to the leisured classes the delectable riches of speculation.

Not for nothing was Arnold to argue that poetry would be the religion of the future. That injunction was devotedly to be pursued by 'modernists' like T.S. Eliot for whom, beginning with the twenties of the last century, the world was indubitably a 'wasteland'. As you would expect, the cure for the unvarying 'human condition' was to be found in the Church. All that just when a revolution had happened in the then czarist Russia, and when Gandhi, the Congress, and the revolutionaries in India were making big strides to alter the 'human condition' in the colony – and, as a fallout, in some two-thirds of the colonized world.

(It is another matter that when 'free' India came to establish its first Education Commission, its recommendations duly reflected the same ruling dichotomy: skills for the masses and the Humanities at tertiary levels in order to keep ruling spirits within the bounds of 'sensitivity.')

Thus, when the American, John Dewey, wrote in 1920 that the true aim and purpose of education is education, he was articulating a seeming abstraction (what education?) that had behind it a whole concrete history of class interests.

III

International corporate capital has since made killing strides. It no longer needs the pretence about poetry (read 'poetry' as a metaphor for the Humanities, the Social Sciences, the Arts, and for critical thought generally). The more it gobbles up the globe, the greedier it gets. In education also, therefore, it is to be push-pin all the way. The least moneys spent on 'poetry' seem unconscionably unwarranted according to the most advanced principles of that despicable thing called Commerce. What used to be commerce between human beings – remember those 'pointless' hours spent in the coffee house? – is thus superceded by commerce between computers which make the world a 'global village' even as they draw oceans between human being and human being. Since you can email, where is the need to meet face to face?

The captains of 'utility' who move the levers of 'knowledge' at the WTO, think that there is no more need to think. Since all the thinking that the world needs is done in the board room, educational processes *ipso facto* invite to be geared to proliferate armies of the new conformism who in turn may be trusted to function as untroublesome engines of profit-maximisation. When the GDP grows, the stock market booms, the middle class expands and fattens and comes into possession of commodities which advertising can then fetishise as the new age gods, pray where then is there any more need to think and speculate?

How many of us know that education (it must still be called that, per necessity) is today, globally, the third most lucrative trade worldwide, after drugs and armaments? That being the case, teaching shops that come from far-off lands come necessarily in order to set up franchises at zero levels of investment that the 'market' may lap-up at hundred percent profit. And those comprise utility items, not 'poetry.'

IV

Alas, whatever is picked-up at school/college/university/institute had better equip young people to earn a keep. But would it not be nice if we should also have learnt (and not picked-up) that which makes of those of us destined to become appendages of the ruling hippopotamus 'warm and tender as can be'? And if that seems like a hopeless reversion to the class-based 'humanist' argument, so it is. Paulo Freire was to write, after Satre, that education must rid us of the 'fear of freedom.' Alas, only in Latin America do we now seem to have regimes that may encourage the 'populace' to do so through their systems of schooling. For the rest, it is still Cuba. Where are the movements elsewhere that have the least object or likelihood of making education coterminous with that recovery of our humanness which the world craves?

Again I reflect how the Bard, as always, knew a great deal about such matters. Recall that when Macbeth's masculine nerve rather wobbles at the last minute, his neocon consort dares him: 'thou wouldst be a man if thou durst do it' (that is, kill the king, inter alia, invade iraq, kill Saddam and so on). And how telling, although pathetic, a riposte Macbeth delivers unto her: 'I dare do all that may become a man;/ who dares do more is none.'

How that thought nails the monetary economist, the corporates he spawns, and the Neanderthal neocons (and they are not just in the United States of America) piercingly in the belly button. But of course, as Henry Fielding would have said, shame is the first meal these kinds eat before they go for breakfast! They leave the business of being human to the rampaging Evangelist/Mullah/Mahant, who in turn teach that being human means being victorious in battles of various kinds. God has no room for 'losers' they say. Blessed no longer are the meek but the mighty, for their's is the oil and the uranium. It is a weak prophet who says turn the other cheek.

V

Indeed, what does it mean to be human (and no ontological debate is intended here)? Recall the days not too long ago when walking down the pavement and noticing a self-contained person some distance away, you remarked to your companion 'such a good man; she/he thinks of everybody.'

But as the world advances, capital has taught us the truth about that person – a 'waster, shun him.' Good is the human being who minds his own business at all costs. He does not stop to look at the fellow just come under the wheels of the latest Chrysler; he does not let his mind waver from the shady deal to be signed at the golf club. He if anything formulates the most efficient plan yet not for the alleviation of suffering but for the eradication of those who are no- good sufferers. Ah, the fruits of education! The least mongrel on the hobo street has lessons we could learn in order to become human. But we are on the road to progress and have ears only for the next announcement at the stock market, eyes only for the next piece of lucrative real-estate, and dreams only about the next career promotion or marvel of household technology. Where we once counted children, we count remotes to sundry gadgets. And when a gadget goes Hawaii, we curse the service fellow whose dying wife keeps him from attending our need!

And the evangelists and the godmen, they teach us to mind our own salvation through greater physical fitness so that we tire less in attending to profit-making. Health services for all, community education, shared labour, shared partaking – these are the things that must be avoided like the plague. When you hear such sounds, say 'the reds are coming.' And education that teaches respect for the other, for difference, or, god forbid, begins to examine the roots of our own rottenness, that indeed is the devil's work. That is when you forget the priest and call out the troops.

Thus, if Plato threw the poets out of his republic, we must add to those the humanists, the social scientists, the philosophers, the political activists, the artists, the rebels without 'cause', the 'wasters' who strangely do not value profit-making, the disabled, the old, the needlessly sick, the children who only make demands but add nothing to GDP. And we must make education available only to those who can pay. To the rest we say, god prepares a heaven for you, so why need you the earth.

And WTO will say endorse only those authors, those academies, those entrepreneurs, those middle-men, those commission agents, those publishers, and those governments, who can conjointly make of education not the third-most but the most lucrative global 'service.' In Brahminical parlance, dethrone Saraswati, install Lakshmi as the reigning goddess of learning – which she already is, de facto.

Make of your education a billion-pound note; and then go ask for the Presidential vote. With that note in one hand and the evangelist/godman in the other, you cannot go wrong. You may only end up destroying the world, a small price to pay for success.

As to the world, may be the time for it to end has come anyway.

August 2007

Indian State on Trial

This story has been told before, but can never be told enough.

On the 6th of December, 1992, a majority right-wing Hindutva putsch overcame the majesty of the Indian state.

With the full and open collaboration of the then BJP government in Uttar Pradesh, and the measly connivance of the Congress government at the centre, the fascists succeeded in overwhelming and demolishing out of existence a five-hundred year old mosque in Ayodhya.

That putsch was effected despite written commitment on affidavit made by Kalyan Singh, the U.P. Chief Minister, to the Supreme Court of India that the State would not allow any damage to the mosque.

As the mosque was reduced to rubble, the most front-ranking leaders of the BJP were caught in full view of cameras – of the BBC especially – hugging one another in ugly glee. There was no end to the sweets that were distributed to mark the 'victory' both over Indian Muslims and over the state.

II

In the city of Mumbai, the 'victors' celebrated the humiliation of the Muslims by taking out cycle rallies.

In the inter-community rioting that this led to, 900 citizens lost their lives, 575 of them Muslims.

A Commission of Enquiry was set up under the then junior judge, Justice Srikrishna (since few others offered their services). It was thought a point in his favour that he was after all a 'devout and practicing Hindu.' Sadly for the killers and their instigators, Justice Krishna turned out to be outstandingly courageous and objective in his findings.

As word leaked about the determination of the Commission to be fair and above board, the Commission was disbanded. It must be said to the credit of the then Prime Minister, Atal Bihari Vajpayee, that the Commission was reactivated in May, 1996. Caveat: the terms of reference of the Commission were now expanded to include enquiry into the serial blasts that followed the communal killings!

III

Justice Srikrishna, however, was able to make all-important sequential connections between the demolition of the Babri mosque, the subsequent communal rioting, and the serial blasts that followed:

> The serial bomb blasts were a reaction to the totality of events at Ayodhya and Bombay in December,1992 and January 1993... The common link between the riots and the blasts was that of cause and effect.

Further, the riots during Advani's 'rath yatra' (that had culminated in the demolition of the mosque 'were the distant thunderclaps portending the storm to come.'

Some other crucial pronouncements of the Commission are as follows:

- speeches made at the Ram Paduka Pujans (worship of Lord Ram's feet/sandals), Chowk Sabhas (street square conclaves) were 'downright communal,' 'warning Muslims' that dissent on the Ram Temple issue would be considered 'treachery' for which 'Muslims would be banished from the country'; (it is to be recalled that the issue remains subjudice till date).
- "Hindutvavadis politicized the issue pending in the court of law";
- "celebrating and gloating over the demolition was like twisting a knife in the wound";
- "police mishandled the situation... by their aggressive behaviour";
- "police firing resulted in the death of a large number of Muslims as compared to Hindus";
- that on 1 January 1993 the party organ of the Shiv Sena, *Saamna*, printed an article 'openly inciting Hindus to violence';

- that on 3 January Shiv Sainiks surveyed Muslim houses in Pratiksha Nagar and Antop Hill; (Gajanan Kiritkar and Ramesh More are named here);
- that on 9 January "the Shiv Sainiks mobilized themselves for retaliating against the Muslims. The Shakhas (congregational units)... turned into centres of local command. The attacks on the Muslims were mounted with military precision, with the list of establishments and voters' lists in hand";

Under 'Immediate Causes.' Justice Srikrishna lists 'demolition', 'aggravation of Muslim sentiments by celebration rallies', 'insensitive, harsh approach of the police'.

And then:

> From 8 January 1993, at least, there is no doubt that the Shiv Sena and Shiv Sainiks took the lead in organizing attacks on Muslims and their properties under the guidance of several leaders of the Shiv Sena from the level of Shakha Pramukh to the Shiv Sena Pramukh, Bal Thackeray, who like a veteran General commanded his loyal Shiv Sainiks to retaliate by organizing attacks against Muslims.

The Commission names other top leaders of the Shiv Sena, including Madhukar Sarpotdar, in whose house the army found unlicensed guns (something rather similar to what was found in Sanjay Dutt's house in the serial blasts case).

IV

Quite the other day, court proceedings with respects to all those adjudged guilty in the serial blasts case have concluded; some ten unfortunate people have received the death penalty, and about double that life imprisonment. The pursuit of the serial blasts case has evidenced exemplary political, investigative and judicial will.

Which invites the question as to why to this day the report of the Srikrishna Commission remains not just unimplemented but unadopted. And regardless of which political formations have been in the seat of power, centrally, or locally in Maharashtra.

It is to be said that some English Dailies are beginning to ask this discomfiting question, although noted columnists still seem to fight shy of mentioning the Pramukh of the Shiv Sena, Bal Thackeray even when the Srikrishna Commission does so explicitly as a 'veteran General who commanded his loyal troops' during the Bombay riots (see 'Shhh… Muslim!' lead article by Sagarika Ghose in the *Hindustan Times*, Aug.,3,2007, for instance.)

For the Congress especially matters must be seen to be complicated by the Shiv Sena's support to Pratibha Patil in the just concluded Presidential elections. It must seem forgivable to argue that Bal Thackeray's support to the UPA Presidential candidate may have had less, after all, to do with Maharashran pride, more with the Srikrishna Commission findings. Some weight is leant to this view when one remembers that such Shiv Sena support had not been forthcoming to Sushil Kumar Shinde, another Maharashtrian and a dalit to boot, who was the Congress candidate for Vice-President at the last elections. Was it not an important consideration that at that time not the Congress-led UPA but the BJP-led NDA was ruling at the centre?

V

The Congress, we feel, must ask the following questions of itself:

1. Would its continued appeasement of the Shiv Sena be consistent with its oft-repeated claim that as the genuine party of governance it alone may be trusted to uphold the Constitution and the rule of law?

2. Would such appeasement sit well with the various attempts it seeks to make to remedy and improve the lot of the minorities, Muslims particularly, pursuant to the findings and recommendations of the Sachar Committee? Nor should it be forgotten that the Bombay riots into which the Srikrishna Commission enquired are not the only instance where the victims have received short shrift. The abortive fate of the Srikrishna Commission has been preceded by similarly aborted Commission findings in, to name a few, five other noted instances. These are:

a) the Justice Jaganmohan Reddy Commission (Ahmedabad riots, 1969);
b) the D.P.Madan Commission (Bhiwandi riots, 1970);
c) Vithayathil Commission (Tellicherry riots, 1971);
d) Justice Jjitendra Narain Commission (Jamshedpur riots, 1979);
e) Justice P. Venugopal Commission (Kanyakumari riots, 1982);

In all these cases, the Commissions indicted the RSS; and in all these cases justice continues to elude the victims.

3. Would the Congress-led UPA be able to escape the accusation that, having received Shiv Sena support for Pratibha Patil's candidature, it has no stomach to proceed with the Srikrishna findings?

4. Would the UPA's touted determination to bring legislation to eradicate communal strife and killing have the least credibility if it continues to fail to show the sort of political will with respect to the Bombay riots as has been in evidence in the matter of the subsequent serial blast cases?

VI

The UPA government needs to realize that selective justice may bring relief to a section of the population, but, if such justice is denied to other sections, such a course can only the more justly and forcefully dub it communal than any overt act of commission.

It is now generally recognized that Indian Muslims are poised on a threshold moment; with each day their willingness to participate in constructive measures to accord them due rights and opportunities as equal citizens becomes more evident. At such a moment in the history of India's composite polity, any tainted evasion of justice due to the victims of the Bombay riots – some of whom will indeed be Hindu as well – when such justice has been all-too loudly ensured to the victims of the serial blasts is fraught with potential disaster for the entire polity and for the locus standi of the state.

August 2007

The Unacceptable Excesses of Irreligion

Baski dushvar hai har kam ka asan hona, Admi ko bhi mayassar nahin insan hona.

Mirza Ghalib

How hard, how impossible To do the things one can; Ah that the mighty earthling Is hardly ever a man. (trans., in *Raina's Ghalib*, Writers Workshop, Calcutta, 1984).

It is once again time to speak straight to the point.

An act of the most grossly irreligious cowardice was on display at the Press Club in Hyderabad the other day.

Three elected members of the Andhra Pradesh Assembly belonging to the MIM (Majlis-e-Ittahadul Muslimeen) party barged into the Club where Taslima Nasreen, the self-exiled Bangladeshi writer, now living in India on six-monthly renewable visas, was to release Telegu editions of her works.

On cue, these MLAs, led by Akbaruddin Owaisi, proceeded to pelt the guest author with books, flower pots and other sundry missiles. Television footage of the barbarity clearly showed Ms.Nasreen being hit several times on the head. But for some brave protection furnished by elderly hosts, real physical injury might have been caused to Ms.Nasreen who has been critical of Islamic orthodoxy on several counts, especially concerning Muslim women. As the world knows, umpteen fatwas are out requiring her to be beheaded.

After the event, Akbaruddin was heard to make two loud proclamations to his supporting rabble and to India in general: one, that were Ms.Nasreen ever to visit Hyderabad again, she would be killed as per injunctions of the fatwa; and, secondly, that he, Owaisi, was first a Muslim and only after an MLA.

Well, well; it is clearly time to speak a similarly plain language to Owaisi and those who think as he does.

II

For a start, our citizenship – and all the rights and obligation that flow thereof – do not accrue to us from anything written in the Gita, the Quran, the Bible, the Granth Sahib, or any other scriptural text.

It accrues to us from the Constitution of the Republic of India as by law established.

Thus, if on the one hand, the Constitution furnishes us the freedom to practice and propagate what religious faith we will, it expressly stipulates that whatever hurts or grievances, real or imagined, we may have on this score must be settled through the due processes of law. On no account does the citizen have the right to usurp the prerogatives so stipulated where they concern the sphere of public conduct and controversy.

Those of us who have consistently critiqued and resisted attempts, especially since the demolition of the Babri mosque in 1992, at a majoritarian take-over of the state and its functions through vigilante mobilization and violence have, Mr.Owaisi, no intention of making the least exception of you and your cohorts just because you happen to belong to a religious minority.

And we say to you and your fellow MLAs that if indeed your religious allegiance (if it truly be such, of which we have great doubt) precedes and supercedes your sworn allegiance to the Constitution of India, the least you can do to prove your bona fides is to resign your membership of the Assembly, and then take up the work of liquidating infidels and dissenters in right earnest, unshackled by your secular oath.

And should such an honourable course not be forthcoming from the MLAs in question (as we do not think it will be), we call upon the Election Commission to do the needful as per provisions of the People's Representation Act.

Citizens of the country will also be interested watchers of whether or not the law-enforcement agencies of the state take due cognizance of open declarations of the intent to murder Ms.Nasreen, with the all-important caveat that these enforcement agencies do not, in the first place, replicate the murderous examples set by their professional colleagues in Gujarat and elsewhere. There is after all ample ground to the widespread public distrust of these agencies, and not for no reason are they seen to be often the sources of the grossest lawlessness, particularly in their dealings with underlings of any definition.

III

To those unfortunate followers whom the Owaisis of this world are able to mislead and mobilize, we want to say that whereas we shall continue to struggle by their side towards the furtherance of their genuine material interests and rights, and against their alienation and exclusion from systems of sharing and of justice, we will reject their violent frenzies as decisively as those of the VHP or the Bajrang Dal.

We have consistently pleaded with them to learn the courage to assume with conviction their rights and privileges of equal citizenship that our secular democracy bestows upon us, and to join with the secular majority of the republic who hold the Constitution to be the one indubitably holy book for all citizens of India.

We now wish to make the further suggestion that they learn, and without loss of time, to distinguish between those so-called Islamic voices that at bottom use them as self-serving fodder, and those other learned Muslim voices who speak the truth both about their faith and about citizenship.

Concerning Taslima Nasreen's criticisms as available in her writings, recall what the holy Quran enjoins: 'attack those who attack you as they attack you.' This teaching would require that those who pretend to lead you into the true ways of Islam engage with Ms. Nasreen in disputation and argument, not in unwarranted and unmanly physical attack or threats of murder. That they do not do so tells us that the Owaisis of this world may after all have a negligible knowledge of the faith on whose behalf they commit illiterate and heinous barbarisms. Here is what Maulana Aqilul Gharawi has to say on the matter: "the seeds of democratic reform are enshrined in three key Islamic tenets of Shura, Ijma and Ijtihad." Mr. Owaisi, go read some books.

IV

Do not then permit an Owaisi to hijack the educated traditions of Islam into the politics of fascism. Think how repeatedly the Quran and the

Prophet emphasise the central value of learning; had that not been the case the Arabs may not have given us the marvels of Algebra and Geometry and wondrous architectures and canal systems built to impeccable scientific principles – traditions that need to be deepened and carried forward. Think also that had a Copernicus or a Galileo not questioned Church teachings with regard, for example, to the placement of the earth within the solar system, the modern world in which the Owaisis practice politics and speak freely may never have been born. After all, why is it that the questions Ms.Nasreen has been asking are also being increasingly asked in many countries where Muslims are in vast majority, not excluding Iran? Why is it that there are as many commentaries on the holy book as there actually are? Or so many sects of interpretation among Muslims, just as among Hindus, Christians, Sikhs, Buddhists, Jews and others? Great are the books that grow, become richer, and change their meanings for us with advances in time and collective human experience. Only the limited ones remain tethered to a stagnant stake.

Especially with regard to India, it is not the violent intolerance of the Owaisis and the Togadias that has through the centuries ensured our most unique commingling of faiths and lives. Remember that if Islam flows so handsomely through the nations's blood stream even today, it is to the noble vision of the Sufi orders that we owe such a rich consequence. And simple and long-lasting was their teaching: they refused all discrimination as between faith and faith, they made no distinction between high and low, they spurned the lure of authority and power, they saw the earth as a testament of universal love, spurning dogma and self-serving religious bureaucracies, they sang songs, they danced in ecstasy, and they were one with whatever was loving and noble in man or beast. And they did not think of woman as second to man. And it is for those reasons that a Chisti in Ajmer or an Aulia in Nizamudin or a Nooruddin in Chrar-e-Sharief in Kashmir draw to their resting places the believer, the infidel, the fat, the starving, the sinner and the saint, year after year, century after century. And we are the children of their magnificent union with a Meera, a Nanak, a Raidas, a Namdev, a Narsi Maheta, a Kabir, a Bulle Shah, a Farid, a Tulsi.

There is the heritage that we must acknowledge and own, saying to the Owaisis and the Togadias that, being blood brothers on the other side, they keep their contagion to themselves in a house of common aboard, but far from where our children, sisters and brothers live. Before we set off in umbrage to behead a suffering woman who only wishes to speak as she has experienced, let us recall that our own poets have asked questions and expressed skepticisms that far outdo what Ms.Nasreen might wish to say. After all, it was Ghalib who wrote:

Hum ko maaloom hai janat ki haqeeqat lekin,
Dil ke khush rakhne ko Ghalib ye khayaal accha hai.

(They must be all correct, of heaven The eulogies we hear; But, may God so command that He Is discovered somewhere there!) RG

Ask yourself, has Nasreen gone that far – to question the very existence of god or heaven? And yet, what has happened that Ghalib pleases us no end, while a poor Nasreen so inflames? Ghalib offends nobody when he says of himself that he is only half a Muslim, in that he drinks liquor but eats not pork. Nor are we inflamed that the great predecessor of Ghalib, Mir Taki Mir could say of himself:

Mir ke deeno mazhab ko poochte kya ho unne to
Qashqa khencha, dair men baitha, kab ka tark Islam kiya.

(Why ask of Mir what his creed or religion be? He wears vermillion, sits in the temple, And has long renounced Islam.)

Surely, perhaps Owaisi and suchlike ought to have been demanding a burning and banning of both Mir and Ghalib. Perhaps they haven't heard the names or read these poets. They may yet do so. Have we ,then, forgotten the lessons these and other great thinkers taught us – that no true religious or spiritual impulse can co-exist with intolerance, bigotry, hate, because intolerance, bigotry, hate are always somewhere or the other expressions not of our love of god but of lucre, dominance, and power. And, crucially, far from being protests against 'modernity.' they are in themselves vicious by- products of it.

V

While I am about it, it is time that governments and parties at the centre and the states recognize that the time to play games with bigotry are long past. While they crow about our rising indices of economic clout, they have not a minute to lose in attending with more than the same passion to the matter of citizenship and equality before the law, at the heart of which in a pluralist democracy resides the sovereign right to peaceful dissent. And that right can never be truly protected in a secular democracy unless it includes the right to interpret or question scripture as well. Indeed their mealy-mouthed failure to uphold secular citizenship everyday auguments the maurauding energies of bigotry and enervates the efforts and convictions of those segments that would protect the republic from the atavisms of various kind. Should they fail to put their sectarian lusts on the back-burner, they must prepare for a conflagration in which they will find themselves in fatal embrace. Far better that the embrace is executed here and now along the best principles of non-sectarian humanism.

VI

Finally, one is deeply heartened by the spontaneity and volume of outrage that the Hyderabad incident has evoked from not just 'liberal' Muslims but, more to the point, Muslim clerics and maulvis. Whereas I have many of these responses on my notepad, let me conclude by citing just two or three:

> The attack on her cannot be justified; the attack was against the spirit of Islam. (Maulana Abdul Wahab Khilji, Vice President, Milli Council.)

> We should stick to only lawful means to register our protest against her. (Maulana Khalid Rasheed, Firangi Mahal, Lucknow).

> Our culture and ethos is based on the foundations of a unique secularism, based on the concept of 'Sarva Dharma Sambhava', unparalleled in the world and which is evolving as we speak. This concept could provide a globalised world with certain key answers that it is desperately seeking. (Muslim Intellectual Forum, Mumbai)

> As Muslims of India and the Muslims around the globe, we urge Mr.Owaisi and Mr.Farhat apologize to not only Ms.Nasreen but the Muslims of the world for the audacity of insulting them by speaking in their behalf without their permission. (Mike Ghouse)

August 2007

India's American Dream

Please Let Us Be Great

> The United States is entering the Civilian-Nuclear Agreement with India on the understanding that India 'has a foreign policy that is congruent to that of the US, and is working with the US on key foreign policy initiatives related to non-proliferation.
> (The Hyde Act)
>
> In fact the purpose of the US to sign civilian nuclear energy cooperation with India is to enclose India into its global partners' camp, so as to balance the forces of Asia. This fits in with India's wishes.
> (*People's Daily*, China, August,30)

We are tempted simply to say 'precisely.' It does seem as though all major players whom the impending nuke deal will be of great concern are clear enough about what it implies, except the honourable Prime Minister of India.

And, then again, not so.

For a start, the rather hollow claim that the primary object of signing the deal with America is to ensure the ostensibly bountiful enhancement of electric power for India's growth requirements has by now been conclusively exposed for a sham – never more conclusively than in a paper prepared by the research cell of the Communist Party of India (Marxist).

Basing itself on the government's own statistics, the paper shows that even going by the 'most optimistic scenario' (Planning Commission), the contribution of nuclear power to India's total output (at present 3% or less) will not rise beyond 7-9% by 2020!

The viability of the magniloquent idea is further crippled when it is remembered that the per unit cost of producing nuclear power at the Plant End itself is estimated to be double that of thermal power, as well as the time taken to construct (Rs.8.1 crore to Rs.3.73 crore, and 8 years to 4 in time terms).

Further, the cost goes up several notches more for power produced from imported nuclear Plants. And those are waiting to come in droves.

And, when you add to all that the known and experienced hazards, the de-commissioning costs, and the fatal conundrums of storing nuclear wastes, the least Indian citizen unburdened by vested interest might say, 'hello, why are we doing all this?'

II

The simple enough answer to that innocent question is adequately contained in the little quote from the Chinese People's Daily. Some 40 million globalised Indians (about 3% of the population) now feel that globalization can have but one definition – living the Indian American Dream with gusto. To them Zarathustra has spoken: *thou art the inheritors of the neoliberal bonanza; thou alone may afford nuclear electric power; and in place of plebian pacemakers for thine failing hearts, thou mayest look forward to inserting uranium pellets for longevity. As to the 836 million Indians who spend less than 50 cents a day, enhanced uranium stockpiles thou shalt convert into nutritional pills and batteries, so there will be no more need to grow food, or waste resources on public health services. And think how many more – and more deadly – bombs thou shalt produce and possess, signatures of unmitigated greatness. And when, like the United States, thou graduate to unilateral prowess, and feel bold enough to invade right, left, and centre, who shall say thy superpowerdom is not complete! Hallelujah! Go forth and rise above all nations and thine own people, for thou art the chosen 40 million that shalt be saved in a Uranium Ark when I smite the weak, the disabled, the dark, and the niggling moralisers.*

With a mandate like that, it must be hard to resist destiny, even though for tactical purposes some disingenuous disclaimers must need be peddled.

Among those disclaimers, the primary ones are two:

1. that the civilian-nuclear agreement (123) is limited just to enhancing power output, and has no implications for India's foreign policy;

2. and that the Hyde Act which enables the 123 bilateral governmental agreement has no bearing on the latter, being merely an internal concern of the United States.

III

Looking at the second first, here is what the US under-secretary of state who was the chief negotiator in the deal with India, had to say on July 27, 2007:

> We were very careful when we began these – the latest phase of these negotiations to remind the Indian government that since the President and the Prime Minister had their two agreements of July, 2005 and March, 2006, something else had happened: the Congress had debated over six, seven months those agreements and the Congress has passed the Hyde Act. And so we had to make sure that everything in this US-India Civil- Nuclear Agreement, the 123 Agreement, was completely consistent with The Hyde Act and well within the bounds of the Hyde Act itself.

Clearly, Burns hasn't yet lost his job for making that unequivocal statement, so where may there be the least doubt that the 123 agreement, after all, draws what breath it has from the enabling legal legitimacy provided by the Hyde Act? Any polemic to the contrary must seem like the ignorant argument that the Accession of the State of Jammu & Kashmir to the Union of India is not embedded in and enabled by Article 370 of the Constitution!

Were that not the case, the US-China treaty on nuclear cooperation would not have stipulated that that particular treaty would operate independent of the 'national laws of either country.' Mr.Burns, therefore, unlike our own rather presumptuous ambassador to the United States, clearly has his beans about him and knows how the nuke cookie crumbles. But, alack the befuddling mists of greatness that render the Indian pupil hazy in a self-induced daze of Edorado!

IV

Having gotten that out of the way, just let us remind ourselves of some, only some of the stipulations of the majestic Hyde Act.

Indeed, its main policy thrust is best captured in the entirely no-nonsense injunction cited in the epigraph above. The control mechanisms are suggested somewhat in the following:

- there will have to be an annual Presidential certification reporting to the Congress that 'India is fully and actively participating in US international efforts to dissuade, isolate, and, if necessary, sanction and contain Iran, (104 g/2 E/i);

- that India will participate and formally support the US 'Proliferation Security Initiative', including (illegally, one might add), the policy of interdiction of vessels in International waters (104 g/2 k);
- that if the required Presidential certification is not forthcoming or is unsatisfactory, Congress under the Hyde Act has the right to suspend or terminate 123 for civilian nuclear cooperation; It is to be noted that in the 123 Agreement the word 'certification' is replaced by 'assessment' (tweedledom/tweedledee?) and the right of return is preserved. Listen again to Burns;
- And if so there is any reason for the US to have to invoke the right-of-return, we could certainly do so;
- And more explicitly and comprehensively, the 123 Agreement (article 2.1) states:

> Each party shall implement this Agreement in accordance with its respective applicable treaties, national laws, regulations and license requirements concerning the use of nuclear energy for peaceful purposes;

- As unambiguous a reference to the overriding writ of the Hyde Act within the 123 text as you could get!
- that in the event of such termination, the US will persuade other members of the Nuclear Suppliers Group (NSG) to 'follow suit'.

V

About foreign policy then.

It is ofcourse not the case that the above explicit texts are not explicit enough to the powers-that-be in India. The plain fact is, as the CPI(M) paper amply documents, that this government, continuing and expanding the efforts of the previous NDA regime vis a vis strategic partnership with the US as a 'natural ally', means to seal a paradigm shift in India's foreign policy orientations and traditions. That notwithstanding the stipulation in the National Common Minimum Programme that 'the UPA government will maintain the independence of India's foreign policy position on all regional and global issues.'

The July 18,05 Agreement between the President and the Prime Minister states:

> US-India defence relationship derives from a common belief in freedom, democracy, and the rule of law, and seeks to advance shared security interests.

Some laughter may be permitted here (see my article 'New Ringtones from Condy Rice: Align with Dubya, or Pay Big Price'). The fact remains that having buried the Nehruvian model of economic development, the Manmohan Singh government now wishes to go fast forward and also bury the rich and respectable tradition of India's Independent thinking in foreign relations. Thus while the communists are shoddily accused of harbouring those extra-territorial loyalties (never mind that the 'Gujral doctrine' had stipulated that the chief object of India's foreign policy must be first to forge the best of relations with neighbouring countries, even if that meant offering unilateral concessions), intimacy with the US and the furthering of US interests in Asia is not regarded as anything in the nature of an extra-territorial loyalty but a 'natural' course of action. Ah the semantics of gourmandizing class interest!

And the grim tale is that soon after the July Agreement, India's volte-face on Iran followed; in the IAEA India voted twice against Iran on US 'persuasion.' Indeed, true to the diplomatic subtleties of the American mind, an official spokesman of the Bush administration has recently stated forthrightly that the Indian vote on Iran was 'coerced.' We haven't heard of a contradiction from the Indian establishment yet.

The salt into that welcome wound was to be applied by no less a man than Senator Luger of the Senate Foreign Relations Committee:

> We have already seen strategic benefits from our improving relations with India. India's votes at the IAEA on the Iran issue last September, and this past February demonstrate that New Delhi is able and willing to adjust (ah those sexy euphemisms!) its traditional foreign policies and play a constructive role on international issues.

Be it recalled that the New Framework for India-US Defence Relationship signed on 28th June,2005 stipulates the brazenly military part of the foreign policy shift; it incorporates joint military exercises, joint planning, joint operations in other countries, and defence procurement.

India is set to spend some $40 billion on armament purchase most of which will come from the US!

A Second agreement called 'The Logistics and Service Agreement' (ACSA) is also being currently negotiated. This deal if it goes through will allow refueling and complete access facilities to all US ships and aircraft.

Both deals (Defence and Logistics) inscribe the requirement of 'interoperability' between US and Indian armed forces, involving the use of identical arms! The projected bonanza for the US arms corporates need hardly be imagined!

Then there is the third axis that flows from the above two: forthcoming naval exercises of trilateral countries (US, Japan, Australia) in the Bay of Bengal. You might well wonder who all this is calculated to ward off – our neighbour China, since even in the US-Korea relations peace has been restored. We are then willing to become an outpost of some sort of Asian NATO.

VI

Let me conclude with just three posers:

- Given that our energy needs, both from an output and cost perspective, will continue to depend on coal, gas, and hydro sources, how clever is it to sink unconscionable billions into nuclear power? Remember that the US has thought it wise not to invest in a single nuclear power plant at home in the last three decades! Are we doing anything more than offering a bonanza to US nuclear industry, since the nuke deal will certainly oblige India to first propitiate the US corporates? Let us also remind ourselves that India still has the world's largest coal reserves, and river systems that could be harnessed to electric power rather than let free to flood the country as they presently do.
- Given that the world's largest gas and oil reserves still lie in West Asia, how clever a foreign policy would it be to alienate that part of the world by overtly aligning with the US?
- In the context of our problem with 'terrorism', (and our tom-tommed pride that Indian Muslims have remained aloof from Al Qaeda activity), how smart might it be to offer just the catalyst the worlds' second largest Muslim population may need by embracing the US?

VII

The interesting caveat on all this is – one that is now regularly peddled by Indian corporates through the TV channels and the Print media they own that any criticism of American foreign policy tantamounts to 'anti-Americanism,' – a term that is ofcourse deliberately substituted for anti-imperialism. Opposition to America per se (something that the left neither voices nor recommends) draws the bile of the upwardly mobile Indian who can be heard to hum 'Sam O Sam, give us today our daily coke/ and our neck is willing to bear your yoke.'

Thus, some 3% Indians accuse the left (which has some 2% more mandate than that!) of killing the joys of coke, burgher, and Kentucky fried without any mandate for doing so. The left is reviled for its nasty habit of doing home-work on issues and arguing till the cows come home, whereas

The new Indian middle class
Is bored by argument;
Argument so upsets
Its vacuous content.
('Hippopotamus', in Badri Raina, *Modest Proposal and other Rhymes for the Times*, Delhi, 2000)

Given that the sum of the cultural life of this class of neoliberalised Indians is encapsulated by the four-fold devotions to new, cunning ways of multiplying wealth, owning the latest state-of-the-art gadgetry, remaining fashionably well-informed with the latest mush from Bollywood and TV serials, and that covering devotion to gods, goddesses, and godmen, accompanied by obscene splashes of consumption and waste at ritual time (the best of them may hardly be able to locate the editorial page in a newspaper, not to speak of reading a journal article, or, god forbid, a whole book), the nagging insistence on thinking the hard way that the left routinely proffers seems like a toothache that is best got rid of. And, it is hardly a surprise that sections of the media are beginning to produce poll figures that show that the Congress would stand to gain and the left to lose from a mid term election if held now – a gentle suggestion that the Manmohan government may well take up sooner than later.

In the meanwhile, the government remains undeterred by the fact that all sections barring the UPA in parliament are opposed to the nuke deal on one ground or the other, since treaty-making power within the Indian democratic system legally resides not with the house of the people but with the executive.

In the days to come, it may indeed become an imperative to take a desirable leaf from the American system and correct that undemocratic anomaly.

America does have good things to offer; why opt always and only for the bad ones?

September 2007

State of the Nation

Do As You Please

As I ponder India 2007, I am struck how truly free a country she is. You may just do as you please – multiply lucre, or starve and opt for suicide. You may also kill without let or hindrance.

How often does history offer so sanguine, even if largely gruesome, a paradox that the happiest occupy opposite ends of an ideological divide that neither wishes particularly to bridge.

On one end, the establishment end if you like, is the 'growth' brigade. Like Arjun of the Mahabharta epic whose warrior arrow was trained to see nothing but the eye of the fish, this brigade sees nothing but the figure 9. Deeply mystified as you properly must be, let us tell you that 9 refers to the percentage at which the Indian economy is growing, give or take.

Still more properly, this 9 caters to its foundational fraction of 3 – yet another deeply mystical figure as you would know. Know also that the 3 here alludes to the percentage of Indians who are by now so sexily amalgamated with the global economy of consumptive crap. They are the pool that give to us our fourth distinguished place worldwide among countries with the most dollar billionaires! Surely, Coleridge's magical lines may without shame be deployed to define the status of our Prime Minister under whose whiz-kid expertise such a consequence has resulted:

Weave a circle round him thrice,
And close your eyes in holy dread,
For he on honey-dew hath fed,
And drunk the milk of Paradise.

And so puissant is this new 3 that it has the power to obliterate all governmental lateral vision, a gift whereby the other 97% of whom

77% subsist on less than US 50 cents a day (all according to report of government's own distinguished committee – no dearth of those, committees, that is) are rendered invisible. So that what is also made invisible is that this 77% is without pottable drinking water, human sanitation, schooling, health care, housing, or piece of land of whose ancient roots they might eat. Although when all public grain disappears from government shops through diversion to privateers, this 77% is known to take their fill of what grass they can find. And often to sell off their unwanted children, daughters especially, for a pittance against the hunger of the next day. A circumstance that calls for invoking the wisdom of another old English poet, William Blake, who was to point out how

Pity would be no more
If we did not make somebody poor.

In our 9% situation, we may indeed replace the word 'pity' with 'greatness.' Although pity and greatness do also go together: they breed that happy marriage between marauding capitalism and equally marauding religion that we see nowadays on display in large parts of India. Remember that it is no object of missionary activity of any religious denomination to actually eradicate misery; that would be incurring suicide. The whole trick lies in catering to misery on a lasting basis without discomfort to oneself. Unsurprisingly, ever since the Washington Consensus was made to overtake India, the object of religious catering has also shifted without embarrassment to the miserable of the Fortune and Forbes magazine types who, after all, being such harried managers of the world's welfare, suffer all kinds of stress and strain. Thus, among the 3% cabal who drip with lucre you may also count most of India's best-known gurus and godmen.

The 9% yielding the 3% phenomenon has another kind of prowess – such that it routinely propagates through the print and electronic media channels whose list of 'experts' on economic wisdom remains sickeningly steadfast. It is able to show, as the well-known columnist, J. Sri Raman, has recently alluded to ('Pillorying the Poor for Poverty', *Daily Times*, Lahore, September,14), how those bleeding-hearts who speak for the 77% are at bottom 'intolerable populists' whereas those who argue for 'more state concessions and incentives for big business' are indeed 'patriotically progressive.'

With sound instinct, therefore, no less than two scions of the Congress Party have smirkingly pointed out how farmers who commit suicide are in fact the ones to blame for their poverty. In the language of Dickens' Steerforth (see David Copperfield) 'that sort of people' have incurably thick skins and will refuse all succour. What can an advancing India have to do with them. Just let them be. India after all is a free country, and we may all do as we like. Who says the Tories are dead and gone.

II

In a word, a state of impenetrable hubris overlays the 'growth' brigade. And the acme of its inebriated self-satisfaction is the new embrace with the world's only 'superpower', even if that poor superpower does not seem to be able to manage to subdue the least of nations where people have the most grit. With unending supplies of uranium round the corner, the 3% who alone may buy what energy that atom yields aspire to scale the heavens where stores may never be short of brands and vending machines of junk food. Now that India has also graduated to the world's largest buyer of armaments with defence deals sealed and signed with who else but the world's only 'superpower', India's ruling elites are convinced that the state is well-nigh impregnable, and therefore deserving of a place at the high tables of all the world's high tables.

III

Looking quizzically from the other end, however, is the anarchist eye. And it sees what the denizens of the bloated balloon of state do not – a thousand little darts stuck in its thick skin, determined to find a way in. Laughing away the pretence of state, it can almost visualize the combustion whose consummation may after all require no extra-territorial conspiracy.

Beginning at the primum mobile of the state, its parliament, the anarchist eye spies a parliament wherein a sprinkling of earnest men and women are overwhelmed routinely by the cacophony of fowls. Thanks to the very channels that proclaim the hubris of the state, the least is able to see how government business is slipped without discussion inbetween its main preoccupation of pandemonial mayhem, much as corporate TV channels slip in bits of programming between their main preoccupation – commercials. And when the honourable, though so overwhelmed, Speaker is heard to say, equally routinely, that it would be best that the House be shut down permanently, the anarchist heart swells at the promised implosion.

Among the polity, the situation seems everyday evenmore promising: more and more army personnel shoot dead their colleagues and disobey their officers, more and more commit suicide, more and more policemen kill off innocent citizens in fake encounters to collect reward and preferment, organized right-wing extremists go on blood-thirsty rampages at the least imagined insult to one cultural/religious icon or the other, burning public property, bashing public men in office, killing as many of the 'other' in unhindered pogroms of carnage; and in still more organized fashion, armed left-wing extremists capture more and more territory in the hinterlands, running their own governments in line with their own laws. In the 'peripheries' dozens of provinces refuse to acknowledge the majesty of the state, and dozens of ethnic armies carry on their defiance of it.

And, most significantly now, instances of fatal public lynchings multiply dime a dozen as well. In village and town, the high-castes vent fatal justice on low-castes, often for no offence greater than standing upright in their august presence, caste panchayats administer instant retribution to loving couples who transgress caste laws (who cares either about the elected panchayats or the constitutional prerogatives of the citizen), many often beheaded in tandem, or left to hang by the next tree, vagrant teenage 'thieves' are caught and bludgeoned to death as approving voices justify the procedure, including members of the state-apparatus who feel relieved that people take upon themselves the rotten business they were appointed to do. Within a month in just one state of India, half a dozen of these wild-western executions have come to light.

Add to all that the time-honoured killings that are conducted to fulfil ritual injunctions – children cut up by tantrics to propitiate some god or the other in order to obviate immiseration or ill-health, women obliged to climb the pyre as Satis, or be hacked as witches so as their claims to property can be obliterated, daughters-in-law burnt off so that new ones may come with fresh infusions of dowry; and with the mouth-watering prospects of the good life beckoning all and sundry, instances of old parents left chained in cells for months/years in the heart of metropolitan India until discovered, or deposited outside temples and suchlike to be carted off by whoever minds their presence. Thus the anarchist sees in the ever-deepening social atavisms the promise of the state's dissolution.

Most of all, the anarchist delights in the new contagious phenomenon that seems to traverse the length and breadth of the country, namely, collective and violent resistance put up by farmers of all description against the appropriation of their lands by the corporates who cannot wait to maximize their profits thousand-fold in the shortest span of time, and who now know that the state is their buddy, and the law-enforcement agencies their permanent protectors from the people. And the courts honourable allies as well. And should these agencies prove inadequate, there is now, after all, the Nimitz and the Kitty Hawk ready and authorized to shoot uranium pellets from as close as the Bay of Bengal.

What wonder then that the anarchist should snigger: did you think Pakistan was imploding? Just wait till you see what happens here you call home. This here democracy that you laud day in and day out is a giant mannequin; its life-blood has long dried out and now flows in the drains everyday with the greed of the haves and the desperation of the have-nots.

And who can say they misrepresent the situation.

IV

So what of those who have a place neither in the balloon nor in the anarchist corner? They are allowed the freedom to make opinion. For now.

September 2007

Quiet Flows the Gutter Paved with Gold

The New Indian Middle Class
will surely take us far;
from hauteur, humbug, heartlessness
to bloody civil war.
(Badri Raina, *Hippopotamus, Modest Proposal & Other Rhymes for the Times*, Sahmat, Delhi, 2000)

A week or so ago, one Prashant Tawang, a police personnel from the Siliguri district of West Bengal, was adjudged the 'Indian Idol' winner at the end of a grueling all-India music competition.

This achievement of the ethnic Gorkhali, however personal, did not fail to enthuse the community and the Eastern parts of India generally, as indeed it enthused a whole of other Indians elsewhere. In many middle-class homes in the metropolises, nonetheless, the smell of conspiracy was ripe: here was another case of the appeasement of yet another 'minority' when, in fact, the winner should have been the other finalist, Amit. As you would expect, there was nothing either 'ethnic' or 'minority' about the latter. Self-evidently, he belonged to India's meritorious 'mainstream.'

These 'mainstream' sentiments were capped by a jolly disc jockey of the Red FM radio: this yuppy wondered aloud while on air where the country would find its supply of 'chowkidars' (doormen/security guards) if Gorkhas began to become musicians and win big prizes.

Predictably, this so-jocular anxiety on behalf of the country set Siliguri alight, to a point where the local government had to impose curfew and take other harsh measures to prevent extensive damage to life and property.

Inevitably, the government at the centre has had to take note, resulting in a decision to impose a ban on the said radio channel for a week.

Equally inevitably, India's savvy and influential corporate TV channels are now in the fray. In one of the interviews held with a representative of the Gorkhas that I happened to listen in to, the 'mainstream' young lady doing the anchor just could not understand how an innocent 'joke' should have been so misconstrued, and why the government was being such a repressive brute. The lady could not cease smirking at the argument that it might be one thing to make such jokes in private confines (although equally symptomatic of 'mainstream' mind-set), but quite another to do so on air. It may be mentioned that in circa 2007 when India is so so up there, India's dalits continue to be routinely alluded to as 'chamars' (untouchables who work with dead-animal leather, a term that carries a historical load analogous to the term 'nigger') in the lordly conversations among the educated upper castes.

II

This incomprehension of India's globalised avant-garde connects with matching incomprehensions in other areas of social and cultural life. To list out just a few:

- they cannot understand why they are obliged to feel any concern for some 800 million or more (some 77%) Indians who subsist on less than 50 cents a day, since it is self-evident that they show no enterprise and are responsible for their plight; or what indeed India's economic path has to do with producing billionaires on the one hand and swelling the disposables on the other;
- they cannot understand why the state should put affirmative action measures in place to improve their lot, when it is self-evident that they are by nature (read caste) without merit;
- they cannot understand why their own achievements should so constantly be held to ransom just because some two-thirds of other Indians have no access to clean drinking water, sanitation, health care, schools, steady work;
- they cannot understand why farmers should be committing suicide when the world's premier financial institutions so laud India's advancement and GDP growth;
- they cannot understand why the police and other law-enforcing agencies should be held responsible if once in a while they kill

innocent civilians in fake encounters, or come down heavily on Muslims in riot situations, since it is obvious that all Muslims are terrorists and responsible, in the first place, for India's partition;

- they cannot understand why their successful sons and daughters should be held guilty of mowing down riff raff sleeping on pavements, since suchlike have no business to be sleeping on the pavements, or be sleeping at all;
- they cannot understand why multitudes of human vermin who subsist in slums should resist being evicted without notice so that a shopping mall might come up;
- they cannot understand why the governments tolerate busy- body civil society activists who relentlessly thwart the march of the country towards superpower status by obstructing 'development' work at dam sites, in the forests, on farmlands and so on; or, who immiserate the nation's will to be among the elect by constantly bringing up the brutal social oppressions in the hinterland, as though any great damage is done if occasionally a dalit or two are bashed to death, a woman or two raped or burnt off as witches, or a child or two sacrificed by tantrics, or a daughter or two sold off for a pittance by parents in order to ensure the next roti dal, or fatal justice dispensed by lynch mobs on boys accused of petty theft with an approving or complicit police officer on the sidelines; In fact, they do not understand why a democracy should at all need any political party system (or more than just two parties that are at bottom one and the same, since, alas, having only one congenial party would lay the state open to the charge of being a communist state), or why all forms of collective social protest should not be banned forever (since the jobs they need done are best accomplished through back-stage clout), or why the Constitution should not stipulate that the Supreme Court of India may always have the right to override both the Legislature and the Executive;
- they cannot understand why the army is not ordered to eradicate and eliminate various armed insurgencies who stand up for bogus reasons, or indeed because they hate India;
- and they cannot understand what is so wrong with allying with a regime in America that is after all only doing the right and proper by going after the Muslim world on any pretext so long as such regime promises more H visas, more Green Cards, more shopping malls,

super-markets, other latest gadgetries, armaments and, not to forget, the once-in-a-lifetime nuclear deal;

- The itinerary here is indeed a long one, forming a formidable package of advancement.

III

So, is there anything at all this avant-garde needs to improve upon whatsoever?

Indeed there is, much as it might surprise you.

And I was made wise to it by a bright and personable young lady in the family who calls herself an 'Indian patriot.' And not a doubt that she meant well.

The knowledge of how, mind you, the 'system' needs to be 'changed' came in the form of a video email, originating from no less than that ubiquitous hero of the new upwardly mobile Indian, namely, the former President of India, Abdul Kalam.

This 'power point' (I have never quite understood what that means, although the 'power' part speaks for itself) presentation lists out some ten stunning ideas that must be implemented if the 'system' is to be 'changed' allowing India to be among the foremost.

Of the ten I now recall only some: it asks with telling force whether 'you' would litter the street were 'you' walking down in 'Singapore', and answers that you would not; so why do it here at home?

It asks whether it is not true that walking your dog down such a street abroad you would not be obliged to clean up the doggy mess yourself if it happened while on the street, and answers of course you would; then why not do the same here at home?

As I said there are some more points equally momentously directed at changing the system, but do pardon me if I cannot recall the same now. These may have included driving carefully, avoiding corrupt practices, asking what you can do for the country's 'development' rather than what the country can do for you, and so on.

What I can vouchsafe for is that the power points made no mention of any of the things listed in my second section. Clearly those have nothing to do with the 'system' and the 'system' has nothing to do with those either. Is it any wonder that so much hullabaloo should have been in evidence on behalf of India's new avant-garde and the channels that speak for them about setting all convention or propriety aside and giving Kalam sahib a second term as President, if not through proper constitutional procedure then by the 'people's' will. No chocolate for guessing who here were meant by the term 'people.'

IV

India's current state then seems adequately defined by the gutter of my first two sections, and by the gold of the third which is meticulously sought to be paved over it. And it is small consolation for the likes of this writer that in some ways it may not be too different in other parts of the world, including the the United States of America where the Jena Six episode has, for example, raised afresh the question whether, despite the victory of the civil rights movement, the rednecks may not after all be back in business. Not to speak of the role of that regime in decimating 'universal human rights' and values not just world-over but at home as well, even as it promises to make India 'great.' Think that in that patron of democracy today habeas corpus, due process, right to legal representation, to privacy, and the bedrock principle of the separation of powers all remain suspended!

Clearly, Indians (those 'other' two-thirds) will have, in the months and years to come, to find other ways of changing the system with all due deference to the former President of the Republic. So we say get busy, and do not be taken in by the gold. It is mortally fake.

October 2007

Right-Wing Constructions of God

> *Say: 'Unbelievers, I do not serve what you worship, nor do you serve what I worship. I shall never serve what you worship, nor will you ever serve what I worship. You have your own religion, and I have mine.'*
> (*The Koran*, Penguin Classics, trans.,N.J.Dawood, 1956; p.401)

It used to be said that patriotism is the last refuge of the scoundrel; for sometime now, it is the first.

Strikingly, the more it trumpets itself, the more suspect it becomes. Not unsurprisingly, therefore, a fascist construction of patriotism that at bottom reflects the violence-ridden impatience of global capital to gobble up the earth requires a medieval recall for longer life. And what more medieval than the idea of the crusade. Ruling classes everywhere engaged in the most irreligious of brutalities thus project themselves as the chief patrons of religion. And there are those who innocently buy the idea.

I am looking at an article posted on alternet.org titled 'The Relilgious Right's New Tactics for Invading Public Schools.'

In the month of August, '07, the Governor of Texas signed a legislation designated 'Religious Viewpoints Antidiscrimination Act.' This law 'requires every public school in the state to adopt a policy guaranteeing student's right to religious expression. It mandates that schools create 'limited public forums' for religious and other types of speech.'

That this new law is not as catholic or innocuous as it sounds is obvious enough to the best of practicing Christians, not to speak of adherents of other faiths. Kathy Miller, President of the Texas Freedom Network has this to say: "The law is fundamentally at odds with the principle of religious freedom." And more explicitly, "It will force public school students to participate in…proselytising."

II

The proselytizing is of course fully underway, and entirely on biblical lines. A video message now doing the rounds is titled 'you sow what you reap.'

The opening gambit reads: I hope this catches U the way it caught ME.

In the body of the message, one Jane Clayson asks a 'prominent American daughter' the question: 'How could God let something like this happen' (meaning what else but 9/11) ?

Anne Graham's 'profound and insightful answer' proceeds as follows:

- "God... is deeply saddened" that "we have been asking him to get out of our schools... our government, and our lives";
- that there is no 'Bible reading in schools'; because thereby we do not acquaint our children with the injunction 'thou shall not kill' there are shootings in schools; (it should be obvious that the Texas law indeed has just the Bible in mind rather than any of the other religious scriptures.)
- we allow 'abortions' and use of 'condoms';
- that this free riot of sex goes on regardless even of what a 'President does in private' (Democrats to note);
- that pictures of 'nude women' flood the magazines;
- that pictures of 'nude children' also make popular copy;
- that TV shows promote 'profanity and... illicit sex'.

Thus it is that something like 9/11 happens; as God in his fury leveled Sodom and Gomorrah, so the USA is now being punished.

III

Looking at this package of profanity, you might well wonder why God is not seen to mind the following profanities, or why God's punishment must not be seen to be attributable to their commission through American history:

- the genocide of native Indians: ('thou shall love thy neighbour as thyself');
- slave trade (60 million dead: 'thou shall not kill);

- Hiroshima/Nagasaki (millions twisted into molten rubble, and millions more maimed, deformed, consigned to cancer);
- Vietnam (millions consumed by napalm and Agent Orange);
- some 69 regular invasions since the end of world war II and the liquidation of life, property and nationhoods thereby;
- 500,000 Iraqi children killed inch by inch thanks to the sanctions regime;
- the propping of dictators, military juntas, sheikhdoms, even religious bigots of 'other' cultures in pursuit of dominance and material loot;
- the tortures inflicted on innocent and guilty alike in Guantanamo Bay, Abu Ghraib, through clandestine 'extraordinary renditions' – all beyond the pale of the regime of US laws;
- the refusal to sign international treaties that would somewhat ameliorate the catastrophic destruction of the environment;
- the militarization of space;
- not to speak of the readiness to invade other countries on counterfeit pretences, using dirty uranium, white phosphorus, cluster bombs, inorder to assume the ownership of oil, and furnish the armament corporates opportunites to forge newer and deadlier weapons of mass destruction.

As should be obvious, this can be an interminable list; yet the right-wing God does not seem to mind any of it, or think these abominations grounds for punishment. Such crimes somehow do not qualify as 'sins' or become amenable to moral considerations. Just only the body of Eve and what the advertisers do with it are legitimate provocations to God's ire. The inference being that if only the imperialist machine learnt simultaneously to honour God's injunctions about the denigration of 'flesh', all would not only be well, but ideal.

IV

Look where you will, and you may find identical sales campaigns about what does or does not anger God.

Here in India, for example, most Hindutva vendettas have been reserved for the fleshly excesses of the profligate: Valentine 'wantonness', 'bawdy' artworks, inter-religious and inter-caste marriages, especially where the woman be a Hindu,or a high caste; these have been seen to constitute evils beyond the pale. The massacre of the 'minorities' from time to time only add to the credit side of those who do God's work. Nor is it any different with an Islam that continues to be ruled by vested clerics. The chief affronts to God inevitably come from women: assuming 'provocative' dress, intermingling, disobeying patriarchal injunctions and traditions, not to speak of questioning any part of the Sharia with respect to women's lives – these affronts warrant the most gruesome retributions. As to the mangling of innocents in fidayeen attacks, God applauds from above and promises, guess what, lovely houris in heaven. As to the Zionists, they did God's work on behalf of securing the 'promised land' when they initiated modern-day terrorism by effecting the carnage at the King David hotel in 1947. The work that was then done by the Stern and Irving gangs has since been taken over by the state with the full blessings of the God of the United States.

Indeed, the CNN's Christianne Amanpour is to be complimented for underscoring many of these historical formations in her current documentary 'God's Warriors.' A must see experience.

V

Clearly, this construction of God, however richly peddled whether by the Bushies, the bin Ladins, the Togadias, or the Rabbies of the Likud does not meet either the imperatives or the best imaginings of human beings who truly believe God can only be a votary of universal acceptance and universal love. Any God whose composure remains undisturbed by the abominations of the kind listed in section II of this piece must be indistinguishable from the worst Pharos and Feuhrers that the world has known. And any God that fights shy of admiring the nude splendour of the human body, female or male, that he is credited to have created in the first place must be a God of small-mindedness.

The fact, of course, is that God, wherever such a one be or not be, must have rather little idea of all that is going on in his name. Those, however, that forge him (forbid the thought that he could be she) in the image that the video propagates know well enough that they mean to use their representation of him as the ultimate WMD as and when the need arises, be it on their own kind or on the infidel 'other'.

Which must mean that the truly godly among all religions have a job on hand, namely, to salvage God from the stranglehold of the mass murderers.

October 2007

Deal or Democracy?
India at the Crossroads

I.

The Indo-US nuclear energy deal may or may not happen. The contested debate that surrounds it has, nonetheless, brought to the fore issues and allegiances of far-reaching consequence.

Notwithstanding their claims of progressive neutrality, it has become obvious that India's 'premier' print and electronic media, especially the English language ones, have since the state's shift to a 'reform' agenda (1990) tended to tilt pretty whole hog to the right-wing.

During the Thatcherite tenure of the unabashedly comprador NDA regime (1998-2004), this tilt had an unbelievably free ride. This in the sense that there was little in the ideological direction of that regime that India's corporates and the media that speaks for them felt called upon to contest or deride.

Sadly, so they see the matter, the fall of the NDA regime in 2004, as the then 'India Shining' electoral campaign came crashing at the hustings in the face of abysmally harsh mass realities on the ground, yielded a government debilitated from the outset because it was obliged to take outside support from the left to make up its parliamentary majority.

Wretchedly, the National Common Minimum Programme (CMP) drawn up between the formal constituents of the United Progressive Alliance (UPA) and the left as the blueprint for policy and governance announced a rather Keynsian welfarist agenda, even as it retained most of the 'developmental' emphases of the earlier regime.

Grievously, the left, now a millstone around the desired monetarist anarchism of the state at home, could be trusted to thwart at every step the larger goal of an amalgamation as a 'strategic partner' with an American world order that presided over corporate globalization.

II

Thus, after what have seemed to the new consumerist class and their political leaderships three odd years of aborted opportunity, thanks no doubt to the 'Neanderthal' mind-set of the left, the Indo-US nuclear deal has come to be seen as the perfect camouflage to the project of reasserting that class aspiration, namely, a privileged spot in the neo-imperialist sun.

This segment of the Indian ruling class and the left, deeply ironic as it seems, understand one another with pellucid clarity, even as ill-informed or half-baked innocents do well-intentioned middle class jigs around a vaguely-formed 'patriotic' concern for India, all according to what movies they see or what clubs or kitty parties they frequent, or indeed what cricket icons they follow.

In other words, both the ruling compradors and the left have known from day one that the Indo-US nuke deal was never just about an isolated agreement on a single issue between two sovereign states.

After three desultory years, the compradors see in the nuke deal a decisive new opportunity to defeat irritating social impediments to profit maximization, just as the American peddlers of the deal honestly admit that its charms lie in the business avenues it will open up to the US nuclear and arms corporates, even as its other consequences and the other agreements reached, or slated to be reached, between the militaries of the two states on defence and logistical inter-operability ('strategic partnership') promise the realization of the American- Asian era.

Furthermore, the nuke deal, understood as the thin end of the 'strategic partnership' wedge, may be trusted as a larger instrument or metaphor to breach decisively the lingering hold of the Indian left via such residues as the Nehruvain legacies of a socialistic conscience, non-alignment, multi-polarity, a Westphalian allegiance to the concepts of national sovereignty and non-interference in the internal affairs of nation-states. In exchange for, as the American Secretary of State was to throw as noblesse oblige – the promise of 'greatness' that the US would bestow on India.

Thus, the class interests of the globalised Indian have required that the media and the government project those interests as the 'national' interest.

III

Cussedly enough, the left argues that in a country where, according to the government's own statistics, 77% Indians spend less than half a dollar a day, while the list of billionaires among the top 3% burgeons on the other end, where more than two-thirds have no access to clean drinking water or sanitation or assured public health care, or the right to uniform elementary schooling, not to speak of the right to stable, gainful employment, it is not only laughable but rather gruesome to invest in the great- power agenda.

The left insists, therefore, that the economic, political, and the environmental and social consequences-to-follow of the envisaged deal cannot be seen in separation from the pattern of 'development' that the UPA seeks to unleash. And that this is a route not to national prosperity or consolidation but potentially to causing a deepening of the axes of disintegration which are everywhere in evidence among populations that rarely grace the TV screens, or become focal to considerations of the state.

Sensing that a 'victory' conceded to the left at this high noon of ruling class ambition can lead to a perpetuation of its relevance, perhaps even its spread, however tardy, beyond its 'demarcated' bastions, senior scribes ensconced in positions of vantage in the media have been obliged to jettison their customary sang froid and come out with fists flailing.

Day after day, these worthies – with a few honourable exceptions that I shall acknowledge hereafter – , chaffing at the bit, have been failing to remain this side of abuse, rather borrowing thereby from the lowly politicians from the hinterland whom they never tire of denigrating for lack of finesse.

And, even as, expectedly, this falange of opinion-makers seek to dub the left's resistance to the nuke deal as a proxy performance on behalf of big brother, China, the more starkly obvious thing has been their own allegiance to and complicity with American corporate interests! Of course, we are to understand that whereas playing proxy for the non-American world constitutes 'treachery' standing by Sam, self-evidently denotes high patriotism. Slow learners we.

Interestingly, what galls is that the left has chosen the route of painstaking case-building on the issue rather than strident slogan mongering. And that their adroit verbal vulgarities hurled at the left increasingly bite less even among the consumerist class that they ostensibly speak for than the arguments and analyses that the left furnishes with regard both to the cost-benefit features and other negatives of nuclear power investment, and the details and implications of striking a 'strategic partnership' with the US. Making matters worse, nuclear scientists of repute who have at one time or another been incharge of India's nuclear development at the key institutes and installations have minced few words in underling the deleterious aspects of the deal. (see Prakash Karat, *Subordinate Ally: The Nuclear Deal and India-US Strategic Relations*, Leftword, Delhi, 2007).

Nor has it helped the official case that the left should make the explicit pronouncement that even if China were tomorrow to endorse the deal in the comity of suppliers called the NSG, the opposition of the Indian left would remain in place. No better proof, you would think, that the left genuinely believes that the deal will damage the national interest. Or believes that China as well may not be the most trustworthy guaranter of those interests.

IV

Unable to dent the unity or strenuousness of the left opposition, Indian media organizations and high-placed columnists have been taking the other route – to berate the Prime Minister for being 'weak', 'spineless,' 'politically non-existent,' and for holding on to his seat despite having 'egg on his face.' So much for the culture of subtlety and sophistication. A gentleman Prime Minister who till the other day was applauded no end for being above the piss and mire of politics is today being faulted for being after all a political novice and lightweight.

Another gimmick that the media has been unleashing is to effect opinion polls with utter dispatch, all of them showing how the Congress Party would stand to gain in parliamentary arithmetic were the Indian general election, due in 2009, to be held now. Unfortunately, thus far the Prime Minister refuses to take this hint as well, even when the polls he is told show that the left would be severely mauled, and thus ejected from any new coalition. The point being: eject the left however you will from the life of the nation. The only other thing ofcourse, in Brechtian phrase, would be to eject the people. Not likely to happen.

V

But an aspect of this conjuncture that seems of the highest consequence is the one that concerns the enticing sales pitch about democracy.

It is said that nothing would be more salubrious for the current world order than for the two most-best (in Shakesperean phrase) democracies to close in strategic embrace. The ironies here are truly befuddling, once these are seen. But let me say in passing that two gentlemen among the Indian media have expressed democratic anxiety with regard to the implications of sealing the deal: Veer Sanghvi of the Hindustan Times (oddly you would think), and Vinod Mehta of the *Outlook* Magazine. (If there have been others I may not have seen them.) This needs to be mentioned because their demur has value of another kind; both believe that the deal may not be a bad thing for India. What is salutary, however, is that both also believe there are systemic considerations that must not be overlooked.

Conceding for the moment that the Indian and American states are constitutional democracies (there will of course be a spate of argument as to the democratic content of those constitutions, and about the equity with which that content operates among the polity), it must be noted that the idea of democracy obtains variably in the two democracies, owing largely to the variable trajectories of formation.

Thus the central feature of American democracy has been its civil-libertarian ethos, and its emphasis on the rule of law. As to its representational legitimacy, its Presidential system remains overly centralized and inimical to the pluralist social dynamic on the ground. Just as the crucial factor in its Presidential electoral process remains the ability of aspirants to amass campaign funds – something that ab initio closes the door to citizens that can never hope to garner such clout. Equally, checks and balances notwithstanding, once elected to office, the American President rarely faces a circumstance when it has to yield to the Houses of Congress in the making of decisions. Given that the American Constitution mandates a two-party system, (that these tend to be tweedledom and tweedledee has never been more obvious than in the behaviour of the current Republicans and Democrats with respect to the Iraq invasion) the President in effect runs a corporate plutocracy unhindered by contesting political forces, whoever they be.

The Indian parliamentary system, on the other hand, lays heavy emphasis on wide-spectrum representation, increasingly so since the decade of the seventies. Of the three wings of the state, parliament is regarded pre-eminent in that it embodies the will of the people. Nor, even during these bad days, does the power of lucre alone, often at all, ensure entry into its portals. A wide spectrum of social and regional considerations can become instruments of electoral empowerment. As to the civil-libertarian aspects of democracy, and the operation of the rule of law, it may be conceded that these are late entrants to our democratic thinking. Citizens whose right to franchise is guarded as best as the system can are often victims of the grossest violation of human rights, both at the hands of the state and of those that have traditionally exercised social dominion over them.

VI

Imagine now that the argument about the democratic embrace should be proferred at a point of time when the civil-libertarian ethos and traditions of American democracy are in shreds, and when the regime of law seems wholesale to have yielded to the arbitrary exercise of executive power. There is hardly a citizen in America today who is not a suspect, who is not under myriad forms of surveillance, and who may claim even the right of habeas corpus. Indeed, as Jean Claude Paye has recently pointed out, the 'Military Commissions Act of 2006' puts an end to an older form of democratic state: 'It is the constituent act of a new form of state that establishes war as a political relation between constituted authorities and national populations' (see 'Enemy Combatant or Enemy of the Government?' Analytical Monthly Review, September,2007, Vol 5, No.6, p.1)

Indeed, the details of that democratic collapse are by now legion in wide sections of the American mainstream media itself, and need not be belaboured here. Nor is there any dearth of erstwhile high officers of US government or Intelligence who bemoan the occurrence each passing day.

And here in India, we have the circumstance that the government of the day seeks to seal the nuke deal in the teeth of the reality that the Congress Party alone in parliament seems to favour it, while every other party in the house of the people vocally opposes it. Votaries of the deal thus seek to clinch the agreement as a sort of supra-democratic fiat, bypassing the sanctity of representation. The official recourse in so stark a situation to the legality that the Constitution at present does not require ratification by parliament only condemns itself as a grossly undemocratic technicality.

We are now to understand that while both countries make minced meat of the substance of democracy in their own several backyards, together in embrace they will inundate the war-torn world with democracy. Do laugh, if you will.

VII

Look at the matter whichever way, and the nuke deal debate is one that involves pretty fundamental considerations with regard both to the ideological direction the Indian state may or may not take, as well as about the content and modus operandi of the Indian democratic system.

But here is what I find to be a great and potentially lasting positive of the contestation. It used to be said, especially by the BJP, that the NDA they led during the Vajpayee priministership set an example of how to run a coalition. As one recalls, most of that prowess had to do with canny considerations with respect to ministerial and other dues of various coalition partners, rarely if ever involving any contest of ideas or principles.

This is the first time ever in the sixty years of Indian democracy that a debate of such depth and rigour has happened within sections of the ruling conglomerate and among the polity generally. It can hardly be said that the intellectual and ideological opposition the left has mounted has had to do with loaves and fishes of office, since they are not in the government to begin with, nor mean to be. Together, the left and the Congress, in keeping that tough engagement going with research and case-building on either side, have put the substance of Indian democracy on a pedestal that recalls the debates that led upto India's Independence.

One is tempted to say that reclaiming that tradition of debate may after all signify a far more consequential deal for the future course of Indian democracy than the nuke deal with America.

November 2007

Gujarat 2002

Murder Most Theoretical

The German philosopher, Kant, gave to the world two highly consequential orders of epistemology.

In a throwback to Plato, he stipulated that it is within the intuitive powers of the human mind that it can have a priori knowledge of the totality of relations among entities. Further, inorder to give a meaningful ground for experience or to make ethical conduct possible, it can postulate things unknowable to itself (god, soul, immortality), and, on that basis, lay down universal principles that can be construed 'categorical imperatives.'

Remarkably, however, Kant wedded these idealist propositions to a caution that 18c Empiricism and Newtonian science made compelling.

This caution was to the effect that the mind, because of its own nature, cannot know the-thing-in-itself, but rather interprets the data presented to it as spatio-temporal phenomena.

Within some forty years of Kant's death (1804), Marx – like Hegel before him – would locate within the Kantian duality the seeds and promise of a dialectical epistemology.

Briefly, Marx would point out to both Kant and Hegel that the realm of the intuitive was as much material as the rest of the phenomenal world. Indeed that ontological/ethical constructs could, in their changing courses, be understood as projections of specific class interests.

Only thus could the universe of contradictions in human praxis be made sense of, since everywhere in history the supposedly universalist postulates were vitiated/remade by productive human agents.

How else could one explain the fact that gems of 'received wisdom' should so embarrassingly be at loggerheads with their conceptual opposites. Here is a sample:

Wise men think alike/ Fools seldom differ.

Slow and steady wins the race/Time waits for no man.

Doubt is the beginning of wisdom/Faith will move mountains.

You are never too old to learn/You can't teach an old dog new tricks.

Absence makes the heart grow fonder/Out of sight out of mind.

Too many cooks spoil the broth/Many hands make light work.

And so on!

II

In theory you could postulate a supposedly self-evident truth – that all men have certain 'unalienable rights' but vitiate its operation among the bulk of mankind.

You could designate 'democracy' as 'government of the people, for the people, by the people' but phenomenally institute government of the endowed, for the endowed, by the endowed.

You could postulate a supra-human intelligence (god), but in practice fight bloody crusades on behalf of particular versions and particular gods.

You could propogate such texts and a priori injunctions as 'thou shalt not kill,' if slapped, 'thou shalt turn the other cheek,' 'thou shall love thy neighbour as thyself,' 'thou shalt love thine enemy,' 'thou shall not lay thy treasure upon the earth,' 'thou shalt do to others as you would have others do unto you,' or, 'whoever receives one of these (children) in my name, receives me,' but in practice kill left, right, and centre, and justify the killings one way or another; point the gun rather than turn the other cheek; gobble up your neighbour (individual/family/nation) rather than love him/it; seek your enemy, real or imagined, or, indeed, constructed, for retribution in the far corners of the earth and lay your treasure very much upon it, ad nauseum; do precisely that to the other as you would never want the other to do to you, and maim, starve, annihilate children if the 'national interest' so dictated (500,000 in Iraq).

And offer justification for all these that you would deny to the other. Sauce for the goose not being sauce for the gander; rather, one man's meat another man's poison – to cite but one further set of opposites.

III

Take the matter of killing others, for example. Were you to look into the a priori injunctions of any denominational archive and you will find therein a universal abhorrence of the taking of life.

Yet in practice the injunction is obviated by laying down a graded ethics of killing, all subject to a varying spectrum of evaluation, justification, or punishment.

At one end of the scale, you may without qualm of conscience kill in 'self-defence.' Expanding that allowance to a larger consideration, you may kill in defence of family, community, faith, nation and be lauded for the same. Indeed, a Hiroshima may also be justified as having been necessary to winning that final victory for world peace. Especially since, happily, those that die no longer have an opinion that you need to worry about.

Among the non-endorsable killings consider first 'murder.' You will find that not all 'murders' fall into one universal category, or into an undifferentiated Kantian 'judgement.'

A life taken unintendedly in a fit of passion, or out of outrage at some proven great wrong may draw but light chastisement of the law. Remember that there still are among us cultures wherein 'revenge or honour killings' do not only receive community endorsement but are, indeed, mandated, rendering 'categorical imperatives' a site of great colour and variety.

Less forgiveable are murders committed from greed of one kind or another (money, property, preferment, desired paramour). These draw far less consensus. And much may depend on how cleverly your lawyer can subvert the evidence.

Killings that draw the most opprobrium, except of course from those that commit them, are those that seem bereft of tangible motive, issuing rather from some grand principle of theory. Intellectual murders these may be called.

The killers here seem to say to their victims: 'we kill you because you are not us, or that you are the not-we. And that the world may not be improved or rendered pure till you remain in it, sharing our earth, air, bread and butter.

To this category belong the genocides and the pogroms – ethnic, racial, religious (native Indians, slaves, Tutsies in Rwanda, Muslims in Bosnia, Armenians in Turkey, the killing fields in Cambodia, and those six million odd Jews in Germany/Europe).

IV

And to this last category indeed belong the 2002 massacres of Muslims in Gujarat. How intimate the theoretical fountain-springs of those killings has been to European Fascism/Nazism – and lately to the actual workings of American Imperialism and Islamist jihadism – may be garnered by sampling the following pronouncements:

> Only a member of the race can be a citizen. A member of the race can only be one who is of German blood. …Consequently, no Jew can be a member of the race. Whoever has no citizenship is to be able to live in Germany only as a guest, and must be under the the authority of legislation for foreigners. We demand that the state be charged first with providing the opportunity of livelihood and a way of life for citizens. If it is impossible to sustain the total population of the state, then the members of foreign nations (non-citizens) are to be expelled from the Reich. (The National Socialist twenty-five point programme of 1920, pt. 4, 5, 7.)

> The highest purpose of a folkish state is concern for the pre- servation of those original racial elements which bestow culture…We, as Aryans, can conceive of the state only as the living organism of a nationality which not only assures the preservation of this nationality, but by the development of its spiritual and ideal abilities leads to the highest freedom… (Adolf Hitler, *Mein Kampf*, pp. 394)

> To keep up the purity of the Race and its culture, Germany shocked the world by her purging the country of the Semitic Races – the Jews. Race pride at its highest has been manifested here. Germany has also shown how well nigh impossible it is for Races and cultures, having differences going to the roots, to be assimilated into one united whole, a good lesson for us in Hindusthan to learn and profit by.
>
> Ever since that evil day, when Muslims first landed in Hindusthan, right

> upto the present moment, the Hindu nation has been gallantly fighting on to shake off the despoilers...The Race Spirit has been awakening.
>
> The foreign races in Hindusthan must either adopt the Hindu culture and language, must learn to respect and hold in reverence Hindu religion, must entertain no idea but those of the glorification of the Hindu race and culture,i.e. of the Hindu nation and must lose their separate existence to merge in the Hindu race, or may stay in the country, wholly subordinated to the Hindu Nation, claiming nothing, deserving no privileges... not even citizens's rights.
>
> (Golwalkar, *We, or Our Nationhood Defined*, 1938)

It must be hard to imagine that the five injunctions cited above are not made by one and the same author!

It is this historical vision that has inspired so much of what has gone on in Gujarat during the Modi years, and to which the massacres of 2002 have been a proud centre-piece.

V

The attempt now afresh underway, as elections in Gujarat draw near, to equate the killing of Sikhs in Delhi (1984),gruesome as those were, with those in Gujarat (2002), miss this one all-important difference: the Gujarat massacres were meant to serve an alternate thesis about 'nationhood', 'citizenship,' and 'culture', the killing of Sikhs following the assassination of Indira Gandhi was the expression of frenzied communal madness.

Contrary to the texts adduced above – and one may add to them a whole chapter in Golwalkar's other book, *Bunch of Thoughts*, which expounds on why and how Muslims are the country's 'Enemy Number One,' – there is no Congress Party document or any evidence in its recorded history which denounces the Sikhs (or indeed any other group of Indians) as the country's enemies. No part of Congress ideology stipulates that nation-building in India requires the elimination or expulsion of the Sikhs. Indeed, the Party has remained and remains a political force among Sikhs in the Punjab, and with time after the Bluestar operation (firing on the golden temple in Amritsar to flush out Khalistani terrorists), and the Delhi killings the Sikhs have returned to the Congress in a way in which it is umimaginable that Muslims will ever go over to the Hindutva forces

It must be recalled that subsequent to the Bluestar action, Indira Gandhi refused to jettison her Sikh body guards despite counsel from her security agents, eventually losing her life to that assertion of secular faith. Hard to imagine Modi recruiting his body guards from among the Muslim community. Nor has the Congress shied away from offering repeated apologies for the killings in which some of its workers and local satraps were doubtless involved, just as also it has let all the law courts take their course. Accusations that the Party has subverted the operations of law have never been conclusively established, although it may well have happened. The fact also is that such of its workers/leaders whose names have appeared during the course of investigations have seen their political careers within the party dismantled; Modi, on the other hand, whose direct complicity in the pogrom of 2002 has been ringingly testified to by the very people who affected the pogrom on the ground remains the hope and the hero of the Hindutva forces.

Importantly also, whereas the Congress has, successfully in the main, made efforts to reinduct Sikhs into its social and political life, (no small matter that the first Sikh chief of army staff and the first Sikh prime minister should have been installed under a Congress dispensation) the Modi regime in Gujarat refuses obdurately to lift the littlest of fingers to do any such thing vis a vis Gujarat's beleaguered Muslims, remaining content with their seemingly irretrievable ghettoisation, ostracism, and economic disenfranchisement. Nor is it conceivable that any future Hindutva-vadi government at the centre or in a state would foreground a Muslim for primeministership or chiefministership.

Satraps of the Hindutva brigade caught confessing their murderous crimes on tape (proudly recounting details of ripping out foetuses from out of pregnant women, cutting a Congress Member of Parliament limb by limb, all under the desperate eyes of near and dear ones) remain jaunty about having furthered the Hindutva agenda. Cities and towns in Gujarat openly designate 'borders' between the two communities. Road signs still point the way either to 'Hindu Rashtra' or 'Pakistan.'

It has therefore been rightly understood that the Gujarat pogrom, carried out as a theoretical agenda, was nothing less than an experiment in pursuance of obtaining historical transformations of the kind enunciated by RSS ideologues inspired by European Fascism and Nazism, namely, to recast the Constitution, Citizenship, Nation, and State.

It would seem that those who have to this day never coherently condemned the holocaust, those who continue to find self-righteous justifications for the Gujarat pogrom of 2002, those who remain at heart content that Muslims the world-over are under siege have nothing more than a crass political interest in the Delhi killings of 1984.

We who caution Indians about the meaning of the Gujarat killings continue to condemn without reservation the Delhi killings; we also condemn those that may have been complicit in those beastly murders, and continue to demand that they be pursued and brought to justice, not excluding any Congress people or officers of state We recognize that like Indian Muslims, Indian Sikhs have made and continue to make extraordinary contributions to consolidating India's secular plurality, and can claim heroic sacrifices in its defence and preservation.

VI

As elections in Gujarat draw close, should the Congress and its allies heed the canny counsel it is now receiving from media pundits and other tactical whiz-kids, namely, to desist from raising the 2002 issue lest it helps Modi bring back into the Hindutva fold those that are now disaffected? Or, should it take a hint from the ringing course set by Sonia Gandhi at her hugely attended rally at Anand in central Gujarat – a Modi stronghold – namely, to take the fascist bull by the horns?

We believe the latter is the honourable course to follow; what will it gain India if an election is won but the fascist worm is allowed to hibernate? Muslims and other minorities in Gujarat, alongwith, one might add crucially, wide sections among Gujarat's enlightened Hindus among urban workers,tribals and farmers whom Modi has betrayed are watching to see what option the Congress takes.

It is time the Congress acquired the oomph to operate as something more than an understudy to the BJP, not just in Gujarat but everywhere, and on a sustained and transparent basis.

Equally importantly, those industrial interests whom Modi has pampered must consider whether it behoves them to be to Modi as the Krupps were to Hitler, (and we know what happened there), or whether they have as much of an obligation to help recover Gujarat for the Republic as anybody else. Let us recall that Hitler, after all, was a bigger 'developer' than Modi could ever hope to be. And yet; and yet.

December 2007

Reading Nandigram

Where to Place the Bookmark?

I recall a young member of the family who would snatch an Agatha Christie as someone was reading it, sift quickly to the last pages, find out who-done-it, hand the book back, and grin for days with the secret knowledge that the one reading the book did not yet have.

Such are the joys of reading books from the wrong end.

Thus, for many historians of modern Russian history, the only one thing to remember about the Bolshevik revolution is that it led to the Gulag, or that the chief feature of India's Freedom Struggle was the Partition of India, or that it is the madness of 1989-90 that once and for all must define the character of Kashmiri Muslims, never mind that the very same saved both the valley and the Pandits against co-religionist invaders in 1947.

In the same vein, many hold that both Nazism and the Second World War happened simply because Hitler was an evil man, and the Gujarat massacres of 2002 had nothing to do with the history of Hindu-Fascist ideology over a century or so but with the fact that a train caught fire at Godhra.

Nor is there a dearth of readers who believe that the evil nature of science is conclusively established by the single fact of atomic fission; nothing else may be said for science. Period.

Regrettably, some outstanding scholars of history who would not dream of reading any of the above in the manner suggested, have nonetheless felt called upon to read Nandigram as that one day in November when an armed clash took place between two sets of citizens for a small strip of territory (in which four unfortunate people were killed and a score injured). The pages of the Nandigram book that span the previous eleven months or so simply form no part of their outrage. And to top it all, parallels have been drawn with what happened in Gujarat in 2002. Truly, one is tempted to think, when the elite heart bleeds, it tends to lose all sense of discrimination.

II

It is of course true that some events in history do stand by themselves in universal memory: for example, Hiroshima/Nagasaki, the Holocaust, Gujarat 2002, or indeed the Delhi killings of 1984, or the mass exodus of Kashmiri Pandits from the valley in 1990. Or indeed the partition of India.

The question to ask is whether the recent bilateral violence in Nandigram qualifies to that sort of semiotics. Does the admittedly violent return of those evicted for months on end to their home, hearth and land warrant the Gujarat analogy? Let it be said that since January 2006 upto now a total of some 50 lives have been lost in the Nandigram episode. And of these 27 were those who supported the CPI(M).

As a passing thought merely, one wonders how the public-spirited elite who have protested Nandigram might react were the ousted Muslims in Gujarat, or the Narmada oustees to attempt to return to the homes and environs that were once their's, or were Kashmiri Pandits to attempt something similar – with the state standing aside in all cases.

III

In an arrogant disregard of farmer's wishes on the ground, the Left Front announced a Chemical Hub Project to be located at Nandigram. Soon to find out that its monumental victory at the hustings may have rendered it insensitive to what the local farming community thought about this cavalier fiat to acquire their lands for the Hub.After much huffing and hawing, the West Bengal government declared in February,'07 that it was withdrawing the proposal and that no land at Nandigram would be acquired.

And yet, unaccountably as it were, a 'struggle' to 'protect' Nandigram from acquisition took shape under the aegis of the Bhumi Ucched Pratirodh Committee (BUPC) led by cadres of the Trinamool Congress (TMC). Joined in time by cadres of the Hindu-right (Anand Marg) and, little by little, by sworn enemies of the Hindu-right, the Maoists, the BUPC succeeded in evicting some three thousand inhabitants of Nandigram for no other reason than that they voted for the left. A 'liberated zone' was soon to be announced – liberated, that is, from the elected government of the day, and all those duly elected to the Panchayat and other local government authorities in the area.

Those evicted found shelter in distant Khejuri where make-shift camps were set up. Attempts by the evicted to regain lost homes was met with killings and arson.

The government of the day stood paralysed, until propelled by an order of the Kolkata High Court to restore normalcy to the situation.

This the government sought to do by sending in a contingent of the police on March 14. Like the police everywhere in India, this contingent took recourse to firing, not below the abdomen, but recklessly above, killing eight inhabitants. Another six were killed by bullets other than those fired by the police.

Since that day in March, the state has been absent for all practical purposes from Nandigram.

A number of attempts were made to sort out the stand-off through negotiations. The veteran elder statesman, Jyoti Basu, met Mamta Bannerjee of the TMC more than once to plead for a peaceful resolution of the stalemate, but it is public knowledge that these attempts were spurned, despite repeated declarations by the West Bengal government that its plans for acquiring land in Nandigram had been shelved.

In the meanwhile, the forces in opposition ensured that access to the area was made intractable by roads that were dug up, blockades that were set up, and the trenches that were dug in strategic places. An influx of arms and ammunition was underway, and only the other day, the law-enforcing agencies have unearthed in Nandigram not only caches of ammunition and explosives but literature originating from the Maoists – people who have been designated by no less a man than the Prime Minister as the chief threat to national security. An opinion we do not share.

It has been in response to this sort of context that the CPI(M), regrettably we think, chose the option of encouraging its evicted supporters to regain what they had lost, forcibly.

In doing so, the government and the CPI(M) are complicit in encouraging violence among citizens, in abjuring the state's role to prevent violence, and in yielding the constitutional obligation to maintain order among the polity to armed volunteers who have no right to bear arms.

Regardless, we think, of the provocation to have done so. Within India's democratic system, accountability here is called for. We think that, however intractable the situation, the honourable course to follow would have been to organize peaceful dharnas or satyagrahas in full public transparency, and to have drafted the media and other democratic institutions to see for themselves. An information blitz could have been mounted to bring the composition and motives of those leading the opposition to public light. The country's legal apparatuses could have been invoked to seek redress for the plight of those who had been violently and forcibly evicted.

By sidelining such avenues of redress and opting for the forcible course, the CPI(M), and the government by implication, may not only have transgressed democratic values and practices, but purchased disrepute of a kind that may not go away in a hurry. All that when the government's declaration to withdraw all plans of land acquisition and its public apology for the March 14 police killings bespoke its willingness to defer to the will of the farming community in Nandigram and to civic outcry.

IV

Much of the public reprobation of the CPI(M) and the government it leads in West Bengal by prominent citizens – many sympathetic to the left – needs, however, to be understood as a phenomenon that goes beyond Nandigram.

Over time, a distinct skepticism with regard to the political/ideological orientation of the Left Front government has been gathering mass. It has seemed to many that in the name of seeking industrialization of the state, the Left Front has tended not only to sideline its people-friendly protestations, but on occasion gone whole hog to woo social forces that have little concern for a socialist programme/vision of any kind.

This seems particularly unacceptable, given that such sectors as education, public health and sanitation, public transportation, or labour-intensive employment seem in no way to have experienced a better fate in West Bengal than anywhere else. The gauche mishandling of the Nandigram episode seems thus to have brought to the fore a quality of distrust and dissatisfaction that has been simmering. Not to speak of the often-heard critique of the increasing bureaucratization of the organizational and leadership culture of the organized left. Those that are familiar with the work-culture and public immersion of older left leaderships that were products of the struggle for Independence find a vacuum and a hiatus that bespeak the assimilation of the left into bourgeois forms of political practice. For such reasons it would seem many who know better have tended to be more forgiving of forms of politics that are otherwise patently outside the framework of constitutional democracy. It is another matter that critics of the CPI(M) are not always clear as to what tactical or strategic line the party must follow, or how best it should negotiate the present phase of globalised capitalism and, inevitably, conflicts that inform its equations with political forces at the centre that are determined to deepen class-rule as it seeks to ameliorate the lot of the disenfranchised.

Most of all, what most well-wishers of the left find missing is a creative politics that brings parliamentary practice and concerted mass movement together into a radically effective conjuncture, however difficult the enterprise. It seems to many that the habitation of the left within two or three bastions has rendered it effectively grounded merely to protect those bastions, inhibiting its ability to operate as a vanguard in the vast hinterlands of the gangetic and central Indian states where its need may be most acute, as also its opportunities to build a county-wide base among the myriad victims of globalization.

The fraught debate around Nandigram thus offers a wake-up opportunity that the left, especially, the CPI(M), can profit by. The worst course would be merely to close ranks or insist on its own infallibility.

V

Equally, however, those that critique the politics of the Left Front need to place such critiques within the larger framework of the national milieu, and to weigh both the contributions and possibilities of the left within explainable histories.

For example, would we advise the left henceforth to abjure electoral participation and state power, so that it may free itself from the contradictions embedded therein, and engage wholly in mass propagation and mobilization? If not, what concrete counsel would we render in relation to the logic of occupying state power more than the left is able at present to comprehend? How in our view may it the better manage a state and corporate media hostile to it in every fibre, or to relate to the plurality of socio-political formations that India has thrown up since the 1960s? And how may these new formations be brought into alignment with the realities of class rule and class resistance? What suggestions can we make in relation to departures in the organizational principles of left parties? And so on.

The least we need to acknowledge is that these are questions that brook no easy answers. Except to those who persist in armed struggle against the state.

November 2007

Communalism and Terrorism

Two Faces of the Same Coin

I write this on the fifteenth anniversary of the demolition of the Babri mosque by fascist hordes of the Sangh Parivar, consequent upon the pogrom set in motion by Advani's infamous rath yatra.

Few events in the post-independence history of India have outfaced the founding principles of both the Freedom Movement and the Republic as decisively as that wanton and blood-thirsty challenge to the secular state. That was the day on which Mahatma Gandhi was buried ten fathoms deep, and when majoritarian terrorism came to be installed as the new operative version of 'nationalism.'

It was also the day when the party that led the Freedom Movement lost its raison d etre. Not to be forgotten that the then Congress prime minister twiddled his pout while fascist pickaxe took the mosque apart brick by brick in full glare of television crews in a day-long operation.

The coercive influence of that terror may be gauged from the fact that fifteen years to the good, the major political formations and institutional mechanisms of Indian democracy have failed to this day to bring a single culprit to book, either from a cloaked complicity or fear of consequence.

Nor indeed has the state found its way yet to implement the findings of the Justice Srikrishna Report on the communal terror that was unleashed by Hindutva forces in Mumbai subsequent to the demolition – a Report that has held the highest of the high among the saffronites guilty of marshalling the killings like 'Generals' in combat.

All that in stark contrast to the avidity with which judgements have been pronounced against Muslims deemed guilty of involvement in the bomb blasts that took place in Mumbai subsequent to the communal terror mentioned above.

Taken all together, the pogrom that began with the Advani yatra yielded a crop of some two thousand or so human lives.

When, therefore, Sonia Gandhi at a campaign rally in Gujarat made the formulation that 'communalism and terrorism are two sides of the same coin' she gave voice to a thesis that Indian sociology has long needed but been too timid to acknowledge or flesh out. For fifteen years no single event has struck as petrifying a terror in the heart of india's Muslims – and, by extension, its pluralism – as that evil deed in Ayodhya on the 6th of December, 1992. A deed that also made possible Narendra Modi's Gujarat and the massacre of 2002.

II

And now, as if to ratify the validity of Sonia's formulation, Modi, putting his fascist foot in his fascist mouth, has thumpingly endorsed two days after – among a thinly attended saffron rally – the murder of one Sohrabuddin in a fake encounter (acknowledged as fake by the Gujarat government in a court of law in the the face of irrefutable evidence) meticulously and conspiratorially planned by Modi's chief satraps among his police force some years ago.

It is to be noted that the Modi government is currently prosecuting those officers for the murders in a case supervised by the Supreme Court of India!

In saying what he has said Modi has clearly admitted to the following:

- that the killing had his blessings; (a recent sting operation conducted by the Tehelka group has conclusively shown of course that the entire carnage of 2002 had Modi's blessings – this from the horses' mouths.)
- that the cases filed against his officers amounted to nothing more than bowing expediently to the undeniable exposures that were made on hidden camera, and to the consequent pressure from the judicial wing of the state;
- that regardless of those cases being now sub-judice under Supreme Court supervision, his sway among saffronite voters renders him above the laws of the land, and fully justifies him in cocking that public snook at the highest court that is seized of the matter, not to speak of the Election Commission charged with the conduct of the forthcoming Gujarat elections;

- and, as the lawyer, K.T.S. Tulsi, prosecuting the arraigned Gujarat police personnel on behalf of the Modi government has been ruefully obliged to say, not only is Modi now in contempt of the Supreme Court but guilty of inciting the polity to engage in extra-judicial murders of people (read Muslims) whom they suspect of being terrorists. Note that during his brazen confession, Modi posed the rhetorical question to the crowd: 'what should be done with the likes of Sohrabuddin?' Promptly receiving the answer from cronies in the front rows. 'kill, kill.'

This of course is a dimension to Modi-speak that confirms the justice of that other epithet used by Sonia Gandhi for Modi and his killer squads – 'merchants of death.'

Little wonder that Shri Tulsi has decided to disassociate himself from the brief he has been holding on behalf of the Modi government.

III

So, will there be consequences?

Now that the concerned District Collector has handed in his report on the Modi rally alongwith a CD to the Election Commission, will the latter do the right and proper under the People's Representation Act that forbids inciting sectarian passions during election time, and debar Modi from the elections, not for now but the next many years, as the late Indira Gandhi was once debarred?

Will the so honourable Supreme Court of India take suo motu notice of the occurrence and proceed under the law to charge-sheet Modi as an accomplice in the murder of Sohrabuddin and his wife?

Will the Human Rights Commission of India take cognizance of the matter and issue showcause to Modi?

Will the Ambanis, the Tatas, and other industrial tycoons that underwrite Modi withdraw their favours, let go their greed, and exercise their clout on behalf of secularism and the rule of law?

And most importantly, will the people of Gujarat stand up and deny Modi his self-proclaimed right to liquidate all and sundry (all Muslims) whom he designates terrorists? Will they rethink Gujarat and vote to reclaim the region for the Constituion and the Republic?

Alas, such is the state of the nation that nothing may be said with confidence.

It is nonetheless certain that until such time as the state picks up the will and the courage to bear down on communalism with the same resolve as it does on terrorism, there will be no end to either. Although there may well be an end to the Republic in consequence of that failure.

The Justice Liberhan Commission has been enquiring into the culpability of the BJP/Sangh stalwarts in the Babri crime for some twelve years or more. Would you believe that it is after fifteen years of the demolition, that the first witness against Advani and others has finally testified in a court!

Does the state now piloted by the UPA government mean to bring these procedures to conclusion? Or is it intended that the cases remain in pendency till some of the chief culprits live out their natural lives?

IV

In the meanwhile, nothing underscores the unacceptable impotence of the Indian state as starkly as the fact that a self-proclaimed monster should rule the roost in the land of Gandhi on the pretext that he alone can guarantee the well-being of five and a half crore Gujaratis. Did not Hitler think likewise of Germany, believing that the extermination of the jews was, after all, only one necessary step in guaranteeing that well-being.

What Modi has now said clearly suggests that he continues to have a similar use for the Muslims towards the well-being of Gujarat.

December 2007

Gujarat

The Face of India's Misbegotten Modernity

India's misbegotten 'modernity' has won another fascist round in Gujarat.

Unlike the mellow inclusivity of Nehruvian enlightenment that strenuously refused the bastardization of variegated cultural refinement and richness, that resisted a gluttonously rapacious leap for the mainchance, leaving the underdog to his/her own devices, that remained wisely wary of militarizing the nation's psyche, the Modi-propagated version of modernity is a beastly mutant wrought through the unlovely embrace between facelessly uncaring technology and atavistic impulses of the ugliest kind – a creature unsurprisingly midwifed by India's 'reputed' corporate fat cats.

For five unconscionable years Modi's touted 'good governance' has remorselessly operated from a mound of gujarati human carrion; and now for another five the ripped, raped, hacked and humiliated may have little other life than that terrified peep occasionally through cracks in the door, cowering like trapped prey against the predator on the prowl – predators who remain secure in the knowledge that the high-priest of 'good governance' and 'development' hunts not for them but alongside them for the victims behind the ramshackle door.

And multiplying the terror manifold, the desperate knowledge that no organized opposition is ever likely to take up their defence, only a sprinkling of brave but marked civil society groups. A Congress party that readily took on board BJP dissidents who were complicit in the carnage of 2002, that assiduously avoided raising the issue of the mass massacre or the wretched conditions in which the survivors subsist this minute, that infact let it be known that the horrific guilt brought to light through a sting operation was a BJP conspiracy aimed at polarizing the vote cannot but have forfeited all trust.

II

Behind me as I write I hear a TV channel compere pose, in clipped English, the question to the panel – and by extension to the nation through an instant SMS poll – whether Modi is not now, after all, the true face of 'modern India'.

There is of course no mention that this 'modernity' comprises a seated hatred for India's Muslims, a macho-militarist 'nationalism' and a willing subservience to neo-liberal imperialism – all nicely purified by an upper-caste Hindu evangelism that brooks no tolerance for those that dither or demur.

Remarkably, there is complete erasure of the far better claim that Mayawati,a dalit, may be argued to have as a pointer to a new Indian future. It will be recalled that by any definition her electoral victory only some months ago in India's largest state, demographically, Uttar Pradesh, wherein she bested both the Congress and the BJP to win a clear mandate was a monumental feat. But then, as I said, she is a woman and a dalit, while Modi remains the child of a Brahminical India led by the RSS, no matter that himself he is only an OBC.

Furthermore, insofar as India's dominant media and corporates look for a cultural homogenization of the realm, preferably along a religious axis since that axis best serves the purpose of drowning out class issues from the nasty public mind, Modi fits the bill. Mayawati on the other hand speaks now a Nehruvian idiom of inclusiveness, as she successfully brought into cohesion diverse castes and faiths in registering her historic victory on a wholly secular platform and a programme of even-handed economic development.

III

In the Modi order of things, it is the accident of birth that makes Indians either victims or victors. Thus Indian Muslims – and Gujarati ones at that – may be perfectly innocent and law-abiding citizens, but they have the wrong names. Just speculate for one moment that Modi had been born into a Muslim family; it is not inconceivable that he might have grown to be as fanatical a Muslim as he now is as a Hindu. He might have gone to a madarasa instead of to an RSS shakha, and therefrom indeed become a dedicated fidayeen as well. All because he would have been born a Muslim!

To this day Modi has not once expressed a syllable of regret for the carnage of 2002 – a pogrom comparable to a Nazi operation. Ironically, Modi and the BJP do not hide their gaping admiration for the Zionist state, Israel. It is another matter that while the latter, sixty years after the holocaust, continues untiringly to hunt Nazi war criminals and bring them to justice, Modi, BJP and sections of the corporate media never tire of admonishing the rest of us how the best thing to do is to forget all about 2002 so that Gujarat's march to vanguard destiny is not thwarted by unnecessarily divisive issues! And believe it or not, the secular Congress is no hurry to press a contrary point!

IV

Fascist politics in Gujarat has been made possible by some discrete social features.

It has the highest percentage of upper-caste Hindus of any Indian state and, concomitantly, the lowest percentage of Muslims.

Unlike the southern states or the cow-belt states of Uttar Pradesh and Bihar since the 1960s, Gujarat has not experienced any social upheavals driven either by the middle castes or the dalits.

Not surprisingly then, Gujarat has never generated a regional political party worth the name, only the Congress and the BJP. Such processes of secularization – using the term broadly as a politics of opposition to cultural or religious homogenization – as other states have experienced have left Gujarat largely untouched. Its powerful farming community, the Patels, thus did not become a vanguard of middle-caste resistance to Brahminical domination, unlike their caste compatriots in other states.

What working class culture Gujarat has had around the Ahmedabad mills and Surat conglomerates were over time to suffer two decimating onslaughts: one from the steady work over long years by organizations such as the VHP seeking to transform the class orientation of mill workers into a communal consciousness, with the aim of pitching worker against worker rather than workers against employers; and, two, since 1990, from the market-driven privatization thrust of neo-liberal economic 'reforms'.

Taken all together, these factors broadly have left the field in Gujarat open to the machinations of social groups that have always dominated cultural and political life. Especially, since the emergence of Gujarat as a separate state carved out of Bombay, the admixture of a new-found political identity and the Gujarati's traditional genius at money-spinning – according to one source, every second Gujarati in urban areas is a player in the stock market – have combined to yield an aggressively Hindu-militarist regional pride, something that Modi has astutely tapped into over the years.

Acknowledging the truism that all generalizations have 'illicit' aspects and often constitute 'orientalising' whole groups of people, it must equally be conceded that not all therein is 'illicit'; nor is it the case that even those who most deride them – like the atomists or postmodernists – entirely avoid taking recourse to them. With that in mind, it strikes me that the two communities in India that have tended to be most enamoured ot the American way of life have been the enterprising segments among the Punjabis and the Gujaratis – the latter now constituting by far the largest falange of emigrants to that promised land. And yet it is interesting to record a fundamental difference of attitude and provenance in the Punjabi and Gujarati love of America.

What India's Punjabis have studiously admired about America is its 'work ethic' and 'dignity of labour.'

In the case of the forward-looking Gujarati who has rather an upper caste distaste for concepts like labour, preferring to get rich through high-financial skills rather than the sweat-shop route, the American and Gujarati love of lucre combine with a devoted religious Puritanism, one that tends to evaluate worth and 'electablility' in terms of prowess at acquisition. In both cases salvation remains a concern, but one that is inseparable from material success in this world; and in either case it is viewed strictly as a personal and individual agenda – something that makes the Gujarati entrepreneur the 'natural ally' of his counterpart in America and a committed privatiser to boot.

V

What has been happening in Gujarat thus requires to be looked at as a complex phenomenon. Unfortunately, in a situation where the choice between the two main parties – the Congress and the BJP – has been one between tweedledom and tweedledee, where no middle or low-caste social movements have been in the offing, and where the left remains almost wholly absent, the task of building an alternate, secular politics is not easy. The millions of Gujaratis – tribals, low-castes, urban poor, minorities – have thus remained bereft of organization, leadership and avenues of struggle.

More encompassingly on an India-wide scale, all of India's major political formations, not excluding the organized left (after all, the hullabaloo in communist-ruled West Bengal began on the question of the Special Economic Zones) have, willingly or not, come to embrace the neo-liberal agenda. This has meant that the only social groups that remain in active resistance have tended to fall either among the largely innocuous NGOs – those ones, that is who have genuinely sought to resist – or among the armed segments of the outlawed left. All that at a time when one after the other nation-states the world-over seem to go the other way, look where you will. Not a pretty picture.

Even so, let it also be noted that in the elections just concluded, some thirty three seats have been lost by the Congress by margins that were far less than votes polled by one or the other secular third-party or independent candidate! A circumstance, surely, for which the voter opposed to fascist consolidation cannot be blamed. (see chart attached, courtesy ANHAD).

VI

And yet if ever it was imperative to halt the fascist juggernaut heralded by Modi's electoral victory despite all odds, it is now.

Without question the Congress party that never fails to parrot its great secular-democratic legacy bears both the burden of the heaviest guilt and the burden also of rethinking both itself and the policies it has been pursuing. In an earlier essay I had the occasion to underscore the irony that whereas a supposedly 'Islamic' Turkey manages to bring millions out on the streets on the question of secularism, the Congress has not once give such a pan-Indian call, something it alone can do, since the left remains locked into just two Indian states. After the Guajrat rout there are reports that blame games are rife within the Congress, as also a wringing of hands. One report from a Congress conclave held today has it that the party has understood the need to put up a cocerted fight on shoring up secularism. If so, the Congress has not a minute to lose.

In moving in that direction, let the Congress understand once and for all that a secularism that simply pays equal obeisance to all religions will never enable any decisive consolidations of secularism. Secularism must mean what it truly means – that the state, all its organs, all administrative structures, and all the edifices of law give no quarter to religious skull-duggery in public issues and public life. And that government functionaries at all levels, and government offices and other properties do not display religious symbols of any kind.

Is the Congress equipped to make that change? It is a question that most individual Congressmen and women need to ask themselves with rigorous honesty.

VII

There is another conundrum that the Congress and the country needs to ponder – one that Kapil Sibal, an eminent lawyer and a minister in the UPA cabinet has pointed to after the defeat in Guajrat: namely, that 'fascists' can win 'democratic' elections. Do recall how Hitler came to power.

Does there need to be new constitutional thinking with regard to this irony? Is it acceptable that social forces who have a long record of flouting what has been designated the 'basic' structure of the Constitution be nonetheless permitted to participate in democratic elections only so as they may have further opportunity to do dirt on the Constitution? Is it not about time that all organized social and political forces that think otherwise come together on this issue to effect amendments to the Constitution?

For a start, one such amendment could simply empower the Election Commission of India to disqualify any candidate who at any time during a campaign makes a religious appeal to the voter, or a whole segment of voters.

The law as at present constituted does not make such an appeal in and by itself violative of the constitutional order, but forbids it only if the intent is to cause disharmony among religious communities.

Yet, insofar as such an appeal per se violates the basic structure of 'secularism' it would be in the fitness of the constitutional scheme to disallow candidates from participation in the electoral process if such appeals are seen and heard to be made by them.

Fully aware as I am that what is proposed here will find resistance of one kind or another, let it be conceded for now that there atleast is a question that asks to be addressed. Surely all parties that swear allegiance to the Constitution as by law established have an obligation to sit together and find answers that are consistent with the letter and spirit of secular citizenship and democracy.

Modi's victory in Gujarat raises many far-reaching questions. And those questions may not brook procrastination.

December 2007

2008

Essentialising Pakistan

There was that time when Hegel pronounced that India had "no history"; it "is a repeat of the same old majestic ruin," he wrote.

Instructively, not until his full-blooded engagement with India 1853 onwards was Marx to demur with the Hegelian hypothesis. That he was to work his way towards enunciating what he called 'the Asiatic mode of production' as an explanation for the seemingly eternal stasis of India remains evidence of his historical anxiety always to make sense of the seemingly incomprehensible.

Since the emergence of India and Pakistan as sovereign nation-states, most 'indigenous' historians have strenuously questioned both the Hegelian stipulation and the full validity of the 'Asiatic mode of production' thesis.

Especially those who subscribe to a dialectical materialist perspective of time, space, and human agency, it must seem an absurdity, ab initio, to suggest that any human subject, concept, group/community, or nation is ever in a state of coma.

It is ofcourse the case that the pace of historical transformation observes differing momentums from agent to agent, community to community, nation to nation; so that in some instances the 'sameness' seems to make invisible the dynamic, and in others the dynamic overwhelmes the 'givens' frenetically.

II

I have taken the liberty to thus preface my point about Pakistan inorder to underscore an irony that informs much lazy comment post the Benazir martyrdom.

Many among those who have over the years hotly, and justly, contested the western metropolitan project of 'essentialising' India (Edward Said called the politics of that project 'Orientalism') think nothing of proferring the complacent view that nothing ever changes in/about Pakistan. 'Repeat of the same majestic ruin,' as it were!

Such Indian comment from 'experts' and upwardly-mobile beneficiaries of India's 'development' alike barely conceals a smirk.

There is indeed truth to the overview that since the murder of the first Pakistani Prime Minister in 1953, interested forces have sought in every conceivable way to keep in place a stranglehold that has been hard to breach. This ideological and material conglomerate has comprised the AMA – America/Mullah/Army – in a peculiar marriage between the feudal, the theological, and infusions of the technologically comprador.

Yet, it would be a serious misreading of the dynamics of Pakistani history to think that the Benazir murder is a mere repeat of that first murder of Liaqat Ali Khan. Or that the Benazir persona in 2007 embodied merely an unvaryingly familiar personal mind-set and collective history.

It would be readily understood that, for example, Gandhi before and after the event in South Africa were two different historical agents; and then again Gandhi before and after the Champaran Satyagraha.

Yet it is not, for some reason, equally understood that Jinnah before and after 1937 were also two different agents, and two different kinds of Muslim. Or that Jinnah of the moment of the call to direct action and of the first speech to the newly independent Pakistan Assembly were starkly different historical personae.

And from thereon, that Benazir at oxford, and the Benazir of 1988 and then again of 1993 require to be seen as an evolving persona, and a carrier if you like of an accreting history that has now come to roost with her martyrdom.

That accreting history warrants the view that the murder of Benazir should not be looked at merely as a sudden Foucauldian 'rupture' but an apotheosis. An apotheosis that connotes the relegation of forms of control even at the very moment that these seem gruesomely ascendant.

The Benazir of 2007 carried with her a sentience born of intervening contestations internally in Pakistan and of Pakistan's rapidly changing dynamics in relation to outer worlds, both friendly and hostile, that has inevitably burst into a not-to-be-stemmed tidal wave.

Her martyrdom has given expression to critiques and aspirations that have been long in the making, rendering the emperor rather pitifully without clothes. At some earlier marker in Pakistan's history, this may not have been so.

In that context it is crucial to understand that large and largely influential segments of Pakistani society have been freed in a conclusive way from the anxieties of an identity politics whose burden has sat heavy on Pakistan's 'nationalist' psyche.

III

I venture to say that this freeing is powered now by a momentum that promises a decisive redefining in Pakistan of 'community' and 'nation,' as well as of reformulating the character of the state in the years to come. And this for the reason that those unique formative features within sub-continental Islam that have thus far remained relegated in the Pakistani nation-state – always vastly different from Arabic origins – are once again finding a self-confident voice. It is that inherited voice that ultimately bears within it the clout to defeat impositions under which the Pakistani national identity has tended to wither and distort.

When the Benazir of 2007, risking her life, spoke insistently of democracy as the answer to Pakistan's ills, she wasn't, to my mind, speaking merely of a new form of political organization. There was an urgency and extension to her articulation that suggested everytime that what she had in mind was a cultural and psychological transformation of far-reaching dimensions.

Even as she knew she would more likely than not pay for that articulation with her life, it was clear that she also knew that the time for it had come, and that, losing her life, she might succeed in ways that may no more be refused. And is it not obvious that the turn of event since her death points that way?

A three-way catharsis seems underway in Pakistan: reliving the Bangladesh experience, vast numbers across Pakistan are obliged to recognize that the theocratic basis of nationhood bears within itself the seeds of disintegration, as the hands that feed it inevitably become its food; secondly, the glorified honeymoon with the army as the most secure arbiter of national stature and security seems equally in tatters; and, thirdly, influential elites who may for one reason or the other have remained silent over the years on the value of that special relationship, even if one of abject dependence, with the United States, acknowledge, again however privately, that the Nehruvian decision to keep a safe distance from that post-war imperialist power and to build the infrastructure of the new India by painful but autonomous inches may indeed have demonstrated the truth of the story of the tortoise getting better of the hare.

IV

This is not to say that entrenched interests will not continue to battle hard; and yet, they are now having to fight that battle not only against an intractable multitude of contradictions within internal and external structures of power but, most frustratingly, against a wholly new Pakistani citizenry whose disenchantment with the hitherto seems comprehensive and complete, and whose willingness to give battle in return equally dour. What turns and twists that battle might take in the months to come remains a matter of concern. As also the price that a successful conclusion of that battle may entail.

Most significantly, a new modern elite in Pakistan seems today ready and willing for a partnership with India, transcending the ghosts of partition. It may not be an exaggeration to say that just that one fact bids fair to cause a sea-change not just in the affairs of India and Pakistan but of the wider world as well. How imaginatively and caringly a newly aspiring India engages with that paradigm shift will, no doubt, be as seminal to the future of the subcontinent and the world as Pakistan's own transformations.

And in that context, India's success or failure in conducting the affairs of all organs of the state along the basic constitutional principle of secularism must be considered of fatal consequence. As well as the refusal of Indians across the board to give in to the forces of communal fascism.

January 2008

The Treacheries of Words

Those that are learned in the modern theories of language have taught us how treacherous words can be.

For a start, there is no organic relation between a word and the object it implies.

For example, they tell us, there is nothing dog-like about the word 'dog.' Nor is there anything colourfully red embedded in the form of the word 'red.' How true!

Thus meanings are largely a matter of convention and cultural consensus among communities.

Alas, that is not all.

Further complications arise when it is considered that the objects towards which words signal (dog, red) in turn do not always or necessarily mean the same things to all users of the same language, even within closed communities.

Thus 'dog' may to one person suggest something low and derogatory, but to another bring thoughts of loyalty and affection. Just as the word 'red' may equally variously suggest any of the following: blood, wine, a traffic light, a communist, or, in the context of the current troubles in the global economy, just plain indebtedness (being in the red).

II

These unsettling ruminations were to assail me with force just the other day while listening to a premier English TV channel.

The spur to my discomfiture were the words 'carnage' and 'bloodbath.'

Like so many backward users of the English language, I had always thought that these words implied but one thing, namely, the gruesome extermination of human beings in large droves.

So that those of us who keep an interested eye on the affairs of the world have often used these words to describe the bloody consequences of collective human madness from time to time and place to place – for example, in relation to what history tells us happened when Ashoka invaded Kalinga, or during Alexander's campaigns, or the massacres during the centuries of the Crusades, or Ghengez Khan's depredations, or innumerable other accounts of medieval warfare, or the bloody gore in the trenches of the first world war, or the holocaust, or Hiroshima, or the genocides in Iraq, Rwanda, Bosnia, or the inter-communal butcheries that accompanied the partition of India, or the many communal pogroms that followed that event, leading upto the crowning 'carnage' of Gujarat in 2002.

Or indeed the less noted butcheries vented routinely on India's dalits, women, ethnic and religious minorities, and so on.

III

Thinking of all that, it struck me that one has but rarely, if not never, heard India's corporate print and electronic media use the words 'carnage' or 'bloodbath' to describe either the killings executed upon India's 'weaker sections' by diverse dominant groups or by uniformed branches of the state-apparatus. Although, one must quickly qualify that killings executed by what are called India's Maoists or Naxals are often so designated – 'carnage', 'bloodbath' etc.,

Customarily, however, the corporate media operate within a descriptive-linguistic pendulum that goes from 'social disturbance' to 'inter-caste' or 'inter-communal violence' to, at best, 'riot.'

As to the millions who die from malnutrition, preventible diseases, and such like, when did you ever hear any strong words used that might raise concrete visions of the horrors thus perpetrated by a social order that thinks the best way to govern is to look after the elect. Surely who has ever heard a TV channel define a hundred thousand or so suicides by India's imperiled farmers as a 'carnage'? I certainly haven't.

IV

Imagine, therefore, my consternation (I was an English teacher for some four decades or more) upon hearing and seeing the words 'carnage' and 'bloodbath' used with force, and repeated force, by TV channels and the corporate print media to describe the goings-on in the stock market over the past week or so!

Looking to see red blood dripping down the screen, I only saw neat little red arrows in professional graphics pointing downward.

And then when you read the black bordered captions that announced 'mournday' for Monday when the losses happened, you might have wondered too why the three days of butchery in Delhi in 1984, in Mumbai in 1992-93, and then in Gujarat in 2002 never got captioned 'mourndays.'

Which is when, some apprenticeship coming to my aid, I recalled the modern theorists of language. I reminded myself how the same words need not mean the same things to all users of the same language.

Further reflection brought home the lesson how the profoundest transformation wrought by the capitalist way of life has been to make the inanimate animate, and the animate inanimate. 'Transferred epithet' the grammarians call this.

Thus, where you and I might, upon reading news of the stock market crash, think of dwindling currency notes, bank bonds and such-like, the capitalists see reserve armies of investment and profit that keep in place the states they command in high order. And where you and I might see oppressed, imperiled and massacred millions of the human race, the capitalist only sees annoying sods that merely clutter the high road to the globalised summit.

Thus 'carnage' and 'bloodbath' are but inaccurately used to define the liquidation of human subjects. Their proper use lies in describing the liquidation of bank credits, housing markets, FDIs, FIIs and the like. For the best human beings to the capitalists are the crispest of currency notes and share certificates; and those that we call human beings are canon for the fodder.

Truly, the haves and the have-nots of the world speak a different English.

January 2008

On Pakistan Elections

There comes a tide in the life of nations,
Which, if taken at the crest,
Leads to fortune.
(Shakespeare mangled)

Remember those two kinds of people – the ones who always see the glass half empty and those that see it half full?

And, oh, the experts, especially the Indian ones; they never do see the bright side of most things, least of all Pakistan. It is as though you could not be an expert if you ceased to be ifsy and butsy and joyed in innocence for a bit.

All of which recalls that most instructive experiment that the good doctor of Austria once conducted.

Dear Sigmund, we are told, put up an easel with a spotless white sheet plastered over; not quite spotless though, for at the dead centre he planted a needle-point black dot as well.

Then came the ten subjects; and nine of them when asked said they saw a black dot; just one cretin blurted that he saw a white board!

Add to that the other conundrum. Most of us who would hold forth on affairs of the world tend to conflate the end of time with our own particular mortality. So just as we imagine ourselves to be the persons we are today, rather than processes that have spanned a lifetime of making and unmaking, we bear on events not as processes but as products.

And when was there a product that was not first an aspect of processes? To this I have spoken rather more in an earlier article titled 'Essentialising Pakistan'.

II

For the wary, let me say that it is not my incautious case that democracy has finally arrived in Pakistan (when does anything ever arrive finally?). An election, alas, does not a democracy make all by itself.

For that to happen – and I speak only of political democracy, which even where it flourishes, as here in India, leaves the bulk of the populace in economic throe – must require a Constitution that acquires long-term incontrovertibility, a Parliament that is answerable only to such a Constitution, a Judiciary that can breathe on its own and be accepted as arbiter, warts and all, mechanisms of law-enforcement that see the citizen without coloured glasses (as they do not still in India), a fourth estate that remains vigilant against atrocity, even as it most of the time, as here in India, speaks for the material interests of the ruling classes, a sustained order of civil alertness that can mobilize against the worst excesses of the state and dominant social groups and interests – all that as infrastructure to the peaceful transfer of state power through free and fair elections.

Clearly, in the case of Pakistan, that is an agenda for the coming days and months, perhaps many years as well.

So why do I see the glass as being half full?

For one thing, the elections just concluded did not happen merely because Kings at home or across the atlantic decreed it. It happened in deference to a new and compelling Bolivarian impulse among Pakistanis across the board. It came in answer to a moment of recognition (Anagnorisis, Aristotle was to christen so momentous a point of departure from that which has been). And it came laden with a message that the people had put behind them all the fear and trembling that has so tended to thwart the expression of popular secular will in Pakistan.

Secondly, for the first time, not the worst of bigots succeeded in centring these elections either on India or on Kashmir. The significance of that only those know who know a great deal about sub-continental history.

Indeed, if India was invoked here and there among opinion-makers and common Pakistanis alike it was invoked as a point of desirable reference. Time after time one heard the sentiment that, after all the blood that has besmirched the five rivers over some six decades, and after all the machinations that Pakistani rulers of any hue and their comprador promoters abroad may have attempted, it is only Pakistan which has been made to suffer while India seems to have gone on more sure-footedly.

And that a credible democracy, in addition to other things, seems to have had a great deal to do with the outcome.

Notwithstanding secular Pakistani's genuine concerns with Hindutva bigotry, thus, it is that other recognition which has forced the everyday Pakistani to ignore appeals to denominational passions and defeat the Mullahs even in the North West Frontier Province. A secular assertion of awesome proportions indeed. And, if anything, in Balochistan, several left-of-centre politicians seem to have succeeded in winning the trust of the voters!

I see the glass half full because, excessive and precipitate as this may sound, I see the beginnings of a turn-around that suggests that the lessons of the loss of erstwhile East Pakistan may be seen to be registering within Pakistan itself. Namely, that the edifice of a viable nation-state cannot be built on the brick and mortar of religious persuasion. That the problems of Pakistan's troubled areas are as much born of ethnic and linguistic oppression as were those in East Pakistan seems now undeniable. As is the further fact that those oppressions should have remained wedded to the same scale of economic exploitation as East Pakistan had suffered.

To the extent that Kashmir has tended to remain at the focus of so much Pakistani consciousness on account primarily of religious affiliation, the transformations underway in Pakistan itself could not but logically force a different perspective on the issue. Quite just as more and more Kashmiris recognize that the one factor that overrides any other in Pakistani history has been that of ethnicity rather than of Islam. And if the Pakhtuns and the Balochis, and indeed even the Sindhis, feel as they do about Punjabi dominance, Kashmiris may hardly expect to fair any better as part of some imagined Islamic state. Consider that only some 3% Kashmiris are below the poverty line in contrast to an Indian national average of about 26%; and that in contrast both to the Kashmir on the other side of the LOC as indeed to Pakistan itself, Kashmiris are rather beginning to relish the cut and thrust of a vibrant political democracy to boot. And also consider that these are by now facts that have percolated deep and wide among most Pakistanis, whatever public statements may be made from time to time. Indeed, a steadfast Islamist like Syed Ali Shah Geelani must wonder what future his brand of politics might have in the face of the rout suffered by the Islamicist parties in the Pakistan elections.

The project to annex the valley then through theocratic mayhem is seen not just to be guaranteed to fail; it is perhaps beginning also to be seen as a goal not particularly of great moment to the real interests of Pakistani citizens. Indeed, Pakistan's generation next that has no felt understanding of or allegiance to the history of partition would much rather get on with the good life that India's generation next seems so much to revel in. And as to those who, like the millions upon millions in India, lack the bare essentials of living even the contingent life, the Mullah/Feudal/Army/America combine seems to have delivered little else but economic and ideological servitude. If then they have spoken as they have, they have not done so from mere pique – an occurrence that promises much to alter the life of the subcontinent in constructive ways.

I hear the expert smirk rather in that knowledgeable way and say of me as Caesar said of the soothsayer, 'he is a dreamer; let us leave him.' I might mumble 'O but the Ides of march will come for Musharraf/Mullah/Feudal/Army/America as they did for Caesar.' Have no fear.

Although they may not come this march or or the next, or in your or my lifetime, but come they will. Let each Indian and Pakistani ask of herself which side she is on, and then be on the side of the future, and then work for that future with selfless resolve. That done, those Ides may come sooner than you think.

III

And what of America? They wanted the PPP, but got instead a serious-minded democracy!

And just as in Palestine, the victory of Hamas in one of the most watched and supervised of recent mandates in the world did not square with democracy for the neo-imperialists, so also the good showing by Nawaz Sharief's party in contrast to the rout of the official PML (Q) must seem a cruel distortion of the democratic agenda desired by Bush and company.

No wonder that with customary shamelessness and lack of principle the American establishment seeks openly to engineer a government in Pakistan that may exclude Nawaz Sharief's party and indeed do dirt on the mandate. The great surprise would have been if the Bushies had indeed done anything else.

What must be understood is that the Pakistani electorate has not vanquished the Mullahs because America so wished them to do; far more significantly, they have done so because, born of neo-imperialist machinations in the first place, the Mullah parties were assessed to have done as little good and as much harm to the people of Pakistan as America itself.

So it is I see the glass half full.

IV

Ah, but what of the Indian establishment that is now so enamoured of America, the world-leader in democracy and warfare?

From what evidence exists, there is little ground for assuming that India sees fraternizing in any far-reaching way with her immediate geo-political world as of greater consequence than striking that 'strategic partnership' with the bully in Washington.

We say to our establishment, thy ides of march will come too; just wait till you get your particular comeuppance a year or so from now.

In that context, how diverting the fact that even Advani, that drooling Prime Minister-in-perpetual-waiting, takes recourse to a left-of-centre discourse in his recent public pronouncements!

He reminds the nation – at bottom himself – that close to 80% Indians subsist on about 50 cents a day, and that some 20 individuals possess as much wealth as some 300 million Indians.

When those sorts of noises issue from the frontline friend of the neocons and the Israelis, be sure that the ides of march are waiting.

And just as the people of Pakistan have demonstrated, here in India as well at the next General elections our own bigots need not think they will fare better than the Mullahs have in Pakistan. And should they not, remember that the quality of results in the Pakistani elections would have had much to do with that eventuality, notwithstanding how hoarse the right-wing throat may have become from shouting about 'terrorism.'

V

Time then for the billions of sane Indians and Pakistanis to come together in a new partnership – one that drives the marauders into the cells they belong in, and intent on assuming a new secular brotherhood and a new history of peace and creative oneness.

Let that resolve pour into the glass, drop by determined drop, and show the frozen expert and the interested sceptic alike that the glass grows full, not half full.

And let the millions of sane Americans likewise force upon their power and greed ridden leaderships that what was once the new world , full of ideals and dreams, has been rendered a decrepit old eyesore, but that it may yet join in with the others to forge another new world that comprises humanity everywhere.

And all that had best happen before the earth takes its revenge and drowns out all the worlds together without regard to wealth, armaments, or colour of skin.

And if that is rhetoric, it is such that an Obama might not mind, nor the people who follow his fortunes in increasing drove.

February 2008

Fascists Attack the Communist Party Office

The Sharpening of Ideological Contention

Ever since the Hindutva right-wing, led by the top leadership of the Bharatiya Janata Party (BJP), demolished the Babri mosque in Ayodhya on Dec.,6,1992 in brazen defiance of the Constitution and the rule of Law, the question has been asked whether, after all, the BJP can be regarded a legitimate participant in India's parliamentary democracy.

A litany of subsequent pogroms since then have, if anything, lent force and urgency to that poser.

These have included violent vigilante attacks on artists, art products, films, text books, institutions, minority religious establishments, and the unforgettable carnage of Muslims in Gujarat in 2002.

That this party has no more than a scant and expedient relationship with parliament is borne out again by the fact that eversince the defeat of the BJP-led NDA coalition in 2004, the BJP has done one of two things as the leading opposition in the house of the people – either disrupt or boycott its proceedings.

And if it has raised its voice there, nothing has been farther from its intentions than to underscore issues that touch the vast pauperized mass of Indians.

These circumstances have yielded a rather unique consequence – that of obliging the left parties which support the UPA government from the outside to function in crucial ways as the most credible opposition within the House.

The overarching fact that it is within the left that the chief antagonist of the BJP resides has thus tended to be sharply emphasized.

The axes of that antagonism become apparent if one were to encapsulate the major planks of the right-wing BJP agenda for the nation:

- Majoritarian hegemony;
- Hinduisation of culture in toto;
- Minority bashing;
- Privatisation of national wealth;
- Militarisation of the state;
- 'strategic partnership' with neo-imperialism of which Zionism is seen as crucial part;

to name just the principle coordinates.

Of these, the 'centrist' Congress – or, at any rate, those within it who for now run the government – supports fully the last three. As to the first three, the attitude of the Congress has been riven with ambivalence, often upright in public pronouncements but fatally prevaricating on the ground.

The left it is that has, much carping notwithstanding, stood firmly against the aforesaid agenda, however effectually or not.

II

It is not a surprise, therefore, that the Hindu right-wing has been venting its fascist ire against the left.

The culminating event in that project has been the naked, broad daylight attack on the central office of the CPI(M) in the heart of the capital city.

Led and organized by some of the top leaders of the Delhi BJP, trucks carrying stones and other missiles were to arrive at the party office, and within a jiffy not only was glass from windows and cars flying all over the place, but five members of the CPI(M) Central Committee which was in session inside were to receive bloody injuries. Incidentally, some of the trucks belonged to the local municipality which is controlled by the BJP whose mayor was among the attackers.

Those that remember may recall the Battle of Cable Street (London,1936) that involved the communists and Mosley's supporters; or indeed the street fights of Berlin prior to Hitler's coming to power.

Nor have they been thwarted by the public and media outcry; more such attacks continue to take place in other cities (Dehradun being one such).

This fascist attack on the office of one of India's recognized National Parties must then be seen as veritably an attack on the Democratic system per se, since it is a system which grounds itself in the concept of democratic political organizations.

The BJP needs to answer why this attack may be regarded any differently from the attack on the Indian parliament during the regime that it led.

III

These vignettes from contemporary Indian history ought to help remind us that, far from being one and the same as centrist elites never tire of propagating, fascists and communists have been mortal enemies from the first.

Let it be recalled that Italian fascism (from whence the RSS in India imbibed all its major ideological predilections as Mussolini met Munje, and Munje passed on to Hedgewar) was infact forged as a countering response to the forces unleashed by the October Revolution of 1917.

Such are the facts that have come down to us from the horse's mouth, as it were.

Here are some snippets from an article that Giovanni Gentile wrote and Mussolini signed in Encyclopaedia Italiana (1923):

- fascism is a "rightist movement to attack the organizations of the working class, parties of the left and Trade Unions";
- that fascism must seek to "partner with big business leaders" and "seek to unite Labour and Capital, to the Labour's ultimate detriment";
- that Unions be replaced by Guilds "which were heavily weighted in favour of the corporation and the owners";
- that "fascism negates the doctrine of scientific Marxian socialism and historical materialism";
- that a corporative organization would eliminate "the clash of economic interests' and thereby neutralize 'the germ of class warfare";
- that "fascism is the complete opposite of Marxian socialism";
- that "fascism now and always believes in holiness and heroism; that is to say in actions uninfluenced by economic motive, direct or indirect";

- that, "above all, fascism denies that class war can be the preponderant force in the transformation of society".

Hardly a surprise then that Marxists and Trade Unionists were the first targets of attack of both Mussolini and Hitler once they came to power.

IV

How closely majoritarian religious organization has from the first favoured the fascists both in their social emphases and in their idea of the totalitarian state is suggested by the stipulations of the Encyclical, Rerum Novarum, that was issued by Pope Leo XIII in 1892.

The Encyclical criticized the socialist conception of class struggle and the elimination of private property.

It urged solidarity between upper and lower classes.

It endorsed nationalism as a way of preserving traditional morality, customs, folkways.

It proposed corporatism – a term that came to encapsulate the whole ideological/class package of fascist organization.

Any surprise then that a treaty could be signed between the State and the Holy See (The Lateran Treaty) in 1929 whereby the Papacy was granted temporal sovereignty over Vatican city, Catholicism was recognized as sole state religion, in return for acceptance of Italian sovereignty over the Pope's former dominions.

The first anti-semitic laws were passed in 1938.

How uncanny the resemblance of all that to the phenomenon we now call Hindutva.

It must be added that similar trends have sought to surface and take hold among the Muslims lately, as the Salafi/Wahabi sects have taken to propagating against those strains in sub-continental Islam which have always upheld secular and syncretic community and the role of Sufis, saints and other intercessors between god and man. The attack on the shrine at Ajmer Sharief and Chrar-e-Sharief, to name but two instances, fall into this pattern. As does the Hindu right-wing- like animus of the Islamists to socialist ideas.

Which is not to say that healthy democratic initiatives from within conservative and dogmatic Islamic organizations are not in the offing. The fatwa recently issued on these matters by no less than the Darul Uloom of Deoband is a major positive event – one that deserves to be followed up more generally, if a further assimilation of the Muslim polity into democratic and progressive India is to happen more rapidly. Even as the communalist opposition of the Hindu right-wing to state-driven programmes aimed at aiding the Muslim community in a far-reaching way in education and employment must be defeated at all cost.

V

To return to where we began: as the electoral prospects of the right-wing recede further (the frustration of the RSS in Kannur in Kerala has after all had everything to do with their inability to succeed at the hustings there), more fascist mayhem and disruption of constitutional and democratic life and governance ought to be anticipated.

Given that context, the Congress will need to rethink the axes of its equation with the BJP and the left. On one side is a class base and class interest that makes it see in the BJP something of a kin. On the other, the Congress will want to evaluate without blinkers the role of the left in preserving the nation-state itself – somewhat in the tradition which its own past has bequeathed to India.

Immediately of course, till so long as it runs the government, the Indian police and other state-apparatus will deserve to be given some very unambiguous directions as to how to deal with fascist and vigilante violence on the bedrock institutions of democracy, among which must also be counted secularism and the freedom of expression. Indeed heartening that the honorable supreme court has only the other day pronounced at unusual length on the alarming negative trends in these areas, and advised that such attacks on freedom must be put down with 'an iron hand.' The Congress must know that its credibility has been the most damaged precisely in that area.

March 2008

Salwa Judum

The State as Instigator of War Between Peoples

It has been one of the criticisms of the Left Front government in West Bengal that at one point during the Nandigram episode the state stood aside while two groups of the farming community engaged in armed violence.

That this did happen for a week or so is true enough, the defensive shamefacedness of the West Bengal government notwithstanding.

What is, however, deeply disingenuous is the fact that the raucous hullabaloo about that lapse should have been and continues to be raised by political forces that have demonstrably instituted a civil war among tribal communities in the BJP-led state of Chhattisgarh. All true to the British-colonial pattern of killing two birds with one stone; namely, getting Indians to fight among themselves while creaming off the fruits of their labour.

For more than a year now the government in Chhattisgarh, supported, it must be said, by some local Congress stalwarts, has quarantined some fifty thousand tribals in make-shift camps away from their homes, provided them arms of primitive make, and obliged them to fight the Naxalites – all against their will.

These marginalized unfortunates are thus used as human shields behind whom the state hides both its impotence and its unwillingness to redress the circumstances which make Naxalism possible and which oppress the tribal communities seamlessly.

The armed groups thus formed are called *salwa judum*.

It is instructive to recall that the great successes of the right-wing Hindu majoritarians in the state of Gujarat owed to similar protracted indoctrination: there the disenfranchised mill workers and deforested *adivasis* (aborigines)were told that their misery owed not to the exploitation engendered by class-rule but to the Muslims who were usurping all their opportunities of employment and trade.

II

In pursuance of a report on the goings-on (salwa judum) submitted by a group of public-spirited civil society intellectuals, the matter landed in the supreme court of India,

Most hearteningly, the court has now pronounced that the state in Chhattisgarh is clearly guilty of criminalizing society and of abetment in the crimes thereof. Interestingly, some print media who remain entirely in sympathy with the neo-liberal economic policies of the government in Delhi and in the states, have lauded the court pronouncement editorially (*Hindustan Times*, April 2).

Yet neither the honourable supreme court nor those sections of the urban elite who sense the dangers inherent in such a collapse of 'order' and of the legitimacy of the state, unsurprisingly, go as far as to entertain any macro-historical question bearing on such a collapse.

Be it the dispossession of tribals from forest rights, or of small farming communities from land rights, or the guzzling of mineral and water resources in the hinterlands by multinational corporations who have now acquired a fatal stake in the seeds and food industry, none of this is seen to be at the bottom of the violence that now afflicts sizeable parts of India. Such a read is duly ascribed to leftist propaganda which is then seen to be instigating the 'red terror' called Naxalism.

The state is thus faulted just for its failure actually to put down such terror by a concerted force of arms – a demand that, incidentally, is never made in the case of the fascists pogroms routinely conducted by the right-wing Hindutva forces against religious minorities. Be it Guajrat, Orissa, Madhya Pradesh or Rajasthan where Muslims and christians are constantly subject to one harassment or the other, often involving the desecration and arson of their places of worship, laws continue to be passed making the freedom of worship and propagation – guaranteed by the Constitution of India – as hazardous as can be.

III

These historical concatenations involve a tragic paradox.

At a time when the 'developed' western world is beginning to see and to rue the ravages wrought upon the earth by unmitigated capitalism, the ruling classes in India wish to do nothing as much as to repeat all those procedures of capitalist social development that inform the history of the modern west. We resent very much the fact that we should be asked to abort that grand opportunity in cutting down on greenhouse emissions and other unsustainable forms of production by those who have had their day in the sun, and, truth to tell, who even now are unwilling to practice what they preach.

There may well be the truth of envy and of accumilated historical wrong in such resentment; the fact nonetheless remains that the luxury of replicating the history of the 'developed' west is no longer an option that countries like India can afford.

For one thing, the resource base neither of land nor of water allows the thought; for another, so gruesome has become the hold of multinational corporate wealth over these as well as elementary sustenance levels of food that the ravages of international finance capital, if permitted the play that 'globalisation' intends it should, spells doom to the very existence of the nation-state and to its soverign rights to manage its own affairs to the good of the mass of its population (supposing that to be an object at all).

Indeed, the argument strenuously propagated by international finance institutions – all at the service of American national interests as those interests are conceptualized by the American establishment – that joining in with the global gravy train promises to bring most bonanzas to the 'developing' world has now run thinner than thin; to the extent that notable erstwhile advisers to the World Bank and the International Monetary Fund, including some Nobel laureates, are no longer willing to buy their own best advice of yore. In political terms, the repudiation of that paradigm is nowhere more in evidence than in the sequential victory at the hustings the world over of forces that have thus far been in the doghouse.

IV

The two major political formations in India – Congress and the BJP – nonetheless remain wedded to the dream of superpower greatness which we are told ad nauseum necessitates a continued recourse to 'reform' (read a faithful implementation of the terms of the Washington Consensus of 1990).

No surprise that perfectly sold-out private channels and other print media ascribe such things as the violence and vigilantism in India's hinterland not to neo-liberal economics but indeed to a deplorable insufficiency of it. In one and the same breath, cocksure but amusingly ignorant anchors thump the microphone to charge the government of the day for being queasy on 'reform' and uncaring of the poverty that afflicts some three fourths of India's population who spend less than a dollar a day.

Just as, in the meanwhile, the government sloganises about the common man while fully implementing the agenda of the super-rich.

Where then is the surprise that Naxalism and the ever-widening rash of social unrest in not just far-off swathes of India but here in Delhi as well is seen not as a problem related to or issuing from India's chosen political economy but as a law -and-order problem. To an extent that scions of India's new middle-class when polled by media channels endorse wholeheartedly the practice of 'encounter killings' by 'ace' cops – instant liquidations of human beings who have neither been brought to trial nor pronounced guilty by a court of law.

The whole idea is to clean the realm of such nuisance as impedes the full and free reign of the 'meritorious' entrenched. Organised vigilantism is thus seen as the need of the hour. And none better than the salwa judum kind which pits one nuisance against its counterpart, leaving the 'developers' to do the job they do best – fleece on all sides.

What is not sufficiently registered is the fact that vigilantism can happen from both ends of the social spectrum. As indeed is happening with feverish pace.

If to the corporates the state loses legitimacy when it fails to orient policy to its garguantian appetites, to the mass of Indians it loses legitimacy when it fails to deliver either equity or justice, as seems to happen most of the time. The result of that is that the sphere within which the state carries any conviction dwindles with every passing day: it loses to globalised predators, and it loses to its own people. And its pathetic balancing rhetoric as between the requirements of 'development' and of 'inclusive' growth increasingly seems just that – pathetic rhetoric.

V

It is to be much doubted that states like India, all the hype notwithstanding, can escape major upheavals unless the hitherto unquestioned assumptions behind the capitalist way of life are subject to critique and amelioration (at the least); and by amelioration is not meant some cosmetic doling out of benefits towards hustings time.

For this rethink to happen, no time seems more propitious than now when the American economy – that indubitable model – is in recessionist doldrums, and when, perish the thought, 'regulation' seems to have overtaken its free flight.

Nothing short of setting and pursuing altered social and community goals, of reconceptualising the value of labour, land, forest wealth, the distributive agencies and institutions that are thus far mere pawns in the hands of those that succeed evermore in centralizing capital, the reassessment of the cosequences that must ensue (indeed are ensuing) if adequate water and food sustenance is denied three fourths of Indians, and if they continue to be consigned to ignorance and ill-health without credible recourse is likely to address the situation that bids fair to spread from the hinterlands to the metropolises.

When the corporates are so told, their predictable riposte is to snigger that a recipe for redistributing poverty is yet again being peddled.

It is time they pondered that the tiger is now roaming the cities, and salwa judums are but a poor remedy.

April 2008

Cricket as Surrogate Kill

Turn on any of India's up-market corporate channels, and you will find therein but just one lead: the IPL, or the Indian Premier League of 20x20 cricket.

It is as though that magic potion has been found at last that snuffs out all our troubles. Yet my migraine gets only more acute.

Watching these gladiators do relentless violence to the round little ball (and, in a moment of defeated frustration, to one another), you are not to think that anyone in India is houseless, diseased, unemployed, starving. Or that rape and murder, suicide and sell-out, insurgency and civil war are anywhere in evidence. Presto, just watch the league matches and yell with the next bludgeon. And should some superior snoot ask the question, just firm your jaw, look him in the eye, and say 'why not'? Why not do as we do do from one gratification to the next? Who says there is anything better to be done with life than feed the appetite and chill the brain? Every rapists thinks the same.

II

Having played some years of state-level, first class cricket myself, I ought to belong to the gladiator party.

Alas, that since that time I should also have done some reading and some worrying. Look where that has got me. Indeed, what follows must declare me an unforgiveable spoilsport. Being stakeless, nonetheless, encourages me to say what I think for now. Not a small satisfaction in these empty, glittering times.

III

Just as behind the falling of the apple lay a whole world of considerations – which, once worked out, gave us aviation and a new world altogether – so, it must be said, behind the 20x20 lies a history of human endeavour that it does no harm to understand. For what seems is hardly ever what is.

When capitalism came to the world, it brought in its wake a great deal of enlightenment.

Its facilitating intellects sat long hours through plague and punishment to examine and expose the manifold nastiness of feudal forms of social life.

Success could not have come to capitalism had its strenuous new rationality failed to persuade wide swathes of people that monarchy and landlordism, buttressed by an absolutist and absolutely corrupt church were houses of oppression and evil.

Where the feudal triumvirate simply assumed its right-to-oppress, the new capitalist class pressed into service a whole barrage of critical and analytic proof on behalf of a new future for mankind. In the process, many lost their lives.

Thus the story of the western world between the century that produced the loom and Protestantism (that made the teachings of the Bible amenable to the interests of the capitalist class) and 1871 (when the possibilities of extending the new rationality to embrace the fate of millions of others who stood to gain little from capitalism were brutally extinguished) was to be the story of the ascendance of capitalism.

However, once ensconced in power, the very career of enquiry and critique that had helped dislodge the old order came to be seen as a liability.

Enquiry and critique were weapons that could be used against the new class as well. Thus if capitalism had to ensure a long enough life for itself, these weapons had to be denied to those who now viewed it with suspicion. All the more so since with time it became apparent that its protestations notwithstanding, capitalism represented not the interests of mankind but of a class. And that indeed those interests could be furthered only if the bulk of mankind was now to be exploited in new, sophisticated ways.

Thus while the method of science remained integral to the career of capitalism towards the expansion of productive capacities, the exploitation of nature, and the maximization of profits thereby, science, this class recognized, was a dangerous tool if allowed to be fairly applied to an understanding of social and cultural issues.

No wonder that this conundrum has obliged capitalism to forge its own proliferating repertoire of superstition, myth, and unreason – a task in which its control of technologies has constantly come to its aid.

IV

Thus, if the career of capitalism required assiduous homework and enlightenment, once in power it saw that in order to thwart the world from thinking beyond capitalism it needed to jettison enlightenment for entertainment.

In literary parlance, capitalism now needed to rewrite the 19C novel into a sexy quickie, knocking out reflections upon processes for the mesmeric event, complete with blood and gore, with a ghost or some extra-terrestrial monstrosity thrown in for kicks. Nowadays ofcourse this menu has been further extended to include creatures, especially in the common fare from Hollywood.

It needed to produce a social order that would displace the thoughtful walk in the country, garden, or bylane by the frenetic rush of jogging.

It needed to emasculate language into digital ejaculations, chop grammar into animal grunts, castrate conversation into a time-saving hi and bye.

And to dethrone the warm contexts of tea-brewing and tea-drinking in favour of the stand-up cup of instant coffee.

It needed to numb the least moment of creative pain with the placebo of the next comfort available in the market.

It needed simultaneously to resist the backward call of religious dogmatism as well as keep afloat the religious sentiment, chiefly for two reasons: one, to keep the dregs of the earth from wandering into class-consciousness, and to make available to the corporates another perennial avenue of profiteering. Remember that more money is made from religious rituals than is from other forms of industrial life.

And it needed to cut to size the complex cadences of test-match cricket and instal the bestial gratifications of 20x20.

Gratification. That is the name of the game. The idea being to return mankind to those hunting-gathering primevals of life – food, sex, and violence. All made easy to hand by the professional skills of the technical and managerial elites who are made to believe that their labours are worthwhile in proportion to the packages they get. Or, vice versa.

And the underclasses are taught in school and market-place that only two classes of human beings exist – not the rich and the poor, but the winners and the losers. The winners are those that prostitute their hearts and minds to the capitalist project, from the shop-floor to the Board, and losers are those who either fail to do so, or opt out, or foolishly offer resistance to the criminal barbarism of capital. Religion comes in handy to teach them that human beings in fact are created unequal, and each must accept his/her destiny.

Thus everywhere capitalism teaches that men may do whatever they set their heart upon and become equal to the highest on high, while in practice it ensures that the vast mass of mankind remain in thrall, and seek to alleviate their misery with the next piece of entertainment. In the mud houses of India's slums, I have seen slum urchins derive great joy from pasting colourful Cadbury chocolate wrappers on their walls. It makes them feel they might belong.

V

When these days things get a bit over the hill even for devoted votaries of entertainment, some corporate channel is sure to do a programme that asks 'is India become too materialistic'?

So 'materialism' (projected as a general human propensity to acquisition) is identified as the villain, never capitalism.

Just as Naxalism is thought to be the 'greatest threat to India's internal security', never the material conditions that produce it.

Same with other forms of violence in the hinterland, or 'terrorism', or indeed what is now called urban 'road rage' wherein motorists simply kill off each other for not yielding the right of way.

Please, therefore, let us not talk just of our cricketing gladiators who were before the commencement of the IPL publicly 'sold' and 'bought' in the full glare of corporate channels in an auction to various franchises owned by those other gladiators of a resurgent India, the film stars and corporate moghuls.

For whatever grand notions a Dhoni or a Harbhajan might have of their worth and status, they are at bottom the anthropomorphic versions of the breed cattle and camel that are routinely auctioned in India, here, there, and elsewhere.

And why should they mind? Without a thought in their heads beyond the next gratification, without a decent book-read in their profile, they make more money for swinging a barbaric bat for ten odd minutes than an Aristotle or Erasmus could ever imagine existed. Look how justly Marx lived and died in penury for being critical of capitalism. Served the carbuncular nuisance right.

VI

I leave you, though, with a thought that he (Marx) left us in the Third of his *Economic and Philosophical Manuscripts of 1844.*

And he left us that thought in the words of one of his adored English writers, name of William Shakespeare, who, in his play, Timon of Athens, spoke thus of the power of money at the heyday of England's transformation to capitalism:

Gold? Yellow, glittering, precious gold? No, gods,
I am no idle votarist: roots, you clear heavens!
Thus much of this will make black, white; foul, fair;
Wrong, right; base, noble; old, young; coward, valiant.
... Why, this
Will lug your priests and servants from your sides;
Pluck stout men's pillows from below their heads;
This yellow slave
Will knit and break religions; bless th'accurst;
Make the hoar leprosy adored; place thieves,
And give them title, knee and approbation,
With senators on the bench: this is it
That makes the wappened widow wed again;
She whom the spittal house and ulcerous sores
Would cast the gorge at, this embalms and spices
To the April day again...

Thus, my fellow commentators, rail not at 20x20; rail rather at the world that makes such an obscenity desirable.

April 2008

Anti-Globalist Zeitgeist

CPI (M) Breaks New Ground

> '…the party congress held recently at Coimbatore had decided that the CPI(M) should directly take up social issues.'
>
> (Prakash Karat as reported by *The Hindu*, May 8)

As I sit to write this comment, I have before me a long-winded draft that took a whole day to do.

I now think my requirement for the task here must be to underscore without baggage or ambiguity the point I wish to make.

As to the first part of my title, much comment is already available internationally, especially within American writing itself, that establishes the endgame status of neo-liberal globalism that was installed as neo-imperialist world policy by the Washington Consensus of 1990 (put in place by the World Bank, the International Monetary Fund, and the American Development Bank).

For example, Kevin Philip who looked forward to a republican future – by which he had meant a regime of openness and democracy wherein enterprise would be fairly rewarded without lapsing into totalitarian consolidation – in his book Emerging Republican Majority (1969) now acknowledges the betrayal of that dream in a new book, titled *Bad Money: Reckless Finance, Failed Politics, and the Global Crisis of American Capitalism.*

In short, the book concludes that American republicanism has after all turned out to be a handmaiden to Wall Street, and that the long battle to rein in big finance that began from the time of Jefferson has been lost.

And with that has also been lost the hegemonic pretensions of American democracy.

Indeed, no less a man than Martin Wolf, chief economic commentator of The Financial Times was to say that 'the dream of global free market capitalism died' the day that Bear Stearns bailout was announced.

II

This failure has happened despite invasion, war, brutal repression, denial of every conceivable liberty within the anglo-saxon world and in the invaded territories, and the most unthinkable forms of inhuman and degrading torture, not to speak of the loss of hundreds of thousands of innocent lives.

And it has been accompanied by the ascendance of left or centre-left regimes world-wide.

In the erstwhile 'backyard,' namely South America, there are now but one or two regimes still holding on to the imperialist apron-string. The latest to go red after some 61 years of right-wing dictatorship is Paraguay, and as if to drive home a point, Fernando Lugo, the new communist President, is a former Catholic Bishop to boot.

In Europe, it is Spain and Cyprus that seem poised to shape the political future.

Not only do the playboy French President's ratings plunge to some 30% from some 70% in less than a year, but one local election after another gets lost to the socialists. Same in Germany. And in Britain, New Labour must now be thought to be dead.

Closer home, the combined perfidies of imperialism, theocratic monarchy, and upper caste Indian establishments friendly to it have failed to stop the march of the left in Nepal – an eventuality that this writer had rather foolhardily prognosticated as early as june 10,2006 (see 'India and Nepal').

To cap all this, the world now hears agonized calls from besieged corporates and financial institutions for that hated thing called state interventions to save the sinking ship, even as the fuel and food crisis puts paid to the free-wheeling criminalities of free-trade.

Only in an aspiring India do the new-money ruling classes continue to be inebriated with consumerist inundations, as their shallow and oblivious Podsnappery merrily disregards some three fourths of their fellow Indians who spend less than fifty cents a day. They remain secure in the knowledge that the government of the day is headed by renowned free-marketeers who will not be persuaded that the water may be seeping from under the crevices of the gateways of state.

III

So the question that is uppermost in many minds: how well is the Indian left poised to assume these histories to advantage – for the left and for the people of India.

For a number of concrete reasons, the work of the left in post-independence India has not been easy – and not always for the fault of left praxis.

Where all of Latin America speaks either Spanish or Portugese, and all countries in Europe use pretty much one or two languages, and all of China – over 90% Han – the same, and all of Russia, Russi, known proficiently also to territories that comprised the erstwhile Soviet Union, India is a Babel by contrast. By itself not a compelling argument about why the left should have been tardy, but taken with the fact that language habits in various regions of India remain inseparable from chequered and entrenched local histories and perceptions, a matter of considerable difficulty.

Similarly, the fact that the left has crucially yielded to sectarian/regional/casteist forces in Hindi/Punjabi speaking regions where it had strong organizations and a record of militant sacrifices through and after the national movement for freedom from colonial rule owes as much to weaknesses within the left (especially after the division of 1964) as to the consolidation of landlordism and caste identity politics both by the Congress and upper and middle castes opposed to bourgeois-English-speaking rule from the Centre. A further dimension of difficulty has been added since the ascendance of right-wing Hindu politics since the demolition of the Babri mosque and subsequent anti-minority pogroms. Over the last two decades, fascist forces have made the fullest use of the ordinary Indian's propensity towards the mythic, the occult, and the mysterious – fertile ground for literally thousands of 'godmen' whose public businesses flourish, including on India's corporate TV channels.

Not surprisingly, rationalist/humanist calls for struggle and unity against exploiting classes has tended to fragment against a slew of imperatives that have seemed more immediate and existential. Political consolidation has seemed available to only such political forces that have proceeded on the strength of some emotive slogan or the other – anti-colonial record of nationalism, cultural nationalism, regional/linguistic pride, caste affinity and so on.

Skirting all these, the left has found it an uphill task to mobilize vast number of Indians on issues bearing exclusively on class exploitation.

Capping all this, India's unequal and often lumpen-bougeois 'development' has tended to generate new middle classes whose concerns and allegiances remain a far cry from middle classes that were in the vanguard of the anti-colonial freedom struggle.

Within such a mind-bogling complex of factors, all modulated with unique specificities in various regions of the new nation, the appeal to class has seemed a far-away abstraction. Often the very 'toiling masses' including copy-book wage-workers, have both participated in left-led movements as well as gone and voted for their caste or community candidates during elections. As much was admitted to me some years ago by an important local leader of the CPI(M).

This woefully thumb-nail sketch may suggest that the work of the left in India, however patriotic, has tended to suffer from a lack of imagination, or, conversely, a rather lordly refusal of social and cultural pluralities that frustrate class consolidation of any straightforward kind.

The fact is that in India, even as class-rule remains the abiding source of immiseration, the conditioning of vast numbers to imagine any alternate system of the production and distribution of wealth has tended to render calls to a humanist essentialism across fractious identities something utopian in contrast to more concrete invocations of realities that have seemed rooted in lived and deeply traditional forms of being.

Often, these entrenched sources of oppression have been attributed to cycles of karma and deserved rebirth into unequal stations in life.

Thus, vast numbers of Indians have tended to experience their social and cultural identities as issuing from a priori and unchanging sources, unamenable to historical transformation. And often not without reason. Consider that, theoretically atleast, a wage-worker may not always remain a wage-worker (which is not to challenge the truth that within the capitalist wage system, educational possibilities and other forms of socialization are ruthlessly controlled to ensure the reproduction of the existing relations of production), but a dalit or a woman or a Muslim remains a dalit or a woman or a Muslim even after she has succeeded in jumping class. Pretty much as happens to many black people in that other great democracy, America.

Having taken to the parliamentary route after the failure of the armed struggle in Telengana (1946-51) – a struggle that was to yield considerable electoral fruit to the left in the first-ever elections in Independent India in 1952 – left politics would seem to have been debilitated by a twin-failure: of disregarding for the most part those a priori forms of consciousness spoken of above, and failing to mount militant challenges of country-wide magnitude purely on issues of class.

Clearly, the left is not too well placed today either to return to the 'Calcutta Thesis' of 1943 (armed struggle), nor to reap through appeals to class oppression alone the kind of electoral dividends that have accrued to the communists in Nepal.

This is the context that lends great meaning to the decision of the CPI(M)'s 19th Party Congress at Coimbatore to address social issues directly.

IV

I may be permitted the indulgence to reproduce a bit from an article I had written on the eve of the CPI(M)'s 18th Party Congress:

> ....social cultural inequities in the mofussil cannot be automatically incorporated into class-struggle. The left will need to devise ways of ingress here which fully recognize the relative autonomy of these inequities, even as those inequities are transformed over time into class consciousness. The left need not fight shy of finding itself engaging in dalit temple-entry movements...since vast masses that suffer social/religious oppression of one kind or another must first be approached at the first point of exclusion and ostracism before they can be expected to see the linkages between those oppressions and class-rule. To the extent that ruling class ideology in the form of accreted myths that have functioned as 'grounds' for discriminatory and inegalitarian histories retain a hold among the disenfranchised, the meaning of that Leninist text – class political consciousness can be brought to the workers only from without, that is only from outside the economic struggle (1902, CW 5, p.422) must be considered as an injunction to free the mass of Indians from ideological oppressions. (see my 'Left Renewal: An Opportunity', *Mainstream*, April 30, 2005).

I had concluded that article with the following insight from the British Marxist, Terry Eagleton:

> The proletariat in ancient society were those who were too poor to serve the state by holding property, and who served it instead by producing children (proles, offspring) as labour power. They are those who have nothing to give but their bodies. Proletarians and women are thus intimately allied, as indeed they are in the impoverished regions of the world today. The ultimate poverty or loss of being is to be left with nothing but yourself. It is to work directly with your body, like the other animals. And since this is still the condition of men and women on the planet today, it is strange to be told that the proletariat has disappeared. (see his *After Theory*, Allen Lane, 2003, p.42).

At another time, indeed, I had the privilege to write to the then General Secretary of the CPI(M) on the subject of the location of women within class struggle, making the simple point that so long as it is the case that not all oppressions suffered by women across the board can be cognized exclusively in class terms, any Marxism that proceeded on the basis of refusing that reality in this day and age could not draw much credence. This especially at a time when the left has been in the forefront of demanding 33% reservation for women in Parliament!

V

What the CPI(M) has thus achieved just the other day at Uthapuram in the Madurai district of Tamil Nadu in pursuance of the Coimbatore resolve signifies far beyond the particular event.

At Uthapuram its cadres, supported by state agencies, demolished a part of a wall that has been built by upper castes to keep dalit communities from using common facilities.

In breaching that wall, the left has symbolically pulled down a bigger wall – its resistance/hesitance thus far to address issues of social oppression as an autonomous revolutionary activity from, in Lenin's above-cited parlance, 'without... the economic struggle.'

Clearly this is the way to go if sufficiently puissant mass struggles are to be waged over the next decade that can begin to relegate the politics of status quoist capitalism, however welfarist it may sound, or however congenial to forms of inherited slaveries.

The Karat statement cited by *The Hindu* of May 8 includes two other significant perceptions: one that political struggles must not remain wedded to concerns of immediate electoral dividend, and, two, that the organized left now must take up the sort of work that has tended to be done in recent years by voluntary organizations.

It is this sort of praxis that, if conducted with diligence and conviction over a decade or so, truly bears the promise of hollowing out the humbugs dished out by 'mainstream' political formations, and substituting in their place a more lasting and substantial politics of equity.

May 2008

The State, the Seminaries, and the People of India

Over the last month or so, India's most influential Islamic seminaries – Deoband, Bareilly, Lucknow, Hyderabad – have been holding well-attended public meetings/conferences with a single-point agenda.

Namely, to make it known that the so-called 'jihad' being practiced by 'terrorists' is 'un-Islamic.'

Whatever may be the particular skepticism employed variously to evaluate this development, these meetings and conferences clearly constitute not just bold interventions on behalf of sagacity but, crucially, a thought-out purpose to disempower indiscriminate violence and killing by denying it any religious sanction or justification.

One of its fall-outs must also be to rob right-wing Hindutva fascism of the enabling propaganda that 'terrorism' has authorized theological approval. As well as, most importantly, to lend strength to moderate/liberal voices among Muslims who routinely suffer the blight of being seen as the 'other' of Islamic authority on the question.

And, interestingly, this Islamic disavowal comes while Hindutva forces continue to draw legitimacy for their brand of terrorism from the exploits of sundry gods and goddesses. Consider that the Bajrang Dal, to which the notorious killer, Babu Bajrangi, belongs, is named after Lord Ram's most devoted follower, Hanuman.

It needs to be recalled that the fascist snarl against madrasas had this covert agenda of maligning Islamic education as contributory to 'jihad.' All that despite the fact that no governmental or other agency has thus far brought any proof that madrasas have anywhere in India been complicit in the matter, although ample proof exists that the Shishu Mandirs and other such educational establishments run by the Hindutva forces under the tried and tested leadership of the RSS routinely spew and teach hatred against the Muslim community for having 'oppressed Hindus' over eight long centuries, and being responsible for the partition of India in 1947.

A corollary yield of the intervention by the Seminarist leaderships must be to disoblige India's secular opportunists from engaging in what the Hindu right-wing calls 'appeasement' of 'terrorism' calculated to win the electoral approval of India's 150 million Muslims.

Of course, the Seminarist intervention may best be understood as recognition of the fact that, however genuine and gruesome the sufferings of Muslims at the hands both of the majoritarian fascists and a complicit state, it is still the case that not violence but the the pressures of democratic mobilization, of informed opinion, and trust in the institutions of India's democracy, no matter how little deserving, offer a better prospect than mindless violence that affects all citizens alike, debilitates the citizen's stake in democracy, and renders the secular sentiment alien even to those who wish India's Muslims well.

II

Not unsurprisingly, sensing the magnitude of the initiative taken by sundry Islamic authorities (imagine the Pope calling the Templars un-christian), the response from the 'jihadis' has been quick and fierce.

The Ullemas who have pronounced the 'jihadis – work 'un-Islamic' have been called a 'bunch of cowards,' 'puppets of Hinduism,' 'ullema-e-kuffar' (clergy of the disbelievers) and so on.

Indeed, evidence seems to suggest that 'terrorism' directed at India may no longer be a foreign-inspired phenomenon merely. An eventuality that lends piquancy to the pronouncements of the Indian Islamic authorities.

An email received by an electronic channel after the most recent Jaipur blasts purports to come from 'Indian Mujahideen' and as the 'Declaration of Open War Against India.'

Who, the email asks, are the terrorists – the 'Hindus who killed the Muslims in Gujarat (and) Maharashtra, or us who took revenge (qisas) through serial blast in Mumbai local trains?'

As to the killing of innocent civilians, the mail argues that all Indians are culpable insofar as 'they have willingly elected their leaders and representatives in Parliament who draw up the policies which murder our children, dishonour our women, occupy our homes, and plunder our wealth.' Further, the text contends, Hindus 'fund the terrorist organizations like Rashtriya Swayamsevak Sangh, Vishwa Hindu Parishad and Shiv Sena' (it is to be noted that one agency of the U.N. does infact list the first, RSS, as a 'terrorist' organization).

But most significantly for our consideration is the view the email expresses of how the state handles the terrorism unleashed by the majoritarian forces; it notes that those responsible for anti-Muslim violence (in Gujarat especially) 'got promotions and are enjoying good government support.' The Gujarat Chief Minister, Narendra Modi 'who gave the orders to kill the Muslims in Gujarat in 2002 won two consecutive terms of Vidhan Sabha. Babu Bajrangi who killed the Muslim women in their pregnancy and kept their child on spear is moving freely in Gujarat.' On the other hand, 'modest Muslims who went for the revenge of the demolition of the Babri Mosjid were arrested and tortured.'

What is striking is that the email enumerates precisely the reality that the Intelligence Bureau of India has, we believe, communicated to the powers-that-be, namely, that the demolition of the Babri mosque in 1992 and then the massacre of 2002 in Gujarat have scarred the Muslim psyche (a safe enough generalization here, except that one would like to add to that the psyche of many thousands of Hindus and other Indians as well with respect, especially, to the role of state agencies in these and other matters) in watershed ways.

Most galling and difficult to swallow is the continuing fact that, notwithstanding noises to the contrary, and noises also about new laws that might render culpability in communal rioting a most heinous crime etc., the Indian state remains blatantly partisan in the way it looks at majoritarian shenanigans and what it calls 'jihadi terrorism.' Amazingly, Nehru's defining caution that majoritan communalism is likely to be taken for 'nationalism' while communalism of the minority is just that – communalism – still remains the chief informing piece of analysis of the situation. And not just among the Hindu communalists but, one would hazard the guess, among many Congress people as well.

Imagine that of the 242 people indicted under the draconian POTA in the Godhra/Gujarat episode, all but one are Muslims; and that other is a Sikh! And, despite public knowledge now that in some cases of recent 'terrorist' violence members of the Hindu community were infact involved (Nanded, Tenkasi, etc.,), the state's first assumption always remains to cast blame on some or the other Islamic outfit without, needless to say, the sort of evidence that stands up or brings about a conviction. For the most part, conjecture reigns supreme.

III

Islamic Seminaries having made their position clear and explicit, the question to ask is how does the state aim to proceed from here.

It is true that the present UPA government has – consequent upon the findings and recommendations of the Sachar Committee Report – initiated proposals that are directed to address the specific educational and financial problems that Muslims in India face. On the ground, although, there is little agreement that these initiatives are sought to be pursued with purpose and alacrity.

There is however little evidence that the state is willing to see Muslim (or, for that matter, Naxal) unrest owing entirely to ascertainable and remedeeable causes of a just nature. Its chief conviction remains that these are matters best left to strong-arm methods. And when pressure mounts from the reactionary right, the Congress party which leads the coalition finds itself saying that they have and will never 'compromise with terrorism.' Whether, on the other hand, the law-enforcement agencies will be taught or encouraged to deal even-handedly with those guilty of violence remains a matter of conjecture. As to the judicial system, only at the apex level does it seem that victims of right-wing fascist violence may expect justice, however delayed.

To state the matter plainly: it is time that the state understood that its own record and procedures in dealing with sectarian violence may actually have come to be the most crucial determinant in the matter whether or not 'terrorism' of any kind will or will not abate.

Secular dispensations whose actual operations are seen to match at most points the preferred prejudices of communalists can no longer guarantee the safety of the realm against loss of hegemony and exponential violence.

And 'socialist' secularists whose theory and practice in the matter of the political economy infact more than apes the preferred options of the honest-to-god capitalists and free-marketers have small chance of halting the onslaught of armed agrarian fighters.

And taken together, such a state must everyday only be witness to escalating and open resort to violence by ordinary citizens in town and country, now on grounds of failed justice, now on grounds of corrupt bureaucracies, now in the knowledge that law-enforcement agencies never speak for the disenfranchised, and now because some godman or caste-leader says such is the course to adopt.

Thus, even as state functionaries and other fortune hunters bask in the knowledge of an Indian democracy that is glorious and forever while others around us cannot see their way through, it is probable that the joke may be turning upon the Indian state itself.

And time may just be running out.

May 2008

Justice Sanjay Kishan Kaul

The Republic Needs More Like Him

Without going into the question why some artists/painters are designated greater or more important than others, or why a vase made lovingly by the potters' deft fingers fetches less than a painting made of it by some renowned painter, it is acknowledged that Maqbool Fida Husain, now a nonagenarian, is justly India's best-known and best-selling painter.

Like a long line of painters through human history, Husain has often painted the nude. Painters, we are told, seek to penetrate beyond man-made encumbrances to celebrate how god made the world in the first place. Far, then, from being a lascivious fetish, the nude has often designated an emblem of purity, and a tribute to the skill of that greatest of artists, however you call her/him/it – Nature, DNA, Creator.

Some years ago, Husain painted India partially in the figure of a nude, legs bent backward at the knees to form the peninsular conical, hair flowing laterally to imply the Himalayas, head thrown back in a gesture of distress, and one eye shedding a tear. Many years later a collector christened the painting 'Bharat Mata' (Mother India).

All that was enough for the majoritarian fascist lobby to go to town, attacking Husains' work wherever they found it, smashing exhibitions, and slapping some seven court cases in diverse states of the country against the painter on charges of obscenity and insult to the Hindu veneration of the motherland.

Consequence: this man who loves his motherland and everything in it, most keenly its Hindu mythological heritage, had to go into exile.

II

Now, just recently, the Delhi High Court, Justice Sanjay Kishan Kaul presiding), has pronounced on three of the cases against the artist:

> In view of the aforesaid, the summoning orders and warrants of arrest issued against the petitioner in the complaint cases are quashed and the revision petitions filed against them are allowed leaving the parties to bear their own costs. (section 121)

And the 'aforesaid' of Justice Kaul's seventy-page judgement it is that must make for a landmark interpretation not just of the laws that pertain to the suites in question but of the implications of all such fascist attacks on the most dearly-held values of India's republican constitution and democracy, and on the most prized attainments of the human spirit everywhere through history.

III

On point of law, Justice Kaul draws upon a breath-taking swathe of legislation and judicial pronouncement on the issues of obscenity and wounding of the religious/patriotic sentiment from America, Britain, Canada and at home.

Reproducing a facsimile of the impugned painting, Justice Kaul then makes applications of those legislations and pronouncement to Husain's work, and at each point of contention refutes the allegations as wholly inappropriate to the work in question. Amazingly for someone whose calling is not that of a connoisseur or a professional art critic, Justice Kaul, arguing how one and the same art work continues to be viewed differently by different people, produces a reading ot Husain's use of the nude in the said painting which speaks for an extraordinary perspicacity into and empathy with the inner world of the artist's concerns:

> The artist's creativity in this painting is evident from the manner in which the artist by way of a tear and ruffled, unkempt, open hair of the woman tried to portray the sad and the dispirited face of our nation who seems to have suffered a great deal of anguish and agony. A woman's sorrow has been described by the way the woman is lying with her eyes closed, with one arm raised on her face and a tear dropping from the eye.
>
> The object of painting the woman in nude is also part of the same expression and is obviously not to stimulate the viewer's prururience but instead to shake up the very conscience of the viewer and to invoke in him empathy for India and abhorrence for the culprits. (section 100)

Truly, one might say, a people's Daniel come to judgement.

Having, upon strenuous examination of the laws, the pronouncements and of the painting, dismissed the charge of 'prurience' and 'tendency to deprave', Justice Kaul takes on the subject of human sexuality, especially within the Indian context, with a healthful and candid attention to cultural history. Noting that India continues to be called the 'land of the Kama Sutra,' Justice Kaul recounts how in our founding traditions,

> way back then…people led exotic lives dedicated to sensuality in all its forms. It was healthy and artistic. They studied sex, practiced sex, shared techniques with friends, and passed on their secrets to the next generation. All in good spirit. Sexual pleasure was not behind closed doors or a taboo; it was in the air in different forms. There was painting, sculpture, poetry, dance and many more. Sex was embraced as an integral part of a full and complete life. It is most unfortunate that India's new 'puritanism' is being carried out in the name of cultural purity and a host of ignorant people are vandalizing art and pushing us towards a pre-renaissance era. (section 110; emphasis added)

Indicating that the charge of 'prurience' could well lie on the charger's foot, Justice Kaul notes that

> the literature of India, both religious and secular, is full of sexual allusions, sexual symbolisms and passages of such frank eroticism the likes of which are not to be found elsewhere in world literature.

And, specifically speaking to Hinduism, Justice Kaul instructs its fanatic and fundamentalist votaries that

> being the world's oldest religious tradition (Hinduism) incorporates all forms of belief and worship without necessitating the selection or elimination of any. The Hindu is inclined to revere the divine in every manifestation, whatever it may be, and is doctrinally tolerant. A Hindu may embrace a non-Hindu religion without ceasing to be Hindu, and since the Hindu is disposed to think synthetically and to regard other forms of worship, strange gods, and divergent doctrines as inadequate rather than wrong or objectionable (a brilliant enough discrimation there), he tends to believe that the highest divine powers complement each other for the well-being of the world and mankind' (104)

This writer is tempted to think how the Trika view of Hinduism, popularly referred to as Kashmiri Shaivism, suffuses Justice Kaul's readings of the world and its divinity here.

IV

Fully cognizant that the motivations of the assault on Husain do not lie in the charges made – prurience or insult to Hinduism – Justice Kaul takes on the politics of the charges head on:

> Our greatest problem today is fundamentalism which is the triumph of the letter over the spirit. In a free democratic society tolerance is vital especially in large and complex societies comprising people with varied beliefs and interests. (115)

> A real democracy is one in which the exercise of the power of the many is conditional on respect for the rights of the few. Pluralism is the soul of democracy… there should be freedom for the thought we hate. Freedom of speech has no meaning if there is no freedom after speech. (113, emphasis added)

It should be obvious from the passionately terse formulations cited above how steeped Justice Kaul is in the founding principles of democracy (a Voltaire, a John Stuart Mill come to mind, although his allusion to Plato in section 112 seems that little bit ironical, since a Husain may not actually have found a place in the Republic of that philosophers's contemplation!)

Making a special mention of the requirements of the Liberal Arts, Justice Kaul admonishes that

> the practice of tolerance in our multi-religious, multi-cultural nation must be regarded as a fundamental duty of every citizen and must be actively encouraged and performed if we are to make our pluralist democracy a living robust. (117)

I have on purpose cited the Kaul judgement in extenso inorder to register the uplifting and salubrious fact that Justice Kaul's concerns in toto coincide everywhere with the agonized concerns of so many of us who have over these fraught years of mayhem argued against 'fundamentalism' and its deleteriously inimical consequences for the Republic and the Democracy that 'we the people' gave to ourselves. In that regard, it is hardly possible to underplay the macro-historical import of the Kaul judgement as one that refuses to limit itself merely to the technical points of jurisprudence. In every word that Justice Kaul puts on record, he comes across truly as an intellectual whose concerns embrace a totality of relations and issues, and who cares about the health of the realm with an intensity and a breadth of vision rare among professionals adept only at speaking the language of their particular discourse

But that is not all. Justice Kaul also speaks to another issue which civil society has repeatedly underscored – namely the fascist tactics of registering such cases in scattered courts with the single despicable intention of causing as much harassment to the victim as can be:

> These days unfortunately some people seem to be perpetually on a short fuse, and are willing to protest often violently, about anything under the sun on the ground that a book, or painting, or film etc., has 'hurt the sentiments' of their community. These dangerous tendencies must be curbed. We are one nation and must respect each other and should have tolerance. (117)

and, most consequentially:

> ...criminal Justice system ought not to be invoked as a convenient recourse to ventilate any and all objections to an art work. (117)

The Judgement notes that the dirty trick of slapping suites all over the place is nothing more than a tactics not to secure justice but to cause the greatest harassment to the chosen victim of fascist ire.

V

Let me conclude by extrapolating from Justice Kaul's text but one sentence that I suggest should stand for a talisman to all and sundry who bear any pretence of being votaries of democracy anywhere in the world:

> Freedom of speech has no meaning if there is no freedom after speech.

Prior to the neocon era in the western world generally one would have thought this was a principle that was largely held sacred. Not so since.

We have indeed a long way to go to meet the standard of thought and practice that Justice Kaul enunciates in that sentence. But it is equally true that unless we do meet that standard we have scant business to be trumpeting our democratic system.

And the culprits here, as we have seen lately (Taslima Nasreen has done that much for us – see my 'The Unacceptable Excesses of Irreligion'), the best of us – individuals, organizations, parties, governments – tend to fail that test. We must remember that, at all times, we cannot point fingers with any conviction if an odd finger can be pointed back at us.

What then will Justice Kaul's historic Judgement achieve? Will it put an end to the suffocating and violent elimination of dissent within our body politic? Not to be thought. But, it will most surely carry the weight of accreting history, and remain a precedent guaranteed to cause hurdles in the way of those who wish to carry on with the kind of pogrom that Husain has been victim of purely on account of being a Muslim, let it be said. It is for civil society organization from now on to ply Justice Kaul's monumentally helpful pronouncement in the continuing secular and lawful struggle to establish a culture of tolerance and pluralism. For a start, efforts must be redoubled to secure an end to the other four cases pending against Husain so that this lovely human being and artist can return to the home he longs for. We also enjoin upon the fraternity of the bench to attend closely to the Kaul analysis and judgement, and set a collective leadership in this regard.

One more thing: en passant, the Canadian law on the subject of 'obscenity' that Justice Kaul alludes to carries within it a moral dimension that many of us have dearly argued for:

> The Canadian Criminal Code defines obscene material as any publication a dominant characteristic of which is the undue exploitation of sex, or of sex and any one or more of the following subjects, namely, crime, horror, cruelty and violence, shall be deemed to be obscene'. (section 18, emphasis added)

The very question we wish to ask: why is it that obscenity/morality tends to remain restricted to the arena of sexuality alone? Why are corruptions of other kind that have far worse and extended consequence as enunciated in the Canadian code not deemed to be universally 'obscene'? Does this fact point to significant features of class rule? Because that provision does not exist in either the American or the Indian code, neither the invasion of iraq and the genocide thereof, nor the routine cruelties vented here upon dalits, women, and children are thought of as 'obscene'; it is high time we say that they should be so designated, and appropriate provisions incorporated in our system of jusrisprudence.

But, in the meanwhile, Justice Sanjay Kishan Kaul, you deserve our admiration and our thanks.

May 2008

Fatwa Against Terrorism

A New Leadership Initiative from India

May 31, 2008 must rank as a very consequential day in modern Indian history.

Indeed, it might be said, in modern Muslim history as well.

On that day, in a public gathering at Delhi's historic Ramlila grounds, hundreds of thousands, mainly Muslims, received a fatwa from the Darul Uloom, Deoband – a seminary that played a leading role in India's secular anti-colonial freedom movement – declaring terrorism 'un-Islamic.'

Considering the fact that the gravest provocations notwithstanding, Indian Muslims – the second largest in the world – have remained aloof from terrorism, the question might be asked as to why the need for such a fatwa was felt in the first place.

One reason clearly was to make it known to the nation at large what seminaries teach their students in private confines – that the Koran explicitly forbids the killing of a single innocent human being, of any faith whatsoever, equating such killing with the murder of all humankind.

A second: to send a message to the state and its agencies, as well as sections of the media and civil society, that Muslims do not take kindly to the frequent use of the term 'Islamic terrorism.'

The point was made that whereas the terrorism of the IRA, the Mizos and the Nagas was never called Christian terrorism, or of the LTTE and the ULFA Hindu terrorism, or of the Khalistanis as Sikh terrorism, or of the Irgun and Stein gangs as Jewish terrorism, the term 'Islamic terrorism' could only be understood as a political currency floated by imperialists abroad and their collaborators in India who seek single-mindedly to destabilize western Asia and the Middle East inorder to install puppet regimes there and obtain control of the oil wealth of the region.

It is to be remembered that of the forty or so groups designated 'terrorist organizations' by the Indian state, only six have Islamic nomenclatures.

Indeed, it has been obvious for sometime that those who persist with the 'Islamic' nomenclature ('all Muslims are not terrorists but all terrorists are Muslims,' never mind that the gravest acts of terror in post-independence India have been perpetrated by non-Muslims, namely, the murders of Mahatma Gandhi, Indira Gandhi, and Rajive Gandhi) have but one objective in mind. This is to keep in place the convergence of the interests of 'communal nationalism' in India and of global anti-Muslim imperialism. Communalism and terrorism are thus sought to be deployed inseparably as a hegemonic strategy to alter the character both of the Indian Republic and the World Order at large.

Thus a concomitant objective of the Deoband initiative must be to defang majoritarian fascists whose political well-being has for decades now rested on keeping alive the myth that India's Muslims are not good enough nationalists because their primary loyalty remains allied to the Muslim ummah worldwide.

Remarkably, no questions are asked when the Vishwa Hindu Parishad (Global Hindu Organisation) worries day in and day out about the fate of Hindus in all corners of the world. It might be noted that the collapse of the Hindu state and monarchy in Nepal has caused less hurt to the people inside Nepal, more to the imperialists in America and theVHP/RSS/BJP in India! Or, at the fact that millions of dollars are received by these organizations – all unaccounted – from Hindu NRIs in America and elsewhere in the West purely for the purpose of refurbishing temple trusts and the political prospects of India's Hindus qua Hindus.

And far be it for anyone to question why Jews globally should be willing to stake everything for the well-being of the Zionist state in faraway Israel.

Yet, Indian Muslims are advised to suppress whatever opinions they may have with regard to a predominantly Muslim Iraq, Iran and so forth – all in their own good interests (see Harish Khare, 'Indian Muslims and their Linkages', *The Hindu*, June 6, 2008). Truly a communal argument unbeknown to the writer, it would seem. Ergo, it may be alright for non-Muslim Indians to pronounce on those matters, but not for Indian Muslims, since they would immediately run the risk of being branded 'terrorist sympathizers'. Expressing a middle-class, centrist view of the matter, Khare – a political commentator who has generally stood out for his sensitivity and perspicacity – goes on to further advise Indian Muslims to be wary of those 'progressive' elements in India's polity and political system whose 'ability' or 'intention' to help Indian Muslims out of their 'ghettoized existence' is to him questionable.

Simple correction to that view: it is majoritarian communalism, expressed variously through hate-filled propaganda and brutal killings, and the failure of the state to be non-partisan that keeps Indian Muslims 'ghettoized', not 'progressive' thinking among Indian secularists. Misjudging that reality, even if for a well-intentioned purpose, is fraught with implications that everyone had better understand.

II

The fact is that the painful ferment among the world's Muslims has more than one simple cause.

There are of course those who wish to establish Islamic theocratic states worldwide. So that their 'anti-imperialism' is at bottom a fake one, wishing to replace one regime of tyranny with another. This falange is then properly understood as one that remains unreconciled to the fruits of modernity and liberalism – ideological archives of which secularism is an integral component.

But there are those as well who have been fighting what are essentially 'nationalist' struggles against a so-called globalization which seeks essentially to neuter the sovereignty of states. The justification for this sort of struggle can be found dime a dozen in the ravages and betrayals effected by western powers in vast swathes of the Middle East, South-East Asia, and South Asia, and indeed of Africa. Not to speak of South America where most countries have already defeated the hegemony of the imperialists.

A third cause that is the one germane to a country like India has to do with the relegation of Muslims from the due rights of equal citizenship and opportunities thereof.

That such relegation is an Indian fact has been eloquently testified to and enumerated at least by two high-powered government Commissions – the Gopal Singh and Sachar Reports.

The dastardly trick, however, employed by the Hindu-right has been to pooh pooh the reality and substance of such relegation, to propagate that catering to findings that establish it is tantamount to 'appeasement,' and, most sinister of all, to deflect such relegation towards the wholly unsubstantiated polemics that in fact Indian Muslims fall within the first category of Islamic oppsition – one that has the objective of turning India into a theocratic Islamic state.

Thus Hindus are everyday reminded that if Muslims continue to be allowed polygamy, a day is not far when the demographic profile of the country will be reversed, to wit, when Muslims will grow from their current 14 or so percent of the total population to being some 80 percent or so – namely the current strength of the Indian non-Muslim population.

Before you laugh at that, you must pause and note that wide sections of middle-class Hindus, chiefly among the educated, propertied upper castes, lend willing allegiance to that fear! A stock on which the BJP has been basing its venomous anti-Muslim politics ever since its first beginnings in the Jana Sangh.

III

Now that two concomitant facts are to the fore – the multiple axes of Muslim relegation, and the open and public denouncement of terrorism by the most influential of Muslim clerics and seminaries – the major planks of Hindu right-wing communal politics must be deemed to be faced with some roadblocks.

And yet, all this may come to nothing for one simple but, in the end, all-important reason. Namely, the will of the state and its agencies, especially the law-enforcement ones, to heed these facts and developments.

Hurt by some repeated calls on behalf of various political segments that the best thing for India would be for the two major national parties, the Congress and the BJP, to join hands in the governance of the realm, an argument that encapsulates the ruling-class desire to see a two-party system enshrined wherein both parties equally cater to the interests of the fat-cats, an articulate and civilized spokesman of the Congress party, Abhishekh Singhvi, (see 'Never the Twain Shall Meet', *Hindustan Times*, June 4, 2008) has posed the question whether the visions of a Hedgewar and Golwalkar on the RSS/BJP side and of a Gandhi and Nehru on the Congress can ever be reconciled.

It is indeed the key question to ask. Yet, it also remains a frustrating reality that whereas the Congress continues to project a socially inclusive, secular vision, its doings have been repeatedly found wanting where it has concerned the injustices meted out to the Muslims.

A long story this, but just three recent instances will suffice to underline the point.

One, when the Babri mosque was set upon by fascist hordes of the majority community in 1992, the then Congress Prime Minister remained somnambulant throughout the day-long proceedings of wanton assault. Indeed, it is well-known that he was popularly referred to as the first BJP prime minister of India; and a chief accused in that mayhem, Lal Kishen Advani, continues to strut the stage and aspire to be the next prime minister of India.

Two, post the riots in the then Bombay, following upon the demolition of the mosque, wherein some seven hundred Muslims were butchered, the findings and recommendations of the Srikrishna Commissions which courageously named culprits in high places, such as Bal Thackeray, have remained in limbo despite the promises made by the Congress to bring the guilty to book; where prosecutions have taken place, chiefly of low-level hoodlums, the accused have been found not-guilty, ostensibly for want of evidence, but truly because of a total absence of will either to find the evidence or to press a credible prosecution.

Third, no recent pogrom against Muslims has blown apart the secular credentials and credibility of the Congress as conclusively as the Gujarat massacre of 2002.

As the mayhem went on for three whole days, taking the life of the Congress's own Member of Parliament, Ehsaan Jafri, the party both in the state and at the national level found itself paralysed into a complicit submission.

Those, therefore, who tend to see the BJP and the Congress, at bottom, as a tweedledom and a tweedledee may not be much blamed. After all there has to be a reason why the country's law-enforcement forces remain deeply infected by the communal virus, or why Congress dispensations one after the other have sought to do precious little either to rectify that social reality or to enact other police reforms conducive to credible and non-discriminatory policing. As the Sachar report points out, the percentage of Muslims in such law-enforcement agencies remains a pittance primarily because they are not trusted to be any part of law-enforcement.

Suffice it to say that the agonized introspections of Indian Muslims notwithstanding, or the scale of the latest Uloom initiative conducted in a massive public meeting in broad daylight, unless the state, now led by the secular UPA, shows the will and the verifiable conviction to translate policy initiatives into implemented programmes on the ground, all this may not come to much.

It remains a sorrowful and damaging fact of Congress history that, however it may protest, it does willy nilly come to see India's Hindus as a vote-bank much as the BJP.

This fundamental failure to conduct politics on the ground of non-discriminatory citizenship and to fight electoral battles on those principles continues to play into the hands of the Hindu right-wing.

It is to be much hoped that the historic event at Ramlila grounds can lend to India's secular parties the inspiration to take the communal right-wing head-on, just as one hopes that secular citizens across communities can find it in themselves to become the bedrock of a new configuration of humanism and fairplay.

Were it to happen that the state fails to rise to the momumental initiative taken by India's Muslims in publicly denouncing terrorism, the consequences can indeed be distressing in the extreme.

Conversely, can it be expected that an Advani-led BJP will answer the Deoband call in equal measure, and in a similar public meeting declare a new covenant – that the majoritarian right-wing will henceforth abjure all recourse to minority-bashing, to hate-agendas, to the the communal poison taught little kids in shishu mandirs and ekal vidyalas (schools run by the RSS in the thousands that routinely teach an anti-Muslim bigotry), to 'Islamic terrorism' and the demand for draconian laws, and support nationalist movements that seek to thwart the hegemony of militarist imperialism?

Will the leopard change his spots? Time and the consolidation or otherwise of the secular forces within the polity and of fairplay on behalf of the state alone will tell.

But kudos to the new leadership initiative that makes these introspections possible

June 2008

The Chieftain State of Gujarat

Where the Republic Ends

When, after the massacre of Muslims in 2002, the electorate in Gujarat voted the butcher of Gandhinagar – the capital city of Gujarat; but think of the enormous irony of that oxymoron – back to power, they effectively declared their secession from the Republic of India. If the founding principles of the Republic are 'secularism' and 'democracy,' Modi's victorious constituency used the latter to spit at the former.

Just as the Germans had done in 1933 – use democracy to install dictatorship.

Always to remember when we speak of Gujaratis that nearly a half of the electorate voted against him as well. Such are the ways in which franchise makes or unmakes, especially in an electoral system where all you need to do is to first pass the post. Much of the time, indeed, in such a dispensation it is the minority that rules the majority! Yet it is all we have for now.

Employing a diabolical double-speak, Modi berated the secularists for feeding off the Muslim 'vote-bank' while simultaneously consolidating first a Hindutva constituency and then a regional/Gujarati one.

Effectively, Gujarat has come to be reconstructed as an alterity to the Indian nation-state. Not Kashmir, but Modi-led Gujarat.

And not just as a rhetorical flourish.

Operating as the endorsed Chieftan of a triumphalist tribe, the Modi 'government' – for want of another word – has, since that ineffaceable butchery in 2002 – sought, every single step of the way to shield the Hindutva satraps (who were knee-deep in blood at the behest of the Chieftan) from the operations of the law, and brazenly to bring back into positions of authority publicly implicated high-ranking police officers, and atleast one judge, name of Mehta, who was spoken of by the ripper-in- chief, Babu Bajrangi, in a sting tape as the judge that Modi brought back to secure the self-confessed ripper from the hangman, after two other judges had honourably refused to do the dirty work of granting him bail. Indeed the same 'Justice' Mehta has now been drafted as part of the Special Investigation Team (SIT) that the Supreme Court of India has assigned to look into the merit of some cases that are asking to be opened and reinvestigated!

As a result, lawyers working for the victims of the massacre have taken the only recourse of opting out of the proceedings in protest against the inclusion of Mehta and challenging his inclusion in the Supreme Court.

Among these worthies who have been recalled not just to life but to brazen authority is the police officer, Mathur, reinstated as the Police Commissioner of Ahmedabad.

And what could be a more ringing declaration of separate nationhood on behalf of the Chieftan state of Gujarat than that this same Mathur should now have instituted a charge of 'sedition and treason' against the editor of the local edition of the Times of India (by any reckoning, one of the country's most widely read and puissant corporate English Dailies) for a story it did on him.

It must be understood that the charge of 'sedition' may be brought against a citizen of the Republic only by the highest political/constitutional authority of the land, and only for actions provenly prejudicial to the security of the state. In post-independent India, such charge has been brought, as far as we can ascertain, only against some officers in the military for allegedly leaking Intelligence to the 'enemy.'

Clearly, therefore, Mathur could not have been the sanctioning brain/authority behind such a charge. By no stretch even of the fascist imagination could a police commissioner be deemed the equivalent of the state. The defiance and the daring must belong to the Chiefton whose dirty work he has been brought back to do. Ergo, 'sedition' not against India, but against ' Modiland.' Since Modi alone may say with Louis xiv of old, 'I am the State.'

And basis for the charge?

True to the ethics and oath of the Fourth Estate, the *TOI* story drew attention to evidence that this Mathur has had links with the criminal underworld, and thus cannot be deemed eligible for the responsibility bestowed upon him by his obliging Chieftan.

As reported in The Hindu of June 2, '08, the basis of the *TOI* story on Mathur's antecedents was a statement given by an underworld denizen that the Commissioner was at one time on the 'Don's payroll.'

Whereas Mathur may well have instituted a case of libel/defamation against the *TOI*, remarkably the case filed accuses the newspaper editor of 'sedition and treason' against the state.

Not even during the dark days of the state of Internal Emergency imposed by the then Indira Gandhi government (1975-76) was, to the best of our knowledge, any member/organ of the Fourth Estate charged with 'sedition and treason.'

Indeed, two infamous instances that come to mind both pertain to the days of colonial rule.

I refer to the charge of 'sedition' brought against Lokmanya Tilak and then Mohandas Karamchand Gandhi, in both cases for writing articles calculated to cause 'disaffection' against the 'legitimate government of the day.' A charge which both those honourable men proudly acknowledged.

In Gujarat of our day, however, 'sedition' has come to mean any word or act that contradicts the myth of 'good governance' cheekily floated by Modi and gladly bought by his constituency, or any attempt to use public institutions to hold the Modi government to account.

Only two years ago, the editor of *Surat Samna*, Manoj Shinde was charged under section 124 A ('sedition') for commenting on the ineptitude of the authorities in handling the waters of the Ukai dam, which caused flooding in the city of Surat. The charge spelt out was that Shinde had instigated people against a duly elected government! (*The Hindu*, 30 August 2006).

Animal Farm? *1984*? Take your pick.

And to think that Orwell imagined that totalitarian habits of mind existed only in 'totalitarian' states. Consider in passing that a Tory Member of Parliament in Britain, name of David Davis, has resigned his membership following the adoption of the new draconian law that will allow the state there to hold in custody anyone for 42 days without trial. The vote may have passed by a majority of just nine, but many in Britain are alarmed that with a plethora of draconian laws in place, including the world's largest data base of citizens's DNA , an I-Card dispensation, and CCTV cameras reaching literally into bedrooms, liberty in that mother of democracies is losing out to the state. David Davis now goes into a bye-election of his choosing to test how Britains feel on these issues. We, on behalf of those who wish the world to be free, also wish him luck.

Alas, no such prospects in Gujarat.

II

You can be sure that nothing that has been said thus far qualifies as hyperbole. The Gujarat Chieftain has now ventured a bolder leap forward in announcing that his realm, after all, may remain autonomous of the union and the constitutional regime of laws that govern its operations.

He has dared the Indian government at the Centre to withhold grants to his state, and be prepared to suffer the loss of tax revenues due to it from Gujarat. Any student of india's pre-Independence history will recognize that such indeed used to be the nature of hostile discourse among the then autonomous Princely States and Subbas and between them and any central authority that might exist for the time being.

As has been rightly pointed out by some political and constitutional spokespersons, if there be any smell of 'sedition' in the air, this must be it. So what does anybody do ?

III

The central government of course can always take recourse to the provisions of article 356 of the Constitution, declare the Modi government in violation of constitutional governance, and lawfully sack it.

This was something that many well-wishers of the Republic would have gladly endorsed had such a recourse been taken to at the time of the Modi-endorsed Gujarat massacres.

But ofcourse with a friendly NDA regime, led by Modi's own BJP, then in power in Delhi, nothing could have been farther from expectation. Famously, Atal Bihari Vajpayee, the then Prime Minister, went the length of recommending that Modi in Gujarat follow *Raj Dharma*, i.e. the ethics of good rule. It was a good laugh, streaked in many places with the blood of innocents.

Since that time the politics of the country has taken several new twists, but chiefly a lurch to the right in which Modi's BJP and the Congress party are equally complicit.

The Congress particularly has been rendered weak by a string of electoral losses especially to the BJP, as the country's middle sections, in town and country, viewing market 'reforms' with a gluttonous eye, draw away from the Congress for initiating a string of social programmes directed at the welfare of the minorities, Muslims in particular, and other weaker sections of Indians.

The proverbial idealism of the young – especially those that have any saleable value – directs itself increasingly and rather exclusively to what 'packages' the corporates have on offer, or what opportunities are to be exploited in the western world. Those that can play cricket look to the IPL (Indian Premier League in which each side plays just a quick-fire twenty overs each against enormous sums of money paid) as the possible high point of a successful life. Conversely, many young students who fail their examinations or do not do to 'expectations' commit suicide, thinking that life can have no success to offer.

Cannily, Modi has during the last assembly elections especially (2007) cast himself as the messiah of 'development', never mind that such development leaves the bulk of Gujaratis as out of reckoning as ever. For those that wield social and economic clout, the admixture of lucre and Hindu pride – visible everywhere in the shape of a sock-in-the-eye display of religiosity, is the winning formula, one that seems to promise salvation both here and in the hereafter. All mightily bolstered by the tribe of NRIs abroad (some 40% of the American ones are Gujaratis) who see this fusing of money and mantra as the way to hegemonise all of the Indian middle classes generally.

No time then would seem more inappropriate/inauspicious for the Centre than now to take recourse to dismissing the Modi government.

IV

If Gujarat is to be reintegrated with the Republic there is only but one way to go: the hard way.

Given that the Congress, the main political opposition in Gujarat, has been effectively reduced to impotence as the constituency for secular politics has shrunk, in no small measure owing to the complicity of the Congress itself, and to the extent that the Congress has long forgotten the culture of mass mobilization through effective organization on the ground and sweat in the doing, there is little to be looked for there as of now.

That fact indeed brings into sharp and admirable focus the toils of those in Gujarat who have through these six years sought on the basis of relentless home work and fearless conviction to bring the Modi dispensation to book – civil society groups and a configuration of socially sensitive, journalists, artists and other intellectuals for the most part. Aided, no doubt, by the highest court in the land.

Working through the Supreme Court and the media – some sections of it – their achievements in unraveling the horrendous excesses and transgressions of Modi-rule constitute the high-watermark of the history of human rights struggles of the last decade or so.

Yet, this is only a resource; the antidote to the misuse of democratic franchise and legitimacy by Modi can only lie in mounting a more cognizant polity in and outside Gujarat.

Unless, beginning now, for a whole year or more, an integration and consolidation of media power, social service resources, labour power, and party-political rethinks happen, such as are able to produce a questioning centre-left transformation on the ground on the concrete issues of livelihood and equity, and so long as Modi remains at the helm of the BJP in Gujarat, the secession of the state from the Republic will only deepen.

Gujarat, after all, has come to represent for the RSS the possibility that the more the Congress goes into somnambulant and aristocratic dotage, the more unable it is to distinguish itself from the ideological contours of the BJP, the more reluctant it remains to ally with the left in launching mobilization against fascist formations without thought to party constituencies, the more Hindutva fascism can forge ahead towards reconstituting India into an erstwhile Nepal – a Hindu Rashtra (Theocratic Hindu state). Recall that it has been in the past the position of the RSS that the best thing to happen to Bharat would be for the Hindu Kingdom of Nepal to take the country into an amalgamated oneness!

V

For now, the charge of 'sedition' leveled against the *TOI* in Gujarat – and another case under section 153 (A) (B) of the IPC – causing schism among communities – against the well-known sociologist, Ashish Nandy, for an article he wrote, also in the *TOI* bemoaning the character of the middle class with respect to Gujarat, an experience that might help this particular intellectual to rethink some of his favourable consideration of Hindu religious identity and distaste for left politics – do provide an opportunity for wide sections of the polity to launch a campaign for the restoration of secularism and fundamental freedoms in Modi's Gujarat.

It is a circumstance that could assist media corporates who have habitually held up Modi as the ideal future Indian hero (for three understated reasons, it might be noted: his friendliness to big business, his rabid hatred of the left, and his ability to galvanise Hindu-communal politics to ward off both labour consolidation and keep potential 'terrorists' in fear and trembling, leaving the local terrorisers under his command to do their work unfettered) to cry off a bit, and suggest to Modi that secession on his behalf is as unacceptable as anywhere else in the country, if not more. Having now added draconian daring to fundamentalist/communalist politics, the media ought to make it known that Modi may not after all be such a darling.

After all, for many of them it is still in fashion to revile the late Indira Gandhi for her 'authoritarianism'; who more so, she or Modi? She did not cry 'sedition' even when the draconian Emergency regime could have legally allowed her to do so; he it seems can do it in broad daylight and with fearless impunity against those whose job it is to keep democracy and the rule of law in place.

If Modi can haul up something like the *TOI* with a charge of 'sedition', pray who is safe?

VI

Note that in Maharashtra one of the most respected and fair-minded senior journalists, editor of Loksatta, Kumar Ketkar, was attacked in the privacy of his home by fascist hordes who did not like his advice to the local government that, rather than spend hundreds of crores on erecting a statue of Shivaji somewhere in the sea, the moneys could be better spent on relieving misery among the people.

Subsequently, the Editors' Guild of India took up the issue and made out a decent statement.

Yet, why the 'sedition' charge leveled against the *TOI* in Gujarat seems a rather muted item is tough to understand. It is ofcourse possible that unbeknown to this writer some strong things are afoot.

One certainly hopes so; and afoot in many places and conclaves.

June 2008

Three Men in a Quandary

Democracy, Who Needs It?

Ah, the travails of high office.

The cruelest thing being that, once elected, Presidents and Prime Ministers should be expected to honour what a majority of the citizens feel or think about issues.

Nothing more debilitating than that the exercise of executive power should be cribbed and confined by the nit-picking sentiments of petty reason and common sense.

Nature may break the levees and uproot whole populations, but Presidents and Prime Ministers may not. You might well ask what is a President or Prime Minister for, if the little fellows should cussedly latch on to the sandbags of suspicion and sanity.

II

George W. Bush: ah, would he not give the remainder of his brain for that world-historical strike on the 'evil empire' called Iran. Imagine, if that other past President who was a True Man could blast away in Japan, thereby rendering the world free of a whole wrong-headed nation, why can't George W. do the same?

Having so conclusively cleaned up the evil in Iraq and Afghanistan, what a grand finale Iran would make.

No more black turbans, no more terrorists; only Exxon, Shell, Chevron and so on everywhere, carrying forward the story of human advancement.

Alas, but no, because an undemocratic majority of some 70 per cent fellow countrymen will not stand for it. And do you know why? Because more Americans feel dispirited now than at any time since the great Wall Street Crash. Indeed the death of patriotism, what else?

Recent polls show – damn those pollsters – that the always bubbly, always forward-looking Americans seem baffled that destiny no longer seems to obey American diktat.

The Associated Press-Ipsos poll has only some 17 per cent thinking that their country is going in the right direction; a figure that sinks to only 14 per cent in the ABC News-Washington Post survey.

Thus, at the least, some 83 per cent Americans seem to have chickened out, and for the pettiest of considerations:

- rocketing gas prices;
- sinking home values;
- astronomical air fares, college tuitions, health care;
- long term food scarcity caused by diversion of cropland to alternate fuel feeds;
- tripled price of rice, leading to riots and rationing in some places;
- defeat and disaster in Iraq and Afghanistan, and the loss of precious white American lives;
- the loathing with which America is now viewed in most parts of the world, with only the Indian middle classes and NRIs standing firmly loyal;
- and, as some sort of divination, the great Mississipi and sundry rivers breaking levees one after the other, storms and tornadoes rampant, destroying millions of acres of cropland, not to speak of whole habitations.

Not for a minute do Americans stop and think that whereas, now in his last year of office, there is little that their President may realistically be expected to do to remedy these petty-fogging irritations of common life, he may at least be encouraged to order that last ride of the B-52 and drop that cleanex over Tehran so that a lastingly unforgettable contribution is made to the peace and well-being of the world.

Democracy, thy name ought to be headache. None of which of course means that the almighty President cannot say to himself how democracy ends when elections conclude, however flamboyantly Floridal. After that, the American President may say, as American Presidents often have said, 'I AM THAT I AM.'

III

Here in India are the two cases of a sulking Prime Minister, and another also sulking because he would be Prime Minister.

More than a year ago, taking the full load of national worry on his economical shoulders, Prime Minister Manmohan Singh went to America, where else, and signed off a 123 Agreement with George W.

Suddenly, we were invited to see the uranium lights left, right, and centre: cars and buses, trains and aeroplanes, running on uranium batteries; domestic gadgets, even children's toys in time, powered by uranium cells; computers and machines, turbines and turnstiles running non-stop on uranium chips; and lots and lots of uranium left over for bombs dime a dozen. Result: end of pollution, endless energy, end of the Chinese threat, all of India incandescent with uranium bulbs and chandeliers. And all of that with only some seven-to-nine per cent of India's total energy output coming from uranium by circa 2020! Ah, Reason, thou art gone among the beasts.

Narry for a moment could he imagine that this particular world-historical signature could come up for as much cacophonic outrage as it has since done. Ah, again, the nettled darts that lurk everywhere in the dark corners of democracy. And most of them against the self-evident 'national interest'.

Questions asked:

- What of the Hyde Act that disallows reprocessing, mandates Presidential certification every year, forbids testing, – or if you do test, we shall take back whatever uranium and other stuff we may have given to you, – ordains an Uncle Sam-dictated foreign policy (thou shalt not side with Iran, sign agreements on energy with them even when that might indeed be the better option for you, thou shalt recast thine foreign policy always to be 'congruent' with American interests, ensure 'inter-operability' of thine military with American forces, training thine soldiers to use American weapons to facilitate such 'inter-operability', send them wherever Sam thinks they are needed, especially wherever the 'Islamists' need to be liquidated, always keep thy infrastructure readied for use by American airforces and such like, give preference to American corporates in the matter of setting up nuclear reactors, embrace American sailors and retailers alike – Walmart shalt make thee smart)?

- Is it so clever to rely so exclusively on a country that has the world's most brutally poorest record of reliability? One that relies on us to refurbish its economic well-being and to spread its tentacles throughout Asia, shooting from an obliging Indian shoulder, or more expeditiously, from the Indian hip?
- Is it not more sensible to mend our fences and deepen our cooperation with our neighbours, especially in the Middle East, and tested allies, both for economic and political reasons?
- Why is it we refuse to sign the tripartite gas procurement deal with Iran and Pakistan, when patently not nuclear energy but hydrocarbons alone can in the foreseeable future guarantee our overall growth?
- Why do we not mine the large stocks of uranium we have in Meghalaya and elsewhere, if uranium it is we need?
- Where is our sense of urgency about the well-thought-out three-stage thorium technology?
- What do we mean to do with the massive stocks of coal we have, if not use them to produce energy? And what of harnessing our inexhaustible hydel sources?
- How affordable will be whatever energy is produced by nuclear reactors? At present calculations, three times that from thermal and hydel? Who will buy it – Indians, some 77 per cent of them – who spend less than fifty cents a day?
- And are nuclear establishments so safe only because you say so? Why doesn't America have more of them than they do? Do you know that they do not explore more than some 6% of their territory even for hydrocarbons-one reason why the conquest of the Middle East is so crucial to them? Why spoil your greenery when there is a whole world to despoil, eh?
- And should you, Mr Prime Minister, be so adamant about this deal when it is backed neither by Parliament that gives you legitimacy, nor by people at large, except of course the classes that have fattened on neo-liberal economic policies to the detriment and immiseration

> of the masses, and who rarely get out to cast their vote, so serious-minded their commitment to democracy? What, after all, is your take on the meaning of 'democracy'?

Alas, for now, our Prime Minister seems only to be saying, give me my nuke deal, or I shall pack my wherewithal. And Democracy? Don't worry about that one; hasn't America taken upon herself/himself/itself to guarantee democracy throughout the world? What else has George W. been doing since that day in September?

IV

Tailpiece: third man in a quandary.

L.K. Advani, formally the Leader of the Opposition in Parliament, and informally the head of the Bharatiya Janata Party, is past eighty. So, come on India, I ain't got much time. By general consensus, I am the cunningest of them all, so make me Prime Minister please any which way you like. If it is the Hindutva hardliner you like, such I am; if some secular façade be needed, remember I went to say hello to Jinnah!

And do not forget that that Justice Liberhan Commission which has been looking into my (Advani's, that is, folks) culpability in the crime of the demolition of the Babri mosque, and the courts in Lucknow and Bareilly doing the same, could soon turn in a verdict of guilty. Then what happens, I ask you?

Surely, the only best way to forestall all that is that you make me Prime Minister first.

And that wretched monster, Democracy, is still unlikely to oblige. Indeed, in nearly all polls conducted over the years on the question as to who are the fit candidates for the post (of Prime Minister), Advani has usually brought up the rear between one and nine per cent – cuttingly, below even that neophyte, Rahul Gandhi.

Which is why the classes invariably say how democracy is always inimical to merit, and has neither eyes to see nor a brain to consider.

And the people? They surely need to be changed, in both great Democracies of the world – America and India. Else, better that the aliens come.

June 2008

India's Roughshod Ruling Class

Manmohan Goes Washington

I may not be accused of ever having written a good word about L.K.Advani, the leader and now projected prime ministerial candidate of the Hindu-rightwing Bharatiya Janata Party.

Now is the time to make amends.

In an elaborate interview given to the redoubtable N. Ram of *The Hindu* (12 July 2008) – easily the most literate of India's premier English Dailies – Advani has rightly pointed out that, in contrast to the current UPA regime, the NDA under Vajpayees' premiership desisted from pushing such agendas that did not form a part of the manifestoes of any constituent party of the NDA coalition.

The nuclear explosion at Pokhran, for example, was undertaken by that regime because the BJP's wish to 'go nuclear' had first been vetted and endorsed by its partners in the NDA.

Contrarily, Hindutva-related items such as building that Ram Temple at Ayodhya at the site of the demolished Babri mosque, enforcing a Common Civil Code on all Indian citizens (in substance, imposing Hindu social laws on India's Muslims), and deleting Article 370 from the Constitution (thereby ending the 'Special Status' of the Jammu & Kashmir State – a covenant on which the accession of the state to India was established in the first place) were scrupulously left out of the NDA's programme of governance.

Notwithstanding the political effort of the BJP to keep such issues alive and ready-at-hand, mainly through propaganda and pogrom, it must be conceded that the NDA regime made no attempt formally to implement communal agendas that were unacceptable to its participants in government.

II

Now.

Contrary to my inability through the years to favour anything at all that L.K. Advani (and his party) have stood for or done, in or out of government, I have on more than one occasion spoken up for the President of the Indian National Congress, Sonia Gandhi, both when her *locus standi* – culturally and politically – has been under crude racist and xenophobic attack, and later in praise of her selfless concern and dignity on behalf of the nation and its deprived masses.

Alas, in the context of the Indo-US civil nuclear deal, and the parting of ways with the left parties without whose support – as she has acknowledged just yesterday in a meeting of the UPA coalition – the present government could not have been constituted in the first place, that she should have allowed herself and the party to be sulk-twisted into a course of action that formed no part of the Common Minimum Programme drawn up with the left, that one feels goes against her best reading of where the welfare of the Republic resides, and that is likely to affect a disastrous paradigm shift in India's sense of herself and of her equations with the rest of the world.

And all that by a Prime Minister who has yet to be elected to the House of the People, the Lok Sabha. (See my 'Deal or Democracy' for a detailed comment on these issues.)

It should be recalled that the nuclear deal arrived at between the Indian Prime Minister and the American President (July 18, 2005) happened just one unseemly month after a report in the USA Today (June 19, 2005) which read as follows:

> More than 26 years after a near melt-down at the Three Miles Island nuclear power plant, the Senate is considering an energy bill that includes financial incentives for construction of nuclear plants. It's the latest sign of the industry's quiet rehabilitation. (See J. Sriraman, 'A Raw Deal for India', *Truthout*, 9 July, 2008).

The USA Today further noted that "the Nuclear Energy Institute's political action committee had contributed $76,376 to (Congressional) candidates so far" the bulk to Republicans but also to Democrats like

Tom Carper of Delaware, Ben Nelson of Nebraska and Mary Landrieu of Louisiana.

Sriraman notes that the "Energy Policy Act of 2005 included an array of incentives, amounting to billions of dollars, designed to promote nuclear power."

Nuclear 'experts' contended that business with India and China would usher in a 'domestic renaissance in nuclear power.' These experts also argued that nuclear cooperation with India would promote India's 'strategic power' as a counterbalance to China – something that Indian experts remain skeptical about.

Is it any wonder then that the Bush administration should so assiduously push the Indo-US nuclear deal, knowing that its corporates (who have not built a reactor at home in 35 years) stand to make a killing they haven't made in half a century. Or that sundry nuclear corporate CEOs should be camping in India for more than a year now, and, in coordination with the American embassy in Delhi, be arm-twisting Indian policy makers to get on with it.

Secondly, the deal bears the promise of inveigling India into the non-proliferation regime, even as the stipulations on the non-use of plutonium issuing from imported uranium puts paid to, or effectually retards, India's thorium technology.

And most importantly, the macro-contexts of the deal further promise – as explicitly provided for in the enabling Hyde Act – to draw India into a lasting 'congruence' with American foreign policy interests worldwide.

III

So what does India get out of the proposed deal?

If by India is meant some 78% of its people who live on less than 50 cents a day, the answer is zilch.

That for the reason that, even after everything were to go as projected, the output from nuclear energy would be some 7-9% of India's total energy output by the year 2020!

And the cost of that energy, as has been pointed ad nauseum in recent debates, would be three times that of energy sourced from thermal or hydel materials.

Indeed, even India's famed middle classes may remain outside the requisite purchasing power. And India seems in no hurry to exploit its year-long sunlight for solar power, or its abundant wind resource for wind-driven power, or to prize its vast coal reserves for clean coal technology, or to harness its abundant water resources for enhancing hydel power. Indeed, the question has been asked as to why India refuses thus far even to mine the considerable uranium finds, if uranium is what she wants. Or why it is so embarrassingly tardy in clinching the Iran-Pakistan-India Gas pipeline project. Or in securing enhanced petroleum resources by participating in the ventures that beckon in Central Asian states through the aegis of the SCO.

But if by India is meant its corporates, much may be said for the deal. A projected enterprise of some 40 billion dollars is in the offing tantalizingly, and the 'new India' of global ambition waters at the mouth at the thought.

Not to speak of that other aspect of India's global ambition: by reserving some eight of its reactors for the 'strategic' sector, India desires now to multiply its bomb-making prowess to a point where, with strategic American collaboration it is in a position to bomb China out of existence.

And it is the very same India (is it, though?) that floated the vision of a non-nuclear world through universal disarmament even as late as 1988.

IV

The left in India has consistently argued that the nuclear deal is merely the thin end of an imperialist wedge that seeks to dismantle decisively what is left of India's posture of independence in the matter of conducting its foreign relations.

However righteously this may be protested by the present Indian government, the statement made by the Indian Prime Minister after his meeting with George W.Bush on the sidelines of the recent G-8 summit in Japan lets the cat out of the bag:

> Dr Singh said that he was 'very pleased with the state of our relationship, which has truly acquired the characteristic of a genuine *strategic partnership*' (emphasis added; *The Hindu*, July 10, 2008).

It is an instructive irony – one that illuminates the sanctity that the Manmohan regime attaches to commitments made to the supporting left at the time of government formation – that the phrase 'strategic partnership' was with mutual consent dropped from the draft of the Common Minimum Programme which was to become the covenant between the left and the UPA!

Manmohan went on then to detail some aspects of that partnership:

> We have made progress in all areas. We have progress in nuclear cooperation, space cooperation, defence cooperation, educational exchanges, our working together in multilateral institutions for the success of the Doha round (Ibid.)

That is an enumeration which ought to leave no one in any doubt that the new corporate-led India means squarely now to climb the American bandwagon, to draw military and sundry corporate stature from such a climb, and inevitably to conduct its foreign relations in close embrace with America and the Zionist lobby. Indeed, and ominously, the collaboration on making a success of the Doha round of the WTO negotiations potentially menaces the already besieged agricultural sector in India to the terminal detriment of those that live off agriculture and those that find agricultural produce already beyond their means.

Thus, if beginning 1990 the then Finance Minister of India, Manmohan Singh, inaugurated the liquidation of Nehruvian welfare economics that sought to draft the state on behalf of those that most needed its humanist interventions, in 2008 Manmohan Singh, now the Prime Minister, is busy liquidating that other falange of the Nehruvian legacy (one that did wonders in keeping Independent India safe from the predatory policy reach of both the West and the East), namely non-alignment and the sovereign right to pursue its foreign relations in the best interests of its impoverished peoples. (See Vijay Prashad, *The Darker Nations*, 2007).

Clearly, the much-abused concept of 'national interest' now comes to connote the interest not of the impoverished but of the rapacious consumerist classes. And the 'invisible hand' instead of 'trickling' only clenches more and more into a fist.

It is to be noted that inbetween, another Congress Prime Minister, the late Narasimha Rao, was to preside over the liquidation of that third of Nehru's articles of faith, namely the preservation at all costs of the secular state. Rao, often called the first BJP Prime Minister of India, was to quarantine himself in considered seclusion as the Babri mosque was pick-axed, piece by piece, by Hindutva hordes in a day-long uninterrupted operation, a crime against the constitutional Republic for which nobody has yet been punished some 20 years after!

V

I said at the beginning that these paradigmatic shifts have been underway during the leadership of a Prime Minister who has never yet been elected to the Lok Sabha.

No surprise then that the Indian democratic system per se seems now hostage to a new order of legitimacy.

Not the people but a clutch of CEOs drawn from across both the political and entrepreneurial segments succeed with each passing day in usurping the democratic space of governmental legitimacy.

Even as the left has withdrawn support to the UPA, well-known satraps of the new supporting party, the Samajwadi party, are already busy seeking changes in ministerial portfolios at the behest of known industrial magnates. Indeed, the remainder of the UPA tenure seems set to witness a contest among windfall-profit-making corporates, mediated through the Cabinet.

And we thought sovereignty rests in the people. More fool we.

It has been noted that India's political system remains severly handicapped by an absence of inner-party democracy (with the exception of the left parties); it should not be hard to imagine what further damage to the very idea of democratic legitimacy and democratic governance may be wrought by the new culture of authority that corporate clout and an obliging political system seem conjointly willing to impose on the Republic.

All that betokening cliques and lobbies whose interests require that as little of policy making is made transparent to the people as can be. No more resonant instance of that than the current fiasco wherein the Congress-led UPA sought the allegiance of the left parties to the nuclear deal without as much as showing them the draft of the agreement drawn between the Indian government and the IAEA. The pretext that the draft was a 'privileged/classified' document has now been exposed by no less than members of the IAEA board of governors – past and present – who have clearly stated that such documents become privileged only when the text is adopted by the IAEA board. Prior to that happening it is for the member countries to do as they like with the draft!

All this by a government which is rightly lauded for having given to the Republic its first ever Right to Information Act!

VI

These shenanigans around the nuclear deal, though, have performed one useful function: they have pushed into the background the misery confronted by India's poor – some 78% of the population – as a result of galloping inflation and rising food process.

A circumstance that speaks eloquently to where the priorities of the government lie.

The less said about the state of policing and law and order in town and country the better.

It will be interesting to see how the electorate of India in the coming general elections pronounces on these occurrences. Will they simply go from frying pan into fire and vote the right-wing BJP, or can the left stand to gain from a fight it has put up through a staunch adherence to principle and argument. Or is India doomed to produce another pot pourri that may nicely become amenable to further ravages of opportunist dismantling.

Be it said that the elections of 2009, supposing that the Manmohan government survives the trust vote due to take place on the 21st and 22nd of July, will be a watershed one.

July 2008

Georgia and the End of Unilateralism

> Saddam Hussain, of course, deserved to be hanged for destroying several Shia villages, whereas Georgian leaders who have wiped out towns and villages, and sent tanks rolling over women and children, must be taken under protection.
>
> Vladimir Putin

As the Soviet Union collapsed under the combined auspices of internal folly and external manoeuvre, the world was suddenly left with but one single dinosaur in the jurrasic park.

Over the last two decades or so, its unbridled big foot has been rampaging beyond land and sea, foraging without let or hindrance.

Recalling its mentor, Nietzsche – rather than the disingenuously invoked Jesus – its maw, full of teeth, has been yelling out to the world how ethics and morality are weapons of the weak, and how the pre-eminently strong must forge ahead to fulfil their 'manifest destiny' and rid the world of those that whine but do not win. After all, Dionysus ordained that true justification underwrites only those that have the power to annihilate.

And how indeed this lone dinosaur has been annihilating.

II

It is said that once the devil sat in the front row of a class on moral philosophy. At the conclusion of class, he said as follows to the illustrious speaker: "thanks, sir, for telling me all about moral philosophy; now I know what to avoid."

Nothing glosses as well what the military-corporate American state has been doing to the farewell lecture that Eisenhower gave to the nation in 1961:

> This conjunction of an immense military establishment and a large

> arms industry is new in the American experience... We must not fail to comprehend its grave implications. Our toil, resources, and livelihood are all involved; so is the very structure of our society. In the councils of government, we must guard against the acquisition of unwarranted influence, whether sought or unsought, by the military-industrial complex. The potential for the disastrous rise of misplaced power exists and will persist. We must never let the weight of this combination endanger our liberties or democratic processes.

It is to be noted further that in the penultimate draft of that address, Eisenhower used the term 'military-industrial-Congressional complex,' thereby underlining, prophetically indeed, the role the Congress plays in propagating the 'military-industrial complex.'

For two decades now, the Pentagon, the neo-con White House, and the 'patriotic' Congress have been implementing an agenda that has constituted as frontal a reversal of Eisenhower's message as the one voiced by the devil in the moral philosophy class.

III

And much of that has been done as the devil quotes the Bible – namely in the pursuit of 'democracy' and 'freedom' throughout the world, but chiefly in those parts where the oil and the gas have been the thickest.

It is no coincidence that the collapse of the Soviet Union and the forging of the Washington Consensus should have been closely overlapping events.

All guns now firing without fear of reprisal, all that the neo-con military-industrial state needed to do was to put in place an 'international' accord that would allow the freest rein to American corporates to ravage the resources of the world.

Thus 'globalization' came to be a sexy euphemism for the unfettered pursuit of American capitalism, construed no doubt as the American 'national interest.'

The new diktat being that finance capital (but not labour) must have free access to all parts of the globe, nation-states and national sovereignty must be rendered anachronistic concepts, capital must establish its obliging clients among governments of the world, and wherever resistance occurs, the dinosaur must leap, maim, kill, and gobble. All of which it has been doing with relish.

IV

The faithful can, however, take heart from the formulation that however Nietzsche strives he does run again and again into some likeness of Jesus.

That likeness was first to be brewing among the American people themselves; over the years they have come to recognize that the 'military-industrial-Congressional complex' has after all done them no great good. Far from strengthening democracy, security, and prosperity, it was endangering and depleting all three at home, even as it was making a bonfire of all three in the wider world which it was claiming to save.

The final and unkindest fruit: an astronomical rise in fuel and food prices and a full-blown recession in the land of the brave and the free. Thus much for the touted economic fruits of the Washington Consensus and Globalisation.

A further assertion of the moral law was to come forth in the shape of puppet-dictators ('our sons of bitches,' remember?) tumbling all over, first in the 'backyard' in South America, then everywhere else. Indeed, the last of these next door here to India, a man called Musharraf. Consider that nothing that the neo-con states' satraps could do was to prevent the congenial Hindu monarchy in teeny-weeny Nepal from falling into those hated red hands. And replacements for the falling puppets nowhere in sight either.

Curiously, and with fitting poetic-political justice, these realms were indeed to go over to genuine democracy (unlike the sponsored colour 'revolutions' in the erstwhile Caucasian regions) – something that the 'complex' had not intended in the least.

And small thanks from the Iraqis and the Afghans for neo-con labours of love . So much for gratitude.

And now, news from Georgia reads to say that the good St.George may after all have turned coat and gone over to the 'enemy' as well. But didn't we say that the gods desert the losers as much as sundry rats do? So no surprise there too.

V

This practitioner of quotidian concerns had vouched some two years ago that the safety of the little man is perhaps best guaranteed when the jurrasic park remains inhabited by at the least two Dinos instead of just a prodigal one. (see my 'Give Us Back the Manichaean,' *Mainstream*, Vol.

xliv, No.28, New Delhi, July 1, 2006). Say what you like, but democracy flourishes only when there are two sides to a question. After all, to be human means to be racking one's brain in some perpetuity between God and Satan. Were there to be more sides in course of time, how much better that would be.

It now seems that the Russian Federation, studiously avoiding any relapse into an erstwhile Soviet Union, has nonetheless acquired again the size and shape of that second Dino. A steady happening that seems to have left the other in Washington rather in the dark as to its newly-confident proportions.

The Georgian event suggests that it now answers not as the mating call of a 'strategic partner' but rather more gruffly to recall to its other that day in Yalta when the big three had agreed to divide the world into 'spheres of influence.' And to say that the Caucasus was indeed too far from Washington to be construed any part of the latter's sphere of influence.

Thus, poor Saakshavilli has been discovering that not only was it a folly to undertake the shenanigans that he did in South Ossetia at he behest of a mentor far far away, but that the European Union that falls inbetween will not as much as criticize Russia for giving him such a bloody nose in double quick time. Here is how Stefan Steinberg was to report on the meeting of the EU foreign ministers in Brussels:

> Despite intense pressure from a number of Eastern EU states, supported by...Great Britain and Sweden, the declaration issued by EU foreign ministers meeting in Emergency session in Brussels on Wednesday to discuss the conflict between Georgia and Russia refrained from any criticism of Russia. (World Socialist Web Site, 15 August 2008)

Indeed, the German foreign minister, Steinmeier, made it clear that 'stability in the Caucasus' could be achieved only through cooperation with Russia.

And a good reason too why the EU says what it says; after all, close to 40% of all its Gas and Oil supplies now come from Russia through the Caucasus pipelines. Unable or unwilling to do an Iraq in Georgia, the EU sensibly decides that it is best to co-exist with things on the ground.

VI

On its part, the Russian Federation seems to have made up its mind to stand up to the Dino in Washington. Remembering Kosovo, it justly argues that the very same cookie crumbles in South Ossetia and Abkhazia. And if the Washington Dino dares send its brood into those parts then so be it. Music indeed to helpless ears.

What we say is how lovely that some balance of terror is back in reckoning after two decades of unmitigatedly one-sided loot and mayhem. A renewed cold war anyday better than a unilateral neo-imperialism gone berserk. And as Medvedev and Putin get ready, Hu Jin Tao cannot be far behind, since they do have in place that thing called the Shangai Cooperation Organisation.

All this, of course, must leave that belated neo-con adulator in New Delhi somewhat out on a limb. Imagine that the Dino in Washington should be losing its teeth just when the whiz kids in New Delhi were hoping to emulate something of its bite. Johnny come too late, it transpires.

But what we say to the good man, Manmohan, is think again. Never too late to retract a folly.

As nation-states are set to be back in contention, as globalization crumbles from within and without, as masses of people everywhere, including in America, see through the neo-imperialist smoke-screen and resolutely gather in revolt (all you need to do is to look around any Indian city or state to know the truth of that), the wise man is one who backtracks and returns to safe and acceptable ground.

Georgia after all has proved the messy marshland in which the Washington Dino's big foot is now caught many fathoms deep.

If Hindu philosophy teaches a Spenglerian lesson – that the Cartwheel turns and turns, and each time returns to where it had touched ground – then the bright minds in New Delhi's South Block may have that lesson awaiting them from the Georgian event.

And no one as bright as the one who learns in time.

August 2008

Conversions

Now, as Miss Austen would have said, it is a truth universally acknowledged that India is the world's largest democracy.

What, however, is less well-known is that it is also the most sinuously adjustable.

Take any of India's political parties – excluding the ossified left which remains unprofitably wedded to principle, although the principle may change from circumstance to circumstance – and you will find that its elected legislators may, whenever the paramount 'national interest' so requires, leave the party fold and conscientiously defect to a more winsome outfit.

And since all parties are happily agreed, atleast in private, that the 'national interest' does often demand such selfless departures, few questions that may tend to a negative read of such 'necessity' are ever seriously entertained.

For example:

Is it right that a politician elected on one platform of public trust jettison his/her covenant with the voter who elected him/her, or jettison his covenant with the particular party that gave him a ticket in the first place, and go over to another party that he/she may have infact roundly castigated during the campaign?

Should the democratic system permit such betrayal of public trust?

Or, put another way, allow political 'conversions' where public faith and hope are involved?

It may be the case that in that mother of all democracies, Great Britain, such conversions are pretty much unheard of; indeed there they have a party – the Liberal Democrats – who never seem to ever want to do anything nimble enough to bring them close to state power. Backward child of long standing.

But, in the scheme of evolution, Indian democracy is a later species, and one more adept at the all-important principle of survival, chiefly personal.

It is true that when legislators offer the supreme sacrifice of conversion from one political allegiance to another, the public cry foul. But it is equally true that few political animals worldwide are as adroit at persuading the public to the contrary as the Indian politician. Which is why, more often than not, they are re-elected from a new party, on a new ticket. Until the next one beckons.

II

Same is the case with the denizens of the companies and the corporates.

They may liquidate or merge with each other upon deep expert and managerial considerations, dictated, no doubt, by the country's best interests, even if often at lethal cost to the share-holders who aid them in the first place to come into existence.

As to the high-ups who run and flaunt these companies, who indoctrinate new recruits with the best principles of my- number- one, complete with frontier echelons of advertisers, commercial artists, and IT whiz kids, one never knows when the supreme economic well-being of brand Bharat may require any prominent CEO to be, Coriolanus-like, conferencing on behalf of corporate A in the morning and a rival corporate B the same afternoon.

Indeed, a superior executive who is seen to be hanging on to the same company for longer than time X invites the suspicion that he/she may not have much more to contribute to the health of the nation than is worth his/her current pay and perks package.

Like the enterprising politician, the company executive must be seen to be on the move, converting from one school of principles to the next, even if diametrically opposite ones.

Thus, among the money-makers and idea-spinners too 'conversion' is seen to be altogether of the greatest utility and consequence to the body politic.

That the body politic may know next to nothing of these rarefied goings-on, or may know that which contradicts the claims of the converted, or may often indeed be at the gruesome receiving end of clandestine entrepreneurial Chinese chequers (in the shape of lethal gas leakages, or polluted drinking water, or manipulated shortages and prices, or fraudulent medicines in the market, or financial transactions that bring several edifices down) only goes to prove that what we in a democracy call the true sovereigns, namely the people, are nine out of ten unteachable and best remain so.

III

Indian democracy has, however, repeatedly demonstrated that the one domain where 'conversions' are taboo is the that which involves neither public trust nor party loyalty but is a matter of exclusive personal persuasion. A schema sanctified by the Constitution of the Republic of India. That book of common prayer says that, contrary to the barbarisms of old, what gods you worship or do not worship is entirely your business and nobody else's.

Yet, when a citizen of India goes over from one religious faith to another, then it is, paradoxically you may well say, that the very foundations of the nation-state are shaken; then it is that public anguish may be wrought to a pitch that blood may flow, habitations go up in flames, and innocent men, women, and children be cut up like mutton for some conquering carnival.

If you don't know how, take a trip to Kandhamal in Orissa. There you will find the Gujarat of 2002 replicated with a fury that refuses to abate, and that the powers-that-be seem in no hurry to abate either. All too familiar.

And you thought India was a secular state. More fool you.

IV

The killers of Kandhamal answer as follows: they will not tolerate conversions brought about through 'inducements.' That is, all except their own kind. Naturally.

To wit, we are to understand that conversions from one political platform to another may well be humongously induced ones, conversions that through the years have, termite-like, gnawed into the very edifice of the state and polity, but since these can be argued to be in the 'national interest' no objection can be made.

We are likewise to understand that conversions of CEOs and whole conglomerates may indeed be even more humongously induced – often with ramifications that make inimical foreign agents stake-holders in the life of the Republic – but that the business of business, after all, is business. Think that after all India may be the only civilization where wealth is worshipped as a goddess rather than derided like Mammon. So when a Nano car runs down the highway, the occurrence not only may stir national pride but equally inspire the rag-picker to say 'vande mataram. What blessing that I am a rag-picker of this 'mahan Bharat' rather than of some lesser country.'

V

The conundrum of course is that unlike the top echelons of political outfits or of corporate board rooms who frequently turn coat themselves in the 'larger interest', the gods and prophets who have spawned various religious corporations never do put in an appearance.

It is thus their politic and permanent absence which leaves no choice to the managers of various faiths but to hold fast to red lines that were seemingly laid down forever. And to order murder and mayhem whenever such lines are deemed to be crossed.

Thus, how truly the Bard did say:

As flies to wanton boys
Are we to the gods;
They kill us for their sport.

And the gods having so decreed, how may a home minister here, or a chief minister there meddle in these matters. A loyal republic is one that must wait the next incarnation. Then, automatically, police reform, judicial reform, educational reform, administrative reform, ideological reform shall descend upon the South Block, and the letters s e c u l a r i s m be rendered sufficiently incandescent for the government to see.

Pending that momentous happening, you may not convert from one faith to another, even if we grab your land, burn and slash your patch of forest, rape your women if you do put up resistance – or even if you don't, bar you from our drinking water well, and from entry into the temple (which god knows why you wish to enter in the first place), deny you education, food, medicine, or kick your teeth in if you dare be standing while we pass.

You are neither a politician nor a CEO; so you will not convert upon inducement even of a loaf of bread, a word of dignity, a promise of brotherhood, an assurance of nursing in your disease, or of equal right to a pint of water when your thirst so maddens you.

And if you do, our hordes shall surely descend under full protection of the majesty of the state.

Then when you come crawling, we shall spit on you and convert you back – all in one spiritual go.

September 2008

Fighting Terror the Terrorist Way

Who doesn't know how the capitalist social order has worked from day one?

By first causing monumental social upheavals in the pursuit of profit maximization, then recommending quick-fixes guaranteed to spawn still worse upheavals so that more profitable quick-fixes are in turn rendered 'necessary.' And all these rooted in technologies of the newest kind that tell us what we always needed to solve our problems.

In those processes of declension, is it any wonder that the final quick-fix that we are offered should be the gun? After all, let us please remember that the biggest enterprise worldwide is the arms industry, and the biggest insurance for the continuance of this order of things not the end of warfare but its assured continuance in myriad forms and theatres. The better things get for the capitalist class, the more they must remain the same for all the rest. And nothing ensures that result as well as warfare in perpetuity.

The coterminous 'spiritual' trick that capitalism of course employs is to ascribe all social upheavals to the 'sinful' nature of man – those opposing capitalism more sinful than others – rather than to its own ascertainable doings. An ancillary part of capitalist ideology, so to speak, that then finds a central role for church, mosque, and temple, and takes the wretched of the earth away from either addressing rationally the sources of their condition or putting up a fight.

II

Thus it is that a resurgently capitalist class in India is today howling for a new, 'tough terror law' that would forever make propertied India safe for super-powerdom. Switch to any corporate TV channel, especially the ones in English, or read most corporate print media, or visit any upwardly-mobile urban elite home, and you will find but one strident recipe for fighting terror; namely, be like the terrorist and give them their own medicine. Only the Muslim terrorist of course, needless to say. Are there any others?

This would be fine if only it worked.

The minute, however, you pose that question another ready answer follows: look at America – not a single terrorist strike there after '9/11'. Ergo, why can't we be like America in every conceivable way, down to the colour of the toilet paper?

Not that we are not getting there, with the 'strategic partnership' (read military collaboration) now in place, buttressed by junk consumerism, instinctual anti-Islamism/pro-Zionism, contempt for socialist ideas (retaining nonetheless the appellation 'socialist' in the preamble of the Constitution, rather like the residual tailbone at the end of the human spine), a mighty embrace of an increasingly lethal majoritarian religiosity, professional therapy for stresses and tensions, the neighbourhood gym or godman as the answer to moral fatigue and vacuity, belief in infinite possibility for the 'endowed' and karmic fate for the misery-ridden, waving the flag in the face of the sanest criticism and so forth.

Most of all, avoiding at all cost the reading of needlessly complex or critical materials that do not straightforwardly endorse the American life-style, or that drag us into considerations that have no understandable bearing on our corporate pay packages, or cloistered dens of comfort. Or, that dampen gratification with any insidious invitation to gravitas, or take our plastic smiles and sniggers away even for a bit. To wit, hey, why can't we be like animals – kill, eat, defecate, copulate, and leave all the rest to god and nature. Gargantua, Gargantua, thou art the best.

It is another matter that, as we write, god and nature (Lehman and Hurricane Ike?) seem yet again confronted with the 'spectre of Marx.' Although, be sure, we can well meet all that with a strike on some other part of the disloyal world, which, after all, remains happily full of 'enemies' but with assets we can use. Why else are we 'strategic partners' I ask you? Lehman may sink, but Pentagon is forever.

III

But, while we are about it, let us examine somewhat the 'let-us-fight-terror-as do-the-Americans' howl.

For a start, unlike India, America has never suffered a demographic division based on religious strife. Were you to mention the natives, that contention has been too conclusively resolved (the world's first ethnic genocide) to be considered an issue.

The American analogy, if one must be drawn, to the Indian Hindu-Muslim partition of 1947 resides in the American civil war fought on the question of race (concealing of course more nitty gritty interests, such as that of the north American need for cheap labour).

And if some sixty years after partition India is still saddled with a Hindu-Muslim question (thanks to those whose political cookies bake best in keeping that question alive), so is the race question in America some century and a quarter after the slave owners were defeated.

Indeed, where India's Muslims obtained rights of citizenship alongwith all the rest as the Constitution was framed, American Blacks had to wait for their's till a century after the end of the civil war.

And just as the Indian state remains, de facto, a Hindu-majoritarian one (everyday that passes reinforces that operative reality, especially since the demolition of the Babri mosque in 1992, the Constitution notwithstanding), the American state likewise remains, de facto, a White, Anglo-Saxon, Protestant state.

As to Muslims, whereas they constitute but some 0.5-1.00 percent of Americans, India has the world's second largest population of Muslims – a fact we need to remember as we speak of 'Islamic' terrorism and how the two countries must address that problem, if such it is.

In passing, another fact of great significance: while America battles 'Islamism' in the wide world, its own miniscule Muslim citizenry is treated with as little or as great favour by the state as any of its other immigrant minorities. Result: America has next to no 'Muslim problem' at home. One has met American Muslims who infact know as well as any other that what neocon America has been fighting is not 'Islamism' but the pre-emptive right to all the world's resources. Simple. All credit to them.

Therefore, our quality of engagement in that fight – if 'fight' it must be – is ab initio precluded from replicating procedures that America employs. After all, it is only the Indian lunatic fringe that recommends that, emulating neocon America vis a vis Iraq and Afghanistan, or the Zionists vis a vis the Palestinians, India as well should invade a Pakistan or a Bangladesh and rid itself of terrorism forever. Apart from the lunacy of the recommendation, don't we know how the invasion of Iraq and the conclusive murder of Saddam has ended 'Islamic' terrorism forever? Not only do we and the world know, but so do the Americans themselves! History's lessons are not lost entirely, even on the most thick-headed. It infact becomes clearer by the day that the whole purpose was not to defeat terrorism but to cause it – as in Afghanistan of the Soviet days.

Not only, then, is the Muslim situation in America nothing like it is in India, our vastly differing geo-political locations render all talk of let-us-go-the-yankee-way a pathetic expression of imbecility.

America on the north is contiguous with a friendly (friendly in terms of race, religion, and history, by and large) Canada, and in the south by a compliant and tamed Mexico. All the rest around is either the Pacific or the Atlantic. As to India I leave you to think.

IV

Then there are other fatally significant distinctions to be drawn.

Most independent assessments, including by associations of American Muslims themselves, suggest to us that America's Muslim citizens are not even by a long shot its most disgruntled or discriminated segments of population. That privilege continues to remain with Black Americans – a fact, as we know, of considerable interest and consequence in the American Presidential race now under way.

Alas, however, several official Indian reports (Gopal Singh and Justice Sachar reports, to name two of the most authentic ones) tell us that India's 160 million Muslims are both the most discriminated and disgruntled among Indians, indeed in terms of the bulk of basic livelihood and human development indices worse than Indian dalits (in older parlance, the Untouchables). And only the most thick-skinned would say that this situation owes entirely to India's Muslims themselves, even as Muslim-Indian leaderships do bear substantial guilt in the matter.

The brute fact is that the state, its law-enforcement agencies, its economic mechanisms and bureaucratic universe, its educational policy, its cultural vision, and its civil society – all have failed the Muslims in India.

To a point where only the other day one of India's most renowned citizens, actors, social activists, member of the upper house of parliament, and diehard secular daughter of a legendary diehard progressive and secular poet (the late Kaifi Azmi), namely, Shabana Azmi was reduced to voicing the personal fact on a TV channel that she has been unable to obtain a house in Mumbai because she is a Muslim!

Not to speak of the repeated majoritarian pogroms, culminating in the massacres of Gujarat in 2002. And the blatant partisanship of investigative agencies and governments at state and central levels to deliver chastisement as by law decreed to fearless vigilante fascios of right-wing Hindu organizations, or in rehabilitating with care, impartiality, and sustained comprehensiveness victims of the pogroms in question.

Never once have the state and its agencies sought in the last sixty years to generate mechanisms of democratic negotiation with Indian Muslims, barring of course pandering to their sectarian leaderships from time to time, especially when elections are due.

Never has any Indian government sought to enforce reforms and retraining among its policing apparatus with a view to giving to the Republic a law-enforcement structure that is decolonized, secularized, pluralized, and rendered sensitive to the social and human needs and realities of India's Muslims. Or for that matter of the bulk of India's downtrodden masses across communities.

Never in sixty years has India witnessed civil society movements driven by the long-term goal of social and cultural integration as between Hindus and Muslims inorder to facilitate their de-ghettoisation. Except of course of making the stereo-typical show of communal oneness at times of ritual and religious festivity. Were you to ask ten middle-class urbanite Hindus whether they have a Muslim friend, or have visited a Muslim home, you might at best get one to say 'yes.' And I may be exaggerating.

V

To return to the howl for the ultimate terror law, then.

In the late eighties and early ninetees there was in India such a terror law, called Terrororism And Disruptive Activities Act (TADA).

It stipulated preventive arrest, the presumption of guilt rather than of innocence, the admissibility of confessions made to the police during investigations (read third degree), the denial of bail and so on.

Result: conviction rate of less than 1% but unconscionable brutalization of human rights, as twelve year olds were booked for petty theft under the law, and left to rot without redress.

The Indian political party then to ask for its repeal was the right-wing Hindu, Bharatiya Janata Party (the party of Advani and Modi), then in the opposition.

Then came the NDA regime in 1998, led by the very same party; and promptly a new terror law was passed called POTA (Prevention of Terrorism Act).

While that law was on the books, India saw some of the most iconic terror attacks – on the Parliament, on the State Assembly in Kashmir, on the historic Red Fort in Delhi from whose ramparts the Indian prime minister gives his or her ritual speech come every Independence Day (August 15), on the Akshardam temple in Gujarat and the Ragunath temple in Jammu.

But it was in Modi's Gujarat that POTA was put to full use. Following the Godhra train burning and the Gujarat riots, some 298 citizens were booked under the law; of them 297 were Muslims. The other we believe was a Sikh.

As at the time of the TADA, all that raised great stink; and the UPA, after it came to power in Delhi in 2004 repealed POTA as well.

So why now this renewed howl from the Hindu right-wing and its entrenched media sponsors for a new terror law?

Two objectives suggest themselves: one ofcourse to polarize the polity along communal lines and designate the Congress as an appeaser of the Muslim minority; all that because elections are due in four Indian states and soon to the Indian parliament as well.

And secondly, true to the capitalist pattern enunciated at the outset, to argue that Muslim terrorism bears no relation to relegation, ostracism, pogrom, injustice on behalf of state and polity but is plain and simple. wickedly and ahistorically ideological, seeking, would you believe it, to transform India into an Islamic theorcracy. Best thing therefore to pick them, whoever you can find, and lock them in, emulating Guantanamo and Abu Ghraib, without recourse to the liberal procedures of normal jurisprudence. Did not Indiana Jones once say, only good Indian is a dead Indian?'

Thus the quick-fix of the gun, disguised as the new 'tough terror law.' Not that the absence of such a law was to deter Modi in Gujarat from assenting to those infamous 'encounter' killings some of which planned murders are now before the highest court in the land, since Modi's police at the highest levels and the courts as well were found to be hopelessly complicit in delivering justice in all cases pertaining to the 2002 pogrom.

Logically, as the BJP seeks to foreground Modi – as at the just-concluded party National Executive in Bangalore – as the shadow Home Minister, he it is who is the loudest to demand that a 'terror law' passed by his Gujarat Assembly be granted assent by the central government in Delhi. To wit, the majority-Hindu vote bank is to see how things could change once Modi was at the helm of law-enforcement in the country. Frightening thought.

Simultaneously, the right-wing Hindu fascists who have been now caught in terrorist bomb-making of their own (in Nanded, Tenkasi, Kanpur, to name just three proven instances) are to be designated as 'nationalists' admirably meeting the 'terrorists' (read Muslims) on their own ground, and hence outside the purview of punishment under any sort of law. Just as currently they have been administering instant incendiary justice to Christians in Orissa and Karnataka, both states ruled by the BJP.

Like the invasion of Iraq, the purpose of the howl for a new terror law is not to address the problem, but to generate it more stridently. Once that happens, the Hindu right -wing can demonstrate how Muslims can never be trusted to be loyal citizens of the Republic of India.

VI

Till so long as India's problem with 'terrorism' was one whose sources lay outside Indian territorial boundaries, one instigated by the ISI in Pakistan, for example, there may have been an argument for the gun.

As Muslim resistance, born of a near-total distrust of the state's willingness or ability to deliver justice to them, builds within the country – not that there is to date any proven case of an Indian Muslim involved in a terror attack, myriad speculations to the contrary – the Indian state, political party system, think-tanks and the polity generally better think hard.

Does India need a new 'tough terror law', or is it time to look our horrendous culpabilities (enumerated by official reports, and known to everyone who cares) squarely in the eye, and to begin to recast the Republic and its institutional operations on a footing of uncompromising fairplay? Do we intend to be one with India's Muslims, or do we mean to make of them an 'other' for perpetuity, practicing a de facto Hindu Rashtra (Theocratic Hindu state)?

Especially, parties like the Congress must decide whether a quiescent pusillanimity and a regard for religions are sufficient anymore to qualify as 'secularism,' or whether some demonstrably hard departure needs to be made. To its credit, thus far it continues to argue against the howl for the terror law; but such is its malleability that there is no telling when it may say 'okay, if that is what you want.' And is its current resistance owing merely to its new alliance with the Samajvadi Party which banks on Muslims in Uttar Pradesh, or is there some further conviction that informs the Congress's resistance to the howl? Or, given the 'strategic partnership' it has forged with Bush's America, whether that may not oblige it to complement militarism abroad with a tough anti-Muslim terror law at home? Time will tell.

As to investigating terror, can a police apparatus and intelligence-gathering agencies that have next to no representation of Muslims at any mentionable levels of decision-making (even as none other than the right-wing Hindu BJP never tires of mouthing the politic cliché that 99.9% of Indian Muslims are loyal to India) be trusted to obtain the kind of human intelligence that alone can yield results adequate to prevention of episodes? Have we forgotten that Sikh-separatist militancy – was it called 'terrorism' then, or was that term made current and obligatory only by the event of '9/11'? – was defeated in the end not by the gun as much as by the cooperation and trust of the Sikh masses in the Punjab?

VII

A wider debate, then, needs to be conducted around the terror-law howl, a debate that goes beyond just the question related to Indian Muslims.

What sort of state is India, or does it wish to become? Why are those million mutinies brewing and in operation in state after state, mutinies quite unrelated to Muslims? Are some 800 million or more Indians simply ungrateful wretches, or has Indian Democracy failed them? Does the unabashedly wholesale tilt to the right and the unashamedly brazen subordination to neo-liberal imperialism bear the promise of redressing that failure or will it infact bring matters to a head from where few escape routes may remain? And does this nation-state have the will to take on those questions in rational, non-partisan, and non-sectarian terms, above and beyond party-electoral considerations?

And those questions are not being asked just by India's Muslims; they are also being asked by India's Christians, dalits, women, forest-dwelling tribals, disenfranchised oustees, landless farm labour, ethnic minorities. They are in the eyes of the hundreds of thousands of children who suffer malnutrition, abuse, denial of education, and whose lives expire prematurely from labour and disease. They are being asked, in short, by some 77% Indians who spend less than fifty cents a day.

Twenty percent India that howls for a 'tough terror law' will need to answer those questions, one way or another, sooner rather than later. For the shadows are lengthening, and Delhi is obviously not too far anymore.

September 2008

Sweet Time For the Left in India

This a short and quick one.

As the American neocon state borrows a whole sheaf from Chavez and other despised socialists, and stoops to nationalizing – yes, nationalizing – the great and invincible bulwarks of American capitalism, it underscores a theory of state that says government must stay out of business, but be ever and devotedly ready to bail it out of despair when its profit-maximising lust gets the better of it and the whole financial system.

In either circumstance, the common citizen must remain the chief guarantor of the profiteer's career. And, in any eventuality, profits must remain privatized, and losses patriotically distributed among the those that pay the tax dollar. The classes make profits out of the masses, and the masses save the classes when their Mammonite chips desert them. A man no less than Joseph Stiglitz has drawn the analogy: as the Berlin Wall was to Communism, the Wall Street has yet again proved to capitalism. Marx, are you there, and chuckling?

Whether or not the Indian neocons say it publicly, the shamefaced thought must certainly occur to them how fortuitous, after all, might have been their dependence on the left parties over some four years of its governance. Indeed, the Indian Prime Minister may privately be thanking his stars that he, in his own words, was a 'bonded slave' of the supporting left parties.

II

Think of what the Indian neocons wished to do when the UPA came to power in 2004, the very same things that the defeated BJP-led NDA regime had been busily doing and wanting to do with greater relish everyday:

- in line with the Washington Consensus and the class interest of the corporates, transfer as much national wealth as they rapidly could from public to private control;
- throw open the banking sector to foreign 'players' (never a more apt discourse than that – they who 'play' with people's earnings as children do with insects);
- throw open the Insurance sector similarly;
- make ordinary indians' hard-earned savings like Provident Funds available to the private 'players' at the stock market;
- disinvest government equity from the public sector in manufacturing and other sectors of the economy, and pass on equity to private investors;
- effect the convertibility of the Indian rupee on capital Account, so that instant hot moneys could be both brought in and taken out of the country as profits stood to be made or not in any part of the world; remember the East Asian bubble burst of 1997?
- bring in labour 'reform' so that moneys 'needlessly' spent on assured work -force could be cut by billions through contract hiring and firing, leaving still more for the private profiteer, a measure already in operation in many sectors;
- make land and infra-structure available at minimal costs to private builders in Special Economic Zones to do with as they like; a matter of great contention as we write;

and then think if all that had been allowed to happen without let or hindrance.

And what calumny the supporting left had to undergo day in and day out from sold-out pundits on sold-out corporate TV channels for standing firm on principle!

Which is why, as I said in another place recently, the left was in 'knowledgeable' metropolitan middle-class homes and the 'knowledgeable' media they frequent called an 'ossified' and unpatriotic roadblock to India's tryst with greatness (see my 'Conversions').

Kudos to the left – which could loudly take credit at this moment for having prevented India from sinking alongwith the new 'strategic partner'

– for not gloating 'we told you so' but, consistent with its admirable anxiety on behalf of India's national future and well being, simply feeling happy at duty done. Not that its battles in this regard are by any stretch of the imagination over.

III

If the neocon Indian leadership indeed has any shame left, or the least strength of mind to embrace some self-criticism, now is the time to acknowledge the above, and, equally importantly, to open its comprador mind to the left at home on another impending issue.

Namely, the matter of the nuclear 123.

Once again, after all the disingenuous water has flowed under the Indo-US deal-making bridge, Bush in his now much commented-on letter of determination to the Congress has confirmed to a hilt everything the left has been saying about the true nature of American intentions.

For a start, Bush makes the brazen declaration that the 123 agreement is merely a 'political framework' rather than a 'legally binding' document, notwithstanding what the Indian government may think or mouth everyday.

Thus, no assured guarantee of perpetual fuel supply for the reactors that American corporates are dying to ink, no rights of reprocessing spent fuel from such reactors, and no reprieve from perpetual safeguards even after the deal may have been terminated. Indeed, the prospect is one of buying another ten barren Tarapurs, if reports that a Letter of Intent has been given by the Indian government already for such purchases are to be believed;

Not just that, under pretence of doing India great and unique favour, the Bush regime means only to curtail its sovereignty with respect to nuclear strategic issues and bring it into an internationally-controlled non-proliferation regime.

It means to use this so-called favour to draw the Indian state into a military embrace fraught with the gravest long-term consequences for India, the region, and world balance of power. And, yes, 'balance of power' should be seen truly once again the germane way to describe what is rapidly happening to East-West relations and world-wide reverberations thereof. (See 'Georgia: the End of Unilateralism'). Something Indian policy-makers need to think about with alacrity as well, since it has bearing on the 123 deal and much else besides.

IV

As the Marriotr hotel in Islamabad burns at this very minute, consuming several foreign diplomats, and as the Indian bear-hug with Bush gets tighter, India – as much as Pakistan – needs to understand that such a hug is not a recipe for resolving the 'terrorist' problem but for exacerbating it.

As the left has consistently pointed out, India's incautiously wholesale tilt to the right is a recipe for comprehensive disaster.

It immiserates more and more millions everyday, and simultaneously lends force to racial and religious paradigms of nationalism, a phenomenon alienating in the extreme. And all that in turn fuels concrete grievances into active explosions of violent resentment.

The Indian ostrich had best take its head out of the sands of obdurate imbecility, and revise all its reigning theses as to why these things happen.

It is not to the neo-imperialists and its own military and para-military might that it must look to for 'crushing' terrorism.

The Indian state needs without loss of time to return to its own people and look for a new order of trust and negotiation, bolstered by non-partisan and prompt justice-delivery systems. And, most crucially, to restructure wealth and opportunity through visibly equitous institutional arrangements. Indeed, its covenant with the people must brook no fear, favour, or discrimination on behalf of those segments of the polity who exercise clout of any kind.

Most of all, it needs to demonstrate to India's 'minorities' that the state is as much theirs' as of the corporates and those others who coerce governance on behalf of majoritarian fascists (see my 'Fighting Terror the Terrorist Way').

Thus, just as the left knew provenly better in the matter of the political economy, it is equally on the button in the matter of the nuclear deal, its implications for security and sovereignty, and for the social harmony of the plural nation-state.

V

When, therefore, the Indian Prime Minister goes to Washington soon, were he to sign on the dotted line of the 123, ignoring what Bush and his minions have openly, candidly, and brazenly averred about what the deal means to them, he would diminish every Indian who is proud of being an Indian and wishes to remain so.

Indeed, even such ones who only till the other day were firmly for the deal – people like the erstwhile, America-friendly, ambassador, Lalit Man Singh – are now saying what we are saying here, and have been saying for more than a year.

Surely, the Indian Prime Minister needs to retain some allegiance, after all, also to a legacy left to him by many previous incumbents in the matter of sovereignty vis a vis imperialism.

In the meanwhile, it is indeed a sweet time for the Indian left. The country can use them for a long time to come. May they go from strength to strength.

October 2008

India's Failed Secularism

A Recipe for Disintegration

As I suggested in my previous column ('Sweet Time for the Left in India') events on Wall Street have shown what a fortuitous circumstance it was that the Indian Prime Minister, in his own words, remained a 'bonded slave' to the supporting left parties until the other day.

Had he had unfettered freedom in matters economic, India would be sinking today faster than a tanker.

Likewise, how fortuitous for India's beleaguered Christians that the good Prime Minister had to suffer 'embarrassment' while traveling Christian lands recently. Think that in France, the spunky Sarkozy called the Kandhamal mayhem a 'massacre' to his face.

Thus, superceding the travails of the Christians in Orissa, it was the rebuke to india's 'image' that registered powerfully. A circumstance that makes you think how much 'nationalism' is often a matter of image and how little of any actual concern for the people who inhabit the nation.

That 'embarrassment' has at least yielded some concrete threats to the BJP/BJD government in Orissa after the many politic secular noises about the arson, rape, and murder there. Will it lead to a constitutional dismissal of the government, though? Think again; elections are round the corner in many states. And, as always, the Constitution must give way to canny political considerations. Remember that Modi was allowed to carry on despite the total and proven complicity of the state in the butcheries in Gujarat in 2002

Speaking of which, how unfortunate for India's Muslims that no country in the world that the Indian Prime Minister has visited or is likely to visit should want to embarrass him about the excesses committed against Indian Muslims. Something that suggests the colossal helplessness that has become their lot.

II

I have suggested elsewhere that the secular protestations and pretensions of the Republic of India have remained a paper-provision through the years of India's existence as a sovereign nation-state primarily owing to the failure of the Congress party to honestly and fearlessly embrace and enforce the Republican principle of citizenship.

All its rhetoric notwithstanding, the Congress remains reluctant to transcend the denominational identity of Indians in political and governmental practice.

From day one, its electoral traditions have tended to be guided by considerations of the social identity of candidates – as much as of any other party – with scant effort made to transform the given and inherited biases of the polity.

Just as the Congress incorporated rather than confronted feudal social practices and formations through the 'freedom movement,' it has sought to cater to rather than educate out of existence those formations in the electoral career of independent India.

Not surprisingly, this social and intellectual failure has coloured the ways in which India's law-enforcement and investigative agencies, indeed often its juridical institutions, at lower levels especially, have operated in approaching the culpabilities of the 'majority' and 'minority' communities variously.

Consider, for example, that the bail plea of under-trials in the matter of the Godhra train burning of 2002 locked away under the draconian POTA (Prevention of Terrorism Act) was heard by the highest court in the land in February-March of this year, but the judgement remains in abeyance. In the meanwhile, one more under-trial, Hussein Mohammed Dhobi, age 65, has died there in custody – the fourth fatality in the matter. Nothing has appeared in public as to how those detainees are treated.

Think also that only the other day a CNN-IBN/Hindustan Times countrywide Poll revealed that 87% of Indians think that the police force is communal (read sectarian on the side of the 'majority'). As well as an Amnesty International finding that the most corrupt institutions in India are the Police, the Politicians, and the Lower Judiciary! Why Amnesty should either have not looked into the bureaucracy and the corporate sector, or found nothing there remains a surprise.

These facts taken together help explain why it is that the Congress party which never tires of tom-tomming its role in formulating a secular-democratic republic has never yet given a nation-wide call for mobilization on behalf of the secular principle. Something that contrasts rather tellingly with the preparedness of people in Turkey to congregate in the millions whenever that principle is there seen to be in jeopardy. One would have imagined that,learning from Gujarat, and witness to the 'majoritarian' rage now in evidence state after state, now would be a good time.

III

Thus it is that when the local head of the Bajrang Dal in Uttar Pradesh makes the public pronouncement that the strategic objective of this terrorizing arm of the RSS is to transform the secular republic into a 'Hindu Rashtra' (Hindu theocratic state; see *The Hindu*, October 2, 2008) no cognizable offence is seen to have been committed. Not to speak of treason against the state as by law established.

Imagine, on the other hand, a call coming from some Muslim organization that they mean to turn India into an Islamic state. Within seconds, the organization would be banned and its members locked up as jihadi 'terrorists.'

The crude and abiding fact is that the Congress party never really internalized the fatal truth of the insight that Jawahar Lal Nehru, India's first Prime Minister, had voiced as far back as 1937.

Writing on 'Hindu and Muslim Communalism,' Nehru had warned that whereas the communalism of the 'minority' is patently what it is – sectarian banding together of a defensive nature – that of the Hindu 'majority' is always likely to masquerade as 'nationalism.' (See *Nehru On Communalism*, ed. N.L. Gupta, published by Sampradayikta Virodhi Committee, 1965, p.9). And, needless to say, that is then but a short step to fascism.

It is ofcourse a well-recorded fact that within the Congress leadership of those times, more than a few were not only members of the communal Hindu Mahasabha, but believed at heart that Indian social pluralism of centuries notwithstanding, India was at bottom a Hindu nation.

The penetration of the communal virus of those times must suggest something of the quality of the intellectual, cultural, and political battle that Nehru and a few others that notably included Muslim leaders (Abul Kalam Azad, Rafi Ahmed Kidwai, Saifuddin Kitchlu, Asaf Ali, to name but a handful) and organisastions (Jamiat-e-ulema-e-Hind) put up against sectarian obscurantisms that disfigured both communities to ensure the founding of a secular republic.

It is to be noted that secularism was subsequently to be designated by a Constitutional Bench of the Supreme Court of India as one of the 'basic' features of the Constitution not amenable to amendment by parliament.

Indeed, in an interesting book titled Nehru's Hero, Lord Meghnad Desai records how during the Nehruvian phase of Independent India, the Nehruvian emphasis on progressive secularism and social pluralism was constantly reflected in the cinematic products of the Bombay Film Industry.

IV

This faint-hearted lip-service to secularism on behalf of the Congress party after Nehru's death in 1964 has meant that its fight against the fascist RSS and its hydra-headed front organizations has always been just that – a faint-hearted, proforma protestation, bereft of any stern ideological conviction or political will to confront it either through mass education and mobilization, or any hard operations of the state apparatus, however enjoined by the Constituion.

The politics of the Congress to this day suggests that much as it may berate the RSS/BJP of fomenting sectarian rioting come election time (Commission after Commission since 1947 has found the RSS complicit in communal rioting), the Congress nonetheless remains as cognizant of Hindus *qua* Hindus as a vote-bank as the BJP.

What is to explain the fact that no attempt has ever been initiated, not to say carried out, by the Congress organization, to dent or alter the socialized prejudices of India's police forces?

Or the fact that these forces and the concomitant investigative/intelligence agencies have to this day next to negligible representation of Muslims, especially at higher echelons of decision-making?

Or the fact that challenges to the state that come from either the left extremists or the Islamists are dubbed 'terrorism' while such challenges when they come from the Hindu right are willy nilly regarded as 'nationalist' mayhem, and dubbed wrong-headed at worst?

Or the fact that whereas Muslim Indians arraigned in violent and 'anti-national' activity are promptly enough dealt with, cases,, when they are instituted at all, pending against Hindu majoritarian marauders never seem to come to any conclusion? Or that police officers at the highest levels found complicit in pogroms against the 'minorities' may be suspended for a while, but eventually are not only reinstated but promoted as well? A case in point here the findings of the Srikrishna Commission into the communal riots of Bombay, 1992-93; officers indicted by the Commission are well and truly in place and promoted under the aegis of a Congress-led government in Maharashtra. Not to speak of Gujarat.

V

With the incremental collapse of the shaping energies of India's liberationary, pluralist, egalitarian ethos that informed the anti-colonial struggle, with the incorporation of India's new upwardly mobile urban elites into market fundamentalism following the Washington Consensus – the Congress largely responsible in both instances – India's secular nationalism came to be displaced by one based on adherence to race and religion (See Vijay Prashad, *Darker Nations: A Biography of the Short-Lived Third World*, 2008 for an incisive exposition of this transformation). After the criminal demolition of the Babri mosque in 1992 by fascist hordes of the VHP, a pogrom in which the best known leaders of the BJP were visibly participant, 'cultural nationalism' came to be the new slogan of the Hindu right-wing.

Designed to alter the definition of the 'nation', this variety of 'nationalism' was equally meant to keep in place the hegemony of the Hindu upper castes over the downtrodden Hindu masses, forestalling the possibility of their banding together on any alternate platform of social and economic exploitation.

It needs to be understood that what irks high-caste Hindus most about 'conversions' is the suggestion that such a transfer of allegiance springs from the abominable oppressions of the caste hierarchy and its religious sanctions within Hinduism. And that Christianity should be seen by dalits and tribals as offering them an archive of existence wherein a modicum of social equality and avenues of educational and medical caring become available.

The Hindu upper caste crusade against 'conversions' has thus nothing to do with Hinduism per se; it has to do with asserting social dominance and answering the rebuke that is administered when another faith is preferred as a life-option.

Indeed, were this crusade to involve any introspection, the whole business could be sorted out by the RSS issuing a fatwa against the caste system, and declaring that Hindus of all castes will henceforth enjoy equal social and religious rights. Not about to happen.

Nor is it anything but a pathetic travesty to think that the crusaders against 'conversions' truly believe that a grave demographic turn-over is in the offing. Even the RSS knows that the census of 2001 has actually shown a 0.6% decline in the overall population of Indian Christians!

So where are these hordes of converts? To this day not a single case of conversion by allurement has been actually demonstrated. If anything, evidences of 'reconversion' to Hinduism on the strength of brute threats to life and limb have been publicly voiced by unfortunate Pana Christians in Kandhamal on India's electronic channels. Remember also that such 'reconversions' are in the first place a misnomer. The tribals thus 'reconverted' have never been Hindus in the first place; they have always called themselves 'Animists.' Nor is it ever made clear what caste these 'reconverts' are meant to belong to after they are made Hindus.

VI

Notwithstanding the public boast of the head the Bajrang Dal in Karnataka that he has been responsible for the anti-Christian mayhem there, or by the other BD local leader in Uttar Pradesh that the man who died while bomb-making in Kanpur had been a BD man, or the half dozen or more proven cases of bomb-making activity by BD cadres, the Dal proclaims loudly that not until the courts find them guilty may anyone raise a finger against them. Not even against those who have committed rape and murder in public view.

That argument on behalf of 'due process' however, we are told, does not apply to Muslims or Christians.

For example, despite a publicly stated acknowledgement by the Maoists in the 'badlands' of Orissa that they are the ones who killed Swami Laxmanananda, the Bajrang Dal has concluded from day one that Christians are the killers of the Swamy.

Indeed, at other times in recent history the Sangh Parivar has vociferously taken the position that matters of faith are not at all subject to judicial examination or determination.

This was to come most ringingly to the fore at the time of the demolition of the Babri mosque. Even the BJP aspirant to Prime

Ministership has consistently avowed that the courts cannot decide on the Ayodhya dispute since it is a matter of faith. That it may be a matter of faith on either side is simply dubbed an 'anti-national' argument designed to placate the Muslims.

Same about the Ram Sethu issue down south, where the Sangh takes the position that since, self-evidently – and scientific/archaeological evidence be damned – the sethu (Adam's bridge in British times) was built by Lord Ram to cross over to Sri Lanka to fight Ravana, no secular, scientific,or legal determination can be made of the matter. Such privilege, needless to say, is however not available to the 'minorities.'

VII

The latest episode in the career of 'cultural nationalism' (more responsibly, racist and religious fascism) is the one that concerns the recent 'encounter' killing of two young Muslim students of the Jamia Milia Islamia university – an institution that goes back to Gandhi and Azad, and that has throughout functioned as a secular icon in Indian academe.

Despite penetrating holes punched in the police narrative about the incident by civil rights activists who include some of the country's most reputed legal luminaries – if the police knew they were 'terrorists' why wasn't the place, which has but one exit, surrounded, and the 'terrorists' challenged, or forced out by throwing in all the gases used in such cases, why was the deceased police officer not wearing a bullet-proof vest? And if the police did not know they were actually 'terrorists' how did they so discover just by killing them off without the least interrogation or investigation? If they were 'terrorists' why would they have reported on official police form, duly stamped, all the correct details of personal identity when renting the house? Why have no bullets been found that ostensibly killed the police officer? Why, as the forensic report says, were there no signs of scuffle, and why were some 21 and 17 bullet wounds found in the bodies of the two killed young students? If two 'terrorists' escaped , as the police claim, where did they go and how did they escape, since there was but one exit and entry to Batla House? – despite all that, anyone asking those questions is to be understood to be abetting 'terrorism' and demoralizing the police force. Indeed, one young man now in custody was provenly taking his exam at the time of the incident. He rushed to a premier TV channel office to report the incident, and was promptly picked up from the channel office itself as having been involved in the conspiracy.

After the arrests, all guidelines laid down by the supreme court in the matter of the rights of the accused in custody were strenuously flouted. And such redress had to be obtained by a civil rights lawyer from the court as explicit directions to the concerned authorities.

Nobody knows whether these young people are guilty or innocent; but surely nobody also has the right to skirt 'due process' and pronounce them guilty ab initio, purely on the strength of religious affiliation.

Thus the Vice-Chancellor of Jamia Milia, a historian of high repute and a man of impeccable secular credentials (who had a few years ago been actually at the receiving end of Muslim obscurantism and had to leave the university), who has stood by the students, offering legal aid to them from funds collected voluntarily for the purpose, is likewise vilified as a protector of 'terrorists.' Never mind that article 39 of the Constitution of India enjoins that legal aid shall be provided to any and everyone arraigned in any crime. Never mind also that it was the VHP which provided such services to their man, Dara Singh, again in Orissa, who was accused of burning alive the missionary, Graham Steins and his two children, and subsequently sentenced to life in prison.

Somehow, the whole argument about no-finger-to-be-raised-till-proven-guilty is not meant to apply to anyone who does not belong to the Sangh Parivar.

It needs to be recalled that in recent years the number of people arraigned as 'terrorists' and then let off by the courts as innocents is a litany. Even when the draconian TADA and POTA laws were in place, the conviction rate never crossed the 2% mark! Nor for that matter has experience been any different world-wide.

On the contrary, the bravehearts who kill suspects in 'encounters' dime a dozen are to be regarded as saviours and heroes. That some famous ones – Daya Nayak, Pradeep Sharma, Rajbir etc. – were subsequently found to be in the employ of builders' mafias, killing designated people for hefty sums, and passing them off as 'terrorists' also makes no dent in the 'nationalist' position.

The greatest danger to the constitutional and law-abiding operations of the state and its agencies comes indeed from the instant approval that this 'nationalist' position draws from the yuppy classes, and from a few electronic TV channels as well.

VIII

If by the 'secular state' we mean that whole ensemble of operations that ought to be based on non-denominational citizenship, equality before the law, fair investigative procedures, and a demonstrated administrative and juridical culture that entertains no regard for religious affiliation, plus a civil and media back-up that refuses to take things on faith and never shies from asking the tough questions, India may well be a rapidly failing state.

It is a problem that is severely compounded by the inability of the organized left to do anything more than make the right noises, with a proforma protest meet thrown in.

Any concerted attempt at a mass secular mobilization is conspicuous by its absence. That leaves only the conscience-keepers among civil society organizations to fight the menace. Indeed, in recent times, the likes of a Teesta Setalvad, a Prashant Bhushan, a Shabnam Hashmi, and the choice souls that work with them have borne the burden that rightly belongs to the state and the government of the day.

The all-important question is: how long?

October 2008

Simplicities

What lovely times those must have been when a rose was a rose by any name?

Many must have thought so, although I doubt that the man who wrote that line actually thought so, or why else would he have also asked 'O Romeo, Romeo, wherefore art thou Romeo'?

Same with the rose. Ask the orchid lover, or the one who loves the cactus best.

In post-Freudian times, we know of the case of a young man who actually died from allergy to the rose.

Best be wary of the truths we are told; such as, for example that the stock market equals the fate of India. Exactly 3% Indians dabble in its fortunes and, now, salutary misfortunes. Or, the banking system: 70% or more Indians do not bank!

II

So what is 'terrorism'?

Engaging in indiscriminate violence? You must be joking. That would make the American chief executive by far the prime terrorist of past, present, and – safe assumption – future times.

Killing innocent human beings? Same conclusion. Name me one event or all events taken together that killed more innocents than 'little boy' in Hiroshima. And, not to forget Nagasaki.

Killing without cause, or in the name of some spurious cause? Like the invasion of Iraq in the pursuit of the non-existent WMD?

Killing in the name of religion? Don't say it, unless you mean to refer to pretty much all of western history upto about the beginning of the 19C. And later as well in places like Ireland.

That which the puissant call 'terrorism'? More to the point.

Think that crashes among currency notes on the stock market are designated 'carnage' and 'bloodbath'; and the millions who die from malnutrition, preventable infection and such-like – millions, that is, of human beings, not currency notes – mere inevitable victims to the 'inexorable laws' of economics and Nature.

III

Thus, what were 'terrorists' till yesterday in relation to the Godhra train burning in Gujarat, 2002, have today been kindly denotified as ordinary enough criminals who acted out of 'sudden provocation.' If indeed they did.

This, thanks to the findings of a Review Panel on the subject of the 120 or so accused (Muslims) who have been rotting in jail for six long years without trial or bail as per provisions of the since- repealed POTA (Prevention of Terrorism Act).

Findings now upheld by the highest court in the land which has pronounced that these denizens of the Indian Guantanamo cannot after all be tried under the said draconian Act since they are not 'terrorists' in the first place.

All that should bring good and bad tidings, severally, to two honourable retired Justices of the Supreme Court.

Good tidings to Justice U.C.Bannerjee who headed a committee set up by the Railway Ministry, and pronounced pretty much as the Review Panel now has; and bad tidings to one Justice Nanavati who has been heading another Commission and has only some weeks ago furnished an Interim Report (an illegal procedure, since as per law governing Commissions of Enquiry, only complete findings can be submitted) concluding that the train burning was an act of 'conspiracy'.

Since the Interim Report was all- too- obviously tailored to enhancing Modi's political standing and prospects, Justice Nanavati went further forward to proffer just the conclusion to the still non-existent Part of the Report that will concern the Gujarat pogrom that followed the train burning, namely, that neither Modi nor any of his hench agencies bore any culpability in the matter. Hallelujah, we say; three cheers for brazen gumption and bold untruth.

This is the same Justice of whom it was heard in a sting operation recording of a conversation with a Modi satrap 'he is our own man.' Provenly so.

But something after all does work in the state of Denmark, although despite the judgement now delivered by the Supreme Court, we may not put it past the Modi dispensation to go in appeal. It may thus still be a while before those that yet survive the Sabarmati jail are granted bail. But who said India is perfect, and then Gujarat.

And yet, what a tribute to the exertions of the tireless tribe that will not take fascism lying down. The vicious triumph, as has often been said, only because the well-meaning opt out.

IV

So, what is 'terror'?

Just those clandestine bombs going off, killing anything from one to a hundred people?

Make a computation and you will find that the total victims of bomb-terror in recent decades in India is but a miniscule percentage of those butchered, burnt, and banished in the pogroms conducted in acts of mob-terror – and all invariably with the state watching in silent connivance.

Not to speak of the fact that mob-terror derives its howling, animal energies from ideologues who sit high among both the polity and government, and directs its depredations against chosen targets among the populace. And the further fact that it does not hide its face because it thinks it is working its murderous business in the interests of the nation, and because it knows that any number of worthies will promptly flood the TV channels to pronounce that same 'patriotic' sentiment. And that the channels will find this distinction between 'terrorism' and 'patriotism' as compelling as the worthies aforesaid.

Even as the blood gushes and hacked limbs lie aground, the face of this terror exults in triumph and apes the famous blood-curdling victory call of Tarzan.

Sitting in their up-market homes, the successful Indian heaves grunts of satisfaction that some people there are who are thus boldly forth to cut down 'evil', and that the state has the sense to stand aside. Indeed, that, thank god, somebody will do what the state is too pusillanimous to do. How else is India, the new super-power, to be saved?

V

After all, throughout history, what is remembered is what the puissant dish out to us.

Everybody knows how many Stalin sent to the Gulag; how many remember that some 8 million Russian soldiers and 20 million civilians gave their lives to defeat Hitler and Nazism? Or, that had Hitler not opened the Eastern Front, Nazism may well have triumphed.

Interestingly, where German historians will tell you so, the Anglo-Saxons ones will not.

And, think about it, how many actually believe that Hiroshima was the single most unforgiveable, 'evil' if you like, thing that modern men have done to other modern men?

Not to speak of the umpteen and countless wars unleashed upon all regions of the world by Imperialism in the pursuit of material ascendance?

Or, how many remember that the Taliban were 'freedom fighters' when they were put up against the Russians and became 'terrorists' when they turned the gun the other way?

Thus, India's mob-terrorists may well come to be remembered and recorded as the heroes who saved India from 'terrorism.' Very few may venture the truth that the two remain inseparable complementarities.

VI

For now, nonetheless, the happy development in relation to the Godhra accused brings hope to those who insist that a rose is never a rose just by any sort of name. And that, whatever the frustrations and the systemic collusions, there is good work to be done on behalf of democracy, justice, the rule of law, and equity. Even plain human decency.

October 2008

Notions of the Nation

Legitimising or Delegitimising Violence

Within hours, literally, the world will know whether the nation-state in America as decreed by the American Constitution has or has not triumphed finally over the competing, even if subterranean, notion of the nation as race.

If indeed Obama wins the Presidency, the American voter would have set an example to other regions, India included, where constitutional stipulations with regard to nation and citizenship continue to be bedeviled by racial and religious supremacists who contest the ideal of secular equality under a commonly accepted regime of laws as stipulated by the Constitution at any given time.

These impulses of course work severally: they can be pressed into service to seek from the state a redistribution of largesse by privileging one identity or the other, internally.

Often an identity that has been reviled previously finds itself elevated to favour subsequently (today's Maharashtra offers a fine instance; for now, neither South Indian lungivalas nor Marathi-speaking Muslims are the targets of Maratha chauvinism); More ominously, a reformulation of the notion of the nation-state in toto becomes the object.

Which of course is not to say that the nation-state is already too evolved to be meddled with on behalf of those that derive rather little participation in or benefit from its decisions and operations.

Occasionaly, intermediate forms of racial privileging detrimental to the idea of the nation-state also surface with strident insistence on behalf of some sections of the citizenry, without overtly challenging the nation-state per se.

A fine current example of this in India is the pressure built within Tamil Nadu on behalf of fellow-Tamilians in another country.

Members of the Indian parliament from this state have thought nothing of making a gesture of resigning their parliamentary memberships if the Indian state fights shy of intervening in Sri Lanka to protect the interests of Tamilians. Never mind that in that beleaguered country, the government of the day is battling the world's first and worst terrorist outfit, banned in most countries including India, namely the LTTE.

Not only did this outfit invent the suicide bomber, it also murdered an Indian Prime Minister, Rajiv Gandhi, using such a bomber.

Tamil parties in India, with the honorable exception of the AIADMK, supported also by bevies of film stars, have thus expressed their primary allegiance to their racial tribe in another country rather than to the Indians who elected them to the Indian parliament.

Not to speak of sections of more vociferous racists among them who have clandestinely supplied munitions to the LTTE for many years, and who make no bones about going to war on its behalf.

Given all that, the Indian government which depends on the support of the Tamilian parliamentarians has felt obliged to send its foreign minister to Colombo to do some talking, and to make repeated statements on behalf of Tamilian refugees in Sri Lanka.

Speaking of which, imagine how the government of India would react were Sri Lankan Muslims to issue statements with respect to real or imagined excesses perpetrated on Kashmiri Muslims, or Muslims in Tamil Nadu itself. Unbearable thought that. Not to speak of Indian Muslims expressing the least anxiety about Muslims anywhere else. That would be pure treason.

Thus, in short, much like many Muslims the world over who privilege the Muslim nation, or the Ummah, over the nation-state, India's Tamilians feel that the 'Tamil nation' takes precedence over the Indian state when push comes to shove.

As to the Vishwa Hindu Parishad (Global Hindu Community), it is on record as believing that 'in pre-Christian times, all people, everywhere in the world, were Hindus' (see H.K.Vyas, *The VHP*, Communist Party of India Publications, New Delhi, 1983). And yet, it only sees enemies everywhere, including in India. You might well wonder why.

II

Dating from colonial times, of course, the most concerted challenge to the notion of a secular-democratic Republic wherein the ideals of equality and non-discriminatory justice, with due consideration for the preservation of the specific needs of non-Hindu Indians – some twenty or so percent of the population, all taken together – against hegemonising oppression, either by the state or the majority community, would define and inform citizenship has always come from the Hindu-Fascist right-wing.

That at least a third of the so-called 'Hindu majority' feel as oppressed by the hegemonising brahminical upper-caste minority of Hindus is of course another little- discussed matter. Indeed, one thoughtful dalit intellectual was to feel impelled to write a whole book, explaining why he does not regard himself a 'Hindu' (see Kancha Ilaiah, *Why I Am Not A Hindu: A Sudra Critique of Hindutva Philosophy, Culture, and Political Economy*, Samya, Calcutta, 1996.)

But, to return to the 'Hindu/Muslim' question:

Before you bring up the question about the Muslim League, let it be reiterated that the earliest formulation of a two-nation theory was not to come from the League but from Savarkar.

Explicitly in his pamphlet, *Hindutva: Who is a Hindu?* (1923), Savarkar was to say that India comprised two distinct nations, 'Hindus and Muslims'.

As has been often noted, Hindutva for him had little or nothing to do with the Hindu religion (not that the Hindu religion is any one identifiable monolith either, although those that have hegemonised it over ruthless millennia is). The man claimed to be an atheist and did not approve of the Hindu caste system.

Hindutva for Savarkar constituted purely a racial thesis; only those could be regarded genuine Indians who were both born in India and whose places of worship lay within the territorial confines of India. That most of these places of worship do lie within India is of no account, since Mecca remains outside, a fact sufficient to negate millennia of Hindu-Muslim syncretism.

This formulation has since become the source of the call on Indian Muslims either to fall in line or accept without question the primacy of the 'Hindu Nation.'

In modern parlance, the RSS/BJP call this 'cultural nationalism' – a racial concept which is deployed to question and dislodge the ideal of secular citizenship, bedrock of the constitutional Republic.

In 1939, Golwalkar was to write about the 'minority problem' thus:

they must 'merge…in the national race and adopt its culture, or to live at its mercy as long as the national race may allow them to do so and quit the country at the sweet will of the national race.'

This he called the only 'sound view on the minorities problem…that alone keeps the nation safe from the danger of a cancer developing into its body politic of the creation of a 'state within a state. –

(see *We, or Our Nationhood Defined*, Bharat Publications, Nagpur, p.47)

Remarkably, as has often been pointed out, the entire ideological equipment of the Hindu right which prides itself for representing the essence of Indianness, was imported from Fascist Italy where Munje, who was to become head of the Hindu Mahasabha, met and imbibed Mussolini, and from Nazi Germany. (Interestingly, it was also in 1923 that Mussolini's Doctrine of Fascism appeared.)

Munje, whose great friend Hedgewar was, passed these thoughts to the RSS which has ever since not just lauded Hitler and Nazi Germany for the height of their 'race pride' but sought to impose this notion of nation on independent India.

III

As visuals now of 'Saffron terror' splash across some Indian tv screens, the occurrence does not surprise those who are familiar with Hindutva history and ideology.

And if the exposure has taken so long to become public, it is for the simple reason that the Indian state, however secular its protestations, has never really on the ground practiced even-handedness as between Hindutva violence, be it mob-terror or bomb-terror, and violence inflicted by non-Hindu militants/insurgents/terrorists – call them what you will.

As we take in the 'shock' of the current revelations, such as:

- a 'sadhvi' implicated in the Malegaon blasts of September 29, 2006, remarkably, two years after the event, something that goes to suggest the alacrity of state agencies when it comes to 'Hindu terror';
- alongwith her a retired army major, Upadhyay;
- a serving, no less, Lt. Col. named Purohit;
- a whole Military Academy at Bhonsala in Nagpur, headquarters of the RSS, its director, one Raikar, now also hauled up for questioning, since

the school, it is acknowledged, had been very kindly handed over to the Bajrang Dal for military training for a full two weeks;

- an organization called Abhinav Bharti run currently by, guess who, Himani Savarkar, – the daughter of Nathuram Godse's brother, Gopal Godse, a co-accused in the Gandhi murder, and niece also of the good old Savarkar, – who has made bold to state publicly on tv channels that Hindu reprisals are justified, we must remember that militarism and violence, often of a secretive and Masonic variety, have been part and parcel of the fascist ideology of the Sangh.

The Hindu right-wing has always berated Hindus generally for being 'pacifist', Golwalkar going to the extent of saying that Ashoka's preaching of 'ahimsa' (non-violence) after converting to Buddhism subsequent to the carnage he wrought at Kalinga in Orissa (3rd century, BC) 'makes cowards of Indians.'

Although Gandhi's murder at the hands of the Hindu- right remains the most telling instance of its willingness to commit to violent terror, more shady details are also on record pertaining, disgustingly but revealingly, to its own internal culture.

For example, Balraj Madhok, the founder of the Jana Sangh, recounts in his autobiography, *Zindagi ka Safar*, how the shady murder of the President of the Sangh in 1968, Deen Dayal Upadhyay, was sought to be passed off as an 'accident.'

Upadhyay's corpse was found on 11th February, 1968 at the Mughalsarai Railway Station. The then S.P. and S.S.P. refuted the theory that the death was the result of an accident.

Pointing a finger squarely at Atal Bihari Vajpayee and Bala Sahib Deoras – who became, respectively, President and Secretary of the Sangh after Upadhyay's murder – Madhok records how Vajpayee admonished him to float the accident theory. Refusing to do so, Madhok was asked to resign from primary membership of the Sangh.

If since India's Independence the chief violent recourse of the Sangh has been to instigating and effecting mass killings of Muslims in one pogrom after another, (Commission after official Commission over the last six decades has found the Sangh complicit in these pogroms) it has now obviously taken a further leap to engage what it calls 'Islamic and jihadi terror' with its own brand.

Having done so, it invites us shamelessly to desist from calling this brand 'Hindu terror.' The pronouncements of Himani Savarkar and Bala Sahib Thackeray notwithstanding. Remember that the latter, not too long ago, had publicly expressed the view that Hindus also need to prepare terror squads that would do more than measly damage to Muslim areas.

Uncannily, it is pushed to gurgitating all those protestations and arguments which Muslims have thus far sought to present to the world: to wit, presume innocence till proven guilty, do not brand whole communities; do not view terrorism as a religious/Islamic phenomenon etc., – arguments which have found little use as far as the fascist Hindu right-wing is concerned.

As Kavita Krishnan speculates brilliantly in an article on the subject, just imagine that the 'sadhvi' was not a sadhvi but a 'maulvi'; the discourse of the Sangh would have been blood-curdling in the extreme. (see Countercurrents, 'The Tip of the Iceberg', October 10, 2008).

Likewise, her further charge related to the role of the state and its investigative agencies in suppressing the facts regarding the Malegaon blast for full two years is both germane and indicative; as is the further charge regarding the quiescent nature of the state's response to the other known recent instances in which Bajrang Dal activists have been found bomb-making, and have indeed also been found dead as some of those bombs went off in their own hands. Complete with the discovery of false beards and 'Muslim' attire hidden in their houses. Not to speak of venomous anti-Muslim and anti-Christian printed materials littered in their hide-outs.

IV

Nothing, it must be emphasized, spells more cataclysmic prospects for the Republic than any attempt on behalf of the state or any of its agencies to become complicit in legitimising one form of terror as an 'understandable' form of violence – reprisal, if you like, and 'patriotic' in intent, don't you know, and delegitimising some other as ab initio 'anti-national.'

And, indeed, the reprisal theory must anyday yield a better argument to India's Muslims than it can to the Hindu right-wing. One long look at all the pogroms that have been affected since 1947 and the meaning of that becomes clear. On the contrary, it may well be asked, what is it that India's Muslims have done to the Hindus which calls for 'reprisals'? Ask for equal citizenship, contrary to the edicts laid down by Golwalkar?

Or are we here to understand that the 'reprisal' theory is meant to apply to the long, secular, and creative rule by Moghul monarchs in India? Or against the insistence of the Gandhi-Nehru-led and Communist-supported freedom movement which defeated the Hindu-fascists' collaboration with the British to forge a theocratic state, and against their success in placing the Republic on a secular and pluralist footing?

It is something of a pity that the secular, pluralist, egalitarian, and anti-colonial impetus that impelled the freedom movement led by the Congress party should be finding exhaustion even within that august bastion; and that the Congress should frequently also be seen to partake of a version of nationalism that, however surreptitiously, yields pride of place to a so-called Hindu culture and religion. No dearth of cabinet ministers who sport idols of gods and godmen in their very office spaces that belong to the secular state.

The sooner this oldest of parties readjusts its coordinates, and rediscovers its sources of creative hegemony among India's labouring and secular masses the better for everybody. And it may not have much time either.

A test of all that will be how it deals, and is seen to deal, with the terrorism that comes from the Hindu right-wing. And where it places considerations of electoral failure or success in so doing. And whether or not it remains undeterred in the many constructive initiatives it has taken to improve the lot of the Muslims.

Likewise, the test of India's upwardly-mobile urbanites who have tended to see in the BJP a guarantor of their commercial and cultural aspirations, together seen as a formula for hegemonising the labouring and the low-caste and putting the Muslims in 'their place' in close embrace with American corporate imperialism, will be to take their blinkers off so they may see beyond their thoughtless , sectarian and self-regarding noses.

They would do well to recognize that two of the accused in the Malegaon blasts have been members of the BJP, just as Sadhvi Pragya Thakur was a member of the RSS student wing, the ABVP.

They should also learn to stop pointing an instant finger at one kind of imagined 'terrorist' outfit even before a crime has been committed, and to be more tolerant of those in civil society who raise questions that are contrary to their world of a priori certainties. Precisely as we do not pronounce on the guilt or innocence of the Sadhvi and the rest before the courts have adjucated.

They should also understand that law-enforcement in India is not such an untainted procedure as they wish to believe when it suits their predilections, and that more repressive laws in the hands of tainted enforcement agencies, far from mitigating terror, provoke it many times more.

It is also to be hoped that the discovery of the Sadhvi and, with her, the clan, will bring some perspective back into the flourishes with which our globalised media channels often glibly pronounce on the menace of 'terrorism.' Or, huckster-like, demand to be told by the police and the politician that some or the other Muslim organization is involved even as a blast goes off.

That shift and correction in perspective should oblige a far deeper acknowledgement of the concrete sources of disaffection among diverse segments of the polity than an impatient, money -and -news-spinning culture of 'modernity' seems to enjoin.

Even blame games deserve to be fairly distributed and explored. And the truth to be nailed, however such an occurrence may hurt our own innards.

November 2008

Hindu Terrorism

The Shock of Recognition

> ...underlying these religions were a common set of beliefs about how you treat other people and how you aspire to act, not just for yourself but also for the greater good
>
> (Obama in his interview about Religion given to Cathleen Falsani, March 27, 2004; cf. to his mother's teaching about the validity of diverse faiths and the value of tolerance.)

So, now, India is home to 'Hindu' terrorism.

Departing from the more usual banner-appelation, 'Saffron Terror', I wish the fact to be registered that saffron is drawn from the stamin of a delicate and indescribably pretty mauve flower grown exclusively in my home valley of Kashmir, and exclusively by Muslims. My inherited memories of it are thereby sweet and secular to the core.

Also, saffron when used to grace milk products, Biryani, or to brew the heavenly Kehwa is a thing of the gods truly.

It is only when it is coerced against the use of nature to colour politics that it rages against the sin. Then, don't we know, what gruesome consequences begin.

I think it proper, therefore, to stick with the more direct and honest description 'Hindu' terrorism, since, much against their grain, even India's premier TV channels are now bringing us news of 'Hindu' terrorism, so compelling the materials gathered by the investigating agencies thus far.

This despite the fact that in my view the term 'Hindu' trerrorism is as erroneous as the term 'Muslim' terrorism. Even though not a religious man myself, I am able to see that being Hindu or Muslim by accident of birth has no necessary connect with how one's politics turn out to be in adult life. A plethora of specific contexts and shaping histories are here provenly more to the point.

II

It was way back in 1923 that Savarkar, never a practicing Hindu (indeed a self-confessed atheist) had first understood that from this benign term, 'Hindu,' could be drawn the toxic racial concept Hindutva, and made to serve a forthrightly fascist purpose. That Brahminism had always been a socially toxic form of Hinduism was of course an enabling prehistory to the new project.

He it was who established Abhinav Bharat in Pune (1904), that theoretical hotbed of twice-born Brahminical casteism against which low-caste social reformers such as Phule, Periyar, and Ambedkar were to struggle their whole lives long.

Such casteism was made the instrument of communalist politics to serve two major objectives: one, to overwhelm and negate the specific cultural and material oppressions of the low-caste within the Hindu Varna system , and two, to elevate the low-caste as a warrior of a common 'Hindutva' army against the chief common 'enemy,' the Muslim.

Such an army has been seen to be needed to salvage the 'real' nation from this so-called common enemy who continues to be represented to this day by the RSS and its hydra-headed 'educational' front organizations as an 'invader' still bent on seeking to convert India into an Islamic theocratic state.

Aided in these mythical fears and constructions by the British during the crucial decades leading upto Independence, India's majoritarian fascists continue thus to keep at bay all consideration of secular oppressions based entirely in the brutal social order of capitalist expropriation.

Savarkar thus counseled how a resurgent nation could result only if 'Hinduism was militarized, and the military Hinduised.'

Clearly enough, the serving army Colonel, S.P. Purohit and the other retired Major, one Upadhyay, who the Mumbai ATS (Anti-Terrorist Squad) tells us, are at the centre of the Malegaon terrorist blasts of September 29, 2008, alongwith Sadhvi Pragya and the rogue-sadhu, Amreetanand – and very possibly complicit in half a dozen other blasts as well – seem to have heeded Savarkar's advice to the hilt.

Indeed, in his Narco-test confessions, Colonel Purohit, sources have told some TV channels (Times Now), admits to his guilt and justifies his actions as retribution for what he thinks SIMI (Student's Islamic Movement of India) have been doing. He is understood to have further indicated that the rogue sadhu, Amreetanand, nee Dayanand etc., has been the kingpin and chief coordinator and devisor of several other blasts carried out by this cell, including the blasts at the revered Ajmer Dargah (Mausoleum of the 12th century Sufi saint, Chisti, which to this day draws devotees across faiths the world-over), and at Kanpur.

The ATS are now busy exploring the routes through which huge sums of money have been brought into the country for such terrorist activity as Hawala transactions, and whether the RDX, suspected to be used in the Malegaon blast, was procured by Colonel Purohit through army connections. It is to be noted that Purohit has been in Military Intelligence, and serving in Jammu & Kashmir, where it is thought he made contact with the rogue sadhu, Amreetanand.

(Indeed, as I write, news comes of the ATS claiming that Purohit actually stole some 60 kilos of RDX which was in his custody while doing duty at Deolali, and that in his Narco-test confession he admits to passing it on to one 'Bhagwan' for use in the blast on the Samjhauta Express train in February 2007.)

Needless to say, that alongwith the courts, we will also require that the ATS is actually able to obtain convictions rather than merely pile on evidence which may not be admissible in law.

To return to the argument:

As I suggested in my last column, 'Notions of the Nation', Hindutva militarism since the establishment of the Hindu Mahasabha and the RSS has been inspired by the desire to emulate and then better Muslim 'aggressiveness' seen as a racial characteristic that defined 'Muslim' rule in India, and rendered Hindus 'limp' and 'cowardly.'

Thus, if Savarkar established Ahninav Bharat, Dr.Moonje, an avowed Mussolini admirer who in turn inspired Dr.Hedgewar to establish the RSS on Vijay Dashmi of 1924 (victory day, denoting the liquidation of the Dravidian Ravana by the Aryan Kshatriya warrior, Ram) established the Bhondsala Military Academy at Indore (1937). It now transpires that this academy has been playing host to the Bajrang Dal for militarist training routines etc., and its director, one Raikar, has put in his papers.

Unsurprisingly enough, both these institutions are now under the scanner.

III

Over the last decade, terrorist blasts have occurred in India across a wide variety of sites and in major cities and towns.

Many of these blasts have taken place outside mosques and known Muslim- majority locations, as well outside cinema halls that were thought to be showing movies inimical to Hindu glory.

Briefly, these sites are: cinemas in Thane and Vashi in Maharashtra, Jalna, Purna, Parbhani, and Malegaon towns, again all in Maharashtra – and all areas of high Muslim density, in Hyderabad outside a famous old mosque, and in Ahmedabad and Surat in Gujarat.

Curiously, in the Surat episode, some sixteen odd bombs were found placed along the main thoroughfare in tree branches, on house-tops, on electric poles and so forth. Not one of them however exploded. This was thought to be the result of defective switches. Curious circumstance that; besides the wonder that Ahmedabad's Muslims could find such sprawling access to such strategic locations without Modi knowing a thing.

Yet, regardless of where the blasts have taken place, almost without exception the Pavlovian response of state agencies as well as, sad to say, media channels has been invariably to point fingers of suspicion and culpability towards one or the other 'Islamic' outfit.

Often, young Muslims men have been rounded up in the scores and held for days of brutal questioning without the least prima facie evidence. Nearly in all such cases, however reluctantly, they have had to be let off.

The most recent case is that of some fifteen young Muslims picked up after the Hyderabad blasts. Tortured with electric shocks, they have nevertheless been found to be innocent and let go.

Indeed, after the gruesome blasts in the Samjhauta Express – a train service of reconciliation and confidence-building between India and Pakistan – in which some 68 people were burnt to cinders, 45 of them Pakistani citizens, fingers were immediately pointed towards the SIMI.

Yet, the ATS of Mumbai now suspects that this may also be the doing of the 'Hindu' terrorists in custody. These speculations have been raised by the circumstance that the suitcases that held the bombs had Indore labels on them.

Just as the ATS now suspects that more than half a dozen blasts (the two at Malegaon, in 2006 and 2008, at the cinemas in Thane and Vashi, at Jalna, at Purna, at Parbhani, provenly at Nanded and Kanpur) have all been the handiwork of 'Hindu' terror groups.

IV

For some years, reputed civil and human rights organizations, and individual members of civil society that have included journalists, judges, lawyers, writers, artists, teachers, students, and labour organizations, besides organized Muslim fora and left parties, have been cautioning both state agencies and media conglomerates to:

- desist from the Pavlovian haste with which some one or other Muslim group is immediately named and labeled literally within an hour of the occurrence of a blast, thus contributing to the maligning of the entire Muslim community;
- to consider the possibility that groups other than those involving Muslims could be involved;
- to refrain from covering up prima facie evidence which points to such possibilities; indeed, where such evidence seems conclusive, as the complicity of the Bajrang Dal at Nanded and Kanpur;
- to ponder the question as to why Muslims should effect blasts within their own localities or outside their mosques;
- to weigh the consequences for the Muslim psyche of the failure of the state to prevent repeated pogroms against them, and to find or punish the guilty; not to speak of active state connivance in those pogroms (Moradabad, 198o; Nellie, 1983; Hashimpura, 1987; Bhagalpur, 1989; Mumbai, 1992-93; Gujarat, 2002, to cite just the more recent ones);
- to permit transparency in the matter of police investigations with due regard for the constitutional rights of those held in custody – such as visitation, access to legal defence, norms of the recording of confession and other evidence etc.,
- to respect the obligatory presumption of innocence until anyone is juridically found guilty.

Time and again these cautions and rightful prerogatives have been trampled under foot.

Aided by the loud biases of the corporate media which have tended to reflect the predilections both of free-market imperialism and comprador urban middle class sentiments in India's metropolitan towns, India's state agencies and that 'all-knowing' species, the Intellegence expert, who seems ever present to reinforce anti-Muslim prejudice, have tended to feed massively into the politics of the Hindu right-wing.

For years on end, India's chief malady has been sought to be seen to reside in 'Islamic' terrorism, and in the complicit refusal of the secularists to allow draconian preventive laws to be brought back on the books. Not in poverty, malnutrition, disease, absence of health care or clean drinking water, or lack of steady work among the urban poor, or the ousted tribals, disenfranchised farmers, chronic failure of primary schooling and so forth among some 75% of Indians. And most of them belonging to the Muslim, dalit, and tribal communities.

And to repeat for the nth time, this three-fourths of Indians able to spend just or under Rupees Twenty a day, all according to the governments' own Arjun Sengupta Committee Report.

Not to speak of the venomous communalization of the polity, the alienation and ghettoisation of the minorities, and the state's failure or unwillingness to carry through schemes that could redress these maladies.

As to new terror laws, the government of the day may protest that it has all the laws it wants, and more; as well as the fact that the worst terrorist attacks took place when laws like the dreaded POTA (Prevention of Terrorism Act) was on the books during the tenure of the NDA regime led by the ultra-'nationalist', BJP. Small dent is made by any regime of empirically-founded facts, or fair-minded arguments on the right-wing fascists and their fattened constituency.

V

Now, of course, a radically transformed milieu is unraveling.

Photos and Videos are doing the rounds that show the 'Hindu' terrorists currently under investigation in close and intimate proximity to top leaders of the RSS, the VHP, and the BJP as well.

Had POTA indeed been on the books today, such evidence would have authorized the police to put them all behind bars on the charge of associating with those under investigation for 'terrorism.' And all that without any recourse to bail either.

Predictably, nonetheless, after some days of dumbfounded crestfallenness (remember that the main electoral plank of the BJP in the elections now under way in several states and in the soon-to-be-held parliamentary polls is the failure of the Congress to eradicate 'terrorism' because of its 'minority appeasement' policies), the right-wing fascists are back to brazen form.

Even as the projected Prime Ministerial candidate, Advani (the high-point of whose career remains the successful demolition of the Babri mosque) seeks to strike a stance of caution, party hard-liners have taken to peddling outrageous theories.

As a complement to the well-known Pavlovian hunch that 'all terrorists are Muslims,' we are now told by the likes of Rajnath Singh, the party President, that 'no Hindu can be a terrorist,' that is to say even when he or she is found to be one.

This for the reason that what the ordinary man calls 'terrorism' is infact 'nationalism' where any Hindu be involved. Live and learn.

Other than that, it is both interesting and laughable that spokesmen and women of the BJP are today reduced to gurgitating every single argument that Muslims and civil rights organizations have to this day voiced:

- presume innocence until found guilty;
- desist from the 'political conspiracy' to malign a whole community;
- do not let enemies of the Hindu -right propagate fake evidence against them, since all evidence against them must be fake in principle;
- and most outlandishly, do not communalise terrorism; that from India's rank communalists who have done nothing but communalise terrorism ever since we remember!

VI

Even as these new developments point to a potentially mortal combat among 'Hindu' and 'Muslim' terror groups, I venture to think that the situation also offers opportunities of far-reaching redressal for all three axes that matter: the state and its agencies, the party-political system, and the polity generally.

First off, if, as has been the case, the Congress's secular credentials have consistently been vitiated by, willy nilly, playing second-fiddle to Hindu-communalist appeasement, the denuding of the Hindu- right offers it the opportunity of a lifetime to assert the supremacy of the constitutional scheme of things, without fear or favour.

It is indeed a circumstance that can now help the Congress and other secular parties to come down like a ton on communalism of all shades that underpin the fatal subversion of the secular republic without the need for apology.

In this endeavour, its greatest inspiration must come from two factors on the Muslim side of the issue:

one, that over the last year every single major and influential Muslim cultural and religious organization has publicly, and repeatedly, denounced through speech, act, and fatwa 'terrorism' as un-Islamic and a rightful candidate for punishment under law;

and, two, that without exception they have pleaded only and ever for fair and just treatment at the hands of the authorized instruments of state, both when victimized by pogroms and suspected as culprits; and for credible pursuit of those that persecute them.

Not once has any Muslim organization worth the name suggested that Muslims have any claims that override the Cosntitutional regime of laws and procedures pertaining to all citizens of the Republic.

All that in stark contrast to the refusal, however camouflaged or strategised, of the RSS and its affiliates to accept either the secular Constitution or the notion of secular citizenship.

It is to be recalled that the RSS tactically acquiesced to acknowledging the primacy of the national flag over its own saffron one in 1949 as a quid pro quo to its release from the ban imposed on it after Gandhi's murder.

To this day it seeks to overthrow the Republic as Constituted by law and to replace it by a theocratic Hindu Rashtra wherein the prerogatives of citizenship will be determined not by secular, democratic equality but racial difference among Indians (all that brutally codified in Golwalkar's two books, *We, or Our Ntionhood Defined*; and, the later *Bunch of Thoughts* which explicitly designates Muslims as the nations's 'Enemy Number One' in an exclusive chapter.)

However Hindu cultural politics may have come to infect sections of the fattened urbanites, the Congress must show the conviction that none of these in this day and age would be willing to back what is explicitly 'terrorist' activity, indistinguishable from any other, once the matter is proven.

This then is a fine moment to release a new energetic politics that recharges the conviction and inspiration of the non-discriminatory humanism that informed the leaders of the freedom movement, and thus to disengage whatever popular base the Hindu- right has built over the years since the demolition of the Babri mosque from its fascist leaderships and cadres.

Just as, infact, many BJP supporters are busy thinking whether they are indeed willing to carry their love of Muslim-haters quite to the point where those other dreams of Indian super-powerdom are seriously jeopardized by a war of competing terrorisms.

It is also a golden opportunity for the Congress-led UPA, should it come back to power, to take a hard look at the communalist virus that has infected law-enforcement agencies over the decades, and to make bold to effect reforms of a far-reaching character, such as include the recruitment of Muslims and other 'minorities' in due proportion to the forces, and not just among the lower ranks.

Speaking of the army, some 3% Muslims are today among its ranks – some sixty years after Independence. And I won't make a guess as to how abysmal might infact be its share among the officer core, colonel and above. And wouldn't I dearly like to take a peek into what sort of Indian History is taught India's future officers at Khadakvasla and Dehradun. Truly; and who does the teaching as well.

VII

As to the BJP: it has another opportunity as well; namely to reconstitute itself as a secular party on the right, bearing full allegiance to the Constitution in letter and spirit (remember now that among other things on the street-level, the NDA regime led by the BJP did constitute a Constitution Review Committee – an ominous enough move that, thankfully, was duly aborted in course), and shunning once and for all its enslavement to the RSS and its fascist vision of India, its history, culture and state.

Failing to do so, the BJP may succeed in causing further mayhem; but it is highly unlikely now to attain the sort of ascendance it seeks through fair means and foul.

Most of all, the BJP must understand that the Muslims of India, and Christians as well, have the inalienable right to live and work in the country on the terms set by the Constitution, not by the RSS or the Sangh Parivar.

And, conversely, that the BJP itself is as subject to those constitutional stipulations as any another collective of Indians who practice their beliefs and politics.

Let the BJP notice the epigraph chosen for this column; it comes from the new President-Elect of the one country that the BJP adores. Or will it now, with a black man at the helm?

A different voice floats from there.

Time for the BJP to change its langoti, and say 'yes we can' also be peaceable and law-abiding citizens of the Republic of India. And to prize and protect its magnificent plurality like all sensible and humane Indians.

November 2008

The Quest for Purity
Another Name for Fascism

> *I am not a fascist only when*
> *I decimate all other kind;*
> *I am a fascist when first I think*
> *It is purity I have in mind.*
> (Badri Raina, *Modest Proposal & Other Rhymes for the Times*, Sahmat, Delhi, 2000)

These are confused times for India's political Hinduism.

As the hours go by, the proverbial cunning of its leaderships across its many falanges experiences an exhaustion that surprises most of all the Sangh itself.

Having fooled millions over a century, it is astonished to find that it may at bottom have been the most fooled.

Adroit as it has been at double-speaking its way out of double-speak, the alleged involvement of its scions now in acts of terror renders it the mirror-image of those it never ceases to construct and condemn as its 'other.'

Worse still, it is abjectly reduced to proffering in defence every single argument routinely proferred by its 'opposite' number. And its self-righteous bluster that no Hindu can, by definition, ever be a terrorist rings hollow even among its loyal constituency, rebuke as such bluster does even the lowest form of common intelligence.

How much dent all that will or will not make in its electoral base must depend on some collateral factors, chiefly the further successes of investigative agencies, the fate of the cases in courts of law, and the quality of exertion on behalf of secular civil and political agencies to bring home the facts to the nation at large.

II

My ruminations here are occasioned by a statement made by the spokesperson of the All India Hindu Mahasabha (that most ontological of theoretical Hindutva over which Savarkar presided as the chief ideologue), Pravin Sharma to *Times of India*, online on 22 November 2008.

This statement characterizes the BJP as 'an opportunist political party playing politics over terrorism': clearly, neither the Congress nor the left could have said more.

It then goes on to say: "Please ask the BJP, VHP, Bajrang Dal, RSS and Abhinav Bharat as to what contribution they have made for Hindus and Hindutva so far." Fascinating stuff.

Taken together with media reports of confirmation of the truth of the allegation that the Sangh scions now in custody, alongwith an endocrinologist who works at a reputed private hospital in Delhi, were indeed plotting to murder two leaders of the RSS (see *The Hindu*, 23 November, p.10), the Congress seems well-placed in saying that there is currently a 'civil war' under way within the Sangh Parivar.

But to return to the disillusionment expressed by the Hindu Mahasabha with all other falanges of the Hindutva brigade.

Just within a year of the framing of India's secular-democratic Constitution, the RSS (Vatican of the Parivar) decided that it was not enough merely to engage Hindus in acts of 'cultural' transformation towards hard-core Brahminical practices.

Such work needed to be done politically as well through the party-political system and electoral participation.

Thus was floated the Jana Sangh in 1951.

Sadly, the Hindu 'purity' of its programmes (read anti-Muslim agenda) failed to yield any more than two seats to the Indian Parliament up until the end of the 1980s.

A declension from 'purity' was thus indicated; and with that realization the BJP was born.

The BJP in turn was to discover that it did not have a constituency large enough even among India's Hindus to reward it with an absolute ruling majority in the House of the People.

Indeed, it remains a significant pointer to the secular heart of India that this pro-Hindu party has never yet managed more than some 29% popular vote in any general election. And given that not more than some

3-5% non-Hindu voters are ever attracted to it, the conclusion is that some 65 or more percent of the Hindu electorate do not vote for the BJP.

Despite every species of public and ideological manoeuvre that the BJP and its individual leaders have attempted since the infamous Rath Yatra led by L.K.Advani, an aggressive Hindutva putsch that was to culminate in the watershed demolition of the four-hundred year old Babri mosque in 1992, the BJP has been unable to achieve state power in Delhi except in alliance with a plethora of other parties who hold no allegiance to the Hindutva telos.

Thus, if successful political intervention in transforming the Republic into a saffron hue has entailed a mitigation of its sectarian agenda, it has simultaneously found itself at the receiving end of purist injunctions from the RSS -Vatican in Nagpur, reminding it with frustrating insistence that its existence in the first place was to Hinduise the procedures and genius of the institutions of Indian democracy.

III

Imagine then the enormity of a situation where a still higher custodian, however self-assumed, of Hindutva 'purity,' namely the Hindu Mahasabha, now feels impelled to find even the RSS fallen into impurity. And to a point where the alleged culprits now in custody felt warranted to do away with two of its leaders for doing little on behalf of Hindutva.

Another way of conceptualizing the dynamic of this narrative – the ruthless impulse to return to 'purity' – is to say that it maps out vividly how democracies are sought to be shrunk from the expanded base of the political pyramid to its fascist point at the top.

And, European history of the last century teaches us how such impulses are sought to be validated by the 'self-evident' and 'transcedant' claims of some legend/myth of past glory, or some past wrong-doing, or, some self-assumed supremacy of race or religion, even biological purity, all peddled as unimpeachably pure 'nationalism.' A whole package of 'purity' that in turn warrants without proven mandate violent voluntary vigilantism, and triumphalist war once the state is captured.

What matters is that the illusory victimhood of the majority is first established, and then ascribed to the sinister scheming of the 'other' who is seen to 'pollute' the 'purity' of the 'real' nation's life at every point.

That history also teaches us that these coercive shrinkages of democracy and the concomitant centralization of political power then go hand in hand with the centralization of capital into a handful of monopolies.

And as the state and its economic arrangements defeat plurality and competition, the Dionysian 'purity' of self-justifying authority is born.

In our time, this package of 'purity' has been in evidence as the marriage between the pre-emptive claims of neocon imperialism and neo-liberal market fundamentalism, internationally. Christened 'globalization,' its beneficiaries have been those at the top of the pyramid, and its victims spread over a base as wide as the world.

How much of that may change now remains to be seen. It is no small tribute to the American people that the consequences of that marriage should have disgusted them decisively enough to have joyfully elected as their President a talented young man from among the 'other.'

IV

To return to India.

A remarkable dynamic counter to the re-centralizing, purity-oriented turmoil within the Sangh Parivar is currently at work among India's Muslims. A dynamic that I venture bears the promise of defeating the renewed fascistic call of the Parivar more conclusively than anything else in view.

Ever since the Partition of India which still left this country with the world's second largest population of Muslims (and yet a 'minority'), India's Muslims – with most of the elite gone over to the new country of Pakistan – bereft largely of secular leadership internally, have been at the receiving end of three sources of oppression: the animosity of the Sangh, the clout of Muslim clerical authorities, and the neglect by the state.

Invariably they have answered these oppressions in two principle ways: one, to band together qua Muslims, and to vote for political parties that could at the least ensure their physical safety.

With the coming to age of a new generation of Indian Muslims unburdened by personally experienced happenings of the Partition, the failure of the state to be wholly secular, especially in the wake of pogroms against them, and the rise of their aspirations as citizens to be equal partners in the productive processes of an improved national economy, the two habitual recourses noted above have come to be seen as wanting, even as the way ahead has seemed unclear and unconvincing.

It was with those contexts in mind that this writer had, as far back as 1990, made the following suggestion:

> Indian Muslims must…resist constructing their identities along a trans-Indian Islam. For one thing, it is only when this begins to happen that Hindutva can lose both its twisted rationale and its retrograde mass appeal. Muslims must, instead, join in with whatever democratic forces and movements are in operation in the regions in which they are located as parts of specific civil societies. Just as the critique of and opposition to majority communalist politics come increasingly from within the Hindu community itself, an invigorated Muslim democratic opinion must take on that role, not just in relation to Hindu communalists but Muslim as well.
>
> ('Pakistan, Kashmir, and the Democratic Agenda', *The Statesman*, 6 May 1990)

Recent trends have shown that this is increasingly becoming the praxis that Indian Muslims seek now to follow:

- Muslims now seek secular education up to the highest levels;
- Many young Muslim men and women are beginning to question social practices supposedly ordained by one clerical authority or the other;
- Muslims are increasingly and in great numbers part of civil rights activities that seek to deepen the values and stipulations enshrined in the Constitution, and to reinforce the non-discriminatory exercise of the rule of law;
- everyday, one influential Muslim social/cultural organization or the other, including clerical forums, publicly decry the resort to violence in any form, condemning the killing of innocents especially as 'un-Islamic';
- a joyful increase of Muslim faces is in evidence in the public arena, in the media, and in inter-community life generally;
- Indian Muslims, most of all, are beginning to recognize that it is in pluralist democracy rather than some loyalty to denominational 'purity' that progressive prospects reside both for them and for the nation-state generally.

As should be obvious, all that subverts the fascist construction of Indian Muslims that has through the last six decades so suited the Sangh Parivar.

This particularly so because the new forward-looking, secular orientation among Muslims draws approval from large sections of ordinary Hindus who remain wedded to the principles on which the Indian state bases itself.

Just as the state as well feels impelled to look more honestly at the specific areas of neglect suffered by Muslims and formulates policies to redress them.

V

Sadly, the response of the Sangh Parivar to these developments seems to be to recede further into 'purity' (emulating Muslim instincts up until now), rather than to say 'how good that these changes are underway.'

And this is not hard to understand.

Whatever its rhetoric about Muslim exclusivity, the Sangh has never at bottom desired Indian Muslims to be incorporated into the full life of the nation-state.

Indeed such a prospect fills it with the apprehension that its pristine project of transforming India into a 'pure' Hindu nation (much like the erstwhile Nepal, now so sadly fallen into secular republicanism) may indeed suffer conclusive rejection. If anything, its private anguish is caused by a sense of betrayal: despite the two-nation theory which led to the Partition of India, why should so many Muslims have chosen to stay back?

The BJP, however, to the extent that it is unlikely now to abandon its participation in Indian electoral democracy, wind up, and return to some cloistered Hindutva 'purity,' has some far-reaching thinking to do.

Does it have the will to match the paradigmatic shift in Muslim attitudes and resolves?

Does it have the wisdom to finally own the foundational principles of the Indian Republic as much in conviction as it does in tactics, accepting or rejecting its operations only to the extent that these suit or do not suit its sectarian purposes?

In short, does the BJP have the courage to jettison the fascist 'purity' enjoined upon it by its mentors, some among them now alleged to be terrorists, and rejoice in the tainted but humane, inventive, and inter-communitarian exertions of democratic creativity?

As things are, it may be idle of the BJP to think that the dynamics of an increasingly secular polity will forever keep a constituency of 'purity' ready and available to it.

Consider that this is what was once stipulated in the Katha- Upanishad:

> Hope and expectation, good company and pleasant discourse, the fruits of sacrifices and good deeds, sons and cattle – all are taken away from that person of little understanding in whose home a Brahmin remains without food.
>
> (D.S. Sharma, *The Upanishads: An Anthology*, Bharti Vidya Bhavan, Bombay, 1975, p.43)

Today, many foodless Brahmins are happy to be alongside a dalit Mayawati.

A History worth emulating in many ways.

November 2008

Enough is Enough

Says who to whom?

The Light of the body is the eye: if therefore thine eye be single, thy whole body shall be full of light.
(Gospel, Matthew, 6:22)

My skimpy acquaintance with the Taj hotel in what was then Bombay goes back to 1962.

I had been selected as a rookie sales executive by the then world's largest corporate house, Standard Oil, whose Asia division was called ESSO.

Our offices, also then the only air-conditioned building in Bombay, was at Nariman point.

Such was the nature of my job that on two or three occasions I had to be inside the Taj, full of smiles and business.

Some three years later I decided I wasn't going to sell oil for the next forty years, and I quit cold turkey to return happily to an academic life, liberally enlivened with activist involvements.

In short, the Taj hotel is truly a magnificent structure, although those days it made me happier to look at its magnificence from the outside than wheeling-dealing inside.

Like every other Indian, therefore, I am deeply saddened both by the insane loss of life, notable and ordinary, and by the damage done to this edifice. Especially when I recall that the Taj was the result of a laudable anti-colonial impulse, since Jamshedji had been refused entrance to another hotel reserved exclusively for the British.

II

My thoughts are here occasioned by a programme that one premier English-language electronic channel has been running since last night.

It is captioned 'enough is enough.'

As I have listened to the outrage pouring out from a diverse assortment of some celebrity Mumbai citizens whose haunts habitually remain restricted to the affluent South Mumbai – a zone of peace and prosperity that has had its first rite of passage to the ugliness that afflicts the rest of the city, indeed the rest of India, and rest of the world – I find myself asking the question 'who is it saying 'enough is enough', to whom, and why now'?

And how credible is the slogan of unity- at- any -cost that now so invigorates the fortunate classes in the wake of this traumatic experience?

And why should these imperious syllables calculated to shut off debate be received with unquestioning compliance when the mind is wracked by instances when South Mumbai-India has failed to employ the same 'single eye' to pronounce on other murderous and murderously divisive events?

Today, thanks to the exemplary courage and discipline of India's security forces, the Taj may have been disfigured and damaged, however brutally, but not demolished – something that seemed to have been the intent of the terrorist attack.

But, alas, some sixteen years ago a four-hundred year old iconic mosque was axed and hatcheted out of existence while the forces stood and watched, as did the whole nation on television.

Neither that fateful day, nor once in the last sixteen years, has the cry gone up 'enough is enough' on behalf of those that are now so outraged. Educated noises have been made, which is not the same thing as saying never again should this country countenance social forces that brought that watershed calamity about.

Only conscientious citizens have struggled since to bring succour and justice to the victims, often suffering opprobrium from elite India that sees them as busybodies.

Indeed, the worthies that were visibly culpable in inflicting that blood-thirsty catastrophe on the nation continue to remain in good favour with influential sections of the corporate media which may have carried on a debate on the issue but never admonished 'enough is enough.'

Some two hundred lives have been lost to the terrorist attack in Mumbai. Yet when, following the demolition of the Babri mosque, our own people killed a thousand or so of our own people in the very same Mumbai, the debate never ceased, and has not to this day.

Nor has the same terminal urgency that is now in evidence informed elite comment as to why those found guilty in that massacre (1992-93) by a high-powered Commission of Enquiry have not been given their due deserts

And what of the Gujarat massacres of 2002? No terrorists from outside there too, but our own good citizens, secure in the knowledge that they had the blessings of the top man in the job. The very top man who continues to be the darling of many elites who do not fight shy of drooling over what a wonderful chief executive he would make for the whole country, full of 'development' and profit maximization.

No wonder that Mr.Modi should have been the first to hold a press briefing outside 'ground zero' (am I sick of that copy-cat phrase) even while the bullets were flying, making it an occasion to deride no less than the Prime Minister.

The same Mr. Modi who until the other day publicly vented his strongest barbs at the ATS (Anti-Terrorism Squad) for daring to enquire into cases of Hindutva terrorism.

Narry an 'enough is enough' there; only a shamefaced disapproval barely audible on the channels.

Indeed, should you ask me, I might say that the most heroic vignette during the current imbroglio has been the refusal of the widow of the slain Karkare, erstwhile head of the ATS, to accept Modi's devious offer of money.

As also an SMS doing the rounds, asking where Raj Thackeray, the great divisive champion of Marathi interests, has been while Mumbai was being butchered? And did he know that it was security personnel drawn from all over the country, including overwhelmingly from the north and the south, who were dying to save his Marathi *manoos* as much as anyone else in the city?

The same Thackeray clan to whom South Mumbai never seems to say 'enough is enough,' cannily remembering that in time of trouble they may after all have no recourse but to their lumpen mercy.

And how ironic that we should then lament how the spirit of a grand unity so eludes us ?

In one brief word, why do we not ever hear an unequivocal 'enough is enough' in relation to the politics of fascist communalism? Or an unequivocal recognition of its intimate bearing on terrorism? Why do these realities remain subjects of TV debates from endless week to endless week wherein the culprits are afforded more than equal time?

III

Speaking of unity, there are other fissures we refuse to acknowledge, not to talk of battle, fissures that reveal equally blatantly the mote in our jaundiced eye.

A former Prime Minister of India died the very morning that Mumbai was attacked.

Not once through these days have I noticed the slightest mention even in a ticker tape on any channel but one. I mean not even the news of his passing.

And not just because our elite channels were so engrossed in bringing to the nation every second of the attack on the Taj and the Oberoi.

Let me say this: had it not been him but another former Prime Minister who is still happily with us, although ill and sidelined by his own party, the channels would at the least have divided their time equally between him and the events in Mumbai.

So why was Vishwanath Pratap Singh so rudely and with such vulgar disdain ignored even in his passing?

Because, I venture to say, there has been no more a hated figure for South-Mumbai India than him who was not merely a man of integrity next only to Nehru, and secular to the same timbre, but perhaps the most imaginative political mind of India since Nehru.

And he was hated because he had the vision and the courage to implement the Mandal Commission Report which recommended reservations in jobs and education for what the Constitution calls India's 'Other Backward Classes' (OBCs). All in consonance with explicit injunctions made by the Constitution itself.

That measure was not seen by India's habitually-ruling upper castes as one intended to bring the neglected into the life of the nation – indeed to cement a more unified nation – but as one deviously calculated to divide the polity. And they never forgave him.

It is another matter that as the years have gone by, that measure has been endorsed, indeed taken to heart, by the very forces that reviled it violently on the streets at the time. No more far-reaching tribute to the historical imperative that he then embraced.

And those whose hands have the blood of the aftermath of the mosque demolition and of the Gujarat massacre on them saw him as the Muslim-loving, 'anti-national' villain whose object it was to divide Hindus.

As though Hindus were not divided already for millennia on end.

No surprise that as V.P. Singh was cremated today, the only political leadership one saw there in attendance belonged to the OBCs and dalits! If there was any local or low-level representation of other parties, who cares. None of that could make up for what the occasion said about the current elite outrage that India must look at India with a 'single eye.'

I surfed all the channels when the last rites were in progress. Not a single channel other than Doordarshan, the official TV outlet, covered the event!

And, it bears repeating, that had it been the other former Prime Minister, I can bet you my last penny they would all have been there.

So much then for the call for unity.

IV

Lastly, I have a message for the perpetrators of the Mumbai attack.

They have circulated an email in which they claim that, among other objectives – killing Americans, Britishers, Zionists – they are acting on behalf of India's Muslims.

I say to them that in doing what they have done, they have committed the most grievous and heinous disservice to Indian Muslims.

There may well be an Indian Muslim here or there who resonates to the violent politics of revenge, as do members of other religious communities, but the great mass of Indian Muslims, as indeed the great mass of Muslims in Pakistan, have been making it abundantly known that instances of such violence and carnage perpetrated on their behalf not only run counter to what they want from life but damage their strenuous efforts to pursue those ends fatally.

Indeed, Indian Muslims have come to recognize, a recognition they have been at pains to voice repeatedly from every conceivable organized public forum, that those who perpetrate terrorist violence are no Muslims in the first place.

In the name of Allah, then, whom you never tire of invoking, desist and do something more useful and humane with your lives, something that true religion might indeed approve of.

Nor must you think that the course you pursue is about to dethrone global imperialism.

If that be your objective, there is no substitute for democratic, mass mobilization, and for an informed and argued strengthening of opinion within what nations you belong to.

In any case, do not involve Indian Muslims in any of your global concerns. And Pakistani Muslims as well.

A fine future awaits them. And many thousands to fight for their cause. Do not be their enemies.

And to South-Mumbai India we say, ask yourself what sort of unity you are looking for? Such as allows you peaceably and happily to continue to cream off India, or a just unity that, seeing with a 'single eye' everywhere, gives in due measure? And a 'single eye' that condemns evil in whatever shade it appears, be it green, red, or saffron. And, most of all, that turns that 'single eye' periodically inward to condemn, foremost, the gluttony that resides there.

November 2008

India's Long But Sure Revolution

Few things about contemporary India have been as consequential as the excruciating churning among Indian Muslims. Consequential, as I suggested in an earlier column, as well for Muslims worldwide (see my 'Fatwa Against Terrorism').

Remarkably, where vested segments among Hindu organizations have sought to move the majority community towards undemocratic closures, it is the beleaguered Muslim counterparts that have been showing the way to greater democratic consolidations.

Transcending a clutch of grievance and hurt, Indian Muslims are today truly in the leadership of Indian democracy – a day I have been wishing for and writing about for over two decades and now live to see.

And this long revolution that is underway is no sham or tactical occurrence. There is stern substance to the Muslim resolve not merely to appeal to the constitutional regime as supplicants but indeed to function as its foremost guarantors in close clasp with secular and democratic Indians across communities.

There is to me something heroic in the way in which India's Muslim citizens have over the last two years especially sought to redefine themselves in relation to the worldwide ummah and the nation at home. All that despite the most irksome provocation.

It is the rigour of that introspection which today translates unselfconsciously into a rejection of ungodly mayhem carried out ostensibly in defence of the faith, even as Indian Muslims alongwith millions of other Indians remain cognizant, as they ought to, of the oppressive forces that alternately both create and denigrate religious and cultural reaction – forces that reside both outside India and among comprador social interests at home.

II

If the discovery earlier of terrorist perpetrators with Hindu names had paradoxically helped to relieve the unmitigated odium vented on Muslims, obliging right-wing fascists, rather abjectly, to mirror a helpless Muslim discourse in their defence, the vanguard role played by Indian Muslims in condemning the attack on Mumbai on behalf not just of common humanity but of India has led to a still more far-reaching historical consequence.

This watershed secular assertion has had the effect of taking the stuffing out of what electoral expectations the right-wing Hindu BJP came to harbour in the wake of the Mumbai attack.

Its emphatic losses in the states that went to the polls after the terrorist strike scream a grassroot rejection of its communal politics. And of the ugly callousness that informs it.

However wedded to the BJP, India's corporate media have had the sense to welcome this occurrence, as it now banners the slogan that terror must never be politicized. Better late than never.

It will not be long before the residual interests of India's capitalist class and collaborative elites in retaining denominational politics, notwithstanding their often disingenuous noises against communalism, will also have to yield to propagating secular democracy in more convincing ways.

Always wary of class consolidations from 'below', India's political class will, nonetheless, sooner than later, find it as expedient to be in the forefront of the fight against communalist politics as they are now against terrorism.

And, as these histories ripen and fructify, the credit in overwhelming measure will go to Indian Muslims and to the leadership they are now furnishing.

Prophesies can come good only as products of dedicated human labour. As India's Muslims now come together with the great mass of other secular Indians, that labour is truly underway and destined to succeed.

III

In the aftermath of the Mumbai attack, this writer, like many others, have received agonizing notes from compatriots in Pakistan.

And they ask the question: can any Pakistanis truly have been involved? Is this again a 'nationalist' outcry from India? Do we not realize how wistfully fragile the democratic experiment in Pakistan is, and how ambushed from all ends?

I say to them that Indian Muslims truly show the way as much to Pakistan now as they do to India.

If their leadership in India helps to render toothless and dysfunctional entrenched evils at home, it carries an equally important message to Muslims in Pakistan.

Do not simply jerk into unanalysed, Pavlonian 'Muslim nationalist' reactions to what has happened.

Go rather back to the insight that Jinnah had voiced in his address to the very first session of the Assembly of the new nation of Pakistan.

In short, however the partition of India may have been brought about by vested interests on all sides, revisit the 'two-nation' theory, revise the Constitution, and be reborn as a secular nation-state. In that future alone resides the well-being of the subcontinent and of much more.

Same must be the counsel for Bangladesh, indeed more especially. Given that the territory could not stay put as part of an 'Islamic Pakistan,' it is an irony that upon that severance Bangladesh should still want to espouse a theorcratic statehood.

If Nepal could do it why not others?

IV

Meanwhile, it is gratifying that the UPA regime in Delhi has thus far not succumbed to the brainless jingoism of the South Mumbai crowd and those in the establishment who view that jingoism with favour.

There is now a political elite in India that requires ATM-like solutions to historical conundrums. Push in that card and pull out the required political currency, as it were. Drop the bomb and warn them not to drop their's etc., All very profoundly slick, no doubt, but eminently ignorable. As in money-making, the shortest of short cuts is recommended – and with educated bluster in the English language.

Nonetheless, it is that Dhoni from Jharkhand who may be trusted with bringing victory to India, because less slick and more astute. And more hard-working as well. As much in politics as in cricket.

Luckily, there does exist a constituency in the Indian establishment that truly realizes that every Indians' best interest is served if India serves the best interests of most Pakistanis. No easy job that, but increasingly both desirable and possible, since answering constituencies also speak up from Pakistan as they did not before with quite the same conviction.

Such a praxis on either side, and conjointly, must seek to isolate from public sympathy, public space, and all kinds of state favour those that find democracy ill-suited to their purposes, but misuse it nonetheless. Or make opportunist disclaimers when it suits them, as Sonal Shah is doing this minute, fearing she may be shunted out of the Obama transition team were she not to do so in time.

And it must equally seek to distance democracy in the subcontinent from superpower interests that work their nefarious way by alternately feeding the cupidities of entrenched classes or threatening disastrous military reprisals.

They ought to be referred back to the problems they have at home, dime a dozen, and indeed encouraged to change course.

In that context, President-elect Obama's resolve to be sworn in not just as 'Barack Obama' but as 'Barack Hussein Obama' is a most worthy and visionary step in the right direction.

It is not that in so doing Obama will have become a Muslim; it is that he will be saying that religious denominations are simply the donnee of individual identity, and need have no bearing on our citizenship or entitlements thereof. As Colin Powell was to say honourably enough during the campaign.

The worry is, as John Pilger has pointed out in a recent Znet article, that Obama's appointments to the cabinet seem thus far to suggest a pattern of 'continuity' rather than 'change.' Surprised?

All the more reason therefore for us on the subcontinent to learn to consolidate our own lives and institutions along principles that bring the most benefit in terms of non-sectarian social and cultural cohesion, collective secular endeavour, and enlightened economic democracy spread amongst the widest commonality.

The more we embrace that sort of historical project together, India and Pakistan can begin to draw away from wasteful militarism that feeds the pockets only of those that retain a value for conflict and destruction, and learn to stand up to threats as two nation-states but one people.

And that includes the Kashmiris as well, who have just been demonstrating their allegiance to the principle of democracy in unprecedented ways.

December 2008

India's 2009 Election

The Ritual of New Beginnings, and the Sameness of Contentions

Hear the voice of the Bard,
Who past, present, future sees.
(William Blake)

When you think of it, there are few things as arbitrary as the naming of time.

Such naming, indeed, might be seen as the first gesture that the homo sapien made towards ordering Time into History.

Thus a new New Year is upon the world, a marker no doubt contested by cultures other than the Gregorian whose beginnings and ends fall elsewhere among the seasons, depending on whether they privilege the sun or the moon.

But till such time as a 'new heaven and a new earth' fructify, the Dollar and the Gregorian fashion our weltanshuuang.

So, what might be in store, generally?

II

In India a general election to parliament is due early next year, and different Indians must desire to see different things happen.

India's power-elite will hope that Indian democracy finally (sic) matures into a suitably de-politicised two-party system, limiting electoral choice to the preferred agendas of the rich and the famous. In other words, a tweedledum and a tweedledee who may often be heard to be fiercely at loggerheads but, at bottom, doing one and the same thing.

However they come by their own riches, they will also want their politicians to be 'morally above-board'; and, if not, then to be dislodged by a conglomerate of CEOs and upright military men who may conjointly multiply wealth and protect it from the marauders, both of the indigenous and the invasive kind. And they will want to decapitate 'terrorism' at one fell blow through improved technology and canny management. If not, then by the war to end all wars.

And they will hope that the bulk of the labouring sort will learn to know and keep their place, and serve the 'national interest' with pride and dedication.

Other Indians of an intermediate variety will hope that their time has come, coterminously with the decline and fall of the Congress and the Bharatiya Janata Party (BJP). They will look to exploiting creative instabilities and remain undeterred by the empty rhetoric of propertied, high-caste righteousness.

And among them, hoping against hope, India's left parties will want to see something of Latin America float over the waves to New Delhi, as neo-liberal market-fundamentalism breathes its last. Even as many literate Indians will also hope that the educated turf wars among various sections of the Indian left will yield to more united recognitions that their chief adversaries lie elsewhere.

In the midst of all that, many well-wishers of Indian democracy will wish to see democracy leap from out the ballot box into the resistant prisons of Indian habits of mind – indeed, one might say, into the ancien regime of changeless hierarchies and received wisdoms.

So that before another sixty years are past, electoral mandates, in addition to spawning new governments, may also spawn a greater willingness to jettison privilege and yield to common citizenship and equality before the laws of the land. Including of those who make the laws and pronounce upon them.

Recent elections to some Indian state legislatures also suggest that working people at large will wish to see religion confined to holy places, like the privacy of the self, the perimeter of the household, and the unobstrusive temple, mosque or church, and spared the profanity of the blaring loud speaker. So that free will is exercised more freely and benignly in matters temporal, such as touch the lives of those preponderant millions whom religious strife in the public sphere promises only untold misery. Often of the so bloody kind.

III

Which is not to say that there will not be other Indians hoping that exactly contrary things happen. Among them an even greater displacement of livelihood issues by passions about social and religious identity.

And that can mean an unsurprising convergence of agendas from ostensibly opposite ends of the organized social and political spectrum.

If Indian corporates and right-wing Hindutva ideologues will wish for a victory for the BJP, so will the Jihadists. Birds of a feather, truly.

And the latter will further wish that the honourable Jaswant Singh once again takes over the foreign office under a BJP-led coalition, a position he held during the NDA regime between 1998 and 2004.

And that for a very good reason.

Think that while the poor Mr.Antulay, Minister for Minority Affairs under present dispensation, was expressing some tactless suspicions with regard to the death of the erstwhile head of the Mumbai Anti Terrorism Squad (ATS), and seeking an enquiry into the circumstances of his shooting, Mr.Jaswant Singh of the BJP was saying that he stood by the correctness of the NDA decision to swap dreaded terrorists for hostages when IC 814 was hijacked to Kandhar.

And who were the redoubtable worthies chaperoned personally by Jaswant Ji to Kandhar? Masood Azhar – source of most of Jihadi Indian troubles since then – Omar Sheikh, and Ahmad Zargar. Funnily, you might say, having reached them home safely, India now wants them back, and no one more stridently than the very people who reached them back home.

Round and round the Jihadi bush gives many people a lot to do.

But, wait, he (Jaswant) was further saying that "I will do the same thing if such a situation arises in the future" (December 18 statement made to a TV channel).

So, for two straightforwardly excellent reasons the Jihadists will want the BJP back in power since such a return might promise a renewed communalization of the Indian polity, a circumstance that offers scope for Jihadist intervention; and, secondly, Mr.Jaswant Singh's reinstallation, since that clears the ground for more hijacks and more swaps, and by his own admission Indeed, as one columnist has recently pointed out, were he now in the saddle, a hijack might have been called for to get the lone

Mumbai attacker in custody out again! (see Neena Vyas, 'A Tale of Two Statements', *The Hindu*, December 25)

As to Mr.Antulay, I fear much that 2009 might judge his faux pas more kindly than the current right-wing hype allows, although even now many, both within his own party and among other parties, have seen logic to his anxiety.

This is how I read what Antulay was saying: dear countrymen, do understand the enormity of the significance that secular Indians, most especially Muslim Indians, attach to the Malegaon probe in which, under the late Karkare's upright investigative endeavours, serving and retired army personnel and college professors, all with Hindu names, besides a saffron-donning sadhu and sadhvi have been found to have been involved in terrorist activity.

Considering that never thus far have state agencies worked up the will to nab culprits brazenly guilty of anti-Muslim pogroms, this one circumstance brought some assurance to Muslims that the Indian state might after all see its way to non-discriminatory investigation and law-enforcement, placing its boast of secularism on more credible ground than heretofore.

Consider also that Hemant Karkare had been receiving death-threats during the progress of the Malegaon probe which was beginning to throw up right-wing Hindutva culpabilities in a clutch of other episodes of terrorism, that while he was about it Karkare was being openly vilified by right-wing Hindutva organizations and individuals, and that the news of his violent death led to shameless celebrations in those same quarters – consider all that and you would know why his sudden and sure death in the very early part of the Mumbai attack might have crushed the hopes of many, and induced suspicions of a plausible kind.

In that sort of context, Antulay, who never questioned the fact that Karkare was actually shot by the terrorists who invaded Mumbai, was making the plea that an enquiry could help to clear up pretty widespread misgivings.

After all, the Kennedy assassination was similarly questioned, and rightly probed by sundry state agencies, including, most famously, the Warren Commission. Although, notwithstanding those exertions, we still can't be sure who wanted Kennedy dead.

IV

While the BJP and allied Hindutva organizations continue to bay for Antulay's blood, I dare say that 2008 will not see an end to this seminal controversy.

Just as Antulay's understandable concern has all these weeks eclipsed the enormity of the Jaswant Singh position on terrorism – thanks in large part to a complicit media – it has also prevented many from noticing how the BJP's own secular ally, the Janata Dal (U) has now sought to extend the scope of Antulay's skepticism.

A much-respected senior leader of the JD(U), Shivanand Tiwari, has sought the removal of K.P.Raghuvanshi, the late Karkare's successor as head of ATS.

And this for two reasons that must have weighed also not just in the Antulay mind but among the wider secular polity:

One, Raghuvanshi "had publicly admitted on November 11 this year to have invited Purohit (the serving army colonel thought thus far to be the king-pin of the Malegaon killings) to the ATS headquarters during his earlier tenure";

And "Tiwari said that when the probe into the Malegaon blasts began during Raghuvanshi's tenure, Muslims were viewed with suspicion and rounded up. He said that it was after Karkare took over that the involvement of Pragya Singh Thakur, Purohit and others in the blasts were unearthed" (see *Hindustan Times*, Decenber 24, 2008)

Imagine Antulay saying all that; india's TV channels would have been up in arms, screaming 'off with his head.'

But now that such apprehensions have been voiced not by a Muslim Indian but a secular-Hindu leader whose party runs the government in Bihar alongwith the BJP, Antulay's misdemeanour must rather pale and seem more cogent than it has tended to be seen, including by some forward-looking and famous secular-Muslim Indians.

Clearly, we have not heard the last of this; and 2009 could be decisively shaped by how these matters, especially the Malegaon probe and attendant right-wing Hindutva terrorist involvements (Nanded, Jhalna, Purbani, Ajmer and others) are conducted by the state.

V

Then there is the all-important poser with respect to what happens between India and Pakistan.

Without question, the Mumbai attack has put India's ruling classes in a bind which they will strive to break even at considerable cost. And the cost will depend on which among the many Pakistans emerges triumphant in the near term – the elected government, its peace-loving civil society and polity, or the Army and the ISI. Easier speculated than prophesied.

Especially when it is remembered that the American stakes in the region are equally riven, needing the Pakistan army to remain loyally engaged on the Afghan front, but also obliged to assure India that it means business on the question of seeking a termination of terrorist outfits and training camps that remain geared to inflicting mayhem on India, without much leverage on Pakistan to ensure that this agenda is realized, given its global concerns.

On its own, having provoked Pakistan to show its nuclear hand after the proud Pokhran II blasts in 1998 (trumpeted to this day by the BJP as the high point of NDA rule) India may no longer be in any position to resort to a conventional-war option. All of which makes for a 2009 that could actually worsen enormously should the Obama surge idea in Afghanistan take place.

VI

And in the middle of all that the real prospects of an economy in recession.

Some 77% Indians who subsist on less than fifty cents a day will wonder how many meals – for want of another term – they might actually manage in a working week.

And should the many social schemes dry up for want of state funds, what might then result: proliferating instances of bread and butter related crimes, or more organized and collectivized expressions of disaffection? Who knows?

Nor must it be forgotten that precisely such conjunctions – receding economy, burgeoning lack of employment, a failing parliament and party political system, provocations of external threat, supplemented by homegrown jingoism – make the breeding ground of recourses to authoritarian/fascist 'alternatives,' as war and 'national identity' are spruced up to deliver the undeliverable.

VII

And how might the Obama presidency bear on all this? Will 2009 see some material realignments among nations and regions towards a more balanced and benign world order, or will it be more of the same, albeit modulated with a grammatically wholesome American presidency?

Will the fallen corporate icons bear with their abject fallenness, or will they seek redress in gruesome ways worldwide, bolstered by a Pentagon that could volunteer for the rescue? Not unheard of, exactly. And will then China and Russia stand by, or feel obliged to demonstrate something of their manhood as well?

And what will be the pace at which mother Nature deteriorates? Or the pace at which replenishments are furnished by the human species? All up for grabs for now.

So, compadres, breathe what clean air you can, make every effort on behalf of peace and sanity, build what dykes of brotherhood and sisterhood you may, shame the greedy predators and the shameless warmongers, institute poetry where the pulpit is, so that the beast is held back from slouching towards Bethlehem. Meanwhile, does Jesus look on this Christmas and not take a part?

We may not have a whole lot of time. Have I ever been this somber before? No.

Am I growing old? Yes.

Pinter, why didst thou go? The world hast need of thee, and the likes of thee.

December 2008

2009

2009

[illegible]

[illegible]

[illegible]

[illegible]

[illegible] Mandal [illegible] of the Indian [illegible]

[illegible] Return [illegible] Spectrum [illegible]

[illegible] Democracy [illegible]

[illegible] Along the Gandhian [illegible]

The Pakistan Problem [illegible]

The Pakistan Problem [illegible]

[illegible] / 408

[illegible] 2009 / 41[illegible]

[illegible]

[illegible] And Europe / 42[illegible]

[illegible] / 429

Bharatiya Janata Party / 43[illegible]

Some Notes from My Visit to North-East / 447

Judge Not the Judges, or Thou Shall Be Judged / 45[illegible]

[illegible] / 457

[illegible] / 461

Something Rotten in the State of Gujarat / 46[illegible]

Old Habits Die Very Hard / 472

[illegible] / 478

[illegible] Extremism / 48[illegible]

[illegible] / 48[illegible]

[illegible]

[illegible] / 492

The Liberhan Report / 49[illegible]

[illegible] and the Mythology of [illegible] / 50[illegible]

Omar Abdullah

The importance of being earnest

The people of Jammu & Kashmir have been justly lauded for the resoluteness with which they came out to vote in the recent elections to the state Assembly.

Their General Will took all parties to the state's and India's political life by wholesome surprise.

Most surprised have been the separatists who had called for a boycott of the polls.

In a bitter inversion, they found the masses separating themselves from the separatist call.

To wit, the separatists are faced with a shock of recognition; they may no longer have a captive hold on the people of the valley, even when it is agreed that the remarkable turn-out – exceeding the national electoral average by some five or more percentage points – need not signify that the voters in the valley have put paid to the larger question, designated the 'Kashmir Problem.'

Unmistakably, nonetheless, they have suggested that they have a mind of their own, and have chosen to address their concerns massively within the available democratic framework. For now, anyway. Which is not to say that such decisions are not often imbued with a dynamic that rolls on rather than rolling back, depending ofcourse on how the totality of factors are brought into operation by sundry stake-holders within the state and polity.

In returning the National Conference as the single largest party, they have reiterated their continuing allegiance to the secular, Kashmiri sub-nationalism which, forged by the great Sheikh Abdullah in the second and third decades of the last century in opposition to Dogra Princely rule, still informs so much of Kashmiri self-awareness in the valley and substantial parts of the Jammu province.

And in rejecting the call of the separatists they have made a telling comment on how they perceive the potential of separatist politics at the current juncture of sub-continental history and within a drastically transformed global milieu.

Whether or not the separatist leaders have imbibed that larger text remains to be seen.

II

It has often been suggested to the separatists that given the failure of violent militancy to detach the valley from the Union of India, it might be a good idea for them to work their separatist agenda through the democratic process.

On my last visit to the valley in July of 2008, I recall asking a senior police officer as to why the separatists do not consider this option.

The analysis I received in response was nothing like you would read in any newspaper.

To wit, the following perceptions were voiced:

- many separatist leaders feared that were they to participate in the democratic process (something that would entail expressing allegiance to the Constitution of India and of the state), this would be seen as the final betrayal by armed militants, and threats to life would follow; a credible enough fear in the light of experience thus far;
- supposing that they did fight an election, sweep the polls, and form the government, there might be little they could in fact do subsequently to implement the separatist agenda;
- that such a failure would tantamount to courting disaster at both ends, since with lost credibility they could neither hope to win again nor return to leading the separatist sentiment from outside the electoral process as they have been;
- that such an eventuality could crucially lead to a drying up of funds that remain available to them from questionable sources.

Their present placement, therefore, it was argued, suited them rather nicely, since they could hibernate comfortably or ratchet up tensions as and when it suited their mentors, alternately, both among the armed agencies of militants and agencies of the state at home.

It was also argued that, as among the country's Non-governmental Organisations (NGOs), Kashmiri separatist leaderships fell into a differentiated spectrum of standing and credibility. Clearly, there are those who remain untainted, above-board, and wedded to principle.

III

The insistent impression, however, is that the priorities and perceptions of the burgeoning elite among a new generation of Kashmiri Muslims – IT whiz kids, management graduates, Ad techies, cultural theorists and artists, doctors and engineers, media professionals and so on – have altered with time.

Most that I spoke to seemed to regard Pakistan a 'failed state' and a non-existent option. Remarkably, hardly anyone thought that religion could ever be a viable basis for nationhood. The case of Bangladesh came up frequently as an instructive example, followed recently by the events in an erstwhile Hindu-theocratic Nepal. Many expressed the view that Muslims in Baluchistan and Sindh provinces of Pakistan, not to speak of the Pakhtoon, were as disenchanted with Punjabi domination as the Bengalis in the erstwhile East Pakistan had been.

Conversely, even as these new aspiring Kashmiri elites recognize 'mainland' India as a space of attractive opportunity, – increasingly so in proportion to the sweeping anti-Muslim weltanshuuang in the western world generally – they see their stakes stymied because a 'Hindu-majority' India continues to see them first and foremost as untrustworthy Kashmiri Muslims.

All that, even as many concede that the number of those who make a successful career in 'mainland' institutions, chiefly in the media and the medical world, is happily an expanding one.

Many expressed the thought that they find themselves unsafe on the Indian street owing principally also to the communal biases of the police forces, especially since 'terrorism' has come to be such a central concern – something that makes normative expectations of the rule of law and due process precariously unsure.

And, remarkably, many also acknowledge that the separatists have developed a vested interest in remaining ensconced within the familiar status quo, and that most have in fact done very well for themselves and their extended families. Jokes are made about how the best facilities of the Indian state – chiefly medical – are promptly made use of at state expense by leaders who spend much of their time fulminating against Indian 'occupation.'

When asked how they interpret now the sentiment for 'azadi' (namely, freedom/independence), most codify this in terms of a desire for full democratic rights, full re-operationalisation of Article 370 of the Constitution that guarantees 'special status' to Jammu & Kashmir, the abrogation of draconian laws such as the hated Armed Forces Specail Powers Act (authorizing the least security man to kill on sight with no accountability demanded), the return of security personnel from their hated and ubiquitous visibility on street and bylane to barracks or the borders, investment in quality areas that can assure employment to high-skilled youth according to the best standards of equipment and remuneration, full transparency in governance and the liquidation of the culture of graft and privilege, the freedom to travel and explore opportunities of trade and employment without fear or discrimination, ideally throughout the sub-continent.

Most wish the Kashmiri Pandits to return to the valley, chiefly as Kashmiris, but without seeking to lord it over the Muslims as their superior education enabled them to do prior to the decades of the 1960s and 1970s.

Despite efforts made since 1990 by Wahabi organizations, most Kashmiri Muslims remain as devoted to the syncretic/sufi inheritance as ever before.

IV

These then are the sorts of contexts that await the young and earnest Omar Abdullah as he takes over the reins of governance in coalition with the Congress party.

Quite rightly he has designated breaching the gulf between the two provinces, Jammu and Kashmir valley, as a chief priority.

The RSS has been at work in returning Jammu, especially the city, Kathua, Samba and Udhampur districts, to the sort of polarized ethos that obtained during the Praja Parishad Movement of 1949-50 (indeed, one of the leaders of the recent Amarnath Shrine 'movement' was Tilak Raj Sharma of that bygone era), and it will want to keep things that way for as long as it can.

The main challenge to the efforts of the new young Chief Minister will no doubt come from this renewed politics of communalism, leading also to an answering denominational politics from the PDP in the valley.

The way to deal with this must be to strengthen the large middle ground of opinion that will be bolstered by transparency and fairness in governmental/legislative decision-making and in the implementation processes thereof. The more the earnestness of the new government extends to incorporating civil society initiatives into these procedures the greater will be its power to show up and isolate the politics of divisiveness and hate.

Wherever imbalances do exist, it will pay rich dividends in the long term to set these on even keel.

Clearly, there is a school that holds the view that the Jammu province is more populous than the valley, and is therefore entitled to a greater number of legislators. A contrary computation also exists, one that has more takers.

The new government would be well advised to engage in a fair and open dialogue on this, and to arrive at a Delimitation Commission that has eveybody's trust. Then let the computation fall where it does. For any political dispensation that seeks to keep the composite state as one, there can be no other choice but to do this exercise fairly, and to abide by the results thereof. Always to remember the lessons of history: Bangladesh set off on its separatist course finally because the eastern wing of the then Pakistan which had won a general election was denied its right to govern.

V

On the larger question – namely, the status of Jammu & Kashmir – it is about time that all parties to the dispute began to address it with a full recognition of the concrete possibilities.

All attempts merely to use the issue as a politics-in-perpetuity must now be sternly excluded from attention and consideration.

I would think – and I have said this before – that the new regime could work towards a praxis of persuasion, aimed to obtain the involvement of all, repeat all, parties to a round table. And let the round table take as long as it takes, keeping in mind the Irish example.

In the eventuality that some/any 'hardline' segments refuse this process, insisting on a priori parameters, I am of the view that in such an eventuality the new coalition government partners must first work out the agreed contours of a scheme of Autonomy, for the state per se vis a vis the Union of India, and for the separate provinces within the state, all in concrete detail, and place it in the Assembly for adoption.

Should it be the case that the Autonomy proposals already formulated some years ago by the National Conference receive endorsement by the Congress, with or without micro-management, then this set of documents can become the basis of a debate and decision within the Assembly.

The debate can be enriched by the additional concerns expressed from time to time by the PDP, so that an overwhelming consensus is built around the proposals.

Clearly, apprehensions within the Jammu province can be answered by the scheme of devolutions thus worked out – something that can go a great way in quelling patently communalist demands wherever they come from.

If the Autonomy proposals are perceived transparently to be instrumental in deepening and democratizing decision-making processes down to the district levels in all provinces, accompanied by mechanism of funding that are equitous, there is reason to believe that the problem can be resolved to the viable satisfaction of all people's of the composite state.

As to the stakes that Pakistan may claim in this dynamic, the best that may now be possible is to open up the LOC as the effective international border to free movement and trade at designated points. Beyond this, after all that has transpired over the years, there is not a great deal more that Pakistan may be entitled to in the matter. Very few Kashmiris today have any illusions about how much Pakistan truly cares about Kashmiris, especially the Kashmiri-speaking ones.

VI

Whoever you speak to in the valley agrees that the absence of the Pandits distorts the exemplary history of the region.

One of the finest ideas that Omar Abdullah has thus far voiced is in regard to establishing a Truth and Reconciliation Commission, keeping in mind the extraordinary contribution such a procedure made in South Africa in healing wounds across estranged communities.

Indeed, such a Commission could go a long way also in scrutinizing cases of the disappeared within the valley, as well as involve the security forces in a dialogue around the happenings of the last two decades.

Caveat: in order to have any credibility or any real chance of success, such a Commission will have to comprise Jurists, Public Eminences, other Intellectuals of proven standing, preferably from within the country and across communities.

And if it be agreed on all sides, Eminences, like Nobel Laureates, wherever they are willing to come from.

The great hope is that the Omar Abdullah-led regime will be seen earnestly to be moving on these departures, whether or not any finalities are arrived at during its tenure. And none of that will be possible until the Congress understands that it and the Indian centre overall has as much at stake here as parties that represent purely regional interests.

We wish the new regime the very best of luck – something it will need in good measure.

January 2009

Satyam
India's Answer to Madoff

Lay not thy treasure upon the earth,
For thieves shall come and steal it;
Lay thy treasure in heaven…
Etc. (Gospel)

Most corporates, of course, do both things – swindle the earth as well as invest in religion. And they take care to bribe the auditors in both places.

Especially in India, where Hindus actually worship wealth as a goddess called Laxmi, and where the acquiring of vaibhav (worldly stature, replete with wherewithal) is an endorsed spiritual goal.

Like religious institutions of the top order the world-over, the Vatican for one, some of India's temple trusts are among the richest corporates going, and the classes and the masses have an appropriately unequal access to their sanctum sanctorums. And those that are out of caste have none, even as many gods that are installed within have not even a human face.

And the priests have ordained that, as among the corporates, there is a pecking order not just among the ruling elites but among the gods and goddesses as well.

You can hardly be any considerable god or goddess if the gold over your temple roof is pasty and thin, and if corporate big-wigs or their political mentors never visit you.

The state shall decree no holiday or festivity in your name.

II

Over the last two decades, following the opening up of the Indian economy per diktat of the Washington Consensus, Indian corporate strides, especially in such things as Information Technology, have been the story to follow, don't we know.

The 'breaking news' now is that the global machismo of India's corporates has indeed arrived at those pinnacles of fraud without which no corporate prowess may be taken seriously, much like the street-corner temple that only the neighbourhood urchins frequent.

The Satyam corporate (the name means 'Truth', would you believe it?) has raised India to the level of a Madoff.

Its founder-CEO, who we are told, had begun his Icarian flight from the humblest of beginnings, has confessed to having systematically fudged the accounts of the company, to the tune of some 7000 crore rupees ($70 billion ?)!

The books have been manipulated to show inflated holdings and profits and reduced debits in order to draw a market valuation wholly incommensurate with its factual standing. All calculated to induce investments that are now not worth the paper they were written on. Some 53000 very hi-tech personnel may soon be fending for themselves.

If you are a sucker still, you are free to think that nobody but the CEO had an inkling. But do consider that the auditors of Satyam have been the one and only Price Waterhouse firm – same that audited Enron. Those are not the types who ever pay for their 'efficiency.' No state is above them. They simply gather their gains and take off, where other meat awaits them.

Big swindlers require comparably big auditors as well, no?

Just as they also require clout among the political class and other scions of the establishment.

No surprise, therefore, that the firm and its CEO had been paraded by an erstwhile Chief Minister of the state of Andhra Pradesh where the firm is located to the then President Clinton on his India visit as an icon of 'shining India.'

And no surprise that the same CEO seems to have received a happy helping hand in land deals of a massive dimension favouring his family by those that govern the state now.

Or that the police could not lay hands on him for three whole days after he made his canny confession – canny, we say, because it turns out that he might have been at risk of losing the firm entirely to other predators if he hadn't done so in time.

Thus it is that India has truly 'arrived'; nobody now may say that our share in globalization is of a low order of chicanery, after all.

III

Some two years ago, the CNN-Ibn news TV channel in Delhi did a series of programmes based on sting operations that exposed the money-laundering shenanigans of some top-level sadhus and sants, many associated with the VHP (Vishwa Hindu Parishad).

This was truly a breath of fresh air.

India's corporate channels have, of course, always had this love-hate equation with organized Hindutva, seeking its perpetuation in order to thwart secular, class-based consolidations among the masses, but wary of its potential to derail the operations of capitalism per se by causing inter-community mayhem and disruption of productive activity.

Be that as it may, I remember at the time (precisely on 15 February, 2006) writing an email to the CNN-Ibn CEO, Rajdeep Sardesai, asking "when will your lenseye penetrate some corporate board-room as well?"

And receiving a chuckle from him, which read 'Desperate to do a corporate "hit"' (16 February 2006)

You see, it is silly to think that the corporates indulge in corruption; such was the meaning I read into the chuckle.

Corporate media channels, in India at the least, routinely bash the politician as being at the heart of India's degradations. They are the only ones, for example, who have spawned a culture of dynastic rule, never the corporates! And, remember, corporate inheritors don't fight any elections either.

Sometimes, very occasionally, the bureaucrats may come in for a swing or two, not for their corruption, mind you, but for the old-world obstacles they often raise to the speedy operations of capitalism. Nehruvian habits of mind, these are dubbed.

But the corporate sector, never.

Indeed the main business of India's democracy is seen to comprise facilitating the so-endless efficiency, the unremitting merit, and the global sheen of the corporate sector.

And now Satyam happens, and wretchedly the cry goes up that this may just be the tip of the iceberg, even as other corporates cry hoarse that one bad fish does not pollute the ocean.

The very same who have had no difficulty in shouting world-wide 'Islamo-fascism' at any single occurrence of 'terrorism.'

And, like it or not, India's corporate media channels are having to take notice of the Satyam scandal. Interesting in the coming days to see what treatment the story receives as the days go by.

And, equally interestingly, corporate conglomerate bosses can be heard on TV to be recommending 'regulations' that were anathema to them until a minute ago. As it is now recognized that elected governments do, after all, have the all-important role to ensure that the baby is not thrown with the bath-water, namely, that the strides that capital has been making are not reversed.

Indeed, all the way from the Lehman collapse upto Satyam, another form of globalization seems afloat – one that screams 'regulation,' and rather insidiously means to hold the governments responsible for corporate shenanigans rather than capitalism itself.

The whole point of this new slogan of globalization is to ensure that the world does not, god forbid, begin seriously to consider alternatives that stink of socialist prejudices.

It has been seen in contemporary India that whenever some notable celebrity is in trouble – facing a jail sentence, or some such – he invariably takes a posse to one or other of the favoured big temples to ask for a manat (boon), which is religiously paid back once the gods have successfully bestowed their favour.

We have nary a doubt that the minute Ramlingam Raju, the troubled Satyam CEO, and his dear brother are out on bail, the first visit they will make will be to Tirupati Devosthanam.

Celebrity CEOs and celebrity gods, after all, do belong together.

We recall that this was not always so.

India's first Prime Minister, Jawaharlal Nehru, had small love for either, and when a scandal did happen (the Mundhra scam), the straightforward result that the then heavy-weight Finance Minister, T.T. Krishnamachari lost his job.

But then Nehru was, if not a socialist, at least a Fabian/Democratic socialist.

Memories of a backward India, truly.

January 2009

Germany, 1933 / Gujarat, 2009

The Triumph of Positivism

> What matters today is to preserve and disseminate freedom rather than to accelerate….the advance towards the administered world.
>
> (Adorno & Horkheimer, *Dialectic of Enlightenment*)

Just the other day, at the 'Vibrant Gujarat' conclave in Ahmedabad, two of India's leading industrialists, Anil Ambani and Mittal, speculated from public platform what a radiantly developed country India could become were Narendra Modi to be made the 'next leader of India' (read Prime Minister).

At which memories of a similar conjuncture in the Germany of 1933 came rather rushingly to the fore.

Jackson J. Spielvogel tells us how Hitler 'knew that to fulfill his foreign policy goals he needed the technological skills of the industrialists and capitalist industry itself.'

Thus he was to appoint Reichsbank Schacht as the new president of the Reischbank, "staunch defender of capitalism, which certainly reassured business and industrial leaders about Hitler's economic direction. Fortunately for Hitler, Schacht was also an astute financier willing to use his many talents to benefit the Nazis" (*Hitler and Nazi Germany: A History*, Prentice Hall, 1988).

Sure enough, the Krupp family and a bevy of other industrialists were drafted to set Germany on the autobahn course, leading eventually within a year to a massive attention to rearming the Reich, and everything that followed, as Jews came to be seen to constitute the sinister fifth column of the Bolsheviks, threatening to capture the German economy and the state.

II

In our own Gujarat, it is not so much foreign policy that Modi has in mind as the domestic ascendance of a Fascist pattern of development that might in course of time yield him the position of the chief CEO of the country.

And, although such thinking has come to permeate the whole Indian state, what makes Gujarat stand out for the captains of industry is the social ground that Modi has prepared since the pogrom of 2002.

Briefly, a graveyard of peace where Modi's administration faces no opposition from any quarter – other political parties, labour organizations, tribals, what-have-you; and where the least voice of dissent from within his own party, the BJP, is put down with no-nonsense repression. Add to that a totalitarian control over investigative agencies, state apparatus, and large sections of the judicial apparatus – the sort of objective conditions that have led the Supreme Court of India repeatedly to intervene in their maladroit operations and to refer both the investigation and juridical determination of cases related especially to the Muslim Gujaratis to agencies outside the state, or to special task forces directly under its own aegis.

As to the media, Gujarat is one place where the most puissant of them can be put into the doghouse: for example, when recently the Times of India did an expose on the Police Commissioner of Ahmedabad, charges of sedition – no less – were slapped on the those who ran the local edition of the newspaper.

State agencies like the Collectorate of Police, the Charity Commissioner, not to speak of party fascios, are used to terrorise individuals and groups who show the gumption to work on behalf of the poor, the minorities, or the other marginalized sections. Not to speak of the intimidation meted out with full state support to artists, film-makers, other cultural practitioners whose work is seen to transgress or question the preferences of a traditional, high-caste Hindu order of things.

Modi's satraps routinely take recourse to the argument that having won elections, Modi has proved his legitimacy – an argument that is denied to the repeated and impressive victories scored by the left in West Bengal, Lalu Prasad in Bihar, Shiela Dixit in Delhi, and so on, victories that have not had the underpinnings of a fascicised, majoritarian produce of hate to propel them. Yet the world knows that Modi's electoral victories have resulted from a Hitlerite polarization of the majority Hindus against, not the Jews but the Muslims?

Nowhere in India, for these reasons, does the road to 'development' and profit-maximisation seem as smooth to the industrialists as it does in Gujarat. As to the living indices of common Gujaratis, and of the relegated sections and victims of communal pogroms especially, how are they material to the story of 'vibrant Gujarat'?

III

Adorno and Horkheimer, seeking in 1944 to understand what could explain the transmogrification of Europe from Enlightenment reason to Fascism, were to theorise how a 'tireless self-destruction of enlightenment hypocritically celebrated by implacable fascists and implemented by pliable experts in humanity' had taken place – a process calculated to to turn 'thought into commodity' and 'language into a celebration of the commodity.'

Indeed, in a whole section devoted to the media. A&H were to show brilliantly, long before Marshall McLulan, how that decline of Enlightenment humanism into reified class interest was to turn the message into the substance, thus scoring a mythical and fraudulent triumph of 'communicative reason' to which such votaries of that reason as Habermas have remained cruelly oblivious.

Given that the Indian bourgeoisie that supported the anti-colonial freedom movement, far from producing any European-Enlightenment moment of opposition, not to speak of sustained opposition, to the social/mythical weltanshuuang of the old feudal classes, simply incorporated the past into both their own lives and into the political manipulations of the anti-colonial movement, the Gujarat variety of fascism could the more easily marry instrumentalist positivism with social stasis and rootedness.

A structure of inherited prejudices and organized corporate religion have, thus, been brought to buttress commodified reason rather than thwart its virulently benumbing operations.

A & H were to point out that 'if enlightenment does not assimilate reflection in this repressive moment, it seals its own fate,' as 'motorized history' furthers the 'oblivious instrumentalization of science.'

And, with uncanny pertinence to the contemporary Indian situation: "in the mysterious willingness of the technologically educated masses to fall under the spell of any despotism, in its self-destructive affinity to nationalist paranoia… the weakness of contemporary theoretical understanding is evident."

This decline of the Enlightenment into an unreflective and despotic positivism ensures that "the flood of precise information and brand new amusements make people smarter and more stupid at once." Brilliant formulation if ever there was one.

Dialectic of Enlightenment (1944,1947,1969,2002, the last in Edmund Jephcott's excellent translation) was thus intended as a "critique of enlightenment...to prepare a positive (rather than 'positivist') concept of enlightenment which liberates it from entanglement in blind domination."

Put another way, this project was to liberate the enlightenment from the extensions it was to find in the work of Kant, Sade, and Nietzsche – all of that leading to Fascism and Nazism.

In our own case, the event in Gujarat suggests the long road still to be taken first to arrive at the Enlightenment moment, and then to disabuse that moment of its instrumentalist, anti-democratic hegemony, both tasks ominously coterminous rather than sequential. And all that almost exclusively the onus of a weak organized left and civil society organizations that often find both the state and the classes that kow-tow to it in concerted antagonism.

IV

Imagine that even as India's leading industrialists think it mouth-wateringly desirable that Modi be set-up as the Prime Minister (by which term they intend really the CEO of the state reconceived as a corporation), here are some facts about common life in Gujarat:

- one of the lowest gender ratios in demography in terms of females to males;
- one of the highest rates of female infanticide;
- girls raped by teachers for better grades, and in govt., hostels;
- boys mysteriously murdered in religious ashrams;
- vigilante violence against young people wishing to cohabit or marry across communities or castes, all duly ignored by state agencies;
- a 'freedom of religion' law that infact punishes change of religion;

- denial of ordinary civic rights to Muslims who are denied both trade rights and housing in up-market areas dominated by Hindus;
- organised lying about developmental indices: e.g concealment of the fact that it is one of the most indebted states in the country; that industrialists are attracted by government subsidies given to them; that no more than some 23% of MOUs signed with them since 2003 are actually in the pipeline; that the waters of the Narmada still do not reach the most needy regions of the state; that thousands have been displaced from the banks of the Sabarmati river to make way for the Sabarmati River Front Development Project; that fisher folk find themselves ruthlessly dispossessed without alternative recourse;
- that dalits continue to live in inhuman conditions;
- that massive numbers of children remain enslaved in the labour force;
- that official school text books continue to be full of distortions of history and other myths and inaccuracies;
- that in contrast to a national average of 66%, only some 59% of rural children can read;
- that right-wing Hindutva groups may put up bill-boards anywhere proclaiming 'Hindu Rashtra';

And so on.

(see *'Vibrant' Gujarat: Lies, Half-Truths and Illusions, The Gujarat Reality Today*, by Fr.Cedric Prakash, Director of Prashant, Ahmedabad based Jesuit Centre for Human Rights, Justice and Peace.)

Yet none of this figures in the calculations of the big-wigs who celebrate 'vibrant' Gujarat.

V

True to this pattern of cutting-edge technological development nestling next to areas of abysmal social darkeness are neighbourhoods like Noida and Gurgaon in the National Capital Region.

These are areas that have some of the highest crime rates in the country, such as include daylight abductions, rapes, robberies, road-rage killings, honour killings of young women – and men – who dare defy the traditions laid down by caste groups and caste panchayats, and other forms of violence engendered by a culture of new affluence married to the prejudices of a feudal world-order.

A pattern entirely to the convenience of investors and industrialists who wish for great leaps in technological development but think any application of the scientific ways of thinking about social and cultural issues first a nuisance and then a potential threat to the flow of their operations.

As Marx had foreseen, the bourgeoisie may have, in Europe especially, made ruthless use of science in dethroning the regressive weltanshuuang of the feudal classes, but once in power, the last thing they desired was to see science carried further forward to scrutinize the weltanshuuang of their own class.

From about the end of the eighteenth century, science had to have but one use: the exploitation and mastering of natural resources for the ploughing of surpluses at whatever social cost. And the chief source of surplus being wage labour.

Gujarat under the Narendra Modi dispensation offers just about the most perfect scenario for so doing. It also boasts one of the lowest rates of wage labour!

What fitter candidate for India's Prime Ministership?

January 2009

The High-Minded Illiteracy of the Indian Elite

No person shall be deprived of his life or personal liberty except according to procedure established by law.

(Article 21, Constitution of India)

The atavistic blood-lust of India's corporate-media elite has again been to the fore.

Same 'premier' English channel; same 'top-billed' programme (viz., *Face the Nation*), same uninterruptibly high-pitched compere, shriekingly anguished about the state's less-than-murderous response to terrorist crimes.

Question posed for the day: should the lone Pakistani terrorist, Ajmal Kasab, now in Indian custody and duly chargesheeted, be given a fair trial? To wit, does he deserve to be so given etc.,

Argument: since everyone saw the chap on video going about his terrorist business, do we not need only to find the most convenient lamppost to hang him by?

Indeed, does it matter what the Constitution of the Republic of India stipulates in matters of life, liberty, or death? And, in any case, should not an elite mob have the privilege to consider the Constitution amended through high-minded soundbyte? A self-evidently patriotic procedure that would save the state much money, and peromptarily assuage the damaged prestige of the wounded clan of celebrities who, after all, speak for the whole nation – slumdog and all; at the least those slumdogs who have now become celebrities.

Interestingly, we have not heard such lawless bloodthirstiness expressed in relation to the accused in the Malegaon terrorist blast case. Recall that those accused are also in custody, and have equally made admissible confessions with regard to their guilt. Indeed, in the latest of those confessions, Dayanand Pandey has averred that the money for the Malegaon terrorist act came from the ISI of Pakistan (no less), and through the agency of two senior leaders of the RSS, under the patronage and protection of the top man himself, namely, Shri Mohan Bhagwat.

A senior advocate on the programme clearly had a hard time balancing his soundbyte on the question posed about Ajmal Kasab, since he happens to be defending the accused in the Malegaon case.

Much as he would have liked to concur with the compere, he must have known how indefensible his defence of Sadhvi Pragya Thakur – allegedly, one of the chief perpetrators of the Malegaon blast – would have instantly become had he been tempted by the force of his cultural sympathies to argue that the constitutional provisions of due process and fair trial need not apply to Kasab. After all, what is sauce for the goose must be sauce for the gander as well – at least for a practicing lawyer!

II

The instructive inference from all this is the following: India's fattened, free-market elite never tire of singing praises of India's democratic system, and of cocking a snook at the poor relations next door in Pakistan and Bangladesh where democracy never seems to take root.

But to this day, some sixty years after the Republic came into existence via the adoption of the Constitution, the further thought that its founding stipulations with regard to freedom and equality are compellingly grounded in the rule of laws and in their impartial and non-partisan application has not sunk in.

Or the fact that even when the rights of people are circumscribed, that too must happen through the enactment of legislative procedures. Something that Indira Gandhi did during the infamous Internal Emergency of the seventies.

And remember what howls that raised among precisely the sorts of people compering the programme I have talked about!

So that when our no-nonsense elite laud the no-nonsense confinement of 'vicious' people in Guantanamo, they do not stop to think why the now thankfully bygone Bush had to find a place for them outside the juridical limits of them United States of America.

Because had they been confined within the territory of the state, they would have automatically, as per American law, become eligible to all the procedures and privileges that American laws furnish to its own citizens.

And that circumstance would have disallowed both torture and kangaroo justice of the kind that our own madam compere seemed to think warranted in the case of Kasab.

III

Indeed, a further compliment is due to American democracy.

Study any American election post the dismantling of racist discrimination and segregation, and you will find that it is never a matter of debate whther laws should apply differently to different people. What those laws should be invariably is the crux of the contentions, in relation either to domestic or foreign concerns.

Alas, we are not there yet.

Thus, in law, white-skinned Americans or Britons or others who have gone over to the Al Qaeda are as much terrorists as those whose skin colour is different, or who espouse a different faith. Those that did the Oklahoma killings found few voices that claimed that they could not be terrorists because they were white and Christian-born. Certainly, no TV channel spoke for them.

India is a different matter altogether: do we not hear from honourable right-wing leaders who aspire to lead the governance of the Republic that Hindus cannot be terrorists, because, being Hindus they must ipso facto be regarded as 'nationalists'?

The sort of reason, after all, why no mention of the Malegaon accused – all Hindus – came up at all in the programme I have alluded to.

Or why the killers of the Bombay pogrom of 1992-93 or of Gujarat, 2002 are sought to be viewed through glasses of another make.

Imagine that even after the Special Investigation Team (SIT) mandated by the Supreme Court of India to reinvestigate some of the more unconscionably gruesome episodes of the Gujarat pogrom has reported on affidavit how the state machinery upto its eyebrows was complicit in the pogrom, how a senior Minister of Modi's cabinet, one thought especially close to him, was on the scene of the carnage, distributing swords to the mob and firing from her own pistol, how two of the most upright police officers swore to being asked by Modi personally to lay off the Hindu leaders of the pogrom, none of India's premier channels has squeaked even to ask for the concerned Minister to resign, not to speak of Modi to be indicted! Do recall that during the Gujarat pogrom, among the rapes and hackings, a woman's womb was cut up and the foetus flung from the point of a sword.

To this day, no one, least of all Modi, has expressed regret, not to speak of owning up responsibility. Even as the chief perpetrators continue to roam free, the state has sought at every step to subvert the procedures and reach of the law – all that testified to by the SIT.

If anything, don't you know, the same Modi is the cynosure today of some of India's leading industrialists, and of TV channels busily projecting him as the most desirable candidate to be India's Prime Minister.

Let it be said that even under the Bush regime, this would never have happened in America.

IV

The Hindu-elite-Indian's take on the regime of laws and jurisprudence is illustrated literally everyday, of course, in one circumstance or the other But here is another notable instance, also pertaining to Gujarat.

Some months ago, the POTA Review Committee examining the cases of some 135 Muslims who have been rotting in Gujarat's jails for seven long years as persons allegedly culpable in the Godhra train-burning episode under provisions of that draconian Act (since repealed by the current Indian government), determined that the Act did not apply to these persons, since the train-burning event did not qualify as a 'terrorist' Act in the first place! The Committee held that the violence ensued as a consequence of an altercation between the karsevaks (the goons who were returning home after demolishing the Babri mosque, and traveling ticketless as well), and the vendors on the railway station at Godhra.

A finding that has since been upheld first by the Gujarat High Court, and now by the Supreme Court.

Any Gujarat heads rolled for this perfidy? Not a one. Any TV channel ask for such a head or two to roll? Forget it. They are all Muslims, after all! And Modi is the engine of a projected Hindu Rashtra (Theocratic Hindu state), one that promises much to billionaire fat-cats out to make further killings in socially neutered conditions.

Futile to recount what screams go up among the channels here when some elite suspect is held by the police just overnight in confinement, provided of course he is not Muslim.

V

India thus, in truth, is a democracy-in-the-making. Thankfully, a vast enough civil society remains fully engaged in ensuring that in addition to voting every five years, this democracy learns to recognize and accept that unless Indian democracy is also to descend to the arbitrary cronyisms of those that it fatuously derides, it must learn to embrace without question the tenets of citizenship, of universal human rights, and the dispassionate and egalitarian principles of equality before the laws, regardless of caste, creed, gender, language, or class which the Constitution mandates.

All this while many well-to-do Indians who have milked Indian democracy to the hilt thus far seem hell-bent to make of it a handmaiden to hate-filled, sectarian agendas, in addition to the interests of the class they represent and speak for.

Consider that everyday some right-winger or other is heard to scream why Afzal Guru, sentenced to death in the Parliament attack case, is still alive; but never asks the same question about Murugan, sentenced to death for the Rajiv Gandhi murder several years prior to the Parliament attack!

Simple enough reason: the one raises the possibility of causing an electorally fruitful sectarian divide among the polity, the other does not. So much for justice. And so much also for the corporate channels who never mention Murugan, even as Afzal is pressed into the service of talk shows and such-like intended to favour the communalists.

That the NDA government, led by the Hindu right-wing BJP (1998-2004) never did anything to carry out the Afzal or the Murugan sentences is of course another matter that concerns the media but scantily.

The fact is that even some Rajas and Mughal Kings of old had a more non-partisan devotion to the dispensation of justice than many of those who fulminate on behalf of Indian democracy in our day. Who more memorable than Jehangir as a dispenser of impartial justice?

February 2009

The Spectacular Return of Gandhi's Spectacles

Gandhi's spectacles did go under the hammer in New York-for money.

And money bought them back for India.

The Mahatma (great soul) wished the capitalist class to perform as the 'Trustees' of the nation's interest.

As the premier Gandhian, Vinobha Bhave, was to write of Gandhi's equation with Scientific Socialism: "Socialism wishes to advance by setting class against class, Gandhism by cutting across classes."

Well, the whisky magnate, air-line and stud farm-owning industrialist, Vijay Mallya, may or may not be a trustee of the nation's interest, but he surely has paid more than a million dollars to retrieve Gandhi's spectacles etc.

India of our days may have only an archival interest in those spectacles, but Mallya surely will benefit. Frontline entrepreneur that he is, his vision is sharp.

He may even set up a huge enterprise cloning those spectacles for the global market. And global celebrities may pay for them more than handsomely as well. And then walk the ramp. Them spectacles could become the best business going.

The powers-that-be, after all the melt-downs, still devoted to neo-liberal economics, may claim during the forthcoming general elections that they did not let the Mahatma's spectacles fall into foreign hands as mere commodity, even if it barely sees eye to eye with the eye that saw through those spectacles.

Asked once how any individual may assess and evaluate the rightness or wrongness of a course of action, the Mahatma responded with his famous talisman:

Ask yourself, he counseled, whether the thought you think or the action you contemplate has any benefit for the most wretched of faces you may ever have seen, and if the answer is 'yes' know that you are in the right path.

As the number of Indian billionaires burgeons, and the gulf of inequity between the top and the bottom widens forever, it beggars the imagination to claim that the Indian state has been a devoted votary of that talisman.

But, on another front, what is a nation without heritage?

II

The word 'memorabilia' is of course a dead give-away.

It connotes at once that he/she whose effects we gather and embellish is a memory, rather than something that impels our present thoughts and actions as a living force.

Yet, the more fallible we are, the more good memories and tough ideals we need.

Plagiarising the poet, Browning, a man's memory must exceed his greed, or what is our striving for.

There are times when a twitch of memory may reclaim us from the excesses we are about to commit. It sort of lends a Kantian distance to our embroiled subjectivity.

And memory expanded manifold is after all what we call history-which is something quite distinct from a chronology of past events.

And it may even now be rather impossible to conceive of India's modern history without reference to Gandhi, however we may work that hermeneutic. Indeed, the more he nags us, even if as an unpleasant toothache, the better our gastronomical functions might become.

III

To illustrate.

I was once asked by a perfectly well-intentioned bigot why I retained my commitment to socialist ideals, since socialism was now all a memory.

Naturally, this was several years before now, when capitalism is fast on the way to becoming one as well, – a memory, I mean – and when *Das*

Kapital is suddenly the highest selling work in Europe and Karl Marx on the cover of *Time* Magazine.

I sighed back in shamefaced agreement, but posed a question back to him as well.

'You seem to me a very religious man', I said, 'and a good one at that'. 'Of course', he shot back with glee, and some satisfaction at my percipience.

'So, do you often go to the temple?'

'Ever since I was a child.'

'That would make it some fifty odd years. Yes.'

'Which means you must have seen god more than once?'

'Alas, that good fortune I haven't had.'

'And yet', I said, 'you keep visiting the temple?' 'I do', he answered with pride.

'In other words, you continue your devotion to something you have never seen, but advise me to abandon that which I and the world have, and which continues to exist in one shape, colour, or form, here, there, and elsewhere?'

That indeed was the end of that.

IV

Which is to say, Gandhi did exist and walk the earth, even when, as Einstein had prognosticated, many find it hard to believe that such a one did so.

And not only did he walk the earth, he led a movement for freedom from colonial oppression in a way that seems today to have come to invalidate other ways of seeking freedom from oppression.

So that the more violence the world sees and perpetrates, without finding the ends that the violence is directed to achieve, the more Gandhi stands validated.

The more that the glaciers melt and the oceans rise, and the forests disappear, and draught and flood answer the sophistries of the profit-maximizers, the more all of that underscores the simple truth that Gandhi enunciated: 'the earth has enough for everyone's need but not for everyone's greed.'

The more that organized bigotry backed by big money takes mankind away from god, the more Gandhi's pluralist pieties seem vindicated, warts and all.

I recall once asking a colleague at Madison, Wisconsin – a seventh-day Baptist he was – what he thought might be Gandhi's fate on Judgment day, remembering that he was one man who carried the Sermon on the Mount everywhere he went, and sought to live Christ's simplicities.

He took not a second to answer that he (Gandhi, that is) would be damned, not having been baptized.

Jesus, are you there, and listening?

Further, the more that technologies calculated to free us from necessity actually bind us into unfreedom, the more we may recall what Gandhi said of freedom:

Ask not what you are free from, but free for.

V

So, what of the warts I spoke of – his insistence that politics without religious inspiration must be evil, that the varna ashram (caste system) has a point to it, barring the reprehensible practice of untouchability, that the cow be seen as a panacea for all kinds of economic and moral maladies, that the rich have a place just as the poor, assuming economic democracy to be neither achievable nor perhaps desirable, that the village system be preserved in perpetuity, and so forth?

Here is my simple suggestion: take a cue from the old man and mount a Gandhian movement against all those warts. And most others as well.

Indeed, what many Civil Society Movements in India and elsewhere in the world seek to do in resisting authoritarian pogroms against democracy and human rights, against the degradation of the earth, against social evils of one kind or another, against corruption in political systems, bureaucracies, and big business, against armaments, polluting agents, war, after all, owe not inconsiderably to the legacy that the Mahatma left the world.

It remains for us then only to extend the reach of that legacy to resist the irrational and uncritical impulse of idolatory, of the impulse to justify his work everywhere without warrant, and to use his methods to rid his legacy of those warts.

Something of course that must require us first to imbibe as much as we can the daring selflessness and freedom from distorting personal ambitions, the conviction to refuse sectarian purposes and self-righteous loathing of the 'other', or the belittling impulse always to claim credit that so informed his life and work.

Now that his spectacles are back with us, how about we recall what he said to the Nawab of Junagarh when he made a gift of those glasses to the fleeing Nawab: "these are the glasses through which I saw my way to the freedom of India."

That seems far more miraculous than anything in Harry Potter.

The paradox is that while India strains to recover those spectacles, it is governments and leaders elsewhere who talk passionately of his vision.

Gandhi said to Louis Fischer that he regarded himself a Communist, and that Communists after Marx had greatly distorted the spiritual force of the latter's work and vision.

Hey, as the meltdown deepens everywhere, how about we begin to see our way to marrying the two – Gandhi and Marx – and see where that takes us.

What is there to lose, more than we have lost?

March 2009

India's Democracy Challenged
The Good, the Bad, the Ugly

THE CONSTITUTION OF INDIA
Preamble
'WE, THE PEOPLE OF INDIA, having solemnly resolved to constitute India into a SOVEREIGN SOCIALIST SECULAR REPUBLIC and to secure to all its citizens
JUSTICE, social, economic, political;
LIBERTY of thought, expression, belief, faith, and worship;
EQUALITY of status and opportunity;
and to promote among them all
FRATERNITY assuring the dignity of the individual and the unity and integrity of the Nation,
IN OUR CONSTITUENT ASSEMBLY this twenty sixth day of November, 1949, do HEREBY ADOPT, ENACT AND GIVE TO OURSELVES THIS CONSTITUTION.'

It is once again Hustings time.

The fifteenth Lok Sabha (House of the People) is due to be elected, and the 16th of May, 2009 – counting day – will tell us what it looks like.

Even as the Indian Republic as duly constituted justly takes some satisfaction at its continuance, transcending a plethora of adverse circumstance, some challenges there are that qualitatively spell more than an ordinary hiccup.

Let me allude to just three.

First, the good challenge:

This comes from none other than 'we the people.'

And they make a simple but incontestable point: namely, that some sixty years to the good, it is clear that they have been at the receiving end of the bad old ruling class trick.

To wit, legitimize the Constitution in the name of 'we the people' but ensure that the state thereof in truth serves the interests of the very few.

This is achieved by enshrining 'Socialist' as the defining USP of the Constitution of India but merrily practicing capitalism of the cronyist and crassest kind.

No wonder therefore that billionaires burgeon on one end, and paupers on the other; that the Republic breaks world records in the numbers of children who suffer malnutrition, preventable diseases, exploitation at home and in the labour market, and untold abuse everywhere; that women have next to no representation in the highest echelons of democratic policy and decision making, and remain unsafe both in the home, in the work place, and on the street; that unconscionable violence and humiliation is routinely meted out to India's dalits by social 'superiors' and members of the state apparatus alike, and often in tandem; that just resistance to excesses of diverse description in vast parts of the Republic is put down by draconian laws, such as the Disturbed Areas Act and the Armed Forces Special Powers Act which empower the least man with an authorized gun to shoot to kill without any questions asked.

No wonder that the requirements of capitalism this day yield a culture of perceptions which enjoins on us to think that those whose assets on the stock market climb down some notches are greater sufferers than those who eat grass or leather or carrion for want of food. Or, failing that as well, kill their families and then commit suicide.

And that the 'growth' of the economy is crucial so that some 77% of 'we the people' can spend at least 45 cents a day!

As to redress of the legal kind, tell me about it. Try going to court against a fatso adversary and soon you will wish you had rather gone to the burial ground.

So much – and indeed the very much more that can and needs to be said – for 'socialism,' 'liberty,' and 'justice' – social, economic, and political.

Yet, as Indians in their millions in one place or another remind the custodians of the state of these facts, their's must be considered a salutary and good challenge.

After all, they only wish the Constitution to be made a universal reality, rather than to be abrogated. And they say: remember, we are 'we the people.'

And many still believe, or wish to, that the ruling interests can be pressed to do so through democratic means.

Not for long, though.

II

The bad challenge:

This comes from very sophisticated quarters who fervently hold that auctioning cricket players to the full regalia of prime-time media, – a spectacle far more engaging than the wretched business of Gandhi's spectacles and the hulaballoo thereof, or of camels and bullocks in the famous event at Pushkar in Rajasthan – and conducting the Indian Premier League (of Cricket, that is) is of far greater consequence to the Republic than holding elections to the House of the People.

And, no more significant fact here than that wide sections of the elite media, often called the fourth estate of the Republic and its chief watchdog and guarantor, concur with these sophiscates to the hilt. As does the right-wing, Hindu party, the BJP, believing that not holding the tournament alongwith the elections only shows how 'weak' the UPA government is against the possibility of terror attacks.

Thus, the government of the day is pilloried for its old-fashioned preference of ensuring free and fair elections to the Lok Sabha over supplying troups to the IPL so that billions can be made and 'we the people' entertained as a corollary.

And, just to remind you, the IPL is a private enterprise solely!

They ask in consternation: what has the Republic come to that it should seriously consider elections to the House of the People more important than cricket and the moneys thereof. After all, if the state cannot furnish food to 'we the people' let them at least eat cricket. And if the government cannot govern the country, let it at least help the IPL honchos govern cricket. After all, what matters more – cricket or the legitimacy of the state?

To wit, this challenge to the republic comes from a new set of Indians who, having thoroughly milked its offers, now feel chagrined that its continuance should so obstruct the hedonisms that they have so earned through smart practices and sharp dealings.

These are chosen ones who pooh pooh the primitive formulations of the Preamble, namely that 'liberty,' 'equality,' or 'justice' either can be or indeed ought to be made available to 'we the people.'

They hold that human beings are not differently able or differently circumstanced but, plainly and simply, unequal and undeserving of equal consideration by the state.

The IPL patrons, wherever they be, simply believe that democracy is a nuisance, the Preamble a joke, and the state their handmaiden. And the electoral process a massive redundance that merely disrupts the smooth flow of money-making and other collateral pursuits. Far more exciting to have the IPL gladiators fight to the kill while they watch and smooch on the grapes.

Which is why they do not bother to dirty their finger nails with electoral ink: after all, when either tweedledum or tweedledee come to power, they only need to make that phone call to get the job done. Indeed, their idea of democracy is to have the same set of people in power, even if under differently-coloured fig leaves.

III

Now the ugly challenge:

This comes from a set of butchers who question the notion of 'we the people' in the first place.

They hold that only some are 'people' (namely, the Hindus) and the rest are 'enemies' (chiefly the Muslims and Christians).

And they are everyday willing to kill for that belief.

A century and a half ago, an English poet wrote of the Lotus Land (where Odysseus's mariners halted during their return home to Ithaca after the Trojan war) thus:

in the afternoon they came unto a land
where it seemed always afternoon.

And of the music there thus:

music that gentlier on the spirit lies
than tired eyelids upon tired eyes.

(Tennyson, *The Lotus Eaters*)

Nothing so sleepy or gentle, though, about India's Lotus wallahs. Here is what Varun Gandhi said of the matter the other day in Pilibhit:

> This is not the 'hand' (of the Congress party); this is the hand of the Lotus. It will cut the throat of Muslims after the elections.

Ever knew the lotus to be so bloodthirsty?

And in saying that with crude directness, he only gave full voice to the teachings of the scions of the RSS.

Those teachings teach that Muslims are 'incomplete, uncultured, demonic.' Further, they are scary like rakshasas (evil demons) and have no loyalty to India because they do not accept their kula dharma, (ancestral duty), towards Hinduism. They are outsiders who must be assimilated to the point where they no longer call themselves Ali, Hassan, John, or Thomas.

And if they will not, here is what needs to be done:

'Parshuram avenged his father's humiliation by offering him libations of blood of those who had insulted him.' 'Likewise, the only way to worship the motherland after she had been defiled' (that is to say by centuries of 'Muslim' rule) would be 'to wash it with the blood of those who dared commit such an act.' (See Jyotirmaya Sharma, *Terrifying Vision: M.S. Golwalkar, the RSS, and India*; see also Siddharth Varadarajan's 'A Stench That is All Too Familiar,' *The Hindu*, March 24, 2009.)

This, then, continues to constitute a challenge to the Republic of a very different sort, albeit one which often conveniently overlaps with the class preferences of the challengers mentioned in the second canto of this write-up.

Put succinctly, these are people who wish to overthrow all the Preambular postulates of the Constitution of the Repulic of India: in their scheme of things, only those who are both born in India and have their chief icons of worship in India (rather than in Mecca or Jerusalem) can be considered 'citizens'; Indian democracy and the nation cannot be 'secular' but one based on Hindu-racial principles, and 'Socialism' as much an excrescence to them as to the IPL fraternity of India's social, political, and economic elites.

And the bad and the ugly together remain opposed to the challengers in the first part who take the egalitarian provisions of the Preamble so much to heart, or seek to cause ruckus on their behalf and behest.

All said and done, not a pretty picture.

But one thing seems for sure: neither the IPL nor 'cultural nationalism' of the ugly holds any promise of redress.

For all that, 'we the people' will need to intensify their humanist struggles, and maybe look to Chavez and the rest of Latin America for inspiration. Not to speak first of Gandhi, Nehru, and the struggles of the Communists and Socialists within India.

If indeed the rational alone can be the right, then those struggles cannot but bear desirable fruit.

"It is patience I need," said Lear.

March 2009

Capitalism is Dead, Long Live Capitalism

What of Religion?

One million Indian lives were consumed by the famine of 1771 in the Purnea district of the then undivided Bengal Province.

Warren Hastings, Governor General, proudly wrote back to the Board of Directors of the East India Company that, contrary to what might have been expected, he had collected more taxes that year than ever before!

This may have pleased the Company but did not please Edmund Burke.

His fulminations about how the Company had devastated flourishing cities like Dacca and Murshidabad and handed the region over to the tiger and the orangutan are of course legend.

So why was he so displeased, and why did he become the chief engine of the subsequent impeachment of Hastings?

Not because his heart bled for the Indians, but because he knew cannily enough that if such depredations were allowed to continue, the Company could not hope to survive for long.

Crucial to the continued exploitation of the colony and to the drain of its wealth was the preservation of the myth that the British were in India to do good to the Indians against their own primitive incompetence. The 'white man' had to show himself a saviour.

Such was also the reason why Burke was to become an implacable enemy to the revolution in France.

It was important to show that the British dispensation at home, however oppressive, was anyday to be preferred to the egalitarian impulse of the French event, and to ensure that nothing of that kind brewed within the shores of Britannia.

Some fifty years on from there, Carlyle wrote perhaps the first three-volume account of the French Revolution (1836).

And the intent was no different. The purpose was to egg the new Whig parliament to effect 'reforms' in good time lest Chartism took on the dimensions of the French happenings at home.

II

Something similar seems to have happened at the London, G-20 summit.

Recognizing the collapse of the Anglo-Saxon model of free-market capitalism, its global votaries have put their heads together to salvage capitalism from its ruins.

The air from London is thus thick with news of capitalist institutions and practices up for pragmatic 'reform.'

Interestingly, if 'reform' since the Washington Consensus (1990) had meant a near-total deregulation of capital flows, banking practices, market mechanisms, and a dissolution of the sovereignty of nation-states to enable the global privatization of wealth and profit-maximisation, 'reform' at the 2009 London conclave seems to have come to mean something rather contrary to all that. Even if only as a change of garb.

We now hear of a global intent to reform the IMF, even as more liquidity is infused into its coffers ($500 billion, precisely), of regulation of banking and other investment practices, of sops to be doled out to those most innocent of the collapse but most affected by it, and of steering clear of 'protectionism' so that the revival of global wealth multipliers are not thwarted by debilitating autarky.

In one word, the captains of world capitalism seem to have come to the view that if capitalism is to be saved for the times to come, it will need to be given the garb of a world-wide Social Democracy for a while.

And, the Sinner of the first part, namely the United States of America, seems to have also come round to the view that it may not hope to lord it over the wealth of nations in quite the unfettered way it has been used to.

Cannily, if the survival of capitalism requires that parties such as India, South Africa, Brazil, and China be incorporated fully into the world capitalist system then so be it.

Better that than give them the breathing space to chalk out political economies of an alternate kind.

And, surely, all of them seem equally elated to be now sitting at the global high-table, with a stake in the pie. And the right to make impressive noises in the world's regulatory committees.

However we may cavil at the subterfuges, the news of the death of the Washington Consensus and of its transmutation into the London Consensus must for now be greeted with some relief, even as the struggle for Socialism must continue to be engaged in with conviction and hard work.

III

The world could, however, also do with another concomitant relief – namely, from the devastating ravages that religion has been subjecting it to.

This writer has often pointed to the integral tie-up between capital and organized religion.

And a full enunciation of that thought is now available in a book called *God Is Back*, written by John Micklethwait and Adrian Woolridge.

Indeed, these two gentlemen, one a Roman Catholic and another an Atheist, concur sentiently on how the adherence to faith and to science-driven capital meet most sweetly in the market-economies of the world. Precisely what we have been at pains to say.

It is another matter that the book shallowly endorses this marriage of convenience, without, as Troy Jollimore underscores in a fine review (*Truthdig*, April 2, 2009), being troubled by any chicaneries and inconsistencies of logic or principle. Including the reality that this unholy tie-up has tended to 'encourage parochialism and hatred of the other, as well as superstition and scientific ignorance.'

As Jerry Coyne says it in *New Republic,* to say that science and religion are compatible because many profit by the conjunction is 'like saying that marriage and adultery are compatible because some married people are adulterers.'

Here is a sampling of what some illustrious souls have had to say on the matter:

> Religions are all alike – founded upon fables and mythologies (Thomas Jefferson)
>
> The Bible is not my book nor Christianity my profession. I could never give assent to the long, complicated statements of Christian dogma. (Lincoln)

> Religion is based… mainly on fear…fear of the mysterious, fear of defeat, fear of death. Fear is the parent of cruelty and therefore it is no wonder if cruelty and religion have gone hand in hand…My own view on religion is that of Lucretious. I regard it as a disease born of fear and as a source of untold misery to the human race. (Bertrand Russel)

> Say what you will about the sweet miracle of unquestioning faith, I consider a capacity for it terrifying and absolutely vile. (Kurt Vonnegut)
> Faith means not wanting to know what is true. (Nietzsche)

> I cannot believe in the immortality of the soul… No, all this talk of an existence for us, as individuals, beyond the grave is wrong. It is born of our tenacity of life – our desire to go on living – our dread of coming to an end. (Edison)

> I cannot imagine a God who rewards and punishes the objects of his creation, whose purposes are modeled after our own – a God, in short, who is but a reflection of human frailty. Neither can I believe that the individual survives the death of his body, although feeble souls harbor such thoughts through fear or ridiculous egotism. (Einstein)

and, succinctly for our consideration of contemporary international life:

> If we believe absurdities, we shall commit atrocities. (Voltaire).

Indeed, the thinker most congenial to the capitalist way of perceptions, Freud, was to call religion an 'extraordinarily useful illusion.'

IV

The fact is that where organized religion before the advent of capitalism presided unmitigatingly as the chief oppressor in league with privileged authority, capitalism, from the Protestant reformation onwards, has found in it a potent tool to neuter the secular concerns and mobilizations of vast billions of human beings, as well as to make of it yet another source of commercialized profit-making.

And when the need arose, to draft whole nations into war through a deadly mix of faith and jingoism. All for the enrichment of the possessing classes.

It is hardly a wonder that the conflict between a rampant imperialism thirsting to appropriate the oil wealth of Western Asia and the Middle

East, and to secure land and sea routes for the purpose was until the other day to find it useful to pitch the contention as a 'clash of civilizations.'

And we were invited to think that the 'civilization' responsible for Hiroshima, the Holocaust, the slave trade, and innumerable other depredations through centuries of aggressive invasions was 'superior' to Babylon and Mesopotamia. Think again.

That human frailty, compounded by immiseration and exploitation, looks heaven-word is perhaps both understandable and excusable.

Yet, that 'global' impulse has nowhere been given a more humane expression than in the saying of those drop-outs from organized 'high-religions' whom the world knows as the Sufis, the Mystics, the Dervishes and so forth.

A tribe of empathy-riddled, non-coveting, and fearlessly loving human beings who placed the least always at the centre of their teachings and concerns.

Happily, such ones were to be found among all of the world's major semitic and non-semitic faiths, and among all of the world's poet-legislators.

They were, and remain, the uniters, not the vicious dividers.

I may conclude by citing just one couplet from the great Mirza Ghalib – a couplet that could bring light and wisdom both to the fraught world of contemporary Islam and their counterparts everywhere, including the right-wing Hindutva fascists in India:

Ham Muvahhid hain, hamārā kesh hai tarke rusūm,
Millaten sab mit gayīn, ajzā-e īmān ho gayīn.

Instantly translated, this might read:

Ghalib, I hold all gods to be one god:
The highest faith can result only
When all discrete dogmas are shunned.

V

At a time now when capitalism is somewhat on the back foot, when the drums of war seem more hesitant, when relations between nations and communities are sought to be 'reset', how lovely it would be if the world were also to be freed of the fatal stranglehold of dogmas, and returned to the noble instincts of common humanity.

After all, what use is it otherwise to say that Jesus, Mohammed, Ram, Budh were indeed the finest human beings – before they were anything else – known to the history of homo sapiens?

Can we expect that capitalist and other warlords will now spare both the earth and the human race from the twin onslaughts of capital and Religion?

April 2009

The Pakistan Problem

Now suppose that the post-Independence Indian state had been constituted as Savarkar and the Hindu Mahasabha, Golwalkar and the RSS had wished it to be constituted – a theocratic Hindu one.

Clearly, secularism would not have been enshrined as one of its 'basic principles'; nor would cultural pluralism have been its endorsed social feature.

Indeed, as had been stipulated by these Hindutva ideologues, Muslims and Christians may have been granted citizenship only if they first abandoned their allegiance to Mecca and Jerusalem, accepting Hinduism as the 'national' faith.

Concomitantly, and crucially, Hindu rituals and 'time-honoured' religious practices would verily have received the sanction of the state.

Sati (widow burning after the death of the husband), child marriages in many parts of India, tantric sacrifices and other forms of voodoo, Hindu religious ceremonies mandated at official functions and in educational institutions, atrocities against dalits (christened the 'untouchables', or those without caste) and much more could all have found an endorsed place within the theocratic Constitution, deriving their legitimacy from a diverse slew of Hindu-religious texts. The killing of a cow may have been inscribed as a more heinous crime than the killing of a dalit (as per, for example, the injunctions of the *Manusmriti*).

And much more, especially in the matter of the entitlement to property as between the genders.

In such an eventuality, however secularists and rationalists might have argued, the 'cultural nationalists' would have pointed them to the nature of the state and the provisions of the theorcratic Constitution as by law established, and put them in the dock as being subversive of the ordained features of the new nation-state.

As it is, if the secularists and rationalists in India have any chance of beating back the Hindutva fascists, it is because they have behind them the authority of the secular state and India's secular-democratic Constitution.

Which is far from saying that the state in India has practiced the stipulations of that Constitution with any great conviction. It is saying, though, that the legitimacy of any governmental dispensation has had to reside in the secular Constitution as upheld by law and the courts.

II

Here is the problem with Pakistan, and it is just as well to face the fact as that unfortunate country is poised to come apart, having already lost its erstwhile eastern wing, now Bangladesh. A stark example that states based on religious principles need not be the most cohesive or lasting ones.

Carved on the grounds of religion, and christened The Islamic Republic of Pakistan, the legitimacy of the argument lies with those who insist that the Republic is not sufficiently Islamic.

That Jinnah, secularist par-excellence, who fathered the theocratic nation had foreseen this possibility and wanted to alter the grounds on which he had successfully persuaded the British to partition India was to become apparent in the very first speech he made to the Assembly of the new nation.

Alas, he died soon after. And Pakistan's first prime minister, Liaqat Ali Khan, who might have effected that sort of transformation was duly assassinated.

So that, ever since, the feudals who were the material force behind the creation of Pakistan, aided by Hindutva 'nationalists' and the British alike, and who have since also included the bulk of its military top brass, were to find in the marriage of theocracy and feudalism an instrument perfectly suited to their purposes.

Even as they did not turn away from the hedonisms that western life-styles had to offer, or from running business establishments and commercial ventures in city and hinterland. A unique army indeed.

Over the last sixty years, a miniscule, English-using middle class has indeed emerged – one that seeks to liberalise the state and polity. And those of them who are now in the forefront of battling obscurantism and orthodoxy are the most grievously trapped. Perhaps even dangerously so. Notice the sacrifices already made by many of Pakistan's enlightened media hands, and the opprobrium suffered by some outstanding human rights activists.

The problem remains that not many are also able to say that so long as the Republic remains 'Islamic' their strivings for a rational modernity stand constantly to lose for want of any endorsed legitimacy on behalf of the state.

And the hope that sections like the Taliban can be brought around to some middle course of a soft-Islamism regardless of the logic of Pakistan's birth as a new nation constantly flounders in the face of their insistence that the 'Islamic' Republic fulfil the full promise of its originations.

After all, they argue, you cannot have a theocracy run on the principles of modern jurisprudence or egalitarian social ideas. Doing any such thing seems to them to make Pakistan indistinguishable from the arch-enemy, India, obliterating the very coordinates of the Partition.

Precisely as would have been the case had the new Indian state become a theocratic Hindu Rashtra.

III

When one considers what an uphill task it still is in India to ensure the unfettered implementation of secular laws and other ' basic features' of the Constitution in the face of centuries of accumulated habits of inegalitarian thought which permeate the lawmaker and the administrator as much as they do elements in society, all despite the authority and the injunctions of state ideology, the task that faces secular-democratic civil society groups in Pakistan must seem stupendously daunting, since their efforts run counter not merely to the order of society but to the stipulations of the theocratic state as well.

The harsh question that democratic Pakistanis, individuals, groups, and political parties alike, must ask themselves is whether it will do simply to defeat obscurantist forces in democratic elections.

Or, whether, however devoted Pakistanis be to Islam, the principles of state ideology require to be rethought and reconstituted. And faith returned to its proper sphere, namely the private spaces of personal and social existence.

Indeed, the landmark elections there wherein the obscurantists were by and large defeated in all four provinces might be construed to offer the opportune moment to remodel the state along lines that the founder, Jinnah, had voiced in that speech to the first session of the new Assembly.

Can liberal and modernizing sections of Pakistanis hope to win the war against the 'Islamists' by simply continuing to fight it within the terms both they and the state stipulate, or is a paradigm shift now an imperative? Do they now need a state ideology that can lend formal legitimacy to the resistance they seek to put up?

To many worldwide, especially to those who wish Pakistan well, it does seem that soon things could go so out of hand that any such retrieval becomes foreclosed.

Is Pakistan's current parliament upto such a task? And does its army have the will to back the shift from 'Islamic Republic' to 'Republic'?

It seems obvious that Pakistan's democracy, such as it is, cannot hope to put the Taliban in the wrong so long as Pakistan's state ideology remains on their side.

And the current effort to marry Republican citizenship and the broad order of things to a continued adherence to theocratic nationhood seems destined to come a cropper.

IV

It would be dishonest not to allude to what seems to remain a profounder problem, one that may be called an intellectual closure.

As has been seen in recent years in India, especially since the demolition of the Babri mosque, a new species of intolerance in matters of debate about religion has come to afflict many Hindus. Violently so.

Yet, if this occurrence remains less than lethal (although the Malegaon event was lethal enough), or this side of overtaking the state, it must be due to the fact that traditions of 'higher criticism' with respect to religious texts in Hinduism have a long history, and can be adduced in support of refutation and critique. Many social movements that have taken place in India, and are taking place now, could not be thought of without those traditions having existed, priestly oppressions notwithstanding.

This seems equally true of Christianity. Consider, after all, that there are Christian denominations that do not still accept the divinity of Christ, but rather see in him 'man-made-divine' The Methodists, for example. Just as some denominations accept the authenticity of the Book of Revelation, and others consider the same as apocryphal. Not to speak of controversies as radical as those that concern the Gnostic gospels (*Da Vinci Code*).

All of those things without fear of losing life or limb, primarily because from the times of Wycliff, Copernicus, Galileo, Luther, and others, a heavy enough price was paid centuries ago to breach intellectual closure.

Perhaps those impulses are now beginning to stir within the world of Islam, but scantily and at great peril. Salman Rushdi and Tasleema Nasreen will know something of what is said here, no doubt.

Considering that Islam within the Indian subcontinent has had an extraordinary preponderance of the Sufi, the sceptic, the downright irreverent, including kings and princes, and fine traditions of Ijtihad (religious argumentation) it should not be such a task to plough those traditions back into the contemporary moment in Pakistan as well, and to put the reconstituted 'Republic' on the footing of a new humanist renaissance.

After all, it is education of the widest sort of latitude that alone, in the end, ensures the deepening of democratic traditions and practices and the strength to meet bigotry with resolve and informed intellectual toughness.

The lesson needs to be imbibed that religious and scriptural texts have always been as much open and subject to interpretation and controversy as any other. And the least demur from 'received' readings or official diktats need not be seen to constitute apostasy punishable with the chopping of limbs, lashing of backsides, or stoning to the death. Current day Swat in Pakistan is a telling example of what can happen when the state's ambiguity about itself becomes its dominant feature.

This writer knows from personal experience with learned Muslim friends that various Suras of the Islamic holy book can be occasions for as much debate and disagreement as any ordinary literary work, even as the Gita and the Bible. Which is why, after all, that such a number of commentaries on the Qu'ran are in existence.

In Pakistan of now, it would seem that an old nation is in death throes, and a new too afraid to be born.

Pakistan is too pretty a place, and its people too intelligent and endowed for that birth to be allowed to be thwarted.

Speaking of which, one must also say that the success of that venture will depend a great deal on whether or not Pakistan learns to forego its claim to Kashmir – a claim that it bases on the ground that it is a Muslim-majority state. As well as to cease to view India as an adversary because it is a Hindu-majority country.

If Pakistan is to make the transition to a secular-democratic state, those grounds cannot hold. What can result from such a transition is its own lasting viability and progress as a nation-state, and the possibility that it can make crucial contributions to the stability and prosperity not only of South Asia but other regions where Muslims face similar conundrums.

April 2009

The Pakistan Problem – II

> Without religion, you would have good people doing good things, and evil people doing evil things. But for good people to do evil things, it takes religion.
>
> Steven Weinberg

Nowhere is the truth of Weinberg's insight more commonly and more globally apparent than during times of inter-community violence in one part of the world or another.

Routinely during India's routine 'communal riots,' it is seen that there are those who, weapon in hand, set out to kill in the name of their religion, and, others who, despite belonging to the same religion, seek to save the hapless victims because they happen to be just good-natured human beings first.

The argument is not that individuals may not practice the tenets of a religion, but that it is only when common humanity sets religion aside that anything good gets done.

If I am writing this, it is because when the first tribal attack happened on Kashmir in 1947, it was our own Kashmiri Muslims who saved so many of us Hindus from the depredations of their co-religionist attackers.

Just as in the Gujarat pogrom of 2002, many desperate Muslims found safety in Gujarati Hindu homes.

On a larger scale, often good people in great office are known to pursue vicious ends with the self-righteous sanction of some self-defined religious impulse.

Voices come to them which decree that this country or that be assaulted forthwith if the world is to be saved for some 'noble' end. That those so-called 'noble' ends often turn out to be crassly ignoble of course remains a truism of organized histories.

Millions, we are tutored by god's own leaders, must die so that other millions be saved for the good life. Or else why would Hiroshima have happened? And, soon after, Nagasaki, without a hint of remorse at or recognition of the meaning of the first catastrophe.

It is for such reasons that the accreted experiences of collective life and strife were to persuade humanist theorists that whereas human beings are free to have and practice religions, the one thing that the state must never have is religion. It would be so much nicer if it also had no armaments. But that is another, though a closely related, story.

That after all was the idea that was to translate into the notion of human beings as secular citizens, subject to secular laws which were made by common consent and with universal applicability.

And made by institutions which embodied the 'general will' rather than some sectarian interest over which only some self-appointed closet Authority had the first and last say.

Pandit, Pope, or Mullah. Or the Dictator blessed by them, blessing them in turn.

Authority which drew its sanction from some permanently unverifiable intimacy with god. For in that scheme of things that which remains forever absent must come to be seen as having absolute sway over everything that is present or available to human determination. And through the unchallengeable agency of god's self-appointed interlocuters.

The pity of it all is that this notion of Authority tends repeatedly to find favour with the high and mighty who fear the cosequences of democracy.

And in many ivy league academies it is not unusual to find high-priests of culture who hold, breathtakingly, the view that whereas poetry must be deeply personal and private, or that literary texts ought to be read principally as coded offerings with transcendant meanings, or as inconsequentially dull or pleasurable distractions, religion we require to suffuse our collective social and political lives, and indeed, when the time comes, to kill and pillage without suffering guilt or shame. Or, indeed, doubt.

That such worthies have often been discovered, finally, to have been on the side of the fascists should be no surprise.

Which is not to say that there have not been godless atheists who have not wrought mayhem upon the world. That they did not do so under the cloak of religious sanction, or at god's command, however, left them rather more naked to scrutiny and opprobrium than those who have killed and who kill in the name of god and religion.

How often and how conveniently they have pleaded that they may not be held responsible, since they had no axe of their own to grind, being mere agents of some divine command. Command that never is susceptible to interception, however evolved the snooping technologies of the world. No satellite thus far that could bring us the gleam in god's hinting eye.

II

Even now there are those in the 'Christian' world who believe that the state should essentially be driven by Biblical injunctions. Meaning of course only those injunctions which suit their class purposes: 'give unto Caesar what is Caesar's,' but never 'it is as difficult for a rich man to go to heaven as for a camel to pass through the eye of the needle,' or 'do unto others as you would have others do unto you,' or 'blessed are the meek, for their's is the kingdom of heaven,' and 'lay not thy treasure upon the earth,' etc.,

Thus many in America still hold to the view that the 'American Dream' has had behind it a divine sanction. especially as deriving from such exegeses of the business of Christianity as provided in the work of the theologian, John Calvin. After all, it must have seemed providential to the Puritans escaping religious persecution in Europe to find a whole 'empty' continent ready and waiting for them.

As to the natives who had been there over millennia, their time had clearly come to yield the continent to god's chosen people!

With an acumen marvelously apposite to capitalism, Calvin was to argue that human beings could not be saved on the day of Judgement either by the 'good works' they had done, or because of the 'faith' they had felt, however intensely, be it. Such matters, he argued, were all 'pre-determined' by god.

And, thus, whereas the homo sapien could never have any free will in matters spiritual, he was totally his own man in matters temporal. From thence you can see how Manhattan came to be.

And that, therefore, like the 'divine right of kings' of pre-capitalist times in Europe, the American state has a similar divine right to make or break all the laws that must govern the fallen world elsewhere.

Yet, the salutary fact remains that over some two hundred years of practicing democracy, it is hardly imaginable that America will be allowed by the American 'general will' to become a theocracy. Thank god for that one certainty.

The Zionists in Israel have of course an even more ancient divine claim to make to the land of Palestine, don't we know.

But even there, all the calumnies notwithstanding, there are enough fissures and fractures and dissensions that may not be stilled violently within the democracy they practice.

That such democracy is most ot the time not to be made available to Arab Israelis is of course another matter. What is to the point here is that the critiques of official dogmas which exist in that state among the Jewish media and intelligentsia, extending sometimes to bold, radical opposition, is not subject to the fear of the loss of limb and life on behalf of the state.

In India, likewise, there are those who wish still to convert the secular nation-state into a Hindu Rashtra. Never a day passes when in some part or the other of the country we do not hear from them, in lesser or greater degree of barbarism. Now vandalizing churches, now demolishing mosques, now chasing and roughing up women in pubs, or art galleries and inimical cultural activists, now going for wholesale loot, burn, and kill pogroms.

Yet, the fact remains that the organized political force which represents that view fails to get the electoral endorsement of some 70% of Hindus. And more especially, thanks to a secular Constitution and to secular institutions of state, their's remains an unrealizable project, because unauthorized by state ideology for now.

And thanks in large measure also to the fact that the armed forces in India have no religious axes to grind.

The fact of India's secular Constitution always puts the Hindutva brigade in the wrong, and lends legitimacy to the exertions of those who seek to foil the totalitarian-racist agenda of Hindutva.

III

In an earlier column on the issue ('The Pakistan Problem') I had argued that, after all the micro-level analyses of the situation in that embroiled country, the fundamental source of what is happening there resides in the Pakistani state's ambiguity about itself. An ambiguity, for example, which does not bedevil Saudi Arabia or Iran who remain full-bloodedly Islamic.

To wit, does the legitimacy of the state in Pakistan derive from secular and egalitarian principles of citizenship and a secular regime of laws and institutions, or must it in turn still seek legitimation from a theocratic idea which supercedes what mere legislators decree?

It should be obvious that the victory of secular parties in recent Pakistani general elections notwithstanding, the question remains a moot one. Or else why would the world be witness to the extraordinary occurrence of a whole swathe of territory being officially allowed to practice Islamic Sharia dispensations rather than the systems of justice available in metropolitan Pakistan?

It is to be doubted whether even a majority, single-party BJP government at the centre in Delhi would formally say to Narendra Modi in Gujarat, 'go, you are now free to institute a Hindu Rashtra in Gujarat, delinked from the secular Constitution of India,' although such may remain its nefarious, subterranean goal. But that is in large measure due to the fact that the Constitution of the Indian Republic is unambiguously secular in the first place.

Just to recall that in Pakistan the Hudood laws brought on the books during the Zia-ul-Haq regime, chiefly to render women disenfranchised chattel, have not exactly disappeared from those books.

And, having tasted blood in the Swat valley of the North West Frontier Province, the Taliban cleric, Sufi Mohammed, has gone on to make a more fundamental proposition – one that informs the anxiety of this column and the earlier column I wrote.

Succintly, the Sufi has postulated that democracy is an un-Islamic system (*HT*, April,20).

And thereby hangs the tale to which I think attention requires to be drawn with more honesty and rigour than seems either available or palatable.

Put simply, it was my argument in the previous column that this is precisely the postulation that all those in and out of governance in Pakistan who stand by democracy need to confront.

To put the matter sharply: having successfully defeated a dictatorship, are they now willing to lose out to theocracy?

It was also another part of the same argument that this confrontation cannot be engaged in or won if the battle is joined on the turf laid out by those who hold that Pakistan being an 'Islamic Republic' must self-evidently abide by Islamic Fiqh (jurisprudence) rather than by such tenets of law and citizenship that derive from the Enlightenment.

And the fact that Pakistan does formally continue to be an 'Islamic Republic' only must lend strength and legitimacy to the Taliban argument rather than to the exertions of those among Pakistan's rights groups and westernized elites who seek a destiny of 'modernity' for their country. Not just in technological terms, but as principles of social and legal behaviour, and of state policy.

Needless to say, the attempt to meet the Taliban argument half-way, as it were, bears as little logic or promise of success in Pakistan as for us in India to grant with any modicum of compromise the perception that India is essentially a Hindu nation.

The difference is that Pakistan seemingly teeters on the edge of a paradigm shift. Sooner than later, that shift will have to happen, one way or another. It may not be able to linger too long in the area of ambiguity.

Depending on what option it chooses, there cannot but be consequences. Should it choose to go over with full scope and honesty to Islamic statehood, we may have losers of one kind. But should it choose to strive for a secular statehood, the losers may be of another kind.

And, depending on who loses and who wins, the consequences for Pakistan, the sub-continent, and the world in general will not but be also suitably momentous.

As things are shaping, it seems less and less likely that Pakistan can procrastinate forever, or find answers merely in a discourse of accommodation, however adroitly articulated. Or, indeed, deflect the problematic by foregrounding its enmity with India as its primary antagonism.

In the final analysis, Islamism and democracy may indeed find themselves at irreconcilable loggerheads, as the good Sufi Mohammed suggests. Religion, we submit may bring solace to the individual soul; it only brings disaster to nations and states when it is made their chief informing principle.

April 2009

L.K. Advani

India's oldest political formation, the Indian National Congress, dates back formally to 1885, a fact that the gauche Narendra Modi has recently scoffed at in his typical lumpen oratory.

It would hardly help to remind him, bruisingly bratish as he is in his paunchy middle age, that he exists in a free India thanks to the fact first that the Congress did start as early as it did. After all, the RSS of which he is such a poster boy, happened only in 1924 – and happened chiefly to stymie the freedom movement led by Gandhi and the Congress.

As to L.K.Advani, the 82 year old aspirant to prime ministership on behalf of the right-wing Hindu BJP, his blood-soaked career may be said to be only as young as some two decades, marked forever by the fascist putsch on Ayodhya, the demolition of a four-hundred year old mosque as he stood on site, and the pogroms that followed in Mumbai and Gujarat.

And by his inability, as the home minister and deputy prime minister (1999-2004) to prevent several terrorist strikes, even as the draconian POTA (Prevention of Terrorism Act) was in place, including the strike on the parliament of India; his acquiescence in the shameful decision of allowing three first order terrorists to be escorted in a plane to Kandahar by no less than the foreign minister of the day, and by his refusal to intervene in Gujarat as Modi's henchmen hacked the Muslims there. If anything, Modi, to whose influence Advani owes his electoral prospects in the constituency of Gandhinagar in Gujarat, remains his hero.

Interestingly, while some Congressmen raise hackles of a media friendly to the BJP for their still unproven involvement in the Delhi Sikh killings of 1984, following Indira Gandhi's gruesome murder, the fact is never highlighted that, unlike those people, Advani is actually chargesheeted under section 153-A of the Indian Penal Code, an offence that can carry a sentence of upto or more than seven years in the slammer.

And nobody who routinely complains here about the law's delay seems to complain that the case against him remains mysteriously in limbo. Or that he should still be allowed to stand for office in the face of that chargesheet while others similarly charged are routinely hounded by the media and other high-minded sections of the Indian elite.

Incidentally, with respect to the Sikh killings in Delhi (1984) for which only the Congress party is held accountable, (that many of its satraps were involved in instigating the killings is not in doubt) it is instructive to read what Nanaji Deshmukh, that most respected of the Hindutva echelon, wrote in the Hindi Weekly, Pratipaksh, in its issue of November, 25, 1984 – a Weekly then edited by no less than the redoubtable George Fernandes, defence minister of India under the NDA regime of 1999-2004.

It was his straightforward view that the killings of the Sikhs reflected a broad-based animus that India's Hindus harboured against them. And, in his view, justly. No wonder that only the other day, Jagdish Tytler, one of the Congress leaders under suspicion, fairly or unfairly, pointed to the fact that some forty or more FIRs (first information reports with the police) still remain in place against individuals known to belong to the Hindutva camp, a feature of the 1984 killings almost never brought to public light.

II

Not heeding Modi's diatribe against gerontocracy – just the other day he has said that the Congress Party is an 125 year old female hag and deserves to be dumped, a fine tribute to the Hindutva tradition of respect for elders and women especially that Hindus are everyday taught in RSS shakhas – Advani, even at 82 wishes to be India's chief executive. A pathetic case of Barkis being more than willing.

A man of little empathy and even less imagination, he now gives us clinching evidence as to why his success in achieving that goal (of which thankfully there is not even a minimal prospect as of this day) could spell the end of the secular Republic of India.

In a letter addressed to some 1000 religious leaders, the bulk of them belonging to the Hindu faith, Advani, would you believe it, has asked for their 'support' and ended his letter to them with a 'shastang namaskar' (to wit, a prostrated obeisance).

That this is much more than merely courting religious communalism and drafting it to electoral success, is underlined by what he says subsequently: "It will be my endeavour (as prime minister of a secular Republic, mind you) to seek on a regular basis the guidance of spiritual leaders …on major challenges and issues facing the nation. For this we shall evolve a suitable …consultative mechanism".

Put simply, the BJP candidate for prime ministership promises to return the secular Republic to an era when India's kings and queens – mainly kings – always had at their royal elbow the religious authority of the dharma guru, and whose counsel on matters of war and peace would be decisive.

A sort of holy Hindu empire, if you like, with Hindu versions of the Wolseys and the Cranmers ready at hand.

That Advani should have so blatantly sought this course must suggest something of the desperation with which he seeks the high office of prime minister, even if in doing so he kicks the fundamental principles and 'basic features' of the Constitution of India down the communal cauldron.

Clearly, unable during the NDA regime led by the BJP (1999-2004) to conclude a successful communal review of the Constitution (for which a high-powered Commission was indeed set up), Advani has thought it best to obtain the same result as part of campaign strategy.

It is much to be hoped that the full significance of all this registers on those well-wishers of the Republic whose life-interests tend to make them lackadaisically certain that cunningly smirking faces do not harbour intentions of the most regressive consequence to India's hard-earned secular democracy and secular citizenship, or to the sequestration of the state from allegiance to any religion or religion-based form of legislative or administrative culture. Or, in the final analysis, of the subservience of secular governance to religious diktat.

Given the continued supremacy of the RSS over the political/electoral career of the BJP, the letter in question must seem an ominous proof of what Advani intends under RSS tutelage, namely to reformulate the nation and the state along Hindutva-theocratic principles of belief and practice.

III

It is to be seen whether or not the Election Commission of India, charged with the task of ensuring that all provisions of electoral law as codified in the Representation of People's Act, and under the primary injunctions of the Constitution, are observed by Parties and candidates at election time, will take notice of the magnitude of offence that the Advani letter comprises.

After all, one of the first injunctions of electoral law in India is that no appeal shall be made to religion or religious authority for electoral gain. That the Advani letter should in black and white give religious leaders the 'assurance' that an institutionalized 'consultative mechanism' shall be put in place by him as prime minister to conduct the governance of the state in deference to their advice surely must be seen by the Election Commission for what it is: namely, not only to alter and subvert electoral laws but the state itself.

Many in India will wait to see what public reaction the Advani move will elicit, and, more particularly, what implications this will or will not have first for his candidature and then for the nature of politics in India. And whether or not Public Interest Litigation, or other legal remedies will be sought.

It will also be instructive to see how the electronic media in India deal with this unprecedented departure from constitutional sanctity and legitimacy.

April 2009

Verdict 2009

India Votes Nehru

Do I contradict myself?
What if I do;
I contain multitudes...

(Walt Whitman, *Song of Myself*)

Were India to speak of herself, she might pretty much say what Whitman famously said of himself.

Which is the reason why so many are repeatedly hard put to make some final sense of Indian social and political realities. And which is why the democratic experiment in India is so very sexy.

Can it be said, though, that Indian democracy is a work-in-progress which, even when it seems to coil upon itself, is always pointing to where it wishes to get?

I hold that such indeed is the case, and the verdict in the just-concluded elections to Parliament is an unmistakeable reminder of the sanities that inform the acumen of the citizen across state and region, community and caste, ethnicity and gender, sometimes even the high and the low.

Always remembering that whatever conclusions we extrapolate from our sea of contradictions must remain mindful both of the contingent here-and-now, and the macro-historical dynamics of the becoming of Indian democracy.

It does seem, for example, that after sixty odd years of independence and some fifteen general elections, the historical sense of the Indian voter has hardened sufficiently not to be hoodwinked anymore by emotive invocations of one kind or another. Fingers always crossed, Whitman would say.

II

You would have read and been told that hardly, but hardly anyone, the Congress party included, would have anticipated the results that came, especially that the party would reach a double hundred score; 206 was to be the eventual tally of the Congress which the infamous Modi had at one point in the campaign called a woebegone hag of 125 years!

And, yet, I could forward you a mail I sent to a friend on the 23rd of April – some three weeks before counting day – which read: 'congress inching towards 200.' Trust me.

Sleight-of-hand? Voodoo? Nothing of the sort.

Let me just share with you a little secret: when you do not find me at home, I am most likely chatting up a rickshaw puller, listening to paan-shop babble, prying out the ordinary Indian around a roadside vendor, catching up with a machine-shop worker returning to his hovel, even smoking out the odd policeman at cross-roads or recharging at a sugarcane squeezer, or conversing with the man in the taxi next to my car at the red traffic light, or borrowing a Bidi – the most plebeian form of rolled-leaf smoke – from a construction worker on site as an overture to some authentic interaction.

Wonderful to go from all that to the piece of paper and make one's computations – a resource far more dependable than wasting time with corporate electronic channels, although I listen to those as well and draw my canny conclusions.

It was that sort of joyful legwork that had brought me to the conclusion in 2004 that the numbers then would be Congress 145, BJP 138 etc., (again a claim still on record) when them channels were blaring with the certitude that the then National Democratic Alliance was set to cross the 300 mark, since India was said to be 'shining.'

Wherever you listened, two sentiments invariably came to the fore: one, that the UPA government led by, most would tell you Sonia Gandhi, was thinking of poor Indians in town and country; and, two, that there had better be an end to the politics of communalism. And that 'terrorism' was something that showed no one political group in any good or bad light. I recall accosting an auto-driver and a Beldar (Mason's helper) who had taken recourse to the Right to Information Act passed by the Manmohan Singh government! Not to speak of the middle classes.

Other things followed: opportunistic alliances, nepotisms, corrupt and criminal practices, the tendency to take social groups for granted, and so on.

In the main, the desire to encourage social-welfarist governance and to return to secular citizenship seemed decisive. Eloquent proof that the country was poised to go forward by returning to the much-maligned first Prime Minister of independent India, Jawahar Lal Nehru, who had understood with searing clarity that India could not be held together unless secular citizenship and governance was considered a sine-qua-non of its being, and unless its economic programmes were calculated to benefit most of all poor and dispossessed Indians. An agenda that required the state to remain firmly in control, rather than abdicate to oligarchies that rule the market, homegrown and foreign equally.

Pretty much what Obama seeks to do now in a beleaguered America – reinsert the state in the economic life of that nation, and attend first to those Americans who have been the most mauled by the insatiable greed of corporate America.

III

It is no secret that over the last two years especially of the Manmohan Singh government, the many schemes of social spending directed at lifting disenfranchised India, including her grossly neglected Muslims, out of economic non-existence were beginning to nauseate corporate India and their customized experts among the media.

Their hope and effort was great to see the BJP return to power.

The BJP, as I have often pointed out, bears a no-nonsense allegiance to neo-liberal marketism, and is seen additionally to have the resource to subvert social unrest on hard livelihood issues by diverting the energies of the resistors towards the comforts of religious-communal bonding.

Apart from subverting class identities among the have-nots, religion as social assertion has the further merit of making available to corporate industry the lucrative opportunity to produce that whole endless paraphernalia of festivities, holy days, and so forth, to the noisy accompaniment of the cymbal and the drum that deter those that would otherwise.

And rare indeed is the policeman who would have the gumption to stymie breakdowns of public order or of civic rights so long as these are sourced in religious activity. Such activity is presumed to transcend the claims of the state and of its regime of laws.

Alas, it has not turned out as corporate India wished it might.

And yet, in a true sleight-of-hand, it is already busy instructing the Congress that its most unexpected good-showing must, after all, owe not to its social-welfarism but to the economic 'reforms' carried forward by it from earlier days when the BJP-led NDA was in power.

And there are those within the Congress Party who will continue to buy this thesis.

There is reason to think, though, that with Sonia Gandhi at the helm both of the Congress and the UPA alliance, economic growth will continue to be seen to have any relevance only when it furthers the inclusion of dispossessed Indians (some 77% of whom are able to spend only half a dollar or less per day) into the economic life of the nation.

That indeed must require the state to remain engaged in the business of increasing farm incomes and wages, consolidating social security safety nets in town and country, enhancing infrastructures basic to the sound health of Indians, such as drinking water, free health care, equal education, investment in housing and connectivity, and special schemes for the absolutely most downtrodden. And safeguarding the mineral and forest wealth of the nation from the marauders who care a tuppence either for the ecology of the nation or the lives of the millions who both live off forest wealth and preserve it for the future.

That in turn must require the replacement of top-down bureaucracies by the grass-root empowerment of people's communities whose decisions must be backed by the financial resource needed to set the nation right where it is most needed. And the will to hold punitively accountable all those who skim off those finances or subvert decision-making at the grass-roots. Most of all, those hinterland husbands who usurp the due empowerment of their elected wives as panchayat pradhans etc., must be publicly flogged. I mean it.

It will also require obliging private entrepreneurs to heed the employment needs of the socially non-networked, and for privately-owned assets, be they hospitals, or schools, to return to the labouring what is owed to the labouring in terms of access and aid. The dirty habit whereby the privateers fatten on the subsidies, overt and covert, made available by the state must end.

And the regulation of India's capitalism will need to include the states's prerogative to disfavour forms of investment that have high profit but low social use (low social use meant to include high ecological damage) and favour forms of investment that are cognizant of the need for productive systems to address their energies to consequences that are fruitful in the widest participatory ambit.

A model of 'growth' that widens forever the gap between rich and poor, making, indeed, the rich richer and the poor poorer, must be avoided as something far worse than the swine flu now aiding and abetting the economic collapse of the capitalist world.

In brief, the verdict of the 2009 seems clearly, at the least of least, for a social democracy that respects and addresses both the political and economic claims of the vast majority of Indians, irrespective of caste, creed, community, or gender.

IV

A word about the left parties:

Much of the comment that has thus far appeared among the national media from 'reputed' columnists or smugly smiling celebrity anchors has tended to be expectedly superior and derisive. Ergo, routinely shallow.

The touching contradiction of the last five years during which the left supported the Manmohan Singh government (till that support was withdrawn because of the government's refusal to buck the nuclear deal which was outside the Common Minimum Programme drawn up as the covenant for left support) has been that the left's interventions were substantially responsible for drawing the policy emphases of the government toward social spending, and away from 'reforms' which, had these been carried out to the full (disinvestment in public sector undertakings, increased FDI in banking and insurance, convertibility of the rupee on capital account, speculating in employees savings in Provident Fund moneys, and so on) could have brought the Indian economy crashing faster than the American. (See my 'Sweet Times for the left in India').

Yet, having brought the Congress party left-of-centre in many important matters, the left itself seems tragically left out for now.

It is useful that the sniggerers also recognize that such marginalization of the left is not bad just for the left but for India as well. Sobering thought, one hopes.

Who is to blame?

Available comment predictably puts the onus on the left on the basis of tactical blunders.

That there is truth in some of this comment is not deniable, even when such comment chooses to wholly rubbish the qualities of concern out of which some of these blunders may have issued.

I have for some years mulled considerations that go beyond the tactical merely – things like should or should not the left have withdrawn support when the nuclear deal became an issue, or, should it or should it not have sought to forge a 'third front' with political groups with which it had next to no ideological affinity, and so on.

Having shared these thoughts with ideologues of the left parties, I can state them here, even if as mere skeletal formulations.

I am of the view that the left's tactical ups and downs can be ploughed back to strategic ambivalences that have dogged the left – ambivalences that have not to our knowledge formed the substance of any major collective evaluation that has seen public light.

To wit, does the Indian left still hold that multi-party Parliamentary democracy in India is reversible, and a single-party hegemonic regime achievable?

Or does it indeed accept the view that such may not be the case?

It has been my case that should the first be true, then a particular form of praxis must follow. It is to be much doubted that the left can hope for such a revolutionary path while consistently participating in state power.

The first strategic option would require that the left dissociate itself from state-power participation (be it in West Bengal, Tripura or Kerala, or voyeuristically at the centre), free itself from the contradictions that such participation must engender, and go into a movement form of politics over a decade or two. Only thus can the left hope to bring the masses to any credible or consistent understanding of the nature of class-based politics. And in so doing, it must learn not just to mouth such phrases as the 'toiling masses' but to put concrete faces to them and *like* to live among them.

This would also require learning to expand the theoretical ambit of 'class' within the plurality of the Indian 'concrete' so that the abstractions of bookishness do not thwart the opportunity to draw greater and greater numbers into a truly Bolivarian/Gandhian movement from below.

Contrarily, if the left does at bottom recognize that multi-party Parliamentary democracy is here to stay, its energies must be distributed between consolidating its hold among those who are at the receiving end of capitalism, and never letting an opportunity go to push class politics from the top leftward

To wit, this would involve learning from social-democratic engagements of the left in Europe and Latin America, on the one hand, and deeply rethinking its evaluation of the possibilities of the Congress Party and other smaller ones for a nation-wide left-of-centre politics.

It would also entail rethinking the principles of party organization, of cadre formation, and the left's overall equation with non-party liberal democrats whose numbers are not inconsiderable.

Indeed, it is to be doubted that, taking the social-democratic option, the left parties in India can hope to dislodge the Congress so decisively as to become its improved substitute.

It is in that context that its experience of the last four and a half-years during which it supported the Congress-led UPA invite to be deeply pondered.

I recall that in 2004, at the time of government formation, many of us had felt that the left should have entered government for the reason that it could both enhance the social quality of government and give the left the opportunity in some ministries of its choosing (panchayati raj, health, labour etc.,) to make its mind better known among greater numbers, as well as profit from the work it might actually have done.

Tactically, this option could have afforded the left the leeway to drop out of the ministries at the time of the nuclear deal imbroglio while still remaining an outside supporter.

I recall that we were told that it would be futile for the left to participate in government until it had enough hegemonic clout to dictate all policy. A clear instance of the ambivalence I spoke of.

There is ofcourse another possibility, one that has not been articulated – namely that the left is happy just to be doing business in West Bengal and Kerala, while picking up the odd gain here or there. A view hardly worthy of left ideology, and one that I seriously doubt crosses any Indian left mind.

It is to be hoped that the pretty bad showing in the recent election where the left has come down from 61 to 25 seats in Parliament will force some of these strategic considerations into open debate.

The left can either be revolutionary, or it can be social-democratic. The attempt to be both seems self-defeating.

V

In the meanwhile, it is no mean achievement that the time-tested shenanigans of the Hindutva parties have been routed. It will be their task to think whether or not to turn their faces on the poitics of cunning, unprincipled polemics, and revisionist and sectarian 'nationalism' and morph into a recognizable right-wing, conservative formation that reconciles itself to the Indian Constitution's stipulations about what comprises its unamendable 'basic features', such as secularism. And its stipulations with regard to the special rights granted to religious and other minorities.

They must know that it is when they cross that line, they dismay even corporate India and the corporate channels that would otherwise wish to see them always in power.

VI

Lastly, a media theme throughout the campaign of 2009 was that it was a campaign bereft of any ideological concerns – something the channels did in fact everything to further.

The sterling fact is that whereas this may have in some measure been true of the participating campaigners, except the left parties, India's 700 million plus voters had a clear ideological line in mind.

Which is what they voted for: a secular, welfare state. They deserve the nation's salute.

May 2009

Indians Down Under

Other Indians Here 'At Home'

The Kangaroos have been behaving badly. Hopping mad, you might say.

This time not on the cricket field, but on the streets, and inside Indian homes and hostel rooms down under.

A number of Indian students studying at Aussie universities have been at the receiving end of hate-violence from young, vigilante gangs – all white and anglo-saxon.

They scream 'you Indians, go home' and suchlike.

All very nastily racist, but racism strangely not directed at other than the Indian race (if it be a single race, that is.)

Which recalls to mind a white Australian couple we used to be friends with in far-away Wisconsin, USA.

Aussies, as you know, tend to be slow and under-stated human beings, but such was our friendship that they did once manage to articulate the view – complaint, if you like – that Indians do not 'mix.'

Which was our own experience as well.

Most Indians we knew there over four odd years tended to keep within themselves (often within regional/linguistic groups merely) as they studied and/or earned. A sort of invisible electric cowl wrapped their social existence, which remained confined to Indian cooking, Indian festivals, and Indian music, mostly of the filmy kind. A sort of profoundly purist insularity of individual and collective selfhood.

Never any sort of osmosis involving the dread of unclean spotting.

No wonder, some Indian electronic channels who are justly inflamed at the goings-on are being told by some experts that Indians are singled out because of two conjoint reasons: one, they do well and earn well; and two, they remain aloof from the natives.

Apparently the Chinese/Malays/Philipinoes and others seem less a threat to Australian jobs, the meaty ones especially, and more reassuringly sociable.

None of which may excuse the patently racist attacks now underway.

And just as the reality of the wantonness of violence seemed to come home to Indian corporate channels and upwardly-mobile metropolitan Indians (for whom Narender Modi remains a shining prospect for a staunch and no-nonsense future dominance of the world) after the Mumbai attack of 26/11 on the affluent icons of south Mumbai, the attacks on meritorious Indians down under have kindled an angry spark against racism.

Better late than never.

The Aussie government which benefits from the Indian influx and whose racism has thus far been, happily, restricted only to their own aborigines had better get busy in earnest. Or else, an Indian travel advisory might follow. Until some influential Indian parents, backed up by organized sponsors among travel agencies, get together to demand its removal so that their wards can go to Australia, study, and be successful in life.

In the meanwhile, the Indian thespian, Amitabh Bachan, emulating the Nobel laureate, Tagore, has taken the crunching decision to refuse a doctorate from the university of New South Wales. Why he should have deserved it in the first place escapes me.

II

On the other side, as the channels say each time they break for that imperiously unchallengeable commercial break from whence their bread and butter comes, just sample the following headlines from Indian papers through just the last five odd years – all random but true:

- the Uttar Pradesh chief minister called a 'chamar' (same as calling a black American a 'nigger') by a member of the Assembly; remember that the said chief minister is a dalit;
- a high court judge has the court premises washed with ganga jal (the waters of the holy Ganges) because the judge he took over from was a dalit;

- upper caste parents refuse to allow their children to eat meals at schools because the cook is a dalit woman;
- dalit children in government school have mid-day meal tossed to them into plates marked out, because they are dalits; the dalit girl students are routinely expected to wash all the utensils after the meal is over;
- dalit boy publicly tortured and killed with police personnel watching; accused of stealing a carcass;
- dalit groom unhorsed and flogged for daring to ride through an upper-caste street;
- dalit girl gang-raped and killed for being friendly with an upper-caste boy;
- two Balmiki dalit young men die cleaning out a soakpit owned by a Brahmin in Fatehpur village; the Brahmin stood by with others but did not attempt to save the manual scavengers because he could not touch them for being dalits.

And, indeed, much more in the same vein.

Ever accost an Indian corporate channel inflamed by such events? Do tell me. Or an Indian thespian actor have his lovely locks shaved clean? Or make even a one-line mention in his blog?

Do you know why? Ah, none of this qualifies as 'racism'; it is mere time-tested casteism with deep religious sanction. Did not even the great Gandhi say that as a 'sanaatan Hindu' he believed in the 'varna vyavastha' (caste system)?

Then what is a mere corporate channel or a thespian with lovely locks?

Recall that at the Durban conference of 2001 (August 31-September 8) where racism was debated by international NGOs, official Indian representatives put up staunch resistance to casteism being clubbed with racism in opposition to the view held by reputed historians that the two were indeed one and the same. (See my 'Caste and Race: Discrimination By Any Name, *Economic & Political Weekly*, August 11, 2001; also listed in www.killingtrain.com/badriraina).

III

Reprehensible as the attacks on Indians in Australia are, it remains instructive that the outrage such events cause now in India most affects the sort of Indians who were outraged by the Mumbai attack of 26/11.

Indians who see themselves as exemplars of a resurgent nationalism backed up by resounding capitalist performance, Indians who are most proud when their wards win something like the Bee spelling contest in America. Indians who expect all other Indians uncritically to endorse the outrages or silences they express or perpetrate.

Indians who view the indigenous battles for social equality and social justice, not to speak of the war on untouchability, as frustratingly inimical to the future of such 'nationalism' as they peddle day in and day out.

Just as they expect citizens and governments of other countries to recognize that the new India is far superior to them all, barring America (and, by association, Israel), and to accept their changed, unequal status (indeed one commentator on an electronic channel the other night pointed out to the Aussies that India is a nuclear power while they are not), they concomitantly also expect lesser Indians to accept that the new 'nationalism' is the product of some select Indians who are extraordinarily endowed, and with whom dalits and suchlike must not seek parity.

Not to speak of the premium that high-caste, svarna (twice-born) Indians have placed from the times of the influx of the Aryans on skin colour.

God may be Light in Christian lore, he is fearsomely bright and burning Agni (fire) in 'mainline', Vaishnavite Brahminism. And the dark-skinned Ravana remains a type of the Prince of Darkness in such Brahminism. Even when, amazingly, Ravana was an erudite Brahmin himself. What scope, then for the dark-skinned dalit?

To this day, when children are born, or daughters-in-law transacted, they had better be light-skinned; failing that, they begin life from a position of great handicap.

IV

Time then for inhabitants of the erstwhile Britannia's penal colony – Australia – to know that things that may be understood or excused here in India (untouchability etc.,) must be put forthwith to end there. Or else.

And we haven't even touched upon what sort of iniquities women – even the most high-powered ones – continue to suffer in the new global leader, India.

Another time.

June 2009

India And Europe

A Tale of Two Directions

Following the severe attrition in the numbers of left candidates elected to India's new parliament, a smug doyen of the Foundation of the Indian Chambers of Commerce and Industry (FICCI) could not contain his corporate glee.

Thus he pronounced on the people's verdict: "a vote for stability, continuity, and the left being left out."

He was right on all three counts, but misread the content of all three epithets.

That it has been a vote for a stable governmental dispensation is true enough; but stability for purposes wholly contrary to how the gentleman construed the matter to be.

Where the FICCI and other corporate conglomerates wish to propagate that stability has been chosen for a continuation of neo-liberal reforms, it is now amply clear that the verdict has been in favour of another sort of continuity, namely, of further expansions of public spending for the upliftment of the common Indian, some 78% of whom spend less than Rupees Twenty a day.

The reforms thus sought by the electorate are those wherein the state further asserts its interventions through financial policy to direct investment in rural employment, health services, education, a pension scheme for the unorganized work force (a massive 95% of the total Indian work force), housing schemes for the urban poor who inhabit vast slums, road networking in the hinterland, building of infrastructure where none has existed thus far through the operation of the National Rural Employment Guarantee Scheme, a qualitatively new attention to the forest rights of Adivasis, water conservation, and renewable energy missions.

Indeed, the government proposes to seriously pursue also reserving a third of parliamentary seats for women, and enacting legislation to prevent/curb communal pogroms. All of these measures open to fine-tuning and amendment.

That in the just-concluded short session of the House of the People, the Prime Minister, replying to the debate on the President's address to parliament which overwhelmingly emphasized reformist programmes of the latter sort, should have devoted most of his address precisely to these imperatives confirms the direction the government wishes to take. Indeed, it is a happy departure in ruling class perceptions that the Prime Minister acknowledged that 'left-wing extremism' has its roots in concrete issues related to land-ownership, land-use, and forest rights. Hallelujah!

Happily, it no longer seems deterred by the fashionable class view that an economic agenda calculated to benefit the vast majority of the dispossessed is bad, 'populist' policy, a mere unconscionable diversion from and depletion of the national resource.

Piquantly, thus, the organized left parties may have been reduced to a third from the numbers they had in the previous House, left agenda, far from having been left out, both won the Congress its impressive numbers, and is seen by the party now to guarantee both its own further successes as well as a just pattern of 'development' in the long term.

The left parties may want to ponder the irony that whereas on the one hand they sought admirably through the life of the previous regime which they supported from the outside to press this agenda, they may have forgotten to administer the same in the states of the union where they held the reins of state power. It is a pity that the gulf between that agenda and the left's closeness to the audience it seeks to benefit should never have seemed more yawning.

Having said that, it is to be much seen how rigorously the new government led by Manmohan Singh seeks to implement the social-democratic vision it has given to itself.

Because it would be a serious mistake to under-estimate the clout of those who, despite all that has happened world-wide to capitalist economies, find it hard to eschew foregrounding their greed – all, no doubt, in the name of 'good economics' and sound 'national interest.'

II

The significance of what is happening in India is most starkly underscored by what has just happened in Europe.

To wit, in the just-concluded elections to the EU parliament, the centre-right parties, including forthrightly fascist ones, have trounced the centre-left.

Ominously, Europe seems set on a path reminiscent of the events subsequent to the Wall-Street crash of 1929.

High unemployment, insecurity about pensions and other social security givens have turned the voter back towards racist/nationalist axes of preference. It is to be noted that many of these right-wing parties have scored victories on unabashedly anti-immigrationist and anti- egalitarian platforms.

In Austria, for example, the extreme right-wing Freedom Party campaigned on an anti-Islam platform, with the election posters calling for 'The Occident in Christian Hands.'

Same with the Geert Wilders anti-Islamic party in the Netherlands.

The singular contribution of the vote in India, by contrast, has been to defeat such forces of exclusiveness and solipsistic bigotry. In addition to a call for an economic vision driven by public investment, the Congress has won on a plank of social and cultural inclusiveness. As did Obama in America.

That India still grows at a handsome 6-7% is an inspiring enough fact to prevent the new government from being pushed towards a policy direction intended to fatten the already fattened, and impoverish further the already impoverished.

History tells us where the European choice is likely to lead Europe, having been there once before. A thought that must further embolden the Indian government to be persuaded of the rightness of what it proposes to do in the coming five years.

Needless to say, that an exclusivist, right-wing agenda at a time of economic constraints can only be a fatal proposition in every conceivable way.

III

Given this ascendance of a left-of-centre agenda in India, it behoves the left parties not just to bemoan their particular electoral losses but to build mass movements in the coming days to ensure the continuance of an agenda they have had so much to do with.

But all that can happen only if they learn not to wish away the concrete failures which led in the first place to their electoral losses. Among these, an ambiguous equation with exacerbating faces of private capital in their own spheres of influence, a style of arrogant, top-down leadership, a failure to amalgamate the multiple axes of distress among the people, and a failure to identify properly and then relate to democratic forces outside of a pristine/doctrinal left ideology.

Indeed, a larger initiative is due – one that offers a historic challenge to the diverse falanges of the organized Indian left.

This is to push the desire for party hegemony into relegation, join heads over a common left agenda, forge a unified left, and let the country have the benefits of a concerted left opposition to right-wing politics.

Such a project could be directed at creating a real, new bipolarity in Indian politics, one where the fake bipolarity as between the Congress and the BJP is replaced by a contention between all right-wing persuasions on the one side and a country-wide alternative of a left-of-centre one.

What the left parties sought to do with a fatal adhocism in the just concluded elections was quite a different thing, one flawed from the outset.

Any initiative in what is proposed would have to come from a unified and refurbished left, refurbished by some years of intimate contact with the masses not just through the agency of shut-down cadres but a more amorphously human dispersal of effort wherein listening long and hard to grass-roots wisdom takes precedence over prescriptive gems of bookish thought.

If such left unity is to be attempted, routinely-held notions of a pecking order would require to yield place to an acknowledgement of concrete contributions on the ground of diverse orders of the left. A sectarian left – a malady that seems to afflict all sections of it – is not a left that can either deliver the goods or that the immiserated masses of India are asking for.

Such a refurbished and unified left would also then require to strike a modus vivendi with progressive sections among other formations, chiefly the Congress party.

It must now seem a truism that India's economic realities and social and cultural plurality demand a caring, left-of-centre politics. A macro-historical imperative that was proved in recent years first by the defeat of the cocky, corporate-driven NDA regime in 2004, and by the re-election of the Congress-led and left-supported regime that followed now in 2009, however depleted the numbers of the left in parliament.

This recognition must continue to fuel left-of-centre forces in India, however the electronic corporate channels may demoralize, or the globally-networked middle-classes scream murder at the least measure to enhance equity.

IV

Meanwhile, it is both instructive and amusing to see how India's metropolitan media are day in and day out busy wracking their analytic heads to advise the BJP how it may best renew its fortunes, even as many of them openly concede that the BJP no longer has either any 'core beliefs' nor a leadership that can put it to the rights.

Contrarily, despite the visible victory of a left-of-centre record and agenda in the general elections of 2009, all of these worthies are equally busy pronouncing the final demise of the Indian left, and wishing that it never return.

Wondrously wonky are the ways of an elite that even though vanquished can stridently and shamelessly argue still.

June 2009

Lalgarh

Poor Relations that the Left Left out?

For some two decades now one fancy area of academic study in the Humanities has been that which is called 'Postcolonial Studies.'

The initial assumption here with regard to the Indian subcontinent would be that colonialism ended here in 1947 with the formal transfer of power.

That over the last six decades colonial oppression has indeed come to an end with regard to some 20% or so Indians – or, indeed, has taken on more subtle and seductive incarnations, often leading to voluntary consent – is true enough.

Alas, however, barring the right to exercise franchise, some 70% or more Indians remain at the receiving end of a homegrown colonial instinct.

And in every sense of the term as well: the 'developers' say to the 'hinterlanders', give us your land, your forests, your waterways, and we shall give to you our culture and religion. As to your livelihood, there is wage labour if and when you are competitive enough to get it.

Thus it is that the oral histories and folklore of India's adivasis, dalits and other relegated communities continue to be imbued with a longing for freedom, often conceived as the right to make life-choices for themselves without the imminent threat of ruling class violence.

A losing sort of yearning, as India's own railroaders, robber barons, and Hindutva peddlers mean everyday to obliterate the native Indians – this time the real ones – in true imitation of the successful conclusions of old across the Atlantic.

'Postcolonial' modernity thus seeks to take on totalitarian dimensions within the framework of franchise, recalling the caution that Adorno and Horkheimer had sounded about the brutally instrumentalist aspects of Enlightenment reason (see *Dialectic of Reason.*)

II

Instructively, however, the legacy of India's freedom movement against British colonial rule, and the subsequent practice of democracy, however coercive and top-down during the first three decades after Independence came to breach the quiescence of the 'hinterland,' leading to the beginnings of armed revolt against the refusal of the 'postcolonial' governments to pass on land-ownership to the real cultivators – a covenant upon which the Indian hinterland had been mobilized by the Congress party.

Interestingly, in the context of the current imbroglio in Lalgarh (which falls within the state of West Bengal), that revolt was also to begin in another part of West Bengal, called Naxalbari. Thus it is that the young idealists who joined that revolt came to be called Naxalites. Idealists who included students from some of India's elite educational institutions.

During that initial decade of 'Naxalism' when the Congress ruled West Bengal, the region witnessed no-holds-barred official repression on the state side, and the killing of 'class enemies' on the other.

It was still largely conjectural where the agrarian masses would position themselves in the contention.

Then the left came back to power in 1977. And to its great credit, it understood that state repression could not be a 'socialist' answer to Naxal violence.

Not until the allegiance of the agrarian hinterland was won could such violence be rendered infructuous. And winning that allegiance had to mean addressing the material cause of the unrest, namely the question of the ownership of land.

Thus it is that operation 'Barga' came to be the flagship agenda of the Left Front government. For the next two decades or more, this government did not just pay lip-service to that agenda, but, despite brutal opposition from entrenched interests, steadfastly carried out the redistribution of agricultural land by according rights to permanent tenancy.

Another vital fact that gave to the new aspiring masses a sense of being true stake holders was the devolution of decision-making mechanisms to Panchayats – a democratic innovation and refinement of far-reaching consequence, and one that the future Congress Prime Minister of India, the late Rajiv Gandhi would pick up and install countrywide through what have proved to be monumental constitutional amendments.

If all too often patedars (those who now had documentary proof of land-ownership in West Bengal) were hauled to the courts, they knew that this was something for which the Left Front government could not be held accountable. It was merely a reminder that what the Left Front government was seeking to do had after all to be done within the constitutional contours of a class state in India – something that the local government was powerless to amend.

The moot point is that land transfers in the Bengal hinterland, hand in hand with the devolution of democratic processes through the Panchayati system precluded any lure that the armed Naxalbari radicals might have held for the land-hungry marginalized.

Unprecedentedly in democratic history world-wide, the Left Front was to be re-elected to power in West Bengal from 1977 to date!

Uncontestably, the Spartan and deeply caring and imaginative helmsmanship of the Left Front by the legendary Jyoti Basu, and the general probity of ministers in government contributed uniquely to this achievement.

That oppositional party-political forces have so long remained out of favour in West Bengal has often been attributed by them to the 'high-handed' electoral excesses of the Left Front, especially of the cadres of the CPI(M). Even 'scientific rigging' of the vote has been claimed.

And yet, the elections to the Assembly in 2006 conducted by the Election Commission of India entirely under the aegis of forces, civil and police, drawn from outside West Bengal produced a still more unprecedented victory for the LF! Revalidating, if you like, the stunning parliamentary victories of 2004.

As comment is made on the failures of the LF, and of the recent depletion of its elected numbers to parliament, it is only just that those histories be kept in mind as well.

III

Having said that, it took one Nandigram episode to bring to a boil corrosions that had been accumulating over three decades of LF rule in West Bengal.

Broadly, the following distortions seemed to have progressively disfigured the idealist impulses of the LF:

- a steady but unremedied breakdown of direct communication with the people, wherein the Panchayats came to be fiefdoms of party sartraps;
- the consolidation of a cadre that now came to be distinct from the people, that instead of facilitating further extensions of the creative energies of the impoverished masses stood like an opaque wall between them and the government, no longer a receptive vanguard, but increasingly a red guard; no longer listening to the mass but telling them from time to time what was expected of them;
- a cadre that became instrumental in installing party over government, in distributing largesse and favour, in construing party hegemony as diktat, and being perceived with some justice as standing above the normal operations of law;
- a party and government that slowly but surely simply habituated itself to taking its mass base as a given, assuming that regressive turn-arounds in economic policy and new emphases in investment would be swallowed on trust;
- askance at the fact that this base did not view the new LF love for the Tatas and other industrial tycoons with the same favour as the party and government;
- a shocking neglect of spheres of social concern such as services bearing directly on the daily lives of millions – health, power, education, employment;
- an attitude towards religious minorities that seemed to replicate the habits of mind of the Congress party – provide physical security and little else to boot, a fact that the Sachar Committee brought to light, and that became a major input into the disaffections among the Muslim farm community in Nandigram;

IV

Rapidly enough, yesterday's Jacobins seemed to have transformed not just into Girondists but pleaders on behalf of class forces that wished to turn their balance now quite the other way.

Little wonder that a left extremism that had defeated its own cause by refusing democracy and choosing to stay with armed struggle has been able to re-enter a West Bengal whose creative LF politics had usurped its legitimacy over the years, while in other parts of India all-too inimical and repressively anti-people regimes have continued to provide space for armed resistance to state policies.

In this renewed context, the West Bengal LF unsurprisingly finds itself in a piquant situation.

Much as it decries the politics of the gun, it now recognizes that the Maoists, all said and done, are taking up causes that are its own, and that somehow it allowed to fall by the wayside during its protracted rule.

It is therefore unable either to condone the violence or to lump the Maoists as just another 'terrorist' organization that can be dealt with simply through a ban.

It is faced with the recognition that if in years gone by it had successfully taken the masses in the hinterland away from the extremists, the latter may now have returned the compliment.

As to coercion and violence, it must be a terrible thing for the perception to grow that between the gun-toting Maoists and the cadres of the LF, the distinction may not amount to a great deal, deeply erroneous as this surely is.

Caught between the state forces and the Maoists, the disenfranchised Santhal adivasis that largely inhabit Lalgarh bordering with Jharkhand seem now to have only some sensitive urban voices to speak for their lives. Here is what some well-known academics and public figures have to say in a letter to the media:

> faulting the WB government for using force to bring Lalgarh back into state control, they hold that negotiations should have been attempted, and that the state has failed to 'differentiate between violent Maoists and unarmed civilians.' Even as they also say 'we deplore the reckless violence of the Maoists, who have exploited West Bengal's post election chaos by using deprived and angry tribal people as pawns and by brutally attacking CPI(M) cadres and offices.' (see letter to *Hindustan Times*, June 22, by Sumit Sarkar and others.)

V

Here then is the conundrum: vast numbers of the Indian intelligentsia who reject both the oppressive, colonial policies of 'postcolonial' governments in India and the politics of armed insurrection had come to invest oodles of hope in the LF experiment in West Bengal especially.

The problem with regard to the Indian hinterland has devolved around an increasingly rampant alliance between state power and marauding corporate interest.

Over the last two decades especially, the state has allowed indiscriminate mining activity in forest areas that have been the lifeblood of the adivasis. And all organized resistance, however democratic, to this pattern of 'development' has been crushed with heavy hand. Throughout the length and breadth of north and central India, oustees from forest and dam sites today have come to constitute refugees who have nowhere to turn. Multinationals and their comprador companies have tended to acquire privileges and stakes that override the livelihood needs and prerogatives of millions upon millions of Indians.

And sadly, far from building concerted mass movements to thwart such depredations, the democratic left has come to be seen as wanting to partake of the pie, however cautiously it frames its polemics in the matter. Not to speak of its failure in addressing forms of social oppression that go hand in hand with such neo-colonial exploitation.

What wonder then that a fillip has been provided to armed left extremists who argue that the mechanisms of Indian parliamentary democracy will never allow class interests to be dented by noises made from the standpoint of morality and fairplay.

Conversely, there remains the perception that sporadic armed resistance to the state promises no lasting debilitation to the state either. Indeed, if anything, it provides a powerful state all the argument it needs to further hone its repressive machineries. After all, even in a state like Nepal, this recognition led recently to the abandonement of armed struggle by the Maoists there in favour of peaceful mass politics within a constitutional democracy. Just as large swathes of Latin America made the transition from insurrectionary resistance to democratic mass politics with sterling successes. That the LTTE in Srilanka should have been so conclusively liquidated militarily must also tell its own story.

Within these macro-historical considerations, the failure of the West Bengal LF to practice and refine democracy is seen not just as an isolated occurrence within one Indian state, but a tragic collapse fraught with far-reaching consequence for the future of Indian democracy and of what may be possible for grass-roots politics within its stipulations.

All of which leads to the question: how irretrievable is the damage done? It is a question of the most relevance to those who seek not just to critique the LF but seemingly to discard it as well.

Contrarily, the West Bengal LF needs to recognize that not all those who critique its career wish it to disappear, but are rather daunted by the prospect of another sort of disappearance, namely, the dream of a vanguard that alone may turn around Indian democracy to the benefit of the last Indian standing.

VI

Does the official left in India have the intellectual and political reserves then to recast its organizational and ideological energies, and to renew its covenant with the people who have stood by it for three long decades in West Bengal, and with Indians elsewhere who look to it not just for holding back the cultural fascists but to reformulate the Indian centre through the power of peaceful mass mobilization?

Particularly, those that feel a stake in the Indian democratic experiment and wish to protect it from armed insurrection must recognize that these goals cannot be trusted merely to the Indian state-apparatus.

Indeed, the armed insurrectionists would wish for nothing better to happen.

Nor can the gung-ho neo-liberal policies of the corporate-led political formations be credited with the power to shame left extremism into compliance and disarray. Quite the contrary.

Upon every conceivable objective analysis, the conundrums of Indian democracy require a democratic politics of the left, meant not simply to cushion the fatcats from extremism, but to help transform and enrich the content and quality of democracy itself towards the greatest good of the greatest number. Remembering that if there can be no democracy without socialism, there can be no socialism without democracy.

Much is at stake in how West Bengal shapes in the months to come. And those that need to realize that the most are the Bengali vanguard themselves.

June 2009

Bharatiya Janata Party
Searching a New Subterfuge?

Wasn't there a playwright who penned Six Characters in Search of an Author?

Well, India has a 'major' political party that seems forever in search of a programme.

It is called the Bharatiya Janata Party (BJP).

But, hang on; unlike the famous play cited above, the BJP's interminable project is, infact, not to find the author/programme but to constantly hide the one and only it has.

That author of its unreal being is the RSS, the so-called cultural organization that was established by India's right-wing, Brahiminism in 1924 in order to direct the anti-colonial freedom movement towards the formulation of a majoritarian Hindu Rashtra, in opposition to the secular and pluralist ideals of the then Congress-led national movement.

Staunch adherent to that time-tested instrument of social and every other oppression in India, the caste hierarchy or *varna vyavastha*, three dominant principles have constituted its raison d' etre:

- an unrelenting hegemony of the uppercastes over Hindu thought and practice;
- an urelenting crusade against the Muslims whom it regards as alien to the land, and chief enemies of India's 'cultural essence';
- a close embrace with militarist imperialism and with the systemic economic underpinnings that make such militarism and imperialism possible and necessary.

Not till 1949 did this organization declare its allegiance to the Indian Tricolour as comprising the undisputed icon of the new nation, and then too under duress and as a quid pro quo to the Nehru government's willingness to release from prison its big chief or sarsanghchalak who had been locked up as a consequence of the banning of the RSS after the Gandhi murder in 1948.

Only then was the RSS literally coerced into framing its constitution and putting on record its allegiance to the flag (national tricolour).

The fact that it still remains unreconciled to the Indian Constitution was borne out when the Vajpayee-led NDA regime (1999-2004) constituted a Constitution Review Committee, designed to alter some of the basic features of the Republic.

Fortunately, India's post-Independence history weighed too heavily against this camouflaged misadventure.

II

This ideological matrix from whence the Bharatiya Jana Sangh – the first avatar of the BJP – was to issue as an overtly political fifth column in 1951, must be seen in conjunction with a more explicit enunciation of a racist/fascist 'nationhood' – that which Savarkar, that self-confessed atheist and non-believer in ritualist Hindu practices or the caste system, gave to the right-wing.

He it was who first enunciated Hindutva as a purely political proposition, related to religious identity only as a tactical ploy of exclusion.

Succintly, Savarkar postulated as early as 1923 – some fifteen years before Jinnah – that India infact comprised 'two nations,' 'Hindus' and 'Muslims.' As to the emerging new state, it was his view that only those who were both born in India and had their chief icons of worship within India could be considered Indian citizens.

Thus a neat stipulation that would exclude Muslims (Mecca) and Christians (Jerusalem) from citizenship was floated

On a TV talk-show the other day, one of the chief spokespersons of the RSS/BJP, Sheshadrachari, when pressed by the smart anchor to define 'Hindutva,' conceded that the only definition available to this day was the one that had come from Savarkar.

He quickly went to add that the RSS/BJP did not, however, subscribe to this definition.

And thereby hangs the tale.

The crude fact is that this definition does indeed remain at the heart of the RSS/BJP political enterprise. And, yet, it is no longer a thesis that they may overtly propound and still hope to practice any viable politics in the India of 2009.

Which is why my friend, J.Sriraman, the reputed columnist, is so right when he says of the current post 2009 electoral rout of the BJP that the 'heated debate (is) over how best to hide the ideology for the wide section of voters outside the 'core constituency – of the Sangh Parivar. (see *Daily Times*, Lahore, june 26, 2009).

Sriraman makes a rapid encapsulation of the various subterfuges that the BJP has sought to employ through time to practice such concealment, now citing one or the other supposedly new idelogical source to their favoured shenanigans. Thus, since its inception in 1980, we have been served with 'Gandhian Socialism,' 'Integral Humanism' (this still on the BJP constitution), followed by 'Cultural Nationalism' (in the wake of the maraudingly anti-Muslim Advani rath yatra of 1990 that led to the demolition of the Babri mosque and pogroms against Muslims thereafter), and culminating yet again in 'Hindutva.'

The one thing, of course, that no scion of the Sangh will do is to make explicit the meaning of that most mythologised term, Hindutva. For reasons not hard to understand. Never has so much benefit been drawn from so much obfuscation.

III

Now the problem that confronts the BJP is that it has to exist and operate both as the thin end of the RSS wedge and as itself.

Unable to make of the Savarkar/Golwalkar (the latter was to stipulate that 'foregn races', read Muslims, who were unwilling to lose their separate existence and merge into the Hindu race could not be granted rights of citizenship) thesis an overt party programme within a secular-constitutional dispensation, the BJP has had the unenviable task of shopping for programmes that might sell more handily among India's diversely plural electorate, crucially without being seen to be jettisoning its Hindu-cultural moorings.

Exactly as among its trader base where the quest must always be to patronize goods and services that have a market for the time being, the BJP has tended to shop for catchy formulations that may yield state power, for no fascist programme can ever succeed except on the strength of a powerful, captive state.

The dynamics of India's democracy over the years, and the fact of a generational shift in league with neo-liberal technological advance have, however, now rendered the charms of the Hindutva project stale, in all its incarnations or camouflages.

Thus it is that the BJP's failed prime ministerial prospect, L.K.Advani, skirting all issues of substance raised in the party's recent conclave, skirting as well his own responsibility for the party's failed campaign, and the responsibility of his chosen coterie who, infact, stand rewarded further, to the understandable heart-burn of others, has typically floated a new formulation of the sort of Hindutva that the party must learn to practice.

This gentleman, whatever his reality, always does have something up his sleeve.

A rose they say is a rose by any name; so can 'Hindutva' be, no?

To wit, he has pronounced that the BJP must henceforth avoid 'any narrow or bigoted anti-Muslim interpretation of Hindutva.'

Amazing, isn't it, how within the fascist camp, stern somersaults of weltanshuuang can happen towards the last minutes of a confused conclave.

Presto, as it were.

But here is what we say.

We believe that coming as this new radical view of Hindutva does from an 82 year old man, hardly in a position to conceive of a future for himself, some deeply felt conversion is here at work, one not subject to any further turn-arounds.

A conversion that inevitably also wraps a confession.

Advani's formulation cannot but simultaneously mean that he acknowledges Hindutva to have thus far been 'bigoted and anti-Muslim.' And on the basis, indeed, of his own marked culpabilities.

The nation might thus say that if the new non-bigoted, non-anti-Muslim view of what Hindutva ought to be is to be taken seriously as a rite d' passage within the BJP, a leap, as it were, into a new being, such a transformation can be made credible only if and when an Advani shows contrition for bigoted and anti-Muslim culpabilities of the recent past, at the least, and apologises to the nation for the same.

After all, precisely because Advani did not think of Hindutva in 1990 as being non-bigoted and non-anti-Muslim did he launch that pogrom on the Babri mosque.

Or, refuse to show remorse for the Muslim massacres under Modi's aegis in Gujarat in 2002.

Which is why we say to Advani ji: notice how quite the other day the American Houses of Congress for the first time under the Obama dispensation passed a formal resolution of apology and contrition for the sins of slavery and racial discrimination.

And thus what better time to emulate the world's other democracy, that iconic strategic partner, that guarantor of freedoms world-wide, and make a public apology to the nation – not just to the Muslims – for having practiced bigotry and anti-Muslim Hindutva.

Short of that, alas, my friend, Sriraman, must remain unrefuted in his astute perception that this is just but another gimmick floated in Goebellesian fashion to further hoodwink India under yet another false pretence.

Contrarily, think that were Advani to actually make that leap, how that might elevate and transform him, his party, and the future of the Republic, leaving a legacy worthy of a superior statesman and patriot.

Indeed, while we are on the subject of contrition, another apology that needs to be made by the Indian parliament is to the dalits of India, for a past bloodied with caste oppression and denial of human rights to a quarter of all Indians. And you may add to that the children and women of India as well.

Let us, therefore, sieze this grand opportunity of national renewal.

The hope here, however, must be tempered with a sense of hard realities. Any scion of the BJP will tell you that the party is 'nothing' without the RSS. Also for the canny reason that it is, after all, the latter organization that has the cadres indispensable to any electoral promise. Not that this is what they will acknowledge. Their point, alas, remains that, the new Advani admonition notwithstanding, the BJP has no raison d' etre except, in the first and last analysis, as a Hindu organization primarily.

Like that chemical, Benzene (C6H6), the BJP retains whatever stability it does only because, as Kekule understood of that chemical with six missing carbon atoms, its serpent's tail remains in the RSS mouth, causing double valencie bonds to occur. The pity is that whereas doubleness gives us a stable and beneficient Benzene, doubleness debilitates and delegitimises the BJP forever, however stable it be.

Take that out, and no Benzene, and no BJP as we have known it to be. A newer and better one may, nonetheless, emerge, not being an inert chemical after all.

India waits with bated breath. As, indeed, does the sub-continent.

June 2009

Some Notes from My Visit to Kozhikode

> As everything natural has to come into being, man too has his act of origin – history – which however is for him a known history, and being as an act of origin, is a conscious self-transcending act of origin.'
>
> (Marx, Critique of Hegelian Dialectic and Philosophy as a Whole, *EPM*)
>
> Both for the production on a mass scale of this communist consciousness and for the success of the cause itself, the alteration of men on a mass scale is necessarily an alteration which can only take place in a practical movement, a revolution…it can only in a revolution succeed in ridding itself of all the muck of ages, and become fitted to found society anew.
>
> (Marx, *German Ideology*)

Teekay, who was professor of English at Calicut university in Kerala, was more importantly one of the relentless critics of stultifying orthodoxy, including, most of all, with respect to India's left parties and politics. Besides being erudite in Marxist theory well into its frontier extensions and amplifications upto his day.

Never one to compromise the integrity of his perceptions, he knew both the opprobrium of dogmatists, and the inside of an Indian jail.

He died at the age of 57, but left behind him a committed following, both among Kerala intellectuals and intelligentsia alike.

It was a great honour, thus, to be asked to deliver the Teekay memorial lecture on the 21st of July, 2009 at Kozhikode on 'The State of Left politics: Theory and Practice.'

Given that this occasion followed upon the rather dismal electoral performance of India's parliamentary left parties in the general elections of 2009, it seemed apposite to borrow some of Teekay's honesty to draw lessons that may even now be pressed into service.

Given also that depletions of left politics in the 'mainstream' of Indian collective life are detrimental not just to the career of these parties but to the life of the nation as a whole, Teekay would have agreed that the times call for a review that goes beyond the tactical here-and-now. Anyone who still feels a stake in the future praxis of India's parliamentary left must square with them, risking, if one must, the title of 'left-baiter' etc., And be equally receptive to criticisms that may issue therefrom.

I

It is with this sort of impersonal urgency in mind that I thought it advisable to record both what got said and remained merely insinuated for want of time.

E.H. Carr, responding to why things are as they are, was to suggest that inorder for the present to have been different – of communities, organized groups, larger histories – the antecedent causes that forged the present would also have had to be different (*What Is History?*).

Clearly, a perception that corresponds to Marx's reminder to us of our point(s) of 'origin'.

Were you to ask a current Indian left leader why, for example, the right-wing BJP is unable or unwilling to be any different than it is, you would most likely be returned to its point of origin in India's pre and post-independence history, and quite rightly be invited to evaluate its class allegiances. For not without a detour into those histories might it be possible to understand why its constructions of nationalism, of citizenship and so forth came to be what they came to be.

It then seems that anyone interested in something more than the fortunes of India's left parties in the strongholds of West Bengal and Kerala might do well to ask similar questions about the point of origin of the left as an intervention into the ongoing anti-colonial 'freedom movement.'

Why should it be that a country where some 77% people spend half a dollar or less a day even in 2009, and which is rated at 134 on the United Nations Human Development Index even in 2009 should remain so inexplicably out of reach of a trans-Indian left politics?

II

Well past the sixth decade of its existence as an independent nation-state, India is still a social and cultural space where, only a dozen or two miles from the capital city of Delhi, caste panchayats in the full presence and with the full approval of police personnel defy and overrule the edicts of the highest courts in the land, and issue community diktats decreeing the public 'honour' killings of adult men and women who are seen to have transgressed the timeless principles of caste organization. And without the fear of any law-enforcement reprisal from the duly established state. Where self-appointed vigilante purveyors of 'tradition' and 'values' think nothing of bashing, molesting, even stripping women in public spaces if declared to be offending high-caste Hindu patriarchal 'norms.'

It is still a country where little children are buried upto their necks come eclipses – all in the belief that such burials remedy their deformities. Or sacrificed to gods for the cure of maladies or in promise of pecuniary gain. Where affluent sections of society use science to detect female foetuses and have the same duly aborted, since successful businesses requires cussed males only, and where daughters are sold off against a bushel of grain.

It is still a country where the waters of the holy Ganges, although provenly full of ecoli bacteria, are thought to bestow good fortune and nirvana. Where talismans and tantrics and sundry sadhus have clients among the most endowed, and where the state itself remains powerless to confront or dethrone forms of unreason which have come to be hallmarks of the Indian way of life and exotic sources of tourist wealth.

And it is still a country where such beliefs and hundreds of the same ilk are held not just by the ignorant masses but by English-using elites in a plethora of high places. All nestling in embrace with the fruits of modern science and the wonders of modern 'development' without the least discomfiture.

From the outset of the first rumblings against colonial rule, (the Indian National Congress was estb in 1885), barring some brave souls, hopelessly outnumbered and out-manouevred, nothing was farther from the minds of most of the leaders of the 'freedom movement' than to ground that movement also in any internal clean-up, incorporating the 'muck of the ages' into mobilizing for a new, post-colonial nation.

Feudal practices and forms of relation between men and the means of production, men and men, men and women, men/women and gods/goddesses were not sought to be confronted and altered; these were simply incorporated into the anti-colonial movement as an enabling cultural back-up which lent uniqueness to the Indian case.

Hierarchies across the board, far from being demolished, came to sense that further enrichment awaited them in a post-colonial India. And they were not wrong. Even the dispossessed erstwhile scions of Princely states do not do so badly, be it in terms of their political fortunes or of the social deference accorded to them even now.

By the time Gandhi happened on the scene, religious mobilization had already become a feature of the anti-colonial impulse, as Tilak drafted the god, Ganesha, into a militant political purpose on behalf of the movement's high-caste vanguard.

By 1922 when Gandhi unleashed the non-cooperation movement, he had already declared himself a 'Sanatan Hindu' and a believer in the *varna vyavastha* (the system of castes), and expressed his abhorrence for any politics that was bereft of the high morality of religion. The out of caste 'untouchables' were denoted by him as 'Harijans' (god's own people) – those for whom the lord hath ready a special table indeed. Blessed are the meek etc.,

Mixing all that with extraordinarily innovative symbologies, backed by personal example, some three years prior to the formal establishment of the Communist Party of India (1925) Gandhi had already both captured and shaped bulk of the popular Indian imagination, and 'rescued' the future of India from the contrary impulses of the 'terrorist' freedom fighters such as Bhagat Singh.

Remember now that Gandhi wrote to the then viceroy to say that whereas he (Gandhi) did not contest the fact that Bhagat Singh and his two other comrades – Sukh Dev, and Rajguru – deserved the punishment they had got (for the killing of the officer, Saunders), namely, hanging, it was his view that greatness often resided in the strength not to exercise the powers vested in us, etc., And hanged they were, bringing to a close an alternative paradigm of freedom and national reconstruction.

III

On the other side of this hostile matrix of history – hostile to insertions of the politics of equity and reason – remember also that whereas the

Communist Manifesto in myriad drafts and clandestine journeys reached many parts of Europe, little of it was heard of in the Indian colony.

Even in czarist Russia, an underground association of 'subversives' came to be in Petersburg, inspiring even the likes of a Dostoevsky to be drawn in for a while. Indeed, wasn't he reprieved from death by firing squad just in the nick of time?

Although in India the 1857 revolt had brought the Hindu and Muslim feudal elements together, obliging all equally to denote Bahadur Shah Zafar as the legitimate political authority of Hindustan, surely towards the end of the century the British and Hindu revivalists were succeeding in dubbing the revolt entirely a Muslim event.

Novelists like Bankim Chandra Chatterjee were to float the view (in novels like *Anand Math*) that the real invaders had always been the Moghuls rather than the British.

Thus was India's future begun to be put into a framework of communal polarization.

While around 1902 Lenin and others were busy in exile working out the forging of a Communist vanguard party (What is to be done?), India witnessed sporadic and isolated attempts by armed revolutionaries to subvert British rule. Till the hanging of Bhagat Singh and the ascendance of Gandhi put a stop to all that.

Thus when Communism came to India, it came chiefly as an invocation from the newly formed Comintern after the conclusion of the Russian revolution. Remember also that whereas Lenin had been able to draft disgruntled Russian soldier peasantries returning from the first world war into forming the foot soldiers of the revolution, Indian soldiers who had fought on behalf of the allied powers had no such historical context or opportunity to do likewise.

The Comintern defined its objective thus:

> to fight 'by all available means, including armed force, for the overthrow of the international bourgeoisie, and for the creation of an international Soviet republic as a transition stage to the complete abolition of the state.

In point of fact, however, the Soviet party undertook to direct operations outside its national borders, issuing authoritative diktats about what 'correct' lines newly floated Communist parties must now follow.

And those correct lines did not necessarily square with the stated objective of the Comintern.

Indian Communists, who, it must be recalled, remained under severe ban by the colonial authorities, and embroiled in one conspiracy case or the other (the two Peshawar conspiracy cases, the Cawnpore Bolshevik conspiracy case, the Meerut conspiracy case and so on), were told that the best course for them was to collaborate with the radical national bourgeoisie in their countries who where engaged in anti-colonial struggle (the United Front thesis, 11th thesis of the 2nd Congress of the Comintern). Even as an M.N. Roy, a delegate to the Comintern from the party in Mexico, had argued that the Comintern must lend support only to the Communists in the colonies.

Remarkably, at the Kanpur conclave (some 500 people in attendance) where the Communist Party of India was formally launched, one of the organizers named Satyabakhta had pleaded for a 'national communism.' He was promptly expelled. All that while the Soviet party, now under Stalin, was infact consolidating interests that contributed chiefly to its national and international hegemony. Remember also that despite the declaration in the Manifesto that the 'proletariat has no country' it was the sad case that during the first world war, many socialist parties in Europe did infact end up siding with the 'national' interest. Just as the events leading upto the second world war showed a similar tendency among working people to support the race idea over the class one under the relentless onslaught of Nazi propaganda.

Refutations, as it were, of the soundly reasoned internationalist argument that obliged new Marxist thinkers to examine factors other than class that impinged on the ways in which even alienated and expropriated victims of capital might respond to historical events and contradictons.

Indeed, in a must-read book, *Darker Nations: A Biography of the Third World*, Vijay Prashad has recently shown how in the subsequent years the bulk of Soviet support in the newly liberated countries was to go not to the Communist parties but to the 'liberatory' bourgeoisies in these countries.

When in 1927, the Kuomintang in China turned against the Communists, a new diktat was unleashed by the Comintern. There was now a question mark on all alliances with national bourgeois elements, and Indian Communists were directed to expose and combat 'national reformist leaders', oppose the reformism of the Indian National Congress, and oppose Gandhian pacifism (6th Congress of the Comintern).

It also denounced the Workers and Peasant's Parties, directing the communists to dump the same. As they left, these grass roots possibilities also collapsed.

In 1934, some radical elements within the Indian National Congress formed the Congress Socialist Party, while remaining members of the Indian National Congress – a turn of events opposed by some Congress leaders such as Vallabhai Patel.

Result: another twist in the line; the Comintern floated the 'popular front' thesis; Indian communists were now expected to alter their relation with the INC and join the CSP.

Through the years between 1934 and 1942, the CSP constituted an unlikely conglomeration of Fabian socialists, Anushilan Marxists with roots among the 'revolutionary terrorist' factions), Marxists loyal to the Comintern line, Gandhian pacifists and so on.

Although at its inaugural session in 1934, flags of the Congress party fluttered next to portraits of Karl Marx, and 'comrade' was adopted as the common greeting, the internal contradictions were far too real for the synthesis to last.

At the Tripuri session of the Congress (1939), Subash Bose walked out of the Congress to form the Forward Bloc, and, soon, the Anushilan Marxists parted company to float the Revolutionary Socialist Party (RSP).

This new collaboration between Indian communists and the socialists within the Congress reached a peak towards 1937. But only in Kerala did the Communists obtain decisive majority within the CSP.

Courage was in evidence at the Ramgarh session of the CSP (1940); the CPI, calling for a 'proletarian path,' suggested a general strike, no tax, no rent policies, and preparation for armed struggle.

Promptly, the National Executive of the CSP expelled all communists from it.

When the CPI was legalized in 1942, it immediately ran into the opprobrium of opposing Gandhi's Quit India call – a turn of decision from whose consequences Indian communists continue to suffer in the popular imagination.

Which is not to say with emphasis that it was the communists who had consistently formed the most credible vanguard in the Congress-led anti-colonial movement. Indeed, episodes of the heroisms of individuals and secret groups here are too numerous to recount.

On the eve of Independence, a Paris Commune was attempted in Telengana in the then Madras province, ruled by the Nizam. And it suffered the same fate as that other Commune. The then general secretary of the CPI was dethroned for having pursued too 'revolutionary' a line.

All of that led to the embracing of the parliamentary/electoral route in 1952. Despite these chequered histories, it remains a tribute to the exertions of the Indian communists that in the general elections of 1957 they came second only to the INC, and indeed were the first communists in world history to be voted to power in Kerala.

IV

The point, however, is that from the first (1925, with Stalin and Gandhi ascendant in Russia and India), Indian communists rarely ever were either allowed or allowed themselves the breathing space to work out lines of action from the soil, as it were, against the press of two adversaries – the diktats of the Comintern (Gramsci and the Italian communists had similar difficulties), and the political/cultural consolidation of a Gandhi/Congress-led anti-colonial movement.

Inevitably from hindsight, it would seem that two great opportunities of forging a credible and ideologically lasting mass base were lost.

One, instead of tying up with the CSP, the failure to link the communist movement with the Ambedkarite critique of the dominant culture. An option that had the promise of marrying class struggle to powerful cultural impulses against forms of ideological and social domination, which, while they lasted (and indeed still last), frustrated any straightforward successes of orthodox class struggle;

And, two, after Gandhi, to take the politics of the left to that overwhelmingly vast mass of Indians who had been astutely marginalized by the Gandhi/Congress-led freedom movement, namely, agricultural workers, poor peasants, unorganized urban poor – those that to this day constitute the bulk of the 77% who subsist on less than half a dollar a day. Although it may be argued that those that were poor peasants then are abysmally indigent farmers today.

Sadly, it cannot be said that the official Communist parties have any great hold among these sections even today. An all-important fact, one would venture to think.

Indian organized communism instead inserted itself among the miniscule organized proletariat, students, teachers, lawyers, bank employees and such like – sections that after all can only be characterized as petty bourgeois at bottom. Sections who may indeed be radicalized from time to time on specific issues, but whose class allegiance rarely allows, qualitatively, any considerable transformation in the nature either of the 'muck of the ages.' or of the political economy.

It must also be acknowledged that Indian communism till recently has failed in another crucial task, namely of engaging critically with that plethora of subjectivities in India which make the forging of class politics such an uphill task. Indian communism did not think it necessary to work out its own Frankfurt school.

Is it not the case that till recently Indian communist ideologues simply refused to acknowledge that such things as social identities of diverse description could also be the proper subject of communist analysis? I recall an interaction with a lower-level sartrap who, in a moment of rare honesty and courage, admitted to me how often workers of the party union, even as they go out in marches under the communist flag, quietly go and vote for their caste brethren come hustings time.

The same about the peculiar oppressions specific to women; how, after all, can any exclusively class analysis explain why between a husband and wife team of workers at a construction site, the woman should be paid differential wages, why the baby should be her burden even as she lifts the brick and mortar, or why, after work, the husband should spread out on the cot while the wife sits on her haunches blowing the coal that cooks the roti, or should receive chastisement, even physical violence, should the roti turn out over or under cooked?

Same about the perceptions widely prevalent among ethnicities that find themselves at the receiving end of majorities who tend to ascribe authenticity only to themselves. The Gorkhas and the Santhals in the state of West Bengal may be cases in point. Even as the Muslim farmers of West Midnapore have their own grievances about the Urdu language, etc., Is it thinkable that the old confusion about 'nationalities' (whether India is a nation comprising many identities, or whether each identity constitutes a 'nation') remains ideologically unresolved? Or that Indian official communism has gone too much over to the other side, impatient that social and ethnic diversity should so often stymie the 'nationalist' project?

Not to speak of India's dalits to whom class struggle must first take the shape and form of elevating them to some status of 'human' equality.

That some of these considerations have now been under the left analytic scanner, leading also to forms of struggle freed from doctrinaire persuasions is thus a welcome happening.

V

There has we think also been another area of scant review, namely the reading and propagation of the central perceptions of Marxism itself, in contradistinction to the smug and centralized habits of Stalinist party structures. Especially, the inadequate consideration given to Marx, intense attention to the specific features of history in diverse geo-political spaces, and his lifelong work to understand the historical possibilities of those specificities, so that appropriate lines of practice are forged to effect heterogenous scales of transformation.

Sadly, over some three decades or more of interaction, it has been a debilitating experience to find among party cadres, even among students and teachers, the readiness to substitute party programmes for ideological training, and the contingent 'correct line' for Marxist analysis.

All of that made decisively counter-productive by scant effort to move from being cerebrally de-classe, if that, to liking to be emotionally one with the 'toiling masses.'

Not for a long while have I seen an Indian communist leader whose most radiant experience is to be among the downtrodden, or who truly believes a dialogy of listening/learning is possible with the lowest of the low. In this context, it remains a tragic fact that lessons that could have been learnt from the Gandhian movement were loftily discarded by the Communist movement in India. Not to speak of the failure to match even the grassroots work of some of India's most dedicated and credible NGOs, or to forge strategies of collaboration with them.

It seems also the case that long years of exercising state power in just two or three states have bred a form of complacency which makes it psychologically secondary for official Indian communism to do much more. Or to recognize that any and all of its critique of the dominant class politics is weakened by being obliged to suffer the contradictions of sharing state power (we recall how upset the Chinese were when Namboodripad formed the ministry in Kerala), and, simultaneously, the failure to forge any consequential resistance to the victims of dominant class politics. The failure especially to build left organization and do left mass work in India's Hindi heartland must be seen as a severe limitation.

The official left looks to enhancing its clout within parliament so that its hegemony might increase, but is unable to forge a base that may make such ambition a reality. It desires to enrich democracy, but practices centralism of the doctrinaire kind that robs its cadres of all initiative and, despite the elaborate skein of the fleshing of lines, leaves effectively only a top-rung in charge of dictating policy for each falange of three years. Practicing social democracy, it makes doctrinaire blunders that hand over its social-democratic successes to other secular parties, chiefly the Congress, and, as in Lalgarh, it leaves grass roots mass needs and politics for the armed left-extremes to plough. It opposes global capitalism but finds itself compromising with capitalist developmental priorities in its own areas of governance, risking mass alienation. The recent events in Nandigram being a costly example.

No wonder then that the official left is seen today so embroiled in tech-savvy ventures, small-time seminar conclaves among the like-minded, unable to turn out even a few hundreds on to the streets except in the bastions of West Bengal and Kerala. Bastions equally under siege.

Worst of all, there seems little evidence that major strategic considerations, both in ideological and organizational praxis, are seen as anything more than mere tactical mistakes, rectifiable by the next 'correct line.'

VI

Returning to the two indices cited at the outset – India even now being 134 on the Human Development Index, and 77% Indians subsisting on less than half a dollar a day, is it idle to expect that a grand council of all segments of the Indian left is attempted? One aimed at mounting a concerted and credible all-India resistance to right-wing policies and reactionary cultural emphases.

That instead of being riven by internal wars of hegemony, all segments rise to the stature of the people who need them?

That, over some years of dedicated immersion, even if invisible to the corporate media, a mobilization of those 77% is realized, and, as a result, even if the state is not overthrown, that 77% is empowered in a gathering Bolivarian revolution that marginalizes the endowed minorities who rule India repeatedly without the majority mandate of 'we the people'?

That party functionaries are dislodged from being the bureaucratic cell-structures they are at present, or, variously, from remaining embroiled in sporadic armed extremism which holds sway not as much through open mass allegiance as out of fear of the gun, and turned into foot soldiers of a democratic revolution?

Not doing all that, what future may the left envisage for itself or for the 'toiling masses' it so agonises about from the precincts of party offices?

July 2009

Judge Not the Judge, or Thou Shalt Be Judged

(satire)

During early days I used to think 'ah, if only I were Sherlock Holmes'! Which was my idea of being invincible.

Now I say 'god, let me be born a judge in a higher court in India.'

There is no better ticket to absolutely unchallengeable freedom, even as I would have the satisfaction to send all sorts of wicked people to their just deserts. And they could include Sherlock as well.

But this thing called democracy – it is such an unthinking leveler; India is now engaged in an uninformed cacophony that demands that judges should be accountable as well. Not realising that they are accountable to each other – the most testing form of accountability. Just as atheists must answer to their own conscience without help from divine intent, or other forms of remote control.

They say Caesar's wife should be above suspicion, but they do not specify who is Caesar, who the said Caesar's wife. After all, there are hardly any wives on the bench. Only Caesars.

They say if those that make the laws declare their assets to the nation, surely those that merely adjucate laws should do the same – a clear instance of where mechanical applications of low-level reason can take you.

Ask them if the requirements of fairplay could be served if everyone in the land knew what a judge possessed? God we say owns all of creation; so judges must be understood to possess and own all of justice, no? Which is why the good book says 'judge not lest ye be judged.'

After all, faith is not faith if it asks proof. The highest form of faith is that which commands unquestioning submission. Ask Asa Ram Bapu than whom no greater saint exists.

It is only when judges know that they can never be questioned – after all, only litigants and witnesses are meant to be questioned – that they can deliver justice without fear or favour. It is those that at bottom desire favour who ask to know how a judge got what he got, because then he can the better know how to try to give. Why else should anyone desire a judge's assests to be made as public as anyone else's? Only to suborn the justice system.

The more clever ones do what they always do – refer us back to America.

After all, you do love America and everything about it; so why not accept that in America judges are appointed after severe grilling by the Senate and the media. Before a judge gets appointed, the good American gets to know everything about the appointee.

As if such knowledge advances by a jot the quality of justice in that land of the brave. Ask the Hispanics and the African Americans.

In India, we are both brave and sagacious. Our accumulated wisdom coming down from long long ages before anyone had ever heard of America teaches us that men must be spared as much of the truth as possible. Truth is simply not everyone's kettle of fish. Think of the storm currently underway on the subject of a reality show that invites people to tell the ugly truth about themselves.

In India we have always known, for example, that homosexuality pervades both our holy books and our human history. But, for that reason, how smart is it to say so in public, or to decriminalize such ugly adult behaviour? And what were carpets made for anyway?

Similarly, so what if there is a judge here and there who likes a bit more than he rightly gets. Do we therefore go about saying so, or make laws to restrict such behaviour? And how do we know, as ancient wisdom teaches us, that the next man may not be smarter? Which is why again the good book says 'be content with thy lot.'

Just what does democracy and suchlike have to do with justice, after all? The fact is that god in his wisdom placed us in unequal situations, and the demand for equality of this and that is what brings god's unfathomable purposes to grief.

Tell me, have we ever made the demand to know how sundry godmen have come by their assets? Then why discriminate in the case of judges, who after all are also secular godmen charged with the onerous responsibility to set us to rights, all for our own good.

I say, therefore, let a stop be put to this mob-like clamour for judges to be made transparent so that judgements are made transparent as well. Which is why I support the Bill that the government of the day means to bring to parliament, mandating that judge's assets be known only to the chief judge, and not made available to any authority, least of all the people in whose name the Constitution was made and who are designated the true sovereigns of the realm.

This Bill will make it clear that between the word and its meaning must fall the shadow of sagacity.

Not suffused with the deep mysteries and conundrums of our philosophical traditions, western democracies suffer the consequences of always wishing to marry words to their meanings.

As a result they get the transparency and the justice they deserve, while we know man lives neither by bread alone nor by probity alone.

It is karma that rules what lives we live and what assets we accumulate. And if judges are obliged to nobody's vote, why should just anybody get their goat?

A judge is a judge who can, if pressed to come clean about himself, as Moses did God in Exodus, return the answer 'I AM THAT I AM.' And then roll out in stupefying awe, the tablets of the Law. Can the law have majesty and the judge none at all?

Please let us not thus be such mindless sticklers for democracy. When we flounder in cacophony we can only be rescued by unimpeachable impunity.

August 2009

For Aung San Suu Kyi

A Single Slender Woman Who Terrifies an Army of Generals

In Burma resides a dame,
Terra Firma is her name;
They lock her indoors,
But her pitying smile soars,
And the Generals are rendered lame.

Thomas Carlyle, that prophetic voice of the 19C, delineated in Heroes And Hero Worship (1841) what he thought were types of world-historical individuals.

Among them he projected Cromwell as a type of hero whose strength lay in a species of obdurate conviction that had no need of any flamboyant oratorical skills.

Two other figures from the 20C/21C spring to mind as further exemplars of the type, namely, Mohandas Karamchand Gandhi and Aung San Suu Kyi.

No more true metaphor for them than the grass, which Whitman called the 'handkerchief of the Lord,' fusing in a magnificently visionary way god with democracy.

The grass, it grows everywhere, however you trample on it. In its fecund unendingness, it symbolizes and manifests the will-to-life itself, and in its undefeatably cussed humility, it is the spirit of universal freedom and common democracy that refuse to be quelled.

And, as any good gardener knows, the more you cut the more it grows.

Which may be why the sensible British did not heed Hitler's counsel in 1938: When Chamberlain went to reason with him, he mentioned Gandhi and how troubled the empire was by him.

Uncomprehending, the Feuhrer asked, 'why don't you shoot him?'

And had they done so, nothing might have brought about so early a collapse of the empire – and in predictably brutal ways.

Clearly, the two-penny tyrants in Burma who strut about in a prison of their own making – if Suu Kyi cannot leave her house, the Generals may not leave Burma, for they are reviled everywhere, including in those parts of the world who have shabby deals with them – have understood that much.

Thus, for their own wretched safety, they desist from doing that Hitler on her. So, we ask, are they winning or losing Burma? Losing, we think. And over that knowledge, Suu Kyi's smile arches like that of angels, seeing far far beyond the events of any single day, beyond even her own life.

II

Meanwhile, the merchants of commerce and pelf the world over – a mining interest here, a military interest there, all clothed as high policy – speak from both sides of the crooked commercial mouth all at once.

Shamed by the radiance and the stature of the slender lady in Rangoon, a twitch of whose eye can bring all of Burma to the streets, they laud her spirit of resistance, remembering even that, after all, she had gone to college in India, but under the table, their grubby fingers make grubby transactions. And these include those in India who did the same to Gandhi. (Or to our own iron lady, Irom Sharmila, who remains on a forced, drip-driven hunger strike for close to a decade now.)

As though he (Gandhi) had not seen through their salivating cupidities. How he was to turn away from them just when they were prancing on the stage of a bloodied 'freedom,' wanting not even to be told of it as he busied himself in quelling the butcheries in Bengal.

And those that proclaim themselves the ordained agents of the spirit of democracy, and cry hoarse how it is so throttled in Iran, China, Russia, Cuba find canny arguments to perpetuate tyranny in Burma, Saudi Arabia, Honduras and wherever else their greed so commands. And no Christian country as Christian and god-swearing as their's. Even as they make sure Suu Kyi is awarded the Nobel prize for peace.

III

But here is what we say: no military uniform, however starched, in Burma can expect to snuff out the grass forever. Under their very nose, it grows and grows. And all the little millions of the world make of their opprobrium a clarion call.

You may think that the fate of a Prabhakaran in Sri Lanka and Baitullah Masud in AFPAK augurs well for the tyrants in Burma.

But think again. Using the gun, they made it easy for the guns on the other side, and difficult for the people who wished them well.

Not so the lady in Burma. She could not hurt a fly, but her patient, fearless eye bears the portents of a cloud-burst that, when it comes, shall sweep from sight the starched uniforms and the little men in them as though they never had been.

With some liberty of emendation, here is what the Bard might have said:

It will come, it will come,
The Generals must perforce
Prey on themselves,
Like monsters of the Deep.

IV

In the meanwhile, the well-meaning millions of the world must sharpen and deepen their noble contempt, until such contempt becomes too much for the oppressor to live with. And combine that with the force of argument, proferred daily in conclave, city square, street side, and among masses of men and women gathered to protest tyranny . And deploy on behalf of that contempt and argument those histories from the collaborating world which shame both the collaborators and those they collaborate with. For, be not cynical about shame. The power of shame is great. It hollows the innards of spit and polish, and renders the General a mere mannequin in time to come.

To the lady in Rangoon we say, we salute you. For your pitying smile renders your oppressors mere wanton boys who know not what chastisement awaits them.

What greater proof of your victory than that the mere thought of your free movement through town should send shivers down the military spine. Generals, little Generals, dressed in little, brief authority – they would much rather have preferred that you came swirling the sword like some modern Joan of Arc. Alas for them, your brahmastra (weapon of weapons) is a smile that is everyday fresh as creation, and a soul that knows no doubt. And an eye that forgives even in the hour of despair. And a spirit that waters the grass even through the brick and mortar.

They held Mandela for twenty six years. Look where he is now. You are but young, both in age and in confinement. And the future is yours, your people's and of the world that stands by you and them.

August 2009

The Democracy Flu

Breaches in the Bastions

Things fall apart,
The centre cannot hold;
Delicious democracy is loosed upon India.
(With apologies to W.B.Yeats for the distorted third line.)

Ah, how often in human history have bastions of one kind or another sought to thwart the march of the rational, always without success.

And what more rational than democracy.

Recall that after the leveling tendencies of the Reform Bill of 1832, and the ominous mass assertions that accompanied that zeitgeist, some famous Oxford dons got together to demand that English Christianity return to its Roman roots.

Ostensibly directed against liberalizing movements in theology, Newmanism and Puseyism were at bottom terrified responses to those mass democratic assertions for full realizations of the principle of equality.

The mutely stated assumption was that the Protestant Reformation had broken the embankments of the infallibly centralized authority of the Pontiff, and thereby let loose the demons of anarchy. Thus their call (1933-1845) to reintroduce medieval liturgies into Church doctrine, and to return to Rome. Which Newman did in 1845.

History, nonetheless, carried on, consigning the Tractarians and their many Tracts to a residual past that could have no future.

Same with the Arnoldian prescription that only the classical 'best' ('Culture,' he called it) could salvage the depredations wrought by undeserving little men seeking parity with the elect. Thankfully, over the last century and a half, Culture has been inundated by cultures, and men and women everywhere in the world express themselves severally, freed from the diktats of self-appointed arbiters od conduct.

II

That magnificently democratizing Russian genius, Mikhail Bakhtin (who, among other things, coined the term 'dialogy'), writing in not so democratic, Stalinist times, conceived of authoritarian historical milieus as 'monologic' eras, when only a single, centralized voice holds sway, be it in politics or in culture, or in the novels of Tolstoy.

But only so long as other voices have not gathered enough force to breach that sway.

And when those times arrive – times always in the making, however suppressed – the 'heteroglossia' of new urges breaks the authoritarian barricades, and delicious 'polyphony' spreads into nooks and crevices, and then on to the mainstreets of history. Then it is that the closed circuits of philosophical, literary, cultural forms come apart, yielding to new forms of knowing, living, and relating. The 'timeless' authority of the 'classics' crumbles, and the fecund outpouring of ordinary human prose assumes the realities and requirements of the contemporary world.

Suddenly, what had seemed 'forever' becomes a dysfunctional part of the archaeology of knowledge, and highpriests of this and that find refuge in the coves and grottos of myth and mystery.

III

Such is the delicious polyphony that now assails two of India's hitherto godlike institutions – the Judiciary and the RSS (mentor and manipulator of India,s second largest political formation, the Bharatiya Janata Party).

Who doesn't know that the Judiciary must always remain above and beyond suspicion.

Yet, alas, many instances have recently suggested that there may be one thing more puissant than the Lordships on the bench, namely, the lure of Commodity.

Calls have thus gone up, led heroically by a voluntary organization of democrats whose chief mover and architect is a frail-looking but steely advocate, Prashant Bhushan (truly a catalyst of India's future Judicial history), and one that includes some erstwhile judges of the highest court, that a small step forward to curb the lure of commodity might be to oblige judges, like the politicians, to make a public declaration of their assets.

But, no, says the voice from the monologic pulpit; such declarations, the voice says, would bring unnecessary harassment to the Lordships on behalf of deranged and ill-motivated litigants/citizens, rendering them incapacitated, and compromising their independence.

Yet, lo and behold, so forceful can the rational be that a polyphony of judicial voices now rise to contradict the pulpit. Following Bakhtin, they say no single pulpit can have the right to represent all judicial voices. And some have indeed gone on to declare their assets as well.

Others point out that the Right to Information Law cannot make an exemption of those who administer the law, and that only those judges fear declaration who have anything to hide. All the more reason that their assets be known, including any mis-statements thereof, so that the fair ends of justice are protected.

A Protestant reformation is thus underway among the Lordships, and it hardly seems that any demand for a return to Rome is likely to win the day either.

IV

Then there is the RSS.

Born some eighty years ago with the purpose of centralizing the then Indian freedom movement towards a monologic Hindu state wherein but one cultural voice alone would be permitted to be representative of the world's MOST diverse polity, it has sought to spawn political fronts through the decades into which it inducts its disciplined swayamsevaks (voluntary workers).

Thus within the current day BJP (established 1980, superceding the erstwhile Jana Sangh) a whole bevy of fifth-column RSS workers occupies leading space.

The unvaryingly grounding mythology of the RSS/BJP has been that Jinnah was the lone communalist during the freedom movement, and that Jinnah was alone and singularly responsible for the partition of India in 1947 along communal lines.

On another axis of mythmaking, having had no role in the fight for freedom from colonial rule, it has sought to fill that massive hollow in its 'nationalist' pretensions by appropriating that life-long Congressman, Sardar Patel, for its own man. All because Patel, ostensibly, was sympathetic to the Hindu cause (although they will not say so), and played a stellar role in uniting the Princely states with the Provinces.

Alas, the facts of Patel's career bely this myth everywhere. Never more so than in his bold decision to ban the RSS after the murder of Gandhi at the hands of Hindu fanatics.

The RSS, whose man Gandhi's murderer was (all according to no less than the recorded account of Godse's own brother, a co-conspirator, recently released from jail), propagates that Patel affected the ban on Nehru's say-so. Alas, again not true, not true.

Consider what Patel then wrote to two scions of the RSS, Shyama Prasad Mookerjee and Guru Golwalkar.

Letter to Mookerjee (dated 18 July 1948):

> As regards the RSS and the Hindu Maha Sabha, the case relating to Gandhiji's murder is subjudice, and I should not like to say anything about the participation of the two organizations, but the reports do confirm that as a result of the activities of these two bodies, particularly the former, an atmosphere was created in the country in which such a ghastly tragedy became possible...The activities of the RSS constituted a clear threat to the existence of the government and the state...Indeed, as time marched on, the RSS circles are becoming more defiant and are indulging in their subversive activities in an increasing measure.

Letter to Golwalkar (dated 11 September 1948):

> The RSS did service to the Hindu Society

but the

> objectionable part arose when they...began attacking Mussalmans.

> All their speeches were full of communal poison...As a result of the poison, the country had to suffer the sacrifice of the invaluable life of Gandhiji...Infact, opposition (to the RSS) grew...when the RSS men expressed joy and distributed sweets after Gandhiji's death.

A staunch secularist and Congressman to the end, the RSS would have been as inimical to him as cheese to chalk.

Yet a founding member of the BJP, Jaswant Singh, has now been summarily expelled from the party overnight, without as much as the courtesy of a show-cause notice, and without anyone really having read the book he has written, ostensibly for having reinterpreted Jinnah and bad-mouthed Patel.

Thin end of the wedge.

With each passing day news now arrives of someone or other of the BJP leaders jumping the boat, the erstwhile adviser of Advani, Sudheender Kulkarni being the last one, shortly it seems to be followed by the cunningly redoubtable Arun Shourie.

The fact of the matter is that after the two successive electoral defeats of 2004 and 2009, the fascistic BJP has been unable to sustain the loss of state power. If Vajpayee held it together, he was largely able to do so because the BJP was the leading party in the government through 1998-2004.

With him gone into obsolescence, what had seemed impregnable turns out now to be humiliatingly cacophonous and deranged.

And no matter what the monologic RSS does to stem the rot, the rot multiplies.

Those that abandon boat proffer the most unlikely reasons for doing so. Kulkarni pleads ideological differences, believing that the BJP can survive and thrive only if learns to be all-inclusive (to wit, accepting of Muslims) and liberal.

Yet the same Kulkarni never as much squeaked a protest when Muslims were massacred in Gujarat (2002), or more recently, when during the campaign of 2009, Varun Gandhi volunteered to cut off Muslim hands were they raised against Hindus.

Arun Shourie, who made the most scurrilously illiberal attack on Ambedkar in one of his books, shouts with Mao that the BJP can be redeemed only if the Headquarters are bombarded, all top leaders dumped and recruits inducted from the mufassil.

Ridiculing the current BJP president, Rajnath Singh, by name (a known RSS appointee) as a mere 'Alice in Blunderland' and a 'Humpty Dumpty' to boot, he is canny enough to proclaim that the same RSS should now openly take over the BJP. Even as he also opposes the ouster of the Rajasthan BJP chief, Vasundhara Raje Scindia, whom the RSS wants out.

Why this seemingly and maddeningly nonsensical heteroglossia within the BJP?

For the reason that the RSS brand of religious/racial citizenship and nationalism no longer has many buyers among India's new, upwardly-mobile classes.

And those that would wish to break away from the RSS know that all the BJP's cadres really come from it.

Yet, after the loss of state power, and the continuing reluctance to revisit decisively the formative axes of its ideological being – contradicting tomorrow what it says today on any subject of consequence – the BJP seems now overwhelmed by the contradiction between its regressive umbilical attachment to the pulpit in Nagpur and its desire to be designated the party of the futurist free-marketeers.

It will thus remain to be seen where the Protestant Reformation within the Sangh Parivar leads its fortunes. The point, though, is that the force of history today renders cacophonously polyphonous what was deemed a hermetically centred political formation. All to the good, we say, of the further evolution of Indian democracy.

Sinking as it seems into a free fall, the BJP's descent into chaos unnerves two powerful influences within Indian political life – a reason why India's electronic channels seem to want to devote all their time and energy to working out its problems.

Sections of the Indian bourgeoisie are truly terrified at the thought that with the disappearance of the BJP some other political formation, even more left to the mildly but problematically left-of-centre Congress may come to take its place.

Were this to happen the space of the right-wing privatisers in collaboration with just that sufficiently distracting modicum of religiosity – distracting, that is, from the return of the labouring classes to any classical left-wing orientation – would be grievously lost.

A day might come when indeed the appellation 'socialist' that sits in the text of the Preamble of the Constitution of India becomes something more than a dead gesture to 'we the people.'

It is to be expected, therefore, that the RSS and this section of the bourgeoisie will leave no stone unturned to revive the fortunes of the BJP.

The trouble is that the two must then have to come to some modus vivendi as to how the BJP must in the years to come play out Hindutva while devoting itself fully to enhancing the fortunes of the urban rich, a formula that may find sufficient general acceptance to return the BJP to power.

This modus vivendi will necessarily have to be short of either the RSS giving up its stated goal of reworking citizenship and nationhood, and of the bourgeoisie jettisoning its modernist devotion to technology and profiteering, with all the concomitant transformations in the world of 'values.'

Easier said than done.

But the pulpits shake, and heteroglossia wins the day.

Hallelujah!

August 2009

Something Rotten in the State of Gujarat

I have supped full with horrors;
Direness, familiar to my slaughterous thoughts,
Cannot once start me.
(Macbeth Modi)

Indeed, great is the temptation to write this account wholly in Shakesperian quotation.

Four new skeletons now rattle for justice in the Modi cupboard. And well might he be saying to himself:

the time has been,
That, when the brains were out, the man would die,
And there an end; but now they rise again,
With twenty mortal murders on their crowns

A judicial magistrate in Ahmedabad, one good man Tamang, has held that the killing of the nineteen year old college girl, Ishrat Jahan, and four others in June, 2004 was , after all, yet another 'fake encounter' executed by high-ranked police Modi loyalists to curry favour with him and obtain preferment.

This on the heels of the earlier murder of one Sohrabuddin and his wife, Kausar Bi, acknowledged in court by the Modi government to have been 'fake encounters.' And by the very same police personnel as well, two of whom are now in the slammer for that killing. At least for now.

Speculation is rife as to how many official murders may have been effected by the Gujarat state since 2002, when the Gujarat massacre took place.

Speculation that has obliged the Supreme court of India only yesterday to persuade the Gujarat prosecution, one, to transfer the Sohrabuddin case also to the Special Investigation Team that is enquiring into some of the more gruesome killings of 2002, and to come clean on all cases of fake exterminations that still lie stashed away in the Gujarat govenment cupboard.

Persuations stubbornly resisted by the Gujarat prosecution. Imagine a Macbeth, a Caligula, a Nero, a Hitler, or a Stalin agreeing happily to self-incrimination.

You must be joking.

And, pray, were such disclosures to be made, what would happen to the 'vibrant Gujarat' project for which Mr.Modi has just been earmarked by the FDI magazine of the *Financial Times* group in London to be bestowed 'The Asian Personality of the year 2009' award?

Clearly, the British of today have little use for their own greatest of thinkers. Long years ago, even at the point of the birth of capitalism, Shakespeare had seen that one of its most inhuman consequences would be to 'disjoin remorse from power' (JC). And that 'conscience made cowards' of the Faustian man who was now set to conquer the world.

Not the British but an exiled German jew saw the profound pointers in Shakespeare's enactments, causing him to cite a whole long passage from Timon of Athens to explicate what capitalism was slated to do to the human essence. (See *Early Writings Marx*, Introduced by Lucio Colletti, Penguin Books, 1975, p.376).

Thus, the FDI establishment argues that capitalist 'efficiency' must entirely be divorced from considerations of 'remorse,' or else how does one effect the killings of 'power'?

And we have no doubt that these must be people who are conscientious church-goers.

II

In the meanwhile, the Gujarat government is busy on electronic channels making the point that even the Central government in Delhi has acknowledged on affidavit, dated 6 August, 2009, that the four victims of the 'fake encounter' had links with a terrorist group.

That the Judicial magistrate has repudiated that contention is seen to be of secondary importance. Indeed, great is the animus of the Gujarat government against good man, Justice Tamang, for having delivered his verdict on the killings with unnecessary dispatch, even as not a day passes when the delays of the law do not come for reprimand.

It is also conveniently forgotten that the investigation of the latest fake killings are infact as old as five years, and all that Justice Tamang has done is to do his duty by the people of India with commendable commitment.

Which is the last thing that the Modi regime desires.

The Central government, thankfully, is underscoring the point that, regardless of what may or may not have been the antecedents of Ishrat Jahan and the other victims, extra-judicial killings on behalf of the state as by law established contravene the very raison d' etre of constitutional governance.

Were the Gujarat government's propensity to kill off people without trial or due process to be held valid, then the lone captured terrorist caught red-handed in the carnage of Mumbai, 26th November, should have been hung, drawn and quartered on the very day he was captured.

Thankfully, to the great glory of the Republic of India, as by law established, Ajmal Kasab is now being tried in Mumbai with all due right and opportunity to defend himself.

Which raises another question: should a lawfully constituted Republic enact draconian laws calculated to defeat lawfully the very purposes of a lawfully constituted democracy, such as the right to life (article 21 of the Constitution of India), and the right to innocence till proven guilty? What we have in mind here is the Armed Forces Special Powers Act (AFSPA), in operation in places like Kashmir and the North East, that entitles the least man in uniform wielding an official gun to shoot to kill without fear of being held to account?

Monstrous contradiction there, and the sooner corrected the better for the Republic.

For when a state behaves like a rogue, it accords every credibility to those who seek to oppose it in like manner.

III

Whenever Narendra Modi has been asked any questions about the massacre of 2002, or the state of Gujarat's Muslim citizens, a glaze overtakes the cocky sheen in his eyes, and not a word escapes his lips.

A state of impregnable and implacable hate that freezes the more you seek to melt it down, recalling to us Lear's magnificently moving speculation with regard to his own daughter who has thrown him out of home and hearth:

Let us anatomize Reagan to see
What it is in nature
That makes these hard hearts.

How dearly we would like to know the answer to that one.

Is it to be thought that a day might come when Narendra Modi, as in the movies, or like history's emperor Ashok, finally overwhelmed by self-loathing, and unable any longer to wash the 'damned spot' may truly donn some real saffron, abdicate his thrown, and go off into a gurukul to expiate his doings?

Or will he reason with Macbeth 'I am in blood/Stepped in so far that, should I wade no more,/Returning were as tedious as go o'er' ?

Who knows but Narendra Modi, who, after all, is an honourable man; or thinks he is.

Perhaps only so long as he is able to brew and press into service the power of collective hate.

Perhaps the decisive loathing will come from the very people that he has thus far plied and profited by.

September 2009

Old Habits Die Very Hard

India's Ugly Underbelly

He that will not reason is a bigot; he that cannot reason is a fool; he that dare not reason is a slave.
H. Drummond

India's Tamilians have always considered themselves a distinct race. Distinct from the Aryans who, history tells us, displaced their Dravidian ancestors after the conquest of the Indus-Valley civilizations. The Tamil language and script are perhaps of greater antiquity than Sanskrit and have remained largely free of its influence. Not to speak of Tamil literature which may be the richest India has to offer, both in depth and scope.

Which is why Tamilians break into passionate protest when any Tamilian anywhere be perceived as being under siege. Sri Lanka offering a prime example, as well as the situation of Tamilians in Malaysia.

So, would it be right to infer that Tamilian civilizational homogeneity brooks no breach?

Wrong.

In the Peraiyur taluk of Madurai district in Chennai is a place called Uthapuram. And there, for the last two decades a ten foot high wall segregates Tamilians from other Tamilians, namely, caste Tamils from those without caste ('untouchabes').

This wall was built to deny access to casteless Tamils of Uthapuram to public places and facilities frequented by caste Tamils on the other side.

Indeed, at one point recently, a live electric wire was attached to some iron scaffoldings in the wall to deter any attempt to scale the wall.

Another wall was to come up to prevent the authorities from providing a bus shelter to the dalits, something that was demanded by the Tamil

Nadu Untouchability Elimination Forum (TNUEF), an organization that had first drawn attention to the electrification of the Uthapuram wall.

This internecine conflict between Tamilians in Uthapuram is apparently of old vintage, indeed some 75 years old.

Over the last two years matters have come to a head. To their great credit, the CPI(M) with some help from the Karunanidhi government succeeded in demolishing some 150 ft. of the wall in April, 2008. (see my 'CPI(M) Breaks New Ground').

Owing to efforts made by the TNUEF, the electric wiring has also been removed, and Brinda Karat of the CPI(M) alongwith the All India Democratic Women's Association (women's front of the party) have been agitating for the wall to be fully demolished, and the ugly apartheid to be ended.

Interestingly, Tamil Nadu is governed by a largely OBC-led formation – intermediate social castes who vanquished the caste oppression of the Tamil Brahmins during the social reform agitations led by Periyar and Annadurai, mentors of the current leadership.

Yet, such is India's social reality that those who fought and defeated Brahminism seem at best lukewarm in defeating caste oppression of the Pillai OBCs in Uthapuram against fellow dalit Tamils.

Thumbs down for 'pure reason.'

Let us recall that, although the inception of the Congress party in 1885 was accompanied by the establishment of the 'Social Conference' as well, political reform was always given precedence over social reform. Here is what W.C.Bonnerjee had to say in 1892 at the 8th session of the Congress:

> I for one have no patience with those who say we shall not be fit for political reform until we reform our social system. I fail to see any connection between the two.

That, by and large has remained the position of the Congress on the issue, although at one point in the thirtees, Gandhi was to feel pressured enough by the Ambedkarite movement to launch his movement for the eradication of untouchability. A purple patch which did not have the objective of eradicating the caste system to which Gandhi subscribed in however a 'rational' mode.

The irony then is that those sterling social reform movements which arose and came to decisive ends in the southern states of India should now have lost all their will and steam. Something that the Karunanidhi government in Tamil Nadu may ponder.

The irony seems explicated by the fact that state formation anywhere and anytime seems inevitably to be accompanied by the desire of the dominant to hold the balance of class/caste forces in an equilibrium that best suits them. Encouragement to radical movements for equality from 'below,' however these might issue from the very ambit of the ideology used by the dominant to come into dominance (equality/liberty/fraternity) runs the risk of undermining the new class consensus. As Lassalle was to say in 1862 to a Prussian audience

> The constitutional questions are in the first instance not questions of right but questions of might. The actual constitution of a country has its existence only in the actual condition of force which exists in the country; hence political constitutions have value and permanence only when they accurately express those conditions of force which exist in practice within a society.

Needless to say to the dalits in Uthapuram in Madurai, and indeed everywhere else, that the Indian political arrangement may be decentred only when india's social reform movements acquire a clout forceful enough to nudge that arrangement. And, however, onerous the ask, democracy carries within it the logic that allows the downtrodden to harbour the hope of achieving that decentring. Through massive mobilization and persistence, and a dogged shaming of the dominant through the very arguments they have used to achieve their present position.

There are of course those sociologists and clinical psychologists who argue that India's modernizing project should skirt the bland deracinations engendered by the legacy of the Enlightenment. In their view such store of riches from the past as religion, race and caste must be incorporated into the equality project rather than done away with, so that india's modernization does not merely ape westernization.

Needless to say, very few of them are either dalits or women.

II

Speaking of women, let us turn to the *khap panchayats* of north-western India.

Preponderately a *kshatriya* phenomenon in ancient times, this form of social organization where the Jats of the western belt would, in aggregates of 84 village communities (khap meaning 'all castes'), meet to deliberate upon how best to defend their terroritories against internal and external threat/aggression, these wholly unelected panchayats with no locus within India's constitutional regime have since come to represent extra-judicial, alternate village governments where it concerns the rights and social freedoms of members of the community.

And not surprisingly, the chief objects of its upper caste oppression remain women and dalits.

What is noteworthy is the fact that its edicts are delivered without the least fear of the law of the land, and in complete contempt of the elected *panchayats* duly empowered to oversee village governance.

As India's modernizing 'development' makes breaches among the iron-clad regimes of the khaps, chiefly in the challenges made to it by young men and women who seek to register their personal/sexual freedom, the khaps have been lately, especially in the state of Haryana where the Jats dominate both socially and in land and other assets ownership, driven to issuing murderous *fatwas* against young couples, many of whom have then been actually done to death.

Zero tolerance is thus asserted against anyone transgressing caste/*gotra* (*gotra* being an intra-caste category within Brahminism, and an intra-*gotra* marriage seen to tantamount to incest, never mind that no blood relation may exist between the boy and the girl) boundaries.

That such a dispensation is at bottom calculated to keep the land and other assets within caste, and to ensure the bonded/chattel status of women as labour class within and without the family is not difficult to understand.

As ever, these sordid considerations are sought to be couched in the language of morality in emulation of the much-maligned Taliban who, after all, are a recent phenomenon. Here, for example, is what Mahendra Singh Tikait, a redoubtable leader of the farming community in western Uttar Pradesh, has said recently:

> Only whores choose their partners.... Recently an educated couple married against the samaj's (community's) wishes in Jhajjar. We hail the panchayat's decision to execute them (reference not to the elected/authorized panchayat but to the khap). The government cannot protect this atyachar (unacceptably immoral behaviour)... (The law of the land) is the root of all problems. ...That's is your Constitution, ours is different.

This Tikait, it should be noted, is as of now a Congress ally. No wonder that the local Member of Parliament, and a young one at that, expressed sympathy for the 'sentiments and local customs of *khap panchayats*.' Not to speak of the police who invariably share the social philosophy propounded by the *khaps*.

Here is the point, though: India's Home minister, the erudite Chidhambaram, holds the view that no special laws are necessary to meet such pronouncements as Tikait's above (remember that special laws do exist prohibiting any form of support to Sati and inducement to dowry); plainly, he thinks, the murders should be treated as murders, as any ordinary murders, and dealt with accordingly.

Never a day goes by when some senior member of the cabinet does not lambast 'internal challenges to the state.' Invariably they have left-wing extremism in mind.

You may well ask why Tikait's explicit rubbishing of the Constitution, followed by assent to the execution of educated and adult and consenting young men and women does not constitute an internal threat and challenge to the state as by law established. left-wing extremists at least by common consent do what they do on behalf of the dispossessed; the Khap does the same but on behalf of the entrenched. And maybe that is why its doings are not seen to tantamount to any internal threat to the state (Lassalle above).

And yet, the ever increasing numbers of young men and women who seem now willing to court the murderous fatwas of this alternate system of tyranny only underscore the certain decentring of the khap. Matter of time, as dominance carries within it the seeds of its own destruction. Those that everyday swear by democracy while wishing to contain it cannot succeed.

Once again, those in the forefront of the battle against the khap brigandage are largely India's women. It is once again the AIDWA (women's wing of the CPI(M)) which has been holding fort in these regions on behalf of those that should but won't.

The following demands have been placed before the government of the day by protestors led by various segments of India's parliamentary left:

- that coercing adults in matters of marriage be declared illegal, whether the coercion come from the Khaps or sections of communal outfits;

- spell out punishments for diktats and death sentences issued by Khap Panchayats, and for Tikait-type justifications of such executions;
- spell out punishments for policing and administrative authorities who collude with the Khaps;
- spell out punishments for parents who falsely dub their wards 'minors' in order to facilitate their separation from their spouses and relegation into Nari Niketans (homes for destitute women).

These specific demands have been made to the honorable Home Minister under the signatures of Kavita Krishnan, National Secretary, AIPWA and Sucheta de, Joint Secretary, AISA, Delhi Unit.

It is to be much hoped that the government will move in the matter, disregarding considerations of electoral calculus, and with a view to eradicating this barbaric and boldly voiced internal threat to the constitutional regime.

Yes, lynch mobs did rule the American west once some century and a half ago, and then again during the era when the Ku Klux Klan behaved like India's *khap panchayats*.

If our strategic friends, the Americans, sorted those things out, how about we do the same.

Not enough simply to grow at 9% per annum, leaving barbarisms to flourish at an even greater percentage.

September 2009

Gandhi at the Service of Mont Blanc

So, is Gandhi great for what ideas he had, or is he great because he can be fetishised and sold?

Clearly the latter, it would seem.

The pen manufacturer, Mont Blanc, now gives us a pen in Gandhi's name worth some 11 lac rupees.

So, even if you wrote a trashy note with this pen it would go into history; not because what you wrote was worthwhile, but because you wrote it with a Gandhi-Mont Blanc golden nib.

On a celebrity talk show just the other day, a young Indian entrepreneur with a pugilists chin was quite clear (those that make money are always 'quite clear' about most things, you must have noticed) that time comes when any icon becomes a 'brand,' and then profitable while it lasts.

The argument being that in this day and age it must be irrelevant to think how Gandhi might have felt about being sold as a pen by a multi-national for a middle-class man's life-times' earnings.

The relevant part is that the needs and genius of capital must always override the content of the icons it presses into service.

Tomorrow if an under-garment multi-national produces a Gandhi logo on its underwear and plasters the same on a Gandhi frame, lovely; it would both contemporanise Gandhi and brings yet more money to the corporate.

Whether that would, however, persuade people to enter the world of Gandhi's moral/ethical concerns is beside the point. The moot thing being that both he and the requirements of capital would have been served, and young people could wear the Gandhi underwear and claim to be doing 'Gandhigiri' (propagating the great man).

A disturbing point was, nonetheless, made on this show by the young actor, Rahul Bose.

He argued with a rustic naivete, it must have seemed to many, that if for a moment Gandhi was to be thought of as a 'brand' then any product stamped and sold in his name should at least bear some relation to the meaning of the brand.

In short, when we read Gandhi or think of his career, personal and political, four ideas would immediately strike us as having informed and impelled his life and work – non-violence, non-discrimination, simple living, truthfulness.

Question, therefore: how does an 11 lac fountain pen or a Philips under garment represent those values?

The idealist actor, of course, did not stop to think that no advertiser of any product ever considers whether the lies propagated – through digital magic – about the product bears any relation to its reality. Thus, for example, current 'brand ambassadors' are shown to be eating or using products that in actual life they neither eat nor use. In canny knowledge that millions of others who see them faking will eat or use the said product Often die in doing so.

Or that billions of rupees and other currency are consumed every day of every year world wide on activity that thinks nothing of projecting violence, untruth, discrimination, and the 'good life' – all of which anathema to Gandhian thought and practice.

Now, the 'honest' profiteer everyday maligns us by saying that our concerns are hypocritical and that we live double lives.

How nice it would be, therefore, if Mont Blanc would come 'upfront' and admit to us that the pen in question was not really honouring Gandhi but indeed looking to my mumber one – ergo, ploughing 'brand' Gandhi only to declare the supremacy of the 'brand Mont Blanc.'

The larger point should be obvious: if Jesus can be peddled as a superstar, who cares about what he said in the Sermon on the Mount?

Same with Gandhi, who once refused permission to a tycoon to use his facsimile on his roof tiles!

In the end, it is the money, stupid.

What a joke, thus, that celebrities should manufacture fassades of disingenuous chicanery in a babble of silken sophistry to convey to us the impression that there may be more to the matter than this gross truth.

Imagine that non-alcoholism was a tenet of cussed faith with Gandhi; but if recently one of India big liquor barons came to the rescue in retrieving Gandhi's spectales from off the auctioneer's table, wasn't he a great lover of Gandhi too?

You will recall that in Milton's *Paradise Lost*, the fallen angels congregate to consider how best to get back at God who has thrown them into hell.

Satan's argument – and Pandemonium was full of ingenious argument – wins the debate: seduce Man whom God has created after his own image and loves to distraction. That seduction knows no end, having become 24x7 corporate agenda.

And, failing everything, take a cue from that other fallen angel, Mammon: pave hell with gold, and make a heaven of hell. That too is rampantly order of the day.

Which is why all good and caring people ought to find ways to draw the waters of the moon to irrigate this thirsty and drought-ridden earth before the Mont Blanc types get up there to set up heavy water factories for thermo-nuclear purposes.

Gandhi would have said so. No?

October 2009

India's Left-Wing Extremism

What Came First, Chicken or Egg?

Even as the Indian state ponders the situation along its international borders with Pakistan, China, Bangladesh, and Nepal, it is increasingly challenged by the spread of left-wing armed extremism at home.

The strongholds of Indian Maoists are, not surprisingly, in the forested hinterlands of central states, such as Chhattisgarh and Jharkhand, where the Adivasis (originary tribals) have through six decades of independent India remained almost wholly outside the consideration of the state, except often as brutal victims of influential land-grabbers and aspiring mining and other corporates, backed by the state in collaboration with multinational companies.

Extremist violence, popularly referred to as Naxalism or Maoism, indeed straddles as many as some 180 of India's 600 or so districts in lesser or greater intensity, along an north-eastern arc stretching from Bihar through West Bengal to parts of Orissa, down to Andhra and Gadchirolli in Marharashtra that touches the Andhra border. With Jharkhand and Chhattisgarh as the heartlands.

Were a map of India's most neglected, impoverished and exploited regions be superimposed on another with the most natural resources, and then again on regions most afflicted by left-wing extremism, they would by and large all sit one over the other. A triad of congruence that tells its own social and ideological story.

That this congruence is less and less amenable to denial is testified to by the recent statement of India's Prime Minister himself: "The growth of Naxalism in central India obliges us to look at what causes this sense of alienation among certain sections of the community, especially the tribal community. It could be indicative of the deficiencies in the pace of development." (*The Hindu*, October12, 2009)

This, of course, is a good question to ask, and not a day too soon.

What must seem problematic, however, is what follows this recognition: '...but groups of individuals have no right to take law and order into their own hands. The designs of these groups are well known and we will take effective measures to counter them' (Ibid.).

The 'designs' part has reference to the Maoist objective to capture the state through armed struggle as opposed merely to seeking amelioration for the neglect and immiseration from the state as at present constituted. That such designs do exist in Maoist literature is ofcourse true.

The further question to ask should have been as to how to persuade the tribals who support the Maoists – being the only state they have known – that India's constitutional regime and parliamentary democracy is at their service as well.

Not an easy thing to do, given that over sixty years of independent existence the state has been unable to reach many of these districts with even the minimal evidence of their inclusion in its 'national' purposes. Not a school, not a dispensary, not a policeman, not a land-revenue dispensation, not a government office, not a road, bridge or culvert, nor drinking water or assured supply of the barest modicum of food is to be found in places like Bastar, Dantewada, Koraput, Gadchirolli and so on.

And over and above all that, vast tracts of forest on which the survival of these tribes has depended are happily demolished to make way for the 'developmental' activities of companies for whose convenience roads and other technical support structures materialize in no time, often with brutal coercion.

With variations, this has been the paradigm in large parts of India's north-eastern states as well where, again not surprisingly, many insurgencies have flourished over the last six decades.

II

Now as the Indian state seems all set to launch a concerted offensive against the Maoists, complete with helicopter gunships, and as phrases such as 'enemy lines' etc., are beginning to sound on India's electronic channels, this may be the only time for both the Maoists and the state to think beyond stated objectives.

If the 'emerging superpower' where some 77% people sustain themselves at half a dollar a day is to be spared wholesale collapse into an anarchy that may further the interests of neither the Maoists nor the state, least of all the interests of tribal populations on whose behalf the war-like contention is ostensibly in the offing, the state may do well to pursue its more sanguine introspections (as evidenced in the Prime Minister's statement above) with due acknowledgement of complicity and failure thus far, even as the Maoists may need to evaluate without unrealistic self-regard the likely prospects of the course they follow.

As I read the Prime Minister's thoughtful poser (what causes this alienation?), I am reminded of the malaria inspector who first brought home to me the scientific fact that killing off any number of mosquitoes does not solve the mosquito-malaria problem. For the simple reason that unless the waters where they breed are rectified, mosquitoes will never end. An insight applicable precisely to all theatres of human enquiry and action – from the smallest individual disability to autism, to cancer, to all forms of collective, social disaffection.

Even in states of great happiness, it is not unusual to hear it asked, ' what causes this happiness?' And, just as the answer to that question can aid our efforts to sustain happiness, the answer to the mosquito question, as overarching metaphor, can help us root out the problem, or, at the least, deal with it where it requires to be dealt with. Simply declaring war on mosquitoes may not do. Especially if the state is with good reason seen to be an instrument at the service not of all Indians but only of some.

Contrarily, the question for the Maoist ideologues to consider is whether armed struggle promises the best dividends for the people they speak for. Can the India of 2009 be justly compared with the China of the 1940s? Pragmatically, is the Maoist movement likely to gather enough support internally and enough reinforcement externally to make the capture of the state a likely possibility in some foreseeable future? If not, what prospects do they see for the poorest of the poor from a praxis of prolonged hit and run killing, in the face of a countering armed repression at an enhanced scale of operation?

In that context, this writer had, in his write-up titled 'India, Nepal, and Left Praxis' made the following submission: 'It would be intellectually remiss of India's Maoists to simply ignore the enormous significance of the choice that their counterparts in Nepal have made.' Three years later, I would still humbly press that thought for consideration.

III

It is entirely possible that some of us have turned timidly finicky about violence in an ontological way. But it does seem a defendable argument to say that, quite apart from the philosophical/ethical dimensions of the question, look where you will, and violence, be it by the state or by forces opposed to the state, fails more and more to meet the objectives of either. Be it Kashmir or India's north-east, violence has produced few gratifications either for the state or for insurgents. Not to speak of Palestine, Iraq, and Afghanistan.

Not that parliamentary democracy has done too much better for India's oppressed; what the praxis of violence has done, though, is to stymie what parliamentary democracy, even of our crass and venal kind, may be made to do through mass mobilization and use of what institutional tools it furnishes, however grudgingly, for its own legitimation, for larger numbers of people in the light of day.

Were the state to initiate back-channel contact with the Maoists, it would need to remember three all-important things: one, that Maoists are not 'terrorists' of the kind that we know; two, that it would pay a heavier price still if parleys were cannily to be conjoined with deception and elimination (as did happen in Andhra Pradesh) – heavier price, that is, on behalf of its own credibility among the downtrodden masses.; and, three, to resist that all-too-familiar paranoia which goads repressive states into suspecting contrary voices to belong to the nation's 'enemies.'

Likewise, the Maoists would make a great contribution by suggesting to the state structural transformations in rural, tribal governance such as bear the promise of ridding the hinterland of venal exploitation both by privateers and state agencies. This could include patterns of ownership and funding calculated both to make people's democracy a workable reality on the ground, and to render onslaughts on it anathema to the nation's conscience – sufficient to produce mass mobilization and proactive revulsion on its behalf.

If it is agreed that neither the state, however it raves and rants, nor the Maoists can hope through violent means to corner the problem of neglect and immiseration to their stated purposes, how much more sensible it might be to stop the killings and achieve something half-way for the people whose fate for now seems to be either to starve to death or to die in unequal contest, often at the hands of their own brethren (like the *Salwa Judum* in Chhattisgarh) who have been made captive antagonists by the state.

October 2009

Does Ideology Matter?

Yes it does!

> There has been a systematic failure in giving tribals a stake in the modern economic system – the alienation built over decades is taking a dangerous toll…
>
> The systemic exploitation of our tribal communities…can no longer be tolerated.
>
> (Prime Minister, Manmohan Singh, *Hindustan Times*, 14 November 2009)

A government report just released on the situation of India's tribals blames the government itself and companies like the Tatas and Essar for the disquiet in the tribal 'hinterlands.' As you would expect, the latter have righteously washed their distinguished hands of the insinuation.

Brought out by the Ministry of Rural Development, the report (some tribute to aspects of Indian democracy) in a chapter titled 'state-connived land alienation' speaks forthrightly of how land grabs in India's mineral rich states – Orissa, Chhattisgarh, Jharkhand – happen with 'direct and indirect participation of revenue officials.' To those must be added the more notorious segments of the political class, now most strikingly represented by the erstwhile Chief Minister of Jharkhand, Madhu Koda, who, by all accounts, is alleged to have made a pile of some Rs.4000/- crores over a span of five or six years of 'rule.' That Mr.Koda is himself a tribal leader must suggest how enticing and promising the dominant paradigms of 'development' are.

That the debate around the issue has penetrated the solid bastions of capitalist theorists is rather hearteningly evidenced by the following sub-heading in the editorial of *Hindustan Times* of November16: 'Tribal land grabs' aren't just an "NGO" theory.'

Conceding that some 40% of all lands used for 'development' belongs to tribals, the report characterises the circumstance as 'the biggest grab of tribal lands after Columbus.'

I may recall that in an earlier column this writer had drawn attention to the significant coincidence that Naxalism afflicts precisely those regions which are richest in mineral wealth, where grabbers are the most active, and where poverty is the most abysmal (see 'India's Left-Wing Extremism').

So you might well ask where ideology factors into the matter.

Look at the epigraph closely, and you would conclude that the statement may well have come from a Maoist ideologue, whereas in fact it comes from the Prime Minister of India.

Caveat: where the Maoist ideologue may have deduced from the language of the epigraph that exploitation and immiseration clearly identify themselves as India's chiefest 'internal danger,' the Prime Minister, having used those words, concludes – and repeatedly – that the greatest 'internal danger' is Naxalism rather than that which breeds it.

Thus it is that ideologues who represent differing class interests interpret one and the same words differingly.

And, doing so, they unleash differing orders of praxis upon the republic, fraught with commensurate consequence for millions of citizens.

II

Having gotten thus far in acknowledgement, the state now demands that it is willing to discuss issues with the Maoists provided they put an end to violence – a stipulation that is made even as unprecedented mobilization of central and state forces is underway to launch on the Maoists in their forested hideouts.

As a confirmed pacifist, this writer endorses every call, whoever makes it, for a world without violence. I am on record as having more than once suggested to the Maoists that however righteous their armed struggle, violence is the wrong way to go about it. (see my 'India, Nepal, and Left Praxis').

Yet, we must all alike countenance the question as to what it is that constitutes violence. Why is it that what is violence to some is often mere administrative fall-out or collateral damage to others, if not just retribution? And are the likes of the Maoists alone in making excuses?

At the extreme philosophical level, Gandhi never failed to underscore his conviction that violence is first born in a violent thought, so that even some of the kindest seeming acts of mankind can sometimes be vitiated by their origins in minds tainted with violence in other spheres of interest and activity. Or that an act of kindness born out of a self-regarding consideration is in itself evidence of a mind still unfree of violence. Often, as Marx was to point out, our charitable acts are ultimately meant only to keep in place disequilibriums of social and economic power. Something that the poet, Blake, was to formulate searingly in the couplet: *Pity would be no more/If we did not make somebody poor.*

But let that be.

Only a month or so ago, the Save the Children NGO brought home to us the following facts:

- one fifth of the children dying in the world are Indian;
- a total of 2 million die before their 5th birthday;
- one child dies every 15 seconds due to neo-natal diseases;
- more than 400,000 newborns die every year within a day of birth;
- one in three malnourished children worldwide is an Indian.

And a great deal more.

Ask yourself whether these are mere statistics or unconscionably violent consequences of state policy?

Whether some Malthusian order of nature can happily absolve the state of this violence?

Whether these and a plethora of other like exterminations – wrought upon dalits, Women, and Minorities, in addition to the tribals – on a daily basis since India's Independence can or cannot be attributed to the active/selective intent of coordinates of governance, of the acquisition and distribution of wealth, in effect to the particular and concrete ways in which the democratic system in India has received guidance?

Whatever be your conclusions will will-nilly trace back to ideological suppositions with regard to what it means to be 'human' and to act as 'human' subjects. Try it.

For now, the question that begs itself is why is it that some forms of violence are never endorsed by the classes as qualifying to be called violence, and if called, duly remedied in lasting ways?

Let me offer just the most obvious reference (as we now consider forms of violence that are obviously active and gruesome, and involve killing and maiming on the instant).

By anybody's reckoning, more numbers in Independent India have been killed and maimed in religiously-driven frenzies and pogroms and in industrial disasters than in Maoist shenanigans. The Delhi Sikh killings of 1984 and anti-Muslim Gujarat pogrom of 2002 alone between them may have vented more gruesome fury upon more numbers than the Naxals have killed since 1967 when peasant uprisings of post-Independent India first took shape in violent form.

And consider that the Bhopal Gas Tragedy of December 3, 1984 at the then Union Carbide factory from leaking Methyl Isocyanate has to date involved, by official account, close to 20,000 deaths. All of India's many insurgencies may not equal that number.

Yet we have never heard the state to say that such matters constitute any great 'internal danger,' have we? Or known the state to pursue the agents with any great resolve.

The reason is not far to seek, and the reason is, like it or not embedded in ideology.

Forms of violence that originate from the tactical or strategic requirements of the classes may evince moral outrage from the media, or sections of it, and sections of the citizenry, they are understood cannily, after all, to keep in place forms of social and cultural dominance needed to prop patterns of possession and distribution. Just as they are also useful in ploughing wage workers and other disgruntled lumpen sections of the population back from class issues to helpfully divisive considerations of identity.

Just as the devastation in Hiroshima and Nagasaki on a more impressive scale was intended after all to keep the godly races safe from the evil ones.

Must there not be a reason why whether in India or abroad, violence thus perpetrated by class affiliates rarely draws either justice or retribution upon known and powerful perpetrators? Justice and retribution are inevitably reserved for those whose violence after all proved insufficient and defeatable by greater violence. Examples will suggest themselves dime a dozen.

There is clear understanding, therefore, that whereas the occasional religious pogrom, caste atrocity, state-driven excess can be used to good purpose on the one hand and shamed by pious hand-wringing on the other, what the Maoists are up to seeks fundamentally to overturn the benign dispensations along which India's political economy thrives for the haves.

Far from 'development' being an ideology-neutral issue, it is understood everywhere to be driven by the existing and projected interests of the classes; and all opposition to it equally by the 'anti-national' resistance of the masses.

And no greater ideological tactic than to say that in India all resistance to current patterns of 'development' is ideological, and thus tainted.

III

We may then be excused for our inability to subsribe to sermons about this, that, or the other in the abstract, including about what constitutes violence.

What is clear to me is that nothing suits the Indian state as well as being opposed with the force of arms, just as nothing would have suited the colonial British to have been opposed likewise by the machete and the occasional bomb blast.

A reality that Gandhi understood to perfection.

It is the 'naked newborn babe' that draws the most force from mankind, just as it did in that first of fascist exterminators, Macbeth.

How often is humane intelligence defeated by doctrine is a text worth the pondering.

At a time when from the lowliest to the Prime Minister and the *Hindustan Times* (and what it represents) acknowledges the force of the resistors' argument, what a pity that the Maoists should be unwilling or unable to forge more imaginative and fruitful forms of engagement than peddling arms in hinterland hideouts.

Dig human history where you will, and no social forces have ever succeeded in obtaining all; on the other hand, they have often settled for nothing after great losses of life.

Contrarily, any state that thinks that arguments however potent and acknowledged can be obliterated by the force of superior arms has little cause to think that it embodies the fine principles of republicanism.

And the time to weigh these matters on either side is now.

If indeed the 'systemic exploitation of our tribals cannot be tolerated,' as the Prime Minister has said, does it not follow that the system needs to be revisited?

November 2009

Carting Off Medical Institute to Corporate Predators

> No one can be perfectly free till all are free; no one can be perfectly moral till all are moral; no one can be perfectly happy till all are happy. (Herbert Spencer)

To that talisman you could add another: no one can be perfectly healthy till all are healthy.

At a time, however, when Obama, the welfarist democrat, battles the American Congress, sundry red-necks, and powerful Pharma lobbyists and private medical insurers to bring to beleaguered Americans a guaranteed public health dispensation, his strategic partner, Manmohan Singh, may be about to cart off the All India Institute of Medical Sciences, an iconic symbol of Nehru's welfarist national vision, 'recognized for providing low-cost medical care to large numbers of patients' (Wikipedia) to sundry business interests.

A committee (Valiathan) now recommends that the institute 'should form consortia to develop and transfer for commercialization a range of products and processes.'

It suggests that 'consultancy for Indian industry should be encouraged among faculty,' and faculty 'should be given leave to join industry.' Further that research papers should be monetarily rewarded as well, such as may be 'of great interest to industry.'

In order that these objectives are nicely fulfilled, it recommends that 'industrialists... be nominated by the central government' to the controlling Board 'in consultation with CII, NASSCOM, and FICCII' – godlike conglomerates of India's private capital.

Lest you think that these recommendations have anything to do with enhancing the primary health care obligations of the Institute, please note that for the 12 years that the prestigious India Today magazine has conducted surveys, AIIMS has been ranked number ONE for 11 years!

Just as surveys conducted by the Week and Outlook magazines have named it the best hospital in India overall, as well as best in several individual fields, such as Cardiology, Nuerology, Gasteroenterology, Gynocology, and Opthalmology, ahead of several specialized institutions (Wikipedia).

Thus, even as Obama pays compliment to Castro's Cuba for the care it takes of Cuban's health, Manmohan Singh rushes to emulate the American Republicans who believe passionately (read rabidly) that the least penny spent on public health by the state violates the overriding sanctity of the market.

II

As you would imagine, there is great and honourable resistance to the Valiathan recommendations within the AIIMS faculty, even as many also see in them an opportunity to make a private killing.

A statement issued by no less than a 100 faculty members have underlined all the obvious and right things:

- that even in the US, UK, EU, Japan, there is no practice of encouraging research papers with monetary incentivization – a move sure to lead to fudged research to cater to private wealth; and repeatedly;
- that the best research is always that which has the approval not of industry but of peers;
- that good research should be approved by the Institute and certificates of honour issued to the researchers.

More explicitly, the Progressive Medicos and Scientists Forum has in a letter to the AIIMS' President pointed out that the whole Valiathan exercise is calculated to transform the Institute 'from a people Institute to an Institute serving corporate interests.'

The Valiathan recommendation that 'members of pharma industry and business bodies be empanelled on the research council and decision-making bodies of AIIMS…in consultation with bodies like FICCI, CII, ASOCHAM' can have no other earthly purpose than to subvert the very

Act of Parliament establishing AIIMS which had intended to make of it a premier act of faith to the people of India that the best health care would be made accessible to the *aam aadmi* (common man, a phrase that formed the bedrock of the Congress Party's election manifesto) at low cost.

As shown above, no argument can be made that this intent has over the years brought the professional standards of the Institute low.

On the contrary, the effort now on to gobble up the institute is but another shameful and grisly part of the tenets of the Washington Consensus of 1990 which enjoined that as far as possible public assets must be transferred to private wealth owners worldwide – tenets that the Manmohan government in India seems still devotedly wedded to even after the Lehmans and the General Electrics, and the Goldman Sachs and the AISes and you-name-it giants of private wealth have gone down the drain, breathing now if at all due to the munificence of the state at public expense.

But the abiding lesson of capitalism remains that cannibals will be cannibals until the proposed victims clench collective fists and put the fear of mass uprisings into them.

III

If you didn't know, India already has the world's sixth most privatized health care system.

And you may well wonder why that should be so in a country which in absolute terms has the largest numbers of children dying from preventable diseases, largest numbers of the world's malnutritioned and undernutritioned populations, largest numbers of anaemic mothers, and some 77% citizens who afford an expenditure of only half a dollar or less per day.

You may well wonder at the obscenity that those national indices should go hand in hand with dreams of superpower glory.

I pose that question not as a rhetorical flourish but to register a deeply embedded truth of India's Brahminical culture, one that bears intimately on the svarna (twice born) view of whose life has meaning and whose rights to life are admissible – a theoretical legacy of inequity tailor-made to fit the inequities of the capitalist social order.

And this sordid story is nowhere more thoroughly and trenchantly laid out than in that magnificent piece of research and analysis by one of the world's foremost social thinkers and philosophers, the late D.P.

Chattopadhyay, titled 'Science and Philosophy in Ancient India,' (in *Marxism and Ideology*, Calcutta and New Delhi, 1981).

And at the heart of that exploration we are taught about the greatest tragedy that Indian social and intellectual life ever underwent some 2500 years ago, namely, the systematic decimation of the beginnings of science in India at the hands of priestly law-makers.

With the first emergence of surplus as ancient India evolved to its agricultural stage, two deadly theoretical pincers were floated by the dominant, Sanskrit-using Brahminical class to ensure its appropriation:

One was to say that our endowments or denials have nothing to do with any material principles of social organization but with our karma; and, second, that whereas till as late as the IXth canto of the Rig Ved the object of prayer had remained the procuring of food, all that changed to the attainment not of food but of moksha (emancipation from the cycle of birth and rebirth), something which again could not be hoped for without involving the exertions of the priest class.

Imagine that into such a conjuncture should have stepped in India's first materialist school of thought, the *Carvak Samhita*, which argued that 'everything about purusa or man is established in the body.' And to say 'pranah pranbhutam annam' – 'life is just food transformed into the living.'

From those stipulations issued the science of the Ayurveda, an empirical science that proposed that the body of man comprises pancha bhuta, five elements (much like the western theory of cholers), and that good or bad health had reference merely either to the sound or unsound proportion in which the elements inhabited the body. And, following from that, the praxis that cure could not be caused by priestly rituals but by the administration of elements procured from the physical/natural world.

Is it difficult then to understand the mortal threat that the new science posed to the dominant social groups, or to understand why they should have set about, in unabashedly obscurantist and cruel ways to ensure that the Ayurved was rendered the shudra among the Vedas, and that the new physicians were shunned, ostracized, and ejected from social approval?

As Chattopadhyay writes:

> while the scientists are interested in the theory and practice by which man acquires mastery over nature, the law-makers are interested in the theory and practice by which man may acquire mastery over man,i.e. to keep the large masses of men under control or as law-abiding people

which in the ancient Indian context, concretely means people submitting to the model of Varnasrama society (loosely, the caste hierarchy, where the word Varn means, interestingly, colour – the first enunciation of a racial principle). Understandably, therefore, the ancient Indian law-makers find their basic purpose totally incompatible with the promise of positive science.

Thus, just to give you a taste of what is meant:

- the law-codes of Apastamba declare that food given by a physician is too filthy to be accepted by members of the higher castes;
- Gautama's law-codes assert that a Brahmin may accept food from a 'trader who is not an artisan,' but he must not accept food from an artisan or a surgeon who belongs to the group of the intrinsically impure persons;
- the law-codes of Vasistha fully concur food offered by the physician is as impure as that offered by the harlot, etc.

Note that the Gita stipulates that 'one's own duty (*sva-dharma*) is relative to one's social status' (see Shri Krishna Saksena, 'The Story of Indian Philosophy,' *A History of Philosophical Systems*, ed. Virgineus Fern, New York, The Philosophical Library, 1950.)

Thus it is that these legacies continue to inform the policy preferences of India's current Brahminical major domos, preferences that gel nicely into the preferences of private capital.

Those preferences conjointly hold that not all human lives have equal worth or equal claim, and that being so, institutes like the AIIMS have but been squandering expertise and resource on those whose claims to health and happiness are denied by the best principles both of India's Brahminical philosophy and of the diktats of private capital.

In recommending what he has recommended for the reconstitution of the institute, Valiathan is but only being faithful to those converging principles.

And, yet, now that we understand more than we did in the years gone by, it is about time that somebody stood up and showed him the door.

'We the People' of our times are no longer the dumb-driven lower orders of times past, and there are physicians among us, like the 100 signatories, who now possess both the theoretical and social clout to defeat social and economic Brahminism.

All power to them and to all the others who are on their way to join with them.

December 2009

The Liberhan Report

What Should It Mean?

On December 6,1992, hordes of right-wing Hindutva extremists (called karsevaks) took the town of Ayodhya hostage with the full and willing connivance of the then state government of Uttar Pradesh and in physical presence of most of the top leaders of the Sangh Parivar (the RSS and its affiliates/fronts like the Vishwa Hindu Parishad, the Bajrang Dal, the Shiv Sena, and the Bharatiya Janata Party).

By evening of that fateful day, the 460 year old mosque built there by one of Babar's lieutenants, Mir Baqi, was razed to a heap of rubble on the grounds that the mosque was built over a temple which enclosed the birthplace of the god, Ram.

To this day, there is no evidence of any kind that a temple of any sort pre-existed at the site of the demolished mosque.

Interestingly, the Prime Minister of the day, late Narasimha Rao, failed/refused to respond to insistent pleas both from some members of his cabinet and many others from civil society across religious communities to intervene to forestall that unprecedently brazen assault on the Constitution and the rule of law.

The local government of Kalyan Singh was to cock a final snook at the central government and resign office after the deed was done, and in daylong glare of television coverage, preempting the possibility of being dismissed from office.

Almost instantly, riots broke out, and Muslims were killed with impunity by Hindutva draftees who saw no obstacle to their exertions. In the city of Mumbai, about a thousand innocent Indians lost their lives. (The Justice Srikrishna Commission inquiring into those Mumbai killings was to squarely hold the Shiv Sena and other Hindutva bodies responsibe for those massacres, and recommend legal action including against the Shiv Sena chief, Bal Thackeray. To this day, however, no action has followed, although the state of Maharashtra has since been ruled by the Congress/Natiionalist Congress Party combine with only an interregnum of Shiv Sena rule.)

Justice Manmohan Singh Liberhan was appointed in January of 1993 to enquire into the sequence of events that led to the demolition of the Babri mosque, and to fix responsibility.

After seventeen long years, the Liberhan report is in. Over a thousand pages long, the Liberhan report concludes that 'the RSS was the author' of the carnage, and all 'logistical arrangements' were 'coordinated between RSS, VHP, Bajrang Dal, and the BJP,' calling the latter 'a front of the RSS'-the worst-kept secret of India's modern political history.

Characterising the event as the result of 'tailor made' and 'meticulous' conspiracy rather than a spontaneous outrage, the Liberhan report draws up a list of 68 names whom it holds culpable of the same, names that include almost every scion of the Sangh Parivar. Significantly, it lists the erstwhile Prime Minister, Atal Bihari Vajpayee, at number 7, holding him responsible of taking the 'country towards communal discord.' A day before the demolition, Vajpayee had been recorded on video making a public speech in Lucknow, the capital of Uttar Pradesh, expressing the need for the ground at Ayodhya to be 'leveled' inorder to facilitate the karseva (collective religious activity) the next day.

Justice Liberhan exonerates the then Prime Minister, Narasimha Rao of responsibility on the ground that he was duped by sworn affidavits submitted by the chief minister, Kalyan Singh, to the Supreme Court of India, undertaking to see that no harm would come to the mosque. Liberhan also accuses the Sangh leaders of duplicity in having 'lulled' him and the central government into complacence through their misleading pronouncements. While this is true enough, not many are convinced that this fact alone forestalled any action on behalf of the Prime Minister.

There is substantial evidence that one or two of his own cabinet ministers had warned him of the RSS plans for December 6 well in advance. One of those ministers, Makhan Lal Fotedar-a distinguished Kashmiri Pandit secularist-has revealed how the then governor of Uttar Pradesh was instructed by Rao not to recommend President's rule till asked by Rao to do so. Fotedar claims he was told about this by the then President of India, Shankar Dayal Sharma-another distinguished secularist Brahmin – whom he found in tears on the day.

Whereas Justice Liberhan has not recommended any specific action against anyone, it has noted some correctives, chief among these the need to have laws in place punishing the use of religion in political activity.

II

Mysteriously, the Liberhan report was leaked to the media before it was tabled in Parliament. Both the Home Minister and Justice Liberhan deny responsibility for the leak.

The BJP which has been in tatters recently as a result first of its electoral reverses, then of the most unedifying internecine discord, and finally of the open and overt take-over of its decision-making prerogatives by the RSS, its puppet master since inception, has sought to unite around two issues: a fake outrage at the naming of Vajpayee (whom both the RSS and Advani have wanted out for long), and at the leaking of the report.

It has also sought to make much of the report having been submitted 17 years after the event-a detail that in the BJP's view renders it only of academic interest, warranting no follow up.

That, even as it continues to demand action against the perpetrators of the Sikh killings of 1984-eight years prior to the Babri demolition-and even as it admires the Zionists no end for pursuing Nazi war criminals some half century after the second world war. Having led the assault on the mosque on the grounds of a four-century old 'dishonouring' of a 'Hindu nation,' it advises that there is little point in revisiting the Babri demolition some 17 years after the demolition! It utters not a word of remorse at the dishonouring of Muslim sentiments.

Privately the BJP hopes that the submission of the Liberhan report and the recorded culpability of the Sangh Parivar may help to portray the Sangh, and with it the BJP, as martyrs and warriors in the cause of 'cultural nationalism,' and revive its political fortunes which stand now at nadir.

III

There are, however, fatal reasons why the demolition of the Babri mosque by a fascist, Hindutva putsch must never be relegated as just one communal episode among many in post-independence India.

The controversy whether the Babri mosque site was indeed the birthplace of the Hindu god, Ram, has for a hundred years or so remained a matter of localized and legal contention, as 'title' suites are still being argued in courts to determine whether the Muslim Wakf Board or some Hindu organization had rightful claim to possession of the site.

Till as late as 1983, nobody outside Faizabad District in Uttar Pradesh bothered a great deal about what was going on in those suites. And not many did so even in Faizabad and Ayodhya which, paradoxically, had remained bastions of age-old inter-community harmony. Indeed, many of the plethora of temples in Ayodhya were managed and run by Muslim devotees of Ram.

It was between 1983 and 1992 that the Sangh decided to convert the Ayodhya issue into a cause celebre of 'cultural nationalism,' leading to the assault on December 6, 1992. That as a ploy to enter Parliament with some seats more than the humiliating two it had got in the elections of 1984.

In projecting the issue as they did, the Sangh had a macro-historical enterprise in mind, something that had little or nothing to do with the Hindu god, or with the purity of faith.

One, the project was to assert the majoritarian premise that India, notwithstanding its secular constitution, was first and foremost, a Hindu nation-state.

So that as the pick-axes rained on the domes of the mosque to the accompaniment of the grossest communal abuse, the fury of the doing suggested that it was not a mosque that was being demolished but, verily, the very body-incarnate of Islam. The subliminal rage of the erasers might have suggested that it was not a dome they were bashing but the head of the Moghul, Babar. Very much as in demolishing the Berlin wall, the body of the wall was seen to represent not an entity that separated two parts of a city but as an entity that embodied Communism.

Far from being just one vandalising episode at the hands of sectarian hordes, the assault on the mosque was constructed and propagated as a campaign to vanquish the secular Constitution of India and to shame it once and for all as being at bottom tilted against Hindus, and violative of racial principles of nationhood-an idea for which the erstwhile RSS ideologue and President, Golwalkar, was to be full of praise for Hitler and the Nazis.

Never reconciled to the secular Republic, the RSS thought to make of the campaign an occasion to reverse the principles of secular and pluralist citizenship that India had chosen to give to herself after Independence in 1947.

Two, the campaign was calculated to register the view that the will of the majority community superceded all the institutions of state, an initial gambit towards turning India into a theocracy, or a Hindu Rashtra in consonance with the well-laid out ideology of the Hindu Mahasabha and the RSS (see Golwalkar's *We, or Our Nationhood Defined*, and Savarkar's *Hindutva: Who Is a Hindu?*). A mirror image of the hardline Islamic idea of nationhood and state!

It should surprise nobody that the Sangh has a standing list of thousands of mosques which are slated to be demolished and replaced by temples, some 36,000 at last count. The question is never asked as to how many temples stand at sites that used to be Buddhist or Jain stupas.

And, not the least, to catapult the BJP as being the primary 'nationalist' political formation of India, and relegate the Congress and the leftists as essentially 'appeasers' of Babar's progeny, the Muslims, whose right to Indianness was to be formally damaged by the construction that they continue to be non-indigenous and disloyal progeny of invaders.

IV

India may have come a long way since 1992; yet so long as the BJP remains a mannequin to the RSS, so long as it fails or is unwilling to transform itself into an autonomous 'political' formation, so long as, willy nilly, it harks back to 'cultural nationalism' as its chief raison d' etre of political existence, remaining thereby unreconciled to secular citizenship, minority rights, and equality of opportunity and equality before the law, so long as, in one word, its chief point of political reference remains its visceral hatred of Muslims, it would be fatal to forget the lessons of the Babri demolition.

In that context, the indifferently evolved secular convictions of the Congress party after Nehru pose no small obstacle to any forthright firming up of the constitutional regime. It cannot be said that many more than half a dozen top leaders of the Congress hold Nehruvian secularism to be sancrosanct, especially when votes are in question.

And the Congress has only one way of disproving those reservations, namely, to grab Liberhan's injunction about the separation of religion and politics, and to put in place legislation that may heretofore brook no heinous mixing of the two.

Legislation, it must be noted, that is then backed up with the legal resolve never to pussyfoot any instance of communal appeal to the polity, and to come down with the full majesty of the law and the state on instances of communal violence instigated by political agents, whoever they be, or however high or mighty.

Taking a cue from the Liberhan recommendations, the Election Commission of India, a constitutional body beholden to no political or governmental regime, may consider the time ripe for laying down that any political use of religion would be ground for derecognition of the party found culpable.

This must include due and prompt punishment to all those who, in school, pathshala, madrasa, or wherever else seek to frame curriculi around communal perceptions of history and polity, calculated to undermine the rights and prerogatives of secular citizenship or to instill antagonism towards other religions, and a ruthless denial of all attempts to grab public spaces for unauthorized communal/religious use/propagation (something that the Supreme Court has recently enjoined) as well.

Even if the current UPA dispensation forgave all the designated culprits of the Babri crime (very few believe that the state has the will to do otherwise) but made the long-lasting redressals suggested by Liberhan and listed above, the generation of Indians to come might inherit a worthwhile democracy in regard at least to the matter of a non-negotiable secular citizenship and a country free of 'internal dangers' far worse and debilitating than pockets of insurgency floated around issues of livelihood.

And if none of that were to be done, the Liberhan exercise would indeed have been a criminal waste at tax-payer's expense. And, worse, an incentive to further depredations along the lines of the Babri crime.

December 2009

L.K. Advani and the Mythology of 'Sadness'

An Eyewitness Account

Ki mere qatl ke ba'd us ne jafa se tauba,
haye! us zud pasheman ka pasheman hona
(Mirza Ghalib).

(She swore she would no longer tease
When she had me slain for fun;
That remorse should have so stricken her
After the deed was done.)
(Raina's Ghalib, 1984).

On December 6, 1992, when the Babri mosque was razed to rubble, Ruchira Gupta was a journalist with Business India.

She was at the site of the carnage, where she met L.K.Advani and the other indicted (by the Liberhan Commission) leaders of the Sangh Parivar who sat 'in a mood of excitement on the terrace as if waiting for a celebration.'

At a commemorative meeting on December 6, 2009 organised by SAHMAT, Ruchira gave a first-hand public recital of what she saw and heard on that fateful day in 1992 – evidence that she had given to the Liberhan Commission, having flown especially from New York to do so where she has been working for a UN organization.

The specifics of her evidence, however, do not find any place in the Commission's voluminous report.

In regard especially to the much-touted remorse that Advani was later to claim to have felt, some of the direct snippets of her interaction with him on that day must seem revealing in the extreme, even though that claim may never have anyway won any credibility among Indians at large, with or without any direct evidence.

Here is what Ruchira had to say, and in her own voice from notes taken on December 6, 2009:

> When I heard the slogan '*kasam Ram ki khate hain/ mandir wahin banayenge*' (we swear by lord Ram that we shall build his temple at the very same spot), I asked Advani what this meant. He said to me "when you reach there you will find out what the slogan means" (this episode during his infamous rath yatra).
>
> On the day of the demolition, I heard Advani direct Uma Bharti to advise "the boys to come down (from the dome) because the dome would come down anyway." Needless to say, the latter half of what he says here puts a whole different colour on his much-propagated anxiety at the violence to come.
>
> Uma Bharti in the meanwhile was busy shouting '*Mussalmanoun ke dou hee sthan/ Pakistan ya Qabristan*' (there are only two places for Muslims/ Pakistan or the graveyard.)
>
> I saw Murli Manohar Joshi carrying statues, clearly to be installed after the demolition.
>
> I heard Vijay Raje Scindia say '*ab meri aankhon ko shanti milegi*' (now my eyes will have rest).
>
> I went inside the mosque, crowded with marauding *karsevaks* (religious draftees).
>
> Someone shouted 'Muslim'; people began choking and molesting me. Shouts of mar dou (kill her); another shout '*yahan nahin*' (not here) because this is the '*garbha grah*' (the place of Ram's birth).
>
> They took me to the trench outside, where a karsevak recognized me and shouted '*yeh patrakaar hai*' (she is a journalist). '*Hindu hai*' (she is a Hindu.)

> Released, I went back to the terrace where I saw Chandan Mitra and Swapan Dasgupta, two senior journalists, were also sitting.
>
> I pointed Advani to homes burning at some distance; he said, '*yeh Mussalmaan ghar jala rahe hain muavze ke liye*' (these are Muslims burning their own houses for compensation.)
>
> And then: '*Itna badda din hai, cheeni khaao*' (it is such an auspicious day; have some sweet.)
>
> I noticed Mark Tully, S.P. Jain and some other journalists being attacked.
>
> I said to some TV journalist, 'Psycopaths.'
>
> Which is when I began to be hounded; character assassination, hate mails, whisper campaigns were unleashed.
>
> During the Liberhan hearings, the defence lawyer was to ask me, 'do you smoke? Do you act in TV serials? What gods do you believe in? Why did you not run if you were molested?'
>
> The very next day, the campaign to propagate the mythology of Advani's 'sadness' began to be floated in the media by journalists allied to the Sangh.

Ruchira also said that some journalists were "pressurized not to testify, and others were bought off."

As said above, none of this testimony finds a place in the Liberhan report.

But, we salute Ruchira for the strength of commitment which obliged her to make a clean breast, and in the best national interest.

Will the state bring the psychopaths to book?

December 2009

2010

A Future India Must Do Without

Genius: a person who has a strong influence upon one for good or ill.
(Advanced Oxford Dictionary)

All of the year gone by, India's corporate classes – in sundry areas of material control, including the media – have been pushing and prodding the Bharatiya Janata Party (BJP) to return from the dumps to health and vigour. Editorially this Hindu right-wing formation has been reminded how the nation cannot do without them.

Alas, at the end of it all, its unedifying, even if highly diverting, internal squabbles have been for now set to right, not by its own autonomous political exertions, but per diktat of the RSS – a fascist outfit wholly extraneous to the constitutional scheme of the Republic.

Brushing aside the many hopefuls within the BJP, Nitin Gadkari, a self-confessed RSS devotee who has never yet won an election to an assembly, not to speak of the parliament, has been installed as President of the BJP vide explicit decree of the RSS.

Within seconds of an installation which violated all the inner-party constitutional procedures and mechanisms of the BJP, and violated also the democratic party-political norms of organizational recognition as required by the Election Commission of India, Shri Gadkare made known where he comes from and to what end.

To wit, much to the dismay of media and other elites sympathetic to the BJP who have been wishing and hoping that the BJP would, after the drubbings at the hustings through the year, learn to rercognize and acknowledge the new India of young, secular purposes, Gadkari announced the party's return to the RSS-dictated theme of 'cultural nationalism' (read a Hindu nation wherein all non-Hindus must learn to think and behave as though they were all Hindus as well, and do honour to Hindu forms of worship, ritual, and to Hindu gods and goddesses, as explicitly set out by the great Guru Golwalkar in his fascist handbook, *We, or Our Nationhood Defined*).

Well aware of the chagrin many hard Hindutva adherents within the BJP have felt at the relegation of Narendra Modi (who, incidentally, still is unable to find a country that will give him a visa), Gadkari has now said that he envisions a major role for Modi in the days to come, presumably both within the BJP and in national life.

Great have been the propogational exertions made since the Gujarat Muslim-massacre of 2002 to float the view that the Modi of then and the Modi of now are, after all, two different personae. By inference, the Modi of then may well have been a murderous anti-Muslim bigot, but the Modi of since has been a shining emblem of a 'vibrant Gujarat' given wholly to 'developmental' purposes, garnering huge foreign investments, and showing the way that India must go.

Alas, though, when are leopards known to change their spots. All evidence since 2002 continues to point to the vibrancy being an all-encompassing phenomenon, informing the congealed infrastructure of hate as much as the infrastructure of investments.

II

It has been repeatedly pointed out by humanist Indians, Gujaratis included, that not once in the last seven years has Modi initiated the least exercise to heal the social/communal divide in Gujarat's cities and towns. Verily, Gujarat's polity continues to be viciously fractured into a Hindu Gujarat and a Muslim one.

To a point where, as a recent write-up in one of India's most respected dailies, *The Indian Express*, brings out, Muslim Gujaratis have been obliged to masquerade under Hindu names inorder to have any hope of finding work.

Thus, in the diamond-cutting town of Surat, Mehboob Pathan took the name of Jayenti Bhatti, his son, Mushtaq, that of Mukesh, Samina of Sharmila and so on.

That the police outfits in Modi's Gujarat have learnt no lessons either is testified to by another recent story of the brutalization, including sexual outrage, perpetrated on a slew of Muslim women in Godhra on charges of alleged rioting and stone throwing.

Proof positive that the vibrancy of Modi's anti-Muslim hate has received scant competition from the vibrancy of his efforts to affect a personal make-over by drafting sundry business tycoons and foreign investors to his realm.

III

To put that hate into a context which Modi's well-wishers wish us direly to forget all about, an episode from the hearing before the Special court of Justice B.U.Joshi must clinch the issue.

The Gulbarg carnage: the year and half long testimony of the second eyewitness to the episode in which the Congress Member of Parliament, Ehsan Jafri, was also hacked to pieces along with some ninety other Muslims.

- Rupabehn Modi (lest you think all Modis are of the same vintage) confirmed to the SIT that Ehsan Jafri had made several desperate calls, including to Narendra Modi, who, N.Modi, that is, had abused him rather than promise help;
- that she had pleaded with the then Commissioner of Police, Pandey, for help but received none;
- that Police Inspector of Meghninagar, K.G. Erda, now an accused, had taken her to two other accused, Atul Vaid and Bharat Telli, promising her the return of her missing 13 year old son, Azhar, but forced her to sign a false affidavit (a heart-rending movie was to be made of this episode of Rupabehn's life, titled *Parzania*, which, however was viciously attacked by Sangh Parivar vigilantes, and not allowed to be screened within Gujarat).

Rupabehn was to break into uncontrollable grief as she recalled the last words her son had spoken to her: "mummy, do not put your hand out; they will cut your hands like they cut up Aslam uncle."

Azhar remains missing to this day.

This testimony before the court of Justice B.U. Joshi in cases being monitored by the Supreme Court of India.

May we, therefore, ask the following question of our Media houses, especially the electronic ones:

Engaged as you have been, admirably let it be said, in hounding people in high office – in the Jessica Lal murder case, the Priyadarshini case, the Nanda case, the Nithari case, now the Ruchika case – including chief ministers like the erstwhile Koda, and others like Shibu Soren of Jharkhand vintage, and the likes of Jagdish Tytler and Sajjan Kumar of the Congress (for their alleged role in the Sikh killings of 1984) governors of the likes of N.D.Tiwari, cabinet rank ministers like Raja, and many others on counts of alleged complicity either in corruption or in criminality, what is it that prevents you from taking Rupabehn's testimony to heart as proof of Narendra Modi's direct complicity in the massacres of 2002?

Plus on the basis of a plethora of recorded evidence to the same effect other than that of Rupabehn?

What is it that makes of Narendra Modi a special case for amelioration and forgetfulness? Why should the past sins of some qualify for pursuit, and those of Modi for relegation? Or, of his entire state-apparatus that continues to this day to vitiate in whatever way they still can the judicial probes that the Supreme Court was obliged to order, thanks to the tireless perseverance of groups like the Citizens for Peace and Justice? Why should the sins of Modi be consigned only to such valiant groups, groups often at risk from fascist goons and outside the pail of media attention, and indeed in their secret bad books?

May there, after all, not be some truth to the Pew report (mentioned in the Times of India) that characterized India as being as communally riven as Iraq?

Is there something subliminally puissant within us that still regards Modi as a true 'nationalist' hero because a darling of sectarian Hindus who, like the Zionists, are to be inwardly applauded for taking on the 'Islamic' menace?

Since much that may or may not happen to India in the coming year must remain entwined with what may or may not happen to and in Gujarat, our vanguard media mughals have an obligation to ponder the meaning, indeed, the continuing meaning, of Gujarat for India's stated desire of achieving super-powerdom.

IV

And what sort of Hindus does Modi speak for anyway?

The answer to that one is furnished in the substance of an interview with Manjula Pradeep, Executive Director of the Gujarat-based organization, Navsarjan.

Snatches of that interview given to the Dalit Media Watch hereunder:

- most prevalent discriminatory practices in Gujarat (total number of villages covered 1655 over three long years) are related to right to equality in religion and religious affairs;
- in more than 90% of the villages, dalits are not allowed temple entry or to touch the idols and other articles of worship; not allowed to participate in religious processions and other rituals;
- dalits are not allowed to sit on the chair or a cot where any non-dalits are present;
- dalits are never invited to community meals; they are served tea in separate cups, ironically christened Ram patras;
- untouchability is practiced against dalits in such matters as use of drinking water, use of ration shops, vegetable shops where they are not allowed to touch the merchandise;
- postmen do not provide services to dalits;
- milk sellers from the shepherd community do not sell milk to dalits during the Navratra festival;
- in some villages, when a Rajput dies, dalit men have to shave their heads to mourn the dead.

V

It is ofcourse just as well that the truth about the BJP is today out in the open and for all to see, including those whose 'Hindu' hearts and corporate purposes melt at the thought of its so pathetic fall from grace. That the BJP stands exposed, and overtly and undeniably, as a puppet political instrument of the fascist RSS must have its own reconstructive consequences among the polity.

But where is the reason that Narendra Modi, the chief architect of that fascist vision which he has sought to implement with ruthless brutality and in defiance of the Constitution of India, be somehow saved, salvaged, and repackaged as a glorious prospect and alternative to the mainline Congress version of nationalism?

The reason, let it be said, lies in the class interest of those who wish to propogate that economic development of some 15% Indians constitutes the best of politics, that 'development' has little to do with matters of social and cultural equity or with the egalitarian promises and injunctions of the constitutional regime, that a 'globalised' India, linking with the exploiters of the world, has a priori privilege over the ragamuffin majority, and that being 'Hindu' must unanalysedly be deemed coterminous with being democratic and forward-looking.

It is not a vision that India of the coming year or years either needs or stands to profit by. Indeed, it is a vision which, if allowed unfetterd sway, promises ruin to India and to the sub-continent.

January 2010

Why do Extremes Unsettle Our Comfortable Middle Ground?

Poor naked wretches, whereso'er you are,
That bide the pelting of this pitiless storm,
How shall your houseless heads and unfed sides,
Your looped and windowed raggedness, defend you
From seasons such as these? O, I have ta'en
Too little care of this! Take physic, pomp;
Expose thyself to feel what wretches feel,
That thou mayst shake the superflux to them
And show the heavens more just.
(Shakespeare, *King Lear*)

You may recall that these words are spoken by Lear as he is caught in a storm on a heath, having been denied refuge by the daughters whom he loved to distraction. Although, in his erstwhile feudal ways.

Could there be a more eloquently acute talisman for anyone in power who professes to be doing politics not to enrich the already enriched but the dregs of the realm?

You may have noticed that Lear's painful realization of misery falls into two conceptual concerns: one, what hope have the 'naked wretches' against the storms of dispossession, given their 'houseless heads and unfed sides' and their 'looped and windowed raggedness' (some two hundred Indians have already died from the current cold wave in north India for lack of food, shelter, and clothing), followed by his agonized self-reproach at having 'ta'en too little care of this!'

And, following from those admissions, the invocation to 'pomp' (a metaphor for all varieties of self-absorbed blindness born of authority) to 'take physic' (medicine remedying that blindness) and 'expose thyself to feel what wretches feel' as a morally enabling resolve to disgorge themselves of 'superflux' (the manifold trappings of acquisitive greed) and thereby be better placed to implement god's just purposes.

II

So why am I suddenly taken with this context in Lear's movement from hauteur, complacence, imperial noblesse towards a revulsion against self-absorption born of endowments, and towards empathy with those who have been at the receiving end of that self-absorption?

Reading what our well-intentioned Prime Minister said in his address the other day to Speakers of sundry parliaments from the Commonwealth countries, the Bard sprang to my mind, as he so often does in so many contemporary contexts.

To wit, the otherwise piety-ridden Manmohan Singh expressed deep apprehension at the vile attempts of some 'extremists' to cause unacceptable imbalances and dethronements in the orderly project of the peaceful enhancement of mainline developmental concerns, piloted no doubt by men in power who know best.

So it struck me, not for the first time, how little a part of that enhancement seemed, despite politic pronouncements from time to time, meant to touch the lives of the 'poor naked wretches' of whom India still comprises some two thirds of its population.

It struck me that none of those politic pronouncements ever carry the agonized charge of Lear's 'O, I have taken too little care of this!' Or the least resolve to 'take physic' in order to 'feel what wretches feel.'

It also struck me how negligible a recognition obtains in our power structure of the 'extreme' nature of the mainline model of development so dear to our Prime Minister, since what else but 'extreme' would you call a model that fattens the fat all the time and impoverishes the impoverished all the time as well? For example, just today's bitter news in India: sugar will now sell at Rs.50/- a kilogram! So no longer even the comfort of that warm and sweet cup of tea for some 70 or more percent of Indians as the cold solidifies into needles and pins.

I also recalled the defence that has often been proferred by those who measure progress in terms of the gross national product, namely, that 'extreme' conditions (drought, flood, global warming, market crashes) call for 'extreme' measures on behalf of those in charge. Yet, why that same argument may not extend to 'extreme' recourses taken by the 'naked wretches' in India's orphaned 'hinterlands' I do not know. As Mr.Podsnap might do in Dickens' magnificent novel about the workings and consequences of finance capitalism at its point of inauguration in the middle of the nineteenth century, such questions are simply not to be admitted even if such refusals bore holes in the official logic itself.

It is easily conceded by the establishment that a team of explorers sent to the ant-arctic's 'extreme' conditions must be suitably equipped with clothing and other wherewithal that may seem awful and outré in ordinary circumstance, but that is needed in those 'extreme' conditions for survival. Or, that a party that goes bear hunting must be equally equipped for the 'extreme' exigencies that might surely offer themselves. Do recall that some two decades ago a plane crashed into the Andes mountains. For two whole weeks the survivors had no morsel. And then it was that their 'extreme' condition led them to feed off the passengers who lay dead in the ice.

Thus, 'extreme' responses, after all, do imply 'extreme' aggravations. It is a comfort yet that millions of Indians who find little or nothing to eat for many months do not yet eat the dead, but make do with grass, or leather, although sometimes carcases of dead animals as well.

Yet it is not conceded that 'naked wretches' with 'houseless heads and unfed sides' and 'looped and windowed raggedness' – extreme conditions by anyone's reckoning one would think – might be equally justified in taking recourse to 'extreme' measures for survival. Don't know why.

Or why it is that those who admire the anti-establishment rebel heroes in Bollywood movies (whom they also often honour on stage) who are often shown to liquidate the policeman, the politician, the businessman, the judge in a rage against injustice in extreme disregard of the sanctities of the 'system' feel great revulsion when those cinematic enactments of 'extreme' careers surface in the actual rough and tumble of everyday life. Don't know why. Why is it that we find all those bravados 'true to life's conditions' but bring to bear every unjust chicanery to quell such bravados when they are attempted off screen?

At such times it is not unusual to be told how, after all, that 'our basest beggars are, in their poorest things, superfluous' (Lear again). Things are hardly as bad, we say, as the radical rabble rousers would have us believe.

III

Every regime that seeks at bottom to consolidate the endowed middle ground of the power structure and the polity nevertheless also, in a democracy, requires popular legitimation every now and then. Thank democracy for that much, even if those legitimations remain illusory and perfunctory (no government in India, except once since 1950 has ruled with a majority mandate yet.)

Thus it is that such projects as the Indian 'National Rural Employment Guarantee Scheme' come into being to ameliorate the 'extreme' pressures generated by the race for higher and higher capital accumulation, that race for the GDP which in capitalist societies defines status and prowess.

'Poor naked wretches' are thus handed out just enough to remain this side of absolute starvation, even as their labour is appropriated at a vast scale to raise infrastructures without which no GDP may grow any further. Marx and Marxist thinkers after Marx saw in this a strategy to do two things: reproduce the relations of production (wage labour to capital) on a continuous basis, and simultaneously to claim to be addressing the 'extreme' conditions in which the masses subsist, if at all.

But when you remember that the NREGS is now also christened the 'Mahatma Gandhi National Rural Employment Guarantee Scheme' another thought springs to mind.

Gandhi was once asked how one could determine the rightness or wrongness of a thought or course of action. Which is when he proferred his admirable talisman: "ask yourself if the thought or the course of action you contemplate would bear benefit to the most wretched face you may ever have seen; if the answer is yes, then you are on the right path."

It may well be argued that this precisely is the object behind the NREGS; and given the 'extreme' conditions in which India's 'poor naked wretches' subsist from hour to hour, the argument may not be all too fallacious. The question to ask, though, is whether this objective informs the totality of India's model of development – which is what Gandhi would have asked as well.

With the enlightened King of Bhutan, Gandhi might have said that human growth in the collective ought to be measured not as Gross Domestic Product but as Gross Domestic Happiness, a wholly different perspective about the purposes of wielding political power.

And Gandhi would have agreed that 'extreme' forms of behaviour among the polity cannot be remedied until such time as the 'extreme' nature of sectarian objectives we propose to ourselves as principles of 'development' and governance do not yield to systemic efforts to generate happiness in the 'widest commonality' (in Wordworthian phrase).

And he would have pointed out that no just dispensation denies the truth of an argument which it finds congenial in its own defence to others whom it disinherits.

Why then should not the piety-ridden chief executive of this land of many spiritualities (and what spirituality condones discrimination, injustice, or exploitation, not to speak of an unequal use of force to suppress 'poor naked wretches'?) recognize the ethical and human superiority of the concept of Gross Domestic Happiness over Gross Domestic Product? And in doing so, revise his thesis about the many 'extremisms' that beset the land?

He may recall that even the Congress party that led the movement against colonial oppression at one point found itself divided between what came to be called the 'extremists' and the 'moderates' (Jacobins and Girondists?). And the 'extremists' were led by no less a figure than Bal Gangadhar Tilak. And it was their position that constitutional methods or modalities alone could not be trusted to deliver freedom.

It is after all a poor argument for any state to make to the 'poor naked wretches' that, however genuine or extreme your conditions, obedience alone defines your status as citizens. Think how often that argument has been made, and how often it has had to bite the dust.

January 2010

A Tale of Two Chief Ministers

Long years ago, at the conclusion of my doctoral work in America, pressure was put on me to stay and teach there. Twice, in fact. Each time I made excuses. Pressed hard to explain I had the following to say:

> Admittedly, staying on there would yield me every facility to write half a dozen books, but once outside the confines of academe, what would I be a part of? By 'what' I meant what sort of active political involvement. It did seem to me that the 'end of history' thesis justly applied to the United States. With few resistance movements on the ground, post-Vietnam, only centrist politics remained available. And who doesn't know that the Republicans and the Democrats are, all said and done, tweedledum and tweedledee, espousing at bottom one and the same class interest. There has rarely been an occasion when American history in the contemporary moment seemed to offer any major openings beyond what has always obtained – individualism, market economics, puritan exceptionalism, a commitment to 'just' warfare, and a near-universal abhorrence of socialist thought and of any skepticism with respect to god's purposes.

In contrast, I pointed out, history in the Indian sub-continent is far from finished. In proportion to the myriad contestations – social, cultural, economic, political – agonisingly real choices confront thinking Indians, and even those that desire not to make them end up declaring choices one way or another. I shared the imperative I felt to be in the middle of those histories-in-the-making. And so I have remained.

One obvious evidence of what I mean is furnished by the ideological spectrum that organized Indian politics spans, even as in the last two decades strenuous official attempts have been made to say that, having liberalised the economy, history ought to be understood to have ended here as well. No amount of peroration to concomitantly reduce Indian politics, America-like, to a two -party system where the so-called two parties rotate as surrogates from election to election thus succeeds.

Notwithstanding the enlightened 'nationalist' endeavours of ruling class ideologues to unite the nation around the market, and then around the global ruling class, contradictions within an acutely inegalitarian and plural Indian polity remain sharp and imbued with precipitate consequence. All that despite also the for-now decline in the electoral fortunes of the Indian left.

Needless to emphasise that such a cauldron of contentions renders cosy concealments even among the beneficiaries of liberalization difficult. Often enough, as electronic talk shows often demonstrate, civility is shattered by the strength of challenge from the opposite camp, and stakes are foregrounded as fatally real. Dialogy is disfigured by contradiction, and the art of 'conflict resolution' is rendered null. Habermas is everywhere relegated by Marx.

And, among the Intelligentsia there are those who seek a closure, and those who seek to push the frontiers of 'consensus' to enable new histories to emerge and fructify.

That necessarily means that any standardized evaluations of public figures and their record in and out of office refuse to gel nicely into any trans-ideological or trans-national agreement. One man's meat remains another man's poison – within homes and neighbourhoods, social communities, professional and non-governmental organizations, reaching, however clandestinely, even into sections of the bureaucracy and the political power structures. What some laud, others vilify, and vice-versa, all according with where they find themselves placed.

Indeed, something of this contentiousness seems to have found expression in America only at the conclusion of a black man's ascension to the Presidency, as something of the riven content of Indian politics comes to afflict its composure. More of that another time.

II

The sharp polarization of stance among Indian opinion-makers has recently nowhere been more in evidence than in the way in which comment has been offered with respect to two contemporary political figures – Jyoti Basu and Narendra Modi., one a communist and the other a fascist, both obliged to do their life-work within a liberal-democratic constitutional regime, interpreted severally by either.

Jyoti Basu, now sadly late (and the 'sadly' should tell you where I stand on the issue), was elected to seven consecutive terms to the West Bengal Assembly, and headed as Chief Minister a coalition of twelve parties for an unprecedented 23 years in office.

So what did he achieve for his people (as you will see, there is no consensus on who constitute the 'people' in question here) during that marathon stint as head of government?

As an approving voice, I would list the following:

- that he truly became a lodestar for secular politics in India, translating the stipulations of the Constitution into realized reality on the ground; not a single Sikh in West Bengal was harmed after the carnage that took place in Delhi, Kanpur and many other cities following the murder of Indira Gandhi at the hands of her Sikh body guards whom she had refused to change for non-Sikhs despite advice to the contrary; not a single Muslim was touched likewise after either the Babri Mosque demolition in 1992 when anti-Muslim killings spread like wild fire, or at the time of the Gujarat massacre of 2002;
- that he implemented agrarian reforms of an unprecended scale and finality, giving ownership or permanent tenancy rights to millions of peasants and share-croppers over millions of acres of farm land previously owned by Bengali Jotedars; as a consequence, raising agricultural output by an unheard of 7.4% and turning West Bengal into a food surplus state, and taking 'people' in the hinterland away from any temptation to go the Naxal way;
- achieving grass-roots democracy through the Panchayati Raj system, a dispensation that enthused the late Rajiv Gandhi enough to adopt the measure as an all-India innovation through amendments (73rd and 74th) to the Constitution; although, to this day, only in West Bengal have elections to the Panchayats been held with unflinching regularity;
- setting an example of probity in office that remains without parallel, a rather mind-bogling achievement when you think how power corrupts, especially in India, and over 23 years at the helm;
- enhancing power generation from an abysmal low to a near-surplus status;
- respecting labour laws and the rights of labour even at the cost of disenchanting investors.

And, yet, it is possible for other opinion-makers to say that Jyoti Basu ruined West Bengal. And you can guess why: because his tenure saw the flight of industry from the state, since his governance over the years made the demand that statutory labour laws be protected, which include the right to strike.

Clearly, in this estimation, the people who returned him to office interminably over two decades or more do not here constitute 'West Bengal' or qualify as custodians of its welfare. Only the urban elite are seen to represent West Bengal, and however miniscule they may be, to the extent that he did not go out of his way to pamper their dreams, Jyoti Basu unambiguously ruined his state.

That said, secularism, prosperity on the farms, social stability and harmony, grass-roots democracy, or the stunning fact that dalits in West Bengal own some 54% of the land – none of these can be counted as achievements. Indeed it is said that farmland prosperity has been one of the worst outcomes of his reign, since Bengali farmers will not part with their fertile land for industrial purposes.

Besides, you do not get to see impressive, world-class roads in Kolkata, or shopping malls that may justly compare with those in other cities. And does it matter that those other metropolises may have become dens of crime and sectarian violence, and nightmares for the commuter? Or rape capitals of the world? Looked at from some distance, they do shine after all.

Remarkably, the disapproving voice does not pick on two indices where Jyoti Basu's rule may justly be seen to have failed, namely, in educational and health reform. But, even if his record here had been as outstanding as in the areas I have listed, it is to be doubted that the disapproving voice would have been much dented. Who cares for education and health for the masses anyway?

In the ultimate analysis, it is the good of the profit maximiser that matters, stupid. And nothing good can be said about governance that does not keep him foremost.

III

Which is, after all, why Narendra Modi in Gujarat draws the approval of the voices that disapprove of Jyoti Basu!

- Does it matter that the Modi regime has the blood of some thousand innocent Muslim lives on its hands?
- does it matter that Modi has torn the secular principle of the state (mandated by the Supreme Court of India as an unamendable, 'basic' feature of the Constitution) to smithereens?
- does it matter that Gujarat's cities and towns have effectively been riven and partitioned into dominant Hindu majority metropolitan areas and decrepit and frightened Muslim ghettoes?
- does if matter that Gujarati Muslims after the carnage of 2002 are often obliged to masquerade under Hindu names to have any hope of obtaining jobs?
- does it matter that Modi's police force has been provenly engaged in fake encounters of innocent Muslims, dime a dozen?
- does it matter that the Modi government has done everything to vitiate and stymie the labours of sundry investigative agencies, including those set up directly under the aegis of the Supreme Court of India, to bring the guilty men to book?
- does it matter that human rights activists and agents have often to fear for their lives at the hands of Modi's goons?
- does it matter that, thanks to piling evidence, the skeletons in Modi's murderous cupboard are now reaching for his throat, no less, as he is due to be summoned for questioning?
- does it matter that most of his claims of having brought water and development to the hinterland have been shown to be fake?
- does it matter that, far from encouraging inclusive democracy at the grass roots, his own party men and women accuse him of ruling like a czar, to the disregard of party mechanisms?

No siree; none of this matters, you see. What does matter is that a line of profit maximisers are gleeful at investing in Gujarat because no impediments exist – no unions, no labour laws, no bureaucratic bottle necks, no hindrance to appropriating fertile farm lands, no social unrest; the most perfect peace of the graveyard, such as made even the exemplary Ratan Tata say in 2007, "you are stupid if you are not here." The deader the skeletons the better fodder they make.

And the other day, the great Amitab Bachchan, India's most successful popular film icon, found himself saying after his recent meeting with Modi that no, none of all that matters so long as Modi grants him tax exemption for his latest film. Besides, having seen broad roads and lush greenery, it is clear that Gujarat, as a part of the Indian story of advancement, is doing more than its share.

And, more honest and upfront approvers say that in having consolidated the politics of aggressive Hindutva, Modi has contributed greatly to strengthening Indian 'nationalism' and in warding off 'Islamic Jihad' and 'terrorism' thereof. Does it matter that no country thinks Modi fit enough to be given a visa for travel abroad?

Remarkably, whereas Jyoti Basu's secular Bengal hardly ever saw any 'terrorist' onslaught, Modi's strongly Hindu Gujarat has been a repeated victim! The He-Man Modi notwithstanding.

IV

Behind these evaluations and counterevaluations, then, lies the story of India's unfinished nationhood and un-concluded democracy. The finishers are unable to finish it enough, and those that would open it up to embrace the 'people' (some two-third or more Indians who spend less than a dollar a day) remain engaged in a mortal struggle to question its presiding definitions and claims, and to force it to acknowledge the betrayals of its promise.

A fascinating, even if much of the time, brutal contest unfolds each passing day – on the street, in offices, courts, and among the dispossessed in the 'hinterland.'

Where greed propels a rapacious minority to appropriate governance every which way they can, need awakens millions to make breaches in that sonsolidation.

Depending on which side your bread be buttered, you are either with Jyoti Basu or with Narendra Modi.

And no syllables of impeccable, convent school English can for now paper over that combat.

January 2010

You the Fascists, We the People

History now and again offers moments of hope that seem small and fleeting but, placed in larger contexts and taken at the tide, promise reconstructions of far-reaching magnitude.

What happened in the city of Mumbai today was one such moment.

The fascist Shiv Sena had threatened not to allow the screening of the film My Name is Khan till such time as Shah Rukh Khan, the main actor in the movie and a Bollywood icon, had apologized for having expressed the view that Pakistani cricketers should have been participants in the forthcoming Indian Premier League. Shah Rukh, to his great credit, refused to do so – indeed the first Bollywood personality to have thus defied the Sena. With the exception, as I recall, of Mahesh Bhatt.

It needs to be remembered that Shah Rukh Khan's father had not only been a freedom fighter during India's anti-colonial movement, but uniquely a Muslim who chose after the partition of the country to leave the new nation of Pakistan and relocate his family in India.

The right wing Shiv Sena whose politics over the last two decades or more has been fuelled by hate campaigns against non-Marathis and Muslims, dubbed Shah Rukh as a Pakistani sympathizer. (See my 'Constructing Shah Rukh Khan').

Over these two decades of Sena mayhem in Mumbai, the state, even when governed by the secular Congress and the Nationalist Congress Party, has had a record of repeatedly letting down the citizen by abdicating to the hooliganism of the Sena, not wishing to alienate the Marathi voter.

Until some weeks ago the young and no-nonsense, Rahul Gandhi, took it upon himself to call the Sena's bluff.

Defying the Sena's boast that he would not be allowed to enter Mumbai, he not only did so, but cocked a fatal snook at the fascists by actually traveling through the Sena strongholds in the local train, for which he bought his own ticket.

It was as though without uttering a word of bravado, Rahul Gandhi let his Gandhi-like deed of a modern-day satyagraha speak for himself, his party, the government and the ordinary citizen of India.

The effect of that has been electric. Most of all in giving the local Congress/NCP government the courage to stand upto the Sena's lawless lumpenism.

On the 12th of February, the scheduled date for the release of the film, India was on tenterhooks, not knowing whether the Sena goons would again succeed in holding the citizen and the regime of law to ransom.

As it turned out, the government of the day in a veritable rite of passage, came upfront to assure both the Mumbaikar and the exhibitors that they would be accorded full protection.

And the government kept its nerve and its word.

Result: the people of Mumbai came out in the thousands to see the film, even as the sporadic attempts by the Sena fascios to prevent the release were purposefully thwarted by the state police – with not a single short fired or injury reported.

It was as though the battle that had been lost to the beer halls of Germany in the thirties of the last century had been won in the cinema halls of Mumbai.

And won in tandem by a state that asserted its lawful and constitutional authority and by the ordinary people of Mumbai who thus made explicit their rejection of the fascist politics of the Sena.

The suburban hordes of ordinary Ghatkopar Mumbaikars had made up for the historic defeat at Guernica.

After years of cowering and capitulation, a clear and consequential demarcation between the people of Mumbai and the Shiv Sena goons was visibly effected, and the Sena's boast of representing all of Mumbai exposed for the fiction it has always been. A fiction strenuously propagated by the Sena despite losing all state elections bar one!

II

For the Congress Party this ought to be truly a moment of far-reaching recognition.

Recalling some pertinent histories, just as it was the Americans and the Pakistan state that had set up the Taliban in the eighties to fight the Russians and oust the communist Afghan government, it was largely the Congress party that had spawned what came to be called the Shiv Seniks in the sixties in order to liquidate the hold of the unions in the mills of the then Bombay. This by displacing the hold of class perceptions and class politics by an emotive, identity politics.

An experiment that was replicated by Narendra Modi with great ruthlessness in Gujarat. As mill workers in Ahmedabad and other industrial cities came increasingly to be threatened with loss of jobs under the compulsions of the new market fundamentalism, Hindu workers were persuaded that their chief antagonist was not the mill owner but the Muslim worker. Under a relentless denominational onslaught spearheaded by the Vishwa Hindu Parishad among the labouring, including the Adivasis, class politics came thus to yield to communal politics as the Congress watched and dithered.

It must be remarkable, for instance, that the two Sena parties in Mumbai have never targeted the many non-Marathi tycoons who have over the years contributed to making Mumbai the financial capital of India. The Sena crusade remains restricted to the labouring classes, be they taxi drivers, local vendors, blue collar workers, slum dwellers, and other segments of the unorganized proletariat of south or north Indian extraction. Reason why a cosy relationship has always existed between the bigwigs of Mumbai and the Sena supremo, Bal Thackeray. And all rather ominously reminiscent of how the Krupps and other industrial families of the Germany of the thirties felt about Hitler and the Nazi party. Same with the movie industry as well, with honourable exceptions.

Same in Modi's Gujarat, about which the industrialist, Rattan Tata, was to say 'if you are not here, you are stupid.' And that despite what Modi had done to the social and inter-community fabric of Gujarat.

For the Congress in Mumbai, the wheel thus seems to have come full circle, as it has for the Americans and the Pakistanis in Afghanistan and the border areas of Paksitan.

Driven by the Rahul Gandhi impetus – one that seems increasingly to find resonance among India's generation next – will the Congress party now learn to turn away from the periodic temptation to appease denominational players whose politics remains anathema to the secular, democratic and constitutional foundations and imperatives of the Republic?

Time will tell.

One thing is certain: that just a one-time stand against the fascists is not the answer, although 12th of February has set a precedent both for the party and the state.

We think that unless India's political democracy extends meaningfully and on a sustained basis to an economic democracy as well, unless the Congress slogan of inclusiveness acquires the dimension of rethinking the state in drastic ways – which is to say, rethink the principles of the production and distribution of wealth – the ruling class impulsion to return to a praxis both of a divisive, identity politics and state violence to quell social upheavals, however deservingly grounded in livelihood imperatives, may continue to remain its recourse.

III

What this day in Mumbai ought to have conveyed to both state and non-state well-wishers of democracy (and I mean here to include the left-wing extremists as well) is that the best way to bolster the politics of equity and the regime of law against the menace of the violence perpetrated by fringe fascios is always to persuade the people at large of the rightness of what you think and do on their behalf.

And that cannot happen unless those who represent the voice of the people (as distinct from those who merely get a majority of their vote, or succeed under the present first-past-the-post electoral system to cobble up majorities as coalitions) are made as much participants and stake-holders in the making of policy as the tycoons and their lobbyists.

Not incorporating that as a steady conviction, the happy assertion of sanity seen in Mumbai today may remain just a sporadic high point.

There is reason to think that under the current UPA dispensation, India's work-in-progress democracy has seen some desirable accretions of accountability and transparency.

The question that must be confronted is the following: what use are 'human rights' if these do not first and foremost include the universal needs of human beings – among them the right to livelihood, to clean water and shelter, to sanitation, to health care, to education, to fair and speedy justice, and the free expression of talent and opinion? Can it be said that there exists a single human being who hasn't these needs, and thus hasn't a right to their fulfillment?

Is it after all possible to contemplate the 'right to life' in separation from those listed above?

On the subject of identity politics – along denominational, linguistic, ethnic, and other axes – I believe the Shah Rukh film (that I have not seen yet) has something telling to say. It involves a young man named Khan who seeks to meet the American President just so he can say one simple thing to the world's most powerful man: 'my name is Khan but I am not a terrorist.'

The Sena and other chauvinists can be brought into a wholesome unity as Indians only when the rights of citizens are regarded, protected, and dispensed without a thought to denominations, and only in consonance with the dictates of the constitution and the majesty of the law, and only when the state at every point makes explicit the will to be seen to be so doing without regard to electoral calculations.

India's political formations next need to learn the lesson that you may win some and lose some, but principles of equity and fairplay cannot be bargained. And that if and when you lose an election, there is much work you can continue to do among the people at large.

Only such a sustained dialectic between the people's human needs/rights and the elements of political and state power can firm up a polity that may in the years to come become a better guarantor of democracy than its formal entrapments.

Let us hope, therefore, that the lessons of the day in Mumbai do not remain occasions merely of self-congratulation but pointers to how a more long-lasting future for the country may be reconstructed.

Should those lessons be followed up with resolve, democracy-to-come will spell all the annihilations due to those who disfigure it.

As to the beleaguered city of Mumbai where outstanding Indians of all hue live and work, its elites must teach themselves to think that all just causes must draw them out, as opposed to only those that affect their comforts the most. And just causes preeminently comprise those that bear on the lives of its relegated millions regardless of which part of India they come from.

Same indeed for the elites of all other parts of India. Do let us remember that Hollywood stars are known for standing firm on causes. Now that the state has come forward to push back the fascists, there is no reason why some of the most notable stars, be they actors or others, should prefer to make peace with the local high-priests of muscle and mayhem rather than aid the duly constituted authorities to run a lawful regime. After all, it is just that bit contemptible to be acting heroic roles in movies and cowering and compromising in real life. And then berating politicians for their perfidies.

Finally, our salute to the Mumbaikar for having said that resounding 'No' to the goons.

Our salute also to those ordinary citizens of Bangalore who have today delivered comeuppance to that Pramod Muthalik who some years ago attacked and molested five young women in a pub on Valentine's day. We do not approve of what they did on their own, but we welcome the symbolic assertion against self-appointed moral vigilantes who shelter under the protection of complicit governments.

Having done what they have done – blackened his face – they should be willing, Gandhi-like, to embrace whatever punishment the law prescribes for them.

Excelsior democracy. We have patience.

February 2010

India, Australia

What is the Difference?

The Victorian police chief, Simon Overland, has finally found the answer to the attacks that Indians have been subjected to down under.

'Try to look as poor as you can,' he advises Indian immigrants to Australia: 'don't display your iPods, valuable watch, valuable jewellery.'

The implication here is explicit: if you don't flaunt, you will not tempt.

Thus, the onus that the state and law-enforcement ought to bear is neatly transferred to the victim on a principle of the call of 'nature,' if you will. To wit, men will be sinners; so the best course is to seduce as little as possible.

The Indian community has characterized this approach to crime as 'ridiculous' – with justice.

I have no doubt we shall soon have fiercely outraged debates on Mr.Overland's take on crime here on Indian TV channels.

But do ask yourself: how is Mr. Overland's advice here any very different from what Indian women are routinely advised by our own custodians of morality? Or custodians of morality in large parts of the world?

If you flaunt, you invite rape – and on the same principle of 'nature' that informs Overland's counsel to Indians down under. Thus, bigots of all hue argue that it is not the rapist and the molester who is out of order but the women who are thus raped or molested.

Which is why young Indian women are customarily beaten and bashed by lumpen right-wing vigilantes, and told to keep off pubs, Valentine celebrations, public parks, and suchlike, and Muslim women reminded that their bodies bode no good for the peace and quiet of the community, or the world at large.

And lest we think that Mr. Overland is a peculiar sort of police chief, do remember that when Indian women are thus often chased and chastised by self-appointed custodians of the right and proper, they do so in the sound knowledge that the Indian police more than shares their take on what women should or should not wear, do, or say.

Perish the thought, but imagine for a moment that some Australian woman tourist in Goa suffers these sorts of ignominies (as German, Russian and other women recently have), and the local police chief is heard to say that Australian women must learn to dress with modesty, or else. How might Mr.Overland and sundry other Australian authorities respond to such an eventuality?

II

Indeed, this readiness on behalf of state agencies to bypass the state and put trust in other forms of authority, besides personal rectitude in public display, is on offer today in Indian newspapers. And, coincidentally, again involving Australians.

You may be aware that the redoubtable patriarch of the Shiv Sena, the right formidable Bal Thackeray (made formidable precisely because of the withering of the state in Mumbai) has let it be known that Australian cricketers will not be allowed to participate in the forthcoming Indian Premier League of Cricket.

The Sena (literally, 'army') of course has a record in this matter, having more than once dug up cricket pitches on the sly to prevent Pakistani cricket teams from playing in India.

So what does the Indian state do? Even as the Indian Home Minister declares that the state shall provide full protection to whoever comes to play in the IPL, the President of the Mumbai Cricket Association, Sharad Pawar, one of the senior-most members of the cabinet, expressing rather scant trust in the Home Minister's official assurance, goes and visits the Shiv Sena godfather to plead that the latter permit the Australians to play in India.

And the godfather graciously promises to consider the 'request.'

Lest you think this is the nadir of the state's collapse in the matter, "Thackeray has asked for a detailed presentation on the issue which we will be providing in couple of days and thereafter he would consider our request."

Thus it is that the godfather's authority – entirely extra-constitutional and hooliganist – is accorded the privilege to override the onus and the assurance of the state. And neither the Minister nor the head of the BCCI (the Indian Board of Cricket) feels the least shame in the matter. Just as Mr.Overland in Victorian feels not the least shame in passing on the onus of the Australian law-enforcement agencies to the Indians down under.

Were some Australian player indeed to be roughed up by Indian goons during the course of the tournament, I doubt me that Mr.Overland would not hold Indian law-enforcement responsible. And rightly.

III

Remarkably, India and Australia are both constitutional democracies, founded on the principle that certain rights are fundamental, and that the right to life includes the right to liberty in dress, demeanour, speech and other forms of expression, in matters of faith, without regard to gender, demomination or colour of skin. Unless of course the exercise of such fundamental rights impinge on the fundamental rights of other citizens.

In that context, one would think that it is not the Indians down under who offend but those who overreach the law to impinge on their right to wear or flaunt what they wish to without causing any sort of bodily harm to others, however vulgar such display might seem to many.

After all, consider that worldwide if there are those who are offended by the burqa worn by some Muslim women, there are others who are likewise offended to see women in skimpy attire.

A democratic state can be democratic only if it allows the liberty to both to dress as they think fit, and if it is prepared to quell unlawful mayhem on behalf of others who may think such liberty cause enough to set the state aside and take matters into their own hands.

It would seem from recent events that India and Australia

have equally to ponder these issues in diverse spheres of contestation. Much better do that than unleash disingenuous blame games or threaten retaliation.

And a sentiently self-critical media in either country here seems greatly the need of the hour.

February 2010

Too Small A Country for One Great Artist

Kitna hai badnasib Zafar dafn ke liye,
Do gaz zamin bhi na mili koo-e yar men.

How ill-fated Zafar, Denied two yards of ground
For burial back in native soil, Among native sight and sound.

(Bahadur Shah Zafar, the last Mughal King of India, (1775-1862); exiled by the British to Rangoon in 1858 after the failure of the revolt of 1857; lines written from exile),

Zafar, who knew only India for home, was exiled by the British imperialists at age 83. Since Moslems and Hindus had equally acknowledged his legitimacy and rallied against the colonial power under his uncontested leadership, the British were only too right to think that letting him return home would thwart the new imperial policy of divide and rule.

Thus it came to be that one who had been king was denied six feet of ground for internment in the only earth of his love.

A century and a half later, another iconic Indian, and a monarch in his own right, the renowned painter, Maqbool Fida Husain, has had to exile himself at a still more advanced age, driven this time not by some imperial power from the outside but by self-appointed 'cultural nationalists' at home.

A determined falange of bigots were to discover some few years ago that a Husain painting was in existence which represented India partially in comely female form. That the painting in question dated back some three decades or more, and was titled 'Bharat Mata' (Mother India) not by the painter but by an exhibitor were set aside as material facts to the case. Not to speak of the many and stunningly articulate and powerful Husain representations of many Hindu deities over the years, deties that he had grown up with as a lad and come to love, venerate, and joy in – none of this mattered to the 'cultural nationalists' who had suddenly landed a meaty 'desecrator of Hindu gods and goddesses.'

That the ubiquitous erotica of so much of 'Hindu' art and sculpture, including temple art and sculpture (Khajurahu, for instance, one of the biggest tourism money spinners), bespoke a philosophical/aesthetic tradition of extraordinary complexity, intellectual reach and metaphysical speculation did not matter either.

Indeed, asked the other day to comment on this reality of 'Hindu' history and tradition, especially the eroticism of so much temple architecture in India, the head of the Rashtriya Swayamsevak Sangh (RSS) pleaded that these were products of another age altogether, based on the conditions prevailing then (*The Hindu*, February 26, 2010).

A position that begs the question as to why the Sangh Parivar had thought it necessary to demolish the Babri Mosque, which, after all, also was a product of another age, based on conditions prevailing then. Or, if that demolition was justified, why such 'shamefully' erotic temple architectures should also not likewise be removed from sight.

To his eternal credit, Justice Sanjay Kishen Kaul, a Kashmiri Brahmin, was to raise and scrutinize these sorts of questions with a lucidly erudite and liberal sensibility in his historic judgement on some four cases filed against Husain (see my 'Justice Sanjay Kishen Kaul'), all of which he dismissed, enjoining upon the state to ensure that the nonagenarian painter was home and happily painting again.

Husain is now 94. Imperiled by a slew of legal suits filed with cruel intent by votaries of 'cultural nationalism' in many different jurisdictions in the country, by threats to life that remain in active status, and not the least by a luke-warm state characteristically reluctant to do more than the minimal right and proper on his behalf (assurance of police protection etc., but with no hope held out that the cases would be withdrawn, or his berators hauled up for their brazenly communal defiance of the laws of the land, and for having vandalized his work more than once, or for holding out threats to his life), Husain we understand has now accepted the offer of citizenship made to him by the Emirate of Qatar.

To wit, if no exertions are made by the authorities in India to persuade this foremost Indian painter who is thought to rank among the world's most notable modern painters to return home to India, he may equally be denied the soil he has loved and painted with maddening energy and passion for some seven decades for his last resting place.

II

A feature of Indian secularism, like it or not, remains this most pusillanimous attitude towards claims of outrage made periodically by some segment of one community or the other at something that is said or done by someone or the other that is seen to be offensive to 'tradition' or some article of 'faith'.

Thus, Indian secularism which prides itself on a seemingly unique and uniquely sagacious self-definition (not a separaton of church and state, but equal regard for all faiths on behalf of the state) often finds itself in knots and conundrums, spending much of its peace-making energy in balancing one communalism against another, or indeed, one casteism against another. And in so doing, is invariably engaged in rendering the legal edifices of the constitution weak and wobbly. Not to speak of the quality of politics which its party formations carry and convey to the polity at large.

With sickening repetitiousness, it turns out that the claims of some self-anointed purveyors of this faith or that acquire privileges that transcend the majesty of the state and of its system of secular laws. With canny electoral calculations intermeshing with the modalities that are then used to negotiate those claims.

If Husain is today at the point of the Hindutva gun, Tasleema Nasreen of Bangladesh was a welcome exile among us because, after all, she had been exiled for berating the then Islamic state for its shabby treatment of Hindu minorities in a novelette titled Lajja. What could have better qualified her for the affections of the Hindutva brigade.

But what of Indian Muslims? Aha, they had/have small use for her, as she was duly assaulted at a public conference in Hyderabad. So how did the state in India handle Tasleema as she sought asylum? The Left Front government in West Bengal did indeed put her up for a while, but soon found that it was thereby losing the good opinion of its considerable Muslim citizenry (some 25% of West Bengal). So slowly but surely Tasleema was persuaded, first gently, then not so gently, to pack her bags. Which this mediocre writer but brave woman did.

Husain now offers the obverse of that case. However above board the Congress party, its gingerly correctness in the matter concerning his fate suggests yet again that it is not as indifferent to the Indian Hindu vote, qua 'Hindu' vote as it would like the country to believe. And, no less ironically, the left parties are more boldly forthcoming in speaking for Husain than they might have been in dealing with Tasleema Nasreen. After all, and thankfully, the left could never hope to placate the Hindu right-wing ever to consider the left anything but a sworn enemy.

III

There is another aspect to this matrix of compromises.

Quite the other day, another Muslim Indian artist, the equally iconic film star, Shah Rukh Khan, was sought to be pilloried for having allegedly expressed pro-Pakistani sympathies (see my 'Constructing Shah Rukh Khan').

And contrary to expectations, and unlike many other stars afore now, Shah Rukh stood his ground with exemplary self-belief and courage.

Over the charged week or so while this was going on in Mumbai, Shah Rukh's refusal to kowtow drew increasingly articulate support from some fellow artists, media organs, other opinion-makers, and eventually from the state in Maharashtra.

To the delight of the secularists and those who wish the tenets of the Constitution and the laws thereof to be always implemented without dithering, fear or favour, the Putsch of the fascists to prevent the screening of Shah Rukh's new film was successfully thwarted.

This needs to be strongly underlined because it is after decades of dithering that such an assertion on behalf of the state and in defence of the rights of a citizen without regard to creed has been witnessed. Something to the accomplishment of which Shah Rukh's personal courage and conviction was the necessary centre-piece.

One would therefore have thought that in the matter of Husain the Congress-led government at the centre might have been more boldly forthcoming. It might have seized on this opportunity come on the heels of the Shah Rukh episode to consolidate the hold and the preemptive call of the state to not just offer protection to a beleaguered citizen – and one all of 94 years of age, and a ntional icon to boot – but to resolutely intervene to seek quick legal redress for him against the vexatious and patently sectarian harassment and threat meted out to him.

Indeed, it may have done more, and sent its envoy to meet Husain in Qatar, and bring him back home with full assurance that no nuisance would be allowed to happen that might impede his creative endeavours.

We would like to think that the state is, however sheepishly, considering these measures, especially now that a PIL has been filed in the Supreme Court of India by a doughty legislator from Jammu.

But equally, I must make another honest averment. Simply put, M.F.Husain, in the full knowledge that articulate and bold support existed on his behalf here in India among civil society groups, various segments of the intelligentsia, many non-governmental organizations, sections of the bench and the bar, and influential sections of the media, might just have considered, much like Shah Rukh Khan, coming home at this late hour to do India and the subcontinent another yeoman's favour.

Even at the risk of some annoyance, and some irritability at interrupted work, he might have made available to a legion of steady strugglers on behalf of secularism, constitutionalism, and the rights of citizen's liberty within those bounds a powerful conjunction to carry the ascendance of these articles of democratic faith and life further forward.

Dear Husain sahib, I would be dishonest to say that I, and perhaps many others, do not feel that little bit let down by the option you have chosen to take, even as we fully appreciate the suffering you have undergone. Nor do I think that in days to come you will remain untroubled by the decision you seem to have made to jettison home and citizenship, offering a somewhat ugly victory to the bigots who hound you and will hound others unless the majority of the sane take time to stand firm rather repeatedly.

Perhaps things are still retrievable, and all parties to the occurrence will come together and work another miracle. In the meanwhile, your exile is as much a heartbreak as was that of Zafar.

March 2010

A Parliament of Women as Much as of Men

As is well known, the semantics of equality entered western intellectual discourse only as a result of the writings of the French Philosophes, whereas previously the acknowledged universal paradigm had been that all human beings were created unequal. Thus there were those who were 'privileged' by birth, and those who were not.

Indeed, in passing, it was only Buddhism in India that could be said to have genuinely offered a world view wherein equality made no exceptions. Some reason why it became fatally important for Brahminism to eject it at all costs.

The new European classes whose material interests were thus enunciated by the emancipatory writings of the Enlightenment claimed, as Marx was to note, that they represented not just their own interests but those of all 'humanity.' A classic example of false consciousness, since, as Marx theorized, every new class that challenges older social formations needs such universalist claims to garner sufficient clout for the overthrow.

The fact of course was that the notions of equality, or rights ('unalienable' ones, you may recall) that came to be floated as potent ideological legitimisers of the aspirations of new dominant interests effectively left out of the ambit of these notions slaves, all labouring classes, and, you guessed it, women. Indeed the men who were inscribing the concepts of unalienable rights were untroubled slave owners themselves. Jefferson for one.

Within the expressive world of what came to be called 'liberal humanism' the reference to 'all men' etc., in well-known redolent phrases meant just that – all men. To a point where indeed not even the world's first industrial proletariat asked for the right to vote for women as they submitted their Charter to the Whig parliament in 1832. Their demand was 'one man, one vote.'

Not until 1928 – only some two decades prior to India's political independence from colonial rule – did English women obtain their right to franchise, as a result of their protracted struggles aided by sections of truly liberated men.

And, as has so often happened in the history of democracy worldwide, those accreted gains elsewhere helped new, post-colonial Indian rulers to provide for universal adult franchise from day one.

II

Obtaining the right to vote ofcourse did not translate in equal measure to an equality of representation in parliament and the legislatures.

As in the case of Indian men, only some women who had the pedigree, of birth or class, came to be given the occasional ticket to stand for elections. Universal franchise thus has remained a grossly anomalous adoption, having left out effectively half the population of India from any stake in decision-making at state and national levels.

Over the last two decades especially of the expansions of consciousness among newly assertive and literate groups and elites, men and women, the demand that a certain percentage of seats in parliament and the legislators be set apart for women qua women has been gaining force. A movement that may be conceived as the third rung of the evolution of Indian democracy into a credible representative system of consent and governance. The previous two having been the success of Indian dalits and ethnic tribals to have won the principle of reserved seats in proportion to their population as a result indeed of the Ambedkarite movement of the 1930s, and the success of India's Intermediate middle castes (often referred to as Other Backward Classes – OBCs) in the northern states to capture political power consistently since the mid 1960s.

For some fifteen years now, the proposal to accord 33% reservation to Indian women has been the most consequential and contested issue in India's political discourse. Not surprisingly, the ruling party apparatuses have found themselves caught in that classic pincer which the idea of democracy has so often presented the world with; namely, the imperative to seem wedded to the notion of universal representation but to be socially unwilling that the ideal see the light of day.

Capitalism, suffused and mediated by patriarchy, remains unwilling to redistribute political power among the genders, just as it remains unwilling to redistribute the right to the ownership of economic assets.

As any number of India's TV soaps will testify, especially since the beginnings of India's neo-liberal, market fundamentalist shift (coterminous with the Washington Consensus of 1990), middle class indian women (the only kind who are visible on TV) are sought to be drafted for two conjoint purposes: one, as consumers of what the cosmetics corporates have to offer, and two, as vehicles simultaneously of ideas of moral/ethical/religious traditions, all of which issue from patriarchy and Brahminism, and seek to hedge and confine women within joint families as the principle torch bearers of culture.

Typically, thus, the soap serials present lavish sets, even obscenely lavish sets, where upon brocaded and bejeweled daughters, mothers, daughters-in-law and mothers-in-law walk about in leisured and gingerly cadences unspoilt by the least hint of labour even about the household, unraveling fatal decisions wth regard to the conduct of various, and endless pujas, engagement ceremonies, weddings (and their consequences), and all interspersed without relief with rituals, ritual fasts, ritual obligations bearing almost wholly on the women. And laced with heavy doses of superstition.

In all these, money remains unmentioned as a given of which we are never told how it is made or how much of it exists. What defines these offerings is a relentless and relentlessly devious ideological tie-up between seemingly unlimited resources and religious iteration. And if ever a woman with a mind of her own surfaces, she does so invariably as a threat or a menace, and thus an object of rejection secured by showing her up as out of line with the best traditions of accumulated culture and received patriarchal wisdom.

Indeed, a woman who chooses to dress plainly or un-selfconsciously is equally a no no, because such a stance then is seen to rebuke the labours of the corporates who know best about what women with money need and how they look best in various situations.

The movement for the reservation of seats for women thus accompanies this matrix of decrepit social muck, all of which accompanied India's 'modernity' through the movement for freedom, and has now gotten insidiously collaborative with corporate capitalism. Religious occasions – dime a dozen in the Hindu calendar – help the corporate world and the corporate state in two all-important ways: one, it is big business (according to one UN study, religion is currently the world's fourth largest enterprise, after armaments, drugs, and education), and it helps to mute and neutralize class consolidation as individuals and communities are projected primarily as religious entities and identities rather than as secular- historical victims or agents, or economically dominant or relegated communities.

Yet, it is suggestive of the irresistability of the dynamics of democratic ideas that this press towards taking another historic step in the equity agenda obliges India's major and otherwise antagonistic political formations (the Congress, the BJP, and the left especially) to collaborate in seeing to the introduction of the Women's Reservation Bill in the upper house of india's parliament (the Rajya Sabha) tomorrow, as the institution of the 8th of March as the International Women's Day completes a centenary. And all that despite the bickerings among the party system as well as the considerable dissent within each party on the issue.

And despite also the often violent opposition of the OBC-controlled parties who insist that the 33% quota for women be further broken down into reservation for OBC and minority women.

That the male leaderships of these parties have thus far failed either to make such a provision for OBC women within their own party office bearers, or to apportion 33% party-electoral tickets to OBC women is another matter – but one that underscores the hypocrisy of the resistance they offer.

Already, one influential OBC Chief Minister (Nitish Kumar of Bihar) has demarcated his own position from that of his party, acknowledging that times have changed, and that he now thinks it is inadvisable to oppose the measure.

Such are the crevices through which the winds of rational historical transformation often creep. The pity being that often those rational winds have to battle barricades set up by even those who should know better.

III

Here is what we say: should the Bill after all be successfully introduced in the Rajya Sabha on Monday, the 8th of March, 2010, it will be our view that Indian democracy will have made qualitatively a great leap forward. The polity all across the nation-state will experience a new energy and conviction, such as will not but invigorate its contributions in many diverse ways, and facilitate the opening of further doors to further areas that remain dark and iniquitous.

In that context, I may enter a caveat.

There are those who still hold to the 'nature' view of gender. Many men and women honestly believe that women are by 'nature' less prone to violence, corruption, chicanery, more inclined to tenderness and empathy, and so on. Many take the view that women are best kept away from such prosaic and hard things as finance, defence, industries, and allied areas of governance, if they must be incorporated as bureaucrats or as ministers. Many also believe that given their 'natures' women must remain incharge of households to which their commitment brings cheer and spiritual light, since women 'naturally' take to the ways of piety and tradition. And many honestly remain unaware that all these things that they say reflect not what women think, but what men of a certain kind think about women.

Some support their greater presence in the legislatures because they believe politics will then see a great ethical upliftment, and so on.

This writer remains of the view that be it in potential or performance, discriminations based on gender are fallacious. Men and women tend to be equally ambitious or not, canny or not canny, self-regarding or not self-regarding, callous or not callous, competent or incompetent, ethical or unethical, violent or not violent, even murderous or not murderous.

Many men are often more tender as parents than many women, and many women are often more gamesome as parents than many men. Many women better drivers of cars and buses than many men, and many men better cooks of meals than many women, especially cooking of the kind that pays. Sometimes women heads of institutions prove to be more inimical to gender justice than male heads, and perfectly of a feather with male corporate counterparts, and sometimes they are seen to be more sensitive to issues of social discrimination among both men and women than their male counterparts. Same in all spheres of prowess and sctivity.

Since we hold to that view, it is preposterous that some 98% of the world's wealth should remain in male hands, while women share the rest of the 2%. And in large measure due to the fact that gender discrimination based on assiduously constructed myths, traditions, and systems of knowledge and control has kept them out of the institutions of law-making and of governance where such constructions can be addressed and changed to the betterment, let it be said, not just of women but of humankind.

We also recognize that women are as prone to social prejudice, inherited bias, and class antagonism as men are. But, we believe that these prejudices, biases, antagonisms are best attacked jointly by men and women both in positions of responsibility and in social movements outside the ambit of the state. And that, most crucially, such an eventuality requires that women be first of all accorded all those transformative, constitutional spaces over which the state presides which have been the fiefdom of men. Tragically thus far in India, this necessary historical onus has been denied to women on one disingenuous pretext or the other. And as a result, we are the nation we still are.

These fingers are therefore crossed as they type. Tomorrow may be a day I shall truly celebrate, not as some teleological end of democratic history in India, but as the victory of a democratic idea and imperative which has been delayed for far too long, and out of which many good things will come for those who are still at the receiving end at many points of the social maze.

Thumbs up for the Bill. And may sense dawn on those male heads that are used to be habitually headstrong without much thought.

March 2010

Women's Reservation Bill

Nearly a hundred years ago, the truly path-breaking Russian social and linguistic theorist, Mikhail Bakhtin, had underscored how during moments of compelling historical transformation monological received wisdoms give way to the prose of multi-tongued contestation (see 'The Politics of Language and Genre,' www.killingtrain.com/badriraina).

At such moments when the deja donnees of old come to be unraveled for what they often are – ideological legitimations of sectarian power-grab – pathetic, comical, and so-obviously disingenuous defences of the status quo find themselves obliged to come forth rather nakedly.

Something of this now occurs in India with frenetic concern and energy with respect to the determination of the Congress-led coalition government to reserve 33% seats for women in parliament and the legislatures, a measure that saw historic adoption by the upper house (Rajya Sabha) of parliament just the other day (see my 'A Parliament of Women as much as of Men').

Sensing that the measure, were it to become law, may spell more than merely reformist changes in the way in which Indian democracy and its institutions may come to be reconceived and redirected, a cacophony of rather frightened voices seek to embroil this deepening of representative democracy in doubts and distractions rather than in any worthwhile critique. A regressive enterprise that spans responses from downright honesty to insincere subterfuge.

II

First, the most honest. Put simply, a large enough number of male parliamentarians fear the loss of livelihood, indeed of existence. This because most do not come to politics from any flaming passion to set the realm right, but from a recognition that during the current phase of India's democracy, success at the hustings translates often into power, pelf, and patronage (PPP). And when it is remembered that most lack any autonomy of skill or competence, the loss of a seat in parliament tantamounts to a return to a boorishly undistinguished non-existence. Where politics is the only calling a man has, what else is there to go back to? Having tasted of sectarian adulation among captive constituencies, the loss of a seat denotes the extinction of what prestige they command.

Then there is the insistence on behalf of those who belong to Other Backward Classes (OBCs). They argue that unless a sub-quota within the stipulated 33% is fixed for OBC women, the measure will only lead to an influx of up-country, English-using women, relegating the socially and educationally deprived women further into oblivion.

Remarkably, these gentle males have never once thus far pressed for any overall reservation for OBCs within parliament and the legislatures where only Schedule Castes and Tribes have seats reserved for them in proportion to their population. Ergo, in the absence of any such provision, there is no way in which seats may be reserved for OBC women alone unless a constitutional amendment is first separately adopted to introduce OBC reservations – something for which male OBC stalwarts have never yet striven. Nor do they tell us why it is that they may not put up OBC women candidates for the seats now proposed to be set apart for women if they so wish to do. Thus far, whenever they have put up any women in general category seats, they have invariably been close relatives of the presiding OBC patriarchs.

Most interestingly, endorsement of the 33% measure has come from a Hindu organization whose constitution stipulates that women cannot acquire its membership, namely the male and military RSS. Work that out for a switch.

The fear within the RSS as always is that breaking the 33% into sub-quotas will not but fracture the monolithic consolidation of India's Hindus – something the RSS holds fatally necessary for the preservation of Indian 'nationhood.' Thus, if you cannot enforce within the Indian constitutional system the same blanket refusal to admit women into the fold as you practice within your own organization, then the next best must be to prevent sub-quotas based on casteist (read divisive) considerations.

What of the Muslim minority? A shout has gone up that the 33% measure will surely spell doom for minority representation. We don't know why. Especially since thus far Muslim patriarchs have practiced a studied refusal to foreground Muslim women in electoral politics. However sanctimonious this shout may seem, the reality appears to be best captured in the statement made to an electronic channel the other day by a Muslim cleric to the effect that 'god intended women primarily to produce a race of good and proper men, and that it was not god's wish that Muslim women should be seen shoulder to shoulder with men in public/political life making speeches' (Nietzsche/Nazis close ideological mentors there?). Indeed, the experience thus far has been that Muslim women – and there are any number – who have made a mark in public/political life in post-colonial India have more often than not been seen as threats to Muslim culture and identity.

En Passant here, do note that a bill has been introduced yet again in the Jammu & Kashmir Assembly that proposes to take away the rights of Permanent Residency (which include the right to acquire property within the state and the right to vote) from Kashmiri women who marry outside the state. Kashmiri men ofcourse may do so without fear of such loss. Did you say Patriarchy rules the roast? Well, it does. On this rather brazenly discriminatory measure we still have to hear from spokespersons of the Muslim leaderships who live outside Jammu & Kashmir. Especially those who seem so concerned that the 33% Bill will relegate Muslim women!

Remarkably, all that in the full knowledge that exclusively Islamic states like Pakistan and Afghanistan already have mandated provisions for women's reservation in their legislative bodies! How effective those are in the matter of defeating gruesomely misogynist laws in those countries is ofcourse another matter, although the prospects of achieving those victories in the years to come can be envisaged, if at all, only because women do have an assured voice there in the first place – a fact that must be considered historically preferable to not having any women at all positioned to strive so.

Then there is the argument that given the rotationary provision in the Reservation Bill, only those women will be put up by Party supremos who they can rely upon to keep the seat warm for their return. Thus, we may see only daughters and daughters-in-law being accorded tickets for the women constituencies.

The argument is adduced to caution the polity about a prospect, namely, cronyism, that has characterized Indian democracy for years on end. That such cronyism disfigures the Indian representative system regardless of gender is an argument readily admitted. Yet we are not told why this prospect may be especially lethal now when women of any sort are slated to enter parliament?

Perhaps the most disingenuous argument is the one that is proferred by sundry 'successful' women. They seem mortified at the thought that women should at all require a leg-up from the system, and thereby be demeaned as a sub-species that cannot stand on their own.

The presumption here is that any 'successful' men or women within the scheme of things have made it or can make it all on their own. Alas, if only this were the case.

The fact is leg-ups come in various modalities. The fact that most are adroitly managed out of sight and in back rooms is too well-known a feature of career advancement in India across genders to need iteration.

Thus the further argument that India adopt a system where political parties allot a percentage of seats for women remains a pseudo-rationalist argument. Had this been as self-evidently possible and painless a recourse, it might have been adopted freely by parties thus far. That this has not happened testifies to the fact that patriarchy rules the party system, to a lesser or greater degree. And, were the measure to be adopted, we are not told why this measure would not lead to one or both of those prospects which are otherwise decried – tickets given either to daughters, daughters-in-law, or to dispensable women in losing constituencies. The consequence then might be that either crony winners enter parliament and the legislatures or most women lose out in hopeless constituencies, defeating the very purpose of enhancing women's representation.

An overarching skepticism is also to the fore (and, interestingly, voiced by many 'successful' women in various areas of public life). To wit, that there is never any guarantee that women in power necessarily either espouse or push concerns that afflict women as citizens.

To this there is an obvious truth. Yet, the obverse of that argument is to say that men alone may thereby be trusted to do so. And when we remember that male legislators often enough do not pursue the interests of the voting communities which endorse them as strong support bases, why this infirmity again seems lethal only in the case of women begs more than a question.

III

The fact is that be it men or women, the genders are everywhere riven by intersecting loyalties – of class, caste, ethnic identity, linguistic affinity and so on.

Given that macro-sociological reality, it remains unforgiveably discriminatory that a half of the population should remain outside the ambit of decision-making at the highest levels of national life.

Even as it is agreed that there is no guarantee that gender justice necessarily issues from gendered leaderships, it is a probability of the highest order that when men and women are pitted together in law-making, preposterous blatancies of policy must receive their due rectification and come-uppance. It is a monstrous argument to say that a good number of women in legislative bodies will not in due course have the effect of critiquing social and economic decisions inimical to women as a whole, and to offer correctives, more than a wholly male-dominated dispensation might.

The simple point is that if at some point the world did acknowledge that democracy without women's franchise was a sham after all, the time to acknowledge further that democracy without women's assured representation as well is equally a sham has arrived.

It is in the fitness of modernity that entrenched Neanderthals who often masquerade as exemplars of equality persuade themselves to push the species forward.

After all, if political moralities and democratic convictions do not evolve to keep pace with strides made in other spheres of human attainment, the world can relapse into crude authoritarianisms of a lethal kind, given the extent now of access to frightening instruments of control and repression.

We firmly believe that democratic victories scored on behalf of or by women do not redound to the benefit merely of women. These victories promise a better life for all mankind.

Let India's parliamentarians then not be caught on the wrong side of history. As the Bill comes up in the Lok Sabha (the house of the people) for adoption, it is our hope that the frightened and the disingenuous will yield to the enlightened and the selfless.

The future of India's democracy is a much larger issue than the future of male constituencies.

March 2010

Troubled Times for Advani & Modi

Will the State Desert Them to Justice?

Satyameva Jayate.
(The Truth is ever victorious).

It suits India's elite opinion-makers always to characterize the Bharatiya Janata Party (BJP) as India's 'principal opposition party.'

Principal opposition, presumably, to 'the natural party of governance,' namely, the Indian National Congress.

The years have shown that such characterization on fact is patently erroneous, especially over the last two decades of Independent India's existence. Be it market fundamentalism, or militarism directed at 'terrorists' and 'Naxals' or love of American imperialism there is little daylight between the Congress and the BJP.

Even on that 'basic' postulate of the Constitution of India, 'secularism,' one has always known that substantial sections among the Congress party covertly share the majoritarian impulses of the BJP, even as the party as a whole swears by the principle of secularism as an article of faith and a feature of its long history. Which is not to deny that other sections within the Congress continue to remain laudably wedded to Nehru's vision of a welfare state of which secular citizenship was envisaged as a founding bedrock. Without question, this section within the Congress has the great good luck of having Sonia Gandhi as a bearer of that legacy.

Meanwhile, corporate India and the elites who are their ancillaries continue to pursue their pet agenda of reducing the Indian democratic system to a two-party structure, where the parties in question (Congress/BJP) alternate governance but essentially govern to the same purposes.

Which is why other parties that do in sharp ideological terms deserve the rubric of 'opposition' to the Congress/BJP together never make that grade in official political discourse of which India's 'mainstream' media remains a bulwark. And notwithstanding the fact that such parties regularly poll a half of the Indian electorate come hustings.

II

As we contemplate the current troubles of the two front-ranking BJP stalwarts – Advani and Modi – one who could not be prime minister and one who is slated to be, it is good that we keep the above backdrop in mind. Yes, as the adage has it, the truth does prevail, but it prevails in two different sorts of ways: among the people at large who always know, and, less frequently, as a consequence of legal processes over which the state puts its official stamp.

The Babri Demolition:

Who doesn't know that Lal Kishen Advani was after all the chief instigator and architect of the demolition of the Babri mosque, not just in the two years leading upto December 6, 1992 but on the very day itself, as the entire top brass of the BJP sat, smirked, and watched in glee the domes falling one after the other?

That is the truth that the whole country witnessed on television; yet a truth that was hardly transparent to the state and its agencies as legal proceedings began to be initiated.

Over interminable years and contestations, charges of conspiracy and direct culpability against Advani and the other top leaders were emasculated, and then dropped, until reinstated in a separate court at Rae Bareilly in 2005.

Then came the Liberhan Commission Report which, however belatedly, nailed the lies that had been deployed both in party and public circles. All that despite the fact that Justice Liberhan did not in his Report take note of the most damningly direct and trustworthy evidence against Advani – that deposed before it by Ruchira Gupta who had been a reporter with Business India and a ringside witness to the event of the demolition (see my 'The Mythology of Advani's Sadness').

Yet, sadly for Advani, just the other day witness no.9 at the Bareilly court, one Anju Gupta, a very senior Indian Police Service officer at the time of the demolition, and then incharge of Advani's securiy, came forth to testify boldly to the truth to which she had consistently testified before.

And at every point of her deposition, the testimony of this brave policewoman made independent corroboration of all the salient points Ruchira Gupta had made to the Liberhan Commission.

To wit: that Advani had made an inflammatory speech on site, thundering that the Ram temple was going to be built at the exact site of the mosque; that far from being sad or despondent, he had wanted the dome breakers to step down inorder not to save the mosque but their lives, since he knew that the mosque was being brought down from the inside the more effectively to collapse the domes; that as the domes fell, he like everybody else was cheery, as sweets went round in celebration; that at no point did he attempt to instruct either the complicit police force or the karsevaks (the labouring hands of the Sangh) to prevent the atrocity from happening.

With another forty odd witnesses still to depose, who knows where the case will go from here? Already, the BJP, that party of dharma, is busy propagating in true Goebbelesian fashion how the IPS policewoman, Anju Gupta, is Anju Gupta Rizvi and hence a motivated witness! Never mind that on affidavit her name is Anju Gupta merely, and a devout Hindu to boot.

Which is not to say that had she infact been a Muslim, her evidence would have been any less truthful or damning, or worthy of admittance.

It thus remains to be seen whether at some point in future, in the Advani case, the Indian state will endorse the self-evident truth that the whole country witnessed in the years between 1990 and 1992.

III

The Gujarat Massacre:

It will be fair to say that rarely in the history of lawful governance has any democratic state in the world sought to subvert the ends of justice as Gujarat under Modi since 2002.

The story is by now too well-known to require painful belabouring. Some salient facts that are by now out in the open, thanks to the unprecedented perseverance of common citizens, voluntary organizations like the Citizens for Justice and Peace, damning sting operations conducted by the Tehelka media group, and the bold public disclosures made by upright officers who were then in the know of things, we know:

- that not without Modi's say-so could the bodies of the burnt victims of the train disaster at Godhra have been brought all the way to Ahmedabad and paraded for public attention;
- that on the 27th of February, Modi took a meeting of his key ministers, aids and police officers, and instructed that Hindus were to be allowed to vent their anger against the train burning;
- that Modi's erstwhile cabinet colleague, Haren Pandya who came to be suspected to have leaked information of this meeting fell into disrepute and was soon enough also found murdered; note: to this day, his father accuses Modi of being behind that murder;
- that the outstanding police officer, Sreekumar, has testified to illegal orders being issued which he for one refused to obey, incurring the implacable vendetta of the state affecting his status and service;
- that, despite the Bandh call given by the Vishwa Hindu Parishad, no instructions were issued to prevent the mayhem that was intended, especially in Ahmedabad;
- that key operators like Babu Bajrangi were given personal assurance by Modi that the law would not reach them, and judges were repeatedly transferred by the chief minister until one was found who issued bail orders to Bajrangi – the animal who, self-confessedly in the Sting tape (which has been declared admissible evidence) ripped Kauser Bi's womb, took out the foetus on sword point and flung the same in the fire;
- that a key aid, Haresh Bhatt is plainly heard to say in the tape that without Modi's clearance and support, nothing could have been done, since the rioters would have surely been bashed by the police and prevented from carrying out the butchery;
- that victims of the massacre, those that survive, have publicly stated from diverse platforms how the police, even as they put in an appearance, blandly either lied to them, or told them plainly that they were slated to die;
- how at the Gulbarg Society massacre, where the then Congress member of parliament was dismembered to smithereens, the said M.P. Ehsan Jafri had made close to two hundred calls, including to Modi, for

protection; how Modi abused him, and how alongwith him another 68 people were put to the sword and the fire; regrettably, to this day, the record of calls made on the 27th and 28th of Feb.,2002, including by and to Modi, remain to be examined.

- that one of his erstwhile cabinet colleagues, Maya Kodnani, has already been found complicit and sent to jail, and three others are willing and ready to testify to the truth (Nalin Bhatt, Goverdhan Zadaphia, Jaideep Patel).

Indeed, the revolting episode comprises by now too many sordid narratives to recount here.

And yet, these things were, if anything, only to steel further the resolve of Modi's adulators to stand by him, and the BJP to laud him; not once has either he or the party expressed the barest remorse for the massacre, not to speak of admitting responsibility, or seeking reconciliation with Gujarat's Muslim citizens who remain ghettoized, ostracized, and discriminated in work-related issues.

And throughout the investigative/legal proceedings, the Gujarat state agencies have sought at every conceivable stage and in every conceivable way to deflect the due processes of law – reason why the administration of justice there has had finally to be literally taken over by the Supreme Court of India which, besides, transferring some key cases outside the state and ordering retrial in more than a thousand others, appointed a Special Investigation Team to re-try some eight of the most horrendous cases, among them the Gulbarg Society massacre.

Ehsan Jafri's widow, Zakia Jafri, thus sought to file a complaint before the then DGP of Gujarat (june 8, 2006), in which she desired, among other things, Modi to be investigated as 'accused number one.'

Rejected.

A writ was then filed before the Gujarat High Court with the same plea. Rejected in November, 2007.

Which is when Zakia Jafri and the Citizens for Justice and Peace filed a Special Leave Petition before the Supreme Court of India directly (SLP 1088, 2008); this time the plea was admitted and the SIT appointed previously by the Supreme Court directed to investigate the charges made in the SLP.

Thus it was that Modi was summoned to appear before the SIT any day between March 21 and 31.

IV

Summoning at first pliable sections of the media to his aid, Modi sought to make much of some confusion in the dates on which he was to appear. As his party drummed up the so-called controversy.

We now know that he sought to persuade the SIT to examine him either at his home or in his office. The plea was rejected.

Finally, on the 27th of March, Modi made another record; he became the first serving chief minister of an Indian state to be summoned for quizzing on charges of criminal conspiracy in a massacre.

We now know that he was grilled for some ten hours or so in two separate sessions, and that, if need be, he could be asked to appear again.

Any chief executive worth his salt may in such circumstances have offered to demit office till cleared by the enquiry; not Modi. Never in India has skin been so thick or conscience so wholly atrophied as not to exist at all.

The chief of SIT is due to submit his report on the investigations to the appointing authority, the Supreme Court of India, by end of April; and there is reason to believe that this will be done on time.

But here is the million dollar question: will it transpire that Modi has provided magical answers to what must seem allegations signed and sealed by an already existing preponderance of evidence, direct and circumstantial, demolishing the case of the butchered, the victim survivors, the people, or will it truly turn out that the truth that has been out in the open for years now will also be inscribed in the report that will go to the Supreme Court?

On the answer to that speculation may depend much more than the fate of Modi and Gujarat. Indeed, should Modi's corporate and celebrity admirers and closet communalists in high office succeed in doing dirt on the ends of justice, India's polity and state may be seen to kiss good bye forever both to democracy and to secularism. Indeed, the continued unity of the realm may itself come into real question.

If on the other hand, the truth does prevail in law as it does in common knowledge, India would have struck a decisive blow on behalf of secularism, democracy and the rule of law, lifting the polity to a level of belief that may bear the promise of legitimizing and consolidating the lawful state and lawful institutions to unimaginably salutary consequence.

Never may as much of a nation-state's future have hung in the balance on the contents of a single report as it does on the Report of the SIT,

And never may have any group of a dozen or less investigators into collective criminality stood to lose or win as much verity and honour as does the SIT.

So low has been brought the esteem of probity in Indian national life that it would be a recklessly naïve citizen who would say on this day that the right and proper is about to see the light of day.

The country trusts them to know that rarely has the fate of so many depended on so few.

Should justice come to be disfigured, it may transpire that those who have eyes only for India's Gross National Product will see both India and its GNP come crashing in sad and irreparable ways.

March 2010

Destitution

India's Greatest Internal Danger

The Hindustan Times is a leading herald of the developmental path that the current Indian government vows to carry forward in the main. Namely, the route that goes through free-market fundamentalism, fiscal prudence, and greater and greater transfer of wealth into private entrepreneurship. Which includes disinvesting public equity in what it sees as inefficient, corrupt and retarding Public Sector Undertakings (PSUs). Never mind that precisely the PSUs prepared the ground over some four decades of Independent India for the industrial and technological prowess that corporate India never fails to flaunt. For example, by making such core inputs as coal, oil, and steel available to a nascent national bourgeoisie at subsidized rates! No problem with subsidies then.

So when you notice that this Daily has been running an admirably laudable series on hunger in the hinterland, complete with brutally honest statistics, you cannot but acknowledge how dire Indian destitution must be.

And it does not matter a jot what its motives might be.

Do recall that Edmund Burke did not for a moment wish the British empire to be liquidated; which is why he was to become the most trenchant arraigner of the Company's barbaric excesses in the colony. And who can say that he made a mistake in initiating impeachment against Hastings.

Or that it was that arch Tory Prime Minister, Benjamin Disraeli, who first coined the phrase 'two nations' in an unreadable novel called *Sybil, or the Two Nations* (the 'two nations' being the rich and the poor). Or that Thomas Carlyle wrote some of the most moving tracts on behalf of 'reform' because he was terrified that were the Whigs not to make a gesture towards British destitution, the French Revolution would surely happen in England. And what could have been worse. And remember that it nearly did during the 'hungry Forties' but was averted by a combination of the gestures, the sticks, and loot from the colony.

Thus, recognizing the ideological history which *The Hindustan Times* replicates, we are thankful that it has made the no-nonsense disclosures it has; and for the reason that coming from it rather than from the Indian left or the myriad non-governmental civil society activist groups, the fact of Indian hunger has a greater plausibility among India's heady, consumerist elites who swear by this English Daily. Though it is much to be doubted that they will lose much sleep over the disclosures.

All that, even as *The Hindustan Times* also remains routinely and rather sniggeringly contemptuous of what right-wing opinion calls the 'hand-outs' approach to social upliftment, often critiquing the recent policy initiatives of the government (under pressure, it must be noted, of the Congress President, Sonia Gandhi, now also again the head of the re-constituted National Advisory Council, a policy think-tank derided in past years for recommending higher levels of social spending) to invest at impressive scales in schemes that are meant to benefit the lowest of the low. Impressive merely in relation to past practice of course, although in absolute terms, still a pittance.

Thus, even as it unleashes an editorial war on hunger ('Treating the Poor Like Dirt,' *HT*, April 6), it doesn't quite know where to go from there, except to recall, most amusingly, that, among other things – 'sovereign,' 'secular,' 'democratic,' – India also denotes itself in the Preamble to its Constitution a 'socialist republic.'

A clear case of the Devil quoting scripture, since the Daily's diatribes at anything sniffingly socialist remain its raison d etre.

II

So, why this new-found concern for the destitute?

Clearly because there is now a recognition of the fact that things are so abominably inequitous that merely upholding the suigeneric prerogatives of the state, or mouthing pious deprecations against social unrest and violent recourses by sections of the polity may not stem the tide.

And what could be more fatally threatening to the nation's aspiration to super-powerdom via the corporate route, which will now increasingly include strategic corporates from afar as well.

After all, even as the numbers of dollar billionaires grow exponentially at one end, a half of India's children – a whole half – are malnourished to a point where a whole new generation of Indians is faced with slow but certain extermination well before it grows into adolescence.

In fact, where the French Queen had recommended cake for the sancullotes, children in India have been discovered by the Daily to be actually subsisting on mud laced with silicon.

You read that right – mud.

When you remember that even in 2010 – some six decades into Independent existence – India harbours the world's largest numbers of poor people in absolute terms, mud has great prospects.

Where mud is available, that is.

Even this minute some canny corporate might be working out the idea of manufacturing mud cakes at affordable prices, for all you know.

It is another matter that these numbers range from some 27% to 77% of the population in various officially constituted findings, giving policy-makers a headache as to which figure to authenticate as it formulates schemes like the 'Food Security Act' etc.,

III

What is of importance in the attention that hunger receives in the *HT* is the recognition, however unstated and denied otherwise, that a polity so execrably unequal (because exploited) is a natural breeding ground for all sorts of mayhem.

Thus, contrary to the oft-repeated mantra of the Prime Minister that 'Naxalism' is the greatest internal danger that India faces, there is an unacknowledged and shamefaced realization that in fact it may be destitution that lies at the root of the problem.

And that this destitution, far from being an other-worldly imposition, is very much the yield of policies pursued, especially over the last two decades of 'reform.'

Now, *The Hindustan Times* and the material interests it espouses and projects would die before ascribing India's destitution to the political economy of free-market fundamentalism.

Which is why its panaceas encompass the well-worn moralisms of ruling class elitism: root out corruption, reign in the bureaucracy, de-hoard the grains, invest in storage facilites, encourage more private initiatives in the food industry, accept BT technologies, eliminate middle men in retail, let in corporates directly into trading food, and put down civil unrest with a firm hand. But at no cost pull down the private mining corporates who busily and illegally rob millions in the hinterland of their right to forest wealth, to land, to water, to livelihoods which have sustained them for centuries.

And at no cost make any public acknowledgement that Naxalism is causal. As in the case of 'terrorism' condemn it several times a day as being without cause and merely an expression of metaphysical evil. And waiting to be bombed out of existence.

IV

As I write, the government's touted 'Operation Green Hunt' against the Maoists has received an ugly jolt in the jungles of Dantewada in Chhattisgarh – a state ruled by the Bharatiya Janata Party: some seventy five soldiers of a hunting Central Reserve Police Force party have been wiped out in a cannily orchestrated attack. And most of those killed perhaps as destitute as the Adivasis among whom Naxalism breeds.

The no-nonsense Home Minister of India, P.Chidhambaram, has shaken his erudite head and pointed to the indescribable barbarism of the Naxals. Nothing here about the failure of the state government, whereas only two days ago he was pleased to berate the Chief Minister of West Bengal for the failure of his administration to curb Naxalism in Lalgarh, reminding him that the buck must stop at his table.

So much for the politics of the issue. And no mention of where the buck may stop after today's massacre.

The Maoists who are accused of wishing to overthrow the state and the constitutional regime are told that all their grievances will be heard if they abjure violence. But it is not explained why those who routinely espouse allegiance to the Constitution while espousing the cause of the destitute are routinely done violence to by the state. Except of course that they are suspected to be Naxal 'sympathizers' rather than committed to the cause of the destitute.

And the test of loyalty to the realm is univocally held to be everybody's unequivocal readiness to condemn Maoist barbarities while upholding the right of the state to the course it follows, as all debate on the issue of destitution is sought to be reduced to a 'you are with us or you are against us' formula. Familiar Bushism. Not for nothing was he so well-loved in India.

Some time back the Maoist made an offer of a cease fire for seventy two days (a riposte to the official assertion that it would be willing to undertake talks within seventy two hours if the guns were silenced). That offer was expectedly accompanied by the stipulation that the state would put a hold on the ravaging corporate activities in Jharkhand, Chhattisgarh, Orissa, and declare an adherence to the forest rights of the tribals as by Statute established.

There of course is the catch.

Many voices among India's civil society ask why it is that in dealing with the problem born of destitution the state is unwilling to respect laws that indelibly protect those rights, to take cognizance of the bandit corporates who care a tuppence for the laws and the Constitution, and carry out their depredations with full connivance of the local authorities, or to enlist democratic voices who may be willing to bring the parties to the table on terms which are seen to be fair by contending interests.

Not surprisingly, such unwillingness is construed as the state's class commitment to private marauders out to make a kill. While, India's children blunt the edge of their hunger by eating silicon-laced mud.

Nor is there any acceptance of the fact that making war on its own destitute may not solve the problem. After all the days when genocide could be visited upon native populations with any conclusive prospect – the Native Indians in America, or the Aborigines in Australia – are long gone.

One would think that at a time when India has its hands full with depredations visited upon it by inimical neighbours, and when elements within the state do seem to favour a wider investment in social programmes, it would be good policy to unite the polity behind sound national purposes.

And that would require a bold acknowledgement that mere militarist or moralist bravado may not meet the situation. Rather a paradigmatic recognition that social violence that afflicts large parts of the country issues from policies that are brazenly calculated to fatten the already fat at the cost of those that eat mud.

Exactly as the state does now recognize that the social unrest among its religious minorities issues from causes that are and have lately been firmly identified as well. For example in the Sachar Committee and the Ranganath Mishra committee reports with respect to Indian Muslims.

What is it then that prevents the state from according similar credence to dozens of its own reports on the extent, nature, and causes of destitution, and the remedies thereof?

Might it not be the case that whereas inequities that relate to caste, religious community, gender, linguistic and ethnic allegiance, are seen to be negotiable by the state in one way or another, sooner or later, and often profitably, those that relate to class remain simply non-negotiable?

If indeed so, a great task awaits India's social theorists in determining as to how the Constitution of the Republic may be squared with so blind a refusal to address inequities rooted in a non-negotiable devotion to capitalism which seems to make its own laws and write its own Constitution.

And whether, should that devotion remain unmitigated and rather drunk with the prowess of the state-apparatus behind it, violence can ever be conclusively put down.

April 2010,

Mirror Mirror on the Wall, Who is the Corruptest of them All?

I have a grouse, and an axe to grind with the 'International Agency ' which has recently placed India at just number 4 in the list of the most corrupt nations in South and South-East Asia.

Clearly, there seems a conspiracy to deny us our deserts even where we justly deserve the top spot.

The Christian world believes corruption to be endemic to the human race as a result of the Original Sin; we Hindus make our own corruption without the acknowledgement that duly should be ours.

Remember now that whereas Mammon was consigned to Hell, at least by John Milton, we are the only culture in the world who worship wealth in the form of a goddess, name of Lakshmi. And, since the inception of the neo-liberal economic 'reforms,' just how!

It is the Washington Consensus of 1990 that finally aligned the world of enterprise to the teachings of the Hindu Shastras which enjoin that man (read here upper caste men in high places) must strive in life to achieve *vaibhav* and *khyati* (opulence and fame) by exercising any of five options over the adversary, namely, *saam*, *daam*, *kaam*, *dand*, *bhed* (negotiation, buy-out, seduction, force, division among the enemy).

Rarely have a philosophical archive and free-market vandalism been so matched and married as above, you would agree. Calvin came much much later, linking salvation to property. Although it should be obvious why, after all, the land of Sam and the land of Laxmi have come to be such strategic partners.

Having kicked out sham notions of socialist equity, we are now finally on the same glittering page, armed with the knowledge that there are but only two kinds of people in the world – the winners and the losers. The chief arbiter being the 'bitch goddess' (borrowing from D.H.Lawrence, lest calumny should follow), Money.

And what can money not do, as Mr.Dombey was to instruct his little boy, Paul, who had just lost his mother.

And, alas, money did not bring her back, the child noted irritatingly.

But that was then, in the 1840s; now, among the moneyed, what mothers care for what sons, and what sons for what mothers. All together and severally care for the latest brand equity.

April the 23rd this day, when birth and death both came to the Bard. How he had thought of the Washington Consensus- to- come when he made Timon say what he did about the power of money.

So powerful and prescient that Marx could use it for his own purposes some centuries after. Alas, it seems, to little end. Not until money ends the world, as may be on the cards, may our animus reach conclusion. And thereafter, again, who knows but only those that had the money would enter heaven, leaving the carping billions to stew in the swelter of their moral iterations.

But, if there is a god other than the goddess, Laxmi, whom we Indians worship, it is called Cricket.

And now that money is seen to have so corrupted this god, will there be forgiveness? Most likely, yes; because, as stated at the outset, corruption is the least corrupt concept in the historical memory of we Hindus. Nothing more corrupt than the failure to be corrupt with flamboyant cunning.

And nothing so heroic as to say to the silly officers of the law and to that nuisance of a book called the Constitution 'I obscenity in the milk of your virginity' (Lawrence again). Ha! Ha! Ha!

Have you forgotten we are a democracy, and may do as we like?

II

Unitl the other day most Indians might have thought that the Indian Premier League of Cricket (IPL) was, after all, another one of the innocent diversions of the rich and the famous, harmless and even pleasureful in the main.

Much as you might have told them you could not stir them from their allegiance to their favourite teams, and stars.

Alas, didn't Marx teach us that in the political economy of various ages, that of capitalism particularly, everything is always linked to everything else, but adroitly made discrete, and the nuts and bolts equally adroitly concealed from view?

So it has turned out.

Name any of the major scams and scandals of the last two decades and they may all pale in comparison to what the current enquiries into the IPL are fast revealing, a million a minute.

Tax haven unaccounted moneys, *hawala* transactions, underhand deals, insider information networks, mysterious and also non-existent holding companies (ah, Vladimir Illych, how you had spoken of these in chapters III and IV of *Imperialism, the Highest Stage of Capitalism*), broadcast channels neck-deep in graft, ministers and minions sunk in muck, politicians, administrators, film stars, relatives and hangers-on thereof, all out for the kill, and all feeding of the blood and sweat earnings of the duped millions who flock to see the matches played, gaping in wonder at the heroisms displayed, or sighing in pain at failures of those to whom the game has been but a diversion to the main business of making them horrendous piles of money, and partying with the rich and famous of other spheres of India's ten percent predators.

And to think that when I played my cricket, some four decades ago, and two decades or more before neo-liberal emancipation from scruple and shame, what sacrifices we made to buy the least of our equipment. But that was merely unevolved and shackled welfare capitalism then, when games were games and profits profits.

As I write, one revelation and one scandal stumbles o, the foregone, news bulletin after news bulletin, swapping space only with the only other archive of matching scandal and scam – the shenanigans of our 'godmen' And the same cast of characters there as well – celebrities, politicians, bureaucrats, entrepreneurs, replete with private jets, private yachts, fleets of BMWs, acres upon stolen acres of public land used for haremite purposes, and billions of moneys, appearing and disappearing as in some giant display of trick and treat.

Ah, thou unenlightened moron, dost thou not know that all this is but the illusory play of Maya – a mere spume to which thou shouldst pay narry any heed, leaving such questions to the men in safaris and in saffron.

III

Yet, I say, is there not perhaps an x-factor somewhere that we are actually getting to know of these matters and to see of it in the light of day?

Is it not the case that where ten almighty rogues are hell-bent on doing us all in, a hundred others are devotedly striving to take the clothes off the emperor?

Therefore, O destitute billions that belong to the BPL (Below Poverty Line) India, wake up even now to what IPL India is doing. Refuse them your hard-earned pennies, and lend might to the instruments, however shackled and compromised, that are now seeking to unravel the boxes of gold in which their perfidies are stashed.

Most of all, learn to withhold your pathetic adulation and to spit on their grandeur.

For even at your least, and in your greatest suffering, you hide more worth than they do in those boxes.

Know thyself, and vow that you will lend no hand in building ever new idols, but rather seek ways to get back your own.

In the days to come, let BPL triumph over IPL.

For that to happen you need no guns.

Just make up your collective mind.

April 2010

Rewriting Proverbs

Sauce for the Goose is not
Sauce for the Gander.

Unlike my friend, J. Sriraman, the reputed columnist, I am no expert on matters nuclear.

As a lay student of contemporary international history (where 'contemporary' goes back , for purposes of this note, to the second world war), I agree with some six billion others that nuclear weapons are unacceptably evil in a usually acceptably evil world.

Everybody of course says so, including those who remain in control of the largest stockpiles.

Yet what stares you in the face is the unconscionable gap between the ethics of the issue which hardly anyone denies, and the record of performance through the decades.

And strikingly here, those that bear the most onus, even opprobrium, seem the most self-righteous.

Which is, after all, what the reviled President of Iran, Ahmedinejad, underscored in his recent appearance at a nuclear disarmament conclave in America.

As I said, on the nuclear question this writer holds no allegiances. So let us ask why was he wrong when he pointed out that America which currently seeks to put him and his country in the doghouse is thus far the only country that has actually used nuclear weapons? And, one might remember, used much more to see that the weapon actually worked than from any real need to use it, besides the collateral intent to show the communists in the then Soviet Union what powers America had.

Why was he wrong in stating the fact that the same United States has thought nothing of using dirty uranium and agent orange weapons in Vietnam and then more recently in Iraq on millions of perfectly innocent human beings? And on pretexts that were to be found to be a hundred percent spurious?

Why was he wrong in pointing out that America therefore may have the least moral right to lecture the rest of the world about the dangers of weaponising?

Did I say 'rest of the world'? Wrong.

Why was he wrong in underlining the brazen double standards the United States exercises in determining where to saber rattle and where to wink? For example with respect to the Non-Proliferation Treaty?

Why was he wrong in insinuating that non-signatory weapon-states like Israel and India continue to receive its recognition, support, and strategic partnership, while signatories like Iran are to be denied even those rights that the NPT allows, such as the right to enrich uranium for peaceful purposes? And, in the process, merrily violating the NPT to the hilt while accusing others of doing so?

And were the matter to be polemicised beyond the lawful, for instance on grounds of reliability or record, whose record remains the most questionable – those that have actually used nuclear weapons or those that don't even have them?

And among those that have them, does anyone doubt that, like their permanent and permanently uncritical benefactor, it is the Zionists who might not think twice of using the weapons they have, and entirely in pursuit of illegitimate claims?

As to the Islamic world, how is it that the country that never had these weapons, Iraq, came to be annihilated on the basis of a despicable campaign of lies, whereas the other country that has them and that even uncle Sam recognizes to be the 'epicenter of terrorism' and the home of the Al Qaeda remains such a darling ally?

Very uncomfortable questions those, and such as only Ahmedinejad could ask, since, however foolishly, he, like some others in Latin America, seem never to want to kowtow to Sam, or beg for his favours.

It would be disingenuous of me not to also point out that American hypocrisy in the whole nuclear question is bettered perhaps only by the aspiring super-power (which harbours the greatest number of the world's poor, malnourished, and anaemic), India.

Think of the cheek that India, a non-signatory to the NPT but a great beneficiary on the sly, should lecture Iran about how it must adhere to the provisions of the NPT!

Ah, as the chicaneries of India's unshackled capitalism multiply, you can see how she learns all the tricks that Sam has practiced throughout the decades since 1945.

What better proof of the greatness waiting to descend on the land of Gandhi.

It should be obvious that no greatness resides in peace-making, in allying with those whose growth rates do them no credit, and whose armies are but pitiful adversaries at bottom.

And no greatness resides in diverting funds from the missile and moon mission, from massive military investments, from astronomical capitalist waste and glamourised episodes of sleaze to eradicating hunger, malnutrition, disease, illiteracy, shelterlessness, and rural and urban squalor and jobessness; or to investing in systems that might provide clean sanitation, clean drinking water, assured farm incomes, tribal rights, and the social upliftment of some two thirds of Indians. Or in recovering from the fatcats the billions of public moneys they owe, the billions they steal, and the billions they still borrow without the least fear of comeuppance.

And no greatness resides in just being merely a South Asian country in friendly and creative communion with other South Asian countries, or to other countries in the region.

The one indubitable source of greatness lies in shaking Sam's murderously solipsistic grasp across the seven seas. Even as its grand banks and financial institutions sink in their own perfidy, taking the world with them.

And in nodding agreement when Sam says what a dangerous lout Ahmedinejad is, how clever the Israelis are, and how the beleaguered Generals in Pakistan deserve our cooperation, even as they keep the terrorist factories on the boil.

Few things offend as much as when the votaries of power recommend reason to all the others.

May 2010

Return to the People What is the People's

Verdict Long Overdue

Now if you haven't heard of the brothers Ambani you clearly cannot be a citizen of the world.

Ask Forbes; they are right up there among the hundred or so who rule our global destiny.

Being super-rich, they are powerful; being powerful they get richer. As the grapevine has it, close to a hundred members of the Indian parliament are their trusted collaborators in nation-building. Else, how do you think we got where we are?

Petroleum, gas, steel, telecom, and a zillion other embroilments keep their riches going. Name any pie and they have a finger or two in it. Thus, considering how much the nation depends on their exertions, not for nothing are they captioned the Reliance group of entrepreneurs.

Somewhere on the precincts of Parliament House, (I forget where) you might find the lofty Upanishadic averments: *tamaso ma jyotirgamaya* (lead me from the darkness to the light), *asatyo ma satyam gamaye* (from untruth to the truth), *mrityo ma amritam gamaye* (from mortality to deathlessness).

However self-evidently these injunctions guide India's democratic life, there might be a hidden fourth which in point of fact is the primary engine of its onward march; thus it may be formulated: *daridrita ma vaibhav gamaye* (lead me from rags to riches).

Truth to tell, it is this fourth hidden one which famously informed the asteroidical rise of the Ambani patriarch, alas now no more. But the brothers Ambani, Mukesh and Anil, carry forth the torch that he lit and fuelled. And, since your curiosity is by now more than whetted, may I recommend a book that sets out the Ambani story in full detail and devotion: do read (if you can find a copy, since it is believed that all its prints were promptly bought by the reliable Reliance brothers at the very moment of its release) *Reliance: the Real Natwar* by Arun K. Agrawal, New Delhi, 2008.

II

Wretchedly, as is known to happen among the rich and famous clans, some years ago the brothers Ambani fell out with one another, as a consequence of which their businesses and sundry assets came to be bifurcated through the enlightened intervention of their beloved matriarch.

Thus the Petroleum Gas business fell to the lot of the elder Mukesh, and the Energy interests to that of the junior, but smarter and handsomer, Anil.

As a new source of Gas was dug up off the coast of Andhra (the K basin), the brothers quickly closed ranks to come to an understanding, entirely privately, as to how the elder would supply the Gas to the younger, and at what rates, for his power producing units.

Alas, yet again, as also happens frequently, the supposedly agreed-upon price of Gas became a bone of contention while the nation and the state watched in awe.

The matter went to court.

Until, just the other day, the honorable Supreme Court of India opined upon the matter in a most curious and unsmart (because non-neo-liberal) pronouncement.

III

Here is what the honorable Court said:

> Natural resources must always be used in the interests of the country and not private interests. The broader constitutional principle, the statutory scheme as well as the proper interpretation of the PSC mandates the government to determine the price of the gas before it is supplied by the contractor.

Further:

> Due to shortage of funds and technical know-how the government has privatized such activities…It would have been ideal for the PSUs (Public Sector Undertakings) to handle such projects exclusively.

And, on the question of the sanctity of the MOU signed between the two brothers, here is what the Court said:

> The MOU was signed as a private family arrangement or understanding between the two brothers, Mukesh and Anil Ambani, and their mother. Contents of the MOU were not made public…it was neither approved by the shareholders nor was it attached to the scheme. Therefore, technically, the MOU is not legally binding.
>
> It is the duty of the Union (meaning the state) to make sure that these resources are used for the benefit of the citizens of this country.
>
> (*The Hindu*, May 8, 2010, p.12).

IV

To encapsulate: that natural resources belong to the people of India; that only the government of the day has absolute jurisdiction over such resources as trustees of the people in whom sovereignty resides; that all arrangements must be such that these resources are used for the benefit of citizens; and that the only way this can be ensured is that these must be placed in the keeping of Public Sector Undertakings rather than handed over to private profiteers.

So we say Hallelujah! Because every single word spoken by the highest adjucator of the land endorses what ordinary Indians and bands of dedicated non-governmental organizations have been saying with respect not just to Gas but, as the Court avers, to all natural resources, citing, for example the (b) and (c) provisions of Article 39 of the Constitution of India, which read:

> (b) that the ownership and control of the material resources of the community are so distributed as best to subserve the common good;
>
> (c) that the operation of the economic system does not result in the concentration of wealth and means of production to the common detriment.

Is it not, therefore, time that the government of the day, fully embracing the imperative directions both of the Constitution and of the Court's judgment thereof in the matter of India's natural resources extend the implications of both to the troubled spots of Chhattisgarh, Jharkhand, Orissa where, after all, the whole contention revolves round the marauding private expropriations of natural resources (bauxite, coal, gypsum, iron ore etc.,) by national and international corporate hand-in-glove with state agencies towards astronomical profit-making, activities which, in brutal violation of the Constitution and of the Judgment now passed, fleece and usurp the sovereignty of the people over natural resources?

Is it not now incumbent upon the state to rescind all the Ambani-like MOUs that have been signed dime a dozen in these areas between corporates and the state, and to take back possession of these resources into public hands as the Court directs?

That such should be the case is now no longer a matter merely of demands made, peacefully or violently, by citizens who inhabit these areas of the Union, but a legal and constitutional obligation flowing from the averment of the Supreme Court of India in the matter of the brothers Ambani.

So we say, do not listen to the Maoists, listen to the Supreme Court. They seem to be saying one and the same thing.

May 2010

Crunch Time for India

Who Speaks for the People?

As violence in four or five Indian states – Chhattisgarh, Jharkhand, Orissa, West Bengal – comes to a boil, the state blames the Maoists and the Maoists blame the state.

The hardliners in government and outside who advocate using the army and, yes, air-power, in these regions are dubbed bloodthirsty rightists hand-in-glove with national and international corporate interests by sections of civil society opinion, and opinion-makers who counsel against a military approach to the 'Maoist' problem are in turn maligned as clandestine Maoist sympathizers who are deemed to deserve all the rigours of the Unlawful Activities Act.

While these contentions occupy centre-stage in the media, the tribal populations in the affected regions continue to suffer from both ends. And if ever that suffering finds mention, it does so as a very subsidiary incidental On either side of the contention, the fight seems so much more for occupying or reclaiming territory than for the hearts and minds of the people who have lived there for aeons.

The only choice the adivasis seem to have is to make a determination from day to day as to which side they might be more secure for the contingent moment. Even as such determinations do not render them much more than 'flies to wanton boys' who kill them for the larger purpose of either saving the state from those who would overthrow it or of forging a new state wherein they would be equal partners in its ownership.

II

It may be time to record some straightforward perceptions, and hope that these find some purchase among those who are on the side of the tribals rather than of the state or the Maoists.

Yes, there is little doubt that the state over the last two decades has come to represent more and more blatantly the interests of the greedy wall street Gekkos. The money-bags, homegrown and of foreign vintage, who rule its deliberations and its political economy want everything and at any cost. So that whatever laws there exist for the protection of forests, fertile lands in the possession of rightful owners and users, mineral wealth buried underneath that the Constitution stipulates is the natural property of the people (recently so adjucated by the Supreme Court of India in back-to-back judgements), for environmental protection of all these and water resources as well, are deemed to be a rank nuisance standing in the way of 'national development' and rapid GDP growth.

Such interests require that the state not interfere with this marauding activity, but be nonetheless at the ready to quell 'misguided busybodies' who resist their operations. A form indeed of homegrown colonialism wherein an unequal ownership of resources is thought coterminous with the laws of nature, and where the state apparatus have but the one task of keeping the natives in their place. The natives in this case being the real natives called the adivasis – if you like, analogues of the native Americans of the nineteenth century. Those were 'red,' these are considerably darker, and thus even less deserving from a racial point of view.

It is not a wonder that elements even within the ruling party not only see the truth of this, but off and on have been picking up courage to make the point, to the chagrin of the current Minister of Home affairs who seeks a broader mandate from his government to go hammer and tongs at the Maoists, army, airforce and all, but thankfully doesn't get that mandate yet.

Even more hearteningly, in two recent landmark judgements, the Supreme Court of India has boldly enunciated these truths – one bearing on the internecine feud between the Ambani brothers (see my 'Return to the People What is the People's'), and the other since, calling upon the state to make 'land losers beneficiaries of acquisition' (*The Hindu*, May, 17) by dumping the colonial Land Acquisition Act of 1894, and orienting industrial and mining activity to the benefit not just of the marauders but of the local populations as well by making them long-term stake-holders.

III

The questions that the Maoists must ask themselves with greater selflessness than they may have are the following:

Is a hinterland warfare calculated to overthrow the state best suited to altering 'the condition of India'?

Does such warfare in any objective assessment of the state they oppose stand a chance of success in any teleological sense?

Or is it more advisable to weaken not the armed might but the hegemony of the state by working patiently to build a peaceful. democratic mass movement in these regions, and extend that movement to link up with oppressed peoples through the length and breadth of India?

We do not think hinterland warfare is the answer to the perfidious content and operation of the Indian state.

We think that far from any real prospect of overthrowing the state, such insistence only risks more and more alienating masses of Indians from those who may have their welfare at heart, both because violence is abhorrent in itself, and because such violence is realistically seen to have no objective prospect of success, except in according greater justification to the state to unleash greater violence.

And, in a country as big and as diverse as India it would be nothing but abysmal cynicism to argue the case that the more violence the state unleashes the better the prospects of defeating it through armed struggle.

Not less significantly, not many are clear as to what dispensation might emerge in the unlikely possibility that the state truly is overthrown. And not without reason. Like it or not, there are few examples available here to enthuse those who share the critique that the Maoists offer of the state. Nor does China offer a heartening instance. How does it help the cause of justice to have a state under totalitarian political control but dedicated to profiteering on a humongous scale? Like it or not, the collapse of the Soviet Union did lead to exposures of unlovely things in the erstwhile 'socialist' world, such as have tended to make bourgeois democracy a lesser evil, warts and all.

As far back as 2006, this writer had pleaded with the Maoists to ponder the events in Nepal ('India, Nepal, and Left Praxis'). It can hardly be argued that Indian Maoists are better placed in a subcontinental land like India than their counterparts were in a small and vastly more homogenous country like Nepal.

IV

And the questions that the state must ponder are the following:

- How much longer do you think you can run a democracy only in name?
- Are you not struck by the prophetic admonition that Ambedkar had given you on the very day the Constitution was promulgated in 1950 – that precisely what we see happening now in 2010 would inevitably happen if India remained merely a political democracy, yielding one person/one vote but refusing to graduate to a social and economic democracy as well, wherein one person/one vote/one value would transmogrify into one person/one vote/one value as well?
- Do you imagine it is the Maoists alone who are fighting you? You say you allow democratic opposition; but what is the fate of those who have chosen to oppose you democratically and peacefully? Do you not relegate and trample over them? Do you ever remember an Irom Sharmila who has been fasting for a decade on one single just demand in Manipur? And what of those thousands who have sought to peacefully resist your marauding onslaught as you build unconscionable dams, protect the murderous perpetrators of genocide, be it in Bhopal or Gujarat or wherever, or who face you with bare bones in Orissa to protect their land and inheritance from the tycoons who would rape the land for wealth?
- How long do you expect to run this democracy which leaves half its children malnourished and incapacitated for the right to life, which leaves half its women anaemic and illiterate, where in absolute terms the poor outnumber the poor of any country in the world? Where indeed some ten billionaires own more assets than some 400 million Indians?
- Where upper castes still rub the lower ones in the dust, where kangaroo courts of puissant jats decree death sentences to those that would live their own lives as the law of the land allows them to, and draw cabinet ministers to their support?
- Where farmers commit suicide by the lacs while you argue the case for multinationals who seek to appropriate Indian agriculture by the jugular?
- Where despite your legislations, more than two-thirds of Indians cannot go to a doctor or buy the medicines they require, not to speak of adequately nutritious food?

- Where the biggest of big fish skim off thousands of crores of public money without the least hair loss?
- Where all your claims on behalf of rationality and science are done in by scoundrels who amass millions as 'godmen', drawing sustenance from the allegiance of the highest on high?
- Where whole communities feel at the receiving end of prejudice, while perpetrators of other hue find succor, protection, and excuse?
- And where those who speak for justice are dubbed enemies of the state?

V

It should be obvious that India needs to be reclaimed and rescued both from the state and those who engage in self-defeating hinterland warfare.

What would Gandhi have done?

Walk from end to end of this beleaguered country, building bonds of self-respect, courage, love, and peaceful mass reistance.

We believe whether or not he would have succeeded (at Champaran he did, would he have at the Poscoe site?), that is the way we need to go. The cure for the ills of democracy is not a denial of democracy but insistently more democracy.

And more democracy can happen only when masses of people shame the state from its own hypocritical postulates and shame it into yielding economic control of the wealth of the nation besides the right merely to cast the vote. And when men and women of all castes and all religions come together to say 'NO' to brutal obscurantisms that flourish at the behest of the haves who can provide money for unleashing both caste wars and religious riots.

And when men and women, remembering Gandhi, face those bullets, lose lives, but refuse to descend to the cruel bestialities practiced by oppressors of all persuasions and denominations.

Let the Indian democratic revolution begin.

May 2010

The Zionist State at it Again

So What?

Tweet: 'Yes, unarmed activists attacked Israeli commandos – RIGHT! With bread, eggs, and bananas; it surely was an onslaught.'

And you thought the Somalians had a monopoly on piracy. Think again.

They are still but neophytes next to the Zionists.

65 kilometres beyond Israel, in international waters, 'commandos landed by helicopters on the boats and immediately opened fire' (Greta Berlin, spokeswoman of the aid flotilla).

'A warlike attack against aid ships and deadly shooting at peace and humanitarian activists' by a 'crazy government' (Uri Avnery of the Gush Shalom organization, and former Knesset member, in a press release).

09 killed; the rest abducted. The fate of the abducted 'is in their own hands' (Zionist spokesman). To wit, cooperate and be freed, or else.

Some ten years ago I wrote a poem on Netanyahu. Two quatrains hereunder:

Netanyahu is no funny name –
It means the Zionist Jew;
He does not mind the Arabs much,
If elsewhere they remove.
The Netanyahus like Palestine
Kosher and occupied;
So peace demands that they revile
Those they have exiled.

And Uri Avnery agrees that the Israeli disclaimer of having 'disengaged' from Gaza notwithstanding, the occupation continues. It continues until that provision in the Oslo accords which said a deep water port would be built in Gaza to allow free movement and trade for the Gazans is not fulfilled.

So it is not just the exiled and the occupied who are reviled, but whoever stands up against the 'siege, starvation, and massacres in Gaza' (Justin Podur, www.killingtrain.com).

And it does not matter who they are. In this case, among the abducted is a Nobel Peace Prize laureate, Mairead Corrigan, 1976, several European Union legislators, and, yes, even a Holocaust survivor! Real hero of our times.

II

And Mairead Corrigan must be whispering in her own ear – since the abductors have cut off all communications – how this mightily indefensible act of war, following on the certified war crimes of 2007 (certified by the Goldsmith Commission) must offer the last Nobel Peace Prize winner, name of Obama, a golden opportunity to show that he deserved the honour.

Ha! Pity the innocence of the peacemaker. Corrigan forgets why the Zionist is so oblivious of punishment in the first place. Because, Obama or no Obama, and the Nobel regardless, every President of America is first and foremost the Jinn who stands behind the Zionist criminals. Gili Gili, and presto, the Jinn appears to shoo off the world of little men, in or outside the Security Council.

And remember, the redneck part of America may be anti-semitic to the bone marrow, for now it is the 'Islamist' who takes pride of place as chief bête noir.

And then there is the pro-Israel lobby. And the next election is never too far.

Thus, this round too shall pass.

As to world-wide obloquy, the Zionist skin is far too thick to worry about suchlike. They have seen it all before.

So, when the noise is over, it will be back to business as usual.

But consider, just for a minute consider, that not the Zionists but the Iranians had stopped, only stopped, a flotilla in the straits of Hormuz. Baby, it would have been war on the instant, and Teheran burning.

And to think that them Iranians have never attacked anyone yet, and do not even have a nuke.

That privilege belongs to the god's chosen tribe of Israel alone.

As does the other honour of having been the originators of 'terrorism'. Surely the world has not forgotten the Stern and Irgun gangs – to which such stalwarts as Moshe Dayan, Begin, Sharon and other worthies belonged, and who wrecked havoc in the David hotel in Tel Aviv long before Palestine was divided, blasting some 90 or more Britishers and others to holy smithereens.

But shout all you can, and the gods are deaf. And just about dumb as well. Don't you know, they have expressed regrets, but will not accept an international enquiry into the attack. That is for the Israeli government to do. After all, the booty belongs to the thief.

III

And what of India, the land of ideals, of Gandhi and Nehru?

That was then.

Now it belongs to Manmohan Singh and the RSS. For them no country as marvelous as Israel. For being America's all-time pet poodle, and permanently anti-Islamist. And for a glorious record of no-nonsense militarism. Go anywhere, anytime, and kill.

Alas, that poor India is not able to do the same, much as it would like to. Thus, teeny weeny Israel remains more puissant than the emerging world power, India. What could be more galling. But, all things considered, best to be on the same side as the Zionists. They have the weapons. And they have impunity that stretches from here to eternity.

Next to all that, ideals are a sissy. Neo-Liberalism has no use for them. The world will always be unjust and unequal – men will always count for more than women (Taliban and the Hindu right wing agree), Jats more than dalits (witness Mirchpur in Haryana), and Hindus, Christians, and the Jews more than the Muslims. Plain enough. Your problem if you can't see that much.

And, lest we forget, the haves more than all the have-nots, flotilla or no flotilla. To them belongs the land, the forest, the mines, the water, the food, the hospital, the university, the job-market, the perks, the ports, the airposts, the swanky hotels, corporate conglomerates, technology, creature comforts, the law, the police, the government, the state. All in one destined swoop.

And do you know why? Because of their karma in births of yore. So, if ye be woman, low-caste, dark-skinned, illiterate, diseased, hunted, dispossessed, and mightily hungry, compelled to eat mud, blame your karma. What does policy have to do with such things?

Remember, there are elections, and there are the Elect. So, elections or no elections, it will always be the Elect who rule.

And who more Elect than the children of Moses who were promised their land?

So when Obama, the colour of his skin and his middle name notwithstanding, made that speech in Egypt, seeking like Moses, to cut a way through to Muslims, what he did not mean at all was that justice would prevail.

Only that the Zionists would continue to ride rough shod over the Arabs, come what may. And, if the Muslims acquiesced, the next attack (after Iraq and Afghanistan) would be delayed till it could no longer be delayed.

And even Egypt and Saudi Arabia nodded agreement. Which tells you why the Iranians are such a pest.

But then, they are only Shias, and no real Muslims. Surely the Sunnis will understand, as they have always done.

Netanyahu, yahoo! Have fun.
Cozy up to Manmohan.
You are much loved in Washington.

June 2010

India, America, Israel

The Three Amigos

That both under the erstwhile NDA regime, led by Atal Bihari Vajpai of the right-wing Hindu BJP (1998-2004) and the UPA regime (s) led by Manmohan Singh of the Congress Party (2004-2009, and since) a central feature of India's foreign policy has been to draw closer to both the United States and Israel is not such a hidden feature of India's post-reforms history anymore.

The more than considerate attentiveness to the interests of American corporates of course has been a long-term constant.

What I seek to do here is not so much to detail these histories as to draw a skein related to diverse episodes, one that seems intricately revelatory of a coherent macro policy intent, always latent among the Indian ruling classes but now more than ever in full bloom.

The Bhopal Mass Murder & Indian Collaboration with Carbide:

The details of this are by now too well-known to require iteration. Suffice it to say that on the night of December 3, 1984, lethal quantities of Methyl Isocyanate escaped from the Union Carbide factory, as water entered tank no. 610.

Within hours, some 2500 citizens, most of them poor Muslims, lost their lives.

Since then, a total of 20,000 are estimated to have perished, and hundreds of thousands either maimed, or rendered permanenly disabled.

The only known antidote to the lethal gas, Sodium Thiosulphate, could not be reached the victims for one disingenuous reason or another. Forensic experts, fudged their reports, causing distortions in investigations over a long period.

The Central Bureau of Investigation (CBI) did, however, manage to file a chargesheet against Company officials in 1987. The charges included one under section 304 II of the Penal Code, 'culpable homicide not amounting to murder' punishable by upto ten years in jail, a charge based on prior knowledge of the Company management that lacunae in the safety regulations at the plant, which did not correspond to safety features of a similar Carbide plant in West Virginia, could lead to disaster, and on their refusal to rectify the same despite admonitions and demands made that they do so. Ostensibly, to keep the costs of running the plant in check!

Whatever the other details, all in the public eye now several times over, the point of interest here is how Warren Anderson, the then CEO of UCIL was dealt with, and, secondly, how the highest court in India chose to view the matter.

That Anderson managed to escape the country is common knowledge; but only now do we know how that ignoble escape was facilitated.

And this we know from no less than the then Collector of the city of Bhopal, Moti Singh., from the officer who manned the airport at Bhopal, and the pilot who flew the plane that brought Anderson to Delhi, literally the very day the disaster happened.

Without mincing matters, the honourable Moti Singh has gone on record to say that on the evening of December 4, while Anderson was in local custody, Shri Singh received a call from the Chief Secretary, the highest ranking bureaucrat within the Indian system of government, to the effect that he wished to confer with Singh and the then Superintendent of Police.

At that meeting, Singh and the S.P were directed to release Anderson and to take him to the airport where a plane was waiting to fly him to Delhi.

It turns out that the state-owned plane was made available by the then Chief Minister of Madhya Pradesh, Shri Arjun Singh. Arjun Singh, it may be said, has always foregrounded himself in politics as a staunch secularist, and a diehard opponent of Hindutva communalism. Most of the those killed in Bhopal were Muslims.

Just today, an Arjun Singh acolyte and erstwhile chief minister of Madhya Pradesh, Digvijay Singh, has told the media that Arjun Singh was not to blame for Anderson's great escape. He has pointed a finger at the then central government, led by the late Rajiv Gandhi, and at American 'pressure.' Even as other Congress leaders, such as Satyavrat Chaudhary who was a Legislator in the Madhya Pradesh Assembly have said that it is for Arjun Singh, the then Congress chief minister, to break his silence to the nation.

It is a matter of interest that never in the last quarter century has such a demand been made by anyone,whether in the Congress or the BJP, a clear pointer to the fact that collaboration with American corporate interests cuts across party lines (leaving out the left) and speaks for the ruling class per se.

One Indian media house claims now to have accessed a CIA file on the issue that records that Anderson's exit was authorised by the then central government inorder not to jeopordise American corporate investments in India at a time when such investments were direly needed.

Were one to think of a parallel to the obscene escape of the Carbide CEO from the country and from liability, what comes to mind is the great escape of the whole Bin Laden clan from Texas, hours after the twin towers were hit, all in a plane made available by the Bush family. Indeed, it was the only plane allowed to leave the United States in the wake of 9/11.

Thus, if the Indian rulers obliged the American corporate, the Americans obliged the Saudi oil bigwigs with whom the Bush family had intimate business relations.. Cute, cosy, and consistent with how global capitalism works.

In Delhi, Anderson reportedly had a meeting with the then President of India, Giani Zail Singh. Next anybody knew, Anderson was off to safety in the United States where he has been spotted living a rich and comfy life in a mansion in New York.

Thus, although he remains an absconder-accused, prime one at that, and although an extradition treaty exists between India and the United States, the world has not exactly been turned upside down by any subsequent government in India to seek his return to face trial, nor is the US government likely to send him over. Indeed, recent statements of US spokesmen suggest in no unclear terms that such is farthest from their minds. Even as they also argue that Union Carbide, America, has no liability in the matter, nor Dow Chemicals which cannily took over Union Carbide India Ltd., inorder that further culpability of the UCIL could be snuffed in legalese.

In that endeavour, it now turns out, they also had support from within the government of India, Kamal Nath and Chidambaram, two influential ministers thought to be close to the United States and votaries of market fundamentalism, having forcefully argued against others that

Dow should not be hauled up if investments from American corporates are to be encouraged.

Dow chemicals operations continue in the state of Maharashtra, ruled by the Congress, and in Gujarat, ruled by the BJP, and a ban on the corporate has never been on the table.

Tail Piece: The sordid conspiracy to favour the corporate found its final expression in a ruling of the Supreme Court which held that the principle of vicarious responsibility did not apply in the case, and proceeded to water down the Chargesheet to ' criminal negligence'(Section 304 A) as it quashed the charge of 'culpable homicide not amounting to murder.' This in 1996.

The then Chief Justice subsequently took over as lifetime chairman of the Carbide–funded Bhopal Memorial Hospital Trust, set up under the aegis of the Supreme Court of India. He is not embarrassed.

Thus, after a quarter century of the event, some seven or eight of the management of the then UCIL have been found guilty of 'negligence' and convicted to a maximum of 2 years in prison!

But, not to fret, they are also promptly out on bail.

One other thing: the medical data from the disaster was consistently sought to be suppressed by the Indian Council of Medical Research.

In the meanwhile, thousands of victims in Bhopal still have no redress to sustained medication, some 325 tons of toxic waste remains at and around the site (statement by the current Minister for Environment and Forests, Jairam Ramesh) as the water pipes continue to receive that lethal contamination.

Not to mention the other perfidy; an out of court settlement with the corporate to the measly tune of some 470 million dollars, amounting at last count to some 300 dollars or less per affected victim! A half of the declared victims yet to receive any.

When the Exxon Valdex spilled oil off the coast of Alaska (1989 – five years after the Bhopal disaster), the damages were fixed at one billion dollars. Clearly, bird life in America was of greater value than the 20,000 human beings who died in Bhopal and the many thousands who have been maimed across generations.

And now, when after the BP spill in the gulf of Mexico, Obama seeks to 'kick some ass' and reverse legislation that caps liability in the US at $75 million after the Alaska event under the oil lobby pressure, and to introduce criminal liability provisions, the Indian government is sought to be pressurized to cap Civil Liability for Nuclear Damages through parliamentary legislation at Rs.500 crores.

In other words, were a Chernobyl or a Three Mile Island to happen at a US corporate nuclear plant in India, the damages would be civil only, and about a half of that which was settled for the Bhopal disaster out of court! And, only the 'operator' would be thus liable. Read, the Indian component of the management and not representatives or managers of the supplier company. Not the nuclear Andersons.

In the proposed new Liability Bill, significantly, section 17(b) which asks for 'right to recourse' if a 'nuclear incident has resulted from wilful or gross negligence on the part of the supplier or his employee' is sought now to be dropped under pressure from the American nuclear lobby and government.

The Israeli-Indian State-Hindutva Connect

The total trade between India and Israel in 2001 was $200 million. By now that has grown to $4.1 billion. India is today the world's biggest buyer of Israeli military hardware, to a tune of $9 billion. India is also currently weighing a most-favoured Free Trade Agreement with a country that was during the Nehru era the pariah of the Indian foregn policy establishment. It is thought that close cooperation now exists between Indian spy agencies and the Israeli Mossad, who have been in and out of the country recently.

The most recent evidence of the closeness has come in the form of the statement issued by the Indian foreign office on the Gaza-aid flotilla event. The statement, while deploring violent means to settle the dispute, does not name Israel.

But an even more sinister link has thus far been invisible to the pubic eye – one that concerns a connect between Hindu terrorist organizations and counterparts in Israel.

Between 2002 (the year of the Gujarat carnage) and 2009, a series of bomb blasts took place in

India, curiously all in areas dominated by Muslims:

- 2002: IED found at Bhopal railway station, aimed in all likelihood at Muslims gathering for a Tablighi conclave;

- 2003: bomb blast at Mohammadiya mosque in Parbhani, Maharashtra; and a bomb again found at Bhopal on the last day of a Tablighi meet;
- 2004: blasts at mosques and a Madarasa in Purna, and Jalna in Maharashtra;
- 2006: two Bajrang Dal activists killed in Nanded, Maharashtra, as the bomb they were making exploded;
- blasts at three places in Malegaon, targeting a mosque and graveyard on the occasion of Shab-e-Baraat; 38 killed; Maharashtra;
- 2007: February 18, 68 killed in a double suitcase bomb blast on the Samjhauta Express, a friendship train between India and Pakistan; of those 42 Pakistani nationals;
- in May 16 blast at the Mecca Masjid in Hyderabad city; two Bajrang Dal activists again killed in Kanpur while assembling a bomb;
- October 11: blast at the eight hundred year old Chishti Dargah in Ajmer, Rajasthan;
- 2008: a blast again at Malegaon in Maharashtra, and another at Modasa in Gujarat;
- 2009: two die while carrying a bomb on the eve of the festival of Diwali in Margao, Goa.

In all these cases, the investigating agencies promptly named one Muslim organization or the other as the culprit., hauled up hundreds of young Muslims, and used torture to draw 'confessions.'

Until, that is, thanks to the exemplary and fair-minded efforts of the late Hemant Karkare, investigations revealed the hand of Hindu organizations in the Malegaon blast of 2008, leading to the arrest of Lt.Col. Srikanth Purohit, Dayanand Pandey, and Sadhvi Pragya Singh Thakur.

Karkare's team now began to see that evidence of linkages between this blast and the others surfaced during investigations, such as common source of SIM cards used, common explosive materials and detonative techniques, and so on. A man named Rakesh Dhawre, a counterfeit arms dealer, is discovered to be the link between the Malegaon blast of 2006, of the Purna and Parbhani blasts and the revelatory Malegaon blast of 2008.

Karkare was thus able to implicate several Hindu organizations in the shenanigans, chiefly, Hindu Jagran Manch, Ahinav Bharat, Sanatan Sanstha. ((Since then, in May, 2010, the involvement of two workers of the RSS, Devendra Gupta and Chandrashekhar, in the Ajmer blast has been revealed).

Karkare begins to receive threats to his life, including on the eve of 26/11.

26/11

Three of the best Mumbai police officers, Hemant Karkare, Ashok Kamte, and Vijay Salaskar are gunned down as they are asked to proceed to the Cama hospital, all in the same vehicle, wearing sub-standard bullet-proof jackets that have no protection above the chest as statutorily expected and required.

This while the main terrorist battle-ground has shifted elsewhere.

Ajmal Kasab and his companion terrorist, Ismail are held guilty of shooting the three.

Smelling a rat, and distrusting the official account of their deaths, Kavita Karkare and Vinita Kamle, wives of two of the slain officers, launch their independent investigations.

Vinita Kamle records in her book To The Last Bullet, how in response to persistent Right to Information (RTI) applications she is told that, the three were advised to proceed to Cama hospital on the fateful day by Rakesh Maria, incharge of the control room during the terrorist episode.

Kavita Karkare and Vinita Kamle also find out that Karkare received shots in the neck and along the shoulder, precisely the spots where the bullet-proof vests did not protect him. Somebody had to know that the vests were defective and vulnerable in those areas.

It may be noted that the vests worn by the officers went missing, until under persistent pressure, they were discovered in some garbage bin. All were found defective.

During the Ajmal Kasab trial, Judge Tahaliyani asks pointedly of the Mumbai police as to what happened to the two bullets which passed through Karkare's body?

Not having the fatal bullets, the judge asked, how do we know whose gun killed Karkare? A speculation that continues to rankle.

Now, here is what: the chargesheet filed by the Maharashtra ATS detailed links between Abhinav Bharat and right-wing Jewish organizations in Israel, and that this Hindu organization had been soliciting the approval of those Jewish organizations for its terrorist work.

Hardnews, June 2010 issue, notes in its cover story:

> Israeli covert outfits have been accused even by Americans for triggering off blasts in Pakistan and Afghanistan. Those allegations found expression even in one of the big Israeli newspapers, Ha'aretz: 'the purpose and intent of these blasts, as perfected by agent provocateurs in different theatres of violence, is to deepen the divide between communities, create a sense of anarchy and revenge, and provide retaliation. Hindu terror groups since 2002 have also followed the same model.'

That, however, Hindu terrorist groups in India have had such close contact with Israeli counterparts, that the activities of these groups have been sought to be kept under wraps or to be deflected to the usual suspects, or that it was Rakesh Maria who advised Karkare to go to Cama Hospital, Karkare who had boldly refuted the pavlovian instinct to blame HUJI and SIMI and other Muslim groups for the blast at Malegaon, and then found other evidences of Hindu terrorist involvements in the preceding blasts, that this spelt a highly undesirable turn of events for a particular version of 'nationalism' in India, one closely analogous to a Zionist variety, these things suggest that the Indian embrace of Israel has been far tighter than anyone speculated. As well as collaboration on the ground.

Indeed, reading S.M.Mushrif, *Who Killed Karkare?*, Delhi, 2009, and Vinita Kamle's *To the Last Bullet*, keeping in mind the trenchant observation of the Judge (who has sentenced the terrorist Ajmal Kasab just the other day) on the death of Karkare, recalling how the police fiasco of 26/11 was strenuously sought to be pasted on the senior police officer, Hasan Gafoor rather than on Rakesh Maria and others, and noting what the Israeli newspaper, Ha'aretz has commented without fanfare on the Hindu/Jewish collaboration in terrorism, the favour routinely shown to Israel should hardly come as any surprise.

Conclusion

It therefore should not seem an excessive inference that the three amigos are indeed joined at various hips together – in a general attitude to seek dominance and privilege, in taking the military route to that dominance, in a barely concealed espousal of 'nationalism' as a chauvinist/racialist idea at bottom, in designating a common enemy, and in collaborating in anti-terrorist mechanisms that include a Hindu/Jewish axis as well, and of a terrorist kind, and as the Anderson case previously and the nuclear-cap issue now suggests, in protecting each other's tactical and material assets and interests every which way.

All that informed and propelled by the interests of market-fundamentalist corporates in a deadly package to fend off the rest of the world, especially the Muslim world (notice India's continued reluctance to join the Iran/Pakistan Gas pipeline project, one that potentially bears enormous dividends to the Indian consumer at low cost) and a still-one-party-socialist China.

The dime-a-dozen military exercises among forces, including the navies and the airforces, of the three countries are thus meant to convey to the world that the three amigos intend to encircle the oceans, and aid and abet one another in ground warfare. The Inter-Operability draft agreements are on the table, whereby such forces must come to each other's aid in wars that will be designated common wars, and indeed carry identical uniforms and weapons for facilitating such warfare, besides helping American arms manufacturers to make yet more killings.

Such amigos clearly must be seen to be bad news.

It will remain to be seen how, public opinion in the three countries shapes in the near future. And how that opinion is marshaled by political forces that both see the tri-junctional coordinates shaping up, and recognize the dangers that lurk therein for the common good.

June 2010

India's Globalised 'Godmen'

Placebos for the Rich and Famous

Our vote is not for sufferance,
Denial, drudgery, pain;
We pack pleasure for the body,
And delusion for the brain.
(Badri Raina, 'Moon, Maharishi, Maharaji,' *Modest Proposal & Other Rhymes for the Times*, Sahmat, New Delhi, 2000, p.110.)

Long before the Washington Consensus, and long before the empire began to write back, Indian globalization was first and truly effected by India's 'godmen.'

The writing back, indeed, was preceded by the preaching back. Where, however, Swami Vivekananda was a freak one-timer in the Chicago conference of world religions in 1892, the efflorescence has been a recent phenomenon, coterminous, significantly, with the leaps made by a 'liberated' world economy.

Quite rightly has Arundhati Roy said that two locks were opened by the Indian ruling elites at one and the same time – the lock to the market, and the lock to the Babri mosque, yielding together that deadly mix of religious and developmental totalitarianism which has since informed the life of the nation as a dominant theme.

And mutually reinforcing in a fatal sort of way.

II

The subject came up on a TV talk show debate just the other night, and what follows may be read as a gloss occasioned by the coordinates that emerged. Indeed as regurgitations of cogitations that this scribe has experienced for a good many year (the epigraph, which comes from a nasty written more than two decades ago, being testimony).

Broadly, two sharply articulated positions defined that debate, with the sedate and subtle historian, Ramchandra Guha on one side, and the feisty advocate, Rani Jethmalani on the other.

Guha made the point that since most of India's frontline 'godmen' seemed always to be chasing money and the media, they could hardly be regarded exemplars of the spiritual life. This in stark contrast to a Gandhi who 'democratized' spirituality, first by questioning his own fallibilities and then by sharing the totality of experiences with the hoi polloi. Or, a Raman Maharishi who never stirred from his abode in south India. And, indeed, fed his mongrels even as he ate himself, he might have added.

Jethmalani, a highly successful scion of the legal fraternity, countered robustly to say that there was nothing wrong with so doing. It was her grateful view that these gurus of India were infact bringing succour and release for a whole lot of people who are otherwise too caught up in the deracinated rough and tumble of activity. Yoga and meditation were the way to bring fraught individuals in touch with their inner lives.

III

Now in recent years, 'godman' after canny 'godman' has been found to be complicit in some shenanigan or the other – land grab, hawala transactions (i.e. the illicit and clandestine transfer of unaccounted wealth from place to place), rape, sex orgies, and murder – all exposed by the very media, sections of which never tire of lauding their contributions to the 'national image' as a haven of spirituality.

But there are a few currently who remain as yet clean to the visible public eye, although questions have been raised about dubious medical and labour practices of one, and shots heard recently at a conclave addressed by the other. Both hugely endowed with all that money may do, including exclusive TV channels for propagation.

So why then do the high and mighty continue to patronize these sorts of 'godmen' whose so-called spiritual splutterings never seem to amount to anything more than platitudinous common sense (Guha), often readily available at the street corner paan shop?

I would like to suggest that the answer lies in the epigraph to this piece.

A whole new class of Indians spawned by the berserk possibilities of market fundamentalism know two things: one, that their ancestors never had it 'so good,' and, two, that come what may, the last thing they wish to happen is to lose what they have accumulated, and may continue to accumulate.

Any spirituality, therefore, that enjoins turning away from money-making and consumerism is passé and infra dig. So that the time-honoured pieties of renunciation (tyag) and the simple life centred around the common good and search for truth beyond possessions are decrepitly medieval. Utterly unsuited to a class whose burden now is to see India at the top of the comity of puissant nations.

More heinously, such a course seems a sinister device to reject capitalism and a dirty trick to bring back socialist ideas.

The agenda of this class, thus, is to see that capitalism goes hand-in-hand with painless placebos, that not only bring momentary relief but recharge entrepreneurial energies for further leaps in profit-making.

And the first of the 'godmen' to understand this agenda to perfection was Maharishi Mahesh Yogi who fathered Transcendental Meditation world-wide. It was his explicit boast that fifteen minutes of TM at work place could not only steady the nerve and stem the blood pressure, but, in so doing, make enhanced leaps in productivity possible. Maximum result at minimum inconvenience – never a better corporate commercial than that.

So, there you had it – you could eat the cake and have it too.

Just as any clever movie-maker fashions his cinema to articulate the desired underside of things, the classy Yogi sets out to become a 'spiritual' collaborator in the compulsive drive to the 'good life.'

IV

None of this can happen if the 'godman' is seen to be a 'beggarly' derelict himself.

In the new world that he seeks to skim, it is imperative that all the accoutrement appropriate to the zeitgeist are his in the first place, ranging from palatial ashrams, to limousines, to fabulous and famous hangers-on, to in-favour politicians, to private jets.

For him these are tools that substitute the old relic, hairshirt, and frankincense.

And his unique selling point has to be, as the epigraph claims, that he brings spirituality not as painful questioning of what is, or of frustrating skepticism towards the preferred social and economic environment of his clientale, but, indeed, as an enhancement of the pleasure principle.

And inorder that he sell, he must primarily be seen to be master of that principle himself. Hey, you can't give what you do not have.

No wonder then that you do not see such 'godmen' trudging among the riff raff of the nation, or taking on injustices, or lining up on the side of equity, or bringing hope and ministry to the wretched of the earth.

Thus a spirituality that is adorned with diamonds and plaited with gold can ill afford to be bogged down in ethical concerns, except as vacuous and abstract gurgitations, uttered with tact and a sense of timing. Or upon catching an isolated raised eyebrow in the audience on any given day.

The whole point and purpose of this variety of 'spiritual' intervention is to bolster and justify the 'good life', and, all-importantly, to neutralize and hush the least stirring of the conscience and of guilt.

Inorder to keep its hold on the Elect, it needs always to appear resplendent in a canny mix of the flowing beard, the loosely worn robe, the ever-smiling visage, the arty enunciation of clichés, and always always next to visuals that betoken wealth and intimations of hidden pleasures.

Truly, the art not just of living, but of living to the hilt.

It is thus that a deadly mix of the Freudian and the Lockean inform this 'spiritual' enterprise, inviting the subject in mystifying suggestiveness to look inward to the navel but seated in surroundings that ravish the physical eye, item after opulent item.

What more could the rich and famous ask for?

As for all the rest, their fate it is to labour to keep the opulence in place. Lucky rabble they.

V

For a contrast now, consider this other saffron-clad Arya Samaji mendicant, name of Swani Agnivesh.

On a state television channel he comperes a weekly interactive programme, titled *Vichaar Manthan* (literally, 'Churning Thoughts').

Invariably his audiences are drawn from people readily available on any street, government school, slum NGO, relegated women, minorities, low-castes and suchlike, with a noted authority or two sitting among their midst.

And here is his route to the spiritual life:

- what can we do collectively to redress horrendous social and systemic wrongs, be it sanitation, slum schooling, local health and nutritive care, honour killings and other caste oppressions, inter-communal mayhems, corruption in offices, in politics, among teachers, contractors, shopkeepers, police personnel, godmen, and so on?
- what mechanisms of redressal does the present system make available to the ordinary citizen, be it RTI or any other? How can we educate ourselves and others to use them?
- what new laws, legislations should we ask for?
- what pernicious influences does a money-driven and complicit media perpetrate? What kinds of advertisements bring shame to the ordinary Indian?
- Who makes the money?
- what can be done about children in labour, anaemic lactating mothers, goons on the street whose lack of employment encourages crime against others?
- can injustices cohabit with a religious life? Can any religion be true if it contravenes our fundamental humanity?

And so on. These but some that I readily recall from his programmings.

Therefore, do not be surprised that the Rani Jethmalanis of India would not see Swami Agnivesh as a 'godman' one bit, but indeed something of an irritating, corrupted and radical rabble rouser – mendicant in himself and inviting to a mendicant life. And suspiciously partial to the left. Could it get worse?

What is a 'godman' who dwells perpetually on the externals, and miserable ones at that, and never rolls his eye upward to the 'transcendant' truths?

Nothing more, indeed, than a proletarian Jesus or a troublesome Gandhi.

Would you marry into a family that has no BMW? No. And if you did, it would be your problem if you lost your club membership.

Would you enter a corporate house that offered you less than X plus plus plus? Forget it; what would your peers think?

Would you be seen next to a 'godman' who rode a bicycle? For god's sake, you must have lost your so-spiritual beans.

June 2010

Capital's Surge, Custom's Dike

India's Martyrs to Social Change

Old orders do indeed change, but 'good customs' continue to corrupt and bloody India.

Think of it this way: those young Indians who seek to overthrow capitalism bear the full brunt of the state and social stake-holders in the culture of accumulation and acquisition, down to the least of the kulak farmer in Haryana, Punjab, Rajasthan, Western Uttar Pradesh where 'honour' killings have recently spurted like so many ruptured aortas.

Those other young men and women who merely wish to express a stake in their own private lives (aspirations inseparable from capitalist social development, you would think) equally bear the brunt of the practitioners of capitalism, but this time in order to keep in place the 'good customs' of patriarchy, paternalism, and property control, even as such practitioners embrace the newest of technologies to maximize output and profit.

This, in nutshell, is what segments of 'modern' India are witness to today.

There are killings that draw instant elite revulsion (like those that the Maoists or the terrorists commit), and there are killings which draw instant social approval (like those committed by the votaries of family and community 'honour.')

Remarkably, where one set of killings is ostensibly directed at undermining capitalist political economy (the Maoists), the other set of resistors who are now being butchered in the name of 'honour' seek merely to assert the social logic of capitalism, namely the will to affined person-to-person relations and unfettered sexual consent and freedom.

Thus, the lords of custom wish the state to bloodthirstily kill the Maoists, since economically they are one with the state in wishing to further capitalist modes of production and the new forces of production that enhance that mode, and they affect the other sets of killings with conviction in order that capitalism does not extend to the subversion of traditional forms of social control, even as the state and the political apparatus that runs it dither and demur, shaking their heads at the feudal backlash but too chary and complicit to give it battle.

With respect to the Maoists, therefore, the 'honour' killers express vociferous adherence to the Constitution of India as by law established. But with respect to the killings they order, encourage, or bolster with open approbation, they call the same Constitution an ass. And, remarkably, many party-political stalwarts who get elected, thanks in part to bulk sectional votes, and then swear to uphold the Constitution and the laws nod assent to the wisdom of the ages and to community customs that keep women and male mavericks in place.

So much of the post-Independent life of Republican India has had this contradiction at its infected and schitzoid heart.

Thus, look around and you will find among the managers of capitalist democracy and the constitutional state more than a few who still think of the custom of child marriage as a 'good custom,' or who empathise inwardly with those outspoken custodians of the 'moral' health of the nation who assert, often with fearless violence, that widows ought not to remarry, and are best stashed away in Vrindavan with their heads shaven clean. Not to speak of placing adverts in national dailies to seek brides or grooms for their wards within the same caste and religion. Or enjoining dress codes for women in colleges and in the life of the nation generally, or designating places (the offshoots of a market economy, like pubs etc.,) where they had best not be seen. Not to speak of gay rights and so on, perish the thought.

Remember that the BJP, always in close embrace with market-fundamentalism, and tipped as the 'legitimate' political alternative to the Congress, thinks nothing of asserting that the Constitution and the laws do not apply to the disputed Ayodhya imbroglio; only the customary emotion and will of the Hindus (read the Brahminical classes) does.

In all cases, 'morality' in India has had but one single reference, from the most ancient of times: sexual morality, and that of women only. Men have always had fun, indeed, none more than many gods and deities in the official Hindu pantheon. None of those other matters to which the evolved capitalist world attaches moral significance have ever mattered here – such as lying, cheating, corruption in office, inhuman disregard of other Indians who may be poor, low-caste, victimized on one count or another, especially if they happen to be Muslim. No Indian of any standing ever apologises for such misdemeanours. For crimes they never are.

II

There exists much scholarship that bemoans the historical fact that in India, unlike in Britain and Europe, 'modernity' did not evolve from prolonged social contestations, although prior to the colonial period, such contestations were not unknown, if ultimately unsuccessful in bringing about any major, country-wide, or long-lasting social transformation. Never an easy prospect when one keeps in mind the quite unparalleled diversity of social, linguistic, ethnic and religious identities in India and local histories barely assimilated into any unifying, 'nationalist' narratives till the last decades of the fight against colonialism.

The proto-bourgeois challenge to British and other colonialisms chose largely to evade fighting on two fronts. Far from subverting feudal forms of life, in social practices and belief systems, indeed even in land relations, the 'national' vanguard opted to incorporate feudal leaderships into the fight against colonialism. Notable exceptions to this pattern belonged not to the north of India from where largely the leadership of the Congress party was drawn, but in the southern states and in Maharashtra. Reason perhaps why no 'honour' killings have been reported from those parts of India.

Interestingly, in recent decades a new school of social thought has emerged in Indian academe, and in some think- tank organizations (such as the Centre for Developing Societies, thought to be closely allied to some American social science research organizations and funding institutions) which have sought to offer challenge to the sort of liberal/positivist critique of feudalisms as stated in the previous paragraph.

Clinical sociologists and ethnographers such as Ashish Nandy, for example, and several of his acolytes have sought to underscore the positive features of traditions, worthy of being integrated into a humane capitalism as guarantors of social depth and stability against the atomist individualism that capitalism spawns.

Some have argued for amendments to the Hindu Marriage Act so as to incorporate the demand of the 'honour' killers that marriages within the same *gotra* (village clan descended from some common mythological ancestor) be proscribed, regardless of the absence of any biological nearness of the parties in question.

The question of course must be as to where one draws the line on traditional forms of social living. And whether capitalist 'development,' can either ever be 'humane' or permit some designated forms of the old ways of community living to sustain themselves.

It is within this matrix of historical debate that 'honour' killings in India's badlands take place. Remarkably, the state of Haryana, one of the worst affected, ranks number two in terms of per capita income, and somewhere near the bottom in terms of gender ratio, with not more than some 700 or so women for every 1000 men.

Capitalism, thus, seems only to reinforce social atrophy in regions where no progressive social movements of any kind have been to the fore. Indeed, high growth rates and individual incomes seem, if anything, to reinforce patriarchy in ways more brutal than before. Even among village *panchayat*s where women have been accorded close to 50% representation, men have found ways to subjugate to surrogate control women *sarpanche*s (Heads of *panchayats*) either simply through brute domestication, or some 'authorized' traditional appeal to male prerogatives in running public affairs. It is not surprising, thus, that female foeticide is most rampant precisely in those parts of India where incomes and enterprises have tended to record highs.

III

It can then be seen that unregulated liasons between young men and women in disregard of the customary order of things (caste affiliation, parental authority, family property holdings) are seen as boding fatal threats of disintegration.

Yet, in my view, the brutalities and murders vented on these young Indians are the less significant part of contemporary history in these regions.

Greater significance ought to attach to the scale and spread of the resistance on offer.

Having been sent to school, and often to college, and then allowed to engage in gainful employment, often beyond the reach of the patriarchs, it is as though these young people now wish to say that they understand their own interests best. And to say that as 'citizens' rather than members of this gotra or that, this caste or that, they are in accord with provisions of the Constitution of the Republic which furnishes to them the right to life with dignity and free choice.

Given the frequency with which cases of such resistance now pour into the public view, it is to be much doubted that the dykes of custom will hold back for much longer the surge of capitalist individualism, since Indian capitalism seems only set to go forward rather than usher in some radical reconstruction.

This seems particularly so now that the Indian judicial system has come forward to demand of the state knowledge of what it is doing to stop and punish actions that have no sanction in the laws or in the Constitution. The *khap panchayats*' boast that come what may they will remain the operative law in matters of marital or sexual choice between consenting adults may soon run out ot steam, since no politician, however he may share the social predilections of the lords of custom, can overtly accept the view that custom is above the law and the Constitution so long as he chooses to remain in authorized politics where the money is.

Increasingly also, the sternness of the courts finds reflection in the exertions of civil society organizations, chiefly of women but supported by liberal sections among men, to stand upto the wild-western diktats of the *khap* overlords. Without question also, investigative agencies whose members are often drawn from the same whoof and warf as the *khap* communities, will not but find themselves obliged increasingly to implement the laws in proportion to the determination that the state and civil society show in meeting the brigandry of the *khap* outlaws.

It is for that reason that the young men and women who have thus far been murdered, even in the capital city of Delhi, may go down as martyrs who precipitated one of the most far-reaching and progressive transformations in the social life of India's north and north-west.

As the days go by, we may see more numbers of India's Bazarovs to transgress beyond intellectual combat with the older generation of men, and take the sphere of active revolt fast forward.

We say, however rotten capitalism be, better its libertarian preferences than what Marx once eloquently captioned the 'muck of ages.'

Better that India have more numbers of 'citizens,' however isolated and deracinated, than mere appendages of ruthless old identities.

June 2010

Food or Nutrition?

Life or Life-in-Death?

Do you remember that day in 1836 when a desperately hungry twelve year old English orphan 'asked for more'?

Yes, Oliver Twist I mean.

Neither the honourable Board of the Poorhouse nor indeed the British Crown had ever before encountered a more perfidious enormity than an orphan asking, actually asking, for more 'food' than the three stipulated bowls of watery thin gruel.

Like a bolt of rebellious lightning the word spread. The danger was atonce recognized to be of gargantuan proportions, leading to the sagacious decision to palm off the orphan to work for an undertaker. From whose likely clutches only Providence intervened to save the famished child.

That recalcitrant history seems now to be repeating itself in India, an erstwhile colony who was to learn great and good lessons from the canny practices of the colonizer, chiefly of how to keep the rabble just this side both of life and death. For dying, they bring disrepute to the realm, and living a human existence they threaten its continuance. But being barely alive, they cast that vote, come hustings, and return to beg for more.

As the Indian government contemplates a Right-to-Food Act, whereby some rice and/or wheat might be given to those below the 'poverty line' (which, in diverse computations by the 'experts' ranges from some 27% of Indians to some 77%) at nominal rates, the hungry and those that speak for them are actually asking to be given nutrition as well!

Just how ungrateful can you be!

II

Of the 88 countries on the Global Hunger Index, the mighty Republic of India ranks at 66, with a child malnutrition record worse than that of sub-Saharan Africa.

On the Human Development Index, at 134 (from some 188), below Laos and Bhutan. And in terms of the absolute numbers of the world's poor, absolutely at the top!

But there is the other India, that of the billionaires (49 dollar ones according to Forbes) and the many millionaires on way to becoming billionaires as well.

So who does the state work for?

Where the latter India looms over the G 20 and suchlike with the promise and the delicious threat of greatness, the former, refusing to see the point, open their ever-hungry mouths and bid fare to swallow what greatness is destined to the Republic.

Were you a 'patriotic' Indian, what would you do or say? Precisely what the state is saying: for god's sake, do not hold the nation back from its evolving superpowerdom.

When History's chips are counted, pray who counts the destitute?

Now, according again to the 'experts' it would take India between some 50,000 and 80,000 crore rupees to make nutrition available to its destitute, as opposed merely to rice and wheat (and that if the scheme were to be universalized rather than limited to some arbitrary numbers of the designated poor). As the inimitable Sainath has just shown, this would amount to about a sixth of the tax write-offs effected in favour of the rich in this year's budget alone!

Or just about equal to the moneys purported to be spent in preparing for the Commonwealth games!

The point, however, is this: how conscionable would it be to make such a nutritious food subsidy available to poor Indians when the same money might be used more glamorously to adorn some further high-end 'developmental' schemes matching the best in the 'first world' to which the Republic is poised to belong, at least some ten or fifteen percent of it?

Do not the 'best' economists both at home and in the wide world tell us that the destitute must be taught to stand on their own feet, and aspire, in the celebrated American fashion to outdo the fortunate in time?

For, remember, the rich are the fortunate; they are not the beneficiaries of state policies. Everybody knows how the state in fact bleeds, especially at election times, for the less fortunate. But then, even the mightiest of states has been known to be helpless in the teeth of fortune. The lady who turns that wheel is after all a lady, and fickle at the best of times.

III

The wretched thing, though, is that this necessary evil that legitimates the state, the thing called democracy, will not let the harbingers of greatness go entirely their billionaire way.

Indeed, the demos argues now for much more than nutrition as well; they actually seek clean drinking water, guaranteed and good health care, assured entry into schools, and a right to inhabit the millions of houses they build with their labour. Even the right to gainful employment.

And worse still, there are those now, throughout the realm, who seem foolishly willing to die for what they call their 'rights' as enshrined in that troublesome book called the Constitution.

Some go so far as to say that the book itself requires to be changed, and a new one brought in, so that the causes of hunger and destitution, and of the humongous cleavages between the haves and the have-notes are addressed in earnest. For a start, they insist that the many land-ceiling Acts enacted by parliament and the legislatures decades ago be actually implemented on the ground. Something that would lead to the horrendous consequence of 'leveling' social lives in the hinterland, and robbing the ordained owners of millions of acres of their birth-right to lord it over the landless millions.

That would also lead to a spread of contentment among the demos, rendering India's police and para-military forces jobless in the main, and the arms dealers devoid of lucrative trade. Perish the prospect, we say. Is India to be a Republic in deed as well? Who would have thought of it!

IV

Six decades of democracy has brought this nation to a point where all Indians think they are equal citizens of the realm, and thus have a right to all that the realm has to offer, especially as the millionaires and the billionaires seem to work far less than the sancullotes for a living. They harbour the dangerous illusion that they are meant to be made equal not just politically but economically and socially as well. So much for the flights of reason.

The state is told that the fatcat corporates who in point of fact run it cannot be allowed to go and rape forests and water resources just any which way they see profit. And for some wonky reason, there are those among the judges of the land who seem to think so too, although a braveheart or two just yet. But if the contagion spreads, there may be more.

Imagine then the prospect for the nation if all the Olivers of the land were to be actually accorded not just food enough to survive another day, but nutrition to become hearty and healthy.

A day might come when not all the police and para-military forces, not even the celebrated army, could hold those violent and demented hordes of the demos in check. Indeed, it is thus proved that the greatest harm to the Republic could come from that one source, namely a happy and healthy citizenry.

The wisdom of the ages thus dictates that the poor be fed – if only to buy some credit with the gods – but just this side of good health.

Any charity that overreaches itself cannot but damage its own purposes.

July 2010

GDP vs GDP

The Story of Indian 'Development'

O Brave New India that hath such Creatures in it.

Clap clap, and clap again.

India's GDP is set to grow at 9.4%, sayeth the oracle of the World Bank.

So, where is the high table, and why aren't we on it yet? And what is a mere G-20; it is the permanent membership of the Round Table we seek and deserve. Our knights now shine too resplendentally, O Arthur-Sam. So, move over, you defunct old inheritors of defunct old glory. Our charge now resistless indeed.

Which is perhaps why the evil ones conspire to stymie that charge with ill-intended facts and figures. Familiar colonial perfidy alive and well still, epicentred where else but in that decrepit Oxford.

They now unleash another GDP to undermine our Icarian flight, namely, Gross Destitute People.

Some busybody Director of the Oxford Poverty and Human Development Initiative brings out a Report on world poverty based on Multi-Dimensional Indices, calculated wickedly to show us down.

And it would have us believe that actually, in point of fact, as they say in Oxford, there are an aggregate of more poor people in just eight Indian states than in all of Africa's poorest 26 countries; roughly, more than some 410 million Indians. That them Africans there have better access to 'good cooking fuel,' 'schooling,' 'electricity,' 'nutrition,' 'sanitation,' and so on than eight of our resource-rich states! Perish the perfidy.

And, as if to mock our GDP I thesis, they also rub in the view that 'low per capita GDP income doesn't necessarily mean high poverty.'

Clearly, waka waka Shakira, whom Oxford loves, brand ambassador for the rainbow nation down south in Africa, must have something to do with this inspired computation. We love Shakira too (or do we?) but to say that 26 of the poorest African nations are less poor than Uttar Pradesh, Bihar, West Bengal, Madhya Pradesh, Orissa, Jharkhand, and Chhattisgarh – well who else but the knowledgeable would believe such calumny?

And who cares for the knowledgeable? Certainly not our corporate channels and print media who spread the word on India's GDP of the first order, namely, Gross Domestic Product. Gross indeed.

As to GDP II, did you tell us something we did not know? And is it to be thought that any nation can increase GDP I without simultaneously increasing GDP II as well? Dammit, somebody has got to pay the price for the frontline few to conquer the world.

Progress – it poureth like ungentle torrents from heaven (as it is doing now in India's showpiece capital); and when it does, is it your view that roads, shanties, bridges, trees, electric poles and mobile towers, even neighbourhoods next to where the Primum Mobile lives will not, or should not, be washed away? Or that only a few should lose their lives? Strange notion of progress you must have indeed.

II

Don't think for a moment we are not wise to you and your anti-national shenanigans.

You are of the tribe who filed that writ in the Supreme Court of India, challenging the validity of Section 2 of the Constitution (42nd amendment) by virtue of which the word 'socialist' was inserted in the Preamble of the Indian Constitution.

And who also challenged Section 6 of the Representation of People's Act, 1989, which makes it incumbent on every political party registered in India to pledge allegiance to the socialist ideal, failing which such a party can be deregistered.

So you would blow the whistle on us, would you? You would like to tell the world how we are not a Democracy but a Hypocrisy. As if the world does not know.

You think good governance entails an honest adherence to what we profess rather than what we do. Alas, how Kautilya and Confucious must turn in their realpolitik graves at the enormity of your naivete.

Know then that good governance means first and foremost feeding words to the 410 million, with an odd 'gurantee scheme' thrown in, and wealth to the handful whose accumulations alone may take India to the Round Table. Elementary, my dear nincompoop, who it seems takes too much to heart what ablutions we make to the 'socialist' ideal when them votes are needed.

Just as we pay homage to the Father of the Nation, that naked fakir, when all else fails to mollify the mob. Returning to designer lifestyles the minute the mayhem dies down.

As to those 26 African nations; have you no concern for Africa where, after all Bapu Gandhi first blew the whistle? How is Africa to seem to move forward if we do not step back that little bit? And what is 410 million but precisely 'that little bit'?

Your problem is that you dig for dirt because you are at bottom a leveler. And you think God truly created all of us as equals with them unalienable rights etc., Not true. Read any of our Hindu scriptures and you will know otherwise. Why else would we fall into unreconcilable castes and gotras we ask you? And not a one of those 410 human beings, we tell you, may seek parity with a Garuda, a Ganesha, or a Hanuman, although not even human those. Such is the genius of mystery. Such are the things between heaven and earth that your philosophy will never understand. Your problem entirely.

When in the history of our colonial slavery did Oxford bode any good to us? So, why should it now?

It made us slaves then, and it sheds crocodile tears at the slavery we have made for ourselves as free republicans. Surely, a perfidious second colonization is being forged, using, cunningly, the very tools we supply. To Oxford we thus say, leave us be; our poor are our own, and they understand us better than you do. So do not stir the pot, which is already on the boil anyway. What is a nation where everybody is fed the same ration? A spectacle of dead uniformity from whence no great deeds can emerge. Know that it is *difference*, as the philosopher has taught us, that lends meaning to us severally. Sameness of well being is a mere recipe for sloth and slouching. It is hunger in the extreme that seeks new recipes and transforms the cuisine. Worry thou about quality, not about quantity. And learn for god's sake that Indian 'socialism' is different, pretty much now like the Chinese, and finds directions to glory through indirections of policy. Too much for Oxford to understand.

Which is not to say that we will not send our children to Oxford if Oxford beckons.

July 2010

The Nation at Stake

As the skeletons tumble in droves out of the house of horrors in Gujarat, right-wing Hindutva forces which now openly include the 'main opposition Party' in parliament, the BJP, is up in arms at what it suits them to call a Congress-inspired attack on 'patriotic Indians.'

As per revelations thus far available from the investigations, ordered not by the Congress Party, or the government of the day, but by the Supreme Court of India, these 'patriotic Indians' include business bigwigs, extortionists, extra-judicial killers among the highest echelons of the Gujarat police, and no less than the Minister of State for Home Affairs of Guajrat (read Interior Ministry), now arrested, and under questioning in custody.

Among the documents of the Central Bureau of Investigations (CBI) is a poser (Annexure C) as to the accountability, to use the most parliamentary of terms, of the Chief Minister and Home Minister, one Narendra Modi, since all transfer files of senior Indian Police Service and State Service officers go to him per protocol for decision.

The question: did he know why these officers were being either removed or relocated while the extra-judicial killings were underway? Who all might he have been in steady communication with during the days and hours when some 21 citizens were liquidated, all accused of having 'provenly' connived, don't you know, to kill Modi, the saviour of Hindutva from the 'Islamist' onslaught, and the heroic emblem of the idea of 'Natonalism'?

Time will tell, it seems sooner than later.

But here is the point: of all the coercively homogenizing discourses through human history – male prowess, racial superiority, colonial 'civilizing mission,' the bounties of Imperialist expansion – it is 'nationalism' that seems to have won the day. Globalisation notwithstanding.

Nothing suggests this more dangerously or despicably than even the parliamentary BJP's a priori refusal to accept that crimes, and revolting ones at that, have been committed in Gujarat, or that even the Supreme Court may be granted the leave to investigate into those crimes through the agencies it designates to do so, in this case the CBI.

Another matter altogether that the same Supreme Court and the CBI may be accorded praise and approval when things go or have gone the 'nationalist's' way – as, for example, in Gujarat itself when the government there was absolved by an enquiry of any hand in the murder of Modi's Cabinet colleague and close aid, the late Haren Pandya. Notwithstanding the firm and publicly expressed assertion of Pandya's father that Modi had him murdered on suspicion of having leaked information about a meeting that was held by Modi on February 27, 2002, in which directions were given to the police to let Hindus express their vendetta against the death-by-burning of Hindu karsevaks (helpers in a religious undertaking) in a train compartment at the Godhra station on their return from the admirable 'nationalist' task of having demolished the Babri mosque.

Or, for that matter, for removing the charge of 'conspiracy' against the names of L.K. Advani and six BJP and other Hindutva stalwarts who were gloatingly present while the mosque was being demolished. And partaking of sweet meats and cheerful hugs when the deed was done.

Then too, the decision to demolish the mosque had been taken at a secret meeting at the house of the VHP (Vishwa Hindu Parishad) leader from Uttar Pradesh, Vinay Katiyar.

So if the same CBI brought such succour to Advani while he was Deputy Prime Minister and Home Minister rolled into one, the CBI was not to be accused of bias or wrongdoing.

You see, the 'nationalists' never ever do any wrong, so where is the question.

Thus if the redoubtable RSS is now under the scanner in relation to the many acts of terror committed by Hindutva terrorists, this can only be seen as yet another instance of a conspiracy to malign the pre-eminent 'nationalist' organization of Bharat.

Declare yourself a 'patriot,' then berate the enemies of the nation. Still a going concern here in India.

II

Speaking of 'nationalism' there is of course a secular version as well. This devolves at the moment chiefly around the flashy and extravagant enterprise underway to prepare, 'develop', indeed bedeck the capital city of Delhi for the forthcoming Commonwealth Games.

To date, according to available information, this enterprise has cost the taxpayer some 40,000 crore rupees (and 42 labouring lives) – all in the name of flaunting India to the world as a superpower-in-the-making. It is also sometime said of course that sport is also a part of the enterprise.

Something similar had happened in 1982 when the Asian games were hosted by India.

Remarkably, to this day, however, this country of a billion and more people figure usually only towards the bottom of any international sporting competition result. A reason perhaps why Cricket remains at the focus of the popular Indian imagination.

Then of course, there is the silent cause why these jamborees are indulged – whatever infrastructural development happens during such preparations all go to facilitate rampantly colossal money-making by builders, bureaucrats, politicians – all this only this day brought out in a report by the Central Vigilance Commission. Among other things, medical and allied infrastructural contracts have gone to two companies, one certainly, and in all likelihood, both with blacklisted records as businesses, and equipments bought in some cases at seven times the declared costs of manufacturers.

As TV channel debates rage on the issue, we will ofcourse wait to see how things turn out. Especially since even some Ministers of the government of Delhi have confessed that stadia and other facilities are far from completion with the games only some fifty days away.

But, try as you might, logic, data, empirical evidence both of under-preparation and wrongdoing that you might furnish to the world, all is a waste against the 'nationalist' voice, which holds you culpable of wishing the nation and its pride ill by so grumbling about either the ill-advised decision to hold the games, or the bribes that were parceled out to the sports federations of various Commonwealth countries to vote for India as host, or the humongous corruption in evidence as 'development' works are carried out.

Not to speak of more basic principles.

Those basic principles were relentlessly underscored by the one and only Mani Shankar Aiyar when he was the Sports Minister in the government of India some years ago. No surprise that he was asked to give over the portfolio, something he gladly did.

Among other things, Aiyar had sought to raise the question whether investments in sports should be directed at building extravagant showpieces in metropolitan centres, or in hosting mega events calculated to build the 'image of India,' or in finding, nurturing, training and exponentially expanding talent countrywide, so that over the long-term India could foster a culture of sports from the grassroots upwards, and so that Indian sports people could also figure among medal winners at international games. Essential to Aiyar's conception was also freeing Indian sports, perish the thought, of the mortal embrace of non-sporting busy-bodies among politicians, corporate honchos, and of bureaucratic controls, all of which have over the decades effectively reduced sportsmen and sportswomen to slavery at the hands of authoritarian bosses accountable to no one but themselves, and handing over the job of fostering talent and games to reputed sports professionals.

Incidentally, Aiyar was also then the Minister incharge of Panchayati Raj, making arguments and efforts there as well to make the devolution of developmental decisions to the grassroots Panchayats and Gram Sabhas (village communities) an effective strategy of rendering democracy real and egalitarian, both for purposes of carrying investment and decision-making to the hinterland where it is most needed, and for meeting disaffection of the Maoist kind on a lasting basis by implementing in letter and spirit various existent laws (the Forest Rights Act, the PESA and so on) which were meant indeed to restore to the most neglected of Indians their due rights in assets ownership and the right to formulate strategies of development with regard to forest, water, and mineral resources as would be best suited to lifting millions upon millions out of malnutrition and abject poverty.

Alas, taken together, whether in the Sports arena or in Panchayati Raj, Aiyar was offering models of development that conflicted with the magisterial paradigms set by the state in league with the corporate class.

No wonder that when the other day he, with admirably characteristic candour, stated in response to a media question how it might be a good thing if the Commonwealth Games failed to come off well, since such an eventuality might discourage the state and the busybodies from venturing further into hosting the next Asian or Olympic games, he was promptly dubbed an 'anti-national' malcontent. The chorus of outrage promptly joined in by the super 'nationalist' BJP.

Thus be it in the matter of racial/religious preference (Hindutva), or in the matter of investment paradigms (even if in sports), the 'nationalist' idea remains all-powerful, shaming the dissenters into obloquy.

The point being how dare anyone harbour a view of 'nationalism' that contradicts that of the state as by law established and as by the corporates run.

A public school (read private school) – Bethany or something – has just sent a circular to parents, warning them of how the governments' new policy directive that such schools must henceforth admit atleast a 25% of children from under-privileged sections of society from class 1 onward ,free of charge, threatens to expose their children to the criminalized and vulgar world of the have-nots. The circular drew approval from some parents I heard on a TV debate.

Proof, if proof was needed that in India the bulk of Indians do not quite yet find acceptance as legitimate inheritors of the nationalist ideal. Roughly some 77% Indians who are taught to know their place regardless of the progressive impulses that the government might harbour now and again.

Remarkably, whereas India has laws that render discrimination on grounds of race, caste, gender, or faith criminal offences, there are no laws that make such blatanly class-based discrimination and calumny as perpetrated by the school circular an offence of any kind. Whereby hangs the tale.

'Culture' and 'Development' thus are conjoint handmaidens, ordained to cater to a 20% or so minority of Indians who self-evidently constitute the nation and prescribe the true meaning of 'nationalism.'

And yet, so long as there are those who are now unraveling the house of horrors in Gujarat, and a Mani Shankar Aiyar who can fearlessly heap contempt on the self-appointed custodians of 'development' all may not be lost.

Many years ago in 1859 John Stuart Mill had spoken in his celebrated essay 'On Liberty' of the dangers of the 'tyranny of the majority.' Many years ago also, John Ruskin had envisaged a model of development based on village communities, cottage industry, and so on in a book like *Unto This Last.*

We recall that if Nehru was much taken with the first, Gandhi was to model his own economic paradigms on Ruskin.

We say then to our presiding Party structures, leave room for truth tellers like Mani Shankar Aiyar who have the integrity and the courage to critique your favoured schemes, and refrain from taking recourse to the tyranny of the majority to sideline them (as we write, any number of whistleblowers have been murdered for exposing wrongful shenanigans through their Right to Information), and recall Ruskin-Gandhi before you set upon such well-wishers of 'we the people' (in whose name you framed the Constitution of India) for rubbishing your Commonwealth Games idea.

Just as we say to the cultural fascists, have a thought to the Constitution and the rule of law upon which you take your oath as parliamentarians and ministers, and have the character to admit to gruesome atrocities of the kind that your own have perpetrated in Gujarat – or the propriety to say that you will not obstruct the course of justice through vigilante hooliganism, brazen denial and filibustering , or smashing media houses who report on your misdeeds, and will abide by the results of court decisions when they come.

And to both we say it is time that you learnt to include and rub shoulders with, not as tactics and gimmickry but as conviction, some 80% 'other' Indians, be it as cultural entities or economic have-nots, in your definition of nation and nationalism. Or the time is not far when they will make you do so.

There is nothing common to the Commonwealth; certainly not wealth.

If only you can first construct an idea of 'nationalism' (and that of the Hindu right-wing in India has been so constructed on grounds of race and religion), then be vociferous in its propagation, through myth-making, lies, and violence, all directed against a steadily constructed 'enemy,' (in the Indian case, the Muslims), you give unto yourself the privilege to denounce every legal or constitutional operation that is seen to be inimical to 'nationalist' pride and glory.

August 2010

Kashmir Now Or Never

> Kashmir may be conquered by the force of spiritual merit but not by the force of soldiers.
> (Kalhana Pandit)

So total has been the loss of hegemony of Kashmir's elected representatives, in government and in the legislature, over the last two months, and so desperately brutal the recourse to coercive subjugation of fearless young anger on the streets of the valley, that if ever there was a time to say resistance to authority (sic) deserves to be rewarded with what it seeks, it has been now. If the prospect, that is, of the secession of the valley – since other parts of the state of Jammu & Kashmir desire, contrarily, not secession but more complete integration with the Union of India – were not fraught with incalculable negative consequences not just for India and Pakistan, but for the inhabitants of the valley itself.

To that I shall return.

Just the other day, the Home Minister of India made two significant averments in parliament. One that the Union recognizes that the Accession of the state of Jammu & Kashmir was a 'unique one'; and, two, that, apart of all other things, the Republic and its successive governments had failed to keep promises made to the people of Jammu & Kashmir.

Since the time for pussy footing about Kashmir is conclusively at an end, it would help to flesh out those two averments beyond the Minister's sketchily en passant mention.

Uniqueness of the Accession

It is to be recalled that the two conditions agreed upon as the signposts for India's pre-Independence Princely states as determinants of whether they would accede to India or to Pakistan were the religion of the majority within the states, and the congruity of the states to either Dominion.

In that context, the three states of Hyderabad, Junagarh, and Jammu & Kashmir offered interesting paradigms.

Where the first two had Muslim rulers but majority Hindu populations, J & K had a Dogra-Hindu ruler but a majority Muslim population. Of the three, clearly, J & K, being also contiguous with Pakistan, had the clearest case for accession to Pakistan.

Maharaja Hari Singh, the ruler of Kashmir, however, desired accession to neither of the two new countries, but wished to remain Independent.

Having succeeded in signing what was called a 'Standstill' agreement with Pakistan, it was his hope to do the same with India. Except that the fates intervened in the shape of a precipitate invasion of the state he ruled by tribal warriors from the North West Frontier Province of Pakistan with that states' active support and involvement in late October of 1947.

With next to no means of his own to meet, let alone defeat the invasion, he found himself constrained to appeal to India for military help vide his request for Accession to India, dated October,26, 1947. He wrote to the then Governor General of India, Lord Mountbatten of Burma:

> The mass infiltration of tribesmen drawn from the distant areas of the North-West Frontier…cannot possibly be done without the knowledge of the Provincial Government of the North West Frontier Province and the Government of Pakistan. Inspite of repeated requests made by my Government no attempt has been made to check these raiders or stop them from coming to my state. …I have no option but to ask for help from the Indian Dominion. Naturally they cannot send the help asked for by me without my state acceding to the Dominion of India. I have accordingly decided to do so and I attach the Instrument of Accession for acceptance by your Government.

That much for a Hindu ruler who had been reluctant to join even a Hindu-majority India but for the fact that circumstances forced such a decision upon him. Another matter that even on acceding, the Instrument of Accession he signed stated that the a\Accession in no way bound him to 'acceptance of any future constitution of India' (Clause 7), and that 'Nothing in this instrument affects the continuance of my sovereignty in and over this state' (Clause 8). Stipulations that to this day continue to colour the fraught history of tensions between the Union and the State.

As a result, Article 306 A was adopted in the Draft Constitution, and in course became the much-talked-about Article 370 in the final Constitution of India. Most significantly, the 'special status' thus accorded to the State of J & K, backed by the then Home Minister of India, Patel, (who said to the Constituent Assembly 'in view of the special problems with which the government of Jammu & Kashmir is faced, we have made a special provision for the constitutional relationship of the State with the Union') was accepted without demur also by Shyama Prasad Mookerjee, a member of Nehru's cabinet, later to become the most vociferous and disruptive voice of the Hindu right-wing. More of that below.

But the best part of the 'uniqueness' lay elsewhere, namely in the heroically principled declaration of allegiance to a prospectively secular and democratic Hindu-majority India by a Muslim Kashmiri leader of a Muslim-majority state, Sheikh Abdullah.

Internally, within the Princely State of J & K, a popular movement for the overthrow of the Maharaja's rule had been underway for two decades before 1947, precipitating in the events of July, 1931, when some 21 popular resistors were gunned down by the Maharaja's police force in front of a court house – a watershed event that led to the formation of the 'Muslim Conference' which came to be led by Sheikh Mohammed Abdullah, a post-graduate from the Aligarh Muslim University who was denied a teaching post in the state by the Maharaja's regime at a time when educated Kashmiri Muslims could be counted on finger-tips.

Within mainland India, although the Muslim League came a cropper in the elections to the Provincial Assemblies of 1936, following upon the passing of the Government of India Act of 1935, between that loss and 1946, the Muslim League under Jinnah made huge strides among Muslims in the states of Punjab and Bengal.

It was during this time that Jinnah was to make fervent arguments to Abdullah as to the obvious decision that the Kashmir Muslim Conference must make for joining forces with Jinnah's League, and for the Pakistan resolution which the League had passed in 1940.

Remarkably, however, despite the Kashmir Maharaja regimes' concerted anti-Muslim rule, and despite having forged the 'Muslim Conference,' Abdullah, by then the undisputedly tallest leader of the valley, and indeed the state, and despite the state having been a Muslim majority one, came to reject the two-nation communal thesis of the Muslim League, and declare his preference for the secular-democratic struggle that the Indian National Congress under Gandhi and Nehru had been waging against colonial rule, as he converted the 'Muslim Conference' into the 'National Conference' in 1938, clearly, some nine years before the partition of India and of the tribal invasion of Kashmir.

Abdullah in these years spoke repeatedly to his convictions.

Arguing that the matter of accession could not be left to the whims and fancies of rulers, but must reflect the voice of the people, he gave public expression to the popular Kashmiri view in a speech on October 4, 1947 at a historic rally (some three weeks before the tribal invasion):

> We shall not believe in the two-nation theory which has spread so much poison (cf to the communal killings that had been underway in the Punjab and in Bengal). Kashmir showed the light at this juncture (Gandhi was famously to say that the only light out of the darkness of communal killings he saw was in Kashmir valley where not a single incident took place). When brother kills brother in the whole of Hindustan, Kashmir raised its voice of Hindu-Muslim unity. I can assure the Hindu and Sikh minorities that as long as I am alive their life and honour will be quite safe.

Vide the Maharaja's proclamation of March 5, 1948, Sheikh Abdullah took over as the Prime Minister of the state, and on the next day, he told a press conference:

> We have decided to work and die for India…We made our decision not in October last, but in 1944, when we resisted the advances of Mr. Jinnah. Our refusal was categorical. Ever since the National Conference had attempted to keep the state clear of the pernicious two-nation theory while fighting the world's worst autocracy (*The Statesman*, 7 March, 1948).

On December 3, at a function of the GandhiMemorialCollege at Jammu:

> Kashmiris would rather die following the footsteps of Gandhiji than accept the two-nation theory. We want to link the destiny of Kashmir with India because we feel that the ideal before India and Kashmir is one and the same.

Those ideals – secularism, democracy, end to feudal landlordship – became the basis for the adoption of the 'provisional accession of the State to India' by the National Conference in the same month of October.

II

The Betrayal

Although Accession vide Article 370 which conferred a 'special status' on Jammu & Kashmir had, as stated above, received approval both from Patel and Shyama Prasad Mookerjee, a new situation was to develop as the Abdullah government in the state launched the New Kashmir Manifesto, bedrocked, among extraordinarily progressive pronouncements – equal status of women in education and employment being but one – on the promise of giving land to those who tilled it.

Thus, disregarding Clause 6 of the Instrument of Accession ('Nothing in this Instrument shall empower the Dominion Legislature to make any law for this state authorizing the compulsory acquisition of land for any purpose,' and should land be thus needed, 'I will at their request acquire the land'), Abdullah declared a maximum land ceiling of 22.75 acres, set up a Land Reforms Commission, and set about distributing surplus land thus acquired to those who actually were tillers on the soil. Abdullah was to rub home the point that such land reforms would never have been possible in a feudal Pakistan.

This was trouble royal.

Most of the land then was in possession of Hindu Dogras, and most of the tillers were Muslim Kashmiris.

Thus it came to be that the material loss of landholdings was sought to be converted into a communal question vide an opposition now to Article 370 by a newly organized forum called the Praja Parishad which came to be led by the very Mookerjee who had been a willing party to the adoption of the Article as a member of the Union Cabinet.

Under stipulations of the 'special status,' Jammu & Kashmir had been granted to form its own Constituent Assembly. When elections to the CA took place in 1951, candidates picked by Abdullah's National Conference won all 75 seats. The Assembly met on October 31, 1951. On November 5, Abdullah outlined the major agenda before it:

- To frame a Constitution for Kashmir;
- To decide on the fate of the royal Dynasty;
- To decide whether there should be any compensation paid to those
- who had lost their land through the Land Abolition Act;

- To 'declare its reasoned conclusion regarding accession.'

Abdullah noted:

> The real character of a State is revealed in its Constitution. The Indian Constitution has set before the country the goal of a secular democracy based upon justice, freedom and equality for all without distinction. This is the bedrock of modern democracy. This should meet the argument that the Muslims of Kashmir cannot have security in India, where the large majority of the population are Hindus. Any unnatural cleavage between religious groups is the legacy of imperialism....The Indian Constitution has amply and finally repudiated the concept of a religious State which is a throwback to medievalism....The national movement in our State naturally gravitates towards these principles of secular democracy.

And, on Pakistan:

> The most powerful argument that can be advanced in her favour is that Pakistan is a Muslim State, and, a big majority of our people being Muslims the State must accede to Pakistan. This claim of being a Muslim State is of course only a camouflage. It is a screen to dupe the common man, so that he may not see clearly that Pakistan is a feudal State in which a clique is trying by these methods to maintain itself in power.... Right-thinking men would point out that Pakistan is not an organic unity of all the Muslims in this subcontinent. It has, on the contrary, caused the dispersion of Indian Muslims for whom it was claimed to have been created (a perception first voiced by Maulana Azad in a prescient interview given to the Covert magazine in 1946, a year before Partition).

Abdullah considered the third option of Independence (Kashmir as an 'Eastern Switzerland'), and concluded as follows:

> I would like to remind you that from August 15 (the day of Indian Independence) to October 22, 1947 (when the tribal invasion began) our State was Independent and the result was that our weakness was exploited by the neighbour with invasion. What is the guarantee that in future too we may not be victims of a similar aggression.

All that notwithstanding, the Hindu right-wing assault began also to gather force, as it launched the Jana Sangh (precursor of today's Bharatiya Janata Party, the BJP) in 1951 – the same year as the establishment of the Cosntituent Assembly in the State. And its leader became Shyama Prasad Mookerjee, with the RSS lending two of its leaders for support, namely Atal Bihari Vajpayee and L.K.Advani.

As stated earlier, stung by the redistribution of landholdings, it sought to make the terms of the Accession the issue, and defying the democratic-federal principles enshrined both in the Constitution of India and in their reflection in the trust reposed thereof by Abdullah, it announced a programme ostensibly aimed to strengthen national unity. At its first session, it called for:

- An education system based on 'Bharatiya culture' (read Hinduism);
- The use of Hindi in schools (in full knowledge that, other than Kashmiri, Urdu was the language predominantly used by educated Kashmiri Muslims; indeed, from about the first decade of the twentieth century, the wholly artificial cleavage between Hindi and Urdu had begun to be deployed by communalists on either side to press their claims to 'true' national allegiance;
- The denial of any special privileges to minorities;
- Full integration of Jammu & Kashmir into the Indian Union.

On the other side, in letters exchanged over a period of time between Abdullah and Nehru, the shape of an agreement between the State and the Union was taking shape. That came to be called the Delhi Agreement (1952). It stated:

- Commitment to Article 370
- That the State Legislature would be empowered to confer special rights on 'state subjects' (a right that had been won through the anti-Maharaja struggles of 1927 and 1932 – a form of privilege restricted to permanent residents of the State in property ownership and jobs);
- That Kashmir would have its own flag, although subordinate to the Union Tricolour;
- That the Sadr-e-Riyasat (later on Governor of the State) would be elected by the State Assembly, but would take office with the concurrence of the President of India;

- That the Supreme Court of India would, 'for the time being,' have only appellate jurisdiction in Jammu & Kashmir;
- That an internal Emergency could only be applied with the concurrence of the State Legislature.

Late in the same year, the riposte to this from the Hindu right-wing came in the form of the following slogan – one around which the Jana Sangh sought to mount its attack on the terms of Accession. And the slogan was:

Ek desh mein do Vidhan,
Ek desh mein do Nishaan,
Ek desh mein do Pradhan,
Nahi challenge, nahi challenge.
(We will not accept two Constitutions, two flags, and two prime ministers in one and the same country.)

This communalist right-wing putsch against the principles on which the state had accepted to accede to India began to find resonance also within section of the Congress Party. To Nehru's great chagrin but helplessness, his candidate for the first President of India, Rajagopalachari, was rejected in favour of Rajendra Prasad (who was soon to lock horns with Nehru on the Hindu Code Bill, and to go to the Somnath Mandir,once ravaged by Ghazni, among many other chieftans of old, to effect renovations on state expense – a move wholly in conflict with the secular foundations of the Republic).

Other collateral tendencies began also to surface, such as bespoke scant regard on behalf of the Union of India for the federative principles. In his despondent letter to Maulana Azad, dated 16 July, 1953, Abdullah complained about the usurpations underway, in contravention of what terms had been agreed upon:

> We the people of Kashmir, regard the promises and assurances of the representatives of the government of India, such as Lord Mountbatten and Sardar Patel, as surety for the assistance rendered by us in securing the signatures of Maharaja of Kashmir on the Instrument of Accession, which made it clear that the internal autonomy and sovereignty of the Acceding States shall be maintained except in regard to three subjects which will be under the Central government (namely, Defence, Communications, and External Affairs).

And:

When the Constituent Assembly of India proceeded to frame the Union Constitution there arose before it the question of the State. Our Representatives took part in the last sessions of the Assembly and presented their point of view in the light of basic principles on which the National Conference had supported State's Accession to India. Our view-point drew appreciation and Article 370 of the Constitution came into being determining our position under the new Constitution.

Abdullah pointed out that although it had been agreed that the "Accession involves no financial obligations on the States" such demands were being made; and "the changes effected on several occasions in relationship between India and Kashmir greatly agitated the public opinion."

And on the other source of perceived menace:

A big party in India (the Jana Sangh) still forcefully demands merger of the State with India. In the State itself Praja Parishad is threatening to resort to direct action if the demand for the States' complete merger with India is not conceded.

Abdullah's anguish at what seemed gathering storms on two fronts – the subversion by the Union of the terms of Accession, and a Hindu communalist putsch to undo Article 370, found poignant expression in a speech he had meant to deliver to an Eid gathering on august 21, 1953 (twelve days after his government was dismissed and Abdullah arrested and incarcerated). In that he wrote:

...there is the suggestion that the accession should be finalized by vote of the Cosntituent Assembly.' 'It is the Muslims who have to decide accession with India and not the non-Muslims....The question is: must I not carry the support of the majority community with me? If I must, then it becomes necessary that I should satisfy them to the same extent that a non-Muslim is satisfied that his future hopes and aspirations are safe in India. Unfortunately, apart from the disastrous effects which the pro-Merger agitation in Jammu produced in Kashmir (the valley)...the Muslim middle class in Kashmir has been greatly perturbed to see that while the present relationship of the State with India has opened new opportunities for their Hindu and Sikh brothers to ameliorate their lot, they have been assigned the position of a frog in the well. ...*What the Muslim intelligentsia in Kashmir is trying to look for is a definite and concrete stake in India.* (emphasis added)

As stated, the dye had been cast, and his great friend Nehru had him arrested on the suspicion that he had been hobnobbing with the Americans for support to secede from the Union and declare Independence. Although there might have been grounds for such a suspicion, to this day no proof is forthcoming.

But read the lament quoted above, and there is not a jot more or different that informs the frustrated Kashmiri youth in the valley who are at this minute agitating in the valley, willing to confront police bullets.

It is another matter that long years after in 1974, Abdullah signed an Accord with Indira Gandhi, the then Prime Minister of India which stipulated, among other things, that

> Parliament will continue to have power to make laws relating to the prevention of activities directed towards disclaiming, questioning, or disrupting the sovereignty and territorial integrity of India or bringing about secession of a part of the territory of India from the Union… etc.

When the Indian Home Minister therefore speaks of keeping promises with the Kashmiris, those promises have a much wider ambit than the question merely of amending the vile Armed Forces Special Powers Act, which allows the least army man to shoot to kill without accountabiliy.

Throughout these turbulent years of conflict, never once has any government of India sought to formulate schemes whereby talented Kashmiri Muslims, products of an educational explosion – all thanks to Abdullah's New Kashmir programme, could be made to feel not just safe in the heartland but valued assets in the ongoing story of national 'development.' Not to speak of the communal lens through which Kashmiri Muslims continue to be viewed by Indian society at large, an old malaise made dangerously trenchant subsequent to the era of 'terrorism.'

And, paradoxically, the more that strong- arm methods and vicious prejudices fail to deliver desired results, the more the state means to persist with them. And now that some streaks of recognition seem to dawn on policy establishments, the present-day incarnation of the old Praja Parishad and Jana Sangh are back to the same old perfidies, robbing the secular democratic sections within the Congress chiefly of any will or courage to disregard Hindu right-wing communalism and do right by Kashmir.

III
Azadi

Some 51 teenage Kashmiris screaming for secession have died in the last two months from police bullets in the valley.

Quite apart from the legalese of the question (the Sheikh/Indira Gandhi Accord for one), and apart also from the hard reality that such secession will neither ever be agreed to by any political establishment in India or any government of the day, or accepted by Indians at large, hypothetically, what prospects could be envisaged were the other parts of the state who do not want secession to be persuaded that the valley of Kashmir be bestowed Independence and Sovereignty?

- following such a declaration, demands for *Azadi* could gain legitimacy in Manipur, Nagaland, Assam, to name a few, and be hard to deny once a precedent is set;
- a Hindu communalist backlash could ostensibly engulf India, rendering the lives of Indian Muslims tenuous, and leading to demands that India be declared a Hindu state, since the secession of the valley would have proved the two-nation theory to have been correct after all;
- within Pakistan, first the Baloch, and then the Sindhis might take heart and set themselves the objective to be freed of Punjabi ethnic dominance through secession;
- within the valley, a Bangladesh-like situation might well emerge, namely a struggle among those who will wish to retain a secular democratic state and those who might argue for an Islamic state; it is well to remember that of its forty years or so of independent nationhood, brought about under the leadership of the Awami National Party on secular principles, some thirty years were to see the communalist Leaguers in power; until now when under the present regime again the Supreme Court there has struck down Article 5 of the amended constitution, and thereby once again reverted to denying any religion-based party formations, but after the spilling of much blood.

This writer has often been accused of exaggerating the sufi-secular orientation of Kashmiri Muslims, and of sentimentally misreading acts of personal and individual camaraderie and brotherhood displayed by Kashmir Muslims towards visiting Pandits as representative of the totality.

I have also been kindly once commented upon as a 'Jihadi lapdog' (see Google). But all that notwithstanding, it remains a fact that at the time of the exodus of the Kashmiri Pandits from the valley in 1990, a campaign was in evidence as loud-speakers from mosques blared how the 'Nizam-e-Mustafa' (Islamic statehood) was at hand, how the Pandits must hasten their exodus, taking care to leave their women behind, though. You will also hear the speculation that one reason why elements within the valley do not, at bottom, wish the Pandits to return home en mass is that they do not wish an Indian 'fifth column' to be reinstated therein, since with them gone, the desire for an Islamic state acquires greater facilitation. Much as the Jews in Israel, for example, fear the return of Palestinian refugees into what was once their homeland.

I must also confess to another sort of experience on some recent visits to the valley, namely the chagrin with which any mention of 'Kashmiriyat' (denoting the good old syncretic ways of Kashmiris) now tends to be received there. Indeed, I recall being at a seminar in the university in Srinagar where a senior academic read a one or two page 'paper' titled 'Kashmiriyat' only, in fact, to rubbish the concept, without much substance albeit.

'Kashmiriyat' is now seen as something of a trick to deny the fact that Kashmir in essence is Islamic, something that finds increasing expression in text books on history and culture, as the pre-Islamic period (roughly upto the fourteenth century, A.D.) is sought to be relegated.

Then the incident that happened not so long ago at Pulwama, where a Sikh Kashmiri was surrounded, and asked to speak the Islamic Qalima, failing which some of his hair was shorn off. Let it also be said that the incident, uncharacteristic in the extreme, drew condemnation from all sections of Kashmiri leadership.

Although, therefore, some residual Kashmiri Pandits who never left the valley continue to be protected by their Muslim neighbours, and their weddings and funerals organized with customary syncretic brotherhood, and although their periodic visits from camps outside the valley to age-old Hindu shrines in the valley are greeted with warmth, it would be wrong to deny that after the near-total evacuation of the Pandits, the impulse to forge a Sovereign and Independent valley into a theocratic state might not be altogether a baseless surmise.

Be that as it may, what might be the security logistics of the new state, bordering as it does Russia, China, Paksitan, Afghanistan, and in that situation, India as well? To return to what Sheikh Abdullah had said with regard to this option ('Eastern Switzerland'), how might the new state meet those vulnerabilities?

And how might it be said that Imperialism from you-know-where, already stationed in countries nearby, might not feel that at long last the valley was his for the taking, with all the Afghanistan-like consequences that could follow, both in terms of turmoil and cultural defilement?

Not to speak of the kind souls from Pakistan's wild-western provinces, many in fact now resident in the main city centres of Pakistan? How might Kashmiris resist their call to a jihadist embrace, in disregard of time-honoured ethnic Kashmiri prizing of exclusivity and identity? And if they became insistent despite a polite 'no', who might come to the aid of the Kashmiris?

Kashmiris are insistent everyday as the current imbroglio proceeds that jobs, development, opportunities – these are not the issues. Yet, these might indeed in time become issues of central magnitude for a prospectively landlocked valley to deal with, in the absence of both monetary and infrastructural resources.

Those resources then may have to come from other places with all the attendant implications, be it the Saudis, or the Yankees, or the Chinese. Altogether, a pickle-in-the-making.

IV

If those be not unfounded considerations, what is to be done?

And it is time that the question is addressed with some candid concern.

A good beginning is made, I think, if all parties to the contention recognize that Kashmir is not a problem that may ever be resolved to the satisfaction of all parties. And it would be wrong to think that what is said therein is merely a pre-emptive ploy. I doubt me much that time will prove me wrong.

Let me say atonce that the two options which seem closest to the heart of contending parties – the Union and the Agitators – I see as non-starters, namely the wish on behalf of the Indian state, on the one hand, that things may drag on as before till exhaustion seals a fait accompli, and, on the other, the desire, however fervent, of the young Agitators for a country of their own in the valley.

The first is bad not only because such a fait accompli will not happen, but because it speaks poorly to the founding pretensions of the Republic of

India-chiefly its claim to 'unity in diversity.' And it reinforces a sentiment felt more widely than just in the valley that the Indian state has, since the 1990 beginning of the neo-liberal era especially, become increasingly impatient of both secularism and democracy, and wholly inimical to the rights of a majority of Indians who to this day, in Abdullah's words, feel no 'definite and concrete stake in India.' This applies as a thought to the lives of India's tribal populations, to dalits, and to minorities of various description on a differentiated scale of neglect.

In that context, the Indian state can only be fooling itself to think that sooner than later the Kashmiris will tire and turn around.

And the second is a bad option because, as suggested above, the consequences of the secession of the valley are potentially fraught only with negatives for all parties to the dispute, and to the subcontinent as a whole.

Those recognitions return us willy nilly to salutary reflections on the possibility of recuperating and refurbishing the covenant of the federative promise and principle – something on which the Accession of the State to the Union had been based in the first place, setting a uniquely outstanding example both in terms of plurality of citizenship and of political partnership in opposition to totalitarian impulses in both areas.

This Kashmiri still thinks that the Delhi Agreement (above) of 1952 still offers the most workable and fair point of engagement. With the caveat that with the advantage of hindsight any cool Kashmiri would recognize that extending the jurisdiction of the Supreme Court of India and of the Election Commission of India to the State, far from impinging on the State's Autonomy, would in fact be credible guarantees of protection from excesses and denials.

As to the majoritarian nationalists, they are as much a menace to the rest of India as to any attempt to arrive at a fair solution in Kashmir. That being so, the Indian State and Civil Society must needs muster the strength and the will to defy and defeat their shenanigans, if the nation is to be saved not so much from the Kashmiris as, first of all, from them.

It is good, late than never, that the Prime Minister has made some noises to the sort of effect suggested here. Let his government and society at large understand fully that it is now or never in Kashmir, and therefore avoid going into another decade-long siesta after the current violence inevitabley lulls.

As to Pakistan, I am simply tempted to nod assent to what Sheikh Abdullah had told the United Nations when he went there to plead India's case: "I refuse to accept Pakistan as a party in the affairs of Jammu and Kashmir State; I refuse this point blank."

After what it has done to its own people over the decades, that refusal seems most in order. What the occupied part of Kashmir in Pakistan may do with their fate is best left to them as well. Significantly, the most recent Chatham House conducted poll showed some 58% of Kashmiris willing to formalize the Line of Control between the two parts of Kashmir as the International border between India and Pakistan. That is as it should be. And once that happens, human and other commerce between the two Kashmirs can be put on a sound international footing, all ambiguities and hassles removed.

If initiatives along above lines are not undertaken soon, it may be pointless to write any further on the subject of the Kashmir problem. Not reason, analysis, or conjoint effort may then sort it out, but a conflagaration that may lead who knows where.

Note: Literature on Kashmir is mind-boglingly numerous, and I have sought to look into as much as time and tide allow. But, for purposes of this piece, I wish to record my indebtedness to three authors on Kashmir, chiefly Prem Nath Bazaz, Balraj Puri, and M.J. Akbar, on whose work I have drawn with abandon. The interpretations thereof being entirely my responsibility.

August 2010

What a Piece of Work is Man

> I created thee as a being neither celestial nor earthly...so that thou shouldst be thy own free moulder and overcomer.
>
> (Pico de la Mirandola)
>
> What a piece of work is man, how noble in reason, how infinite in faculties, in form and moving how express and admirable in action, how like an angel in apprehension, how like a god: the beauty of the world; the paragon of animals.
>
> (Hamlet)

Ah the 'Humanist' Renaissance, and what it has come to.

I see the Creation of Adam on the Sistine Chapel, and note the rebuke that Michaelangelo administered to many previous representations which depicted Adam as a dithering little creature over whom God towered like a colossus. Not so. Michaelangelo's depiction not only has God and Man at the same height of head, but Adam a brawny and sexy male of the kind implicit in Hamlet's tribute.

And I recall how in his *Oration On the Dignity of Man* ('Manifesto of the Renaisance' it was called – 1486), Pico, defending his 900 theses, went boldly forth to rubbish the medieval notion of a will-less creature, fixed forever in the negation of sin, and destined to remain embroiled in expiation. Man, he argued, was created not as the other animals, but uniquely as a vessel of possibility, his own 'moulder and overcomer.' Astutely then, depending on what he did with his will and prowess, he could either rank among the angels or sink among the creatures of the netherworld.

Till along came Marx some hundred years later, looked at history of the interim over his canny shoulder, and saw that when Renaissance Humanists spoke of Man, they had but a particular species of Man in mind – namely, the new-age entrepreneur who had overthrown the feudal economies of Europe, and set his sights on exchange and rates of profit maximization. Indeed they understood their destiny as one that sanctioned their towering over 'lesser' men (of women who spoke then?) as God had been shown in the Middle Ages to tower over Adam.

Thus came colonisation, extermination, and the world of 'modern development.' As the 'elect' set about fulfilling that destiny, billions of little people paid the price. Blood, bounty, and the palaces of gold became a configuration that God had ordained in His wisdom.

II

So, when enterprising Indians defeated British colonialism, they took care to absorb all the 'developmental' lessons. The one new thing was the need to remember periodically that the blood, sweat, and hunger of the labouring (in whom 'sovereignty' resided, don't you know) was rewarded every five years or so with a call to elect a new set of rulers of the same old vintage. They called it Democracy.

Never more to the fore in the year of the Lord, 2010, when the democratic state fires away at the little people from one end of the double barrel and prepares to showcase the realm to the world via the Commonwealth Games through the other.

Thus, in a throwback to Pico and Shakespeare, the Indian state displays its faculties of innovation and spending in the works it gets made at less than minimum wage, and, on the other side, plays the beast to man, woman, and child who have, alas, not inherited the pedigree of Renaissance Humanism. Recall the butcheries the Conquistadors were perpetrating as they sought to make of the white race the gold-plated inheritors of God's selective intent; and recall that even as Jefferson was inking the Declaration (all men are equal etc., with them unalienable rights) he, like most of his distinguished peers – Madison, Washington, what-have-you – owned a hundred or more slaves (of whom, Howard Zinn tells us in his *A People's History of the United States of America*, some 50 million died during the slave trade. Some other estimates put the figure at 60 million.)

You may have heard that millions of Indians (what else can we call them?) are at levels of fatal malnutrition countrywide. You may also have heard that the Indian state suffers an embarrassment of riches in terms of stocks of grain, thousands of tons of which grain either are rotting for want of storage (or because the godowns are seen to be storing liquor at lucrative discounts while the grains lie in the open) or are feasted on by rats (objects of worship in some famous temples of India which draw the white tourist to gawk at the 'wonder that (is) India.' (Basham only spoke of 'that was India.')

Wonderous indeed. Especially as you note that, notwithstanding an order now of the Supreme Court to the Executive of the day that the excess grains be distributed among the starving, the 'socialist' state (so defined in the Preamble to the Constitution) takes umbrage at the direction thus given, and in true loyalty to the philosophy of exchange, points out that grain is meant to be sold, like all other commodities, not given. A circumstance that recalls what Hamlet was to go on to say of Man in the epigraph cited above: "yet, to me, what is this quintessence of dust" as he concludes that "man pleases (him) not."

So grain may not be given free to the starving even as it rots, but, wait, something there is that may be given free, namely, mobile phones! At a flashily showcased event in Rajasthan, a mobile company in which the government is the major stake-holder, company officials distributed thousands of phone-sets to uncomprehending country folk who were strangely caught on camera to be saying what use phones when food is what they need! So much for gratitude. They will not eat cake when there is no bread.

Then there is the case of the charming Chief Minister of the capital city of New Delhi, chock a block with pride and glee at how the Commonwealth Games have provided occasion to deck the city like a new-minted bride, with clovers and fly-overs, with under-passes and looped diversions, with shining road lanes reserved for the visitors while quotidian citizen sweats and crawls inch by inch of the traffic jungle, ready to shoot both abuse and gun at the least provocation.

And even as the TV channels show her cavorting to the theme song of the Games – a piece of wretched noise merely – the cameras also show an unknown and unnamed Indian woman, prone by the pavement, in labour for four days, as she delivers unnoticed and unassisted on the fourth day, and dies on the spot. Pray, where be the human being thus born? Really can't say, except that here is another wretchedly unnecessary mouth to fill, provided he/she pays the going rate. No free lunches for infants either, decrees the god of progress, capital.

Such are the ways and by-products of 'humanism', and of the legendary compassion of the Hindu way of life. What does the dead anonymity of a woman know how Pujas are being performed at royal expense to keep the rains and the floods away from the Games (not from the people, needless to say), which just goes to prove how we Hindus are devoted to the gods if not to human beings.

III

Meanwhile, as 'Operation Greenhunt' takes out the rebellious Adivasis in the hinter-heart lands, as teenagers die from police bullets in Kashmir, as the rains and the floods devastate millions of superfluous lives, and as the grains rot for want of buyers, as the Brahmo missiles are tested, as nuclear power plants are about to come up while schools, hospitals, sanitation (in India the owners of mobile phones outnumber those that have toilet facilities), shelters, drinking water, electricity, a decent wage, and other accoutrement of the right to a dignified life guaranteed by Article 21 of the Constitution of India to all citizens, without regard to caste, creed, gender, linguistic affinity (all but class) wait their turn. Whatever is going wrong has nothing to do with the crass cruelties of the well-meaning state; they have to do with the general lack of patriotic fervour and pride on behalf of carping Indians who refuse to see the glories of 'humanism'. Treachery everywhere, chiefly among those who now have a pittance but ask for more. And those who point to the proliferating numbers of dollar billionaires, and will not understand how necessary they are to the practice of 'humanism'.

And then there are those who teach how 'humanism' mortally depends on where a mosque or a temple ought to stand or not to stand. Many already make a computation of how many more thousand urchins must need to be put to the sword if the Court judgement on the title suit of the contested Babri mosque site due to come on September 24 should disfavour the torch-bearers of saffron. Between the chickens that go cooped for slaughter and those that may soon die in city and town is the difference that the chickens may be counted whereas the mystery of uncertainty hovers over the likely human victims. Who knows in what beleaguered spaces may fall the corpses – fodder to the project of building an India of high-morality and noble religious ideals to which Hindutva terrorism dedicates its energies.

Incidentally and en passant, Reverend Terry Jones sets the example in that other democracy. He seems as good a Christian as the Hindutva vanguards are Hindus, or the Jihadis are Muslims. We have a good idea of who pays the latter two; but who pays you, Mr.Jones, a lot, it would seem, to tear the world apart?

All in all, Pico and Shakespeare knew what they were talking about: 'Man' may be both devil or god, but only Marx knew that 'humanism' spawned by capitalism foreclosed the latter probability some five hundred years ago.

So let the Games go on, while the grains rot and the children go hungry or fall to disease after disease born of the elementary deprivations that 'humanism' makes necessary. And national pride.

Always what comes first is India's image, not its reality. Which is why all of Delhi's beggars are to be hidden away from gaze till the Games are over. On the principle that what you don't see does not exist. Such is the contempt we have for the intelligence of the world community. Do you hear a knowledgeable chuckle? I do.

Yes we can make the wood disappear and deck the trees we choose.

Not for long, not for long. I see many millions of skeletal knuckles reach out of the wood, and many hungry wails raise a curse no earpiece may obstruct. And a resistless flood in the making that may take away everything that stands in the way.

September 2010

We Abuse Ram When We Spill Blood in His Name

One of my most soothing childhood memories is of my mother reading aloud the Ram Katha (the story of the ancient, mythical or not, King of Ayodhya).

A woman of the most extraordinarily acute practical intelligence, never easily fibbed or taken in, and always watchful of the disingenuous or scheming charlatan, I recall how that act of reading melted the sharp and mistrusting edges of her intellect, brought tears to her eyes, and transformed her into the semblance of an all-forgiving saint. The radiance from those readings was often such that those in the room that included our Muslim helpers along the periphery forgot we were Hindus or Muslims and were rendered naked human beings struggling for love and understanding.

As I look back, my own socialization in Hinduism resides in those early contexts in which, after all, stories about gods and deities had but one object-to disable hatred and selfishness, and engender a warm empathy towards all things animate and inanimate. The gods seemed mere instruments to furnish enlightened human purposes.

And I believe this would go for most people in India who call themselves Hindus.

All that was sought to be changed in 1990 as India's party of the Hindu right set out to make of Ram a political icon around whom a new state was to be forged, informed not by love or understanding or accommodation, but hatred, exclusivity and physical force. Leading within two years of Advani's abrasively menacing Rath Yatra (travels atop a warlike chariot, with cut-outs of Ram not as my mother saw him but now as a kshatriya warrior with an arrow stretched in the bow) to the water-shed desecration and demolition of a more than four hundred year old mosque. And leading, let it be remembered, to the gratuitous killing of some two thousand Indians who were no part of that politics.

That reality was, in a tribute to the ordinary Hindu, to be repeatedly underscored as the BJP came to lose one election after another, following some initial gains. No more stern rebuke to the Hindu far-right agenda than the fact that to this day the inhabitants of the town of Ayodhya and of Faizabad generally retain inter-communal harmony and bonding of a kind which nothing that the fascist falange could do has impaired. They remain of my mother's party, and wish a pox on the trouble- shooters and hatred- rousers who invade their enlightened social togetherness from 'outside.' And the Hindus and Muslims of Ayodhya also remain seamless at home, on the street, in the work-place both in their devotion to Ram and in their collaborative life and work experiences.

II

Seeking from a platform of medievalist animosity, paradoxically in close embrace with segments both of India's own big-business interests and neo-liberal foreign marauders, to dislodge the state from its mainline constitutional commitment to secular and modernizing democracy, the Hindu right has sought to keep the Ayodhya issue alive, namely its 'nationalist' call to build a grand temple to Ram at the very site of the demolished Babri mosque, since it is their unproven and unprovable claim that Ram was born at the very spot where the main dome of the mosque stood.

Which, of course, is not the real purpose.

The real purpose is to iconically and thumbingly demonstrate to Indian Muslims that India must be acknowledged to be in essence a Hindu nation; and that, more than Mecca, it is Ram that Indian Muslims must do obeisance to. All that true to the teachings of the old RSS chief, Golwalkar, who, picking up from the racist Nazis, had decreed that the Indian state be a racially defined state rather than one that owed allegiance to the history either of the Indian National Movement for freedom from colonial rule, or to those antecedent secularizing and democratizing histories of England and Europe that sought to create non-discriminatory citizenships and rights thereof.

To the extent that Gandhi endorsed and led those efforts of the anti-colonial Indian nationalists while remaining the most exemplary Hindu through all his personal and political concerns, he offered a great difficulty to the fascists. Which, after all, necessitated his assassination.

Yet such is the force of India's syncretic history, and of the conjoint battle for freedom from British colonial rule, that while in power the BJP has had repeatedly to jettison its promise to the electorate that once in power it would see that the grand temple was built at the site of the demolished mosque. For the reason that none, bar one, of its coalition partners in government would stand for it. In consequence, it remains embarrassingly impossible for the BJP to counter the criticism that its main devotion is to political power rather than to the god, Ram. The canny wisecrack will also say that the temple does not get built because Ram would not approve of the proceeding in the first place.

III

All these decades, in the meanwhile, a title-suit has been argued in the courts. To wit, a judicial determination has to be made as to whether the site of the demolished mosque belongs in law to the contending Hindu or Muslim organizations.

For some sixty years that suit, a la Jarndyce vs Jarndyce of Dickens' Bleak House, has seen twists and turns. But, finally, the court in question, dismissing all further attempts to procrastinate, is due to deliver its judgement on September the 24th.

Two decades from the demolition of the mosque, Indian ruling classes have come to harbour a different sort of dream, one that seeks a full realization of the material status that a devoted alignment with a neo-liberal 'reformist' era promises to the endowed and the enterprising. And a whole new generation of young middle class Indians seem on board.

In that changed historical context, only the tea-party segments of the Hindu right seem still to retain that fervent desire to carry the politics of the Ayodhya 'movement' forward.

Given that reality, and the reality that the BJP retains power in states like Bihar, where elections are due in a couple of months, in partnership with allies who do not share its Hindu-sectarian orientation, the BJP has chosen to lie low, without making the unequivocal averment that it will accept the judicial verdict. That in stark contrast to the Muslim organizations who have repeatedly stated that, were their case to fall in the coming judgement, they would go in appeal to the higher court whose final findings would be accepted without demur.

The stated position of the Hindutva forces remains that were the final court verdict to go against them, parliament must legislate that the temple be built, since mayhem, alas, will not do it.

IV

A momentous test for the state and for several other agencies is thus in the offing in a weeks' time from now.

As far as the Muslim organizations and the polity generally are concerned, it may be reasonably assumed that a negative verdict will not yield street violence. The Babri Action Committee has clearly enough made public what they will do, namely, go in appeal to the Supreme Court of India.

Alas, despite the seemingly low-key postures now being struck by even the ideological patron of the Hindu right, the RSS, such an assumption could be fallacious in their case, given the record of its murderously lumpen storm troopers like the VHP, the Bajrang Dal, and the Ram Sene.

The governments of the day, both in the state of Uttar Pradesh and in Delhi may well be tested.

Should there indeed be only fringe protests from the Hindu right, both the Congress party and the government it leads at the centre may pick up courage to quell the mischief without any great opprobrium from the 'Hindu' electorate. Should, however, things blow out of reckoning, the old canny calculations may yet again come into play. And that would tell us that, despite the above-board secular convictions of the Congress President, Sonia Gandhi, there remains within the Congress party an unwillingness to confront Hindutva fascism without regard to electoral considerations.

Contrarily, should the court deliver in favour of the Hindu contenders, the task may be no less trying, for the reason that typically celebratory shenanigans-complete with the distribution of sweets, bursting of fire-crackers, and humiliating gestures made towards Muslims, orchestratedly noisy temple trumpetings, could bring out the same results that might come if the verdict were to favour the Muslim litigants. The legendary and time-tested modalities of engineering communal strife perfected by the RSS could then be set in motion.

For a state and government already besieged with secessionist violence in Kashmir and left-wing extremism in several states, a fresh communal conflagaration might be the proverbial last straw, especially if the fascists succeeded in drawing to their purposes armies of the jobless and sundry other victims of neo-liberal economic immiseration. Such an old and tested modus operandi that, telling such victims that not the political economy practiced by the ruling classes but the cultural and religious 'other' is at the root of their problems.

Perhaps most importantly, given a touted new India, the ones most severely tested would be those that occupy the liberal middle ground. It will remain to be seen whether or not they will come to the fore with the same resolve as they did at the time of the terrorist attack on Mumbai on 26 September 2008. And whether the corporate media that now is seen to strike a 'progressive' cord plays out that cord with full force or does the customary dance of equivocating between parties to the dispute, all in the name of 'fair-minded' coverage of events. What makes that question well worth the asking is the fact that the corporate media retain more than a soft corner for the market-friendly BJP.

Interestingly, a demolished mosque and a likely mosque now trouble the hearts of the strategically partnered democracies of India and the United States of America.

Will the Indian state measure up to the outstandingly principled position enunciated by Barack Obama?

September 2010

The Ayodhya Verdict

Like many others who have made comment on the verdict of the Allahabad High Court on the several suits pertaining to title over the disputed site in Ayodhya, I also have available to me only the excerpts of the operative parts of the Judgement (s) that have seen print thus far.

Having read these with care, and repeatedly, alongwith most commentaries that have appeared, and listened with despair to the many debates on the electronic channels, after some excruciating hours of befuddlement and reflection, I had better get my word in for what it is worth. Not a great deal, I suspect.

I agree with most that the honourable court seems to have with deliberation chosen to operate rather more like a problem-solver than a legal/juridical entity. Attempting thereby to resolve issues that the other branches of the state have thus far failed to resolve. "We decided to take the risk despite some saner elements advising us against it," Justice S.U.Khan has reportedly said in his Preamble, adding that the 'landmines' needed to be finally removed, even if it meant to venture 'where angels fear to tread.'

Now, for long years I have expressed chagrin at those homo sapiens who mope and mull – indeed secretly live off the problems they eternally grumble about – and admiration for those others who trouble themselves to find solutions.

The tricky part, though, can be that sometimes the answers that are found compound the problems rather than solve them. And it is now my view that something of this nature may have been accomplished by the honourable judges, even if against their best intentions. Not that intentions can ever be demonstrable facts. Like the gods, they must be taken on faith.

II

That a 'mosque' stood at the site in Ayodhya for some centuries wherein regular worship took place is agreed to by the two judges who form the 'majority' verdict, although one of the two discounts the theory that a temple was demolished to build the mosque and the other holds to the view that such indeed was the case (Justices Aggarwal and Khan). Justice Aggarwal who thinks a temple was demolished does not allude to any evidence that the supposedly demolished temple below the surely demolished Babri mosque could be provenly denominated the birthplace of Ram.

The dissenting Justice Sharma, whose live interview I heard on the Aaj Tak channel, convinced by archaeological evidence supplied by the Achaeological Survey of India in 2003 that not only did a 'massive Hindu religious structure' lie beneath the Babri mosque but that in a layer below that structure had stood the Dashrath Mahal – palace of the King Dashrath, sire of Lord Ram – and precisely the place where the Lord was born. Citing the Quran and the Hadith, Justice Sharma concludes that since the mosque, so-called in his view, was built after demolishing another religious structure, it could not have been considered a 'mosque' per Islamic tenets.

Justice Sharma, who retired from service one day after the Judgement was delivered, remains untroubled by the many knowledgeable critiques of the Survey Report on which he bases himself, or by such crucial findings that animal bones, glazed potteries, and graves were found beneath the demolished Babri mosque – artifacts that do not point to a Hindu site but a non-Hindu one.

It is also agreed that an idol of Ramlala – the infant Ram – and a few others were clandestinely placed inside and below the central dome of the demolished Babri mosque during the night of Dec.,22-23, 1949, and Justice Khan underscores the fact that it was only some years before that event that Hindu organizations had begun to propagate the belief that the birthplace of Ram lay precisely at the centre of the central dome, whereas through all the preceding times the Ayodhya site was generally thought to contain such a birthplace somewhere or the other. He leaves it to us to speculate why such certitude should have surfaced in the years close to India's independence from colonial rule – decades that were to see fierce ideological contestation about what the new nation should comprise, a secular democracy or a 'Hindu Rashtra'.

That politically reformulated belief about the location of the birthplace, of course, was to fuel the right-wing Hindu putsch that culminated in the wanton decimation of the Babri mosque on Dec.,6,1992, an event that does not find mention atleast in the excerpts of the Judgement thus far available.

And yet, both Justice Aggarwal and Justice Khan are able to certify that the birthplace of Ram indeed stood below the central dome of the demolished mosque. Whereas Justice Khan simply orders that "the portion beneath the central dome where at present make shift temple stands will be allotted to the share of the Hindus," Justice Aggarwal opines: "It is declared that the area covered by the central dome of the three domed structure, i.e., the disputed structure being the deity of Bhagwan Ram Janamsthan and place of birth of Lord Rama 'as per faith and belief of Hindus,' belong to plaintiffs (Suit-5; the Hindu organization pleading the case) and shall not be obstructed or interfered in any manner by the defendants."

Clearly then, the birthplace is so designated by one deciding Judge in deference to the 'faith and belief of Hindus' and the other simply as an act of acquiescence, no legally tenable evidence being cited by either.

Is that a problem larger than the one the honourable judges were conscious of attacking at great risk? It clearly is.

As *The Hindu* editorial of October 1 justly comments, "at one point, from the standpoint of political morality, the verdict could be viewed as partially rewarding those who placed the idol overnight under the central dome of the mosque and those who in 1992 razed it to the ground."

But when the same editorial also goes on to counsel that "Secular India needs to move on and not be held hostage to grievances, real or imaginary, from the distant past," it begs more than a question.

And here is why: just how is 'secular India' to be squared with juridical determinations based not in legally tenable laws and facts of evidence but on any systems of communal 'faith and belief'? Is it not the case that the contract of constitutionalism and rule of law that was broken between the state and its citizens at the times the idols were inserted and the mosque finally brought down by voluntary and extra-constitutional initiatives on the one hand and the state's complicity on the other seems now to be replicated by once again denying to the aggrieved party its due in judicial redress authorized by proof and evidence? And once again to the favour of those who were the culprits in those depredations?

How is the Sunni Waqf Board, fighting the constitutional battle for secularism, to swallow the sleight-of-hand that 'faith and belief' of a community should be deemed to constitute evidence for such a potentially game-changing verdict and the tangible and proven existence of the mosque, of the fact of worship within it till 1949, and of its brazen decimation not be seen to constitute evidence of possession?

How is secular and law-abiding India generally to consider the circumstance that where in 1993, the Supreme Court of India to which a Presidential reference had been made on behalf of the government of the day to make a determination whether a temple had stood beneath the mosque and, if so, whether it could be identified as the birthplace of Lord Ram had thought it prudent to return the said reference on the grounds that it had no wherewithal to make such determinations, the honourable Justices of the Allahabad High Court should have seen no difficulty in the matter whatsoever, feeling no need of proof that could stand the test of law?

And how is secular India to quell its apprehension that the honourable judges, in holding as they have, may have laid a precedent of enormous consequence – one to which many more suits may likewise rise for redress of real or imaginary wrongs by parties long dead and gone?

If I permit myself a reference to what I wrote on the subject of Indian secularism just the day before the verdict was due:

> At the heart of the (problem) has been the peculiar version of secularism adopted by the state from its inception, namely not a separation of church and state, but an 'equal' regard of all religious faiths.
>
> Clearly, where some 85% of all Indians are Hindus of one kind or another, that mandate of 'equal' regard finds its own disequilibrium in the politics of 'mainstream' India. Just as dependable citizenship remains coloured by denominational proclivities and preferences. ('Ayodhya and What it Implies,' www.gtobpost.com; www.liquida.com; www.butterfliesandwheels.org; www.kritikulture.blogspot.com; www.skeptic.ca.za; etc., September 29, 2010)

I fear me much that those innocent speculations have been borne out in the determination that the Allahabad Lordships have made with respect to the claims about the birthplace on the one hand and the defendants of the demolished mosque on the other.

I had concluded that post with the sentence:

> A distinct watershed moment then in the post-Independent history of 'modernising' India which will tell us whether the constitutional clock moves ahead or suffers a circumambulatory regression in time.

The Judgement seems to have answered that one as well but to the trepidation of that vast majority of Indians of all denomination who wish to strengthen pluralism and secular democracy.

III

And yet it is a tribute to the seductive substance of the Verdict apportioning a third of the site to the three contending litigants that voices are heard even among Muslims that the Judgement offers opportunity for a compromise Distinguished Muslims such as the poet, Javed Akhtar, and the other celebrity, Anu Agha, alongwith the Khadims at the Ajmer sufi shrine can be heard to welcome the verdict and see in it the opportunity to bury inter-communal tensions and animosities. After all, a third of the site has been allotted to the Sunni Waqf board where it may now build a new mosque. That speculation, the fear of further bloodshed, and the desire to lunge into the 'development' agenda of a new young India lie behind such an impulse and counsel. Indeed, one distinguished Muslim intellectual, Jalees Ahmed Khan Tareen, Vice Chancellor of Pondicherry University goes as far as to advise that Muslims 'form a public opinion saying we do not support the Board's decision to continue this fight. The one-third land should be gracefully gifted to Hindus to build the temple' (Letter to *The Hindu*, October 1) On the face of it a sort of Gandhian gesture; yet why do I feel that had Gandhi indeed been with us today on his 140th birth anniversary as I write this, he would have rather called upon ordinary Hindus to come forward and build the mosque that the Muslims lost in 1992 to an act of historic hate and criminal vendetta.

But those that earn their bread by logic and law ask the question: if the suit of the Waqf Board has been dismissed by the honourable court, on the grounds presumably that it was time-barred in law, and that the Board could not prove possession, then why have they been allotted any part of the site? And if they have been, then why has their suit been dismissed? Other than raising the main interrogation that has formed the substance of this piece so far: can 'faith and belief' be construed fit legal grounds for any judicial verdict about title to properties? And would the same criterion apply also to the 'faith and belief' of communities other than the majority Hindu community?

How much the urge to put the issue behind has weighed in these matters is movingly explicit in what Justice Khan says in parts of his 285 page Judgement. He writes:

> I remind both the warring factions of the following. The one quality which epitomized the character of Ram is tyag (sacrifice). When Prophet Mohammed entered into a treaty with the rival group at Hudayliyah, it appeared to be an abject surrender even to his staunch supporters. However the Koran described that as clear victory and it did prove so. Within a short span therefrom Muslims entered the Mecca as victors, and not a drop of blood was shed.

And again:

> Muslims must also ponder that at present the entire world wants to know the exact teaching of Islam in respect of relationship of Muslims with others. Hostility, peace, friendship, tolerance, opportunity to impress others with the Message, opportunity to strike wherever and whenever possible, or what? Noting that Indian Muslims occupy the unique position of once having been rulers, and now being a vast minority as opposed to countries where they are either a vast majority or a miniscule minority, they are therefore in the best position to tell the world the correct position. Let them start their role in the resolution of the conflict at hand.

I have cited the text in extenso because it comprises a conglomerate of the most far-reaching consequence and deliberation.

The impulse seems clear enough, namely, to learn how to forge a new and better life and future for the community, and presumably for all Indians, from an act of tyag (sacrifice) or surrender.

Curiously, where Ram is cited for his selfless ability to sacrifice, what is overlooked is that those that speak in his name seem to have imbibed none of those qualities. Note that not one spokesman of the BJP has so far publicly committed that, arising from the tripartite division of the property, the Muslims may now build a mosque on the portion allotted to them, let alone make the gesture that such a task will draw cooperation from their Hindu brethren. Over the last two days we have only heard the chief of the RSS and other spokesmen of the Hindu right to say how everybody must now set their shoulder to building that 'grand' temple.

Simultaneously the event at Hudayliyah seems cleary invoked to inspire Muslims whose solid legal claims have been set aside to emulate the example of the Prophet and help put this festering sore of a problem behind them.

Yet, all that notwithstanding, it must be emphasized that nothing would be more erroneous than to view the Babri site suit as one exclusively between Hindus and Muslims. At its heart reside issues that necessarily bear on the determinations of all Indians who take the Indian Constitution and secular democracy to be founding informants of their lives as citizens.

It is for that reason that, regardless of the possibilities of any out-of-court compromise in the matter, the issues flagged by those that know the law and those that wish to live by it must be carried to the highest Court in the land. What affirmations or revisions of the Allahabad High Court Judgement may there emerge can then atleast be regarded as the law of the land in such matters, however it turns out. It may be said of course that every secular and law-abiding citizen of India will harbour the hope that the Supreme Court of India which had many years ago refused to make any determination on the question of birthplace etc., will no doubt recognize the enormity of what has transpired in the High Court and order due corrections.

IV

Which brings us to the politics of the question. Put in one word, the Hindu rightwing, and the BJP will find it impossible to resist the opportunity (as they see it) to plough their 'victory' in terms of a judicially secular endorsement of their religious sentiment and ratchet up the ante in familiar style, and the Muslim organizations not to be downcast at a denial of their legal rights by an Institution of the state that they have trusted the most in favour of that majoritarian sentiment.

How much that euphoria on one side and gloom on the other may or may not tell upon the life of the nation in the years upto a final determination of the Babri case will crucially depend on how intelligently hoi polloi allows or does not allow the politics of aggrandizement or resentment to influence electoral democracy and cultural pluralism. Not to speak of how the liberal classes, influential sections of the media, and agencies of the state behave themselves in thwarting a dreaded return to the abrasively repulsive Ninetees which saw thousands of lives lost in the aftermath of the Babri mosque demolition.

India may indeed again be on test as it was then. Hopefully, it will not repeat the failure that cost the nation grievously.

October 2010

An Open Letter to Ten Percent India, Myself Included

The Games are over. Our revels have ended for now. Many white people have gone satisfied; some even impressed. What might have been a bland and colourless event elsewhere was rendered magical as the hooded cobras put in an appearance to greet the visitors. In what other country would you have pressed Langurs into service to shoo off mere monkeys. You might say that the abiding world of Kipling rendered what might have been the anasthetised efficiency of gadgetry a seductive, orientalist bonanza. Brand India once again proved itself distinctive, syncretising anti-deluvian flood with exotic food, laid-back timelessness with the flurried event, Brahminical self-regard with the fear of failure, devotion to imagined glory with the shame-faced last-minute attention to reality on the ground.

But the worry about corruption remains, and it shames our sense of our collective self. Canny operators made killings, as too many cooks stirred the froth to gainful purpose. But the screaming channels would have us believe this is the first we have seen of corruption in India. Really? When and where has it been otherwise? Your point must be that this once we were shamed because it was for all to see, most wretchedly the first world media to whom we wished to sell ourselves as something other than we are.

By all means, get at them in the days to come. But do answer me this one question: why, just why does it happen that corruption, understood as take-on-the-sly, so undoes our uprightness while the metropolitan eye carries on winking at the congenitally inhuman depravity that suffuses our soulless self-absorption in the successes of a nation-state where some ten percent of us own some ninety percent of the national wealth, and the 'other' ninety percent or so (whom we hid behind the grand Games posters or shunted out of town) subsist (cruel word) on the rest of the ten percent? Does such an order of inequity protected by systems of orderly injustice comprise corruption? Or should the thought simply perish, while we rail at those among our own kind who did us in? One way of sorting this out might be to say 'crony capitalism no, no; capitalism yes, yes.' Is it that simple?

Of the 8 million or so children worldwide who die before the age of 5, 2 million die in India. 42 % of the world's under-nourished children and 31% of the 'stunted' ones are Indians. Nowhere, not even in sub-saharan Africa, are pregnant and lactating mothers as anaemic and as prone to die as in India. Nowhere else do as many millions defecate in the open for want of sanitation as in India. Nowhere are millions obliged to drink water from chemically contaminated ditches and drains for want of potable sources. Nowhere do as many millions die from preventable gastro-enteric diseases for want of access to clean water and the most primitive of preventive medication. And what of food, since nutrition is out of the reckoning? Do I hear us complain of astronomical food prices, and yet never wonder whether some 800 million or more Indians who have no greater than half a dollar to spend on everything a day eat anything at all? If we do wonder, where is the energy of attention that ought to go into all that in comparison with the righteous anger we spout at low quality of macadam on the highways of the capital city? Or trash thrown uncaringly out of gleaming automobiles? And the lack of promptness with which the menials must be ordered to remove it from sight?

Yet none of this qualifies as corruption; and rightly: would you not agree that our collective disregard, our accomplished Podsnappery, in relation to those details connote something far worse than corruption as we define the term? Would it be wrong to designate an order of things that makes such cruelties of exploitation, expropriation, inequity, the law's oppression, the contumely of policy necessary to 'advancement' depravity and barbarism of a conquistador dimension? And all in the name of pursuing democracy, wherein the legitimating 'demos' is left without a loaf. Or do we have a ready answer for that, namely, dangerously anti-national left-wing voices the sooner quelled the better. After all, we do at bottom think we are the nation, don't we?

II

Another thing: how we have been lauding the fact that so many medals have been won. To that computation you might add won to some 2/3rd measure by our women sportspersons. And of those some 3/4th nameless women from the 'hinterlands' that never seem to form any part of the 'emerging great power' narrative with which we cloy our earholes day in and day out.

Medal winning women from the land of Irom Sharmila who has been on a fast for over a decade in Manipur. When was she last in focus on our TV screens? Medal winning women from the badlands of Haryana where unborn female foetuses are put to the sword by order of the scions of martial patriarchy. Did you hear Krishna Poonia (Gold medal in Discuss throw) allude to that irony? And Deepika Mahato from Jharkhand Adivasi forgotten land (father auto driver) who shot the arrow home for another Gold, leaving the Brits and the mighty Aussies and the New Zealanders behind? And the foursome who raced to that magnicicent Gold in the 4x400 Relay? And many others.

And practically none of them English-speaking.

So is it too much to ask that we might now use the power the state bestows upon us in diverse ways and through diverse means to campaign for the following:

- that the powers-that-be begin to demonstrably include the 'hinterlands' in their grandiose schemes of 'development,' and not just in sports; and not just for electoral propaganda, allowing the women especially on the ground to lead from the front;
- that the *khap* warlords in the badlands of the north where women are either killed off in the womb, or subsequently ordered dead should they stray into thinking for themselves are rounded up and put into medieval torture chambers where they belong;
- that the mettle that these our undemanding and selfless women have shown for us to flaunt to the world now become cause for us to lay siege to political party offices, legislatures, and the parliament until the promised 33% reservation for women in these bodies is made the law of the land;
- that those thousands of labouring hands who put the Games infrastructure in place while the busybodies were busy cutting each other and strutting upon the stage be now given their due in housing, health care, education, dignified wage, and in the hallways where policies are made for the nation; and not just those who thus laboured in delhi (a hundred of them paying with their lives; think of the jingoism that

invades our living rooms at the news of a single soldier's death), but the entire class of famished and degraded workers whose sweat and blood and dour defiance of hunger and pestilence oil the wheels of our modernity and greatness. Can we campaign that their disenfranchised children be now allowed free and full use of the facilities their mothers and fathers, brothers and sisters have built for the glory of India?

- that the cacophony about 'corruption' is somewhat remedied to include our own un-named complicities and culpabilities in the silent ways in which we subscribe to and legitimize the gluttony, greed, and class-based grab which enriches the one and consigns the nine into animal existence, or worse. Can we pick up the courage to remind ourselves and the nation at large that the Constitution enjoins upon us to be not just a 'secular' but also a 'socialist' republic?

Any hard-boiled left ideologue would retort that much of what I ask is baloney bred of unfounded idealism. And he/she would have a point. After all the same middle class that applauds the maverick and marauding cinematic icon, the 'angry young man,' who disregards the rule of law etc., (showing all representatives of the state complicit in the villainous cruelties of the Thakur, the smuggler, or the heinously corrupt and criminal politician), unleashes unconscionable violence, kills off one tainted scion of the state after another, is ready to go for the kill if the 'Maoist' or the 'Naxalite' does the same in real life as opposed to reel life. So the ideologue would indeed have a point. Yet, I say with the Gypsies in Tom Jones, let us try the power of shame for now. Its effects are invisibly slow but often long-lasting.

So, dear ten-percent India, of whom I am one, is it time to say 'yes we should, yes we can'? Ergo, yes we should, yes we can first of all revisit our own socializations and our own loci, a circumstance without which our bark will remain hollow.

Can we acknowledge to ourselves that democracy is not only a matter of free speech wherein the fourth estate stands for all of it, but about the other three estates doing their assigned and foresworn bit to ensure that the dispossessed who make the nation go round have access to the bite which is by right their's?

The Games have come and gone, but let us stop playing the games we play all year round. We no longer fool even ourselves.

October 2010

Eminences of the Bench

Ponderous But Vulnerable

There is that vignette in Marquez's *Autumn of the Patriarch* where the protagonist looks idly out of the window at the bay below and seems to see an array of ships lined there, not all the same but their make and model spanning the centuries gone by.

'Magical Realism' everybody said. Including the best and brightest of teachers in the universities of the world. All except the author himself.

Same was the pedagogic fate that befell the opening fare of *A Hundred Years of Solitude* – two Latino rampagers visiting an Indian village (Indian as in South America), and beguiling the natives with the mysteries of a magnet and a compass. 'Magical Realism' yet again.

Till Marquez in an elaborate interview confessed to doing or meaning nothing magical but being squarely within the realms of the mimetic/realist tradition of fiction-writing. But just how?

On the first count, the composite image of ships spanning the centuries meant to suggest how in Latin American history, accreted layers of colonial oppression were ever embedded in the political semi-consciousness of the average perceiver as one historical whole – the gone-by never quite gone-by.

And on the second count, how the colonizing metropolitan West took hegemony to the hinterlands through technologies (magnet/compass) by claiming magical powers of redress for them, whereas at bottom meant to be deployed as mere instruments of domination. Nostromo, Nostromo?

Most instructive both these contexts, methinks, for those of us who seek to unravel the qualities of change and the complex of perceptions accompanying them now here in India.

II

The second first: haven't we heard every day, every damn day you might say, for the last two decades since the Washington Consensus came to be embraced by our well-meaning nationalist avant gardes how the market, driven, deepened and rendered ever more sophisticated by infusions of gitzmos and gadgetries is guaranteed to annihilate our inherited ills of penury and perverse backwardness?

Only to find that this magical embrace has indeed remedied the penury of the mere millionaires, rendering them billionaires, and elevated some ten percent Indians to world metropolitan standards, while consigning millions more of mere indians to enhanced levels of hunger, disease, and desperation. To wit, the magnet and the compass have all pointed away from the well-being of those in whose name these were adopted, and towards those for whom they were actually meant.

Give unto Caesar what is Caesar's. Those that have shall get. For the meek there is always heaven. As in the myriad Astha (faith) channels on television.

Now to the first: the just concluded Commonwealth Games saga has brought to light, if it ever needed to be so brought to light, the fact India continues to live and jostle among many centuries simultaneously. The slave-driver with the feudal lord with the colonial bureaucrat with the private entrepreneur with the latest whiz kid and his comprador buddies on Wall Street, the turfs now so rattled by the rough and tumble of democratic glare that none of these seems any longer self-sufficient, self-contained, or entirely safe from contention.

III

To a point where lately the Eminencies of the Bench, even on the Supreme Court of India seem open to question, and not wholly able to hold to the legacies of the past, as leveling agents of critique and resistance nibble at their grandeur of old.

On the positive side, the times press on many of them to raise an egalitarian voice in favour of mere rickshaw pullers, common vendors, children in slavery, dalits in thrall, women snuffed out in the womb, and in support of those who argue that laws of contempt are at bottom calculated to muzzle even expressions of the plain truth of things (Justice Shailendra Kumar, we salute you.)

For this our thanks and deep admiration. For we know that such transformations of the psyche, once they begin to happen even in some far corner and from some non-metropolitan Bench, may not be easily reversed. Much of this of course for the reason that increased doses of oppression in India are now also accompanied by a larger constituency for justice among vox populi. Can't put down those NGOs, rights activists, whistle-blowers, however you may try. The need for legitimacy requires that they exist.

But on the negative side, very negligible initiatives yet to address the bold questions that have been raised by the likes of Shanti Bhushan and Prashant Bhushan, the first an erstwhile Law Minister and Senior Advocate of the Supreme Court, and the latter an admirable Senior Counsel on behalf of a spectrum of inequities that plague the common citizen in city and hinterland.

It is to be noted that this father-son duo have actually submitted on affidavit to the highest court listings of what they consider to be substantive evidences of corruption engaged in by no less than eight or so past Chief Justices of that august body. And even raised questions about some determinations made by the current Chief Justice in relation to a corporate house.

An extraordinary circumstance in modern India, truly, glossed with his usual aplomb and magnificence of articulaltion by the redoubtable ex-Chief Justice, V.R. Krishna Iyer, who at ninety plus may yet be our most un-put-downable rebel. I quote him:

> Now it is left to the nation to move on this matter of paramount importance. This is an astonishing event – the rarest of the rare kind (justice Iyer's dark humour in evidence in that phrase, since it is most associated with the law that stipulates that only the 'rarest of the rare' homicides qualify for capital punishment.) If India is not a coward, if its swaraj is not merely soft and formal but firm and phenomenal, an appropriately high-level investigation, with consequential follow-up action that is punitive and reformatory, is imperative. This is no time to hesitate or involve in an exchange of rhetoric. Nor is this the time for a guarded and diplomatic reaction. This is unprecedented: a succession of Chief Justices have been publicly accused by a Senior Advocate of standing, risking his career (*The Hindu*, September, 21, 2010).

The all-important question is who will bell the cat?

Under the present constitutional dispensation in India, judges of the superior courts may only be impeached by parliament upon, first, at least 50 members of the Rajya Sabha making such a request to the Vice President of India. And after all due process, the removal from the bench by a 2/3rds majority of parliamentarians in both houses.

Such a thing was tried once; it did not work.

There is simply no other redress for now.

Here is the further fact: we know that whereas in that land of our 'strategic partnership,' America, nominees suggested by the President have first to pass the test of severe grilling by the House and the Senate, wherein everything about the candidate, down to the colour of the undergarments is up for scrutiny, here in India of many simultaneous centuries, our Lordships happily and in close quarters appoint themselves through the secret proceedings of a Collegium which comprises just three brethren of the fraternity. And none of those proceedings open to question, or to the provisions of the Right to Information Act. A sort of Masonic conclave which thinks it is none of anybody's business how one or the other brother – sister most rarely – is elevated.

This then remains one of those most ancient of ships in the harbour, resisting the transformative gadgetries of modern India. Like all modern gadgetries, of course, the concerns of India's judiciary rarely bear upon the lives of the disenfranchised millions, since they have no wherewithal even to approach this august institution. But if ten percent India now makes a pitch for finding ways to clean those Augean stables, some day, some distant day, vox populi might be encouraged to mumble that the blind-folded Lady with the even-scales has come to some life, and the pronouncements that fall from her lips may be free of fear, favour, or taint.

Clearly, something has got to give. The accusers must either be proved wrong, or the wrongs they underscore be righted. And righted not just in the cases under question, but in ways that can bring the Institution of the Judiciary somewhat more into the ambit of a just and non-discriminatory democracy of which we are so proud.

These are days when the oldest of ships wrecked centuries ago are vulnerable to disturbance on behalf of inquisitive scuba divers and national agencies. And the findings reflect on the quality of lives then lived, and their times are often then evaluated and held accountable by modern day historians. Nor may the magnet and the compass these days entirely beguile whole populations.

Nothing would be more honourable and altruistic and wholly in the 'national interest' than for the Eminencies on the Bench to recognize the signs of the times and to proceed as per the law and the requirements of transparency. Some may be hurt thereby, but India will surely stand to gain.

Tailpiece

This writer, at the end of a talk on India given in 1984 to a group of American citizens in the suburb of Berabou, was asked the question: 'how may we know the real Indian? Since there is no end of languages, religions, castes, regions, ethnicities, colours of skin, what-have-you.'

I recall saying that any real Indian will be heard to say two things: one, 'I know, I know'; and, two, 'not my fault, not my fault.' This across the length and breadth of the subcontinent, and across all communities and classes.

Who else but the unimpeachable brotherhood on the Bench may rescue us from this most Brahminical of legacies?

October 2010

Corruption Makes Neo-Liberalism Go

These are the days for corruption.

India never had so much lucre going around, so big a class of people with lolling tongues and copious pockets, and so little prohibition to illicit money-making on behalf of the neo-liberal state and its institutions.

Thus, why not? Especially when humongous acquisition and conspicuous consumption have come to be conflated with the promise of salvation not just here but in the hereafter.

But let me backtrack, and indulge some esoteric speculations on what corruption has variously been seen to comprise through the times. As I see it, all of the variants invite considerations with respect to the human subject and how he/she constructs collective human endeavours and defines his/her equation with supra-human stipulations. Or, how such constructions are handed down to him/her by authorized agents of social and spiritual power.

II

In the good old classical Catholic construction of these matters, it was to be understood that corruption was born of what Milton was to call 'man's first disobedience,' namely his defiance of god's injunction not to eat of 'the fruit of the tree of the knowledge of good and evil.'

In a pre-Copernican world of ideas, then, the homo sapien was not sent to the earth to have a good time, but to constantly mull his sin, and in his exile from heaven to expiate and self-flagellate in order that his repentance could be rewarded with a re-entrance to the Garden made blissful by god's forgiveness and reinstated love.

In that view of corruption, self-evidently, no one, but no one was free either of sin or corruption, including those who took upon themselves to do god's work in the church and to minister to sinners who came to them for guidance. Or those laggards whom they sought out and not infrequently punished severely for their own everlasting good.

Such a universe of ideas made it a matter of little importance as to who ruled over whom, or how, until of course times changed and such matters acquired enormous and embarrassing importance, often indeed to fatal consequences to individuals, institutions, and nations.

Within 'mainstream' Hindu thought, of course, corruption, corruptibility, and nearness to or distance from the deities were and insidiously still remain related to hierarchies of birth across Varnas. Thus the Brahminical castes could never ever be corrupt, or indeed guilty of other forms of trespass. The political class of ruling Kshatriya kings, if anything, had an obligation to pursue Vaibhav (opulence), obligation which the Brahmins were duty-bound to help further through various Yagnyas (oblations etc.,) made to the chanting of hymns to the gods. It must be an interesting and unique feature of Hinduism that its pantheon includes a goddess of wealth, Laxmi, who is to this day worshipped for the bestowal of prosperity on the best known festival-day on the Indian sacral calendar, namely, Diwali, when homesteads are lighted to welcome the goddess into the favour of the worshipper.

III

The old Christian ways began to change with the advent of what we call the exchange economy. Slowly but surely, the possibilities of capital accumilation, of surplus productivity, and of the leap from what one should produce and consume to what one could produce and consume – all of that incrementally at higher and higher levels as rates of profit increased – seemed to resurrect if not the human soul then the self-esteem of the species, as flesh began to feel not as despicable as the old church had taught. (A matter in which Hindu thought had remained miles ahead in time, until historical circumstances of diverse conquests came to breed squeamishness and denial.)

For groups of men at the helm of affairs, living was now too seductive to be dashed by the teachings of the decrepit old church. Time then to readjust doctrine to suit new aspirations and possibilities. Suddenly the light of a new truth dawned upon the thinking elites of Europe: it was neither the claim of a humble life-style nor of the nature of work done upon the earth in god's name that would justify the human subject to god on Judgement day. Rather, what would count would be the quality of ones' Faith – a category deliciously unquantifiable and unamenable to collective policing.

Much as man's sinful nature remained a constant of Christian teaching, a caveat was now introduced: it was discovered that human subjectivity could be neatly cognized in a duality: that whereas man's Will was fallen, his Wit, or some part of it, remained 'erect.' (Some metaphor there.)

It can then be seen that corruption now began to acquire a moral meaning. It was entirely upto individuals to examine their own ethical lives. Ergo, some may be corrupt, others not, An argument that thus refuted the twin notions that either all mankind was corrupt ontologically, or that corruption ensued necessarily from new and evolved systems of money-making.

Indeed, a Christian theologian based in Geneva was to extend the argument as he struck the last fatal blow even to the possibility or desirability of ethical behaviour. He taught that nothing we did or believed in here on earth mattered a fig to god, since he in his infinite wisdom had predetermined what numbers of us were to be saved at the final account. Such ones were the god's 'elect' (the earliest and perhaps most telling definition of the concept of election, except that democracies only elect the lucky ones to ephemeral glory for short periods of time here on earth, whereas god's election was to be forever.)

So, in that scheme of things, how might you know whether god did or did not have kind thoughts towards you? But of course by the quality of life he granted you in the here-and-now. If you proved to be a 'loser' here, it was most likely that you were meant to be out of god's favour; but if you proved to be a 'winner,' acquiring property, wealth, and the powers that came with all of that, why he obviously meant well by you. Thus no more sure indicator of salvation than wealth. And each episode of well-being then began to be followed by an episode of thanksgiving and prayer (just read Daniel Defoe's *The Adventures of Robinson Crusoe*, and you might find that when his goat gives milk, or when he grows the first grains of wheat, he quickly falls to pray – a paradigm of behaviour which suffused the early strivings of those that came to colonise America, much as Crusoe came to colonise the island upon which he was ship-wrecked., including the black man, Friday. By that reckoning, incidentally, the beggars of the world entirely have a good argument against praying, since they have no thanks to give for anything.)

This American paradigm of the inseparability of acquisition and consumption from prayer has, as I have written in columns before now, come visibly to inform the political and spiritual economy of India's post neo-liberal upwardly-mobile classes, a fact that illuminates the marriage of extreme lucre-lust and flaunted religiosity among the Hindutva-espousing Hindus across metropolitan India, extending rapidly even to the hinterlands. (Within the Muslim world decreed by the Koran, inequalities of endowment are entirely willed by God; corruption enters into the question only if those that have fail in the duty that is ordained on them to part with a certain percentage of their wealth to the needy by way of *Zakat*).

And, interestingly, in the zeitgeist of these classes, corruption is always what the other fellow is doing to outstrip competition. This heinous betrayal elicits much moralizing on TV channels, even as, like the proverbial cat in the adage, the moralizer at heart wishes nothing more than to exchange places with those that are thus vilified.

Or corruption comes to be simply disregarded under guise of a superior cynicism which knows that such has always been the case and will remain so. Clearly, a theoretical option that only the haves may proffer, since corruption makes little difference to their well-being anyway. Unless indeed a campaign against the other man's, corporates', political party's real or perceived corruption bears the prospect of one's own further advancement among the Who is Who list of worthies. Until recently in India it was normal and routine to ask of a match for one's daughter as to how much he earned on the wrong side of the table, salaries being looked upon as an incidental endowment.

Not surprisingly, thus, the object of obtrusively aggressive prayer mechanisms of these classes is not to ask the gods for a peace that passeth understanding, but for the next acquisition that is crucial to self-esteem and social advancement. And to show to the world how much in sync the worshipper is with the latest fineries that the business world makes available to embellish the act of worship.

Berating corrupt practices, these new elites simultaneously will be heard to endorse all and every institutional arrangement conducive to corruption, such as, for example, to address the current moment, corporate lobbying. What is wrong with it they ask the yokels who proffer analyses suspiciously derisive of greed and the philosophy of best-foot-forward.

IV

In a disconcerting book titled *Civilization and its Discontents* the father of the science (pseudo-science if you like) of psychology, Sigmund Freud, was to offer a painful formulation: that the human psyche is driven by two antagonistic drives, the 'pleasure principle' and the 'reality principle,' the first seeking the fulfillment of desire and the latter reminding the subject of obligations to collective social life with its inbuilt constraints. Conclusion: unhappiness is the human lot whether desire is fulfilled or dutifully suppressed. The one may lead to corruption, the other to subtle forms of disease. All that without regard to what the gods will or what arrangements of production and distribution obtain in a given social order. Externalities of equity or inequity bear not at all on the Freudian paradigm.

V

Among the religious archives, it is perhaps in Buddhist teaching that corruption is shown to be the necessary corollary of excess and inequality.

Speaking of which, a final construct suggests to us that, whether or not corruption is a defining characteristic of human imperfectability, its actual operation and ambit relate intimately to what sort of social order we give to ourselves. The less rational and egalitarian a state and its institutional mechanisms, the less fair-minded its systems of accountability and control, the less humane its distributive justice, the less transparent its order of productive life, the less caring and non-discriminatory its thought for the least, the more corrupt it will be.

It is to be learnt that because the American constitutionalists, as good Christians, did not have the faith that any human being could be trusted with the absolutes of reason and benevolence, they opted not for a government by men but government by laws, binding thereby, as it were, all subjects in a common contract of how to deal with fallibility. And who will say that the American system of government has not, give or take, lived upto that originary perception. The presumption here is not that men and women must strive to be morally perfect, or ever can be, but that the law must oblige them not to override the contract with other citizens whose failings and rights must be seen to make them equal in the stipulations of the constitutional contract. And that, if and when transgressions happen, all must ready themselves to take their medicine without regard to status. Thus while a Bernie Madoff is sentenced to 150 years within six months of his infraction, our own Ramlingam Raju of the Satyam scandal detected about the same time as Madoff carries on through the courts merrily from one procrastination to the next. All of which should not be read to mean that equality before the law within the American scheme of things has absolute value on the ground. But the value that it does have may not be as easily or as blatantly violated as it may be in that largest democracy, India.

Here, whereas all the good laws exist on the statute books, the force of cuturally accreted and imbibed notions of inequality among citizens, the most gross to be found anywhere – the persistent subtext that democracy may have decreed non-discriminatory governance, but some must always remain more equal than others, and thus more above the law than others, be it for reasons of birth or access to hereditary forms of power, all reinforced by other acquired forms of clout – continues to bend the formal features of constitutionalism either to atavistic or newly constructed structures of privilege.

Infuse that construct with the neo-liberal free-for-all of the last two decades or more, and it is no wonder that corruption today has swallowed every segment of the power-elite, not excluding that fourth estate watchdog. To wit, even within a capitalist social order, depending on how laws pertaining to asset-creation, ownership, transactions at home and abroad, forms of state regulation are either loosened or made stringent, and depending on how investigative agencies are either allowed non-discriminatory operation or enslaved to the clout of the transgressor who holds the state in thrall, corruption and corruptibility must rise or fall. Put another way, even class states may define a spectrum of allegiance as between the people at large and those whose bidding the state is meant to do. What we have been seeing in India has been a gross infringement of that balance. The result: the last two decades have seen a burgeoning of numbers at both ends – more dollar billionares, and more absolute numbers of people who crawl through forgettable lives.

The question: will the systems correct themselves at whatever cost to the interests of the haves, or will the current crisis of faith lead to other forms of challenge. Not to say that those other forms are not already with us.

There are those like the present writer who would like capitalism, and not just crony capitalism, to go before corruption may. And there are others more canny who know that corruption must go if capitalism is to survive.

Either way, there is a job to be done.

December 2010

2011

Binayak Sen Sentenced to Life Term

A Sessions court judge in Raipur, capital of the BJP-ruled state of Chhattisgarh, has pronounced Binayak Sen guilty of sedition and conspiracy against the state, and sentenced the good doctor to a life term in prison.

So who is Binayak Sen?

An alumni of the prestigious Christian Medical College in Vellore, who had the foolhardiness to turn his back on career both there and in the equally prestigious Jawahar Lal Nehru U niversity in Delhi, follow the lead of the late and legendary Shankar Guha Niyogi – who was murdered some years ago by paid assassins of industrial interests for his dogged and path-breaking, hence dangerous, labours among the unorganized adivasis, dalits, women, and other voiceless denizens of the backwaters of Chhattisgarh against some of the most gruesome exploitation that free Indians have known – and devote the last three or so decades of his still young life to serving among the poorest of the poor.

For decades now, this selfless and saintly man has run a weekly clinic deep in the Sal forests of the region that has drawn tribals from as far away as 30 kilometers for healing. Their only other option a two-day walk through the jungles. Sen trained hundreds of tribals to become healthcare workers, an effort whose sterling success found it acceptance as state policy, christened Mitanin Swasthya Yojna (volunteer health programme).

Inspired by Niyogi, Sen also helped set up the Shaheed (martyr) hospital, one that still operates with donations from coal miners.

Indeed much of his work parallels the sort of immersion in ministering to the wretched of the earth that the world associates with the Nobel prize winner, Mother Teresa.

With one all-important difference. Binayak, unlike the good Mother, did not think there was any great purchase in being meek. Thus it is that he made the grievous mistake of standing up and speaking for the 'human rights' of god-fatherless forest dwellers in the face of the cruelties and denials vented upon them by the state, by its vigilante agency of goons named 'Salwa Judum,' and, if only the judge who sentenced him had listened, by the insurgent Maoists as well.

In particular, Sen's opposition to the displacement of a hundred thousand tribals from their homes and hearths by vigilante goons of the state made the latter saw red. Ostensibly done to facilitate police operations against the Moaist insurgents and for their own safety (sic) such displacement and any resistance to it by innocent tribals has caused unconscionable brutalities to be inflicted upon them, often on the charge that they were informants to the insurgents, and guilty of sheltering them.

As to Sen himself, does it matter that in repeatedly asking for 'equity and peace' whenever querried by the media, he rarely balked from condemning the atrocities perpetrated by the armed Naxalites on innocent men, women, and children.

But in an era of McCarthyism that now seems to accompany the murderous impatience of India's state and corporate combine to enhance private wealth, Binayak's infuriating doggedness of purpose in staying his course in the hinterland among the victims on the ground (had he been, like so many of us, content to combine a lucrative metropolitan career with urbanite activism, things may not have been so dire, either for him or for the state), finally broke the camel's back, as it were.

The official finger went up, declaring the doctor public enemy number one.

II

His crimes:

- ministering to the sullen malcontents among the dregs of the dispossessed, when the state and its vigilantes had ab initio and without requirement of proof designated them Maoist sympathizers;
- visiting a sick 74-year old Naxalite ideologue in jail in the capacity both of a human rights worker (indeed, as vice-president of the well-known People's Union for Civil Liberties), and as a doctor – all with due

knowledge and permission of the relevant authorities both within the jail and outside; never mind that the said Maoist ideologue has curiously himself never yet been charged for being such, or for belonging to a banned organization. He is in jail on a plain murder charge!

- and, ostensibly, (ostensibly because a slew of facts on record point to the fake nature of the evidence here), couriering three letters from the Naxal ideologue to a sympathizer outside; a charge that falls flat in the face of the testimony given by no less than jail authorities to the effect that whenever he met Sanyal, the Naxal ideologue, Sen did so in the presence of the police, and that there is no way in which he could have carried any materials unbeknown to such authorities; further investigations reveal that said letters may indeed have been 'plants,' and that the testimony of the lone witness who claims to have heard someone else say that the said letters were couriered remained uncorroborated hearsay. It is germane here to recall that Vinayak Damodar Savarkar was let off in the Gandhi murder case on the ground that the approver's testimony could not be independently corroborated!

III

The Charge:

The provision of the charge of 'Sedition' was, as anyone would know, incorporated into Indian jurisprudence by the British colonial rulers, like most other punitive provisions as well. And it was under that provision that both Lokmanya Tilak ('freedom is my birthright') and Gandhi were to come to be tried then.

Not many know that during the deliberations of the Indian Constitution-makers, the overwhelming vote was for dropping the provision of 'Sedition' (that Gandhi had called the 'Prince' of all black laws) post-Independence. During those formative debates, Nehru had spoken as follows of Sectiion 124-A (Sedition) of the Penal Code as it was bequeathed to the new nation-state:

> Take again Section 124-A of the Indian Penal Code. Now so far as I am concerned that particular section is highly objectionable and obnoxious and it should have no place both for practical and historical reasons, if you like, in any body of laws that we might pass. The sooner we get rid of it the better.

Retained as it was, shamefully, the Supreme Court of India subsequently added an all-important caveat (in the Kedarnath judgement) to it to the effect that NO act of free expression would tantamount to 'Sedition' unless there was clear and irrefutable evidence of 'incitement to violence' against the duly constituted state.

In the instant case, even if the three fatal letters were indeed couriered by Binayak Sen, none carries within their texts the least hint of any such violent intent.

Which would make sense in the light of the fact that Binayak, as stated above, has throughout his human rights career pleaded privately and publicly for non-violent resistance to the havoc wrought among tribals' lives and rights by marauding mining and other corporates in violation of a litany of statutory laws, such as Schedule V of the Forest Rights Act.

Binayak's great mistake here has been to condemn state-sponsored vigilante violence in the same breath as all other forms of violence.

A fact that goes hand-in-hand with some other facts, namely the sly collaboration of many corporates on the ground in Chhattisgarh with the insurgents, to whom they regulary have paid protection-money, and, if reports are to be credited, passing on explosive materials from factory premises as well. All done with careful deniability.

None of which tantamounts to sedition against the state! And for the simple enough reason that during the neo-liberal phase of India's famed 'development' over the last quarter century, the corporates have come to BE the state. As incontrovertibly simple as that.

IV

Here is what seems to be happening in contemporary India.

Should you have a full-blown fascist under your chassis, you are ok. The fascist after all, as always, is only the political front of the marauding corporate. That this is no piece of leftward polemics has been recently confirmed by the leak of the Radia tapes wherein all the fine meshings of connectivity between industrial houses, their lobbyists, their political benefactors, and other segments of the brokering power-elite among the media and bureaucracy have come to inglorious light.

But if you have under your bed someone suspected to be red (one of such suspicious circumstances in the Binayak case, would you believe it, is reference to the fact that he and people around him sometimes were heard to accost each other as 'comrade') you are best dead. And, beginning with the water-shed official murder of Shankar Guha Niyogi, the long line of perfectly innocent workers thus liquidated in those regions of India is indeed a long one; not to speak of hundreds upon hundreds who rot in the jails, often without trial.

Another way of saying the same is this: no greater enemy of the republic than the one who insists that the establishment is after all obliged by oath to the Constitution to implement its promises of equity in asset ownership and distribution, redolently enshrined in article 39 ('Directive Principles of State Policy').

Here is how that pernicious article reads:

> The State shall, in particular, direct its policy towards securing –
>
> (a) that the citizens, men and women equally, have the right to an adequate means of livelihood;
>
> (b) that the ownership and control of the material resources of the community are so distributed as best to subserve the common good;
>
> (c) that the operation of the economic system does not result in the concentration of wealth and means of production to the common detriment.

Cannily, those that framed the Constitution had the great good sense to stipulate that the 'Directive Principles' would not be enforceable by law! Imagine what might have happened to class rule had they indeed been thus enforceable. The pity is that some mavericks like Binayak Sen insist that these pledges to 'we the people of India' who chose, don't you know, 'to constitute India into a Sovereign Socialist Secular Democratic Republic,' promising 'Justice, social, economic and political,' ought to be implemented if Indian Democracy is to have substance and true legitimacy.

More fool they.

Especially now when India is set on a path of humongous 'growth' and world-mastery. What could be more seditious than to puncture that ruling-class aspiration with reminders of equity and justice, or to conflate 'we the people of India' with the Republic and its future.

Thus if it takes our own McCarthyism to hold back an avalanche of menace from below, so be it. Reason that explains the current onslaught on human rights protagonists of any hue. Indeed, the next internationally recognized (and Padma Shree Awardee here at home) human rights worker facing the prospect of arrest even as I write is no less than Teesta Setalvad of the Citizens For Justice and Peace. Currently, the Pioneer newspaper, owned by a Rajya Sabha member of the Bharatiya Janata Party (the right-wing Hindu BJP) has unleashed a full campaign of calumny against her for the trouble she has taken since 2002 to stand up for the victims of the Gujarat massacres, and to pursue the legal processes of redressal on their side. A campaign of lies aided and abetted by an erstwhile co-worker of her organization, Rais Khan, who has thought it fit for reasons not far to seek to gang up on Teesta on the side of the very Hindutva brigades who remain the accused parties in that massacre.

Indeed, before long, the state might think it fit to go so far in its collaboration with its 'strategic partner' as to set up our own Abu Ghraib and Guantanamo Bay.

Time will tell.

January 2011

Isn't Dissent the Essence of Democracy?

A charge of sedition is contemplated against Arundhati Roy following some statements she made at a meeting in Delhi supporting the demand for Kashmiri 'azadi' (variously interpretable, secession from the Union being one).

No evidence has come to light that she intended to either engage in or incite violence-provisos integral to a charge of sedition. It is her case that she only reiterated what thousands of Kashmiris have been demanding everyday over the last many months in the cities and bylanes of the Valley.

I outlined my understanding of the Kashmir question at some length recently in an article titled 'Kashmir Now or Never.' It formed the 'cover story' of the July-August 2010 issue of the journal, *Communalism Combat*, and was published by *Kashmir Times* as well. That article should make it clear that I do not share Ms. Roy's understanding of either the genesis of the Kashmir problem, its continuing career, or the merits of granting secession to the state.

I also do not subscribe to the view that the Indian state 'annexed' the state in 1947 against the popular will, or has functioned as a 'colonial power' since the Accession of the State to the Union of India. Or that Indian bad faith has been the only obstacle to a plebiscite in Jammu and Kashmir.

Also, despite my having critiqued over the years the viciousness of the doctrine of 'nationalism,' I do not fully share Ms. Roy's anarchist view of the nation-state, or disregard the speculation on what alternatives offer themselves as achievable paradigms. Likewise, where I agree that the prevalence of left-wing extremism in many parts of the north underscores the class-based character of the Indian state, I have been firmly of the view that armed struggle is not the answer to this malaise.

Having said that, I continue to have the highest admiration for Arundhati's courage of conviction and her commitment to millions of Indians – victims to a wide spectrum of iniquities. I have also been fully in agreement with her perceptions of how the state perpetuates conditions that not only breed violence but allow it to justify its own.

The critiques she has been voicing of the state are unique only to the extent of her genius to articulate them in telling formulations; as to substance, much of what she has said has been said by myriads of thinking people on the left of the political spectrum.

It is interesting that the rubbishing of the state from the right has rarely drawn the sort of official umbrage that critiques from the left have tended to – a circumstance that speaks of the character of the Indian state. Were there to be any doubt on this, the recent leaks of the Radia tapes ought to put it to rest. The one theme that runs through them is proof of the common knowledge that in all decisions that matter with respect to appropriation of wealth in India, it is the corporates who rule the roost.

To the best of my knowledge, Arundhati has never openly either endorsed or advocated a praxis of violence. That an intellectual effort to comprehend the rationale of the violence that stalks the land should be construed as seditious activity is pitiful beyond words, and underlines the theoretical poverty of Indian democracy. Besides making it more and more intractable to find resolutions to people's problems.

The Constitution guarantees as a fundamental right to its citizens the freedom of expression, subject only to the caveat that the exercise of such freedom does not imperil national sovereignty or incite violence.

The regrettable fact is that over the last two decades the market-friendly policies have come to dominate the Indian ruling class concerns, and the expression of any views whatsoever inimical to those policies or their consequences for the vast mass of Indians (enshrined in many official documents as well, such as the Arjun Sengupta Report) has been tended to be seen as anti-national activity.

The charge of sedition sought to be slapped on Arundhati thus needs to be seen in a wider context of official intolerance, and seems like the culminating act of the expression of democratic insecurity and argumentative decline on behalf of the state. Recalling Emile Zola, I accuse the state of descending to a new low in democratic self-confidence and intellectual resource, and betraying the universal idealisms that had informed the making of the constitutional Republic.

To Arundhati I say with Voltaire, that however I disagree with you, I will defend to death your right to disagree with me and with the official view of the Indian state and democracy as long as you do not either instigate violent opposition or become violent yourself.

I invite the state to study the First Amendment of the American Constitution, and to ponder over the fact that had American allegiance to a peaceful expression of dissent been as tenuous as it seems to have become here in India, a Michael Moore, a John Pilger, and a host of other opinion makers would long have been in jail. They are not. Just as the American state did not touch the mad man who was readying to burn several hundred copies of a book holy to a billion human beings.

January 2011

Pigeonholing Gandhi

Doomed Enterprise

Like most non-specialist browsers, I have read not more than that 'good bit' of Gandhi and not more than some twenty or so book-length studies of him. *En passant*, let me say, at great risk of injury from Gandhi scholars, that the book that seems to me to understand his enterprises with the most sensitivity and intelligence is Ronald Terchek's *Gandhi: Struggling for Autonomy*, 1998.

Had Gandhi been merely a figure of attempted piety and saintliness, the job of fixing him might have been tractable. That task may have been achieved by referring to just two statements he made in his write-up on 'Hinduism' (*Young India*, October 6, 1921, reprinted in C.F. Andrews, *Mahatma Gandhi's Ideas*, London: Allen and Unwin, 1929, pp.35-42): "I do not believe in the exclusive divinity of the Vedas. I believe the Bible, the Koran, and the Zend Avesta to be as much divinely inspired as the Vedas"; and: "I decline to be bound by any interpretation, however learned it may be, if it is repugnant to reason or moral sense." Thus his abhorrence of untouchability which he regarded as "the greatest blot on Hinduism" (*Young India*, April 27, 1921), and equally his endorsement of the *varnashrama dharma* strictly in accordance with the interpretation he gave to it, namely, that "the divisions define duties; they confer no privileges." And, "it is, I hold, against the genius of Hinduism to arrogate to oneself a higher status, or assign to another a lower status."

And when his conviction took the place of reason, he would not be swayed. For example, he would not be persuaded that untouchability demonstrably issued from the logic of the *varnashrama*, or that the total schema of that social organization was based inherently in disequalibriums of status. To the extent that Hinduism for him comprised chiefly *Ramcharitmanas* and the *Bhagvatam*, did it matter that there was also the 'Purusa Sukta' in the *Rig Veda* or the *Manusmriti*, the most formative Hindu texts on the subject, which made nonsense of Gandhi's construction of *varanashrama* and untouchability.

Such wholly personalized endorsement or rigid resistance to selective historical/textual truths, as Ambedkar was to discover, could only be associated with someone for whom 'reason' spanned many categories of perceptions – a dearly-held sentiment, common sense, observable truth. Thus, if on the one hand "*Varnashrama* is not affected by interdining or intermarriage," "prohibition against intermarriage and interdining is essential for a rapid evolution of the soul," even as "a Hindu who refuses to dine with another from a sense of superiority altogether misrepresents his Hindu religion." (Ibid.) If all that leaves you scratching the wall, no blame accrues to you. Consistency, Gandhi would agree, is the hobgoblin of small minds. Ultimately, as has been often said, the truth of his pronouncements could only be found in his practice rather than in the strenuous demonstrations of theory. And in his practice he was rarely found wanting.

Gandhi was always, of course, superbly honest; and most of all to his perceptions of himself. As in his acknowledgement that he was a practitioner and a politician first and a saint only after.

Precisely the fact that his experiments with scripture and ethics intertwined with his immersion with one of the most complex and conflictual collective moments of modern history makes any evaluation of him a matter of the utmost difficulty, even of frustration.

For example, in eventually coming to lead one of the most consequential anti-colonial movements of the twentieth century, he was clearly engaged in a 'modernizing' project. Yet few practitioners of mass politics have problematized the project of 'modernity' as Gandhi did. Or, concomitantly, of tradition. To those of us to whom 'modernity' unambiguously constitutes a monochromatic episteme, Gandhi offers many hurdles in the ways in which he either endorsed its stipulations or rejected them. No simple answers there as well, either for the modernizers or the traditionalists.

Traditionalists who seek to appropriate Gandhi for an 'anti-western,' and rootedly 'indigenous' paradigm of historical construction must find it hard to square the following facts with that paradigm:

- that, despite taboo and parental and societal obstructions, he traveled not just to England for studies, but thereafter to South Africa and other lands;
- that he made full use of such modern facilities as the railways, the telegraph, the print media;
- that he 'endeavoured humbly to follow Tolstoy, Ruskin, Thoreau, Emerson' and other 'western' thinkers, and never explicitly rejected their teachings or practices at any time;
- that he passed on the baton to a modernizer like Nehru rather than choose Patel for the honour;
- that he wholeheartedly subscribed to the notion of 'equality', faulting any aspect of tradition that contradicted the same;
- that like so many 'secular Hindus' then and now, he saw the Hindu Mahasabha and the RSS as the biggest damagers of the cause;
- that his closest backers eventually came not from the traditional class of landlords but from the scions of the nascent national bourgeoisie;
- that his concern for Muslims seemed to override his concern for his own community, or that his faith project included their scripture and that of other religious 'minorities'; or that, being as devoted to Hinduism as he professed to be, he should have given his life for the secular idea;
- or that he should have so unashamedly made sexual experiments upon himself, lying in bed with young women to test whether his abstinence was achieved.

And the 'modernists' must stand equally frustrated by another set of facts:

- that, his devotion to 'equality' should not have been seen by him to be contradictied by his endorsement of the *Varanashrama Dharma*;
- that instead of encouraging the 'untouchables' to organize and resist, he should have counseled that they live clean lives, bear with the barbarisms inflicted upon them by false prophets, and remember that God loved them especially (which is why he called them 'Harijans'); or that he wished to be reborn an 'Atishudra' (the casteless untouchable) in order to suffer what they suffer and to atone for the sins of their oppressors;

- that he should always have preferred a pencil to a type writer, or argued forcefully against the 'march of technology';
- that he should have fetishized the cow as he did, equating Swaraj with cow protection, or propagated vegetarianism as a high moral principle; or denied the injection of antibiotics to his wife on the principle that it would be a polluting exercise;
- that he should have so opposed the notion and practice of a justly violent and, to many Indians, 'heroic' opposition to colonial oppression as was undertaken by such young idealists as Bhagat Singh and other 'revolutionaries', or done rather little to persuade the colonial masters not to put them to death (barring a letter to the Viceroy, which, even as it requested mitigation, acknowledged that under the law they deserve to be punished);
- or, that having brought Indian women out of their home and hearth to participate in the freedom movement, the extent of his definition of freedom for them should essentially have remained embedded in different stipulations of *Sanatan Dharma*, holding up Sita as an ideal.

It would seem that any understanding of Gandhi both as an individual and as a leader of men and women must take in a fascinating, even if frustrating, complex of often inseparable contraries. Out of the deepest commitment to some orthodoxies emerged some of his most creative unorthodoxies, be it in the religious, the cultural, or the political sphere of thought and activity.

A modernity that seemed frozen in a moment of western history (the French Revolution) was in part endorsed and in part rejected. The endorsement of equality was in turn sought to be ploughed back into aspects of 'Indian' tradition as Gandhi chose to construct them. If technology freed the human agent from soulless labour it was endorsed (the sewing machine); if it threatened to railroad and straitjacket the human agent into automacity, turning freedom and autonomy into mechanistic comfort and slavery, it was rejected. If Nature was objectified and exploited for 'prosperity' it was seen as an evil enterprise; understood as an organic and intelligent entity, it could be drawn on for wholesome benefit to humankind. Remarkably, it seemed of little purpose to Gandhi to examine western modernity as a marriage of reason with capitalism. Or to examine how capitalism as a particular form of social organization vitiated both reason and equality. He would much rather chide the capitalist for being a 'materialist' and appeal to his moral conscience to perform as a 'trustee,' given that god had bestowed munificence upon him. All that while also contending that he wanted the same things as did the Bolsheviks, except that their methods did not appeal to him.

Likewise, any aspect of tradition that stultified the ordained equality of all men and women under god's benign dispensation was abhorrent; or that advocated the supremacy of one religion over another, even as Gandhi's personal devotion to Hinduism remained tearfully transcendant.

Above all stood the power of example – the courage and preparedness to live one's convictions regardless of social opinion or the fear of calumny. The one thing that ultimately must explain the influence Gandhi wielded in a matrix void of conviction. All that wedded to a non-acquisitive praxis, enriched by the demonstrated willingness to partake of the meanest chore and lift it thereby to dignity, and to undertake personal suffering on a sustained basis. Only by thus infecting many millions Gandhi believed could a new nation emerge not as a territorial but as a moral entity worthy of emergence.

January 2011

Modi vs the Constitution

Day of Reckoning for the Republic

To every action there is an equal and opposite reaction.
(Modi)

The Special Investigation Team entrusted by the Supreme Court of India to enquire into the culpabilities (including those of the Home Minister of Gujarat at the time of the carnage of February, 2002, namely one Narendra Modi) with respect especially to the gruesome killings at the Gulbarg Society where a Congress Member of Parliament, Ehsan Jafri, was also hacked to smithereens alongwith the rest has now submitted its report to the honourable Court.

Within days, the redoubtable *Tehelka* magazine found access to the 600 page document, consistent with the era of leaks. Contrary to the propaganda machine of the proto-fascist Sangh Parivar which had been busy spreading the unfounded lie that Modi had been given a 'clean chit,' the findings scooped by Tehelka must seem all too damning to any objective and conscientious citizen of the Republic. Caveat: assuming that the magazine has given us the authentic text of the SIT report, something we have no reason to doubt.

Hereunder a quick wrap in direct quote from the Report as published by *Tehelka*:

- inspite of the fact that ghastly and violent attacks had taken place on Muslims at Gulbarg Society and elsewhere, the reaction of the government was not the type that would have been expected by anyone. *The Chief Minister had tried to water down the seriousness of the situation at Gulbarg Society, Naroda Patiya…by saying that every action has an equal and opposite reaction* (p.69);

- that Modi's statement 'accusing some elements in Godhra (where a coach of the Sabarmati Express train bringing back Hindutva volunteers from Ayodhya had gone up in flames, leading to the deaths of some 59 people; the Justice Bannerjee Committee deputed by the then Railway Minister to enquire into the burning had concluded that there was no way that the coach could have been set on fire from the outside, and that most likely a spark from a stove or a cigarette butt within the compartment had reached the cushions, leading to the smouldering before the fire spread) as possessing a criminal tendency was sweeping and offensive, *coming as it did from a Chief Minister, that too at a critical time when Hindu-Muslim tempers were running high* (p.13);
- his (Modi's) implied justification of the killings of innocent members of the minority community, read together with an absence of a strong condemnation of the violence that followed Godhra suggest *a partisan stance at a critical juncture when the state had been badly disturbed by communal violence* (p.153);
- that in a 'controversial' move, Modi placed two central ministers, Ashok Bhatt and I.K.Jadeja, in the Ahmedabad police station control room, with 'no definite charter,' fuelling the speculation that they "*had been placed to interfere in police work and wrongful decisions to the field officers.*" "*The fact that he was the cabinet minister for Home would heighten the suspicion that this decision had his blessings*" (p.12 of Chairman's Comments); crucial to note that Ashok Bhatt's cell phone record analysis showed that he was in touch with Jaideep Patel of the Vishwa Hindu Parishad, a key conspirator in the Naroda Patiya and Naroda Gaon massacres, and a central culprit in the Ahmedabad carnage);
- that those police officers who had attempted to do their duty lawfully had been subjected to 'questionable' transfers, "*since they* (the transfers) *came immediately after incidents in which the officers concerned were known to have antagonized ruling party men*" (pp. 7-8, Chairman's Comment);
- sample this: "*The Gujarat government has reportedly destroyed the police wireless communication of the period pertaining to the riots*'; '*no records, documentations, or minutes of the crucial law and order meetings held by the government during the riots had been kept*" (p.13); interestingly, the Shah Commission, later Nanavati-Shah Commission which was appointed on the 6th of March, 2002 by the Modi government to enquire into the riots did nothing to first secure the safety of all these records;

- and who were appointed to prosecute the accused? "It appears that the political affiliation of the advocates did weigh with the government for the appointment of public prosecutors" (p.77); it is commonly known that these were men directly affiliated to the RSS and the VHP;
- that the Chief/Home Minister displayed a 'discriminatory attitude' in "not visiting the riot-affected areas in Ahmedabad where a large number of Muslims were killed, though he went to Godhra on the same day, traveling almost 300 km within a single day"(p.6); "*Modi did not cite any specific reason why he did not visit the affected areas in Ahmedabad city as promptly as he did in the case of the Godhra train carnage*"(p.8, CC); all that despite the fact that Ehsan Jafri, the Member of Parliament had been making frantic calls to whoever he could, intimating the incendiary conditions that prevailed;
- that Modi took no steps to proscribe the illegal bandh call given by the VHP for February 28, a call that in fact was supported by Modi's party, the ruling BJP (p.69); the bandh was to become the launching pad for the butcheries;
- that Modi did not impose curfew in Naroda until 12 noon, and in Meghna Nagar (Ahmedabad city) till 2.p.m, by which time the murderers had done the worst;
- that despite recommendations by field officers, no action was taken against inciteful reporting of events in the local media (p.79);
- that shoddy investigations were affected by the state police, overlooking the cell phone records of Sangh Parivar members and BJP leaders involved in the rioting (pp.101-105);
- that compliant police officers such as M.K. Tandon, joint commissioner of police in whose jurisdiction some 200 Muslims were massacred, and P.K. Gondia, also guilty of having willfully allowed the killings, were hugely and consistently rewarded with lucrative career advancement and postings (p.48-50); indeed, SIT has also found evidence against the then Minister of State, Home, Gordhan Zadaphia who reported directly to the Minister of Home, Modi, for his complicity in the riots. Zadaphia has since left the BJP.

Considering the humiliations suffered by him at Modi's hands, we would suggest he (Zadaphia) turn approver for a much larger cause than his own well-being; exactly as the senior police officer, M.K. Amin has recently agreed to turn approver in the matter of the fake encounter killing of Sohrabuddin Sheikh, a murder that also involves another one of Modi's cabinet colleagues, Amit Shah;

- that, come August, 2002, a false picture of normalcy was presented to the Election Commission of India to facilitate early elections, when in fact the state was seething with communal tension (pp.79-86).

Based on just these facts, were we to ask the reader to close her eyes and make a determination of Modi's culpability in the carnage of 2002, and thereby of the state, ten to one, the verdict might be 'guilty.'

But wait a minute, No. Having recorded all these details, the SIT, for reasons unfathomable on grounds either of legal plausibility or plain commonsense, concludes thus:

> the substantiated allegations did not throw up material that would justify further action under the law.

Astounding, to put it mildly. As far as we recall, Hitler was never known to have killed anyone with his own two bare hands, or used a gun, except, appropriately, upon himself in the end. Something he must have done knowing that he was indeed guilty as hell.

We are taught that the law pertaining to circumstantial evidence – supposing all the above to be circumstantial evidence and not the 'smoking gun' – lays down that if all the circumstances of a given case point only in one direction, and are not amenable to any contrary narrative, such evidence is more damning than even an 'eye witness' account, or a confession drawn by force. That for the reason that whereas, in law, even a confession made before a magistrate requires corroborative proof, consistent circumstantial evidence reinforces itself at all points of the circumstance. It can easily be seen that in the points listed by SIT, every circumstance thus reinforces the inescapable conclusion that Modi was not only in the know of everything that was happening, but indeed pulling all the ropes as well.

We pose the question: in what direction do the stated facts as recorded by the SIT and reproduced by Tehelka point? And is it to be thought that even the cleverest misrepresentation of those details could lead to any conclusion other than that the Gujarat killings were fully state sponsored and Modi-directed?

Remember now that the Report also alludes to the fact that a law and order meeting was called by Modi on the evening of February 27. From recorded statements, including by Modi, the SIT has drawn up a list of seven people present in that meeting of which no records/minutes were maintained.

News of that meeting was first shared by one of Modi's ministerial colleagues, Haren Pandya (now unsurprisingly deceased as a result of a murderous attack for which his father to this day accuses Modi as the chief architect) to two eminent retired judges, one of the Supreme Court and the other of the Bombay High Court who comprised the Concerned Citizen's Tribunal. That Tribunal recorded thus: "Pandya appeared and deposed before the tribunal on 13 May, 2002,on condition of anonymity, *that he had attended a meeting on 27 February 2002 night at the residence of Modi in which the latter had made it clear that there should be a backlash from the Hindus on the next day and the police should not come in their way*" (p.18 of that report).

On this most crucial piece of revelation the SIT opines that this fact "is not established" since Pandya being deceased could not testify to SIT, and all the others had either pleaded amnesia, or refused to otherwise confirm or deny Modi's directive, having been either rewarded, or in expectation of reward. Those that had retired did not desire any controversy.

The Strange Case of Sanjeev Bhatt:

An IPS police officer, name of Sanjeev Bhatt, was to say to the SIT that DGP Chakarvarthi had insisted that he attend the 27 February meeting, since it was thought desirable that an officer from the Intelligence services be on hand. And since his senior, GC Raigar was away on leave, Bhatt was asked to fill in.

In his testimony Bhatt argued that since the SIT enquiry was merely a preliminary one, he would not like to testify on the point; but were a criminal case to be instituted he would be willing to tell the truth. The SIT, for reasons best known to it, dubs Bhatt 'an unreliable witness,' although, curiously, at other times during the enquiry his testimony is given due weight.

And sample this: when Modi was asked in his summons before the SIT about the meeting of the 27th, he concluded his statement by averring that Sanjeev Bhatt had not been at that meeting. Significantly, Modi had never been asked any question with respect to Sanjeev Bhatt. The truth as they say will out.

It must be noted that the SIT was deputed the job of a 'Preliminary Enquiry.' It had no power to search, raid, arrest, interrogate in police custody, or compel the state to produce any records.

Its proceedings therefore comprised entirely asking various protagonists to record statements. Yet within such a lame-duck frame of reference it was able to dig such facts as listed above. We wonder what results it might have obtained had its enquiry followed upon the registration of a formal First Information Report – a police procedure which authorizes a full scale police investigation leading to the framing of charges.

Be that as it may, we are speculating that the amicus curiae, Raju Ramachandran, appointed by the Supreme Court, would have in his observations and recommendations submitted to the SC on January 20, 2011 made the inescapable recommendation that a formal FIR be now lodged in the cases that the SIT was entrusted with.

And, indeed, as the SIT Report comes up for consideration of the honourable SC (perhaps in early March), every citizen of India who wishes the 'basic feature' of India's constitutional regime, namely 'secularism,' to be preserved and protected at all costs would hope that the highest Court of Justice would not but take due note of the gravity of the culpabilities relative to the Gujarat massacres across all segments of the then Gujarat state apparatus and of the governing regime, and of the implications these bear on the founding principles of the Republic, and order accordingly.

II

Liberal India has often since 2002 had to respond to the question as to why it seems so obsessed with Modi, since the Gujarat communal killings were not the first nor may be the last that India has experienced.

And this question now needs to be given a truly short answer; in one word, the Gujarat killings were no mere communal killings. The SIT findings now confirm what Liberal India has always maintained: that with Modi's ascension to power in Gujarat, a clear determination of Hindutva fascism came to the fore, namely to attempt a state in Gujarat alternate to the stipulations of the Constitution of India, especially as enshrined in its 'Preamble' which a Constitutional Bench of the Supreme Court has designated its 'Basic Structure,' laying down the law that this structure will always remain outside the ambit of Article 368 of the

Constitution, namely, the power of the Legislature to affect amendments to the Constitution.

And part of that 'basic structure' is the stipulation that India is a 'secular' democratic country where the right of minority populations to equality before the law and to profess and practice their religious faiths will remain guaranteed and protected.

In doing what he has been doing in Gujarat, Modi has sought to draw his legitimacy not from such constitutional injunctions, but from the alternate and arbitray source – that of sectarian legitimacy. Whenever he has boasted of representing the honour of Gujaratis, he has in effect always meant the honour of its Hindu residents – a concealed fact that has found demonstrations in all his political, administrative, and cultural dealings. To this day, Modi has failed to visit any of the locations were the residual Muslim lives from the carnage seek merely to exist, nor once expressed the least regret at what happened. Indeed, the energy of polarized hate from which he has drawn such electoral dividends continues to inform the general tenor of community living in Gujarat, and he moves not a little finger to bring about any change in that situation.

In repeatedly underscoring the Gujarat massacres, liberal India is not merely referring to the criminal culpabilities, but to a regime that has flagrantly spat on that structure of constitutional legitimations which alone can be envisaged within the Republican regime as the authorizers of political and administrative life, to a point where this regime has brazenly at every step moulded the state and its power-elite to subvert what 'secular' India and the 'secular' Constitution thinks, and to dare, browbeat, harass, and indeed liquidate any and all who have stood up to its nefarious project. That we now know as much as we do is thanks in the largest part to those dour civil society organizations that have, against all odds, persisted with their resolve to move all public and judicial stops to get at the truth of Gujarat, 2002. We salute them.

III

Furthermore, liberal India has this to say: looking at Pakistan and now at the Arab world, it should be clear as daylight that only within a fiercely guarded principle of secularism may nation-states find stability, peace, and the inclusive upliftment of all citizens. Even those polities that are preponderantly of one religious denomination are beginning to find that faith is the most fragile building block of nationhood, or else why would there be more than a score Arab countries, or why would the Saudis have been so anxious for America to launch an attack on Iran (Wikileaks). How often do we note the despairing fact that more Muslims have been killed in an 'Islamic' Pakistan by other Muslims and by external forces than in a secular India.

There is no greater illusion than to think that India is a Hindu nation, given that some seventy percent of Hindus have never voted for the BJP in any of India's elections. Or that the Muslims are a 'minority' simply by virtue of numbers. Across communities, if India survives as a vibrant democracy, the miracle can only be attributed to the secular legitimacy of its empowering citizens, and to a secular Constitution that will not allow any other form of transaction between the state and its empowering populace. To the extent that Modi in Gujarat has rougishly sought to overturn those grounding and binding obligations between state and polity, without, albeit, taking up a gun himself, as the Maoists do, the offence strikes at the roots of the Idea of India, and is no less heinous than of those who take to arms with far better justification.

If Pakistan has suffered so grievously by remaining ambiguous about what sort of state it wishes to operate, the least that India must do is to make it explicit that its secularism is not for bargain. And to that purpose, it will not do to soft-pedal Modi's culpability. The SIT Report already seems to have enough in it that the majesty of secular law assert itself in no uncertain terms if an example is to be set for future Neros (the Supreme Court's appellation for Modi) who might harbour the ambition to frame a Constitution of their own.

Indeed, were Modi, reviled at home and refused entry visas abroad, to wish truly to find new life beyond the borders of a Hindu Gujarat, he might take a leaf out of the heroic confession made by the terrorist, Swami Aseemanand with regard to the his and his accomplices's responsibility for the many blasts heretofore ascribed to Muslim youth. It may not be an exaggeration to say that Aseemanand's rebirth into humanity and love within the precincts of a jail, as per his own moving admittance, was triggered by the very Muslim he thought of as his enemy. A circumstance fit to receive a Dostoevskian treatment we think.

Speaking of which, is it too much to hope that many of India's industrial and corporate scions nowadays so taken with Modi's 'developmental' genius (a great part of that as fake as anything else about him) would rethink their greed-driven adulation in the light of the SIT findings, and set something of a secular-moral example to the nation? Is it not a wonder that they and the new middle classes generally should be so holier-than-thou on such issues as corruption, hounding other ministers out of office and into jail, but remain so unmoved by the blood that so obviously stains Modi's hands? After all, it may be fair to ask: what is more heinous, the loss of moneys or the massacre of lives?

And Modi's party, the BJP, might also introspect as to whether it is consistent for an outfit wedded ostensibly to 'values' to remain so brazenly defensive of their Chief Minister in Gujarat? Unless, of course, the party at bottom truly sees in his praxis its own best future of ushering in that coveted Hindu Rashtra of which the now terrorist-tainted RSS never fails to remind us day in and day out.

India looks to answers. And there is no question that the day of reckoning will be when the honourable Supreme Court pronounces upon the findings of the SIT Report.

February 2011

Thus Conscience Can Make Good Indians of Us All

> During my interaction with Kaleem, I learnt that he was previously arrested in the Mecca Masjid bomb blast case and he had to spend about one-and-a-half years in prison. During my stay in jail, Kaleem helped me a lot and used to serve me by bringing water, food,etc. for me. I was very moved by Kaleem's good conduct and my conscience asked me to prayaschit by making confessional statement.
>
> (Swami Aseemanand in his confessional statement to Magistrate. The statement was recorded on December, 18 under section 164 of the IPC, and is thus admissible in evidence. Kaleem, the Muslim boy, has been accused of the crime, namely the blast at the Mecca Masjid in Hyderabad, that Aseemanand says was in fact committed by Hindutva terrorists.)

I was asked the other day what kinds of people I thought to be the greatest danger to the 'idea of India.' Hopelessly enough, as many in the audience must have thought, I came up with a complicated answer, contradicting the clarity that seems rampant these days.

Yet my simple point was that the answer to the question must depend greatly on how one is placed within the nation-state.

Ask the question of a Tata, a Birla, an Ambani, or those that comprise the country's land and mining mafia, or those in politics and the bureaucracy who largely do their work, or those in the corporate media who remain busily occupied in peddling with penchant the ever-more avaricious aspirations of India's upwardly mobile classes, or the endowed non-resident Indians impatient to do away with the uncouth habits of the masses and to pave some ten percent of the 'homeland' (which they have deserted) with gold (that they may also own), and the answer you might get is left-wing extremism, trade unionism, NGO activism, wasteful social spending and so forth.

Ask the other eighty or so percent of Indians who sweat in fields, farms, factories, or vend the day for a pittance, forest-dwellers who are told not a tree, a bush, a patch of land, or a drop of water belongs to them anymore, or millions of children who rag-pick, or slave in shops or homes, who feed on crumbs and get roundly abused and beat routinely and die like flies in the cold and heat, and they might not even comprehend the question you ask, being past all conceivable danger all their wretched lives. The 'idea of India,' – what might that be? Ask those who still scavenge for a living, and get treated like lepers for their labours of keeping the rest of us clean, and they might say that the greatest danger is that they may be dispossessed even of the privileges of scavenging which keeps them just this side of starvation.

And ask the same question of India's religious minorities, and they might say, (however denied they remain in the 'developmental' concerns of the super-power-to-be), the greatest danger continues to be the prospect that the Constitution that guarantees to them, as to others, an equality of secular citizenship and the right to freely practice their faiths may yet be dethroned by a putsch from majoritarian fascists who remain to this day unreconciled to the idea of India as a pluralist space, and to the Constitution and to a system of laws which say that all citizens may be treated equally.

To wit, if for ideological convenience, the danger were to be formulated as the danger to the constitutional regime, leaving aside for now any consideration of the quality of its implementation, such danger lurks not in one quarter but in two.

It may suit the ruler- Indian to say that such a threat comes only from the Maoist communists, but vast numbers of other Indians know, as Jawaharlal Nehru did, that the greater threat remains embedded in the fascist politics of the Hindutva- right, since its exertions are always liable to be mistaken for sound 'nationalism.' And if the first is so obvious an object for liquidation, against which every other sort of considerable Indian might easily be mobilized, the latter is more in the nature of a virus that afflicts even sound secular Indians in some nerve-end or capillary. And being a threat from the economic right, its operations are more prone to be excused, both by the corporate power-houses and by the elites who look upto them. Note how sections of India's influential electronic media are already debating whether an Aseemanand is a terrorist or only a 'zealot' after all. And how ideologues of Hindutva who never tired of dubbing terrorist acts on behalf of Muslim individuals or groups as 'Jihadi Islamism,' now suddenly advise that terrorism has no colour whatsoever, despite the fact that all of the Hindutva terrorists who have thus far been nabbed or identified can be seen clad insistently in saffron robes. Or how, in contrast to the stated and proven disapproval of violent Naxalism by India's parliamentary left, the parliamentary BJP is out brazenly denying that Hindutva terrorism exists, or that investigations and findings in that regard are anything but a dirty conspiracy against the 'nationalist' majority community. Ergo, whereas Muslim perpetrators were to be justifiably held guilty prior even to the most elementary forms of proof, their Hindutva counterparts (which is what they are) are to be thought victims of conspiracy even in the face of piling evidence and confessions made to Magistrates in the full knowledge that such confessions are admissible proof.

Here is the BJP's problem: so long as the connections that these Hindutva terrorists bear to the RSS remained concealed, their shennagans could be attributed to misguided individuals or to 'fringe groups.' But now that Aseemanand has spilled the beans on the lead role of a very senior RSS leader in the series of blasts (Malegaon 2006 & 2008, Ajmer, Mecca Masjid, Samjhauta Express, Modasa, and who knows how many of the others) earlier attributed, per the Pavlovian instincts of the country's police forces and sundry organs of opinion, to Muslim individuals and groups, there is no way that the puppet-BJP can nod in agreement.

And the Congress, as always, finds itself caught in a cleft stick: it may not be seen to be prevaricating, and it may not be seen to be anti-Hindu. It will be no exaggeration to say that the future of Indian political and constitutional life may well depend on how the cases against Hindutva terrorists are either carried to lawful conclusions or muffled and erased.

Ever since the murder of Mahatma Gandhi by a man who belonged to the RSS, and, according to the statement made by his brother, Gopal Godse, on his release from incarceration some years ago, never left the RSS, contrary to such propagation by the RSS, this 'nationalist' organization whose pioneering scions drew their inspiration explicitly from Hitler and Mussolini, has been found to be complicit by a plethora of official Commissions of enquiry in episodes of communal violence against India's minorities. Such violence it knows is one sure way of always keeping in the foreground its racialist thesis about what ought to constitute 'Indianness'. And, at the least, to keep Indian Muslims in the doghouse for as long as possible. Aseemanand, whose Bengali name is Naba Kumar Sarkar, clearly sought to carry forward, as is implicit in his confession, the tradition first unleashed by another Bengali from the nineteenth century, Bankim Chandra Chatterjee, who propagated the view that not the colonizing British but India's Muslims, descendants of the Moghuls, were the real enemies of the nation. And, after him, with theoretical support from the German Nazis, whom he praised no end, the revered RSS guru, Golwalkar, in his two offerings (*We, or Our Nationhood Defined*, and *Bunch of Thoughts*) wrote India's Muslims as 'Enemy Number One.'

Ironically, but understandably, Indian Muslims increasingly realize that the best course for them is not to resort to violence, (reason why in recent years most Muslim organizations of any consequence have repeatedly engaged in public denunciation of terrorism), but to invoke the promise of Indian democracy and the secular, democratic Constitution from whence it draws breath and legitimacy. It is not for no reason that Muslim vanguards have insistently said that whatever be the ignominies heaped on them both by the Hindutva camp and institutional agencies whose biases make themselves evident time after time, they stand by the rule of law. A course of thought and action which indeed, equally ironically and understandably, do not suit the Hindutva agenda, since such behaviour on behalf of Indian Muslims helps their greater assimilation into the mainstream politics of the country, and facilitates greater approval from that vast liberal mass of citizens who seek to get a leg up without frequent mayhem, however their sympathies may lie with the 'Hindu cause.'

Long years ago during Nehruvian India when the secular and humanist, if not wholly socialist, ideal suffused civic and cinematic life (see Meghnath Desai's *Nehru's Hero*), the great poet, Sahir Ludhianvi, wrote a stirring song for a movie. In that song, an idealist Indian who has adopted an 'illegitimate' love-child, seeks to dream for the future of the young one. From that song I have a minute ago on impulse translated but two stanzas as well as I could on the instant:

Such Creed as teaches hate is not yours,
Such stride as tramples the human pate is not yours,
Such temple as has not in it the Koran,
Such mosque that has not in it the Gita
Are not yours;
Yours will be the yearning for peace and harmony,
Human you were born, human you shall be.

And

These merchants of Creed, these traders of the nation,
These that sell the very shroud for a consideration,
Assasins and looters that reside in palaces,
Those that kill the Garden's spring instead of its calluses,
To them your breath shall come
As the clarion of death.

Such idle sentiments then gave offence to no one, and were not censored. Keeping in mind the ugly revelations we are witness to, both with respect to the captains of the economy and the vast network of chicanery they seem to have engendered in brand India's nook and cranny, and now with the revelations of terrorism on 'this' side, how nice it would be to call a halt both to the merciless and marauding exertions of exploiters who may not leave a blade of grass in place in pursuit of profit, not to speak of the whole Niyamgiri hill, and to sectarian refusals to accept India as a garden of plural perfumes wherein not the monsters of hate belong but angels of peace, harmony, equity and conscience.

And thus I have sought on purpose to highlight in the epigraph that part of Aseemanand's confession which relates to the stirrings of conscience. I ask, if a terrorist who set out to unleash 'bomb for bomb,' could thus be affected by the power of innocence and service on behalf of the 'enemy other,' and feel impelled to make atonement even at the prospect of implicating himself to a judicial sentence of death, what should this say to the rest of us. In this most noble moment of realization Aseemanand conveys a message to all of India, and indeed to the rest of the world, one that invites us to find our own humanity and, thereby, that of all others.

Ultimately, there could be no better or finer idea of India than is contained in that existential moment of redemption that Aseemanand has experienced. The question is, will this act of supreme enlightenment shame the RSS into rethinking its dodgy, abrasive and hate-filled existence and career, or will it continue to thwart and stymie the lives of some 180 million peace-loving Indians because they are not Hindus?

Indeed, after the revelations about Narendra Modi's ubiquitous intimacy with all the murderous proceedings of the Gujarat episode of 2002, as encapsulated in the report submitted by the Special Investigating Team to the Supreme Court and scooped by the Tehelka journal, what a lasting service Modi could render to the Idea of India as a secular and pluralist paradise and a land of peace and harmony were he to take a leaf out of Aseemanand's book and confess to his misdeeds, which after all included sheltering the key terrorists of Madhya Pradesh and Indore vintage in the Dang district of Gujarat, most of all, Aseemanand himself, and allowing free play to the carnage that happened in 2002.

Aseemanand is to be applauded on another count as well. In his letter to the President of India he has sought permission to be allowed to travel to Pakistan so that he might attempt a heart-to-heart with the likes of Hafiz Saeed with a view to bringing about in the latter a conversion matching his own.

An aspiration of profound proportions resides in that impulse, one that seeks to do nothing less than to draw the Pakistani Jihadis away from Maulana Maududi, just as Aseemanand's own confession seeks to draw the RSS away from Golwalkar to Gandhi. And this writer for one thinks that the Indian state would rise so far above its own lowly politics of antagonism should it make it possible for Aseemanand to make that trip. That endeavour in itself would constitute a transformative event, regardless of what came of it. It is when the mind weakens in its evil resolve that the sinews go limp as well.

Far from making 'cowards of us all' (Hamlet), an awakened conscience alone can change both personal and collective destinies in ways more far reaching than either realpolitik or the force of arms.

February 2011

The Intimate Zone

The 'Mainstream.'

Ask any ordinary Indian citizen whether the bulk of their elected representatives or members of the administrative tribe ever really can be trusted to square with them on any issue at hand – from the burst water pipeline, to the price of food articles, to any policy issues bearing on domestic or foreign concern.

And you will discover that, among democracies, the Indian political/bureaucratic class scores the lowest worldwide on truth-telling, and absolutely the highest on the fine art of dodge and double-speak.

This is so, Wikileaks now tell us, for the canny reason that India's 'mainstream' power wielders/brokers reserve truth-sharing not for the people of India but for the American Embassy. There is the intimate zone where they bare their hearts out.

Here is a sampling – from the lowly and bumptuous, although not less punishable for that reason, to the venerated sublime:

- in his cable dated August 11, 2009, Timothy Roemer, the US Ambassador, recounting his first ever meeting with the then Indian National Security Advisor, (no less) underlined how the latter had candidly revealed his differences with the Prime Minister, Singh, on issues related to peace with Pakistan; and how Narayanan told him of his retort to Singh's sentiment about the 'shared destinies' of India and Pakistan: "you have a shared destiny, we don't" Narayanan confided as having said. Presumably, the 'you' had to do with Singh being a north Indian and a Punjabi, and Narayanan being a southerner to whom the partition of the country in 1947 carried small resonance. Roemer, with good judgement and reason, concluded that Narayanan's readiness to 'distance himself from his boss' suggested that "Singh is more isolated than we thought within his own inner circle in his effort to 'trust but verify' and pursue talks with Pakistan." With the National Security Advisor of a host country so willing and ready to tell, why would the US embassy need them spooks one wonders.

And not just that; Narayanan left the Ambassador in no doubt as to who he thought was boss: "Narayanan noted that all matters related to nuclear and space issues, defense and foreign policy, should be directed to him." God knows why the Indian electorate gave itself a cabinet and a prime minister.

- Not to think that any lowly joint secretary in the Indian bureaucracy has less grandiose notions of self-importance or is less willing to enunciate policy to the members of the intimate zone. As Hardeep Puri was appointed the Indian Permanent Representative to the United Nations, a mere Gaitri Kumar, joint secretary in the ministry of external affairs, told Ted Osinus that "we should let MEA know if we have any complaints" (against Puri). Making it known thereby that the said joint secretary believed not Bang Ki Moon to be the real thing at the UN but the Americans: Puri, in his turn, went one better, telling the US official how 'his specific brief' was to seek a 'higher degree of convergence' with the US (meeting dated May 1, 2009). The Prime Minister of India or his External Affairs Minister have not spoken. Do the people of India have a right to be told? Forget it. They are too used to being fibbed to be hit with the truth.
- Now to the sublime. Wiki tells us how the redoubtable, Harvard- savvy, Home Minister of India confided to the heart throbs of the real home, the Embassy of the US, that had there been no north or east to the republic of India, but only the west and the south, her GDP growth rate would have been vaulting sky high. What pity that these laggard and slovenly regions cannot be bombed out of existence, India's military prowess notwithstanding. Indeed, India, suitably reduced, might then have competed with the most 'developed' nations on their own terms. Lost opportunity, you would say.

Now we wonder whether the honourable Home Minister would ever have publicly shared this his heartfelt view with the people of India. Much to be doubted. So thank heavens there remains an intimate zone where such inward truths may be told, namely the US embassy.

- But, all this is nothing to the BJP- Jaitley's confession made to the intimate zone and retold by Wiki. That surely takes the cake, and invites millions to rethink India's major opposition party. Not that the millions did not already know, but coming from the horses's mouth, ah, that is something else.

Meeting with Robert Blake, the Charge at the US Embassy, on May 6, 2005, Jaitley, leader of the opposition in the Rajya Sabha, educated the intimate Charge on the true position of the so 'nationalist' Bharatiya Janata Party on the true and profound meaning of 'Hindutva.' This is how the Charge reported on the intimate exchange:

> Pressed on the question of Hindutva, Jaitley argued (whenever any member of this right-wing Hindu party argues, which they do all the time, understand Goebbelesian spin without shame, let, or hindrance – added) that Hindu nationalism 'will always be a talking point' for the BJP.

However, he characterized this as an opportunistic issue (cable dated May 10, 2005).

That being so, Jaitley confided to the intimate zone how opportunism dictates an assessment of when Hindutva may or may not have 'currency' among the electorate. For example, in India's north-east, Jaitley propounded, such currency remains intact so long as the issue of Muslim migrants of Bangladeshi extraction also remains intact. Just to share a fact: the BJP has never objected to the entry of Hindu immigrants from Bangladesh, only the Muslim ones. The very soul of the BJP's sectarian/ communalist politics there for show, if one needed a show.

And note this: now that terrorist attacks seem to have halted, especially on the capital of India, 'Hindutva' has rather lost its 'resonance' in New Delhi (Jaitley again). But, wait a minute and wonder, "that could change with another cross-border terrorist attack, for instance, on the Indian Parliament," Blake reported Jaitley as having said. So does that sound like a consummation devoutly to be wished? We leave you to work that one out, even as we also invite you to ponder the logic and objective of the terror strikes now known to have been conducted by groups and individuals affiliated to the RSS.

Do also recall another Wiki gem, wherein the redoubtable L.K.Advani of the BJP is heard to reassure the intimates that the party's opposition to the nuclear deal must not be taken to heart, since it was meant for public consumption. The intimate fact was that the BJP had no intent to do anything but go alongwith it once they came to wield power in Delhi, or to dilute the strategic partnership with the US.

All very patriotic stuff this, told not to Indians but to the Americans.

But Jaitley, Advani and Wiki are all to be thanked; we now know we were always right. As will, no doubt, many heretofore gullible Indians also get to know that they may have been suckers at the altar of false gods whose commitment to a foreign power and its claims and interests exceeds its commitment to both Indians and to Hindutva.

Indeed, the central tenet of this so 'ideological' party turns out to be a mere piece of cold and callous machination, to be deployed where, how, and when gains are to be made, and to which thousands of innocent Indians have lost their unsuspecting lives.

The Left

Strikingly, but not surprisingly, Wikileaks underscore the reality that it is India's left parties, and the Communist Party of India (Marxist) directly, who, although everyday maligned for its non-nationalist (sic) sins, shine for patriotism, spunk, and ideological integrity in contrast to the private minds of its ideologically fake, right-wing accusers.

Indeed, to make an important point, where the 'nationalists' are shown to have been low both on integrity and patriotism, the left comes off as truly patriotic in being devoted to what it sees as constituting the good of the people of India, even as it remains an ideological critic of the idea of 'nationalism.' Just to recall, this contrast between the vicious nature of 'nationalism' and the honourable sentiment of patriotism was nowhere more eloquently addressed in India's modern history than in Tagore's justly celebrated lecture on 'Nationalism' (see Rabindranath Tagore, *Nationalism* (1917; reprinted New Delhi: Penguin Books India, 2009).

Thus, in his first meeting with US Embassy officials after his election as General Secretary of the CPI(M), Prakash Karat, Wikileaks tells us – see *The Hindu*, March 23, 2011) shared the same truths and perceptions with

Blake (meeting dated May 4, 2005) as he, the party, and the left overall, have routinely shared with the people of India, and until the break with the UPA, with the government it was then supporting.

In that meeting with Blake, Karat as reported by Wiki, held his own on all matters that came up, namely, the nuclear issue, missile defence, retail trade, FDI policy, Insurance, land reforms, stability of the government, and foreign policy generally. Not one word there that could be seen to be out of line with what the party and the left have been saying for two decades or thereabouts. One is able to understand why even a Sonia Gandhi is revealed by Wiki to have so much preferred and been so much more comfortable with the left than with the 'regional' parties supporting or willing to support the UPA. For the reason that the left always told you where they stood so you could know where you stand; and all that without fanfare, deceit, or reckless irresponsibility towards the nation or its governance.

There may have been a time when India's left had the same sort of intimacy with the USSR and their Embassy as our major parties of today have with the US Embassy. Always had, in fact, after the Nehru-Indira era came to a close. What is of importance and of value to common concerns is that the left in India today is in all likelihood the one political force most credibly devoted to Indian people's interests and to the sovereignty of the nation-state overall.

It speaks to the unsentimental toughness of American assessments of men and matters that Blake should have reported of Karat not just that he found Karat 'talented and skillful' but, more fully as follows:

> Relatively young (at 57) he will be a powerful figure on the Indian political scene for years to come, and could play an increasingly important role in the formation of future Indian governments.

Clearly, the assessment of Karat here can hardly be delinked from the politics of the left in general.

It was to be expected of the Goebbelsian BJP that all derogatory references to others in the Wikileaks exposes would be treated and propagated as gospel truth, and, as to its own, as so much misreporting.

Thus the BJP is busy hoodwinking the nation with the spin that whereas the other things said by Jaitley to Blake may be true enough, the 'opportunistic' bit is wholly Blake's own. It is to be doubted that even the BJP's dear ones are now willing to credit Jaitley before Blake. Having already been rendered obsolete by so much that has been happening in a young India, the exposure of 'Hindutva' as mere gimmick, although a deadly one since lately discovered to be aligned with terrorism as well, may contribute to transformations that the country can do with.

For one, these shaming exposes may oblige India's 'mainstreamers' to square first with Indians before they do with the intimate zone, an eventuality that could put Indian democracy on a rather more respectable footing.

April 2011

Communalism Bad, Development Good

Anna Lauds Modi

Anna, the Voice of the Upwardly Mobile

A voice has been raised in India against the venal misdeeds of politicians and, mutedly, of bureaucrats (no mention of the corporates here).

Groups of protestors led by a most unlikely mix of civil society leaderships, ranging from those with staunch secular credentials and proven personal integrity (Prashant Bhushan, Swami Agnivesh, Mallika Sarabai) to those others with known affiliation to right-wing Hindu organizations and dubious claims to probity (Baba Ramdev, Sri Sri Ravi Shankar), raucously foregrounded by corporate electronic channels with barely concealed antipathy to any mass assertion from the left, have been holding fort.

True to pattern and apprehension, the politics of a section of the protestors could not after all hold back mentioning Chief Ministers of two BJP- ruled and BJP-in-coalition- ruled states as exemplars of the India of their dreams. Most significantly, that mention this time came from no less than Anna Hazare himself.

As per Anna speak, Nitish Kumar and Narendra Modi belong to a common category – Chief Ministers who do good development work without being corrupt. More of the corruption part hereafter. But, what of Modi's fingers dipped in blood? Response: communalism is bad, but "I was speaking only of his development work."

To be fair to Nitish Kumar, he, although bracketed with Modi, has sought consistently to resist the equation, and keep the fascist Modi at arms length, disallowing the BJP to unleash him in the last two election campaigns in Bihar, thereby seeking to draw a line between himself (and presumably a section of his party, the JD-U) and Modi at least on the issue of secularism, even if merely to avoid offending Bihar's considerable Muslim electorate.

So, here is the inference (one that neo-Nazis – many of them Indians – to this day make with aplomb and pride): Hitler may have liquidated some six million innocent human beings for no fault other than their racial characteristic, but look he gave to Germany great autobahns and provided fillip to German industrial houses at a time of depression. Whereas what they always mean to say is how Hitler's greatest contribution was to achieve Aryan racial purity. (See Golwalkar's, *We, or Our Nationhood Defined*, 1923, and *Bunch of Thoughts*, 1938 – two texts on which the edifice of the RSS rests.)

This is precisely the hub of the barely concealed support that Modi enjoys among India's proto-fascists; namely, that whereas they may feel on occasion publicly obliged to disapprove of the Muslim massacres of 2002, all under total state connivance, at bottom, in their hearts they are filled with glee that he gave to the Muslims what has been coming to them, setting in motion the Hindutva-fascist project of purifying India racially as Hiter had sought to do to Germany and Europe. Add to that the welcome to the corporate chiselers, and Modi is up on the middle-class pedestal.

Here is what we ask, charitably: if the operative profiles of political leaders can be so neatly and conveniently separated, why wouldn't Anna and those others with him agree that many among the politicians they seek to pillory may be corrupt, but are also known to be fine administrators with substantial records of achievement to their name. After all, many corrupt politicians since 1947 must have done some development work to bring India to her present status among the comity of nations that matter (sic). So why does not the same charitable double-speak apply to them as it does so often and so heinously to Modi? Modi may be a communalist murderer, but look at his developmental activity; likewise, why can't it be said, X or Y may be corrupt, but look at his record of achievement in government?

The Modi Model of 'Development'

There has of course been a studied refusal to question the Modi model of 'development.' Tainted and disfigured by his marshalling of the massacres of 2002, influential sections of his party leadership, closet communalists among the new middle classes, and those in the corporate media who have been busy touting and boosting the 'India story,' the future they desire for Modi has been sought to be pinned on his personal probity and developmental genius. Clearly, those that wish Modi to occupy the high table in Delhi sometime soon use with ruthless dishonesty the Podsnappian fore-arm to deny some pretty ugly truths about what he has done for which segment of Gujaratis. If only they would listen to a litany of facts on this that are in the possession of social service organizations located in Gujarat.

Briefly, without let or hindrance, Modi has sought to parcel out Gujarati assets in land and other natural resources at a pittance to a clutch of favoured industrialists whose every wish takes precedence over the lived requirements of rural Guajrat and of its forest dwellers. Innocent as he may be, Anna Hazare, the part-Gandhian (since, it turns out he is also by his public admission a votary of Shivaji Maratha, by no means an icon of non-violence in the annals of Indian history) needs to know that of all Chief Ministers now operating in India, not one may be more rapaciously anti-rural than Modi. And what would Gandhi have said of that preference in 'development' given his passion for a village-centred India?

Indeed, the Mahuva farmer's agitation in Gujarat was to showcase all of those preferences. Farmers, fishing communities, salt-pan workers, tribals, dalits, industrial workers, minorities – a pretty substantial section of Gujaratis wouldn't you say – all have come to be at the receiving end of those preferences, as gauchar lands and irrigated farmlands have been acquired to be at the service of a club of industrialists, all at throwaway prices. One has to visit rural and tribal Gujarat to register the extent of the loss of livelihoods, displacement and loss of natural resources, and the pace of land grab, with withering consequences for swathes of poor and indigent Gujaratis. And, as to the Muslim minority, read the recent Wikileak US consulate report of how Modi has sought with unmitigated single-mindedness to marginalize and ghettoize the Muslims of Guajrat. And never to this day as much a politic 'regret.' Only continued machinations to thwart and vilify the plethora of investigative mechanisms ordered into the Gujarat massacres and the countless fake encounter liquidations of Muslims by no less than the Supreme Court of India.

Does Corruption Apply to Modi and Nitish?

A recent report of the Comptroller and Auditor General of India, a constitutional body (CAG) has indicted the Nitish Kumar government in Bihar for submitting no 'detailed contingency' bills against 'abstract contingency' withdrawals amounting to no less than Rs.15,850.41 crores! Useful to know that this is the same CAG whose report on the 2G Spectrum goings-on was to bring about the current massive upheaval in how neoliberal economics in India has been proceeding, leading to the arrest of the central cabinet Minister in-charge of Telecom. That being the case, it may be a forgiveable question to ask Anna ji as to why CAG should be so venerated with respect to the central ministry, but wholly side-stepped with respect to Bihar. Remarkably, although a CBI enquiry has been ordered into the Bihar matter, ask any TV-guzzling middle class Indian and he would not have heard of it. For the simple reason that the very media that pillories the said Telecom Minister turns a Nelson's eye elsewhere.

And what of Modi? Three fair-sized scams come readily to mind: the Sujalam Sufalam scam estimated to be of the order of Rs.1700 crores; the NREGS Boribund scam (Rs.109 crores), and the Fisheries scam worth about Rs.600 crores.

And would you know, whereas the whole Anna-led 'movement' has had the institution of an all-powerful Lokpal (Ombudsman) at its focus, Modi in Gujarat has refused to implement the mandatory requirement to install a Lokayukta in his own state, even as he is heard ranting about the need for the Lokpal at the centre!

The less said about the Yog guru, Baba Ramdev, the better. Only a few years ago the world came to know how he refuses to supply correct information about the content of the medicines he sells from his establishment, defying thereby a statutory requirement. The disclosure that those medicines contain human-bone components was to be made in full public view in Delhi by dozens of people who have been working at his medicine factory. Just as it was found that he violates another statutory requirement as well, namely, refusing to pay mandated 'minimum wages' to workers who make his millions possible. Indeed, just last night here in Delhi on one electronic channel, a venerable sadhu maharaj from the holy city of Hardwar had this to say: "Ramdev is the Hassan Ali of Hardwar; more dubious, in fact, because Hassan Ali at least had horses for generating those thousands of crores, Ramdev did not even have a donkey." Hassan Ali, you might know, is the man currently in the eye of the storm as India's biggest tax-defaulter, and thought to have billions stashed away in those Swiss and suchlike other banks.

Corruption vs All the Rest

The fact here, we hold, is a rather ugly one. Crimes issuing from class or caste or community or gender based oppressions have never borne the same purchase among upwardly-mobile Indians as 'corruption' for the two reasons that 'corruption' as enemy brooks no opposition, obliges no self-definition and scrutiny, and can be fashionably deployed to decry not just politicians but the institution of politics per se. It was no mere accident that the Nazis during the twenties and thirties of the last century in Germany made a big issue of 'corruption' with the ulterior purpose of doing dirt on all democratic institutions floated by the Wiemar republic, and dissolving the nation into the state, and vice versa. Keeping those histories in mind, there is more than a valid point to voices today who caution that the Anna Hazare phenomenon has to it aspects which are deeply anti-democratic, and which threaten to void all institutional procedures authorized by the constitutional regime. Recall that only some months ago the left parties came out in even bigger mobilization against corruption on the streets of India; yet one saw nothing of that protest on India's gung-ho electronic channels. What one did see over the last week of the Anna mobilization however, was more than a sprinkling of Hindutva-based icons and groups, making strenuous efforts to float symbols and slogans with barely concealed pedigree. Predictably, one did not see a single shot of supporters of the CPI (ML) who, in their wisdom, had decided to stand with the Anna-led protestors at Jantar Mantar.

Put the question to any of India's current day urban-elite young person as to whether the roots of corruption being talked about lie only in corrupt politicians or in a political economy driven by neoliberal capitalism, and you will be told unambiguously that the latter has nothing to do with what has been happening. Some reason why during the current campaign one has heard no mention of corporate houses whose corruption it is at bottom that has been spilling all over the systems of governance. After all, those corporate fortunes are precisely where so many of the protestors who have been on display hope to find entry as India rises and shines. Not to speak of systems of electoral funding that ensure that politicians must do the pay back. Again, not an issue for the 'corruption'-baiters. And for good reason: make elections state-funded, and the corporates lose what clout they have under the present dispensation. Anna's young warriors might not see that as a desirable prospect, assuming that they have any use for elections in the first place. The eradication of corruption merely and only requires the clenched fist from the right.

You may then well wonder whether we will soon see another Anna-type 'movement' on the subject of refurbishing the governmental draft of a bill designed to eradicate communal mayhems, or an Anna putsch to seek the adoption of the Womens's Reservation Bill, pending in parliament now for aeons. Or to force the government to draft purposive legislations to eradicate female infanticide, atrocities on dalits and adivasis, or to enforce without nonsense the right to food and education. Or how about ensuring clean drinking water, affordable health-care and sanitation, and securing housing, and freedom from police atrocities to some eighty percent of Indians? Or easy and credible access to systems of justice and grievance redressal? Or justice for a Binayak Sen who rots in a Chhattisgarh jail on a charge of sedition, and sentenced without a shred of proof for no less than life. Or indeed a 'movement' in support of an Irom Sharmila in Manipur who has now entered the eleventh year of her fast (kept forcibly alive on drips by a terrified state) for the withdrawal of the draconian Armed Forces Special Powers Act. Not a chance.

I doubt me very much that any such 'movements' are in the offing on behalf of the support base that has been on show during the Anna-led putsch.

And thereby hangs a tale.

Just as well to suggest that in the days to come the ideological content, the active politics, the leadership-profile, and the constitutional consequences of this recent event receive considered debate. Most so among sections of civil society and individuals whom I respect deeply who for idealistic reasons chose to be a part of what they thought to be a single-minded objective (the Lokpal Bill), with insufficient attention perhaps to the surrounding political milieu of the Anna event.

April 2011

The State of the Left

Consternation

After some thirty four years of undefeated rule in the Indian state of West Bengal – often called the 'red bastion' by political pundits of other shades – the Left Front has been voted out of power.

Although the shout has gone up how the left has been 'routed,' the fact is that there is greater disbelief among left-detractors at the circumstance than among the left itself, stridently politic pre-result noises notwithstanding. Those that gloat and experience glee barely believe that the beast has been quelled.

And for good reason. However the 'rout' may be trumpeted, imagine that even in defeat, the Left Front has polled 41% of the popular vote, a million or so votes more than it polled in the parliamentary elections of 2009! And after more than three decades of continuous rule. The question may be asked: when was the last time that either of India's major centrist parties obtained a 40% verdict in a regional or parliamentary election? The answer to that might take us all the way back to the first decade after Independence. Indeed, most parties set to form new governments in the five states that went to the hustings in the current round will do so on an electoral base far smaller than the vote the left still commands in West Bengal. Such are the maverick vagaries of the first-past-the-post system. And yet the left has lost, due mainly to forms of high-handedness which the Trinamool Congress and Congress combined were able to exploit fully among sections of Bengalis, including erstwhile left supporters.

Why Has the Left Front Lost?

Having noted the fact that the left was up against a unified opposition, the question must still be answered: why did such consolidation take place? And, why did a majority 49% vote for the winning combine?

As the left parties mull these questions, they might find that the answers range from the fairly obvious to the more troublesome and far-reaching, all of which the left must address without succumbing to self-delusion, or, contrarily, without sinking into any apocalyptic political/intellectual depression. Here are a few thoughts that come to mind:

- Thirty four years, a record unparalleled in any democracy, come to think of it, is far too long even for the best of marriages, not to speak of a marriage between governments and people; since, unlike China, the Indian political system makes alternate political choices available, it is hardly any surprise that the people of West Bengal opted for a change of guard; if anything, they are to be thanked for having rewarded the excellent work done by the left in the matter of land redistribution, grass roots democracy, and social harmony over three decades or more. Yet, although in other states of India governments routinely change complexion after five year terms, the defeat of the left after thirty four years of rule is sought to be made out to be a catastrophe equivalent to the fall of the Berlin Wall. The underlying supposition being that the left will never return to power, since its governmental defeat is sought to be propagated as the defeat coterminously as the defeat of leftist ideology per se. This must be seen for what it is: wishful thinking on behalf of India's newly spawned propertied classes who imagine that history has come to an end with neoliberalism and with India's strategic embrace with global capitalism.
- Given the peculiar circumstance that the Left Front, after all, had to operate within the larger national framework within which macro-economic policies are laid down by governments at the centre, there is only so much the left could do in West Bengal beyond the unprecedented upliftment of incomes in the rural sector; it could have done more in the industrial sector should it have chosen to succumb wholly to the diktats of the neoliberal captains of finance capital; the left could hardly be berated for raising the questions that any left politics must with regard to the social and accumulative consequences of pursuing neoliberalism – consequences which have mightily come home to roost in the developed world itself since the crash there began with the collapse of giant banks and corporations, all bailed out by you know who – the tax moneys of the discredited public treasury; it was inevitable, therefore, that in the current environment of economic thinking spawned by the Washington Consensus, the left would be faced with aspirational pressures that

it would find difficult to negotiate on quite the same terms as some non-left state governments were willing to. Given the shrinkage of the state-sector, job creation beyond agriculture and state services then came to be a tough ask.

- The Left Front was, therefore, not wrong in determining that jobs could result chiefly from reinvigorating industry, especially manufacturing; as it sought to turn attention to encouraging investments and acquiring land, it ran into a reality that it may have smugly left out of consideration: over time, its equation with the class that it had benefited the most, the small and middle peasantry, had suffered deep ravages. All importantly, land-owning peasants were no longer willing simply to be vassals to the diktat of party cadres. Over long years of control, the cadres had ceased to be one with the people, or to talk with them; a coercive habit of talking-down had set in. Result: despite its pioneering work in installingPanchayati Raj (grass roots democracy), such raj (governance) had come to go out of the hands of the people and into the muscular enforcement of party cadres. Indeed, the malaise stretched beyond the rural sector, encompassing most aspects of public life and service, including the state-apparatus. The cadres came to see themselves and to be seen both as the people and the state. Hegemony had come to yield place to precipitate and overbearing coercion.

Good to remind ourselves that whenever that has happened – no more eloquent instance than the erstwhile Soviet Union – disaster is only a step away. It is my view that the overthrow of the left in Bengal, even as it had to do with episodes like Nandigram which shocked chiefly the Muslim Bengalis out of a habitual preference for the left despite little cause for thanks beyond the land they came to possess and physical safety from majoritarian onslaughts, had to do with the little man's assertion on behalf of self-affirmation against big-brotherly habits that seemed to take their allegiance for granted. The question therefore cries to be pondered: why, and why so often, do people-friendly formations that seek to deepen democracy end up stifling the same?

I have submitted on more than one occasion that the Indian left must diligently seek to rethink the Leninist legacy of a party in total command, and of democratic centralism itself. These legacies no longer seem conducive to the sort of rapport that left politics needs to forge with toiling people on whose behalf it thinks and hopes to work. These are legacies that have hubris written into them, and sixty years of political democracy in India have eliminated the room for command or hubris as the operative axes of relationship between political formations and the masses. Given the complex cultural matrices of Indian social and historical life, leaderships that only understand people's suffering from a safe theoretical distance, however correctly, always have lost to others who share those sufferings on the ground, and on a sustained basis of immersion. There are lessons to be learnt here from the more authentic non-governmental organizations who, slowly but surely, have over the decades, come to substitute the grass roots work that rightfully belongs to organized left parties. And lessons as well from those communist leaders who, into their ageing days into the end of the sixties, observed patterns of personal living and relationship with the people that were instrumental in setting up an influential politics of the left in India when in most other democracies the left had come to shut shop.

Is there a call, therefore, for the left to rethink not just contingent errors of policy and praxis, but its root organizational principles? I think there is. Not until rigid and robotic forms of affiliation between party leaderships and cadres, and between cadres and the mass of people are loosened and freed from mere cerebrated correctness may the left now hope to secure a more willing foothold among wider sections of the immiserated who recognize the authenticity of left concern but who also feel thwarted by high-falutin rebuke.

Thinking Beyond Capitalism

In a recent article, Prabhat Patnaik, the credible intellectual voice of the CPI (M), has rightly argued that the relevance of the left remains a long-ranging one because, alone among India's political formations, it thinks of life beyond capitalism, and has the theoretical equipment to do so.

The question I ask myself is one that Marx would surely also have asked: what does it mean to be fighting capitalism in the India of 2011? Or, indeed, India per se.

As I seek for answers I find no easy ones. The vanguards of India's anti-colonial movement, many impeccably rational and seeped in knowledge of ideologies, did not, often could not (because for every rational leader there were two or three who shared irrational habits of custom and thought) battle the social and cultural content of pre-capitalist material orders. I say that in the plural because there is still little agreement among economic historians as to whether pre-colonial India was uniformly Feudal, or uniformly Asiatic, or indeed offered a spectrum of practices in economic organization.

India's post-colonial 'modernity' thus arrived as a mish-mash of absorptions and compromises. There are those among India's sociologists who think that a good thing, since, thank god, such a consequence has saved us from unilinear models of 'modernity' and its deracinating effects on subjectivity.

The fact, however, remains that economic considerations did not come to inhabit the chief pinnacle of concern among Indians generally, with the exception of those, of course, who came to, and have come to, appropriate the means of production. More than in any other country, the consciousness of class has remained strangulated by multifarious allegiances that have often succeeded in burying the relations of production beneath piles and piles of debris from what Marx called the 'muck of ages.'

One consequence of those concatenations has been that, barring the stipulations laid down in the Constitution of India, it cannot be said that Indians have uniformly achieved the consciousness of 'citizens.' And for good reason: to this day the operations of the state and its agencies do not negotiate with all Indians as 'citizens.' Apart from considerations of class, such negotiation is everywhere coloured by determinations that may be proscribed by the republican Constitution but remain alive and kicking on the ground. To a point where even the extent of torture inflicted on prisoners, or the nature and quantum of punishment given to them for identical crimes is often conditioned by habits of socialization among law-enforcers and officers of the Bench that run contrary to the stipulations of law and the requirements of justice. Indian capitalism and the party-political system that represents it, then continues to plough into these fractured self-definitions, never allowed to gel into 'citizen' consciousness across the board.

I therefore plead that capitalism in India now cannot be confronted exclusively on the single plank of exploitation, but that such a fundamental premise of class analysis requires to be arrived at through a diverse spectrum of negotiations. For that reason I doubt much that Indian capitalism can be fought with any great consequence through a book-ridden route to some pristine proletarian struggle, supposing that anything like a proletariat with a dour class-consciousness exists, or, if it does, carries sufficient clout. I also think that the debate whether or not the Communist parties should formally declare themselves Social Democrats, embrace the irreversibility of capitalism, and carry on from there is little more than a red-herring, although viewed from a ruling class perspective, of great comfort. For a start, dialectical thought which I hold to be a truer representation of the operations of time, space, and human agency than any other I know, rebukes from irrefutable scrutiny the very notion of irreversibility. But on more practical grounds, embracing such a so-called finality can only have the consequence of debilitating the sternness of conviction without which the work of the left can only dissolve into a complacency matching that of well-intentioned Liberals.

I think fighting capitalism at this juncture in India's history must mean engaging with oppressions of diverse definition (oppressions against tribals, dalits, women, children, religious minorities, relegated ethnic groups, displaced populations, victims of state and social/community atrocity alike), definitions that impinge as forcefully on subaltern self-consciousness as economic impoverishment and seem, more often than not, prior to such impoverishment, and seeking to bring those into a unity of 'citizen's' consciousness against the operations of the state and its supportive social elite who seek both to prevent such consolidation and to profit by its lack. Intending not a snuffing out of the colours of the rainbow, but to syncretise them into a light of shared and common recognition that what seem disparate circumstances are everywhere syncopated into the realities of class society. To wit, the hydra may have many heads, but it is one and the same animal. Even as the heads must need be dealt with each in its own location.

And it means, most of all, not just to take up causes for the record, or for media exposure, but devise organizational strategies whereby the left is constantly among the affected people, educating itself about the specifities of particular oppressions, and preparing the conditions for mass assertions that may in time come to identify a common adversary. Because, emphatically, such discrete coordinates of attention must, even as they do their work, at all costs be prevented from ossifying into vested enclaves of specialized activity which over time become bureaucracies oblivious of the totalized purpose to which they must all contribute severally. Those that are assigned the task of cutting off each head must never forget that the heads belong to one and the same brute, and it is a conjoint task they perform; nor should they forget that the capitalist hydra spawns ever new instruments, which sometimes spawns newer heads, especially in so pluralist a venue as India..

Electoral Politics

I have for many years felt that in order to free itself of the contradictions that participation in state power in a multi-party democracy must entail, left parties should go wholly over to mass work for a decade or two. The attempt to work from above and below simultaneously may have brought the left to a point where the loss of a state government seems to acquire the proportions of a calamity. Much as I might wish the left first to consolidate into a unity grounded in a short list of macro-historical determinations, and then to go over wholly to a revolutionary line of mass mobilisaton and education, including self-education, this does not seem likely to happen. Although we may wonder why not.

It should also be obvious that the left parties on their own are in no position whatsoever, especially as I write, to determine the course of parliamentary power. Nor is it foreseeable that the left will become a decisive force in parliament for many years to come, regardless of objective conditions that cry out for left victories.

A question that has repeatedly cropped up in the conclaves of left decision-making, then, is how may the left forge an effective role in parliamentary participation? A question that, like it or not, brings us down to unlovely considerations of an opportunist and contingent nature. Today let me say with brevity that if the two all-important objectives of constitutionalism are social inclusivity/secularism, and as much material and institutional justice as class society and the state it owns may furnish to the people, the left must consider with wisdom and without self-pride which parliamentary and party-political forces to align with and which to confront, all within the ambit of constitutional possibility. Such consideration must need disregard interests limited to specific areas of the nation-state and take a view that keeps the entire body politic in mind. As well as the histories/ideologies of major political players, and their record of governance as instruments of class rule. After all, if the parliamentary exertions and interventions of the left are to be meaningful and consequential, its negotiations and compromises must follow some order of preference. In that context, the left may need to take a second look, however painful, at the Indian National Congress in disregard of the fact that the Congress remains its chief electoral adversary in West

Bengal and Kerala. Even as the work of the left among the masses brings, overtime, the Congress to a fresh evaluation of its own policy frameworks. The left must never forget that forces exist in India that seek stridently to fascicise both state and polity – stridently because wide segments among the new affluent classes support any course calculated to homogenize the nation into a strident social unity, weaken democratic institutions and practices, and set out on a course of abrasive militarism. By common recognition, it is the left mainly that is rightly seen to be the ideological adversary to such forces. But the left must in turn recognize and accept the reality that it is a fight in which it needs both democratic mass assertions on an exponential scale, and organized political partnerships from among the contenders for power.

West Bengal

As the adage goes, every loss conceals a gain. The loss in West Bengal affords the left a fine opportunity to contemplate and interpret. The time to change will surely come in five or less years, given what has taken over in Writer's Building.

Bengal remains a thoughtful and magnanimous place. Those that write off the left after the Bengal debacle need to remember that it still runs the best government in the North East – one that has succeeded in righting innumerable wrongs done by earlier dispensations, and that the CPI (M) still remains the largest single party in Kerala where, but for the spectacular show put up by the Indian Union Muslim League (winning 20 of 24 seats it contested in contrast to a Congress score of 38 from 82), the Left Front government would have been ahead by more than a mite. They also need to remember that the BJP once had just two representatives in parliament, but went on in 1996 to form the government at the centre.

In the coming five years in West Bengal the left must expect to receive provocations galore, and not all non-violent; but as it rethinks its cadres, the left must not be tempted to reply in kind. As in many other matters, the left here has lessons to learn from Gandhi.

May 2011

What is a Temple Minus the Moolah?

Ay, in the very temple of transcendence,
Gold and silver have their sovereign shrine.
(With apology to John Keats)

Between what is universally known and empirically proven even now lies a gasp of disbelief.

Thus, it was one thing to have an idea that temples in India, in a declension of degree, have always been repositories of clinking treasure, and another to be actually shown gold and silver goodies worth, we are told, one lac crore rupees as in the case of the Padmnabhaswamy temple in erstwhile Travancore. I wish someone quickly told me how much that stacks up in dollar terms so as we could equally quickly shame Obama into recognizing how our godly left-overs far outstrip his oily assets.

And, if not matchingly, then, in Nehru's phrase, 'substantially,' a none-too-lowly answer from the inward regions of the Puttaparthi domains of the late Satya Sai Baba of the mesmerizing hairdo. Add all the others, and our godly entrepreneurs have enough to go buy the world several times over. Murdoch to note.

At which point well-meaning people like my friend, Ram Puniyani, make the predictably rational leap to suggesting how all this moolah – god alone knows how many times larger than the measly 2G speculations – might be deployed to vanquish overnight those problems of penury, illiteracy, ill-health, malnutrition, anaemia, what-have-you, that continue to bedevil this land of rishis and munis. And, remarkably, neither Shri Ramdev, himself no pauperly chicken, nor the redoubtable corruption-fighter, Shri Anna Hazare, are heard to say 'yes, let us' to Puniyani's overture. Nor any of the others who routinely berate the politician and the bureaucrat for being such blood-sucking vampires. Suggestion: only the corporates and the babas may save India for its newly opulent destiny.

Of course, things are never so simple; and Puniyani, good man several times over, makes the egregious miscalculation to think that what is sauce for the goose may be sauce for the gander. Indeed, though, to be fair to him, were Shri Manmohan Singh, alongwith Shri Advani ji, to go visit Bhagwan Shri Ram, and ask for instructions in the matter of the clinkery findings, I, as a good Rambakht, have narry a doubt that Shri Ram would say exactly as Puniyani does, namely, go use the loot to serve rhe destitute.

But, there is the rub. To be a Rambakht is one thing and to be a high-caste Hindu quite another. Brahminical Hinduism teaches, first and foremost, that what is or is not given to us in this our current life has nothing to do with the moral or political predilections of the day. It has to do with those our accumulated good and bad points when last we were alive. Thus, be it our gender or caste-placement or our economic location, our unequalnesses are predetermined and mandatory. All we may do is to ensure a better next life by being properly subordinate to baba-teaching in this. Add to this the further thought that our acquisitions in this life are only proof and reward for good things done in the previous one.

That being the case, where is the question that, except in the case of the politician and the bureaucrat, anyone else should be asked to answer for their possessions, least of all those who give gold and silver to temple deities and their anointed staff, and those who preside over the fallen lives of the hungry and the immiserated? It must be understood, that, in the absence of any other indicator, as in Calvinism, it is our wealth that suggests whether or not we are favoured of the gods to have a better life next time around.

Thus, to put the matter succinctly, in high-caste Hinduism, both spiritual and economic salvation are matters of deeply individual concern and consequence, and the latter impinging crucially on the former. It is only in very lowly forms of the Hindu faith – such as among the Bakhti saints, tainted no doubt by their indiscriminate contact with the then Sufi ones – that salvation etc., bear any relation to how we give or not give ourselves to other human beings, indeed to all living beings, insects included.

And within those lowly forms of the faith, gold and silver have as little consequence as the brayings of the high and mighty. Reason why that gold and silver must, after all, remain solidly in the keep of the temple hierarchy, presided over by a compliant deity.

Which leads to this further thought: all those now under the scanner, or likely to be, need but do one smple thing, namely, instantly construct deterring temple structures over their piles of moolah, and claim that the offerings belong to the deity. Enough to send jitters of devotion down the investigative spine. A Hasan Ali could pass on his pile on contract to his friend Taraporewala (or some such) who indeed has the wherewithal to build a bhavya (remember Advani of the Ram Temple fame?) mandir over the takings, security more secure than any of them off-shore no-tax havens.

There is nothing in India's secularism that dare lay a legal hand on such hard-earned acquisitions. And not to forget that our deities far outnumber the puissant sleuths that the state can muster. Pure no-brainer that.

Pity that poor Raja and Kalmadi did not think of all this; fools must pay for their idiocy.

August 2011

Corruption: A Heady Brew

Bliss is it in this dawn to be alive,
But to be old is to be doubting.
(With apology to William Wordsworth)

Maha Kumbh

These are heady days in India. An orgy is underway in many parts, as angels of virtue shriek holy imprecations, ostensibly, to exorcise the demon 'Corruption,' a word that has a nice Biblical-post-lapsarian ring to it. This inventively constituted Ravana of our times, embodied, we are told, chiefly in the conjoint body of the politicians of the day, especially of the ruling Congress party, is now faced with the equally inventively constituted Ram in the person of Anna Hazare. Suitably, this crusader, although he wears the pristine white, topped with a Gandhi cap, opposes the demon in hues which are increasingly more and more saffron as the hours go by (see 'Is Anna's Crusade Changing Colour?' *Hindustan Times*, August, 19). No wonder that some electronic channels seem to have nothing better to do than to pour incandescent ablutions of fuel into the corruption-Kumbh, in the full knowledge of the politics they seek to advance.

The Anna Crusaders

Well-endowed citizens who think nothing of doing their bit of corruption day in and day out – in sale and purchase of properties, in tax-evading clevernesses, in getting their job done, whatever the job and whatever it takes (after all, the Shastras do say that you may employ any one of the principles of *sam, dam, dand, bhed* – where *dam* stands for inducement, aka, bribery), including by flaunting their 'connections' with 'high-ups,' not to speak of corporates (those chief corruptors of national life who find no mention either in the government's Lokpal Bill or of the alternate Anna draft, called the Jan Lokpal Bill) – dip their complicit hands in the Anna-Ganga, certain that all the spots will wash off. Unlike in Semitic faiths, Hinduism provides Uppai (remedial ways of out of any sort of ill-fortune or sin committed, depending crucially on the price paid to the Purohit, except of course in the case of Brahm Hatya, namely the murder of a Brahmin.) So, if only Lady Macbeth had been a Hindu, her 'damned spot' may not have been as intransigent. Unto each our fate.

Anna's faithfuls thus wish the powers-that-be to bring illicit wealth from foreign tax havens back to India, but have not yet asked any serious questions about the unaccounted moneys within the country that constitute a parallel economy to the official one of equal proportions or more. Not to speak of the obscene volumes of wealth stashed away in temples across the length and breadth of the land. These are not exactly suicidal revolutionaries, after all.

Indeed, these are people, as far as the eye can see and experience tell, who see no corruption in the facts that nearly 40% the world's poor are Indians, that a half of India's children are severely malnourished, and a half of India's lactating mothers severely anaemic, that close to two-thirds of all Indians have no access to clean drinking water or modern sanitation, that rates of female infanticide soar in India's prosperous states even as the GDP climbs upward, but mostly into the coffers of a miniscule club of billionaires, some fifty nine or so, who own a quarter of India's total GDP, that communal carnages are routinely vented upon religious minorities, that young lives are routinely taken to protect family 'honour,' that lacs of farmers are driven to self-slaughter because of neoliberal farm policies, that atrocities on low castes happen dime a dozen while the corporate TV channels sing hosannas to the 'India Growth Story,' worried only that 'corruption' wrought by 'politicians' may dent that story and bring back those sad days of leveling boredom (and what would the flourishing diaspora and the western world, however it may be crashing in debt, dust, and war-mongering thereof, think then of India?).

Just let the good Anna declare a fast unto death on any of the above issues and he might find that not a soul of the kind that now deify him – much like the hero in the film, Guide, where the distraught lover-guide is mistaken for a messiah and forced to undertake a fast unto death so the rains may come – walking in his step, all except me. For among the bulk who are now out in the streets are good old casteists, devote communalists, committed worshippers of market fundamentalism, traditional upholders of patriarchy, and unflinching detractors of social welfare policies that oblige the 'appeasing' state to squander 'honest' money on India's have-nots who, after all, are destitute because of their own laziness and karma of previous births, don't you know.

There are of course those as well whose lives are too disempowered to play games, and who see in Anna an avatar come to deliver them of their misery. We wish these honest folks well in every walk of life.

The Anna Agenda

Remembering how the good old Gandhi undertook some of his most strenuous upliftment crusades precisely in relation to matters of caste and communal oppression, would it be too awry to expect that Anna might do the same? But, do pardon me, Anna ain't no Gandhi, and divisive agendas are not for him. Do recall how he lauded Modi of Guajrat 2002 vintage during the course of his first fast at Jantar Mantar (see my 'Anna Lauds Modi'). So, do not expect that he might expend the same sort of energy on seeing an effective Bill to bring sectarian murderers to book as he seems to want to do in the instant case. Especially when you remember that just as a Lokpal Bill awaits Parliament's endorsement as I write, so does another Bill designed to curb sectarian mayhems wrought on various types of minorities by majoritarian pogroms. Or, for that matter, the other jinxed Bill seeking 33% reservation for women in the houses of parliament and state legislatures. Anna's thoughts do not thither tend. Nor Indeed of those who target 'corruption.'

Recalling Gandhi's Champaran Satyagraha on behalf of the then workers on Indigo plantations, how nice it would be to see this Gandhian Anna strike a blow on behalf of the millions of unorganized workers and street vendors who are today the hopeless and helpless victims of neoliberalism. There again, you have another thing coming.

The wonderful thing about 'corruption' and 'terrorism' is that these buzz words unite everybody, including the corrupt and the terrorist. Easy enough to lead such crusades where only the wicked government stands before you, waiting to be dislodged.

August 2011

Parliament and the Anna Putsch

It should be obvious by now that a majority of dalit and Muslim organizations are opposed to the sort of denigration of parliament that seems inherent in the Anna putsch as it has developed over the last few days. Add to that most Other Backward Classes whose leaderships may make opportunist statements but who also remain staunchly wedded to parliamentary supremacy against the claims of 'direct democracy' made by Anna backers.

The social character of this polarization is of the highest significance, and must interest all those for whom Indian democracy is a work-in-progress towards the enhancement of equity and non-discriminatory justice.

In one word, dalits, Muslims, tribals, and large sections of the Other Backward Classes view the attack on parliament as an attack on the only democratic institution wherein they, thanks to the Constitution, have any empowered presence and clout. Not in the judiciary, not in the bureaucracy, not at all within the media conglomerates, and negligible among the state-apparatus.

To put it another way, more than three-fourths of all Indians continue to have an enormous stake in the state, especially the legislatures, since their historical disabilities and lack of influence within the privatized productive assets and processes is close to non-existent.

The sentient sections of the backers who presently form the informing engines of the Anna event essentially speak for a new middle class whose links with the state, thanks to neoliberal transfers of wealth from the state to private agencies, have not only been atrophied, but have come to be seen as an obstructing nuisance. This reality in stark contrast to the middle classes that either drove the main coordinates of India's anti-colonial movement, or engaged in nation-building thereafter, till India came to be absorbed into the Washington Consensus of 1990 under the guidance of the current Prime Minister, Manmohan Singh.

A profound irony then that the very products of that all-important policy-shift should today be demanding that the next step in neoliberal thinking be effected without loss of time, namely, the full-scale dissolution of the state as guardian of people's interests.

dalits, Backward Classes, and Muslims may seem to be opposing Anna and his Jana Lok Pal Bill from restricted, sectarian interests – dalits arguing that the proposed Lok Pal idea and the processes leading upto it have, in a studied way, left them out of reckoning as stake-holders as a typical casteist exclusion, and Muslims deeply distressed by Anna's less than forgettable predilections towards the Hindu right, and his refusal to condemn Narendra Modi – but, underlying those axes of opposition is the far deeper anxiety about the weakening of the state, and its caving in now not just to private wealth but to the social and denominational leaderships that back the private wealth.

It is clear from the twists and turns of the last few days that sections within the political class across party lines do sense this, and do also understand the dimensions of what is at stake for state and polity.

It is time, and imperatively so, that segments of the intelligentsia who share these analyses and anxieties also make their voices heard.

August 2011

The Real Agenda?

Dislogded, did I say. Indeed the word is also doing the round that the point and purpose of the Anna crusade is neither corruption nor the anti-corruption Bill. It is to get rid of a government that has another three interminable years to it, and, according to a recent country-wide poll conducted indeed by one of the corporate TV channels – no friend of the Congress party – the strong likelihood of being returned to power for an, oopgh, third wretched term in 2014. Unbearable thought for those forces who are dying to see India's retail trade thrown open to foreign predators, India's Insurance Companies substantially privatized, the Provident Fund moneys of retiring and retired employees made accessible to the stock market for its 'creative' purposes, arms purchases,including nuclear reactors, ordered in piles and bulks not just from anywhere but the United States of America and its satellite, Israel, all cases of 'terrorist' involvement against good saffron nationalists quashed, the likes of Modi saved for a date when he might be installed Prime Minister of a Subramaniam Swamy-like India etc., What could be more wretched than the fact that the above-mentioned poll showed three Congress leaders occupy the top three places as desired candidates for Prime Ministership, with the likes of Shri Advani – that never-say-enough – is enough aspirant to the post – and Shri Modi polling a measly 5 and 4% respectively! Galling in the extreme. And, yes, let us say like it is: a statement did come from an official US spokesman, admonishing the Indian government to deal nicely with the Anna crusade. Hey, whatever Sam's major domos might effervate from time to time about the Indo-US 'strategic partnership' the sad fact is that at a time when a collapsing US economy needs its Indian partner to 'open up' to its goods, services, and genetically modified seeds, the UPA government seems set on yet more moneys' to be wasted in social welfare programmes that only help the destitute Indian to survive, one day to another, but leave the US entrepreneur holding the sack of debt and likely default. Some 'partnership' that.

Not that influential sections of the UPA government do not wish to do as Sam says. Boy, are both Manmohan Singh and Montek Singh Ahluwalia not dying to do so, egged on by the Sam Pitrodas, the Nandan Nilekanis, and the electronic corporates who salivate at the very thought of having them grace their studios. But there still are contrarian voices within the Congress that go the other way. No such problem with the BJP if the Anna crusade could install it, as the J.P. crusade had done in the middle seventies, if only for a short Indian summer. And incidentally, if both the J.P. crusade and the one led by V.P. Singh after that failed to eradicate either the crass, authoritarian character of the Indian state or corruption, the reasons obviously do not lie in lack of moral fibre and so on, but in the class character of the state – something no crusader wished to do anything about then, or wishes to do anything about now. Including the BJP-led NDA government that was in power in New Delhi between 1998 and 2004.

As to India's left parties, having lost West Bengal, they are loathe to give any quarter to the UPA government, even if it means supping briefly with the enemy of enemies. Sad in the extreme. But, as you would know, they always know best.

About Democracy

The Anna crusade is of course the harbinger of hope of another kind. He and his lieutenants proclaim that the will of the 'people' (O people, I wish I knew who you are at bottom) must prevail over the petty and ill-intentioned machinations of parliament. To this effect a new theory of 'referendums' of which nothing exists in the Indian Constitution, is everyday being floated, as well as the slogan that the crusade is now about a 'second independence movement.'

Both those postulates must bring great comfort to others who have been seeking either 'Azadi' or precisely what Anna opines, a second liberation whereby the state is overthrown and reconstituted. The one difference being that whereas the Anna platform would wish to effect that reconstitution from the right, the Maoists would want to do so from the left. Others wish simply to secede from the Union of India altogether.

As to the idea that such crucial things as the content of an anti-corruptiion Bill had best be settled through a referendum, what gorgeous possibilities lie in that thought. Indeed, here are a few issues on which sections of 'civil society' other than those that comprise the Anna platform might want referendums held and imbroglios settled:

- how about a referendum to settle the issue of whether a magnificent temple should not after all be built on the site of the Babri mosque which was vandalized and demolished equally through another referendum of sorts?
- or to settle whether or not the Kashmir valley be allowed to go its way, and leave the Hindu-majority parts of the state to remain aligned with India?
- or whether more people than less in Gujarat would wish that state to be declared an autonomous Hindu-Rashtra?
- or, whether the upper castes of Haryana, Western Uttar Pradesh etc., should not be allowed to carry on with their time-honoured custom of 'honour' killings?
- or whether the Shekhawats of Rajasthan may not reinstall the hallowed tradition of sati ?
- or, whether female infanticide, caste discrimination, majoritarian citizenship, should not be formalized as practices that Indians may think best for a proper nationhood?
- or, whether mining mafia or forest dwellers have first right to land, water, and other forest products? Gosh, how those primitive Adivasis would be voted out of home and hearth, precisely by the like of citizenry who now dance around Anna ji!

And so on and so on…

Altogether, as I said, heady times; and who knows whether India's strenuous efforts to hang on to institutional democracy despite all odds has any more breathing time, notwithstanding the stark fact that the orgy that is now on would not have had much life had democracy not been the operative episteme of India's political life, and of the, however reluctant, objectives of the state.

Sting in the Tail?

During the course of these most heady days in defence of direct democracy, the Anna campaign has predictably drawn on memories of the Internal Emergency imposed on the nation by the late Indira Gandhi in 1975, albeit, lifted by her within a year when she called for fresh elections. A telling reminiscence of that year was the famous slogan uttered by the Congress leader, Devkant Barua "India is Indira, Indira is India." How charming that our current crusaders against authoritarianism should have sloganeered just the other day "India is Anna, Anna is India." Which tells you how much of what is now on display is about democracy.

Another thing: I ask myself which of the two facts may, after all, be the most detrimental to Indian democracy in the long term: one, the brief preventive detention of Anna, or the insistence of the Anna camp that Parliament must do as the crusaders say. Or else.

Do chew on that, as you enjoy the spectacle.

August 2011

Those That Rule Above and Beyond

It is a common recognition of Indian 'mainstream' politics that however the various off-shoots of the Sangh Parivar may seem to be warring from time to time, they all obey the RSS.

A more macro version of the above is the following: that however the Congress and the BJP may be warring on issue after issue, both these faces of Indian capitalism obey the Ambanis. And sundry other corporates that have any real clout.

Think of the many recent reports on corruption of one kind or another germinated by the Comptroller and Auditor General of India (CAG for short). Apart from the lip service done to this 'constitutional authority' by all sections of the political class, the fact remains that its findings are now endorsed, now not by either of the two major parties, depending on how the reports of this body suit or not suit their realpolitik of the moment. Too many instances here in very recent public memory and media exposure to need recounting.

But, as the CPI(M) has just pointed out in a most instructive Press Release, when it comes to the CAG exposure of the corruption engaged in by the Reliance Group of Industries with respect to oil exploration rights and stipulations in the KG-6 deep water block, a pall of eloquent silence seems to have fallen over both the Congress and the BJP. Not a squeak thus far. True guru bhais in this regard, you may say.

Just to cite three unlawful enormities underscored by the CAG, and publicized by the CPI (M):

- a 117% increase in estimated capital expenditure for the block without any augumentation of capacity involved;
- procurement awards made by Reliance Industries Limited "on single financial bids, major revision of scope/quantities/specifications, post-price bid opening, substantial variation in order quantities, with consequent adverse implications for cost recovery and Government of India's financial stake";
- a contract of $1.1 billion given to the Aker group for a ten year lease against an estimated original cost of $300 million; RIL gave eight such contracts to the Aker group out of ten single party bids on what prima facie seem to be sweet heart deals that enabled it to inflate capital expenditure.

Equally remarkably, one has heard nothing to date on this particular CAG report from Anna and his team who, after all, have taken on the burden of exposing corruption and its sources in modern India. But then, as some have been pointing out, the chief object of the Anna phenomenon seems to be to pillory those that manage the state, not those who actually own it.

Postscript: How many Indians know of the fact that the chief beneficiaries of the Oil for Food programme (Iraq) were not the ones we got to hear of but the Ambani group of industries? A fact concealed and kept from parliament and people with conjoint efficiency by both Congress and the BJP while the country was going after the likes of Shri Natwar Singh. (See Arun K. Agrawal, *Reliance, the Real Natwar*, Manas Publications, Delhi, 2008.)

September 2011

The Abject Desperation of the Right Wing

Modi and the Congressional Research Service (CRS)

Anyone who has studied American political systems for any length of time would know that American Congressmen routinely employ young men and women from their electoral constituencies to prepare functional research briefs for them.

Invariably compiled from selective inclusions from relevant media interventions from region to region rather than strenuously researched on the ground, these briefs speak neither for the American Houses of Congress nor for the American state.

Put another way, these briefs are, more likely than not, attuned to specific special interests who may, at one time or another, wish either to disparage or laud any particular trend or entity in any part of the world through the aegis of Congressmen and women funded by them.

Thus it is that a CRS report (some 93 pages) has en passant praised the developmental efforts in the Indian state of Gujarat during the tenure of Narendra Modi. Although such approbation of Modi's 'governance' from sources aligned to International Finance and Indian capital is not new, the CRS reference has provided grist to India's Hindu right-wing mill, as Modi's party, the BJP, is currently going to town with the polemic that Modi has allegedly now found favour with an uncle Sam who, incidentally, still refuses to issue an American entry visa to this Nero (characterization used for Modi by no less than the Supreme Court of India) of Guajrat.

This groveling need of Modi and the Bharatiya Janata Party to obtain from the U.S. a rescinding of his pariah status at the present moment of India's political effervescence is indeed understandable in more ways than one: widely favoured by the Hindutva hard core as the first among warring BJP leaders for claim to the party's prime-ministerial candidate, Modi's leap from his captive constituency in Gujarat to the national stage cannot be effected unless ways are found to neutralize his humungous culpabilities with respect to the carnage of 2002.

As everyday whistleblowers of high rank and unimpeachable integrity come out with bold resolve to set the Modi record straight (see Sanjiv Bhatt's unprecedented open letter to Modi in *The Hindu*, September,15), and when, with the latest Supreme Court decision to refer hitherto unadmitted materials pertaining to the Gulberg society massacre in which the then Congress Member of Parliament, Ehsan Jafri was hacked to pieces alongwith another 63 innocent Muslims, materials that include the original complaint filed by Jafri's 75 year old widow, and the Citizens for Justice and Peace, the final report of the Special Investigating Team, and the independent observations and conclusions of the Supreme Court-appointed amicus on the report of the SIT, to the trial court for formal legal proceedings against the persons named in the Jafri complaint, names that include Modi, the latter's legal difficulties seem now only to assume the proportions of a formal arraignment. All that contrary to the noisome propaganda that the Supreme Court has actually given Modi a 'clean chit.' Goebbels would yet again have similed.

Given those contexts, it is hardly any surprise that Modi and the BJP should reach for any straw that offers itself, and manufacture others, however disingenuous or indeed laughable. Thus, sections of India's corporate media which wish to see the back of the current Manmohan Singh regime in favour of one led by the 'nationalist' and 'next-generation-of-reforms-friendly' BJP are busy tom-tomming the CRS reference to Modi's prowess at governance (read his ready willingness to jettison the interests of indigent Gujaratis in favour of the aspirations of private wealth) as the final ringing endorsement by the American state and International Finance who are thought to think a Modi vs Rahul Gandhi contest for prime minsitership as the most likely political scenario for India of 2014, a contest which is also ab initio being touted as a no-contest. Ergo, close your eyes, and Modi is the Indian Prime Minister as you open them again!

Thus is the future manufactured.

Modi to Undertake a Three-Day Fast

Now to the hilarious bit.

Narendra Modi is to undergo a three-day fast in an obliging, air-conditioned venue at a university in Ahmedabad, beginning Saturday. The fast is to be undertaken for 'harmony and brotherhood.' It may be noted that the same university had denied this facility to the Congress party on the grounds that the university does not encourage 'political' activity on its premises. So much for the quality of academic independence and integrity under the aegis of the Modi regime.

On both counts, namely, fasting and the desire for harmony, Modi seeks with astounding but rather despicable cunning to take a leaf out of the book of the Hindu right-wings' established bête noir, Mahatma Gandhi.

Throughout his career, the RSS never failed to revile Gandhi for his fasting gimmickries, and most especially when those fasts were undertaken to salvage inter-community harmony. Indeed, you may recall, he was duly assassinated for his heinous secular endeavours by stalwarts spawned by theHindutva brigade.

To this day it is difficult to recall any Hindu right-wing leader who ever went on a fast on any social or political issue – not Golwalkar, not Vajpayee, not Advani, not Deen Dayal Upadhay, not anyone. A record that highlights Modi's genius at tactical innovation. Having just seen how the Anna Hazare fast allegedly against a corrupt Indian political class drew more than impressive media and middle class support, Modi's decision to do likewise, albeit for three days, must be considered canny at the least.

As to the 'harmony and brotherhood' bit: how cute that a chief executive who presided, and, from all accounts, directed, the anti-Muslim carnage of 2002, under whose continuing watch the Hindu and Muslim communities in Gujarat have now become almost totally segregated, who has to this minute disdained every plea and bit of advice, including from the erstwhile BJP Prime Minister, Vajpayee, to speak one word of regret or remorse, who has to this minute refused to visit the Jafri widow, for example, and to commiserate with her fate, and those of the thousands who left behind them ruined families, who has without let attempted to subvert every effort of the investigating agencies and of the courts to bring out the truth and furnish redress, who will in all likelihood return to his hate-spewing rhetoric come the next elections, how cute that this unredeemed and unrepentant Nero should speak of harmony and brotherhood and seek to dramatise the same in air-conditioned comfort to a national television audience.

Ah, said the Bard, "you may smile and smile and be a villain."

The Congress Party

Interestingly, the Congress party in Gujarat has hit upon a rather telling way of calling Modi's bluff. Its leader, Shanker Singh Waghela, is to sit on a parallel fast, an indeterminate one, not at a parallel venue of air-conditioned comfort, but from a well-chosen Gandhi Ashram site.

However disingenuous this fast may also seem, historically the Congress party can claim that fasting has been a long-used recourse in its political and activist repertoire since Gandhi first came to lead it. And, a fast undertaken from a Gandhi-related venue ought surely to find greater salience with the hoi polloi than one that bespeaks a form of luxuriating realpolik from the most unlikely of sources and subjects.

Clearly, one expects that in the days and months to come, the Congress and other secular forces will marshall the factual status of Modi's so-called incorruptibily (note that the Comptroller and Auditor General of India, or CAG, the very same who has been at the centre of the many recent exposures of corruption in high places, has in a report on Gujarat underscored likely corruption running to some 26,000 crore rupees!) and the unlovely truths of his lauded developmental model, for, as long as it takes, it is truth alone that can best bring Gujarat round to 'harmony and brotherhood.'

The Trial Court

In that context, many millions now look to the trial court in Gujarat with hope; having been given a second wind of life to prove its impartial metal after the unflattering episodes when the Supreme Court was obliged to take one case of atrocity after another away from the legal system in Gujarat to other courts in other states, that court, given the reams of evidence newly incorporated, should find little rationale or justice in exonerating, ab initio, anyone from the list of accused furnished in the Jafri complaint, or implicated in the substance of the report of the SIT and of the amicus in his independent observations upon that report.

If the sordid story of the Modi years in Gujarat has to find closure, that trial court may have as much to do with it as all those who seek to foreground aspects of the Modi era, most of all the incredibly brave whistleblowers and non-governmental organizations and activists.

To put it another way, the question still remains whether Modi's Gujarat will shape the future of the republic, or whether the republic will rectify, redeem, and revalidate Modi's Guajrat.

September 2011

Endgame in Gujarat?

The abuse of greatness is when it disjoins remorse from power.
Julius Caesar

There comes a time in Macbeth's bloody-minded totalitarianism when, wishing to control every little mite of time, space, and freedom of action, he realizes that in so doing he has in fact come to lose all control over everything.

Indeed, the one profound and profoundly enacted truth of Macbeth's career is to communicate the fearful irony at the heart of all absolutist ambition, namely, that far from achieving any omnipotent security of selfhood or regime, every successive crime calculated to nail opposition leaves a residue which in course metamorphoses into an uncontrollable destiny. All moral compass lost, a madly irrational anarchy overtakes the tyrant, until his only pathetic rationale for going forward or turning back comes to be which end is physically closer and more accessible: "I am in blood/Stepped in so far that, should I wade no more/Returning were as tedious as go o'er" (*Macbeth*, Cambridge, ed. John Dover Wilson.)

This seems to be the point at which politics in Gujarat may now have arrived.

Sanjiv Bhatt may well be the 'naked new born babe' whose sheer unconcealed innocence and open-ended helplessness bids fair to rouse the 'collective conscience of society' (to borrow that redolent phrase from the Supreme Court's judgement on Afzal Guru), including of the Congress party, into more than just mumbling 'enough is enough,' that there truly has been 'something rotten in the state of' Gujarat that screams for healthful redress and renewal.

As the remorseless arms of tyranny flail in all directions, to strike, as it were, whoever may lurk in the blinding shadows of gathering justice, Sanjeev Bhatt may just be the reincarnated eighth of Devki and Vasudev, blown in with the winds from nearby Dwarka, deriving a charmed life from the spirit of the moment, from, if you like, a post-Anna Zeitgeist. Imagine that in one leading English Daily today (Gandhi's birthday fittingly), Anna is reported to say that "Communal Forces are a bigger threat than Corruption" (*HT*, 2nd oct, 2011). How heartily we agree!

Meanwhile, are you as askance as we are at the constitutional and ethical poverty of a party like the BJP that one segment, it would seem, of its many segments should think, and like us to think, that an intolerant boor, a sectarian warlord, a no-holds-barred extinguisher of non-compliant voices, however selfless and rightful, a rewarder of cronies who trample any and every constitutional or moral principle at his bidding, a democratic pretender who appeals not to the best collective reason but to the basest collective prejudice, is indeed the fittest candidate to be the Prime Minister of the world's most pluralist country! O tempora, O mores!

On this hallowed day of the birth of two of India's noblest souls – Gandhi and Lal Bahadur Shastri – do spare us that ugly thought.

Another thing: we in India say '*Satyameva jayate*'. From where else but this must Hegel have imbibed the insight that "only the rational is the right." Never more true than in a democratic system, however flawed, mangled, or appropriated. And, after long years of seeming victory, the rational one day materializes in the shape of a kashmiri-looking IPS officer who, perish the thought, stands up straightforwardly and says that his allegiance is not to the boss, but to the boss of all bosses, namely the Constitution of India as by law established. Ha, the gumption! But there it is: the same Constitution from whence the canny one derives his own wherewithal in the first place, much as he might say no, no, no, Anal Haq, Anal Haq i.e. I am god, I am god. Not Advani, not any other prani. Just me, just me, can't you see, can't you see.

Alas, will no one rid me of this fear, meaning not Richard but Sanjeev Bhatt.

The time for that sort of thing to happen may well be past, as Gujarat seems poised to emerge from the heart of darkness into the sunshine of common day.

Time to be humble, and time to pray.

October 2011

I am the Electronic Media

America, as you might know, has the Rifle Association. Nobody, but nobody, Republican or Democrat, may touch it. For the reason that the USP of American democracy is that an American citizen, preferably all white, may fire away at any real or imagined threat to the safety of his person or property. The American Constitution, good republicans think, was drafted with the singular purpose of ensuring this right, both at home and abroad.

Well, India now has her own answer to this. Born some forty odd years after India's independence from colonial rule, India's private-corporate electronic TV channels have over the two decades of neoliberalism come to be established, with complicit aid from the state, as the Indian Rifle Association. Holy cow, rogue elephant, mythical albino pachyderm that everybody seeks and fears, it has come to be all of these. And it is the untouchable – from- above that rarely ever notices the untouchable-from-below.

Upto this day, this animal that traverses across the plethora of channels a spectrum of production from the occasionally sober and urbane to the habitually sectarian, tendentious, jingoist, gauche, superstitious, reactionary, callously exploitive of base instincts and illiteracies, and obliteratively noisy, remains formally unaccountable within the institutional arrangements of Indian democracy, answerable only – as some very senior Indian journalists recently pointed out in a talk show – to a handful of private paymasters. In its recent fulminations against 'corruption,' for example, the secret fount of corruption was rarely mentioned, namely the corporates who crony upto political and bureaucratic allies that may do their dirty work.

Even as they routinely scream to hold all state institutions – the political class, the bureaucracy, the judiciary, the state-apparatus – accountable, India's electronic TV channels remain blissfully and shamelessly outside the ambit of any regulatory mechanism, unlike the Print media who are overseen by a Press Council of India, however conciliatory and toothless thus far.

But now, something seems set to change. The new Chairman of the Press Council of India is a recently retired justice of the Supreme Court, Justice Markandey Katju. And as he did while he was on the bench, he means business.

Good old Nehruvaian socialist that he is, as well as one who has a nasty courage of intellectual and political conviction, Katju has been expressing what some polls have shown to be a majority view that the fourth estate cannot by any stretch of constitutional arrangement be deemed to be above the decencies that must always be observed in public discourse, or above the livelihood concerns that affect and inform the existence of some three fourths of all Indians, concerns that but rarely ever surface among the coverages of these channels, except now and then as token offerings. Nor may it be permitted the carte blanche to exhibit slanted presentations of events that betray allegiances contrary to one of the 'basic structures' of the Constitution, namely secularism. Equally, the channels cannot be allowed to hold this party or that guilty, often in denigrative and abusive terms, before the courts have so pronounced them.

His proposal to the government of the day that the electronic channels also be brought under the ambit of the Press Council of India evoked upon the instant the predictable howl that Katju is not interested in any rational discourse on the issue of regulation but is simply desirous of gagging the fourth estate as it was gagged by the Indira Gandhi government in 1975.

Another instructive historical instance of how a power-structure that acquires the character of fascist domination cries the loudest for democracy whenever its totalitarian hold is sought to be questioned or brought in line with answerabilities that apply everywhere else.

And often accompanied by resonant ironies as Katju has now underlined. Writing to the News Broadcasting Association, Katju has asked its secretary, N.K. Singh,

> I would like to know whether the Association is willing to be placed under the Lokpal, which is proposed to be set up in the winter session of

> Parliament. You seem to be reluctant to come under the Press Council. Are you also reluctant to come under the Lokpal?

Further:

> You claim the right of self-regulation. May I remind you that even judges of the Supreme Court and the High Courts do not have that absolute right. They can be impeached by Parliament for misconduct... Lawyers come under the Bar Council and their licence can be suspended or cancelled for professional misconduct. Similarly doctors come under the Medical Council, chartered accountants under their council, etc.,... In the recent Anna Hazare movement, wide publicity was given to it by the media. What is the demand of Anna Hazare? That politicians, bureaucrats, judges, etc. should all be placed under the Jan Lokpal Bill. By what logic do you claim to be exempt from being placed under the Lokpal?...You claim the right of self-regulation. By the same logic, politicians, bureaucrats, etc., will also claim the right of self-regulation. Or do you claim to be so doodh ka dhula (cleansed by milk) that you should not be regulated by anyone else except yourself? What then were paid news, Radia tapes etc.,? (The phenomenon of 'paid news' was uncovered first by that doyen of journalists dedicated to the causes that affect India's hungry and exploited millions, P.Sainath; it involves politicians paying for sponsored copies of adulation but appearing as news, especially during election times. See The Hindu, November, 9).

These, you might well think, are pretty unanswerable posers that the electronic media houses will predictably seek to meet with self-righteous rhetoric on behalf of democratic principles for which they give not a fig in the first place. Most will stoop, in real life, to however low they must in order to pick up that Television Rating Point (TRP).

In the days to come, therefore, despite the many discussions that may take place on the theme – and not all disingenuous – Katju must expect a concerted gang-up for his ouster from Chairmanship of the Press Council of India. If the real purpose of the Anna Hazare-led putsch, as I have argued more than once, is to oust the government at the centre that seems chary of jettisoning its social-investment orientations in favour of further reforms calculated to increase private wealth, the corporates, very same ones who bolster the Anna drive, will also leave no gold-leaf unturned to ensure that this new ominous Katju tendency with respect to their captive hold on the electronic media is nipped in the bud. Pitiful are those senior employees and anchors among these channels who will not but continue to make strident assaults on the state so long as their own slavery to the corporates they serve remains well-paid.

And the hope that a majority of Indians who everyday suffer the inflictions of these channels, often as charmed zombies, and who sympathise with what Katju seeks to do may come out in considerable and visible support must be discounted for now.

To those who are hard put to think where their next miserable meal may come from, the Katju cause, however sane and laudable, will seem not of an order of concern that may relegate bread and butter issues. That bread and butter issues may indeed be inherent in the Katju concern about privately-owned electronic media may also seem a thought remote from quotidian congnizance.

So much the pity.

November 2011

As the Murdered Come Alive in Gujarat

I am sure that in the history of human discourse, somebody must have underlined the great paradox that informs not so much public killings but private murders.

That if the object of murder is to obliterate forever the 'other', the act of murder in fact has the consequence of not obliterating but perpetuating that 'other' forever.

Public massacres have often been legitimized on one high ground of impersonal righteousness or the other: patriotism, racial purity, the moral good of mankind, the call of the divine, what-have-you, and often enough swallowed without much regurgitation by whole peoples and civilizations, and endorsed by the best of high-minded thinkers and philosophers.

But killings effected cloak-and-dagger in pursuit of personal safety or stature carry a troublesome load of universal denunciation, and, however thick-skinned, brazen, or conscienceless the agent that gives the sanctioning nod to murder, he faces his sleepless nights.

Think that in Shakespeare's *Macbeth* (a text I keep returning to whenever I think of Modi's Gujarat) of all the gruesome murders the most gruesome turns out to be that of sleep: "Methought I heard a voice cry / Macbeth hath murdered sleep / Macbeth shall sleep no more."

So is Modi, who now smiles but rarely, losing sleep as he and his obliging minions have yet again been found out in the matter of the killings of Ishrat Jahan and four other young people?

Between 2002 and our moment, some 22 inconvenient human entities have been done to death in Gujarat in order to secure Modi's 'safety' and heroic enhancement so as he may strut the stage rather more stridently, even if shamelessly.

Not to speak of guiltlessly; do keep in mind that since the day his regime began, he has been the Home Minister of the state of Gujarat in addition to being the Chief Minister.

So what makes Modi tick?

Five things:

- one that he has been able thus far to sell private killings, read murders, to about a half of the Gujarati electorate as killings necessitated by the call to keep them safe from the forces of evil (did I hear you laugh?), and thereby as a tribute to his unbreachable local patriotism and machismo;
- two, that wide sections of Indian media to this day continue to buy this construction of eventualities in order not to undermine what they see as the most puissant counter to the prospects of a wholly secular or leftward swing to India;
- three, that in Gujarat there is no party, only neutralized, even dispatched, dissenters and Modi;
- four, that thus far Modi has not been taken on by any organized political force within Gujarat, although this seems set to change;
- five, because when all else fails, there is always the recourse to the time-tested 'Hinduism under siege' hypothesis, one to which both India's corporates and new middle classes resonate, notwithstanding their love of a market-driven modernity.

And, yet, the bards of old were not wrong: things are distinctly closing in on Modi.

Those heroic and recklessly fatal acts of resistance and exposure initiated by the likes of Teesta Setalvad and Citizens for Justice and Peace – the organization she runs – built upon through the last nine years by a gathering mass of caring and fearless citizens, and culminating in the unprecedentedly bold revolt of one serving police officer after another, Sanjiv Bhatt being the most daring protagonist here for now, coupled with the increasingly more forthright pronouncements from investigation agencies and courts of law, and a vastly more damaging national and international climate of opinion against Neros like Modi, – all this streaked with the congealed blood of one murdered corpse after another – bids fare to unravel the long years of Nazi rule in Gujarat.

If I am not mistaken, Ishrat in urdu has the meaning 'happy consequence' or thereabouts.

Will Ishrat's sacrifice prove the final bearer of happy tidings for a sane and secular India?

If it does, tomorrow, the next day, even a year from now, many of us might attempt a canonization.

November 2011

Is Pakistan Coming Full Circle?

What is happening among the Pakistan establishment currently must be regarded as extraordinary by any reckoning.

What had always been known and written about is actually out in the open from the mouths of both ends of a most visible and disabling dyarchy in the power-structure.

The elected leadership feels obliged to go public with the apprehension that yet another coup may be under way to 'pack away' the civilian dispensation on behalf of an army establishment that is squarely characterized by the Prime Minister as a 'state within the state.'

And, refuting the allegation that the army means to overthrow the legitimate government, the Chief of Staff nonetheless adds the caveat that 'security matters' must remain paramount. To wit, the military brass believes security matters must remain its unhindered preserve rather than the concern and jurisdiction of the elected government – a curious position to take within a democratic set-up. And, clearly, 'security matters' must be seen to involve most foreign policy concerns of the state.

No wonder that the Defence Ministry in Pakistan has had the abject imperative to say in court that the military establishment does not really answer to it.

This may indeed be an egregious new year wishful leap on the part of this writer, but I see within the collapsing womb of the ancien regime the promise of a desirable rebirth.

That regime has, since the partition of India and the years preceding that event, been predicated on three postulates:

- one, that Paksitan had to come into being as a theocratic state because Hindus and Muslims could not be trusted to live together in harmony in an independent sub-continent; that postulate automatically was to render religion as the chief denominator of what it meant to be a Pakistani, and to construct India into an enemy, since the preponderance of Hindus could not but be the ill-wishers of Muslims;

- two, that given this self-evident enmity with India, only the military establishment in Pakistan could be the chief guarantor of its security; and that any civilian leadership seen to be seeking a normative political relationship with India must be duly despatched in the larger 'national interest' of Pakistan;
- three, that, given the larger size and resource base of India, Pakistan had to have allies that would help it withstand any ill design on behalf of a 'Hindu India'; thus the early embrace of the United States of America, and security arrangements like the erstwhile SEATO.

The years have relentlessly brought to the fore the bankruptcy of all three of these originary postulates:

- the breakaway of Pakistan's eastern wing in 1971 was first conclusive proof that religious identity could not be trusted to be the unequivocal glue holding a nation-state together; issues related to other aspects of cultural life – language, and all that goes with that – and concrete economic realities that affect the livelihood of common people came to be decisive progenitors of a new national identity. Interestingly, contrary to some speculation, the so-called 'Arab Spring' can infact be seen to be precisely a phenomenon wherein diverse concerns unrelated to denominational identity, and the diversity within Muslim identity itself, are coming to reshape West-Asian and Middle-Eastern nation-states in as yet unpredictable ways;
- the birth of Bangladesh, infact, carried another momentous lesson, one that a General Kayani in Pakistan would do well to pay heed to. Far from ensuring the security of undivided Pakistan, it became a chief cause of its dismemberment. The genocide unleashed by General Yahya Khan on March 25, 1971 left the Bengali Muslims little choice but to seek a separate destiny. A lesson that ought to be kept in mind while dealing with, for example, the province of Baluchistan.
- The events since the attack on the twin towers in Manhattan can be seen to unravel the second foundational myth that the establishment in Pakistan has throughout nurtured: the chiefest enemies of Pakistan can be seen to be after all creatures of its own making. No wonder that wide swathes of the Pakistani intelligentsia have come round to the view that, one, an amicable relationship with India need not rebuke the founding idea of Pakistan, and, two, such a relationship may actually

> help reverse many shibboleths that have rendered Pakistan a state that constantly remains its own and the world's anxiety.

Lastly, a matter of equally profound reconsideration: a celebrity intellectual of Pakistan confided to this writer not too long ago that perhaps the most astute and far-reaching thing that Nehru did with the birth of independent India was to resist all pressures to link India's destiny with that of the United States of America; and that Pakistan's folly was to have done exactly the obverse.

Clearly, the imperialist war on Afghanistan and issues emanating therefrom one after the other have brought home with conclusive force the wisdom of that insight. No wonder that the call to disengage Pakistan from what has been its parasitical but also self-destructive dependence on the American establishment – call currently emanating most forcefully from a party on the ascendant, the Tehrik-e-Insaaf led by the ex-cricketer, Imran Khan – should be drawing unimaginably large public support.

These unravelings ought to bear, seen from a long-term perspective, undifferentiated lessons for both ends of the Pakistani establishment, the military brass as well as the elected civilian leaderships. And, if I say Pakistan seems to be coming full circle, it is for the reason that this indeed does seem now to be happening in embryo.

Nothing could be happier news for Pakistan, for India, for the World.

It is only when the Pakistani state fully ends the ambiguity about its own character which has disabled it over decades, and becomes fully democratic and only culturally Muslim, that too along diverse intra-Muslim axes (with the dominant Sunnis recognizing the right of the Shias, the Ismailis, the Sufis, the Ahmedias, to live without fear of ostracism or oppression, not to speak of the miniscule non-Muslim minority population) with the army establishment fully on board that it can begin to exorcise the ghosts that have haunted its existence.

Given that few Pakistanis, except of course the jihadi institutions and power-structures, now believe that Paksitan is forever at risk of a forced reamalgamation by an evilly disposed 'Hindu India,' the Pakistani military brass, fatally at the receiving end both of the monsters it has bred and nurtured, and of the American power elite whose hug, always questionable, has also now come to be life-threatening, must learn in double quick time to jettison myths that it has indulged and lived by, myths that no longer convince.

There is evidence that this may be happening. That its proliferated vested interests notwithstanding, the Pakistani military establishment may no longer be as zestful in seeking an end to the people's mandate, or in propping up monsters that are now at its own throat. That, coterminously, the democratically elected leaderships may be revising their view of the Pakistan-India equation and the Muslim-Hindu binary in path-breaking ways, and, as a necessary corollary, revising also its hitherto compulsive comprador impulses in favour of greater self-assurance within a sub-continental future.

Astute Pakistani thinkers have also noted the fact that not only have Hindutva communalists within India not succeeded in any consequential way to alter the secular-democratic character of the Indian state, they have also been powerless in preventing the dissolution of the erstwhile Hindu-theocratic state of Nepal. Just as the Jamat-e-Islami in Bangladesh has failed to reconstitute Bangladesh into an Islamic state.

The frequently enough voiced call from time to time to return Pakistan to the vision of its founder, Jinnah, conveys precisely these constitutive elements – chiefly, a secular state with a tolerant and modernized Muslim majority culture that does not engage with the rest of the world only from the frenetic fear of losing the so-called pristine identity which supposedly made it a country of its own.

2012 may indeed prove a happily decisive milestone in the career of the Pakistani state and polity.

December 2011

Just Why Did God Create Us?

Duniyā banāne vāle, kyā tere man men samāyī,
kāhe ko duniyā banāyī?
(whatever got into your head, o creator/ why did you create the world?)

Lines from a film song that have comprised absolutely my mother's most favourite poser. And mine as well.

She has now entered her one hundredth year – you heard that right – and is tough-minded enough to say she still does not have an answer, although her ninety nine have been full of observance and piety.

So, does she not fear death and the alleged aftermath? I suspect she takes cognizance of those things, but refuses to attach herself to an order of constructions that she remains unconvinced about. Mama, I salute the integrity of your mind and heart.

Being of a high intellectual calibre, and honest to the core, she is unable to say that watching cinema in a theatre or drinking a shot of whisky now and then are acts guaranteed to send us to jahanum (hell). I recall her remarking off and on how such injunctions are merely man-made, and entirely meaningless to those that may have felt the presence of the divine.

Which reminds me.

I think the first ever movie I watched at age seven or so was in the then Regal theatre in Srinagar, Kashmir. The film was either *Baazi* or *Jugnu*, and my father was as excited to be in the cinema hall as either of his two boys. Touching and edifying story-lines and heavenly music, ah. How noisy the world seems today.

In the city of Srinagar those days, the most heroic thing that a posse of young Kashmiris – Muslims and Pandits – set themselves to do was to buy a cinema ticket for the matinee of any new movie, even if this meant brawling with milling crowds at the crevice of a ticketing window, or literally scaling the aspirants in a flying tackle to get to the window before anyone else.

The successful Galahad received the awed acknowledgements from lesser combatants, and often the legend of that success did many rounds in galli and mohalla.

Remarkably, through our college careers – naughty times those were of a very sweetly honourable ambience – we Kashmiri young people across communities often visited the cinema without falling into horribly bad ways.

Often, working late nights in laboratories over gravimetric experiments, we sang those Rafi, Noor Jahan, Lata numbers that remain with us even now, and will remain so after all the Mullahs and Pundits have wended their holy ways to heaven. Where else would they be going?

As to liquor, we had our stolen moments, to the accompaniment of expansive verses from the subcontinent's renowned and beloved urdu poets. *Pilā de ok se sāquī gar ham se nafrat hai/ Piyālā detā nahīn hai na de, sharāb to de*, we would sing (pour thou that wine into the hollow of our palms/if you have no tankard, just give us the wine). And we sang of love as well in affected ways: *Ulti ho gayīn sab tadbīre<u>n</u>, kuchh na davā ne kām kiyā / Dekhā is bīmāriye dil ne ā<u>kh</u>ir kām tamām kiyā*. (all remedies fell flat, no medicine ever worked / the heartache in the end did us in).

Yet no domestic or political elder seemed ever to mind, or caution us against the pain of hellfire to stay away from cinema, song, or love; as to liquor or smoke, they had the excellent good sense to know when we were about these things, and to let us find our depths or shallows. If an admonition came, it came as a honeyed word of care, never as some monster doctrine that was waiting to swallow us into satanic oblivion. And such admonitions for that reason were often heeded and effective.

And, look, at the end of all that, we haven't done too badly, have we?

But the onslaughts of the 1989/90 moment were set to change much of how good-natured, caring, secular Kashmiri young people lived and bonded.

The Pandits having exited the valley, barring a few thousand, the demographic field seems more and more amenable to doctrinal fiat.

The return of peace and normalcy do not seem destined to bring back those magnificent swathes of syncretic innocence that made of going to the cinema or visiting a liquor shop – of which Srinagar had many – a matter of ordinary occurrence or conjoint camaraderie.

Many who buy pirated movie CDs or DVDs from ubiquitous street shops and watch them at home, or indeed watch movies off the television screen dime a dozen admonish that cinema houses must remain closed, since cinema is 'un-Islamic.' Think that it never was so for as long as cinema has existed.

Same with liquor: any number of knowledgeable Muslims have recounted to this writer how the Quranic attitude to imbibing can clearly be seen to have evolved over time. An earlier surah alludes to liquor as fraught both with potential 'benefit,' especially for men, and with sin, where sin may tip the scales (Surah Baqarah, 2:219; also Surah Al'Nahal); after an interesting episode of misdemeanour that would take too long to recite here, the injunction was laid not to use liquor during prayer times: 'O Believers, do not approach Salah while intoxicated' (S. Nisaa); a further episode of misdemeanour by an inebriated Ansari youth who threw a bone at Hazrat Saad Ibn Abi Waqqas out of tribal animus led to the more decisive outlawing of intoxicants (S. Maidah). It may be permissible to conclude here is that the injunction has less an ontological basis, more a revulsion against the likely loss of civility and social responsibility.

Think that whereas in a theocratic Pakistan, cinema houses run well and happily, and many of India's cinematic icons draw raging adulation, the valley of Rishis and Sufis seems set to out-Herod Herod. Think also that the Shariat Court in Pakistan ruled not too long ago (2005) that imbimbing was not tantamount to Hadd, and that it is un-islamic to punish the offence with 80 lashes. The recommendation has been made to make the offense a bailable one.

One must thus be pardoned for asking what was the tehrik(Movement) of 1989 about after all? Is the misgiving justified that some influential vanguards may have had more than merely the sanctity of the ballet in mind? Or the formation of a secular state away from India?

I was all of fourteen years of age, and privileged to be included in a Kashmiri cricket team to play an exhibition match with a posse of film stars from Bombay who had landed in Srinagar. These included such legends as Dilip Kumar, Nargis, and many others.

Then when the match ended and the stars came walking out of the Amarsingh club grounds. poor Dilip sahib was all but swallowed by droves of college girls who had come to watch. Unforgettable sight. Yet no solemn Kashmiri voice, or stern newspaper editorial thought the episode sinful or 'un-Islamic.'

How times change, or do they?

I imagine if a Shahrukh, or Salman, or Aamir Khan were to visit the valley this day, and go among the crowds, nothing much might have changed as far as ordinary Kashmiri Muslims are concerned. Indeed, these 'fallen' cinema icons might even be graciously invited into pristine Islamic homes for food and photo ops. And why not.

If the new and uncharacteristic expressions of puritan teaching in the valley are to be believed, some of India's greatest poets and Muslim-humanists, beginning with Mir and Ghalib, are set to be proscribed, no? Little wonder that the one poet who seems everywhere among the valley's literati these days should be Iqbal, and for reasons only tangential to his stature as a poet.

All this seems rather diminishing and sad. And perhaps indicative of what colour Azadi (secession from India) might take if and when it transpires.

And then if Kargil, a Shia majority area of the valley, were to seek Azadi as well on denominational grounds of identity (after all, think of the news that the world brings everyday of the horrendous killings between Sunni and Shia Muslims), would they be wrong?

If I therefore find myself on the side of Farooq Abdullah on the desirability of opening up, it is not out of any mercenary anxiety about wealth from tourism, although anyone administering the state cannot but think hard about that as well.

Rather from a larger consideration about what the future shape of Kashmir is likely or not to be.

Think of it this way: if imitation is the best form of flattery, then Narendra Modi does seem to have many admirers in the valley, endorsing the general right-wing principle that what may be indulged at home is not what may be allowed in public, constitutional provisions notwithstanding. Gujarat, as you know, is a dry state wherein, nonetheless, the grapevine flourishes more than elsewhere. Indeed, the vigilantes of the Sangh Parivar who go about destroying art works, attacking women, and such like might become role models too. And what a shame that would be.

Surely, we deserve to return to being Kashmiris.

December 2011

Selected non-Znet Essays by Badri Raina

The Subversion of Universities, *Seminar* 296, 1984.

Education Old and New – A Perspective, *Social Scientist*, Nos. 196-197, 1988.

CPI-M is Myopic, *The Hindustan Times*, June 29,1989.

The Politics of Development, *Journal of Arts and Ideas*, Nos. 17-18, June 1989

Abject Surrender to Saffron, *The Statesman*, November 13,1989.

Pakistan, Kashmir, and the Democratic Agenda, *The Statesman*, May 6, 1990.

Narmada and the Democratic Movement, *The Statesman*, May 15, 1990.

A Pretty Piece of Orientalism: A Rejoinder to Veena Das, *The Times of India*, October 21, 1990.

Ayodhya and After, *Daily Observer*, November 5, 1990.

The Tenth Avatar of Vishnu, *The Times of India*, February 17, 1991.

Kashmir: A Window to India, *Seminar* 392, April, 1992.

Pursuing Ayodhya is no longer a Compelling Agenda, *The Pioneer*, April 20, 1993.

Questions on Kargil, *The Hindustan Times*, July 20, 1999.

Patriots and Nationalists, *The Hindustan Times*, November 27, 1999.

No Longer A Hidden Agenda, *The Hindustan Times*, February 23, 2000.

Dealing With the Autonomy Demand, *The Hindu*, July 7, 2000.

Thackeray and the Indian State, *The Hindu*, July 25, 2000.

Befooled in Paradise, *The Hindu*, August 24, 2000.

Bangaru Beckons But, *The Hindu*, October 2, 2000.

Fixing the Indian Parliament, *Mainstream*, February 17, 2001.

The Chimera of Hindu Unity, *Mainstream*, March 3, 2001.

Sangma Treads Dangerous Ground, *Mainstream*, April 14, 2001.

Dealing With Kashmir, *The Hindu*, June 20, 2001.

Caste and Race: Discrimination by any Name, *Economic and Political Weekly*, August 11, 2001.

Desperate Times, Desperate Measures, *The Hindustan Times*, December 3, 2001.

Petulance Will Not Do, *The Hindustan Times*, April 1, 2002.

Imperialism and Afghanistan, (Review), *Frontline*, June 22-July 5, 2002

Pushed Into the Footnotes, *The Hindustan Times*, July 3, 2003.

The Valley of Love, *Frontline*, August 1, 2003.

In Bad Faith, *The Hindustan Times*, October 14, 2003.

Silly Sentimentality, *The Hindustan Times*, October 29,2003.

Grand Narrative of Terrorism, *Economic and Political Weekly*, December 27, 2003.

Redefining the Secular Agenda, *Economic and Political Weekly*, January 31, 2004.

Luminiscent Act, *The Hindustan Times*, May 27, 2004.

Patriotism, the Last Refuge, *The Hindustan Times*, August 28, 2004.

RSS and the Gandhi Murder, *People's Democracy*, August 29, 2004.

No More Borrowed Robes, *Mainstream*, October 23, 2004.

Two Notion Theory, *The Hindustan Times*, November 16, 2004.

Identity Crisis, *The Hindustan Times*, December 7, 2004.

History's Mysteries, *Economic and Political Weekly*, February 12, 2005.

Left Renewal, An Opportunity, *Mainstream*, April 29-May 5, 2005.

The Aesthetics of Evil-Doers, *Mainstream*, October 15, 2005.

Recasting India as a Vassal State, *Mainstream*, October 21-27, 2005.

Anti-Reservation Protest: Shoring Up Privilege, *Economic and Political Weekly*, May 20, 2006.

Give us back the Manichaean, *Mainstream*, July 1, 2006.

Heal and Renew (Kashmir), *Kashmir Times*, July 17,2006.

The Darker Nations: A Biography of the Shorlived Third World' (Review), *Frontline*, November 7, 2008.

The Infirmity of Noble Minds, *The Hindu*, August 11, 2009.

Agha Ashraf Ali: Enfant Terrible, *Kashmir Times*, November 14, 2010.

Much Merit in the Fine Print, *The Hindustan Times*, June 23, 2012.

Whistelblowers Hot and Cold, *The Hindustan Times*, May 2, 2012.

Mirror Mirror on the Wall, *The Hindu*, July 12, 2012.

Animal Spirits, *Mainstream*, July 14, 2012.

What Lies Ahead in the Annals of Anna, *The Hindu*, August 07, 2012.

McCarthyism Mamta Style, *The Hindu*, August 17, 2012.

Other Titles from Three Essays

Aijaz Ahmad, *On Communalism and Globalisation: Offensives of the Far Right*

Amar Farooqi, *Opium City: The Making of Early Victorian Bombay*

Angana Chatterji, *Violent Gods: Hindu Nationalism in India's Present – Narratives from Orissa*

Antoinette Burton, *Brown Over Black: Race and the Politics of Postcolonial Citation*

Archana Prasad, *Against Ecological Romanticism: Verrier Elwin and the Making of an Anti-Modern Tribal Identity*

AR Vasavi, *Shadow Space: Suicides and the Predicament of Rural India*

Arup Banerji, *Old Routes: North Indian Nomads and Bankers in Afghan, Uzbek and Russian Lands*

Ashraf Aziz, *Light of the Universe: Essays on Hindustani Film Music*

Barbara Harriss-White, *India's Market Society: Three Essays in Political Economy*

Biswamoy Pati, *Identity, Hegemony, Resistance: Towards a Social History of Conversions in Orissa, 1800-2000*

Brinda Karat, *Survival and Emancipation: Notes from Indian Women's Struggles*

Colin Leys, *Total Capitalism: Market Politics, Market State*

Eduardo Galeano, *Open Veins of Latin America: Five Centuries of the Pillage of a Continent*

Harsh Mander, *A Fractured Freedom: Chronicles of India's Margins, 2004–2011*

Jackie Assayag and Véronique Bénéï (eds.), *Re-mapping Knowledge: The Making of South Asian Studies in India, Europe and America, 19th-20th centuries*

John S Saul, *Development After Globalisation: Theory and Practice for an Embattled South in a New Imperial Age*

John S Saul, *Decolonisation and Empire: Contesting the Rhetoric and Practice of Resubordination in Southern Africa and Beyond*

John S Saul, *Liberation Lite: The Roots of Recolonisation in Southern Africa*

KN Panikkar, *An Agenda for Cultural Action and Other Essays*

Kristoffel Lieten, *Views on Development: The Local and the Global in India and Pakistan*

Meera Nanda, *Breaking the Spell of Dharma and Other Essays*

Meera Nanda, *The Wrongs of the Religious Right: Reflections on Science, Secularism and Hindutva*

Madhu Trivedi, *The Emergence of the Hindustani Tradition: Music, Dance and Drama in North*

India, 13th to 19th Centuries

Meeto (Kamaljit Bhasin-Malik), *In the Making: Identity Formation in South Asia*

Mukul Dube, *The Path of the Parivar: Articles on Gujarat and Hindutva*

Nasreen Ahmed, *Muslim Leadership and Women's Education: Uttar Pradesh, 1886-1947*

Omar Khalidi, *Khaki and Ethnic Violence in India: Army, Police and Paramilitary Forces during Communal Riots*

Omar Khalidi, *Muslims in Indian Economy*

Paul R Brass, *Forms of Collective Violence: Riots, Pogroms, and Genocide in Modern India*

Patricia Jeffery and Roger Jeffery, *Confronting Saffron Demography: Religion, Fertility, and Women's Status in India*

Pritam Singh, *Economy, Culture and Human Rights: Turbulence in Punjab, India and Beyond*

Radhika Desai, *Slouching Towards Ayodhya: From Congress to Hindutva in Indian Politics*

Ralph Russell, *Findings, Keepings: The Autobiography of Ralph Russell, Early Years, 1918-1945*

Ralph Russell, *Losses Gains: The Autobiography of Ralph Russell, Middle Years, 1945-1958*

RK Jain, *Indian Transmigrants: Malaysian and Comparative Essays*

Romila Thapar, *The Aryan: Recasting Constructs*

S. Irfan Habib, *To Make the Deaf Hear: Ideology and Programme of Bhagat Singh and His Comrades*

Shereen Ratnagar, *The Other Indians: Essays on Pastoralists and Pre-Historic Tribal People*

Shubh Mathur, *The Everyday Life of Hindu Nationalism: An Ethnographic Account*

Subhash Gatade, *The Saffron Condition: Politics of Repression and Exclusion in Neoliberal India*

Sunil Kumar, *The Present in Delhi's Pasts: Five Essays*

Sunil Kumar (ed.), *Demolishing Myths or Mosques and Temples: Readings on History and Temple Desecration in Medieval India*

Utsa Patnaik, *The Republic of Hunger and Other Essays*

Vasudha Dalmia, *Orienting India: European Knowledge Formation in the Eighteenth and Nineteenth Centuries*

Vijay Prashad, *The American Scheme: Three Essays*

Vina Mazumdar, *The Mind and the Medium: Explorations in the Evolution of British Imperial Policy in India*

Zaheer Baber, *Secularism, Communalism and the Intellectuals*